MAURITANIA

SEAN CONNOLLY

www.bradtguides.com

Bradt Guides Ltd, UK
The Globe Pequot Press Inc, USA

Bradt GUIDES
TRAVEL TAKEN SERIOUSLY

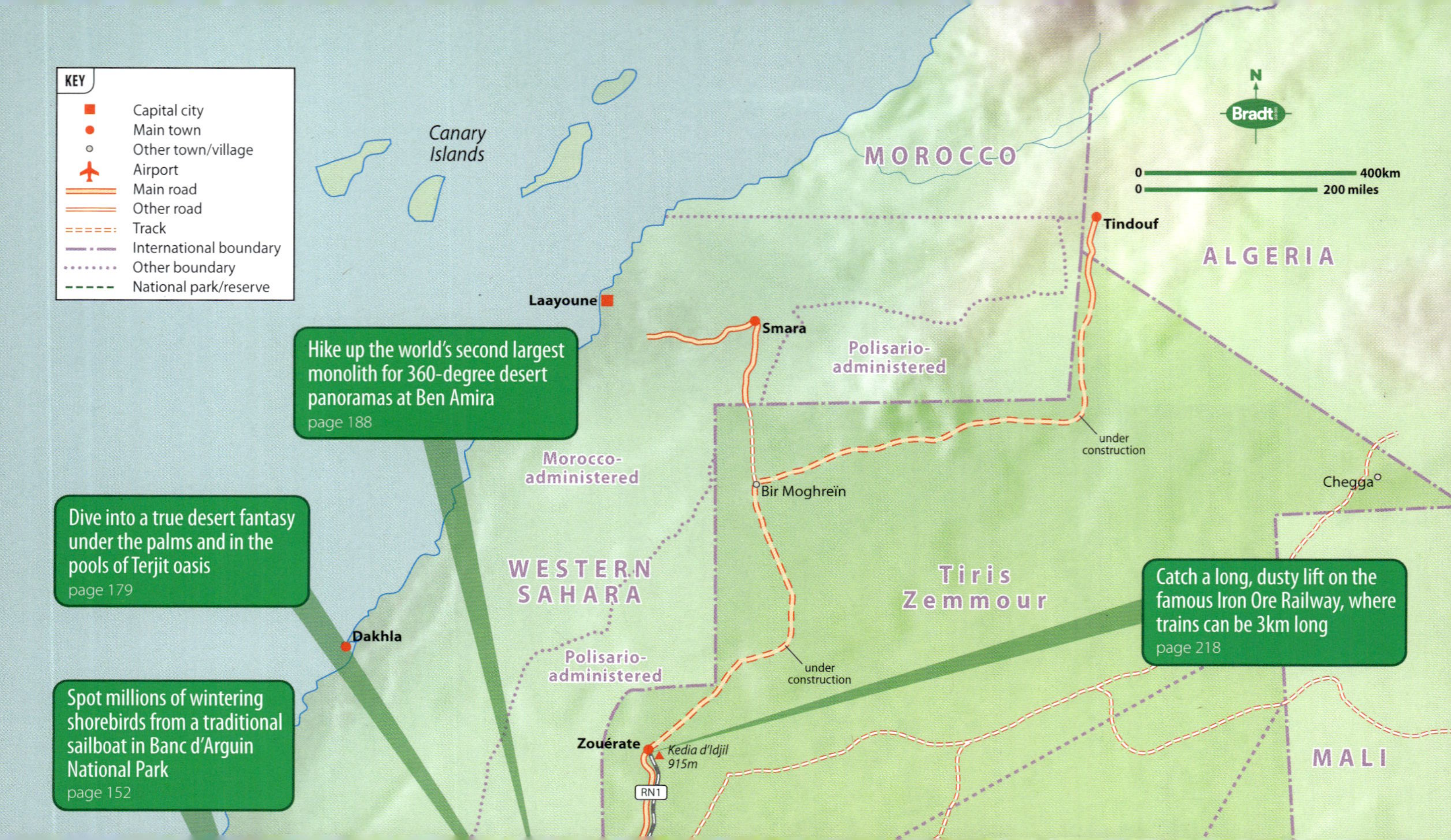
KEY
Capital city
Main town
Other town/village
Airport
Main road
Other road
Track
International boundary
Other boundary
National park/reserve
Canary Islands
MOROCCO
ALGERIA
0 400km
0 200 miles
Bradt
N
Tindouf
Laayoune
Smara
Polisario-administered
Hike up the world's second largest monolith for 360-degree desert panoramas at Ben Amira
page 188
Morocco-administered
under construction
Bir Moghreïn
Chegga
Dive into a true desert fantasy under the palms and in the pools of Terjit oasis
page 179
WESTERN SAHARA
Tiris Zemmour
Catch a long, dusty lift on the famous Iron Ore Railway, where trains can be 3km long
page 218
Dakhla
Polisario-administered
under construction
Spot millions of wintering shorebirds from a traditional sailboat in Banc d'Arguin National Park
page 152
Zouérate
Kedia d'Idjil 915m
RN1
MALI

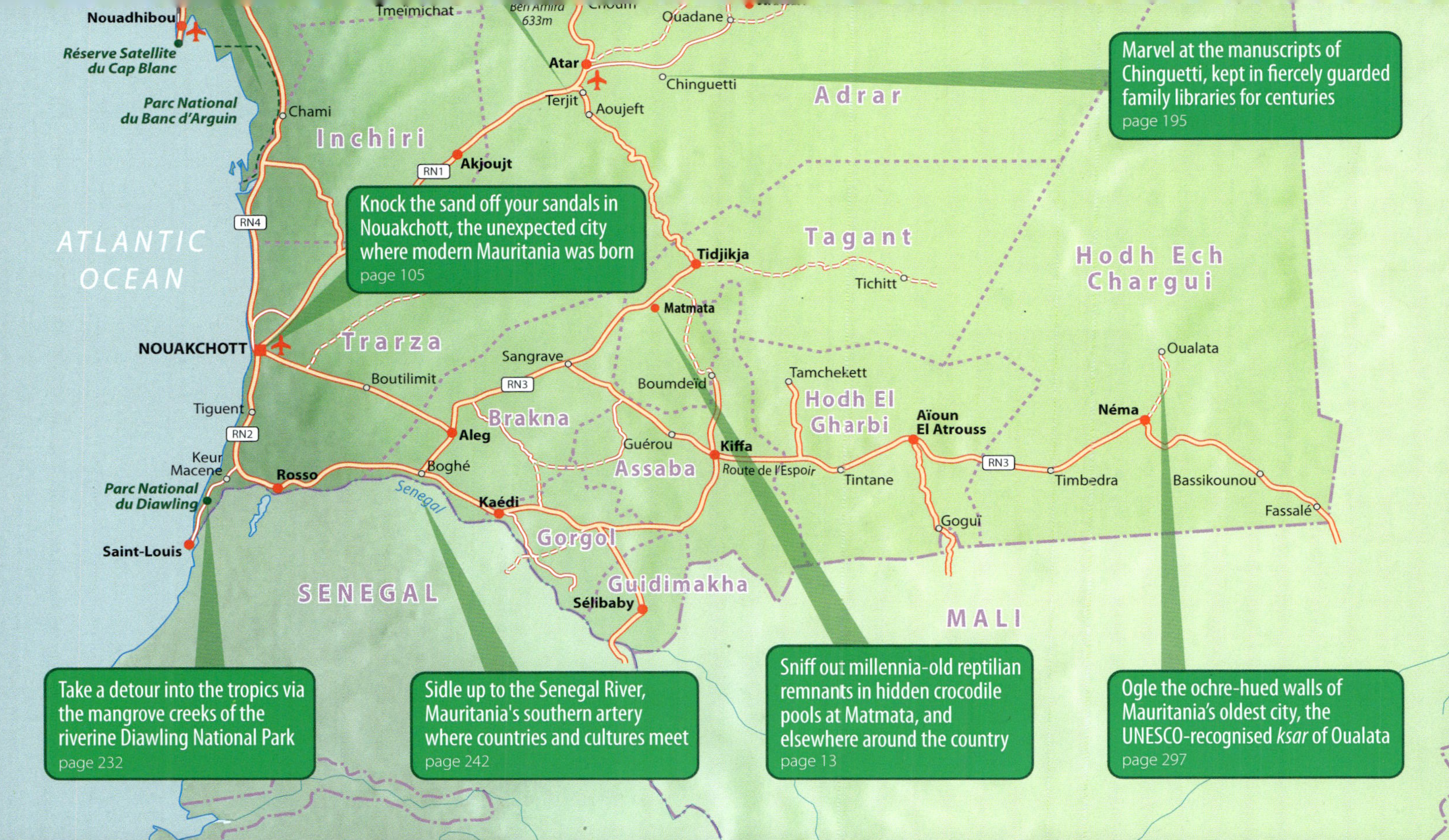

Marvel at the manuscripts of Chinguetti, kept in fiercely guarded family libraries for centuries
page 195
Knock the sand off your sandals in Nouakchott, the unexpected city where modern Mauritania was born
page 105
Take a detour into the tropics via the mangrove creeks of the riverine Diawling National Park
page 232
Sidle up to the Senegal River, Mauritania's southern artery where countries and cultures meet
page 242
Sniff out millennia-old reptilian remnants in hidden crocodile pools at Matmata, and elsewhere around the country
page 13
Ogle the ochre-hued walls of Mauritania's oldest city, the UNESCO-recognised *ksar* of Oualata
page 297
ATLANTIC OCEAN
SENEGAL
MALI
Adrar
Inchiri
Tagant
Hodh Ech Chargui
Trarza
Brakna
Hodh El Gharbi
Assaba
Gorgol
Guidimakha
Nouadhibou
Réserve Satellite du Cap Blanc
Parc National du Banc d'Arguin
Chami
Tmeimichat
633m
Ouadane
Atar
Chinguetti
Terjit
Aoujeft
Akjoujt
RN1
RN4
NOUAKCHOTT
Tidjikja
Tichitt
Matmata
Sangrave
Boutilimit
RN3
Boumdeïd
Tamchekett
Oualata
Néma
Tiguent
RN2
Aleg
Guérou
Kiffa
Aïoun El Atrouss
Keur Macene
Rosso
Boghé
Route de l'Espoir
Tintane
Timbedra
Bassikounou
Parc National du Diawling
Senegal
Kaédi
Gogui
Fassalé
Saint-Louis
Sélibaby

MAURITANIA
DON'T MISS...

OUADANE

A critical stop on caravan routes for centuries, Ouadane's wealth of stone architecture stands witness to this long-lost past PAGE 199

(SS)

CHINGUETTI

With its iconic minaret and legendary libraries, the ancient town that once gave Mauritania its name still holds an important place in the country's national identity PAGE 191

(LH/S)

BANC D'ARGUIN NATIONAL PARK
This wind-blasted coastline, once home to a Portuguese trading post, is a true study in desolation PAGE 152
(FP/D)

OUALATA
The red-and-white bas-reliefs which decorate Oualata's walls and doorways distinguish this remote oasis from similar stone-built settlements PAGE 297
(SC)

THE IRON ORE TRAIN
Take a ride on one of the longest, heaviest – and dustiest – trains in the world for a unique and unforgettable experience PAGE 218
(S73/S)

MAURITANIA
IN COLOUR

above left (SC) The ornate interior of Nouakchott's Mosquée Marocaine, or Moroccan Mosque, one of many mosques in the city PAGE 132

above right (SC) At Nouakchott's Marché aux khaïmas, women sell handmade Mauritanian tents (*khaïmas*) in various colours and sizes PAGE 124

below (SS) The capital's camel markets are home to hundreds, or even thousands, of not just camels but also goats and cattle, which grunt, spit and chew their way through the day while owners vie for the best prices PAGE 125

Nouakchott's most iconic landmark – the twin minarets that tower over the Mosquée Saoudienne, or Saudi Mosque PAGE 132 above left (SS)

Baguette-style *mbourou* loaves are a mealtime staple around the country, and ambulant vendors do a reliably brisk trade PAGE 89 above right (K/S)

The Port de Pêche is Nouakchott's most colourful corner, where more than 1,000 brightly painted pirogues line the shore PAGE 132 below (K/S)

JOIN

THE TRAVEL CLUB

THE MEMBERSHIP CLUB FOR SERIOUS TRAVELLERS FROM BRADT GUIDES

Be inspired
Free books and exclusive insider travel tips and inspiration

Save money
Special offers and discounts from our favourite travel brands

Plan the trip of a lifetime
Access our exclusive concierge service and have a bespoke itinerary created for you by a Bradt author

Join here:
bradtguides.com/travelclub

Membership levels to suit all budgets

Bradt GUIDES

TRAVEL TAKEN SERIOUSLY

AUTHOR

Sean Connolly (Instagram @shanboqol) first travelled to Africa as a student in 2008 and has been returning to the continent regularly to research, guide or simply soak up the ambience in Africa's countless little-visited corners ever since. He's been poring over maps since before he could read them, and working with Bradt Guides since 2011. Along with authoring new Bradt guidebooks to Mauritania, Senegal and soon Guinea-Bissau, he has also updated or contributed to the Bradt guides to Somaliland, Malawi, Mozambique, Ghana, Uruguay, Sierra Leone, São Tomé and Príncipe, two editions of Rwanda, The Gambia, and Gabon. When he's not updating guides, leading tours or discussing the many merits of camel meat, you'll find him seeking out a country's funkiest records or otherwise clacking away at a desk in Copenhagen.

FEEDBACK REQUEST

At Bradt Guides we're aware that guidebooks start to go out of date on the day they're published – and that you, our readers, are out there in the field doing research of your own. You'll find out before us when a fine new family-run hotel opens or a favourite restaurant changes hands and goes downhill. So why not tell us about your experiences? Contact us on t 01753 893444 or e info@bradtguides.com. We will forward emails to the author who may post updates on the Bradt website at w bradtguides.com/updates. Alternatively, you can add a review of the book to Amazon, or share your adventures with us on Facebook, X or Instagram (@BradtGuides).

First edition published November 2025
Bradt Travel Guides Ltd
31a High Street, Chesham, Buckinghamshire, HP5 1BW, England
www.bradtguides.com
Print edition published in the USA by The Globe Pequot Press Inc,
PO Box 480, Guilford, Connecticut 06437-0480

Text copyright © Sean Connolly, 2025
Maps copyright © Bradt Travel Guides Ltd, 2025; includes map data © MapTiler
© OpenStreetMap contributors
Photographs copyright © Individual photographers, 2025 (see below)
Project Manager: Susannah Lord
Copy Editor: Gina Rathbone
Cover research: Pepi Bluck, Perfect Picture

Thank you for buying an authorised edition of this book published by Bradt Travel Guides. For over 50 years, Bradt Travel Guides has encouraged adventurous, immersive and responsible travel, and this is only possible because of the support of our readers. By purchasing our books, you are enabling us to continue to commission expert authors who genuinely know and love the places they write about, and who write their books after thorough, on-the-ground research.

The author(s) and publisher have made every effort to ensure the accuracy of the information in this book at the time of going to press. However, they cannot accept any responsibility for loss, injury or inconvenience resulting from the use of information contained in this guide. All rights reserved. No part of this book may be reproduced, scanned or distributed by any means without the written permission of Bradt Travel Guides, nor used or reproduced in any way to train artificial intelligence technologies/models. Bradt Travel Guides and the author(s) unequivocally reserve this work from the text and data mining exception, as per Article 4(3) of the Digital Single Market Directive 2019/790.

ISBN: 9781804691724

British Library Cataloguing in Publication Data
A catalogue record for this book is available from the British Library

Photographs Dreamstime.com: Aleksandr Katarzhin (AK/D), Fabian Plock (FP/D), Jameswest (J/D), Smellme (S/D); Romain Miot (RM); Sean Connolly (SC); Shutterstock.com: Eric Valenne geostory (EVG/S), GLF Media (GM/S), kaikups (K/S), Lena Ha (LH/S), RobNaw (RN/S), Sergey-73 (S73/S); SuperStock (SS)
Front cover Saif al Islam al Ahmed Mahmoud is the guardian of one of the most recognised libraries in Chinguetti (RM)
Back cover, clockwise from top left The Iron Ore Train (J/D); Al Makhrougat (elephant rocks), near Tichitt (SC); Barbary sheep (*Ammotragus lervia*) (S/D)
Title page, clockwise from top left Alone in the Sahara desert (RM); a decorated doorway, Oualata (SC); manuscripts, Tichitt (SC)

Maps David McCutcheon FBCart.S. FRGS

Typeset by Ian Spick, Bradt Guides
Production managed by Gutenberg Press Ltd; printed in Malta
Digital conversion by www.dataworks.co.in

Paper used for this product comes from sustainably managed forests, and recycled and controlled sources.

AUTHOR'S STORY

We were sitting under a *khaïma*, deep in the cool stillness of the Terjit oasis. I was leading my first tour group in Mauritania, and a few of us had taken up chatting with a handful of mates who had driven in from Nouakchott for the weekend. These well-polished city boys were here to soak up the desert's peace and stillness, just as we were, and we were equally happy for the chance to get to know each other. Twigs of juicy dates were quickly pressed into our hands (along with cream to dip them in), phones came out to double-check our itinerary and make sure we weren't going to miss any of the guys' favourites, and eventually the topic turned to Mauritanians' inimitable style of dress.

In a flash, their billowing blue *daraas* were off – it was time for a game of dress-up, which quickly exploded into a comic-book cloud of hands, feet and elbows as we fought to locate the unfamiliar arm and neck holes of this fantastically unwieldy garment. Once we'd recovered our ***boubou*** bearings, a round of primping, preening, and cheesing for the cameras began. But, of course, one daraa does not an outfit make, and an explanation of the *haouli* headwrap came next. I had naïvely complimented one of the guys' turbans earlier, a striking white-and-blue number which was now securely affixed to my head.

Meanwhile, an enormous platter of *méchoui* barbequed goat emerged from I'm-not-sure-where, and we were hit with an emphatic chorus of '*Bismillahs*' and incredulous looks when I (attempted to) explain that the group was to be fed shortly, just down the road. Unable (and uninclined) to refuse entirely, we started to change outfits back – I had taken off my host's haouli to avoid covering it in goat grease with my unskilled eating – and sat down to tuck into just a little of their gargantuan platter. Our self-appointed hosts, guardians and fashion advisers set about carefully extracting the choicest morsels and placing them in front of each of us.

But eventually it was, despite protests from our hosts and procrastination from my guests, time to move on. We were trading back the last of the daraas when I noticed that the owner of the flash blue-and-white haouli hadn't so much as touched it after I had set it down next to him. As we worked through a drawn-out set of goodbyes ('What do you mean you're not staying for tea?!'), he admonished me for forgetting something – his haouli, of course. After a long round of refusals (in this case, quite genuine – you could tell this wasn't just a throwaway piece), he informed me: 'You can do what you want, but when I leave here tonight this haouli will be sitting right here, as it's no longer mine.'

Thinking I had perhaps taken my polite refusals a step too far, I sheepishly took up the scarf, offering a litany of handshakes and thanks along the way. Since that day, Mauritania has burrowed its way into my life, through a series of tour groups already past and still scheduled, and through the lengthy process of researching and writing this guide. Throughout it all, I've kept this haouli alongside, for both its practical use (they're not wearing them just for style, after all) and for its reminder: to accept hospitality when it's offered, and to reciprocate when you can, as life here has sustained itself for centuries. And even better still, I now know how to tie it – though sometimes with a little help!

Acknowledgements

Having got to know neighbouring Senegal quite well in the process of writing two Bradt guides to the country, I was grateful for the opportunity to discover this enormous and mysterious land to the north. Needless to say, I was not disappointed with what I found.

But without the help, companionship, and advice of the following people, I wouldn't have found even half of what I did, and so many of Mauritania's charms might have remained lost to me in the desert, like the Ma'den Ijafen trove (page 206). My heartfelt thanks are therefore due to Mohamed Ahmedou and Hademine Ahmedou (Time For Mauritania), Baba (T'Ore Mauritania), Sidi (Sidi Tours), Seck Mar Dendou Boulkeir (Atar Voyages), Lupine Travel, Deborah Walker, Sébastien Armand Bouhot (Auberge Triskell), Mamine Evin (Camping-Auberge Du Puigaudeau, and Aziza), Zaïda Bilale (Auberge Vasque), Delahi Ahmed Karashi, Brahim Hbib, Mad Isselmou, Ahmed Sheriff, Phil Paoletta, Matt Christie and Boubacar Tessougue (Scoot West Africa), Andrew Jainchill, Uli (Chameaux Nouakchott), Bakary Tandia and Sean Tenner (Abolition Institute), Victor and Tish (Villa Maguela), Elhadj Dhmine (Terjit Vacances), Sidiahmed (Mauritanides), Isabel Fiadeiro (Zeinart), Jim O'Brien (Native Eye), Ahmed Mahmoud Jemal Ahmedou, Nancy Jones Abeiderrahmane, Katherine Baird, Peter Hudson, Eric Gilbertson, Alassane Ba, Matthew Lavoie, Lucie de Beauchamp, Joost Bastmeijer, Thomas Stricker, Romain Miot, Nick Brooks, Laurent Meillan, Joel Corush, Taleb Elghaly (Maurisert/Diawling), Sidi Ely (Banc d'Arguin), and Jiyid Mahfoudh and Aya Hmeid (ONT).

Back at home, I thank everyone who continues to show me ever so much patience and grace as I endlessly take on more projects than I know what to do with, and often find myself somewhat harried and unhelpful as a result – firstly and especially my partner Line Riis Christiansen, whose unfailing encouragement and thoughtful perspective has made this book possible. Another big *mange tak* is due to Jon Tofteskov, Marta Jankowska and Ellie Taylor for the support and patience on the home front.

And finally my thanks are very much due to my always-superb editors and colleagues at Bradt Guides, most especially for their patience as this book slowly came together, and in particular to Susannah Lord, who has ensured it could finally see the light and shine.

Contents

LIST OF MAPS

Introduction

When you tell your friends and family you're off on a trip to Mauritania, you can expect the conversation to go something like this:

Mauritius! How exciting! Will you be doing an all-inclusive? Scuba?
No, no…we're going to Mauritania.
To where? Is that different to Mauritius?
Mauritania? It's in the Sahara, between Morocco and Senegal.
Hmm, I see. Don't think I've ever heard of it. So does that mean no all-inclusive, then?

And yes, dear reader, it most certainly does mean no all-inclusive. While the two countries might sit next to each other in the atlas, you could hardly find two more opposite destinations than Mauritania and its near-namesake some 9,000km to the southeast. But while Mauritania is more *harmattan* than honeymoon, and more bivouac than bungalow, there's still plenty of opportunity to get sand between your toes here – just not in quite the same way.

In fact, there's a whole country worth of the stuff – Mauritania is among the most comprehensively desert nations on the planet, and the otherworldly landscapes here have a way of turning visitors into armchair geologists overnight. Indeed, the Mauritanian paysage oscillates rapidly between glory and fury, and history stretching back into deep geological time sits within a finger's grasp. The sharp-eyed will find the ground here studded with small treasures: ancient seashells, tortured fulgurite formations (created when lightning strikes the sandy ground), and even chunks of meteorite, often collected by herders in hopes of selling them to the occasional passer-by.

And among these dramatic dunes, mesas and tablelands, a nomadic nation was born. Straddling the line between the Sahara and the Sahel, between North Africa and West, and between the lands of the camel and those of the cow, Mauritania sits *à cheval sur* – on horseback between – several worlds. From the north, Arab and Amazigh tribes brought Islam, and from the south, the empires of the Wolof, Halpulaar and Soninké cultivated the bounties of land and sea.

Together, the two sides developed into complimentary poles of a trans-Saharan trade that would define life here for many centuries, and give rise to the UNESCO-recognised fortified towns, or *ksour*, that Mauritania is famous for today. And while elements of this trade were sordid, with kidnapping and enslavement commonplace, these centres also saw the germination and development of a refined scholarly tradition, manifest in the thousands of priceless manuscripts still secreted away in the country's many hereditary libraries.

Today, Mauritania is slowly putting some of these ghosts of the past to rest, but remains a deeply traditional place that must be taken on its own terms. In the north, stone-built herding villages still live from the goats and the *guetna* date palm harvest; and in the south, planting and harvesting around the Senegal River's annual flood waits for neither man nor beast. Along the wind-whipped Atlantic coast, salt and sun preserve the heroic efforts of the fishermen as they always have.

And still, the old ways and obligations of the desert remain in force – to the extent that even the hotel was until recently something of a novel concept. Here, welcome and care for a guest remains not only a sacred duty, but as natural and obvious as the annual monsoon – though precious little has been designed or adapted to the needs of tourists. This can make travel here difficult, but also makes it immensely rewarding and immersive in ways that are increasingly rare around the world. Just 5 hours from Paris, you can rest your head under a *khaïma* tent, absorbed into a desert world and lifestyle where you'll be warmly welcomed, but which will not be changed on your account.

But not everything in Mauritania remains so stubbornly steadfast: the road network has improved dramatically in recent years, making the further reaches of this enormous land more accessible than ever before. Today, world-beating birding, dunescapes hundreds of kilometres long, and oases straight out of a storybook are all within easy reach of one another. And despite this increasing accessibility, there's still hardly a 'beaten path' here to get off – instead you'll often literally and figuratively have the place to yourself.

As the political and security situation has deteriorated in much of the Sahara over the last decade-plus, Mauritania has so far largely avoided this fate, instead emerging as an unexpected sensation in desert tourism. The country's unlikely social media star, the Iron Ore Train, has played a role in this, but also the simple fact that Mauritania is now among the only places in the whole Sahara where you can freely explore the depths of the desert without excessive security or bureaucratic requirements.

So, while the discomforts of travelling here remain very real, and you may find yourself longing for a hot bath and a cold drink by the end of your trip, you may also find that Mauritania is the type of place that returns to you over and over again. Perhaps when the careless drip of an office coffeemaker recalls the burble of hot *atay*, lovingly poured into tiny glasses, or when morning traffic hearkens to the quietude of a pre-dawn birdsong and murmured prayer. Here, the sweat of the journey is soon forgotten but the sweetness lingers – just as around a pot of *atay*.

Among the first and most storied outsiders to have travelled in Mauritania, Odette du Puigaudeau said this when she began her first journey here in 1933 – one that ultimately changed the direction of her life:

> On setting out we had no prejudices about the country; we had taken no sides. Nor have we since. Mauretania is a huge country, half as big again as France, and shows wide diversity in its landscape, its people and their characters and habits. We have not sought to generalise, but to give a truthful account of what we found, hoping that the reader will be gripped as we were by the beauty of the Western Sahara and the poetic character of its people.
>
> Odette du Puigaudeau, *Pieds nus à travers la Mauritanie*, 1936

We have set out to produce this guide in the same mindset, and hope that today's readers might too be gripped by the beauty and grandeur of this untamed land and poetic people that we have done our best to distill into the pages before you.

HOW TO USE THIS GUIDE

AUTHOR'S FAVOURITES Finding genuinely characterful accommodation or that unmissable off-the-beaten-track café can be difficult, so the author has chosen a few of his favourite places throughout the country to point you in the right direction. These 'author's favourites' are marked with a ✷.

PRICE CODES Throughout this guide we have used price codes to indicate the cost of those places to stay and eat listed in the guide. For a key to these price codes, see page 87 for accommodation and page 90 for restaurants.

MAPS

Keys and symbols Maps include alphabetical keys covering the locations of those places to stay, eat or drink that are featured in the book. Note that regional maps may not show all hotels and restaurants in the area: other establishments may be located in towns shown on the map.

Grids and grid references Several maps use gridlines to allow easy location of sites. Map grid references are listed in square brackets after the name of the place or site of interest in the text, with page number followed by grid number, eg: [114 C1].

WEBSITES Although all third-party websites were working at the time of going to print, some may cease to function during this edition's lifetime. If a website doesn't work, you might want to check back at another time as they often function intermittently. Alternatively, you can let us know of any website issues by emailing e info@bradtguides.com.

KEY TO SYMBOLS

Symbol	Meaning	Symbol	Meaning
	International boundary		Antenna/mobile tower
	Main road		Statue/monument
	Minor road		Nightclub/casino
	Track		Restaurant
	Footpath		Hotel/guesthouse/hostel
	Ferry/boat trips		Church/cathedral/monastery
	Airport		Mosque
	Filling station/garage		Cemetery
	Bus station, etc		Lighthouse
	Taxis/car hire		Beach
	Telecoms		Birdwatching/Important Bird Area
	Ancient city gate		Summit (height in metres)
	Tourist information office		Other point of interest
	Embassy/consulate		Stadium/sports facility
	Museum/art gallery		Dunes
$	Bank		Cliff/crater
	Post office		Marsh/wetlands
	Hospital		Palmeriae
	Pharmacy/clinic		Urban park
	Historic (archaeological) site		Market
	Border post/crossing		

Part One

GENERAL INFORMATION

MAURITANIA AT A GLANCE

Location Straddling North and West Africa, the Tropic of Cancer passes through the northern third of Mauritania.
Neighbouring countries Senegal, Mali, Algeria, Western Sahara (partly administered by Morocco and partly administered by the Polisario Front)
Land area 1,030,700km^2 (about four times larger than the UK and twice as large as Metropolitan France)
Climate Hot and dry, cooler on the coast and considerably hotter inland, with humidity rising as you go south. Short rainy season from July to September, with dry, harmattan conditions prevailing between October and May. Coolest between November and March.
Terrain Overwhelmingly open desert plains, punctuated by rock outcrops and bisected by a chain of sub-1,000m mountain plateaus running north–south. A full third of the country is covered in dunes, with the northern Saharan desert zones slowly giving way to Sahelian grassland and savannah in the extreme south. Agriculture is practised along the Senegal River.
Status Multi-party Islamic Republic
Population 4,927,532 (2023 census)
Life expectancy 68.9 years (2021)
Capital Nouakchott (population 1,446,761)
Other main towns Nouadhibou (173,525), Kiffa (84,101), Fassalé (79,508, including the Mbera Refugee Camp), Kaédi (62,790), Zouérate (62,380), Rosso (61,156)
Economy Offshore gas reserves coming online in 2025 will soon dominate; other major sectors are mining (iron ore, gold, copper), agriculture, livestock and fishing.
GDP US$10.65 billion; US$2,380 nominal GDP per capita (2024); 6.5% annual growth (all 2023)
Languages Hassaniya Arabic is the official language, and there are three other officially recognised 'national' languages of Pulaar, Soninké and Wolof. French is no longer official, but considered a 'privileged foreign language'. Zénaga, an endangered Amazigh language, is still spoken in tiny pockets of the southwest, while a few Bambara speakers may be found along the Mali border.
Religion Islam is the state religion and 99% of Mauritanians are Sunni adherents. The small Christian (Roman Catholic) community is predominantly comprised of immigrants.
Currency Mauritanian ouguiya (redenominated in 2018)
Exchange rates €1=47.23UM; US$1=39.89UM; £1=54.39UM (September 2025)
National airline Mauritania Airlines
International telephone code +222
Time GMT+0
Electrical voltage 220V, 50Hz
Weights and measures Metric
Flag Green field with a gold star and crescent and horizontal red stripes at the top and bottom (the stripes were added in a 2017 referendum)
National anthem *Bilāda l-'ubāti l-hudāti l-kirām (Pays des fiers, nobles guides*; Land of the Proud, Guided by Noblemen)
Public holidays Mauritania officially celebrates a mix of eight Islamic and secular public holidays (page 93).

1

Background Information

GEOGRAPHY

Taking in 1,030,700km^2, Mauritania is the 28th largest country in the world (and 11th in Africa), straddling the transitional zone between the emptiest depths of the Sahara and an increasingly populous and cultivated Sahel. More specifically, the country stretches over five distinct bio-geographical zones including the inland desert, coastal desert, mountain, Sahel and savannah areas. Mauritania is also the world's largest country that sits entirely below 1,000m, topping out at the 915m Kedia d'Idjil mountain near Zouérate. Topographically speaking, Mauritania is dominated by low, flat plains and dune seas punctuated by occasional rock outcrops and cut into unequal halves by a set of four rocky table mountain massifs running north–south along the centre of the country. Starting in the north, these are the Adrar, Tagant, Assaba and Affolé plateaus. There are also five significant escarpments, known as dhars. The dhars Tichitt, Oualata and Néma ring the Aoukar Depression in the southeast, Dhar Chinguetti protrudes northeast from the Adrar plateau, and El Hank dominates the northeasternmost corner of the country.

Mauritania is in fact fully one-third sand dunes, distributed over 11 main sand seas known as ergs. The largest of these include Erg Makhteir and Erg Ouarane, at the east end of the Adrar plateau system on either side of the Dhar Chinguetti. Several other dune systems dominate the far east of the country, including those of El Mrayyer and Ijafen. Erg Amatlich stretches from the western Adrar towards Nouakchott and contains some of the highest dunes in the country at Azoueiga (page 183). Another quarter of the country is covered by regs, which are wide gravel plains covered in stones and sand (also known as Hamada at higher elevations). The largest of these, Ghallamane and Yetti, predominate in the northeast of the country, and the Tasiast (Tâziâzet) reg covers the hinterlands inland of Nouadhibou. The rather prosaic categories of compact soil, bare rock and rocky soil cover another 25–30%, which includes most of the rocky massifs dominating the centre of the country and some of the elevated Hamada plains. This then finally leaves roughly 12% of the national territory covered by grasslands and savannah, all along the Senegal River and southern border with Mali.

As to be expected in a desert country, water resources are extremely limited, with the notable exception of the Senegal River (and its one permanent tributary in Mauritania, the Gorgol), whose annual flood allows for a significant tradition of both irrigated and rain-fed riverine agriculture along the southern border. A handful of shallow, marshy lakes dot the south, some of which are natural (Lac d'Aleg, Lac R'Kiz, Lac de Mâl), while others are manmade reservoirs (Lac de Foum Gleita). In either case, they vary greatly in size depending on the season. Outside of these, water tends to appear in one of a few contexts, including sebkhas (salt marshes or floodplains), gueltas (isolated rock pools, a number of which host relict

SANDSTORM

Katherine Baird

Taanooy's calls became urgent, her panicked arms waving frantically across the darkening lane. Looking northeast toward the rocky hills of Dow Hayre, I now saw why. A gigantic billowing sandstorm, so large and thick it was blotting out the sun, was churning our way. The edges of it were clearly discernible as it plowed towards us, its trajectory and speed unmistakable.

We'd been warned about these winter sandstorms, when blistering winds came swooping down from the Sahara, picking up and depositing vast amounts of dust and sand along the way. Over the decades the region had lost so much groundcover that now these storms had intensified and increased in frequency. So large and powerful were they that each year they carried away something like one billion tons of dust and sand, the particles sometimes winding up halfway around the world.

I rushed inside to close my two back shutters…frozen with both fear and fascination, I remained standing with my door ajar as the billowing orange sandstorm hit. It was darker than dusk, the sand pelting down like a violent rainstorm while unsecured items hurtled by. I couldn't make out my fence located a mere twenty feet away and was oblivious to the fact that by then my clothes had spun away to join in the mayhem.

It didn't take long for my hair to fill with sand, my eyes to sting, and my curiosity to end. I wrestled my front door shut, and with the help of a flashlight, settled in amidst swirling dirt, pelting sand, and an image of Dorothy's house spinning in the eye of a Kansas hurricane. Could these Harmattan winds uproot a mud hut?

Lacking an answer, I stayed put. For thirty minutes the wind howled, the sands strafed, roofs ripped, cast iron pots cartwheeled by, unprotected animals wailed, and my heart pounded. Then finally, utter silence.

From Growing Mangos in the Desert *(Apprentice House Press, 2022)*

populations of crocodile; page 13) and oueds or wadis (seasonal watercourses) which run for some weeks or months of the year, and are often used for agriculture at other times thanks to the shallower water table beneath.

As on much of the African continent (and in the world), the environmental pressures on Mauritania today are manifold, and in many ways the country's environment has never recovered from the droughts of the 1960s–1980s. Ongoing threats include deforestation, desertification, coastal erosion and biodiversity loss, and environmental preservation remains a seemingly low priority for the state. Though some efforts have been made to stem the tide, for example the Great Green Wall (page 8), the Mauritanian economy is overwhelmingly organised around the extraction and export of non-renewable resources, and it will require a paradigm shift at the highest levels before this changes. On the bright side, however, Mauritania is extremely well positioned to take advantage of renewable wind and solar resources, and a number of initiatives are already underway to begin realising this potential.

Administratively, the country is divided into 15 wilayas or régions (regions; three of which comprise greater Nouakchott), which are then subdivided into 61 moughataas or départements (departments) and 218 communes (municipalities). Wilayas are headed by walis or gouverneurs (governors), moughataas by hakems or préfets (prefects), and communes by maires (mayors).

CLIMATE

Except for most of Guidimakha region and the southernmost reaches of Assaba region, *all* of Mauritania is classified as a hot desert climate (with the Sahelian reaches of Guidimakha and Assaba considered a refreshing 'hot semi-arid' instead). Along the coast, the intensity of temperatures is moderated considerably by the winds of the Canary Current, but it remains desert just the same.

Mauritania essentially has three seasons: rainy, cool and hot. The short rainy season, known as *kharif* or *hivernage*, runs from July through September, though

ON CLIMATE

Nancy Jones Abeiderrahmane

The [Mauritanian] climate is harsh, with searing dry heat in summer, and cold winter nights in the bleak Saharan north; the northern fringe of the African monsoon system sweeps across the southern half of the country from east to west between July and October, and then the whole nation lives around the rainfall. Conversation centres on 'Where did it rain?' 'How much?', while no-one risks a forecast or a glance at the clouds lest it attracts the evil eye and dispels any rain. Special prayers are offered if rain is late, because it has always meant the difference between life and death, survival and hunger.

A week or two after the first rainfall, the first shimmer of brilliant green on the sandy landscape is uplifting, provided it rains again soon enough to ensure continued growth: an unseasonal winter or spring rain, or an early monsoon downpour in June, spell hardship if seeds germinate and the new grass dries out without seeding, sometimes heralding several pastureless, hungry years.

About a week later 'the sheep graze' on brilliant new tender grass. Specific words describe the growth stages: gradually travellers report that 'calves are eating', 'cows are eating', and in the East, 'the grass hides the sheep', 'the grass hides the calves'...maybe even Land Rovers.

This riot of green helps to explain why humans cling on through the terrible long dry season: animals get fat, guzzling frantically from morning to nightfall; later in a good season they even lie down in the shade at noon, sheltering from the leaden sun, at last trusting there will still be some grass left in the afternoon. Herders rest from the toil of drawing water out of deep wells, letting livestock drink in ponds instead. Night time is full of croaking frogs.

Then in October, a ten-day-long blast of scorching dry air called todi or alawa turns the grass to hay. The landscape fades quickly from intense green to ochre and later to dun. The next nine months scarcely see a drop of rain; indeed winter rain is feared because it rots the standing hay. By April any remaining pasture has been blown away by hot winds, and livestock gets thinner and moves farther south.

Rains are irregular: some years they are bountiful, some years they are scant, or just do not come. Even in a good year, rainfall may not be evenly distributed.

Desert dwellers have adapted to this unstable climate and its erratic and unpredictable pasture: instead of harvesting grass, it makes sense to leave it standing, to be grazed by herds moving around making the most of what there is. Provided it does not catch fire.

From Camel Cheese – Seemed Like a Good Idea *(2013)*

this varies greatly in length and intensity depending on where you are in the country. In the Saharan north, Nouadhibou and Zouérate get hardly any rain at all, while the Sahelian Guidimakha can see well upwards of 200mm in the heaviest months. Many families decamp to the countryside at this time of year to bask in the vivid greenery that overtakes the landscape and fattens the herds.

The rains taper off in October, when temperatures can briefly spike as the rains dissipate before the relative chill of winter (*shteu*) sets in from November to March. Here, the weather remains (relatively) cool and dry, offering hot but not unbearable days and reliably cool nights; as such, it forms the heart of the tourist season. It is also peak time for the harmattan tradewinds to start blowing Saharan dust over the entirety of West Africa, free of charge. This harmattan dust can leave the skies a dull, soupy grey, and the omnipresent sand is hard on mechanical items like camera mechanisms – photographers take note! The hot season (*seif*) follows, heating up to some truly stupefying temperatures from March onwards until the rains arrive in July.

NATURAL HISTORY AND CONSERVATION

It's probably worth mentioning straight away that anyone primarily interested in seeking out opportunities for mammal spotting in Mauritania may walk away disappointed. The country's terrestrial fauna was dealt a devastating double blow by the massive droughts of the 1960s–1980s alongside increased poaching during the concurrent Western Sahara War, and has never really recovered. But fear not, there's still much to explore for naturalists casual and dedicated alike, and the country boasts an impressive avian checklist, unexpected relics of reptilian life, offshore odontocetes, and new protected areas dedicated to restoring some of its long-lost ungulate populations.

Mauritania's national parks and preserves are managed under the Ministre de l'Environnement et du Développement Durable (45 24 31 38; e dpcid@environnement.gov.mr; w environnement.gov.mr; f Ministere.Environnement.Mauritanie) and there are now three national parks, with the newest only dating to 2016. There are also a few réserves naturelles (nature reserves) and 30 forêts classées (protected forests), principally in the south, though the large majority of these are unmanned and unmanaged, and certainly not developed for tourism. The private or community-run nature reserves common in other parts of West Africa are largely unknown here, with just a couple of exceptions. Birdlife International (w birdlife.org) has designated 25 sites in Mauritania as Important Bird Areas, and four areas have been recognised as Wetlands of International Importance under the Ramsar convention (w ramsar.org). Additionally, the Parc National du Banc d'Arguin has been inscribed as a UNESCO World Heritage Site since 1989.

PARKS AND RESERVES Starting in the north, the country's northernmost reserve also happens to be its newest: the maritime **Réserve naturelle de la Baie de l'Étoile** (page 146) was only proclaimed in July 2024 and covers roughly 12km^2 in a western extension of the Baie du Lévrier north of Nouadhibou, encompassing a shallow lagoon with associated mudflats, sandbanks and a tidal river to the south. Just a short distance to the south at the end of the Ras Nouadhibou (Cap Blanc) peninsula lies the **Réserve Satellite du Cap Blanc** (page 149). This small 210ha (2.1km^2) reserve was set up in 1986 to protect populations of Mediterranean monk seals living at the base of this wind-beaten peninsula's staggering sandstone cliffs; today it's thought to be the world's largest colony, with several hundred individuals present at last count.

Straight east across the Baie du Lévrier is the 'mainland' to this satellite reserve, the **Parc National du Banc d'Arguin** (page 152) – Mauritania's first national park. Gazetted in 1976, it covers 11,700km^2 of coastal wilderness, including 5,400km^2 at sea and 6,400km^2 on land. Taking in enormous beds of seagrass, expansive tidal flats, mangrove thickets and a barren desert hinterland of barkhan dunes, it's a haven for avian and aquatic life including dolphins, flamingos, shorebirds, sea turtles and more. An ancient caste of fishermen make their living between the more than a dozen islands and islets offshore.

Continuing down the coast, the **Parc National d'Awleigatt** (page 135) is Mauritania's newest protected area, only gazetted in 2016. More of a wildlife sanctuary than wilderness area, it covers 1,600ha (16km^2) some 60km inland of Nouakchott, encompassing a large fenced enclosure which serves as a refuge for a range of local and exotic ungulate species, including scimitar-horned oryx, addax, and other threatened desert species. The zoo portion, however, may be more difficult to recommend, with the presence of both lions *and* tigers seemingly more to do with prestige than conservation. (And on the subject, Nouakchott's Parc National Zoologique et Botanique (page 135) is, despite the name, not a national park as such, and cannot be recommended besides.)

Continuing to the riverine south of the country, the **Forêt communautaire de Loboudou** (page 245) is quite minor as these things go, but merits inclusion as Mauritania's first community forest and 'eco-village', where a degraded local landscape has been meaningfully restored. Inland along the Senegal River between Lexeïba II and Boghé, the forest only covers 18ha, but is a commendable example of community-led conservation and reforestation just the same.

Finally, at Mauritania's southwesternmost tip, the **Parc National du Diawling** (page 232) was gazetted in 1991 and covers 16,000ha (160km^2) of dune, mangrove and wetland in the Senegal River Delta. Along with Senegal's Parc National des Oiseaux du Djoudj just across the river, Diawling is one of the most important sites anywhere in West Africa for migratory birds, and hosts hundreds of thousands of waterbirds annually. The undeveloped **Réserve naturelle du Chat Tboul** (page 238) sits just to the north, taking in 15,500ha (155km^2) around a former mouth of the Senegal River. It's another significant birding site, and the most important place in West Africa for the black-necked grebe. Diawling and Chat Tboul are managed in co-ordination with protected areas on the Senegalese side of the delta as part of the Réserve de Biosphère Transfrontière du Delta du Fleuve Sénégal (RBTDS), encompassing 600,000ha of mixed-use land and water.

Mauritania is also home to a couple of 'phantom reserves', which do not exist in any meaningful sense, but seem to have once existed, if perhaps even then only on paper, and have since disappeared altogether – other than popping up in the occasional ministerial or development agency report rehashing age-old data for the umpteenth time, or even being resurrected as proposals for new reserves. Of these, El Aguer (variously listed as either a réserve naturelle or réserve de faune) is perhaps the best attributed, gazetted in 1937 and supposedly once covering 2,700km^2 north of Tintane to protect a population of several hundred elephants living atop the Afollé escarpment (⊕ 16.727, -10.3411). The last of these was reportedly shot in 1964, and the reserve remains undeveloped. Tilemsi is another parcel existing somewhere in the liminal space between former and proposed reserve, covering 7,000km^2 southeast of Oualata in Mauritania's extreme southeastern corner. These same reports also indicate that the **Richat Structure** (Guelb er Richât; page 204) was once under some kind of protection as well; this is certainly no longer the case, as whether to *make* it a reserve of some sort has been an active topic of discussion

THE GREAT GREEN WALL

Since 2007, Mauritania has been part of a project that is perhaps as audacious as it is necessary – the Great Green Wall. Though the concept was first mooted by naturalists in the 1950s, the accelerating rates of desertification across the Sahel led to the idea being picked up in earnest, and this time adopted by a series of 11 national governments, in the mid-2000s. Beautiful in its simplicity, the crux of the initiative involves planting a 15km wide and 7,100km-long belt of trees across the Sahel, which will eventually run all the way from Dakar to Djibouti and form a massive natural bulwark against the Sahara's southern expansion. Mauritania's portion is planned to run 1,100km through six of the country's southern regions, from Keur Macene in the west to Koumbi Saleh in the east. Senegal to the south is also in on the scheme, so in concept it seems there will be two parallel reforestation routes here. All the better!

The project is off-track to meet its goal of 100 million reforested hectares by 2030, however, with only about 20 million hectares of land reforested so far – given the turmoil in much of the Sahel, this remains slow but encouraging progress. In Mauritania, there's a very long way to go, but more than 12,000ha of land has been reforested so far, striking a small but significant blow against the ongoing deforestation endangering the livelihoods of farmers and herders across the country and continent. The increasing accessibility and use of agricultural drones stands to accelerate the seeding process significantly in the years to come.

The Agence Nationale de la Grande Muraille Verte (45 25 29 03; w angmv-mr.com; f ANGMVmr) oversees the project's implementation in Mauritania, and has established a handful of Fermes Agricoles Communautaires Intégrées (Integrated Community Agricultural Farms) along the proposed reforestation route; the one at Meftah Elkheir was one of the first to be set up (16.8133, -16.0707), and is only a couple of kilometres off the main Nouakchott–Rosso road. It's not intended as a tourist attraction, but the gardens (all run by women) are literally and figuratively the seed of something much larger. If you do swing by for a look, close your eyes for a moment and imagine a future touring the protected forests of Mauritania, while someone 7,100km away in Djibouti is on the Indian Ocean doing the same.

If you happen to be around on 17 June, you can see if the national agency has any activities planned for the World Day to Combat Desertification and Drought.

among the environmental ministry and others for years now. As of 2025, there was an active proposal to turn the area between the Richat Structure and El Ghallaouiya into a 2,000km^2 protected area, but it's unclear if and when this might happen.

FAUNA AND FLORA Though there has never been a comprehensive national wildlife survey, when the Ministry of the Environment themselves write that Mauritania 'no longer has fauna in the true sense of the word', you know the situation has become rather dire. And so it must be said right off the bat that Mauritania is not a conventional wildlife-spotting destination by any means, and there's a 100% chance that cows, camels, goats and sheep will be your primary animal sightings here. But it's also worth remembering that even though not even 1% of Mauritania's land area is officially protected, more than 75% of the country is considered by conservationists to represent the 'last of the wild', ie: the areas of the planet where the human footprint is faintest – so there's still a lifetime's worth of wilderness to explore here.

So indeed, Mauritanian wildlife populations, particularly those of larger mammals, have been decimated over the past half-century, largely thanks to a combination of several rounds of cataclysmic drought, the war in Western Sahara, and ongoing pressures including habit fragmentation, deforestation, desertification, bushfires and pollution. These pressures doomed Mauritania's populations of some of the most iconic African species, including cheetah, giraffe and elephant, which were present until the 1970s, roan, kob, reedbuck, bushbuck and dama gazelle, which were all gone in or by the 1980s, and both African wild dog and lion, which are thought to have hung on in the southern Guidimakha region until the 1990s.

But despair not! All is not lost, and there are still several thrilling wildlife experiences to be had in Mauritania, from clocking the silent trot of a fennec fox (*Vulpes zerda*) along a remote dune, spotting an unexpected crocodile (*Crocodylus suchus*) in a remote mountain pool, or feeling the sea spray from a pod of bottlenose dolphins (*Tursiops truncatus*) cavorting in the Banc d'Arguin. And that's without even mentioning the country's avian treasures – which include the largest gathering of waders anywhere on the planet! So while a trip here is nothing like a textbook African safari, only the most jaded travellers could fail to be moved by Mauritania's epically wild landscapes and the hardy creatures that continue to make them their home.

As is common in Mauritania, there is a significant north–south divide between the Saharan and Sahelian parts of the country, and this is equally visible when it comes to the fauna. Among the livestock, you'll notice there's something of a camel–cow border as you traverse the country, and this rough bifurcation is equally true with wildlife, where there is generally a greater number and greater diversity of species present in the south.

Mammals There are roughly 100 land mammal species found in Mauritania today, though these are often present in low numbers and within small ranges, making them quite hard to spot. As such, few places in Mauritania offer what might accurately be called a game viewing experience, but the opportunities for getting out into the bush are nearly infinite, and one need not visit one of the three official national parks in order to do so.

That being said, the new Parc National d'Awleigatt is probably the safest bet for reliable mammal sightings. It lacks the wilderness atmosphere that you might expect of a national park, however, both feeling and operating more like a wildlife sanctuary than a genuine wilderness park. Nonetheless, it's home to several species that have been extirpated (or very nearly so) elsewhere in the country, including antelopes like the endangered scimitar-horned oryx (*Oryx dammah*) and critically endangered addax (*Addax nasomaculatus*), as well as the vulnerable giraffe (*Giraffa camelopardalis*). The park is home to a number of other antelope species, including rhim gazelle (*Gazella leptoceros*), blackbuck (*Antilope cervicapra*), common eland (*Taurotragus oryx*), Arabian oryx (*Oryx leucoryx*), blue wildebeest (*Connochaetes taurinus*), impala (*Aepyceros melampus*), sable antelope (*Hippotragus niger*), greater kudu (*Tragelaphus strepsiceros*), springbok (*Antidorcas marsupialis*), gemsbok (*Oryx gazella*), nyala (*Tragelaphus angasii*), defassa waterbuck (*Kobus ellipsiprymnus defassa*) and the vulnerable dorcas gazelle (*Gazella dorcas*). Outside of the Awleigatt sanctuary, most antelopes are now locally extinct, but with quite some luck it's still possible to see a few red-fronted gazelle (*Eudorcas rufifrons*) in the south and several dozen dorcas gazelle on the Île Tidra in the Banc d'Arguin.

Maybe the most iconic mammal species remaining in the wild in Mauritania today is the leopard (*Panthera pardus*), though its ongoing presence here seems to be just barely on the right side of extinction. Reclusive and hard to spot at the best of times, official sightings only get recorded about once a decade (but in locations as widespread as Banc d'Arguin and southern Assaba region!), so it would be advisable to not get your hopes up. Alternatively, small numbers of hippopotamus (*Hippopotamus amphibius*) are still periodically reported along the middle and upper lengths of the Senegal River. They once lived along the entire watercourse, but disappeared from Diawling and the lower river in the 1960s.

By contrast, the also iconic – albeit in a somewhat different way – warthog (*Phacochoerus africanus*) may be the most commonly spotted mammal in Mauritania. They have been recorded in several parts of the country, but are by far the easiest to spot in and around Diawling National Park, where they are concentrated in the hundreds. (Indeed, unlike the vast majority of Mauritania's mammals, there are still enough of them to support a small hunting tourism industry – for now, anyway.)

For primates, Mauritania sits along the northern fringes of the ranges of several species, and both green (*Chlorocebus sabaeus*) and patas monkeys (*Erythrocebus patas*) live along the Senegal River and in the semi-forested savannahs and grasslands across the south of the country. There are also several hundred or more Guinea baboons (*Papio papio*) living in the central south, scattered across nearly 100 sites throughout the Tagant, Assaba and Affolé mountain massifs. They are typically found near gueltas or other reliable water sources, not unlike the isolated crocodile populations that survive in the same area.

The African golden wolf (*Canis lupaster*) is fairly widespread along much of the coast and the inland mountain massifs, while the side-striped jackal (*Lupulella adusta*) is also present but much rarer. Striped (*Hyaena hyaena*) and spotted hyena (*Crocuta crocuta*) are both present in Diawling and Banc d'Arguin (as well as elsewhere), and both are rare, but striped is more common. A few near-threatened Barbary sheep (*Ammotragus lervia*) may still be hanging out at the outer fringes of the Adrar, near El Beyedh and the Tarf Tazazmout.

Several types of fox are present, including Rüppell's fox (*Vulpes rueppellii*), pale fox (*Vulpes pallida*) and fennec fox (*Vulpes zerda*). There are also multiple cats and viverrids to be found, including African civet (*Civettictis civetta*), common genet (*Genetta genetta*), caracal (*Caracal caracal*), African wildcat (*Felis lybica*), Saharan striped polecat (*Ictonyx libycus*) and sand cat (*Felis margarita*). Recent records also point to the presence of serval (*Leptailurus serval*) in Diawling National Park and a couple of other locations along the Senegal River. A fair number of honey badger (*Mellivora capensis*) also live throughout the south.

There are also a few mongoose species present, including common slender mongoose (*Herpestes sanguineus*) and Egyptian mongoose (*Herpestes ichneumon*), followed by a large variety of smaller but nonetheless charismatic desert creatures including widespread Cape hare (*Lepus capensis*) and African savannah hare (*Lepus victoriae*) populations, plus rock hyrax (*Procavia capensis*) on the mountain plateaus. The crested porcupine (*Hystrix cristata*), four-toed hedgehog (*Atelerix albiventris*) and desert hedgehog (*Paraechinus aethiopicus*) all make an appearance as well.

Smaller still, there are numerous rodent representatives, including the lesser Egyptian gerbil (*Gerbillus gerbillus*), African striped ground squirrel (*Euxerus erythropus*), Western Saharan spiny mouse (*Acomys airensis*), pouched gerbil (*Desmodilliscus braueri*), pleasant gerbil (*Gerbillus amoenus*) and fat sand rat

(*Psammomys obesus*). It can be hard to tell some of these apart, of course, but there's no mistaking the impressively long-legged lesser jerboa (*Jaculus jaculus*).

Given its status as a somewhat artificial slice of territory covering a subset of two much larger climatic zones, Mauritania has vanishingly few true endemic species, though the charming 'roly-poly rodent' called felou gundi (*Felovia vae*) is close, and the Mauritanian shrew (*Crocidura lusitania*) is not an endemic, but carries the national banner nonetheless.

Finally, there are multiple bat species skittering around in the Mauritanian night, including straw-coloured fruit bat (*Eidolon helvum*), hairy slit-faced bat (*Nycteris hispida*) and Egyptian tomb bat (*Taphozous perforatus*), among others.

For aquatic mammals, see page 12.

Birds For whatever it may lack in mammals, Mauritania amply makes up for in avian life. With an impressively long checklist – a full 580 species, according to Avibase (w avibase.bsc-eoc.org) – there's a world of birding to be done here. At least 25 of these species are globally threatened, and Birdlife International (w birdlife.org) has recognised 25 Important Bird Areas in the country.

These threatened species include several bustards found in arid climes – African houbara (*Chlamydotis undulata*), Arabian bustard (*Ardeotis arabs*), Denham's bustard (*Neotis denhami*) and Nubian bustard (*Neotis nuba*); waders like Caspian plover (*Charadrius asiaticus*), bar-tailed godwit (*Limosa lapponica*) and semipalmated sandpiper (*Calidris pusilla*); birds of prey like the saker falcon (*Falco cherrug*), bearded vulture (*Gypaetus barbatus*) and white-headed vulture (*Trigonoceps occipitalis*); and others like the razorbill (*Alca torda*) and black-crowned crane (*Balearica pavonina*).

Most of Mauritania's Important Bird Areas lack any formal protection, with a couple of notable exceptions. Among these is the Parc National du Banc d'Arguin, where more than 2 million migratory birds gather annually, forming the largest winter concentrations of waders found anywhere in the world. The islands and mudflats of the park provide food and shelter, and significant numbers of greater flamingo (*Phoenicopterus roseus*), long-tailed cormorant (*Microcarbo africanus*) and great cormorant (*Phalacrocorax carbo*), and several species of heron and tern all nest on the islands here.

In the southwestern corner of the country, the Parc National du Diawling is also recognised as an Important Bird Area, and actually has a longer avian checklist than Banc d'Arguin, running to no less than 225 species in just 160km^2. The park's expansive floodplains and mangrove estuary support multiple species of pelican, heron and egret, alongside black stork (*Ciconia nigra*), Eurasian (*Platalea leucoradia*) and African spoonbill (*Platalea alba*), pied avocet (*Recurvirostra avosetta*), African darter (*Anhinga rufa*), black-crowned crane (*Balearica pavonina*), and multiple species of ducks, terns and geese. It's also home to the lesser flamingo's (*Phoeniconaias minor*) only known breeding site in West Africa. The area was hit by an outbreak of avian influenza in 2021, which killed some 250 pelicans in Diawling and at least 750 across the border in Djoudj.

The Mauritanian coast is also home to a couple of local subspecies unique to the area, including subspecies of Eurasian spoonbill (*Platalea leucorodia balsaci*) and grey heron (*Ardea cinerea monicae*). For a deeper dive, there are a few useful bird guides available. The 2010 book *Oiseaux de Mauritanie – Birds of Mauritania* by Paul Isenmann, et al, is, as the name implies, exclusively dedicated to the country, along with Avitopia's 2025 *Birds of Mauritania* (Wolfgang J Daunicht). Nik Borrow and Ron Demey have produced two other books that will be of use, namely *Birds of*

Western Africa (Princeton Field Guides, 2nd edition, 2014) and *Birds of Senegal and The Gambia* (Helm Field Guides, 2nd edition, 2023). Despite the latter being focused on the countries to the south, it is still of considerable utility, especially for sightings in Diawling and along the Senegal River.

Reptiles Mauritania is home to more than 85 species of reptile, and their origins mirror the country's north–south split, with roughly half being considered as Saharan species and half being either Afrotropical or Sahelian. But if there's one reptile in particular that's become an unlikely icon in Mauritania, it's the must-be-seen-to-be-believed desert crocodiles found in the centre of the country. In an extraordinary callback to the region's ancient history, the Tagant, Assaba and Afollé massifs are home to a scattered population of West African crocodiles (*Crocodylus suchus*), relicts of a time long passed when the region was much wetter than today. They live dispersed between 80-plus gueltas (rocky pools at the base of a mountain) and tâmoûrts (floodplains), primarily around the southeast. The densest concentration of sites is on the Tagant plateau, and the Matmata site here is one of the largest and the most commonly visited by tourists. Most of the sites are home to a small handful of crocodiles, and depending on the water availability and conditions at each, some crocodiles are even thought to go into a state of aestivation (the summer equivalent of hibernation) during the hottest months of the year. Some of these groups may be permanently isolated, while others may venture out during the rains, where they can encounter other crocodiles and trade a bit of genetic material before the receding waters force them back to their mountainside redoubts. There are also crocodiles living along the Senegal River, with a notable population in Parc National du Diawling.

The dozens of remote beaches and sandy islets of the Mauritanian coast also serve as occasional nesting grounds for numerous species of sea turtle, and Mauritania represents more or less the northernmost limit of their African nesting range. Between the Banc d'Arguin and Diawling in the south, observed species include green (*Chelonia mydas*), critically endangered hawksbill (*Eretmochelys imbricata*), endangered loggerhead (*Caretta caretta*), vulnerable leatherback (*Dermochelys coriacea*) and olive ridley (*Lepidochelys olivacea*) turtles. On land, the endangered African spurred tortoise (*Centrochelys sulcata*) is also present in the south.

Other reptiles include numerous species of lizards and geckos, including white-spotted wall gecko (*Tarentola annularis*), three types of monitor lizard, and southern long-tailed lizard (*Latastia longicaudata*). Snakes include the Central African rock python (*Python sebae*) and Saharan horned viper (*Cerastes cerastes*).

Aquatic life Mauritania's 700km of harsh and largely uninhabited coastline can look positively barren from above, but there's a rich world of life below, most notably around the Banc d'Arguin. Here, expansive offshore shallows and extensive mudflats are a haven for marine life of all types, and the fishing grounds here have not only sustained the Imraguen people for hundreds of years, but have long attracted fisherfolk from the Canary Islands and further afield as well.

Here, enormous seagrass meadows cover more than 400km^2 in the mudflats and offshore, providing nutrition, shelter and other ecosystem services for a wide variety of undersea fauna, including shrimp, crabs, rays, and cetaceans and marine mammals including long-finned pilot whales (*Globicephala melas*) and many species of dolphins and sharks. These include six species of dolphin and 15 species of shark, among them the iconic hammerhead (*Sphyrnidae*) and tiger sharks (*Galeocerdo cuvier*) and the bottlenose dolphin (*Tursiops truncatus*), which is closely associated

MAURITANIA'S CROCAPELAGO

Some 5,000 years ago during the African Humid Period, the Sahara was once lush and green, cut through by an unknown number of rivers, lakes and the like. In the years since, the drying of the Sahara has seen most of the species requiring a humid home either go extinct or decamp to more amenable climes. But not all of them.

Despite thousands of years of unfavourable climate change and decades of increasing human pressures, Mauritania is home to an extraordinary population of relict **crocodiles** scattered throughout 80-some (known) *gueltas* (rocky pools at the base of a mountain) and *tâmoûrts* (floodplains) around the country, primarily around the Tagant, Assaba and Afollé mountain ranges in the southeast. But their remote redoubts mean they also remain under-studied – a 2011 study found 27 previously unknown sites, a 35% increase over what was previously known – so perhaps you'll even find a new one yourself, should you get deep enough into the Mauritanian countryside.

Most of these sites are home to a small handful of crocodiles each – some perhaps permanently isolated, while others may take advantage of seasonal flooding on the *tâmoûrt* floodplains to encounter other crocodiles and trade a bit of genetic material before the receding waters force them back to their mountainside strongholds.

These crocodile hangouts are generally quite isolated – part of the reason they've survived – but there are a handful that are possible to visit without undertaking a major excursion.

Matmata (⊕ 17.8820, -12.0937), near the towns of Nbeika and Moudjéria, is the most commonly visited crocodile site in Mauritania, and is covered in detail on page 278. But it also sits at the heart of one of Mauritania's four Ramsar wetland sites – (Lake Gabou and the Tagant Plateau hydrographic network) – and crocodiles live scattered in at least 20 different sites nearby, across numerous lakes, wadis, gueltas and floodplains. This includes the wetlands of **El Mechra** (⊕ 17.8600, -12.1701) and **Tamourt Naaj** (⊕ 17.9446, -12.2398), **Lac Gabou** (⊕ 18.2716, -12.364) near the abandoned city of Ksar el Barka (page 277), and **El Gheddiya** (⊕ 17.8349, -11.5580), at the east end of the plateau, and soon to be connected along the new Tidjikja–Boumdeïd road.

Other crocodile sites include **El Mefga** (⊕ 16.6873, -10.1921), 35km north of Tintane, on the Route de l'Espoir between Kiffa and Aïoun El Atrouss, and **El Metrewgha** (or Metraucha; ⊕ 16.5373, -10.7414), less than 5km north of the Route de l'Espoir between Kiffa and Aïoun. The swampy Tâmoûrt Bougâri (⊕ 16.5332, -10.7970) is a few kilometres to the west.

There are many others, including **Oued Foum Goussas** (⊕ 16.5487, -12.0077) and **Le Bheyr** (⊕ 16.5597, -12.0779), which are about 8km apart on the west side of the Assaba Massif, some 30km from the nearest tarmac road towards Barkéol.

Keep in mind that some of these crocodile oases are home to just a few individuals and therefore may require quite some patience to make a sighting.

with the Imraguen fishing tradition. (The Imraguen are the only people allowed to fish in the park, but the waters nearby are a sport fishing haven and outfitters in Nouadhibou can take you out angling for barracuda, grouper, hogfish and more.)

On the other side of the Baie du Lévrier, the Réserve Satellite du Cap Blanc protects the world's largest colony of the world's rarest pinniped, the Mediterranean monk seal (*Monachus monachus*), of which several hundred live in the sandstone caves at the base of the Ras Nouadhibou (Cap Blanc) peninsula.

The Senegal River is also home to some significant underwater residents, including small populations of African manatee (*Trichechus senegalensis*) upriver of the Diama Dam – though you'd have to be incredibly lucky to spot one on a casual visit. The lower river below the dam also sees the occasional oceanic visitors, including dolphins like the Atlantic bottlenose (*Tursiops truncatus*), Atlantic humpback (*Sousa teuszii*), or the harbour porpoise (*Phocoena phocoena*), though you're more likely to encounter any of these at the Banc d'Arguin.

Flora On first glance it would be easy to dismiss much of Mauritania as a desert waste, devoid of significant plant life beyond a few wisps of desert scrub, but this would miss a world of small wonders eking out a living in this harsh desert environment – sometimes with a bit of human help. This is certainly the case when it comes to the country's most symbolic plant, the date palm. These populate dozens of oases across the north of the country, and outside of livestock, traditionally represented the most significant wealth held by the people of the north. As such, the management and harvest of these palms remains an important and well-practised skill, and the oases of the north are populated by more than 200 different cultivars of date palm.

When driving around the country, there are a number of species that provide a bolt of colour through the predominant shades of slate and dun. Keep your eyes out for dandelion-yellow flowers of the gum arabic tree (*Acacia nilotica*), the eye-popping pinks of the desert rose (also known as jackal baobab; *Adenium obesum*), or the purple-and-white blooms of the Apple of Sodom (also known as giant milkweed; *Calotropis procera*).

The southern landscape is a fair bit more vegetated than the north, comprised of archetypal Sahelian grassland and savannah. Here, mile after mile of acacia scrub dominates the southern swathe of the country, with irrigated agriculture increasingly predominant as you approach the Senegal River. In the deep south, the landscape is occasionally punctuated by the inimitable shape of the baobab (*Adansonia digitata*), whose gnarled branches, bulbous trunks and seeming invincibility are immediately recognisable to anyone who's spent any time in Africa.

Along the coast, cordgrasses (*Spartina* spp.) are a common sight near the sebkha salt marshes formed in a number of coastal depressions, and several stands of mangrove still survive in a few tidal or riverine locations, such as in the Banc d'Arguin and Diawling national parks.

HISTORY

PREHISTORY The oldest evidence of human history in Mauritania stretches back several hundred thousand years, with deposits of Acheulean and pre-Achulean hand axes and similar artefacts having been found at several sites, most notably surrounding the outer reaches of the Richat Structure.

The Neolithic period, starting 5,000–10,000 years ago, left behind considerably more archaeological evidence, including rock paintings, pottery shards and many arrowheads, blades and other hunting tools. The earliest identifiable group in Mauritania is thought to be the Bafour, who were present in the area as early as 5000BCE. The Bafour presence coincides with the peak years of the African Humid Period, better known as the 'Green Sahara', during which the region was densely

ROCK ART

Mauritania sits at the southwestern fringe of the Saharan Neolithic rock-painting area, and is home to many rock-art sites, particularly throughout the Adrar and Tagant, where there are several dozen recorded sites scattered between the two regions. These are a mix of engravings and paintings (with the former being most common), and most date to within the last 4,000 years. Many tend to be small or significantly degraded, however, and are therefore infrequent destinations for casual visitors.

Nonetheless, the corpus of Mauritanian rock art includes many interesting figures, including creatures still to be found – cows, camels and crocodiles; as well as those long since disappeared – rhinos, elephants, lions and giraffe. There are also many human representations, including hunters and dancers, horses and riders, and even technological depictions like chariots.

Mauritania's most-visited rock-art site is certainly that of Amogjar (page 190). El Ghallaouiya (page 206) is the next most significant, and other noteworthy sites include El Beyedh (page 205) and Mont Guilemsi (page 281). There are other sites to be found near the ancient Tichitt settlements (see below) Taoujafet guelta (page 281) and Tin Labbe (page 203).

The British Museum has a good selection of photographs online (w africanrockart.britishmuseum.org/country/mauritania), and for a comprehensive index of the numerous Adrar and Tagant sites which goes far beyond the purview of this guide, see the (French-language) pages listed below, which contain maps, photographs and descriptions:

w prehistoireouestsaharienne.wordpress.com/2020/05/30/les-peintures-rupestres-de-ladrar-de-mauritanie-les-stations-damogjar
w prehistoireouestsaharienne.wordpress.com/2020/05/30/les-peintures-rupestres-de-ladrar-de-mauritanie-ii-autres-stations
w prehistoireouestsaharienne.wordpress.com/2025/05/10/inventaire-des-peintures-rupestres-du-plateau-du-tagant-2

vegetated and supported hunter-gatherers, who were able to take advantage of large wildlife populations including elephants, giraffes and rhinoceros.

Many of these hunters would eventually adopt a pastoralist lifestyle, first harvesting and then propagating local grains like barley, and Mauritania is thought to be home to one of West Africa's earliest complex societies. Known as the Tichitt Tradition, this prehistoric culture flourished between 2000BCE and 200BCE and spread across several hundred kilometres on the northern fringes of the Aoukar Depression in eastern Mauritania, which at that time was home to expansive wetlands and palaeolakes.

The Tichitt settlements, of which some 400–500 ruined examples remain, sat just above this massive basin, perched on the long sandstone escarpments hemming in the basin to the north and east, today known as Dhar Tagant, Dhar Tichitt, Dhar Oualata and Dhar Néma. The thousands of residents here lived an agro-pastoral existence, herding cattle and harvesting barley, and many of the ruins still visible today are thought to be pens for cattle or other livestock. (For some good armchair travel, many of the Tichitt Tradition ruins are easily spotted with satellite imagery – indeed the technology has allowed for perhaps the first-ever comprehensive cataloguing of Tichitt sites.)

When the lakes at the base of the escarpment began to dry up and they could no longer reliably water their cattle or crops, they began to abandon these villages and move south. Eventually situated in their new southern homes, fact, many speculate that the descendants of these industrious refugees from ancient Tichitt would go on to found another of West Africa's most important states, the Ghana Empire, some centuries later.

For a deeper dive into the prehistory of the western Sahara, see the remarkably comprehensive (French-language) info at w prehistoireouest saharienne.wordpress.com.

THE RISE OF EMPIRES AND SPREAD OF ISLAM (CE300–1200) Just as they do today, north–south linkages and exchange defined the trajectory of ancient Mauritania, and its territory has played both peripheral and central roles to a diverse array of peoples and polities in centuries past.

The **Amazighs (Berbers)** began to arrive in numbers in what is now Mauritania from the Maghreb from about CE300, and arriving with the advantage of domestic camels, they quickly became influential and displaced, enslaved and assimilated the settled Bafour over the next several centuries. **Islam** also arrived in the region from the north and east, starting with the Umayyad Caliphate's 7th-century invasion of the western Maghreb under General Uqba ibn Nafi. The new faith began to percolate south into what is now Mauritania along Saharan trade routes in the 8th and 9th centuries, with many Amazigh groups converting in this period. The main Amazigh tribes in the area (Lamtuna, Gadala and Massufa) began to coalesce into the **Sanhaja Confederation** around the same time. This loose confederacy of nomadic pastoralists and desert traders would soon come to control most of the trade routes across the Western Sahara, including the key city of Aoudaghost, which itself dates to the 5th century and would soon become the most important centre for the Sanhaja, particularly the Lamtuna. Situated at the southern fringe of the Sahara and the northern edge of the Ghana Empire, Aoudaghost was ideally positioned to take advantage of trade from a variety of sources.

By the end of the 10th century, the **Ghana Empire** had moved in to control Aoudaghost. Tracing its origins to at least the 6th century CE, the Soninké-dominated Ghana, also known as Ouagadou (Wagadu), controlled a significant territory in southeastern Mauritania and western Mali, with (from the 10th century at least) its capital at **Koumbi Saleh**. It was a powerful trading empire, acting as a middleman between the goldfields of the south and the salt caravans of the north. Dating to the 7th century, **Oualata** was one of Ghana's most important centres, and eventually overtook Aoudaghost as the preferred terminus of the trans-Saharan trade starting in the 11th century, after which Aoudaghost began a long and terminal decline.

The Halpulaar-dominated **Takrur Empire** was Ghana's contemporary and rival to the west, centred along the banks of the middle Senegal River on either side of today's Senegal–Mauritania border. Positioned at a highly strategic junction for both Saharan and riverine trade, it's thought to have been founded before CE800 and to have been a well-established ironworking civilisation by the time it first appeared in the historical record in Andalusian Muslim geographer Al-Bakri's 1068 *Book of Roads and Kingdoms*. As with Ghana to the east, Takrur's development was intimately linked with its trade partners further north in the Maghreb, and in the first half of the 11th century the Takruri king War Jaabi became the first West African monarch to convert to Islam. Ghana's leadership and inhabitants, on the other hand, remained staunchly animist, a choice that would soon attract the attention of one of the most significant movements the Western Sahara had ever seen.

This movement was that of the **Almoravids**, a politico-religious faction that arose within the Sanhaja Confederacy. The leaders of the Gadala, one of the confederacy's constituent tribes, felt that their people were only nominally Islamicised and sought to rid them of animist beliefs and promote a more orthodox interpretation of the faith. To that end, they recruited theologian Abdallah ibn Yasin to spread the word in their communities, but his severe interpretation of the religion's strictures alienated many and he was soon shunned. Along with some followers, he withdrew and constructed a new base or *ribat* (frontier monastery-fortress) around 1041, which some believe to have been on Île Tidra in the Banc d'Arguin. (This is where the Arabic term for the Almoravids [and the Mauritanian national football squad], *al mourabitoun* or 'those from the ribats', comes from.)

A couple of years later, Abdallah ibn Yasin and his followers returned from their island redoubt with the vengeance of the spurned, forcing the Sanhaja to comply with their austere brand of Islam. He recruited heavily among the Lamtuna and allied with Islamicised Takrur, and within 15 years his fanatical movement had conquered both Aoudaghost (in 1054) and the Maghrebian city of Sijilmasa, hundreds of kilometres away at the desert's northern edge (in 1055). The Almoravids were therefore able to control and profit handsomely from the most important trans-Saharan caravan routes, cementing their power and enabling them to enforce widespread conversions. So despite the fact that Abdallah ibn Yasin continued to alienate many and was killed in a Gadala-Sijilmasa uprising in 1059, his two successors, Yusuf ibn Tashfin in the north and Abu Bakr ibn Umar in the south, would nonetheless manage to found the city of Marrakesh in 1062 (moving their capital here from the Adrar city of Azougui), take Koumbi Saleh from the Ghana Empire in 1076, and even cross the Mediterranean to seize Muslim Andalucia by 1091.

The war with Ghana and sacking of Koumbi Saleh ultimately triggered the conversion of the Soninké, but just as quickly as it arose, the Almoravid movement collapsed, extinguished at the hands (and swords) of the **Almohads** from the Atlas Mountains around 1150. The Almohads were focused on the Maghreb and Iberia rather than the Sahara, so Abu Bakr ibn Umar's southern fiefdom carried on a bit longer, but the writing was on the wall and this too soon collapsed. Though their control only lasted just over a century, the Almoravid cultural impact was significant, leaving behind a uniformly Islamic population following the Maliki school of jurisprudence. The Sanhaja Confederation was much diminished after the ructions of Almoravid rule, but the tribes continued to practise their time-tested traditional occupations of trans-Saharan trade and herding in the centuries that followed.

EMPIRE AND DISINTEGRATION (1200–1600) After the fall of the Almoravids, both Takrur and Ghana were on the decline, and the newly founded (by the celebrated Sundiata Keita) and rapidly ascendant **Mali Empire** captured Koumbi Saleh, levelling the deathblow against a weakened Ghana in 1240. It quickly set about absorbing what was left of Ghana, and this expansionist empire of Mandé peoples would soon become West Africa's most important state. Training its sights west towards southern Mauritania and Senegambia, under General Tiramakhan Traore the Casamance and Gambia river basins were both conquered and incorporated into the previously landlocked empire, offering it access to the sea and plentiful lands for Mandé settlers from the east. The coastal Aoulil (Awlil) saltworks near today's Tiguent (page 240) roughly marked the empire's northwestern limits.

Meanwhile, the **Jolof Empire**'s foundation likely took place somewhere between 1200 and 1350, and it's to here that modern-day Wolofs trace their identity. Founded by a semi-legendary prince named Ndiadiane Ndiaye, the empire's territory was primarily in what is now northwest Senegal, but Jolof's writ also extended across the river into southwest Mauritania, and it eventually controlled much of the land between the Gambia and Senegal rivers. Though directly in the line of its westward expansion, Mali did not conquer the neighbouring Jolof and Takrur empires outright, but turned them into vassal states instead. There was a rivalry between the tributaries, though, and Jolof would soon overtake Takrur as Senegambia's dominant state, occupying it directly in the 15th century.

For nearly two centuries Mali was far and away the most powerful empire in the region, and it remains famous for Mansa Musa (Kankan) Keita's 1324 hajj, where he sent gold prices all along his caravan route to Mecca into a years-long slump thanks to his enormous wealth and profligate spending. Such was the Malian taste for grand gestures that Musa Keita only took the throne because the previous mansa, Abubakari Keita II, had abdicated in order to lead a 2,000-boat expedition into the Atlantic and was never heard from again (though a small handful of scholars argue the seafarers may have reached Brazil).

Just as Oualata began overtaking Aoudaghost as a node for trans-Saharan trade in the 11th century, it was itself overshadowed by the legendary city of Timbuktu starting in the late 14th century. And while it may have had a golden age unparalleled in the region, by the mid 15th century Mali's fortunes had soured and the empire found itself firmly on the defensive. Squeezed from the east by the breakaway **Songhai Empire** around Gao and no longer able to effectively exert its authority over its vassals in the west, Mali lost control of Timbuktu to Sonni Ali's Songhais in 1468. A successor to the defeated Tekrour known as **Great Fulo** (or the Denyanke Kingdom) arose at the beginning of the 1500s and began to fight Mali from the west, and by the end of the 16th century, the empire had all but collapsed. Rival Songhai was even shorter-lived: the Moroccan Saadi dynasty sent troops to sack Gao, Timbuktu and Djenné in 1591 in a successful effort to assert control over trans-Saharan trade routes.

The era of the great successive West African empires of Ghana, Mali and Songhai therefore came to a close around 1600, and the remains of Mali and Songhai splintered into numerous smaller kingdoms and fiefs. The Moroccan sacking of Songhai and years of subsequent instability in the wake of the empires' disintegration was an enormous blow, and was particularly detrimental to the area's religious and intellectual life, as it sent thousands of refugees, particularly Islamic scholars and educators, fleeing.

Many of these learned and lettered refugees arrived in the ancient Mauritanian cities of Oualata, Ouadane, Tichitt and Chinguetti and brought their scholarly tradition with them, hugely augmenting the towns' cultural and intellectual production and reputation. Indeed, the refugees fleeing to Oualata ultimately reversed its decline, and the city began to attract an increasing number of Arab residents from northern Mauritania around the same time. The growing Arab presence and associated changes in population and social dynamics throughout the country would soon touch off a conflict whose effects are still being felt today.

ARRIVAL OF THE BENI HASSAN AND THE CHAR BOUBA WAR North and west of these great Sahelian empires, the Sanhaja-inhabited territories began to see the arrival of Beni Hassan Arabs starting in the 13th century. The **Beni Hassan** (sometimes Bani or Banu Hassan) are a sub-tribe of the Bedouin Maqil Arabs, who trace their origins to the area around Yemen in southern Arabia. The Maqil began a great migration from Arabia across North Africa in the 11th century, eventually reaching the Maghreb and continuing a nomadic Arabian way of life equally suited to Maghrebian climes. The Beni Hassan eventually migrated south, first arriving in Mauritania in the 13th century and over time seeking to gain control of the Saharan trades previously dominated by the Sanhaja. This process was met with fierce Sanhaja resistance, and the centuries to come were defined by this Hassan-Sanhaja power struggle.

The 14th to 17th centuries also saw expanding desertification in the north, spurring migration to the south in search of pasture by Beni Hassan and Sanhaja alike. This increased competition for limited water resources further aggravated the Sanhaja–Hassan relationship, as well as increasing conflicts with the largely black agriculturalists in the southern river valley. Though over the centuries a number of alliances and intermarriages between the Beni Hassan and Sanhaja did take place, the overall trend (and Hassan aim) was towards the entrenchment of Hassani control and marginalisation of the Sanhaja, including the enforcement and collection of the horma, a protection tax levied on vassal tribes. For people of black African descent, the Hassani arrival was even worse, and often meant expulsion towards the Senegal valley or abduction and enslavement.

In this context, the Sanhaja often had 'little choice but to go south or to make peace' in the face of the Hassani invasion, and it was clear that they were slowly being muscled out of most positions of power in the lands and trades where they previously reigned supreme. It was in this context that a Sanhaja holy man from the Lemtuna tribe named Nasr al-Din launched the rebellion that would define Mauritanian social structures up to the present day. As with so many military-political movements in the region, al-Din defined his fight as a jihad against those unfaithful to Islam, but it was in practice as much a last-ditch attempt to stem the tide of Sanhaja subjugation as it was a religious war.

Known as the **Char Bouba War** (or Shar Bouba etc), it was fought in southwestern Mauritania 1644–74, and is occasionally known as Mauritania's Thirty Years' War. Though the conduct of the war itself is poorly documented, there were at least three major battles between the Sanhaja forces of Nasr al-Din and the Hassanis led by Haddi ould Ahmad ould Daman. The last of these, the 1674 battle of Tin Yedfad was a catastrophic loss for the Sanhaja, marking the final nail in the coffin for their aspirations to rule in Mauritania. The peace settlement agreed in its aftermath was the apotheosis of the multi-century campaign to entrench Hassani power.

In the agreement, the Sanhaja were officially vassalised, forced to pay the horma tribute and forbidden from all political and military power. The Arab Hassanis were to be the warriors and emirs from here on out, while the Amazigh Sanhaja became known as 'Zénaga' and were relegated to secondary status.

The Arabisation of Mauritania was also significantly advanced, as many Zénaga sought to abandon their Amazigh identity, adopting the Hassani's language, Hassaniya Arabic, and their cultural traditions, including following patrilineal lines of descent. Others worked to cultivate a scholarly status and took up religious roles, becoming known as **zawiya**, or marabouts, and earning a considerably higher status than that of Zénaga – though still no right to involve one's self in political or military affairs. Given the social advantages attached to Arab lineage, many zawiya found ways to claim Arab heritage over the generations, and today very few Mauritanians claim Amazigh extraction. The hierarchical social organisation of Mauritania today can largely be traced to the aftermath of Char Bouba – for a fuller explanation of the castes that developed in the wake of Char Bouba and their functions today, see page 34.

The aftermath of the war also paved the way for the political groupings that would dominate Mauritania for the next two centuries, from the late 17th to the early 20th. These are four main Hassani tribal confederations known as **emirates**. The first of these to arise was **Trarza** in the southwest, followed shortly by **Brakna** just inland; both of these coalesced in the late 17th century and took advantage of a growing trade in gum arabic with the recently established European trading entrepôts near the Senegal River. To the north and inland, **Tagant** and **Adrar** organised into emirates in the middle of the 18th century; being further from the new coastal trading posts, they continued to rely more heavily on the centuries-old trans-Saharan trade routes. Along the river, the Denyanke dynasty supported Nasr al-Din's revolt, but after its failure continued to rule Great Fulo until they themselves were overthrown during a revolt by the Halpulaar *torodbe* clerical class in 1776. The torodbe founded the revivalist **Imamate of Futa Toro**, which fought against the Trarza and Brakna emirates into the 19th century.

The appearance of Europeans along the coast and the subsequent reorientation of centuries-old trade routes would have enormous repercussions for the region, shifting the balance of power between inland and coastal tribes, and challenging the raisons d'être of several desert settlements.

EUROPEAN CONTACT Portuguese navigator Nuno Tristão captained the first European ship to reach what is now Mauritania. Dispatched by Henry the Navigator in 1441, Tristão's first voyage took him on an exploratory mission down the coasts of what is now Western Sahara, where he encountered another Portuguese navigator, Antão Gonçalves, somewhere around today's Dakhla. Junior in rank to Tristão, Gonçalves had been dispatched to the area not to explore, but rather to hunt the monk seals that were once ubiquitous in the area (and now have their final redoubt at Cap Blanc, page 149). Having successfully filled his ship with skins and lard, Gonçalves abducted a local they encountered on shore. He led them to a settlement, where Gonçalves and Tristão abducted another ten or so Amazigh-speaking captives, among them a nobleman named Andahu. With this, Gonçalves returned to Portugal and Tristão set about rounding Cap Blanc. What was to become more than four sordid centuries of the Atlantic slave trade had officially begun.

Tristão was back only two years later in 1443, continuing past Cap Blanc until he encountered a settlement on Île d'Arguin in today's Banc d'Arguin National Park. Wasting no time in raiding the village and returning to Portugal with another dozen-plus captives, his journey set off a 'gold rush' of several dozen would-be slavers who ransacked the area. The Portuguese set up a trading post on the island in 1444, and despite the area's low population density, ten years later the port at Arguin was sending some 800 enslaved people to Portugal every year. (Tristão, meanwhile, was slaking his greed around Senegambia until he was killed by locals in either the Gambia or Sine-Saloum rivers around 1447.) A stone-built fort, one of the oldest European structures in Africa, was completed at Arguin in 1461. A corresponding inland fort, the Fort d'Agoueïdir (page 205), was supposedly built in the interior around 1487, though at more than 500km straight inland from the coast, the history and provenance of this purported outpost are rather enigmatic, particularly as it lacks any contemporary precedent on the continent. Regardless, Arguin remained a Portuguese outpost dealing in gum arabic, enslaved people and gold until it was conquered by the Dutch in 1633 as part of the Dutch–Portuguese War.

The three ships of the Dutch West India Company, the *Jager*, the *Noortsterre* and the *Regenboog*, had no trouble overpowering the 14 Portuguese soldiers inside, and – other than a few months of English occupation in 1665 as part of the Second

Anglo-Dutch War – Arguin remained Dutch until the French swooped in during the Franco-Dutch War in 1678. They did not occupy the island, however, but instead simply knocked down the fortress and abandoned it.

At the same time, France was busy setting up what was to become their most important post in the region: Saint-Louis, at the mouth of the Senegal River. In 1638, a number of French slave traders, including the navigator Thomas Lambert, built a small outpost on Bocos Island; 21 years later in 1659, after flooding made operations on Bocos Island untenable, Louis Caullier, a Norman trader with the Compagnie du Cap Vert, erected the first permanent buildings on the previously uninhabited Ndar Island, ceded to the French by Djambar Diop (also known as Jeanne Barre), son of the brak (king) of the Wolof kingdom of Waalo. It was soon renamed after the reigning French monarch, Louis XIV, and made capital of the Senegal colony in 1673 (a position it held all the way until 1902).

Though just outside of today's Mauritanian borders, Saint-Louis was still the country's most influential entrepôt, and trade via Saint-Louis completely reshaped the economies of southern Mauritania, the Senegal River valley and beyond. The early settlement was managed by the various mercantile companies based here, and the Trarza and Brakna emirates did considerable business at Saint-Louis (and a series of *escales* established along the river) trading slaves and gum arabic sourced from the hinterlands north of the Senegal River.

Back on Arguin, the Margraviate of Brandenburg (later Brandenburg–Prussia) occupied the abandoned island in 1685, with Captain Cornelis Reers arriving with the *Rother Löwe* frigate and setting up a post to support their slaving efforts between Fort Fredericksburg in their Brandenburger Gold Coast colony (now Ghana) and Saint Thomas in the Caribbean. From Arguin, they also traded in salt, fish and even ostrich feathers. Arguin changed hands yet again in 1721, touching off a decade of Dutch–French rivalry in the area, which ended with the fortifications once again being destroyed, and the island definitively abandoned by Europeans in 1728. They would not return until around 1880, when an abortive French fish factory was built.

It was in 1721 again that, still wishing to maintain its interests in the area and perhaps hedging its bets over Arguin, the Dutch founded another outpost to the south, known as Portendick. The port itself already existed in some form – its name is thought to be from a deformation of a Portuguese name, Porto d'Addi or Portudaddi, after Haddi ould Ahmad ould Daman, who led the Trarza Emirate in the Char Bouba War and was the first Mauritanian emir to establish trade relationships with the Europeans in the second half of the 1600s. But there was little infrastructure here, and the site was only occupied during the gum-arabic harvest or trading season. Dutch efforts to maintain a permanent outpost were short-lived, with France destroying their fortifications in 1724. So while there was no permanent fort or settlement and it was increasingly overshadowed by the growing settlement at Saint-Louis, a number of British, French, Dutch and other traders continued to visit the port and conduct business with the Trarza Moors living in Portendick's hinterlands until the 20th-century French colonial takeover.

THE 19TH CENTURY AND THE BIRTH OF MAURITANIA Though the 1814 treaty of Paris affirmed French sovereignty over Senegal and Mauritania, France continued to be little interested in the Mauritanian territories to the north – just so long as the emirates kept themselves largely north of the river and the desert trade in gum arabic, salt and other goods kept flowing downriver to Saint-Louis. To that end, the Senegal colony exercised some authority in escales on either side of the river, which served as the meeting points between nomadic Moors and French or Senegalese traders, from where goods would make their way downriver to Saint-Louis.

French abolition of the transatlantic **slave trade** began in 1818, reordering trade routes that had become oriented around coastal ports in recent centuries; trans-Saharan routes saw a resurgence in popularity after the oceanic trade was outlawed (though a clandestine trade continued here as well). Slavery remained legal in French colonies until its 1848 abolition in the wake of the French Revolution, and the Mauritanian emirates would continue to practise slavery well into the 20th century.

France first became meaningfully involved north of the river in 1833, when a marriage alliance between Trarza emir Mohammed al-Habib and Ndieumbeutt Mbodj, the linguère (queen) of Waalo (one of the Jolof Empire's successor kingdoms), threatened to cut off Saint-Louis. The French sought to discourage any unification of these two states straddling the lower river and attempted to sabotage the marriage. When it went forward anyway in 1833, they launched a series of punitive campaigns, later known as the **First Franco-Trarza War**; Mohammed al-Habib was ultimately forced to sign away his claims (and those of his descendants) to Waalo in 1835.

Other than this, the first colonial governor to show significant interest north of the river was the expansionist Louis Faidherbe (whose tenure began in 1854), who sought to accelerate the French penetration of the Senegal River and seize control of the surrounding gum-arabic and other trades. To that end, the French built forts in Podor (1854), Médine (1855) and Matam (1857). The **Second Franco-Trarza War** was fought for reasons quite similar to the first, plus a new alliance with the neighbouring Brakna Emirate; its conclusion spelled the end of independent Waalo under linguère Ndaté Yalla Mbodj in 1855, and the definitive relegation of Trarza and Brakna's activities to the north side of the river. The famous **Battle of Leybar Bridge** took place during this war, when Faidherbe was away on a punitive expedition into the Trarza during April 1855. Trarza leader Mohammed al-Habib knew of the governor's plans, and decided to instead take a force to sack an undefended Saint-Louis while Faidherbe was away. Unfortunately for the Terrouzi forces, a new defensive tower had recently been built at the foot of the bridge (the only access to the island city), and the 14 French soldiers left behind here were able to stave off the emir's army and force their retreat from the city gates.

Faidherbe then largely turned his attentions to conquering and securing Senegambia for France, and it wasn't until 1899 that the name Mauritania was first used to refer to what was, at that stage, seen as little more than the empty space between French territories in Senegal and Algeria, and a place to secure the ever-coveted supplies of gum arabic and salt. This amorphous landform had never been given one name (or considered as one territory) before, but rather was known to Hassaniya speakers as two distinct entities, the Trab el-Bidhan (the land of the whites) and the Trab es-Soudan (the land of the blacks). The political landscape began to take its current shape with the French–Spanish Treaty of Paris; signed in June 1900, it delimited the boundaries between the then Spanish Sahara and what was to eventually become Mauritania.

The man behind this new appellation was one **Xavier Coppolani**, an Algerian-born Corsican who, unlike most of his peers, was fluent in Arabic and Islamic customs, and therefore uniquely positioned to advocate for French interests in the Hassanophone hinterlands. He advocated for the so-called *colonisation pacifique*, or peaceful colonisation, and pacification of Mauritania, essentially through the co-optation of Moorish power structures through alliance with the zawiya marabout clans. Though second in power to the Hassani warriors, the zawiya marabouts often wielded considerable influence, moral authority and popular support, and were frequently consulted by Hassanis for religious and social guidance.

Coppolani's proposal to the zawiya was one in which they would not only gain in status as the allies of the powerful French, but equally be unburdened by the internecine raids, succession struggles and other conflicts between Hassani tribes (both within and between emirates) that would often leave their communities in distress; they would be freer to study, propagate Islam, and take advantage of trading opportunities in a context free of conflicts that they derived no benefit from.

These influential zawiya, once allied with Coppolani, would seek to persuade the Hassani leadership to accept French control through the promise of greater returns from trade than raids, and with the implicit threat of French military action behind. Though he consistently advocated for a decidedly hands-off approach to governing Mauritania and an independently directed Moorish society, in Coppolani's own words, the choice offered was between 'co-operation with financial rewards, or resistance with military consequences'.

Being the closest emirate to Saint-Louis, Trarza was Coppolani's first approach on the north side of the river. Having been destabilised during the Franco-Trarza wars of the 19th century, as well as an early 20th-century succession crisis between the French-backed Ahmed Saloum and Ould Sidi Mohamed Fall, Trarza was an obvious first target. Having enlisted the assistance of influential marabout **Cheikh Sidiyya Baba**, soon to become Coppolani's right-hand man, they were able to persuade the rulers of Trarza to accept French control by the end of 1902. The Mauritanian protectorate was declared in 1903 and Coppolani was named its first governor.

The collaboration between Cheikh Sidiyya Baba and Coppolani continued apace, with other influential supporters like **Cheikh Saad Bouh** (son of Fadiliyya Qadiriyya Sufi order founder Mohammad Fadil ben Mâmîn) mobilising the Sufi brotherhoods and their networks in support of the French cause, on the basis that the stability provided by French rule provided fertile ground for the propagation of Islam. With this influential support, French control spread quickly: Brakna was brought under the colonial umbrella in 1904, and Tagant in April 1905.

But it's here that Coppolani's luck runs out. Mohammad Fadil ben Mâmîn had another son besides Saad Bouh, and he was similarly influential, but took the opposite position as his brother, fiercely resisting all collaboration with the French and their agents. This was **Cheikh Ma El Ainin**, who based himself in Smara (in today's Western Sahara) and the Adrar, allying himself with the Moroccan Alawite dynasty and launching a jihad against the French power encroaching from the south. On 12 May 1905, his followers in Tidjikja killed Coppolani at home, ending the era of colonisation pacifique and throwing France's plans to absorb the Adrar into disarray.

The next couple of years saw repeated attacks from Cheikh Ma El Ainin and his followers against France and the emirates and tribes who had allied with France, but they failed in their mission to dislodge the new colonial order, and the 1907 appointment of Colonel Henri Gouraud as governor was the beginning of the end for Ma El Ainin's resistance movement. At the start of 1909, France launched its most significant military campaign in Mauritania, and the colonne de l'Adrar (Adrar Column) began its march from the French-held Tagant. They quickly captured the town of Atar, but a deadly stalemate set in as back-and-forth attacks between the opposing sides failed to land a decisive blow. The French then set about occupying the Adrar's many oases, denying Ma El Ainin and the Adraris the dates and water sources so critical to life in the region and therefore provoking a series of battles where the French were able to best the anti-colonial forces and bring the final of Mauritania's four traditional emirates, Adrar, fully under their control. (The French campaign and Adrari resistance are featured in the Musée d'Amatil, page 179.)

Though pockets of resistance and raiding remained, particularly around the Adrar and among the northern Reguibat tribe, the Mauritania protectorate was made into a full-fledged colony and incorporated into Afrique Occidentale Française (French West Africa) in 1920. The last major razzias (raids) took place in the early 1930s, including the famous one of Oum Tounsi (page 136). But French rule in Mauritania was indirect and largely hands-off, with colonial authorities preferring to leave Moorish socio-political life largely untouched. For example, to bring Mauritania into line with its other colonies, colonial authorities officially abolished slavery in 1905, but the edict went almost entirely unenforced and slavery continued throughout the colonial era.

Therefore, the colonial experience in Mauritania, despite giving the country its current shape and name, has otherwise been described as 'late, turbulent and superficial'. The colony's difficult conditions, fiercely independent people and limited resources (as it was seen at the time) meant that the colonial influence on society in Mauritania was lighter than in many of its contemporaries, and produced cultural and societal shifts that were less profound than those found in other parts of West Africa.

French influence was in many cases limited to little more than the construction and maintenance of military posts around the country, and there was never a colonial settler population to speak of. The Moorish population largely shunned the idea of colonial schools, so most colonial educational infrastructure was built in the south and served the Afro-Mauritanian population. The first teacher training college did not open until 1950 (in Boutilimit), and up until at least World War II, life in the colony looked little different than it might have several centuries prior. Indeed, the colony was so neglected that its capital city between 1920 and 1957 was officially Saint-Louis, situated extra-territorially in the neighbouring colony of Senegal. Geographically, Mauritania took on its current shape in 1944, when today's Hodh el Gharbi and Hodh ech Chargui regions were transferred from French Sudan (today's Mali) to the Mauritania colony during the administration of Governor Laigret.

As with the rest of French West Africa, Mauritania allied with the Vichy regime during World War II and remained under Vichy control until the successful Allied invasion of French North Africa in Operation Torch persuaded the authorities in Dakar to switch sides at the end of 1942. Tens of thousands of African troops, some in divisions known as the Tirailleurs Sénégalais, fought to liberate France from the Nazi and Vichy regimes; Mauritania's small and rural population means that there were fewer recruits than in neighbouring Senegal, but Mauritanians were still represented among Allied troops.

INDEPENDENCE After World War II, questions of independence among colonised peoples began coming to the fore around the world, and France began to expand the political rights extended to its colonial subjects. In 1946, the loi Lamine Guèye (named for the Senegalese politician who was the first African with a doctorate in French law) extended certain citizenship rights to some of France's colonial subjects, including the ability to elect delegates to the French National Assembly and representatives to local Conseils Généraux (General Councils). Mauritania therefore constituted its first political party, the Entente Mauritanienne, and elected its first representative to the national assembly, Horma Ould Babana, that same year. He was unseated by a Union Progressiste Mauritanienne (UPM) candidate, Sidi el-Mokhtar N'Diaye, in 1951. Though N'Diaye had little political reputation, his part-Moorish, part-Wolof ancestry was a potent symbol for the UPM's inclusive message.

The UPM also dominated in the first Mauritanian Assemblée Territoriale (successor to the Conseil Général), which was formed in 1952; the UPM took 22 of 24 seats, with the other two going to the Entente Mauritanienne. The 1950s saw further changes in France's administration of its colonies, but perhaps none more significant than the 1956 loi cadre, which expanded on the loi Lamine Guèye and extended voting rights to all Mauritanians, not just a 'qualified' few. The 1957 Assemblée Territoriale elections were the first to be held with this expanded voter base, but the results changed little, with UPM taking 33 of the 34 seats.

At the time Mauritania's only lawyer and among its only university graduates full stop, **Mokhtar Ould Daddah** was elected to the governmental council in 1957, but had his sights set much higher. Influential thanks to his qualifications and good relationship with the French authorities, he soon sought to use this influence to unify the nascent Mauritanian political scene. Seeking to create the biggest tent possible in his deeply divided country, the influential Daddah convened the nation's political actors at the Congrès d'Aleg in February 1958 at which a new party, the Parti de Regroupement Mauritanien (PRM), was formed out of several previous rivals, with Daddah at the helm.

The French-educated Daddah himself was at first not at all an advocate of full independence, but favoured maintaining continued close ties with France as part of a federal system. He, along with his new PRM party, very successfully (94%!) campaigned for a vote to remain in political union with France during the 1958 referendum in French West Africa, an option only rejected by French Guinea, which would receive an abrupt and punitive independence later the same year.

Still, the winds of change were blowing on the continent, and Guinea's example hastened the demise of the envisioned but ultimately abortive French Union. More than a dozen French territories were granted independence in 1960 alone, and Mauritania was no exception. The new Islamic Republic of Mauritania was the final French territory to gain independence that year, becoming independent on 28 November 1960 with Mokhtar Ould Daddah as its first president.

The new republic certainly had its work cut out. A divided populace, few nationwide institutions, and an enormous and sparsely populated territory with next to zero surfaced roads would be enough of a challenge, but the new nation was also faced with an aggressive neighbour to the north: much like with Western Sahara, Morocco also had territorial designs on Mauritania and claimed it as part of a historical 'Greater Morocco' until long after Mauritania's independence. Rabat did not officially recognise Mauritania's independence for a decade, only establishing diplomatic relations with Nouakchott in April 1970. Though today it's closely associated with the Arab world, the Moroccan threat meant that Mauritania's early years were defined by pursuing much closer relationships with black Africa and France.

Meanwhile, first president Mokhtar Ould Daddah's position was reaffirmed when he was elected unopposed in 1961. Daddah was a self-consciously unifying figure, repeatedly referring to his country as the 'trait d'union', or link, between North and sub-Saharan Africa. But this obsession with unity, perhaps out of fear of the deep social chasms he was all too aware of in the country, would soon show a dark side. Daddah convened another conference at the end of 1961, appropriately enough called the Congrès d'Unité, at which he convinced several opposition parties to form a new unified party under Daddah's leadership. The Parti du peuple mauritanien

(PPM) was henceforth the only legal party, and Mauritania was officially declared a one-party state in 1964. The country's slide into authoritarianism was confirmed at the Congrès de Kaédi in the same year, when Daddah declared that all candidates to the Assemblée Nationale would have to be approved by the PPM's politburo equivalent, the Bureau Politique Nationale.

With the young state's political organs effectively captured, Daddah was free to pursue his authoritarian vision of a unified Mauritania, but was not free from the prospect of unrest, often along sectarian lines. This was the case in 1966, when he announced that Arabic would henceforth be the language of all education above the primary level, touching off protests in the south, where French was strongly preferred. He was re-elected unopposed in the same year, however, and enjoyed an improving economic situation as the iron ore mine in Zouérate was beginning to reliably fill the state coffers. Another election in 1971 saw the same result.

After Morocco abandoned their claim to the country in 1970, Daddah had a freer hand to push back on French interests and pursue the stronger links to the Arab world he desired. In 1973, the country joined the Arab League and withdrew from the Communauté Financière Africaine (CFA) currency union which was closely associated with French West Africa, instead introducing a new currency of their own, the ouguiya. In 1974 came nationalisation of the French-owned MIFERMA, previously responsible for exploiting the iron ore mine in Zouérate.

But Daddah's biggest geopolitical move of all was in fact a collaboration with the erstwhile enemy, Morocco. It would also prove to be his downfall. Signed by Spain, Morocco and Mauritania in November 1975, the Madrid Accords promised to divide the Spanish Sahara between Morocco (two-thirds) and Mauritania (one-third). This agreement entirely froze out the Polisario Front, which had been agitating for the region's independence since 1973. Spain officially withdrew from the territory in 1976, touching off a war between Morocco, Mauritania and the Polisario Front, which has in various forms continued until the present day.

The same year, Polisario began attacking Mauritanian territory, conducting raids as far as Nouakchott and attacking the mining infrastructure at Zouérate. The former may have been embarrassing to the regime, but the latter was striking at what was far and away their number one source of income. Daddah held another unanimous election, this time theoretically including voters from their newly annexed Tiris El Gharbiya territory in the southern Western Sahara. But the territory was at war, and increasingly so was Mauritania itself. Polisario attacks paralysed the railway almost entirely from 1977, dramatically crippling the Mauritanian economy. The situation for Mauritania was so dire that they invited both French air support (Opération Lamantin) and Moroccan ground troops into the country to prop up the regime against the Polisario.

But the threat to the Daddah regime was already inside the house; the Saharan war was the straw that broke the one-party camel's back, and President Daddah was overthrown by **Colonel Ould Salek** in July 1978, touching off several years of military intrigue and political churn. The Mauritanians sued for peace with the Polisario, relinquishing their claims to the territory and signing the Algiers Agreement in August 1979.

The post-Daddah period would see multiple attempted and successful coups. The last of these may have also been at least in part triggered by Sahara policy, as **Ould Haidallah** was overthrown shortly after extending formal recognition to the Polisario-led Sahrawi Arab Democratic Republic (SADR) in 1984. In his place came another military man, **Colonel Ould Taya**, who would rule until he himself was overthrown in 2005 (besting Daddah's time in office by a full three years).

The early Ould Taya years were marked by another great crisis, this time on the southern border. Latent ethnic tensions, suppressed under Daddah's rule, rose to the surface, including the dramatic appearance of an Afro-Mauritanian paramilitary group known as Forces de Libération Africaines de Mauritanie (FLAM) advocating for the overthrow of not only the military regime but of the Bidhani elite in the country. In 1986 FLAM published their inflammatory treatise, Le Manifeste du Négro-Mauritanien Opprimé (Manifesto of the Oppressed Black Mauritanian), and the state cracked down hard; the outlawed group's supporters, or perceived supporters, were rounded up, jailed and tortured (often at Oualata Fort, page 301) in a wide-ranging regime clampdown.

In 1989, these tensions exploded when a localised but fatal conflict between Mauritanian herders and Senegalese farmers over grazing rights touched off a diplomatic feud and ethnic pogroms against those perceived to be citizens of the opposing country, typically along racial lines. Senegalese and Mauritanian interests in Nouakchott and Dakar were torched and dozens killed, the border was closed, and diplomatic relations between the two countries were severed. In under two

DROUGHT AND SEDENTARISATION

Just a few years after its independence in 1960, the fledgling state of Mauritania was thrown into an existential crisis that would profoundly alter not only the future development of the country, but imperil and eradicate the ancient livelihoods and lifestyles that had governed life here for many centuries past. This epochal event was the *grande sécheresse* (great drought) of 1968–73.

On the cusp of this great drought (in fact to be the first of several), 65% of the Mauritanian population lived a traditional nomadic lifestyle. Just over a decade later in 1977, the percentage was almost exactly reversed: 64% of the population was now sedentary. To call this an enormous social change hardly scratches the surface: since time immemorial, Mauritanians have kept their wealth in livestock, which were now starving to death in waves, leaving families bereft and penniless. People who could began fleeing the countryside in droves. Nouakchott, whose foundation stone was laid only a decade prior in 1958, was expected to have 8,000 residents by 1970 – instead it had 70,000. Famine set in and thousands died.

Further droughts followed in 1976, 1983–84 and 1990–91, each one further grinding the country's traditional livelihoods into so much Saharan dust. Nomads who had hung on through the previous crises, often barely, were wiped out once again, and more and more gave up and headed to pitch their khaïmas in the *kebbe* slum districts of climate refugees now surrounding Nouakchott and other major towns. The 1,100km Route de l'Espoir between Nouakchott and Néma was in part built to alleviate difficulties in accessing and aiding the areas of the country hardest hit by drought – hence the name – and even though its presence improved conditions for many, it also facilitated and accelerated the rural exodus already underway. Today, only a small percentage of Mauritanians continue to live a truly nomadic lifestyle.

In addition to their destabilising effect on the people, these prolonged droughts also ravaged the land, triggering a significant acceleration of the desertification process. The 1968–73 drought alone is thought to have expanded the desert by 150,000km^2, and today an estimated 85% of Mauritania is subject to ongoing desertification pressures.

months, an estimated 170,000 Mauritanians and 75,000 Senegalese had fled to their country of origin, and as many as 53,000 Fulbe, Toucouleur and other Mauritanian citizens of black African ethnicities were labelled as foreigners and forced into Senegal. Diplomatic relations were restored and the border was reopened in 1992, but several thousand Mauritanian refugees remain in villages along the Senegalese and Malian borders, even today.

The 1990s saw Ould Taya initiate certain constitutional reforms, and multiple political parties were legalised in 1991. Mauritania's first multi-party elections were held in 1992, and though Ould Taya easily won, were noteworthy as the first Mauritanian presidential elections to feature more than one candidate on the ballot! Elections in 1997 saw Ould Taya and his Parti Républicain Démocratique et Social (PRDS) easily win again, though much of the opposition boycotted the vote, alleging an unfair contest.

THE 21ST CENTURY Despite joining the organisation as a founding member in 1975, Mauritania began the new millennium by withdrawing from the Economic Community of West African States (ECOWAS) regional grouping in December 2000, thereby cementing the long-term reorientation towards the Maghreb pushed by successive governments. (Mauritania is also a founding member of the 1989 Arab Maghreb Union, though disagreements over Western Sahara mean this organisation is effectively gridlocked and inactive.) First president Mokhtar Ould Daddah died in 2003. (His French-born wife, Mariam Daddah, became a beloved figure in the country and lived in Nouakchott until her death in 2023.)

The first few years of the new millennium were marked by increasing dissatisfaction with Ould Taya's long autocratic rule. The June 2005 jihadi attacks on **El Mreïti** which killed 15 soldiers (page 217) aggravated discontent within the military, and after more than 20 years, Ould Taya's reign came to an abrupt end in August 2005, when he was overthrown in a coup while out of the country attending King Fahd's funeral in Saudi Arabia. Colonel **Ely Ould Mohamed Vall** took power as chairman of the Conseil Militaire pour la Justice et la Démocratie (Military Council for Justice and Democracy, CMJD). The CMJD promised a return to civilian rule, and set about organising a constitutional referendum in 2006. This introduced a two-term limit to the presidency and reduced the term from six years to five. It also introduced an upper age limit for the presidency, forbidding candidates over 75 years old. They held presidential elections in 2007, which, true to their word, neither Vall nor any other members of the ruling junta contested.

Veteran politician **Sidi Ould Cheikh Abdallahi** was therefore elected in the second round of voting (against first president Mokhtar Ould Daddah's half-brother, Ahmed Ould Daddah) in March 2007, marking Mauritania's first-ever democratic presidential election. But not everyone was satisfied with Cheikh Abdallahi's rule or the democratic direction of travel, and when he attempted to purge a number of top-ranking military officers in August 2008, a coup led by former CMJD higher-up **Mohamed Ould Abdel Aziz** sent him packing.

Abdel Aziz declared himself president of another military junta, known as the Haut Conseil d'État (High Council of State), promising a corrective to Cheikh Abdallahi's supposedly irresponsible rule and a more robust response to the mounting security challenges in the region (as exemplified by the 2007 murder of four French tourists and their Mauritanian guide near Aleg). Assuring that new elections were imminent, Abdel Aziz stepped down as president of the Haut Conseil d'État so that he could contest these in 2009. Abdel Aziz won with 52% of the vote, representing his newly formed political party, Union pour la République

(UPR). He stood again in 2014, and an opposition boycott saw him walk away with 82% of the vote.

A 2017 referendum abolished the country's bicameral legislature, removing the Senate in favour of a unicameral National Assembly. It also changed the national anthem and added some sporty red stripes to the flag, signifying 'the efforts and sacrifices that the people of Mauritania will keep consenting, to the price of their blood, to defend their territory'. Having served his two terms (and then some), Abdel Aziz did not contest the elections in 2019. Instead, these pitted retired army general **Mohamed Ould Ghazouani** (representing Abdel Aziz's UPR) against anti-slavery activist Biram Dah Abeid. Ghazouani won in the first round with 52% of the vote and, although the opposition challenged the results, the 2019 elections are generally regarded as Mauritania's first-ever peaceful transfer of power. After more than a decade of calm, the 2023 Nouakchott prison break saw the deployment of an enormous security operation, which tracked down the escaped jihadis in a matter of days.

The elections of June 2024 saw a rematch between Ghazouani (now representing a rebranded UPR known as Insaf) and Dah Abeid, in which Ghazouani was re-elected with 56% of the vote. Representing the Pôle de l'Alternance Démocratique, an alliance between the Sawab and Refondation pour une Action Globale parties, Dah Abeid took 22%. Ghazouani's second five-year term expires in 2029, and is constitutionally his last.

In what seems like a victory for Mauritania's democratic consolidation, former President Abdel Aziz was investigated on charges of embezzlement, money laundering and abuse of power starting in 2021. He was ultimately convicted and sentenced to five years on a variety of corruption-related charges in December

ON MODERNITY *Nancy Jones Abeiderrahmane*

To be mobile, the Bidhan live(d) in beautiful tents supported on two long poles leaning on each other at the top like an A. Traditionally, tents were made of hand-spun, hand-woven wool or cotton, and more recently of white fabric lined with brightly coloured patchwork (with layers of old clothes in between for enhanced shelter from the sun and rain). The Fulani move(d) between peanut-shaped grass huts of a summer camp and a winter camp, although recently dairy herders have adopted tents for improved mobility.

Was pastoralism the first form of livestock husbandry, later replaced by sedentary farming, or was it receding rainfall that drove sedentary populations to move? The latter is certainly plausible in the Sahara, which was covered with wet, lush savannah five thousand years ago, as witnessed by crocodiles left behind in some highland pools. Pastoralism should therefore be appraised as an evolved system, not as a relic of the past.

In fifty years, a unique people has leaped through centuries and cobbled together a country of sorts, and, despite the achievement is understandably finding it hard to catch up with the rest of the world.

Deep-rooted Islamic culture and history, ancient wisdom, centuries of subtle poetry and scholarship in a complex language, are losing ground to money, consumption, globalised TV, politics, and a modernised version of the thousand-year-old merchant tradition.

From Camel Cheese – Seemed Like a Good Idea *(2013)*

2023. Abdel Aziz appealed the ruling, but in May 2025, he not only lost the appeal, but was instead re-sentenced to 15 years.

And while significant military involvement and influence in the political, media and business landscape in Mauritania continues – nearly every leader of the country, democratically elected or not, has had a military background – the past few years have shown encouraging signs of a nascent democracy beginning to find its feet, and a teetering security situation begin to stabilise. (Plus a potential natural gas bonanza on the horizon...) How long will it continue? *Allahu a'alam!* (God knows best!)

GOVERNMENT AND POLITICS

Mauritania is one of only three self-declared Islamic republics in the world (the other two being Iran and Pakistan), and the constitution declares that 'Islam is the religion of the State and of the people'. As such, most civil law derives from Islamic Sharia ('the only and unique source of law', again per the constitution), though some elements of French civil law inherited from the colonial era remain.

Though Mauritania's post-colonial political history is predominantly one of one-party rule and a series of military coups d'état, recent years have seen a string of increasingly credible elections, and 2019 saw what is generally considered to be the country's first peaceful and democratic handover of power. The military remains a significant player on the political scene (indeed President Ghazouani is himself a former officer and Minister of Defence), but this is to date Mauritania's longest period of multi-party civilian rule and another satisfactory presidential election in 2024 continued to cement this trend.

Today, the government operates under a unitary semi-presidential system, in which there is an executive president elected by popular suffrage and an appointed prime minister accountable to the country's 176-member unicameral parliament (Assemblée Nationale), which is itself elected using a mix of proportional (88 seats) and majoritarian (88 seats) systems. There are 15 parties represented in the current (10th) assembly, with President Ghazouani's El Insaf (Equity Party) the largest by far with 107 seats. The next-largest parties, Tewassoul and the Union pour la démocratie et le progrès (UDP), have 11 and ten seats, respectively.

The Cour Suprême (Supreme Court) is led by a court president (appointed for a renewable five-year term) and four chamber presidents dealing in administrative, civil/commercial, social and criminal law.

Freedom House (w freedomhouse.org) categorised Mauritania as 'partly free' in 2025, calculating a score of 39 points out of 100 when measuring political rights and civil liberties. On the Economist Democracy Index, Mauritania consistently scores right on the border between 'hybrid' and 'authoritarian' regime, oscillating back and forth between the two categorisations over the last 20 years.

ECONOMY

In 2023, Mauritania's exports totalled just under US$5 billion, of which iron ore and gold each accounted for about one-third of total exports (68.5% together, and 72% including copper). Fisheries-related products account for nearly a quarter, including frozen fish, fish oils, processed crustaceans and more. This all totals up to roughly 95% of all exports, with the remainder a mishmash of agroproducts including melons, cotton, fertilisers and machinery. As such, agriculture is best understood as being of major importance in terms of employment, but is marginal in terms of export value; livestock exports are similarly miniscule. Depending on the year, anywhere between 25 and 40% of exports go to China (primarily iron and copper ore), while Switzerland (for gold) and Spain (for fish) are the preferred export partners in Europe. Canada and the UAE are also popular destinations for Mauritanian gold. Less than 1% of exports go to the UK, mostly iron ore.

And while mining, fishing and agriculture have long been the (unequal) pillars of the Mauritanian economy, the discovery of several enormous offshore hydrocarbon deposits in the 2010s is set to upset this balance entirely, and will soon catapult Mauritania on to the list of top ten Liquefied Natural Gas (LNG) producers worldwide. The country's 6.5% annual growth rate and US$10.65 billion GDP (both 2023) are expected to spike, and Mauritania joined the Gas Exporting Countries Forum (GECF) in 2023.

The Greater Tortue Ahmeyim gas field was discovered 120km offshore along the maritime border with Senegal in 2015. This 33,000km² block is being developed jointly between the two countries (alongside BP and Kosmos Energy), and is thought to contain up to 1,400 billion cubic metres of natural gas. The first well, among Africa's deepest at some 2,850m underwater, was officially opened on 31 December 2024, and the two countries aim to produce up to 2.5 million tonnes per year in the first phase of production. A further 2.5 million annual tonnes is expected in several years during an eventual phase two.

In 2019, Mauritania found another bonanza gas field 125km offshore, known as BirAllah. The deposits here are found nearly as deep underwater, but this time fully within Mauritania's exclusive economic zone. Though it's not set to come online until 2030, it's estimated that this field alone could produce up to 10 million tonnes of gas per year. (For comparison, Russia is the world's fourth-largest LNG exporter, and clocked 31 million tonnes in 2023.) All told, the two fields together could have more than 3,100 billion cubic metres of gas that Mauritania is quite keen to exploit.

Not content to be a débutante in the LNG world alone, though, the Ministère du Pétrole, de l'Energie et des Mines (Ministry of Petroleum, Energy and Mines; w petrole.gov.mr) has also stated they would like to see Mauritania become Africa's largest producer and exporter of hydrogen. To that end, they have begun to distribute exploitation blocks on land: Chariot Energy Group and TotalEnergies completed feasibility studies on their Project Nour in 2024, proposing a 10GW green hydrogen and ammonia plant on a 5,000km² wind and solar park north of Nouakchott. South of the capital, Danish developer GreenGo Energy has a similar project in mind, known as Megaton Moon; they were awarded 1,000km² of land for wind and solar in 2025, soon to power a proposed 6GW green hydrogen and ammonia plant of their own.

Beyond solar and wind, Mauritania also hopes to provide the fuel for nuclear power in the form of uranium. Along the country's eastern edges, the Australian developer Aura Energy received government approval for the Tiris Uranium Project in 2024, which plans to mine uranium from two 'world-class' deposits near Chegga and Aïn Ben Tili starting in 2026. They hope to produce nearly 1,000 tonnes annually, which would also put Mauritania in the top ten uranium producers worldwide.

But as for projects that are actually online *today*, there's no-one place as important to the Mauritanian economy as the Kedia d'Idjil mountain outside Zouérate, which is made almost entirely from impressively pure iron ore, and has been exploited – and almost single-handedly propping up the Mauritanian economy – since the 1960s, when the famous iron ore train first hit the rails. Administered by the Société Nationale Industrielle et Minière (National Industrial and Mining Company;

SNIM), the mine accounted for just under 10% of Mauritanian GDP in 2022, representing 22% of state revenue and 32% of all exports.

The Tasiast Gold Mine north of Chami is another heavy hitter for the Mauritanian purse. This gigantic open-pit mine is administered by Tasiast Mauritania, a subsidiary of the Canadian Kinross Gold Corporation, and has been active since 2010, extracting something like 11.5 million tons of gold every year. But the Mauritanian gold sector is increasingly crowded. Since 2016, artisanal miners have taken up shovels and picks (and quite a bit more) en masse, decamping to the far-flung, uninhabited deserts around Chami, Chegga and Aïn Ben Tili in hopes of cashing in on a modern-day Klondike. The Mauritanian state has approved of the trend, setting up processing and purchasing infrastructure near the miners' outposts.

Though it doesn't dominate the economy like iron ore and gold, copper is another significant Mauritanian export, and has been so for many years. The Guelb Moghrein Mine near Akjoujt started production in 1970, and is today administered by Mauritanian Copper Mines, a subsidiary of the Canadian First Quantum Minerals. Nowadays these enormous open pits produce roughly 13,400 tons of copper per year, effectively all of which goes to China.

Finally, fish and other products from the sea account for nearly 25% of Mauritanian exports, tallying up to almost US$1.2 billion in 2023. Fishing in Mauritania takes a variety of forms, from the artisanal practices of the Imraguen to the traditional pirogue crews seen at the Port de Pêche in Nouakchott. But the most controversial, and economically consequential (to say nothing of conservationally), method is that of the foreign commercial fleets that trawl Mauritanian waters. The Chinese-owned Hong Dong Fisheries began operations in Nouadhibou in 2011, building a US$100 million dedicated facility and launching a fleet of some 170 boats. The Hong Dong port is the largest facility of its kind in the country, processing fish for export and into fishmeal. Depending on the product, Mauritanian fish exports tend to go to different places. Fresh fish often end up in Spain and southern Europe, while frozen fish are popular on the West African market. Fishmeal goes to China and East Asia, where it is used as agricultural feed.

BUSINESS The Agence de Promotion des Investissements en Mauritanie (APIM; w apim.gov.mr) promotes Mauritania in international investment fora and offers a single window system for would-be investors in Mauritania. APIM and the Mauritanian government more broadly are increasingly active in courting outside investment and seeking to develop private investment opportunities in the country.

PEOPLE

A casual visitor to Mauritania is very unlikely to meaningfully unravel what one academic describes as the 'Moorish social labyrinth', but the intricacies of ethnicity, caste and tribe remain consequential social signifiers in Mauritania, and as such it's worth taking some time to get to grips with the broad strokes of social organisation in this diverse country.

At its broadest, there are three primary divisions among Mauritanians to remember. The largest group is that of the Hassaniya-speaking **Moors**, from where the country's name derives. Moors themselves are divided into **Bidhan** (the so-called white Moors) who formed the traditional aristocracy, and **Haratin** (the so-called black Moors) who were traditionally their slaves or tributaries. The Bidhan are of primarily Arab-Berber (Amazigh) descent, while the Haratin are of largely black African ancestry, though these distinctions are not categorical.

There is also a significant non-Moorish, non-Arabised segment of Mauritanian society, whose traditional territories straddle the boundary between Mauritania and Senegal or Mali to the south. These include the Halpulaar, Soninké and Wolof, each of whom has their own language and traditions distinct from those of the Moors. Collectively, these groups are referred to by a variety of names, including Afro-Mauritanien, Négro-Mauritanien, *Mauritanien noir*, black Mauritanian, or the Hassaniya term **Kouar** (Kwar). As Afro-Mauritanien and similar terms might appear overly broad or unclear to a non-local or non-specialised audience, we have opted to use the term Kouar when referring to these groups collectively, as this categorisation is both readily understood within Mauritania and less ambiguous to foreign readers.

The Mauritanian census does not disaggregate information on who belongs to which group, and as such it's very difficult to ascertain with any accuracy how the population is divided between these groups. Given the sensitivities surrounding ethnicity and belonging that exist within Mauritania, and the many associated implications for political power and representation, the numbers are often furiously contested, with little hard evidence available to back them up. With all those caveats in mind, a reasonable estimation might put the numbers at 40–45% Haratin, 25–30% Kouar, and 25–30% Bidhan.

Geographically speaking, Moors are predominant in the north and east of the country, with Bidhan particularly concentrated in the north and Haratin in the east (though both groups are found throughout the country). Kouar live primarily in the south, and as with everything else in Mauritania, all roads lead to the ethnically mixed city of Nouakchott.

MOORS The Hassaniya-speaking Moors are a heterogeneous population, descended from a mix of Arab, Berber and black African ancestors. Though separated by traditional castes, they are united by a common language, culture and faith. The primary division in Moorish society is between **Bidhan** ('white Moors') and **Haratin** ('black Moors'), though this is not nearly as clear-cut as the 'white' and 'black' nomenclature might imply, and the distinction is best understood not as primarily one of skin colour, but rather one of social status.

These divisions have their origins in differing interpretations of patrilineal descent, where the children of a free, Arab-speaking male, regardless of his own background (Arab, Berber or black African), would be considered Bidhan, even if, as was historically often the case, the mother was a slave or concubine of primarily black African descent. Conversely, the children of an enslaved male, no matter his background (or that of the mother), would be considered Haratin. As such, both Bidhan and Haratin are quite heterogeneous populations, and skin colour alone is not an accurate way to distinguish between them. Indeed, you may find yourselves surprised by 'black' Haratin who are fairer in complexion than some 'white' Bidhan.

Bidhan society is largely divided into two 'noble' castes, the **Zawiya** (known as marabouts, clerics) and the **Hassan** (known as guerriers, warriors). This division has its origins in the 1644–74 Char Bouba War (page 19), in which the Sanhaja Berber population unsuccessfully revolted against the more recently arrived Beni Hassan Arabs. Militarily vanquished, the Sanhaja Berbers pivoted away from seeking military control and instead leaned into a scholarly and monastic tradition, providing religious services to the newly ascendant Hassan warriors. This social distinction persists today, with Zawiyas overrepresented among religious occupations, and Hassans in military service. A third Bidhan caste is that of the **Zénaga** (Znaga, Lahma), who represent a tributary or vassal class among the Bidhan, frequently associated with camel herding or other manual labour. (As the formerly

THE MOOR YOU KNOW

Prior to arriving in Mauritania, it's fairly likely that the only Moor you know could be Othello, the Moor of Venice. But Shakespeare's famous character is quite unlikely to have ever passed through Nouakchott. In the Middle Ages, 'Moor' was an amorphous term referring to any Muslim North African (or Andalusian), regardless of their Amazigh, Arab or African origins.

The term's origins stretch as far back as the first century CE, to when Romans conquered and named the province of Mauretania after an Amazigh group they referred to in Latin as the Mauri. This Roman province, founded in circa CE44, covered what is today northern Morocco and Algeria, so like modern Ghana, modern Mauritania takes its name from an ancient kingdom in an entirely different location. 'Mauri' would eventually morph into the 'Moor' of Shakespeare's time, but did not become attached to what we know now as Mauritania until the end of the 19th century.

In the modern era, Mauritania was first used to describe the lands of the western Sahara by Xavier Coppolani, who in 1899 proposed the French take control of the territory between Senegal and Algeria. The so-called Moors living in this newly christened polity (who were indeed Muslim North Africans of Amazigh and Arab heritage) would have instead referred to themselves as either Bidhan (the so-called white Moors) or Haratin (the so-called black Moors).

And while the Bidhan and Haratin designations still have currency, Moor today has grown from an amorphous term into a specific one, referring only to the Hassaniya-speaking group of people who live in Mauritania and surrounding countries. Of course, today's Mauritania is not purely Moorish, and therefore the term for all citizens of the country, Moorish and non, is simply Mauritanian.

enslaved class, Haratins are also associated with manual occupations, but today are more associated with cattle or sheep herding than camel.) Bidhan society is further subdivided into numerous descent-based clans or tribes known as qabil, each of which traces their origins to a putative common ancestor; each qabil is divided further into extended lineages called fakhdh and smaller kinship groups called ahel.

Similar to many West African societies, including those who trace their histories to the Mali Empire, Moorish society also has several occupational castes, who are often socially stigmatised, or at minimum considered subservient or tributary. Most occupational castes are populated by Haratin, but Znaga Bidhanis fulfil these roles as well. The **Mallemin** are traditionally engaged in blacksmithing and artisanal pursuits; a blacksmithing class also exists among the Kouar, where they are known as baylo (Pulaar), tègé (Soninké) and tëgg (Wolof). The **Iggawen** are the traditional court musicians, praise singers, historians and entertainers of Moorish society. Among the Kouar they are known as gawlo (Pulaar), gesere (Soninké) and géwél (Wolof). These praise singers are found throughout much of West Africa, and are best known to outside audiences by the French word *griot*.

Finally, **abid** is the term for a person who is currently enslaved. This, quite predictably, was considered the bottom rung of the Moorish social hierarchy, and a distinct status from Haratin who may have had enslaved ancestors (or had been enslaved themselves), but were now free. Despite the ongoing controversies surrounding the lasting nature of dependent relationships between Bidhan and

Haratin in Mauritania today and which of these might or might not be justifiably described as enslavement, the term is not in common use today (indeed the state's official stance is that there are no abid left in Mauritania), and carries a predictable amount of baggage alongside.

Haratin lives today can look very different, depending on the family circumstances. Many Haratin have cut ties with their 'patron' family entirely and live independently, and there are many small villages throughout the countryside with an almost exclusively Haratin population, where they practise agriculture and raise cows and sheep. As might be expected, these are, on the whole, somewhat poorer than their Bidhan counterparts. Many Haratin live independently in Mauritania's cities as well, engaging in trade, artisanry and other occupations. (An increasing number also now sit in government.) But a significant share of Haratin also maintain a relationship with their historical 'patron' family, in which they occupy a 'client' status vis-à-vis their Bidhan patrons. In these relationships, perhaps somewhat comparable to sharecropping, the Haratin family is free to move, trade or work as they please independently, but will still be expected to perform certain roles for the Bidhan family, which could include housekeeping, animal care, or the provision of a share of the harvest.

KOUAR (AFRO-MAURITANIEN) Within the 25–30% Kouar (Afro-Mauritanien) population, the Halpulaar are the largest group, thought to make up more than half of all non-Arabised Mauritanians. For this reason, they were especially targeted during 'The Events' of 1989 (page 262) in an effort to stymie their political power. The Halpulaar are followed in descending order by the Soninké and the Wolof; the Bambara (page 41) are also sometimes included among the Kouar, though they enjoy no official legal recognition in Mauritania.

Halpulaar Mauritania's largest non-Moorish group is the **Halpulaar**, who form part of an enormous ethno-linguistic group numbering more than 40 million people living in nearly two dozen countries stretching from Senegal and Mauritania in the west to Sudan, the DRC and the western fringes of Ethiopia in the east. Though usually referring to themselves as **Fulbe**, there's quite a bit of local variation in naming, and they're also commonly known as Fulani, Fula and Peul. They speak the Pulaar language, which is also variously known as Fulfulde, Fula or Fulani, again depending on where you are.

Halpulaar is something of a catch-all term used in Mauritania; it simply means Pulaar speaking (in Pulaar, of course), and is employed to include Fulbe subgroups resident in the country, most notably the **Toucouleur**, who are culturally and ethnically similar, but rather than living as nomadic pastoralists as Fulbe traditionally do, they have long been settled farmers and fishers in the Senegal River valley, and as such consider themselves a distinct but closely related group. (Their name derives from a French corruption of Takrur, from the ancient Senegal River empire.) As climate and other factors have encouraged more Fulbe to try their hands at a settled livelihood, the distinction is perhaps less meaningful than it once was, but Toucouleur nonetheless maintain their own identity as a separate branch of the enormous Fulbe family. They began to adopt Islam as far back as 1030CE with the conversion of War Jaabi, the king of Takrur, an empire that stretched along either side of the middle Senegal, roughly approximating the Halpulaar heartlands even today.

Halpulaar/Fulbe society is also highly stratified, with a traditional hierarchy separate from, but in certain ways parallel to, that of the Moors. The noble Rimbé class is divided between the scholarly Torobé and warrior Sebbé, while other occupational castes exist for fishing (Soubalbé) and woodwork (Laobé), and the Mathioubé were traditionally the lowest-caste serfs or slaves.

Soninké Also sometimes known as Sarakolé or Sarakolleh, the Soninké (who speak an eponymous language) are considered among the region's oldest inhabitants, as it's thought that the ancient residents of the Neolithic settlements on the escarpments

SLAVERY

One of the few ways that Mauritania has penetrated the general global consciousness is also among the most sordid. The country unfortunately holds the distinction of being the last in the world officially to ban slavery – in 1981 – and even this was largely symbolic and unenforced. Today the topic remains an extremely delicate issue in the country, where arguments over the nature of enslavement and who can be considered enslaved remain.

The historical capture and enslavement of rival groups was a widespread historical practice in Africa and beyond. Amazigh groups were involved in capturing and trafficking black Africans to the north for many centuries, but the racialised, hereditary character of Mauritanian chattel slavery took shape, accelerated and was religiously codified with the Arab arrival in the Maghreb and the arrival of Beni Hassan in Mauritania from the 13th century onwards (page 18).

Slavery is in fact the institution most responsible for creating Mauritania's current socio-cultural make-up. Africans who were captured, enslaved and Arabised over generations eventually formed a new and distinct cultural identity mirroring that of their captors. Enslaved people are known as *abid* in Hassaniya, but these acculturated descendants of slavery have come to be known as Haratin, or black Moors (page 34). Haratin language and traditions are closely connected to those of the Bidhan, or white Moors, but they nonetheless occupy an inferior position in the Moorish social hierarchy – a position that some modern scholars have compared to apartheid.

The institution was so entrenched in Moorish society that, despite a 1905 French decree forbidding the practice, the colonialists largely considered it more troublesome and disruptive than it was worth to enforce the ban. Despite the independence constitution's promises of equality being seemingly at odds with keeping citizens in bondage, the medieval practice nonetheless continued into the post-colonial era unabated.

The first Haratin anti-slavery organisation, El Hor, was founded in 1978. Starting with the 1981 declaration issued under President Ould Haidalla, the Mauritanian government has taken an uneven series of steps to stamp out the practice. These steps include: the 2003 law on the suppression of trafficking in persons; the 2007 law criminalising (as opposed to simply 'abolishing') slavery, which created a legal framework for prosecutions; the 2013 creation of L'Agence Nationale de Lutte contre les Séquelles de l'Esclavage, de l'Insertion et de la Lutte contre la Pauvreté (The National Agency for the Fight against the After-effects of Slavery, for Integration and the Fight against Poverty; known as TADAMOUN); and the 2015 Anti-Slavery Act, which defined slavery as a crime against humanity and increased penalties against perpetrators. TADAMOUN was replaced in 2021 by Solidarité Nationale et à la Lutte contre l'Exclusion (National Solidarity and the Fight against Exclusion; TAAZOUR).

All of these laws have been hampered by uneven and arguably minimal enforcement, with only a handful of cases ever brought to trial (Minority Rights around Tichitt and Oualata hailed from a group that would eventually become the Soninké. These stone-built settlements are thought to comprise some of, if not the first complex societies found in West Africa, and these industrious ancestors were active in eastern Mauritania at least as far back as 2200BCE. Early evidence of domesticated millet has been found around the escarpment, and Soninké are known as skilled agriculturalists to this day.

Group reports that only 47 cases had been brought as of 2022.) Like some of the legal structures, TADAMOUN and TAAZOUR have also been criticised as toothless, as their official stance is that slavery is over and that their mandate is therefore limited to dealing with its 'vestiges' and after-effects. (Because the practice is regarded as eliminated by the government, many anti-slavery activists have endured state-backed repression for their activities, including jail time.)

The 2022 establishment of a new organ, the Instance Nationale de Lutte contre la Traite des Personnes et le Trafic des Migrants (National Authority for the Fight against Human Trafficking and Migrant Smuggling; w inlctptm.org), promises improved enforcement, though it integrates the fight against hereditary enslavement with more modern forms of trafficking.

Tomoya Obokata, the UN Special Rapporteur on contemporary forms of slavery observed in 2022 that 'Despite the important steps taken by Mauritania, the fact remains that descent-based slavery and other slavery-like practices still exist in Mauritania.' The Walk Free organisation ranked Mauritania as having the third highest prevalence of modern slavery in the world in their 2023 Global Slavery Index, behind only North Korea and Eritrea. They state that 32 in every 1,000 people, or nearly 150,000 Mauritanians (just over 3% of the national population), are living in slave-like conditions, including victims of forced marriage. Hereditary/caste-based slavery also exists in small numbers among the Soninké and other kouar populations, and these numbers also reflect this.

But answering the question of who should be counted as enslaved in Mauritania remains thorny, as relations between Bidhan and Haratin still revolve around a complex and unequal set of material and familial obligations that leave many Haratin in situations of sometimes extreme dependence. The UN Special Rapporteur also observed in 2022 that 'many [Haratin] are still economically, socially, and culturally dependent on their former masters as they are not able to sustain themselves independently.'

There are a number of local anti-slavery organisations advocating for the continued elimination of the practice and for Haratin rights more broadly. These include SOS Esclaves (f sosesclavesmauratanie), Fondation Sahel pour La Défense des Droits de l'Homme (f fondationsahel1) and Initiative pour la résurgence du mouvement abolitionniste (f biramofficiel), whose founder, Biram Dah Abeid, was awarded the UN Human Rights Prize in 2013.

Several international organisations are also active in the fight against slavery in Mauritania, including the Abolition Institute (w stoppingslavery.org; f AbolitionInstitute), Free the Slaves (w freetheslaves.net), Anti-Slavery International (w antislavery.org) and Walk Free (w walkfree.org).

As this remains such a difficult and controversial topic, use your discretion when discussing it in Mauritania – responses may vary wildly depending on whom you are talking to.

The Soninké historical pedigree is further buttressed in the first millennium as they were leaders of the Ghana Empire, which stretched over much of southeastern Mauritania and western Mali for more than 600 years. Soninké were among the first residents of Oualata, and Chinguetti also takes its name from the Soninké language. Ancient Ghana, and thus many of the Soninké converted to Islam in 1076CE under pressure from Almoravids to the north, who had been in a back-and-forth conflict with Ghana for some time.

Around the 12th century, drought and political instability in the waning days of the empire saw many Soninké migrate west, and today the southern Assaba and Guidimakha regions and upper Senegal River are considered Mauritania's Soninké heartlands. Here, the relatively humid climate offers fertile territory for Soninké agriculturalists to ply their trade. Soninké have also been at the forefront of modern

THE HEAVY COST OF BEAUTY

Of the very few factoids about Mauritania that have filtered out to the wider world, that of Moorish men's penchant for very large women is perhaps the most widely discussed, chiefly because of how starkly it contrasts with the Western beauty standards that so many in Europe and beyond have assimilated as 'normal'.

But, as with Western beauty standards, the pursuit of this ideal has often been taken to painful extremes. Almost unique to Mauritania's Moorish communities, young girls reaching a certain age have traditionally been fattened up for marriage through a regime of systematic force-feeding known as *leblouh*, or *gavage* in French – the same term used for how foie gras is made. During this process, girls are force-fed up to 16,000 calories daily, mostly via consuming litres upon litres of camel milk and couscous – sometimes up to a stomach-churning 20 litres a day. Traditionally, the fatter the girl, the more beautiful and marriageable she was considered. Thus, the better a girl ate, the more attractive and well resourced a husband she might hope to attract – a powerful motivator in precarious times.

To that end, girls are sometimes sent away to 'fat camps', where they'll be gorged; many find it difficult to ingest such enormous quantities of food. This is where the coercion begins, and girls are pushed to eat through a variety of cruel techniques, including the use of an *azàyyâr*, a double-pronged wooden tool used to squeeze and pinch the fingers and toes of the offending girl – occasionally breaking them in the process. If a girl throws up, she may be forced to drink her vomit. In recent years, the off-label usage of pharmaceuticals causing weight gain has become a common addition to this extraordinarily heavy mix.

Accurate statistics are hard to come by: the most recent official data are now 20 years old, but in these, 22% of women had been subject to gavage; this percentage rises considerably in rural areas, where estimates range from 40% to 75% of women still being subject to the procedure. It does seem to be receding over time, however, and for a variety of reasons. Some say it was diminishing until the 2008 coup that put Mohamed Ould Abdel Aziz back in power, and his government's subsequent promotion of a reactionary form of traditionalism. But more powerful still may be Western beauty standards: the broad proliferation of global media on TV, Instagram and TikTok (among urban audiences at least) ensures that fashions from other parts of the world are increasingly influential.

The gavage has attracted a fair bit of Western media attention over time as well, but much of this is voyeuristic and tittering at best. By contrast, Italian director Michela Occhipinti's award-winning 2019 film *Flesh Out* (*Le Mariage de Verida*) is global migration trends, with significant numbers of (particularly) men migrating to France in the 1960s and 1970s to fill needs in that country's economy; migration has since become something of a Soninké tradition, and many families are split between southern Mauritania and West Africa, France, or even further afield.

Wolof The largest ethnic group in neighbouring Senegal, Wolofs live primarily in the far southwestern corner of Mauritania, in areas along the northern fringes of what was once the Wolof-dominated Jolof Empire (1200–1549). Their conversion to Islam began in the early days of the Jolof Empire, but took several centuries before the population was predominantly Muslim. Traditionally engaged in farming, fishing and trade, the Wolof are the smallest of Mauritania's officially recognised ethno-linguistic groups, and are closely associated with the neighbouring state

essential viewing, sharing the intimate story of one woman's experience, caught between expectations both ancient and modern.

The difficulties associated with gavage notwithstanding, the long-term health consequences for Mauritanian women are also significant, and there are a number of organisations and activists in Mauritania aiming to support healthier norms and rites of passage for Mauritanian women and girls. Anyone interested in the topic should follow up with Aminetou Mint El-Moctar and her organisation, Association des femmes chefs de familles (Association of Women Heads of Households; f af.cf.1).

French explorer Odette du Puigaudeau observed the leblouh up close in 1933:

> Held by an old woman servant, the unhappy Toutou was struggling on a disarranged faro [lambskin].
>
> I could not at first make out what the man was doing, kneeling at her feet, but creeping closer to the tent I saw that he was pressing the toes of the wretched girl between two camel sticks. It must have been a cruel torture! Every time that his victim opened her mouth to protest he dropped the sticks, snatched up a calabash of milk and made her drink. She dribbled, she cried, she set her teeth; then her torturer began to beat her and to squeeze her hands and feet.
>
> To my astonishment, as he turned towards his old accomplice, I recognized Meïmoun. I could hardly believe it, but Meïmoun it was, Meïmoun, the most trusted servant of the Emir, the nounou of his children. 'Ah,' I thought, 'if only Lalia were to see her precious daughter of whom she is so proud being bullied by this brute!'
>
> But when he saw me step into the circle of the light, Meïmoun, far from being disconcerted, smiled broadly like a man surprised in the fulfilment of his duty.
>
> Toutou, delivered for a moment, readjusted her clothes and murmured *Alik essalam*! The old *hartania* confided to me in despairing tones that Toutou was really not a good girl; that Meïmoun and she had already fattened many young ladies for marriage, but that none had ever given them so much trouble as Toutou had. She was beginning to be beautiful, and a result so satisfying, which showed the favorable intentions of Moulana [Allah], should encourage her to drink her milk.
>
> Then she turned to her charge: 'Toutou, my joy, the apple of my eye, drink to be beautiful, beautiful as the moon. Drink, my dove; do not dishonour your old nurse.'
>
> From *Barefoot through Mauretania* (*Pieds nus à travers la Mauritanie*),
> Odette du Puigaudeau (trans. Geoffrey Sainsbury), 1936

of Senegal, where their language serves as the country's lingua franca and they generally hold the most political power.

Wolofs were also the dominant African population in Senegal's colonial cities, including Saint-Louis, from where Mauritania was governed for many years, thereby cementing their influence in trade and politics. Today they are especially present in Rosso and along the lower Senegal River, and because fishing is one of their main traditional occupations, you will also meet many Wolof fishermen and fishmongers in the Port du Pêche in Nouakchott.

MINORITY GROUPS All told, groups that don't fit into one of the above categories make up just a small sliver of the Mauritanian population; this catch-all category includes a few groups that might not fit the conventional definition of an 'ethnic group', but whom are nonetheless distinguished by their traditional occupations and ancestry, who are peripheral to, or do not fit neatly into, the broader categories of Moorish society, and are simply worthy of note for their distinctiveness. It also includes larger groups found along Mauritania's borders who are a part of larger populations in neighbouring countries but wound up on the other side of a colonial demarcation from their compatriots.

Numbering no more than a couple of thousand people, Mauritania's best-known minority group is probably the **Imraguen**, who live in a series of tiny villages along the north coast inside the Banc d'Arguin National Park. Renowned for their theatrical mullet fishing tradition that once upon a time seemingly solicited the help and co-operation of dolphins (page 154), scholars consider them to be a heterogeneous group with Berber, African, and other ancestors, or the last remnants of the ancient Bafour people who once occupied much of what is now Mauritania – or perhaps a little of both. Today they speak Hassaniya and since the park's 1976 gazetting, have been officially recognised as indigenes to the area; this development means they enjoy exclusive rights to the traditional fishing trade there, and the maintenance of a distinctive Imraguen identity now comes with certain economic advantages.

Mirroring the Banc d'Arguin, Diawling National Park is also home to an acknowledged indigenous population in the form of the **Taghrédient** (Taghridjant). Numbering just a few hundred people, they are not entirely outside the Moorish social structure and the Taghrédient count both Hassans and Haratins among their numbers. Their Hassan status is unusual as they are primarily engaged in fishing and agriculture – occupations traditionally categorically shunned by the noble, landlubbing Hassans. Odder still, they claim both Berber and Arab lineage, where the former is generally studiously downplayed or outright denied among the Hassan. Their origin story involves a feud between mythical brothers Nyarzîg and Rizg, the former representing the ancient coastal Berber populations (likely with some relation to the Imraguen), and the latter representing the Arabs who arrived in southwestern Mauritania in the 1600–1700s.

Inland east of Tichitt, the **Nemadi** are a traditional hunter-gatherer tribe perhaps also numbering just a few hundred individuals. Though also considered as part of the Bidhan, they have historically been a significantly marginalised and looked-down-upon group, but known for their *gueïmaré* hunting raids. They traditionally made their living through keeping and hunting with dogs, but their prey, usually antelopes, ostriches and other desert fauna, has diminished drastically since the droughts of the 1960s, 1970s and 1980s, making their livelihood increasingly precarious and unsustainable, and forcing them to either adopt camel herding or live off the increasingly impoverished returns available in the *bâdiyya* (bush).

A small number of **Bambara**, a Mandé group dominant in neighbouring Mali and related to the Soninké, live in Mauritania, mostly along the Malian borderlands and in nearby cities from Guidimakha region eastwards. One of the many groups formed in the wake of the Mali Empire, the Bambara are today Mali's largest ethnic group, and their eponymous language is used as the primary lingua franca throughout much of that country.

Though the Majâbat al-Koubrâ (page 206) acts as a divider between the Moorish and Touareg worlds, there are now also a fair number of Tamasheq-speaking **Touareg** living as refugees in Mauritania in the wake of the ongoing conflict in Mali, particularly in and around the Mbera Refugee Camp in the far southeast. Traditionally resident in the central Sahara from Mali east towards Algeria, Libya and Niger, the Touareg are also nomadic pastoralists with a mixed Arab-Berber-African background, much like the Moors, though they maintained their Berber-derived language, only adopting Arabic for religious purposes.

Unlike in neighbouring Senegal, there was never a significant **French** population in Mauritania, and even in the colonial era the French presence was largely limited to the military men, functionaries and traders necessary for the functioning of a garrison settlement. This limited population and conservative cultural norms meant that a significant métis population never emerged in Mauritania either. As such, though there is a visible French presence in the country today in the form of cultural institutions like the Alliance Française, the French population remains miniscule and tends to be characterised by either modern-day immigration for business purposes or employees posted internationally on expat contracts.

The presence of **Lebanese** traders so common elsewhere in West Africa is also considerably less noticeable here, but a growing number of **Chinese** traders have set up shop in Nouakchott and Nouadhibou. These two cities are also hubs for a small population of **West African** migrants, including from Senegal, Ivory Coast, The Gambia, Guinea and Mali, and Nouadhibou in particular is home to a notably large migrant population, as it's one of the main jumping-off points for clandestine migrants seeking to reach the Canary Islands by boat. (Nouadhibou also historically hosted a large population of Canarian fishermen who came to trawl the rich shoals of the Banc d'Arguin.) And while not all arrivals to Mauritania are with onward migration in mind, indeed many have come simply to work, many who initially intended to leave never quite manage to do so, instead staying on for years and making a life in Nouakchott, Nouadhibou, or sometimes Zouérate instead.

LANGUAGE

Mauritania's most widely spoken language is **Hassaniya Arabic**, a dialect of Arabic which traces its origins to the Beni Hassan tribes that began to arrive in and occupy Mauritania from the northeast at the end of the 13th century. The Arab conquest of Mauritania initiated a long period of language contact between the Arabic-speaking Beni Hassan and the Sanhaja Berber populations already present in the area, and ultimately the decline and near-extinction of their **Zénaga** Berber language, once spoken across Mauritania. Though there are only a couple of thousand speakers at most left in the Trarza region, Zénaga has had a notable impact on the Hassaniya spoken today: scholars disagree on the specifics, but most estimate that 10–20% of Hassaniya vocabulary may have a Zénaga origin. Hassaniya is also spoken as a mother tongue outside of Mauritania, primarily by the Sahrawis of Western Sahara, but also into southern Morocco, southwest Algeria, and among the Arab populations of northern Mali.

A NOTE ON TRANSLITERATION

As most place names in Mauritania originally come from Hassaniya Arabic, they can be transliterated into Latin script any number of ways to reflect English, French or other orthographical conventions – and they often are: one can find more than ten variations listed for certain place names. (Take the Mauritania–Sahrawi border settlement of **Agounit**, **Aghouinite**, **Aghounit**, **Aghouinit**, **Aghoueinit**, **Agueinit**, **Agüeinit**, **Agüenit**, **Agwenit**, **Agwanit**, **Aguanit**, for example.)

As Mauritania's second working language is French, however, we have opted to use French spellings and transliteration conventions as much as possible, as these spellings are what you are most likely to encounter in-country. That being said, this standardisation also seems to be shifting and certain French spelling conventions are now often replaced by, or used interchangeably with, those that will be more familiar to Anglophones, for example the villages of Doueïrat/Dweiratt or Aouyevia/Awevia/Aeweivya. You may also see Oualata transcribed as Walata or Ouadane as Wadan.

Hassaniya is by and large an oral language. Arabic in Mauritania is not written according to Hassaniya convention, but rather according to the norms of Fusha, or Modern Standard Arabic. This is true for nearly all written texts, including official communications etc, other than perhaps the most informal contexts like text messages or similar. In these contexts, you are also likely to encounter Arabizi, where Arabic is rendered using letters and numerals from the Latin script.

Outside of the Hassanophone population, **Pulaar** is the second-most widely spoken language in Mauritania, followed by **Soninké** and **Wolof**, each of which is spoken by its respective ethnic group. All three languages are considered 'national' (but not official) languages, and though official proclamations are done in Arabic, parliamentarians are allowed to address the national assembly in any of the three national languages as well. There have also been a number of initiatives to introduce primary education in these languages over the years.

The status of Arabic and **French** vis-à-vis one another has long been a topic of some discord in Mauritania. French and Arabic were co-official as Mauritania's official languages from independence until 1980, but at the end of that year, the military government stripped French of its official status, declaring Arabic to be the only official language. Broadly speaking, the French–Arabic tension is a proxy for tensions between the southern Afro-Mauritanian populations, who were more receptive to French education during the colonial era, and Bidhans, who were for the most part staunchly resistant, preferring their traditional Quranic schools. As such, a French-educated class of Afro-Mauritanians emerged as influential in the early Mauritanian state, which inherited many French structures, while the Bidhans were underrepresented here, or at least felt so.

This situation, in which Afro-Mauritanians utilised French as a vehicle towards increased civic power and representation, was something of a rejoinder to their historic marginalisation by the traditional Bidhan elite, and was seen as an intolerable role reversal by the Bidhans, long accustomed to political and economic dominance. Over time, the Hassanophone elite pushed back against their supplantation in the corridors of power, and a push to emphasise their cultural connections to the Arabophone Maghreb and fully Arabise the state began, culminating in the 1980 loss of status for French.

French was, however, given the rather ambiguous legal status of 'privileged foreign language', and though it has not been official for more than 40 years, it remains the de facto working language in many spheres, and most government publications remain available in both Arabic and French. It also remains preferred by many Afro-Mauritanians as a way to resist what is still seen as government-imposed Arabisation, and to maintain their ties to the neighbouring Francophone countries of West Africa. As such, French fluency remains considerably higher among Afro-Mauritanians than within the Moorish population.

Finally, the Azer language, thought to have been a Soninké-Hassaniya-Zénaga hybrid of sorts, disappeared in the 20th century, though some publications still indicate the Imraguen and Némadi as speaking some kind of Azer-Hassaniya mix. This is unsubstantiated by current scholars (linguist Catherine Taine-Cheikh dismisses them as 'langues fantômes'), and these groups are now considered fully Hassanophone, albeit with some specialised vocabulary relating to their traditional occupations.

RELIGION AND BELIEFS

Islam is the state religion and 99% of Mauritanians are Sunni adherents, following the Maliki School of jurisprudence, one of four major schools of thought in the Sunni tradition. Islam first arrived in the region with Arabs and Berbers migrating from the north around the 10th century, and the next two centuries saw the faith spread quickly, with the Almoravids a particularly influential movement.

Today there are several Sufi brotherhoods present including the Tijāniyyah and Qadiriyya, as well as some Mourides, particularly among the Wolof community. Smaller brotherhoods including the Chadeliya and Goudfiya are also regionally influential. There are a few settlements built and organised around Sufi principles, including Maata Moulana (page 267), Maaden El Irvane (page 186) and Nimzatt (page 241).

FGM

Though officially illegal since 2015, female genital mutilation (FGM) remains widespread in Mauritania, though with significant regional variation. The practice, which involves partial or total removal of the external female genitalia, is commonly considered to be an integral aspect of Islamic teaching in Mauritania, though it causes extreme pain and distress to the girls upon which it is performed, and may result in healing problems, long-term health issues, or even death caused by infection. Despite the law, there are seemingly no prosecutions on record against practitioners of FGM.

The overall prevalence remains extraordinarily high: around 64% of Mauritanian women between the ages of 15 and 49 have been cut, and rates are highest in the southeast. But as with so many things in Mauritania, the prevalence of the practice is also mapped along ethnic lines. Research indicates that approximately 90% of Soninké women, 79% of Halpulaar women and 68% of Moorish women have undergone FGM, but only 16% of Wolof women in Mauritania have been subject to the practice.

Oumi Bah Sow and her organisation Alliance pour les droits des femmes mauritaniennes (f ADFM.Mauritanie) have been advocating against FGM, and for women's rights in Mauritania more broadly, since 2022.

One peculiarity you may notice is that Mauritanians often pray directly on the earth and perform their pre-prayer ritual ablutions (wudu) with sand rather than water, an act known as Tayammum. Generally speaking, it's not allowed for non-Muslims to visit mosques in Mauritania, but depending on where you are, it's sometimes possible with a polite request.

The (very) small Christian community is predominantly Roman Catholic, and the Diocese of Nouakchott (w evechenkc.org) administers churches or chapels in Nouakchott, Nouadhibou, Rosso, Atar and Kaédi; their congregations are comprised largely of immigrants.

EDUCATION

Public education in Mauritania is based on the French system and administered by the Ministère de l'Education Nationale et de la Reforme du Système Educatif (Ministry of National Education and Education System Reform; w education.gov.mr). Schooling is officially compulsory and free of charge between the ages of 6 and 16 but, despite this, educational attainment remains low, particularly in rural areas, where schools are ill-funded and overcrowded, and the cost of uniforms, books and other materials remains a barrier towards full school enrolment. Nearly 100% of Mauritanian children today do enrol in primary school, but less than 70% complete it. From here, only half continue to collège (middle school) and 30% to lycée (high school). At the primary level, there is parity between girls' and boys' enrolment, but the percentage of girls begins to drop off at the secondary level. Among Mauritanians 15 and older, the literacy rate is an estimated 67%, including 72% of men and 62% of women (2022 estimates).

Depending on the school, education is done in primarily Arabic or primarily French, and government interest in expanding the use of Arabic has been fiercely resisted among the Afro-Mauritanian populations in the south, who overwhelmingly demand French-language education for their children rather than Arabic. There is also an interest in expanding access to education in the national languages of Pulaar, Wolof and Soninké; these were offered in the 1980s and 1990s but ultimately scrapped.

A new educational decree was promulgated in 2022, which aims to reintroduce these national languages into education, and would require all students to study in at least two of them, ie: Arabic and one other. To that end, the Institut pour la Promotion et l'Enseignement des Langues Nationales (Institute for the Promotion and Teaching of National Languages; f IPELAN) was founded, and though this means that Moorish students will find themselves studying an African language for the first time, some Afro-Mauritanians see the reforms as yet another effort to reduce the usage of French in favour of Arabic (for which a much larger corpus of materials exists than for any of the national tongues). The reforms were just being implemented in the 2024–25 school year, so it remains to be seen how they will succeed.

Religious factors play a role in dictating educational outcomes as well. Despite the fact that Islamic instruction is integrated into the public school system, many parents still prefer to send their children to Islamic schools known as mahadras. Most children will spend at least some time in a mahadra, often before enrolling in public school, while others will do most of their schooling here. There are estimated to be more than 11,000 mahadras in the country, which are recognised by the Mauritanian state and regulated by the Ministère des Affaires Islamiques et de l'Enseignement Originel (Ministry of Islamic Affairs and Original Education;

w affairesislamiques.gov.mr), but most operate informally, without meaningful oversight or established standards.

They are typically led by holy men known as sheikhs or marabouts (serignés in Wolof and thiernos in Pulaar), and coursework typically revolves around memorisation of the Quran (in Arabic) and the tenets of Islam, taught through recitation and repeated writing on a wooden slate known as a lawh. Children studying at these schools are known as télamids or talibés, and, depending on the mahadra, begging for alms may be a central component of their education (page 54). The Mauritanian state has made efforts to extend its oversight over mahadras and introduce teacher trainings in an effort to hedge against violent extremism, ensure a minimum standard of education, and improve the circumstances of the enrolled children, but these are significant reforms requiring significant capacity. Despite these concerns, the mahadra system as a centuries-old institution of community and cultural continuity was inscribed on UNESCO's Representative List of the Intangible Cultural Heritage of Humanity in 2023.

At the conclusion of lycée, students who wish to continue to university must sit the baccalauréat school-leaving exam. Tertiary education is overseen by the Ministère de l'Enseignement supérieur et de la Recherche scientifique (Ministry of Higher Education and Scientific Research; w mesrs.gov.mr). At tertiary level, the Université de Nouakchott Al Aasriya (w univ-nkc.mr) is the country's largest and most significant institution, formed in 2016 after a merger between the Université des Sciences, de Technologie et de Médecine and the Université de Nouakchott, which was initially formed in 1981. There are a handful of private tertiary institutions, including Université Sup'Management, Université Libanaise Internationale, Université Moderne Chinguetti, Université Cheikh Mohamed Lemine Chinguetti (all in Nouakchott) and the Université des sciences Islamiques in Aïoun el Atrouss.

CULTURE

LITERATURE

> Poetry is Mauritania's long-standing national 'sport', and although it is often easy verse, churned out with alarming alacrity by any educated person, there is a tradition of profound, delicate, wistful poetry, and men and women recite pre-Islamic or 18th-century poems as easily as their own.
>
> Nancy Jones Abeiderrahmane, *Camel Cheese – Seemed Like a Good Idea* (2013)

Like much of West Africa, Mauritania is home to a centuries-old tradition of poetry, music and legend performed by hereditary praise-singers and storytellers, known here as **igaouen** (more familiarly known as griots abroad). But despite this national pedigree for poetry and verse, this corpus remains largely out of reach to a non-Arabophone and/or non-Francophone audiences, as only a handful of Mauritanian works of literature have been translated into English (including few, if any, igaouen performances).

The selection is growing, however, and several works from **Mbarek Ould Beyrouk**, perhaps the most celebrated author in the country, have become available in recent years. He is the author of something like eight novels in French, with three of these now available in English: 2015's *The Desert and the Drum* (*Le Tambour des larmes*), 2021's *The Silence of the Horizons* (*Le silence des horizons*), and *Pariahs* (*Parias*), also from 2021. *The Desert and The Drum* won the Prix Ahmadou-Kourouma in 2016. **Moussa Ould Ebnou** is another celebrated novelist who writes in both Arabic and

HASSANIYA PROVERBS

Collected and translated by Nancy Jones Abeiderrahmane

The old man lying down sees more than the young man standing up.
The owner of pregnant camels burps milk froth.
Drop by drop the wadi flows.
The one not in the fight is brave.
Half your intelligence is in your brother.
If you are patient, the shade will reach you.
When one foot works free, the other one gets stuck.
May God grant that we do better than what people think.
If you fill your mouth with flour, you will have to figure out how to wet it.
One hand alone cannot clap.
He went for more, and lost his whiskers.
If someone bites you and you don't bite back, he thinks you have no teeth.
If flour is spilled it doesn't return to the same size.
'Give-me' leaves no friends.
Allah loves someone who knows his rank and sits beneath it.
If someone spreads his cloak for you, don't sit on it.
If someone doesn't see the sky, don't point it out to him.
Rain always does more good than damage.
If you know your camel's character, you don't get thrown off.
Carried by many, a burden is a feather.
Buying poor quality cheap may seem like a bargain when it's a rip-off.
As far apart as knowledge and ignorance.
As soon as water is poured away, you need it.
If you don't spare your steed, you will have to stop.
Man does not appreciate wellbeing until it's gone.
If you have a tongue, you don't get lost.
He broke a year-long fast by eating a grasshopper.
It's like a dumb man's dream.
To fill your bowl, do your own milking.
Lying is a sin…but the truth can't be told.
No man ever left without his family finding how to milk.

From Camel Cheese – Seemed Like a Good Idea *by Nancy Jones Abeiderrahmane (2013)*

French, and his 1994 novel *Le Barzakh* was published in English as *Barzakh: The Land In-Between* in 2022.

Self-published author **Mohamed Bouya Bamba** writes in English and has released two works, *Angels of Mauritania and the Curse of the Language* (2011) and *Outside Servitude* (2019). Also self-published, **Amadou Ndiaye**'s 2014 *Crossing the Atlantic Ocean In Search of Happiness* just about rounds out the totality of Mauritanian literature available in English. (There are also of course a number of academic and non-fiction works on Mauritania in English, a selection of which can be found on page 314.)

Given the extremely limited availability of Mauritanian literature in translation, it may seem unlikely that the most famous living Mauritanian also happens to be a writer. It's true, however, and his path to literary success was about as unlikely –

and difficult – as they come. This famed wordsmith is of course **Mohamedou Ould Slahi**, who was imprisoned without charge at the United States military prison at Guantánamo Bay for 14 years, 2002–16. His memoir of his time there, *Guantánamo Diary*, was written (in English) and published during his imprisonment, reaching bookshelves in 2015 after a prolonged legal battle. It was used as the basis for the 2021 film *The Mauritanian*. As a free man, Ould Slahi has continued writing, and he published his first novel, a fantastical meditation on Mauritanian desert life called *The Actual True Story of Ahmed and Zarga*, in 2021.

Literary magazine *Words Without Borders* (w wordswithoutborders.org) also ran an issue featuring a collection of short stories and poetry from Mauritania in

THÉODORE MONOD AND ODETTE DU PUIGAUDEAU: DESERT DEVOTEES

When we talk about non-Mauritanians writing on Mauritania, a few names loom large as desert monoliths, and none more so than famed French desert scholar **Théodore Monod** (1902–2000). Monod spent decades studying the natural and cultural worlds of the Sahara, during which time he located the lost Ma'den Ijafen cache (page 206), (mostly) disproved the so-called Chinguetti Meteorite (page 194), and recorded more than 80 new-to-science species of plant and animal throughout the country. He published nearly 700 academic articles and numerous books aimed at general audiences, though unfortunately to date none of these have been made available in English.

Another towering figure in Mauritanian studies, the Brittany-born traveller and ethnographer **Odette du Puigaudeau** (1894–1991), offers us one book in English, *Barefoot Through Mauretania* (*Pieds nus à travers la Mauritanie*). Published in 1936, it chronicles her first journey in Mauritania alongside companion Marion Sénones. Here, the two women set out with a decidedly straightforward yet hugely unusual goal: to simply explore the Sahara together on camelback. Mauritania and Sénones would become du Puigaudeau's lifelong companions, and she would go on to publish many works on the culture and customs of the westernmost Sahara.

Even if you don't read French, her books remain compelling documents. *Arts et coutumes des maures* is full of exquisite illustrations documenting all aspects of Moorish life, covering everything from habitations to hardware to haircuts. It began life as a thesis and was cobbled together over decades; the disparate articles and papers were definitively compiled and published posthumously with a foreword by Théodore Monod (also posthumous) in 2002. Her *Mémoire du Pays Maure (1934–1960)* (2000) is another priceless document, full of photographs and illustrations by both du Puigaudeau and Sénones which assiduously capture traditional life, ancient cities (which look shockingly similar today), and material culture from the Atlantic coast to Oualata.

Over time, the two women have also been recognised as queer icons, as explored in Catherine Faye and Marine Sanclamente's 2020 book, *L'Année des deux dames*. Professor Paraska Tolan-Szkilnik and Nouakchott-based artist Amy Sow intend to produce an as-yet-unnamed graphic novel on the two women's travels, only this time telling the story from a Mauritanian point of view, from the perspective of one of their guides (w themarkaz.org/puigaudeau-senones-graphic-novel-on-mauritania-circa-1933).

2021. The collection, called 'Movement and Multiplicity: Writing from Mauritania', contains works from seven different Mauritanian authors, including poet Mariem Mint Derwich, and can be accessed online (w wordswithoutborders.org/read/collection/may-2021-writing-from-mauritania).

There have also been a small handful of non-Mauritanians to publish memoir and travelogue on their experiences in the country, including **Nancy Jones Abeiderrahmane** (*Camel Cheese – Seemed Like a Good Idea*, 2013), **Katherine Baird** (*Growing Mangos in the Desert*, Apprentice House Press, 2022) and **Peter Hudson** (*Travels in Mauritania*, 1990; *Under an African Sky*, 2014), all of whom have a deep knowledge of and affinity for the country and have generously allowed for selections from their works to be featured in and enrich this guide. Finally, famed Aéropostale pilot Antoine de Saint-Exupéry also wrote about his experiences in Mauritania in his 1939 book *Wind, Sand and Stars* (*Terre des hommes*).

MUSIC Classical Moorish music, known as azawane, revolves around the *tidinit* (men's lute), *ardin* (women's harp) and *tbol* (kettle drum). Other styles will also sometimes incorporate the *neifara* (flute) and *rbab* (one-stringed violin). Moorish music is historically performed by a caste of hereditary praise-singers and storytellers known as igaouen (iggawen), who are analogous to the more widely known *griots* found elsewhere in West Africa. The five-part Moorish modal system is wickedly complex, which will come as no surprise to first-time listeners: azawane sounds about as far from Western pop as it's possible to get while remaining on the same planet. For more on azawane's intricate melodies, modes and requirements, see page 50.

Some of the earliest Mauritanian recordings available today are those of Sidaty ould Abba and Mounina mint Eida, who performed as Si Daty et Mounina; Sidaty ould Abba was a widely beloved figure, considered the 20th century's best singer, and their recordings, done in Morocco, are perhaps the first-ever studio recordings of Bidhani Moorish music. Their daughter, Dimi Mint Abba, went on to become arguably an even bigger legend than her father, and released two albums internationally, both in the early 1990s: *Moorish Music from Mauritania* (accompanied by her husband, Khalifa Ould Eide) and *Musique & Chants de Mauritanie*.

Down the generations, there's clearly plenty of music in the family: Dimi's half-sister, Garmi Mint Abba, is a major star in Mauritania today despite never recording internationally; Dimi's daughter Veyrouz Mint Seymali was recently featured on *Music from Saharan WhatsApp 09* (2020); and Dimi's step-daughter, Noura Mint Seymali, has released two international records, *Tzenni* (2014) and *Arbina* (2016), and continues to tour internationally.

Other early recordings include the family band Ahl Nana, whose compilation album *L'Orchestre National Mauritanien*, issued in 2023, contains their only recordings, from 1971. They should not be confused with L'Orchestre National de Mauritanie, which was a tradi-modern national band in the style of (and trained by) those famously cultivated by the Guinean state. Their self-titled compilation of recordings from 1968 to 1975 is now available via label Sahel Sounds.

Otherwise, some of the oldest azawane performances extant today were captured in field recordings taken in the 1960s. These include Ely Ould Meïddah and Mokhtar Ould Meïddah's *Musique Maure* (2002) and the compilations *Musique Maure – République Islamique de Mauritanie* (1987) and *Mauritanie: Concert sous la Tente* (1999). These performances involve poetry, praise singing and the recollection of historical ancestors and events. This repertoire sometimes includes the T'heydinn Epic, which traces its origins to the 16th century and recounts the creation and evolution of Moorish society since. It was recognised on UNESCO's Intangible Cultural Heritage List in 2011.

During these performances, it's not only the performers on stage who participate. The crowd cries out with joy and appreciation, women ululate (*zaghārīt*) and clap, men vibrate their lips (*tberbir*), and the audience pushes the concert along. Spectators will also get up and jump in the circle to perform a variety of freestyle and choreographed dances, including a ritualised stick fight or 'game of clubs' known as *anigur* (*eneygour*). Depending on the concert and the style, dancers can work themselves into quite a frenzy, leaping, twirling, and even twerking – and sometimes spinning a rifle around for good measure.

More traditional azawane albums available online include Ensemble El-Moukhadrami's *Chants de Griots* (2000), Ooleya mint Amartichitt's *Praise Songs* (1998) and Aïcha Mint Chighaly's *Azawan, L'art des Griots* (1997). Aïcha also runs the Musée Ardine in Nouakchott (page 130). Saïdou Ba from the river valley near Maghama plays tidnit (known as *hodou* in his native Pulaar) on three volumes of *Musique de la Republique Islamique de Mauritanie*, released in the mid 1970s.

Though only introduced to Mauritanian music when Sidaty ould Abba came back from a 1962 trip to France, the guitar now sits comfortably in the Moorish instrumental pantheon, and has arguably even displaced the tidnit in many contexts – check out the 2011 album *Wallahi Le Zein!!*, compiled by musicologist Matthew Lavoie (page 50), for a great example of the wild and wonderful ways that Mauritanian musicians have integrated and innovated with the guitar. On the other side of the musical coin, several albums from Malouma are quite intentional in their exploration of cross-over territory, incorporating a variety of Western instruments and styles.

The Nouakchott-based Teranim (page 122) promotes Haratin arts and music and hosts an annual festival of *medh*, a Haratin style of praise-singing. They released an album, *Eski*, in 2019 (which is not online but can be purchased at the Zeinart gallery in Nouakchott; page 125). More medh, this time from across the border to the north, can be heard on the compilation *Medej: Cantos Antiguos Saharuis* (2004).

North of the border in Western Sahara, traditional Sahrawi music also incorporates parts (but not all) of the Moorish modal structure, and is also sung in Hassaniya, therefore making it a natural complement to Mauritanian sounds, though with certain notable differences – including overtly political content that is typically absent in Mauritanian styles. Much like Dimi mint Abba in Mauritania, Mariem Hassan is the unquestioned doyen of Sahrawi singers, and in addition to her several international recordings, she was the subject of a posthumous documentary, *Haiyu*, in 2025. The 2013 compilation *Hassānīya Music from the Western Sahara and Mauritania* (and Hisham Mayet's accompanying film *Palace of the Winds*) is another good cross-border collection. Finally, though they're a fully Sahrawi band, El Wali's 1994 album *Tiris* is also a perennial hit in Mauritania (and a good example of the political nature of much Sahrawi music).

Among the most popular modern styles of Mauritanian music is wezin (also written WZN), which simply translates to 'instrumental music' and is a wild and warbly keyboard-forward style, and a must-have at today's weddings and other celebrations. Its most noted performer is probably Ahmedou Ahmed Lowla, who can be heard on 2019's *Terrouzi* and in duet with tidnit player Jeich Ould Badu on 2017's *Top WZN*. Jeich Ould Badu can also be heard on the 2015 compilation *Nouakchott Wedding Songs*. Another, slightly older style is that of the guitar-heavy Jakwar, which traces its origins to guitarist Jeich ould Abba's innovations during the war years of the 1970s. The previously mentioned *Wallahi Le Zein!!* is a great place to hear it.

MOORISH MUSIC: AN INTRODUCTION

Matthew Lavoie

The music of the Bidhani Moors is a distillation of all of the musical traditions that have swept through the Sahara over the last several centuries: the Chleuh melodies of the Berber from southern Morocco, the lute music of the Bambara of Mali, the repertoires of the Wolof, Halpulaar and Soninké of the Senegal River valley, the songs of the Tamacheq nomads, the rigid architecture of classical Andulasian music, and more recently the melodies of Saudi and Egyptian popular music.

Music-making among the Bidhan remains the virtually exclusive birthright of the *iggawen*, the griot families who jealously protect and preserve their specialised skills and knowledge. Up until the massive droughts of the early 1970s that forever changed Mauritanian life, most iggawen families were attached to the 'tents' of nomadic Bidhan warrior chiefs. The iggawen would entertain their patrons with praise songs extolling their noble ancestors and the virtuous characteristics of their tribes. But, above all, the iggawen were valued for their poetic and musical skills, and among the Bidhan, until very recently, an ear for music was considered one of the signs of nobility. Today, although the traditional bonds between iggawen and 'their tribes' remain meaningful, any music fan can invite any given *vennane*, or artist, to perform, in return for adequate compensation. Contemporary Bidhan vennane make their living performing at marriages, baptisms, birthday celebrations, private concerts and political rallies.

Bidhan music is a modal music, with a deep repertoire of melodies and dances, and ample room for improvisation. The building blocks of this system are a set of five modes, or *bhor*, whose performance is governed by immutable rules. The five modes are *karr*, *vaghu*, *lekhal*, *lebyaal* and *lebteyt*, and they must be performed in this order. As a musician goes through the sequence of the modes, she may not return to a previous mode at any point in the musical event. So, for example, once a singer has left *lekhal* there is no returning to this mode for the rest of the performance. Furthermore, each mode is subdivided into two parts; the black (*lekhal*), which is always played first, and the white (*lebyaal*): it helps to think of each of the five modes as a distinct seven-note scale, and of the black and white sections of the mode as different ways to play that scale, in this case *legato* versus *staccato*. Each of the five modes has different emotional weights: *karr* is associated with the innocence of childhood, *vaghu* with the virility of young adulthood, *lekhal* with the maturity of mid-life, *lebyaal* with nostalgia and the wisdom of old age, and *lebteyt* with the serenity that comes from no longer fearing death.

A Bidhan musical event is a participative one, and vennane will only give as much as they get from their audience. There are, with a few notable exceptions, no Bidhan 'bands', and every Bidhan musician can perform at any time with any other

The music of Mauritania's Pulaar, Soninké and Wolof citizens closely tracks with the music found to the south in Senegal and Mali, and when it comes to music, the Pulaar saying '*maayo wonaa keerol*' (the river is not a border) rings especially true. Indeed, identities are so fluid here that it's sometimes even difficult to figure out which side of the river someone considers themselves to be from. It would be entirely remiss not to mention, as just one example, superstar Baaba Maal, who sings in Pulaar and hails from just across the river in the Senegalese town of Podor. Maal's long-term collaborator Mansour Seck is also from the Senegalese side of the water, but his own faithful collaborator Ousmane Hamady

Bidhan musician. It is not uncommon for larger weddings to feature three or four different singers, each of whom will usually arrive with 'their' own guitar player.

Over the course of the evening the singers will pass the microphone back and forth, each, in turn, rising to sing a song, with each piece lasting only as long as the audience seems interested. The more the women in the audience clap and rise to dance, the longer a 'song' will continue. Encouraged by the audience the singer may repeat a poem several times, sing the praises of a dancer she recognises, or improvise a few lines about the evening's event. The quality and intensity of the music will depend on the state of the sound system, the skill of the dancers, the size of the crowd, the enthusiasm of the audience, the relationship between the vennane and their hosts, and on the amount of money that gets sprayed.

The songs collected on *Wallahi Le Zein!!* present one dimension of a multisensory experience. They do not capture the sensuality of the dancers, the extravagant behaviour of the percussionists, the body heat generated by 50 people packed into a small room, sweating and sticking to each other, the warm greetings and exuberant conversations of friends coming together, or the sweetness and flavour of the mint tea being poured for the musicians. But, they are the closest you can probably get without spending a lot of time in Mauritania.

And while the Haratins are avid fans of Moorish classical music, they also have their own folk musics; most importantly, the Medh and Banjey. The first genre consists entirely of religious praise songs. In its most basic form the Medh, usually sung on Thursday nights, consists of a solo singer accompanied by a chorus, several percussionists, and the handclapping of the audience. The women in the audience frequently punctuate the music with enthusiastic ululations. This Medh is folk music, performed by amateurs singing under the light of the moon in desert encampments.

The popular music most associated with the Haratins, however, is Banjey music. While related to the Jakwar music invented by Jheich ould Abba, the Banjey performed by Haratin musicians is its own distinct genre, stripped down to its nuts and bolts; a new genre that sounds like Black Sabbath playing a desert wedding. Gone are the five modes of the Moorish classical repertoire; all that is left is a trance-inducing riff, repeated until the dancers are exhausted. These Haratin guitar players run their instruments through distortion pedals, home-stereo amplifiers and abused bull-horn speakers, incorporating the inevitable squalls of feedback generated by the equipment into their music.

Musicologist Matthew Lavoie is curator of the 2011 album Wallahi Le Zein!! *and author of blog* The Wealth of the Wise *(w thewealthofthewise.blogspot.com).*

Diop instead hails from the northern shore. With several successful international releases, Daby Touré (who also performed with the cross-over band Touré Kunda) is certainly Mauritania's most renowned Soninké musician, though he's now based in France. Finally, you're sure to hear Wolof *mbalax* hits from Senegalese superstars like Youssou N'Dour and Thione Seck, as well as newer pop acts and rappers like Dip Doundou Guiss.

There are also a number of acts who intentionally seek to bridge Mauritania's cultural divides. One of these is the Walfadjiri band, who you can go visit in Nouakchott (page 121). They have released two albums, *Séhil* (2009) and *Espoir*

(2016), on which they sing in all of Mauritania's national tongues. Reggae-influenced multi-instrumentalist Madani (Mister Mada) also sings in a variety of languages – including English – and Ziza Youssouf's output is in a similar vein.

Though its rap scene isn't as active as some of those found elsewhere in West Africa, Mauritania has also produced a number of hip-hop acts, most notably those rapping in Pulaar. These include the politically active Diam Min Tekky, who have been recording since the early 2000s, as well as Authentique BD and Yero Gaynaako, newer voices from the Mauritanian south and BRMX, who hails from Nouadhibou. Ewlad Leblad rap in Hassaniya, though their output is harder to find online. The first women on the Mauritanian hip-hop scene were Les Filles du Bled, whose early 2000s track 'Komi Debo' means 'I am a woman' in Pulaar.

For a full discography of officially released Mauritanian music, see **w** radioafrica.com.au/Discographies/Mauritanian.html; and for a priceless collection of one-of-a-kind recordings and expert insights into Mauritanian music and culture, see Matthew Lavoie's blog, The Wealth of the Wise (**w** thewealthofthewise.blogspot.com).

FILM Though Mauritania's film industry is quite small, it has nonetheless given rise to more than one internationally acclaimed director, including one who is often hailed as among the 'fathers of African cinema' – **Med Hondo**. Born in 1936 to a Mauritanian mother and Senegalese father, he migrated to France at the end of the 1950s and spent his adult life there, eventually working as a dubbing artist, where he famously became the French voice of Eddie Murphy and Morgan Freeman. His films, however, were fiercely independent of commercial considerations, and his oeuvre predominantly interrogates the French–African relationship and its difficulties, including migration, discrimination, colonialism, corruption and independence.

He directed several highly regarded films, most notably his 1970 debut feature *Soleil Ô*, which won the grand prize Léopard d'or at the Locarno International Film Festival, and his 1986 film *Sarraounia*, which took home the grand prize Étalon de Yennenga at the FESPACO biennial in Ouagadougou. His final film, *Fatima, l'Algérienne de Dakar*, came out in 2004 and he passed away in 2019.

Though unknown internationally, Nouakchott entrepreneur **Hemmam Fall** is responsible for some of the earliest films made inside Mauritania. Fall landed in the director's chair by an unusual route: he was a businessman who owned most of the city's cinemas, eventually deciding to try his hand at the seventh art himself. It seems that most of his output may be lost to the sands of Mauritania and time, but a few clips of his 1975 film *Terjit* are available on YouTube. His unexpected death in 1978 coincided with the overthrow of first president Ould Daddah; the subsequent installation of a succession of military governments decidedly uninterested in the arts was a double blow. His cinemas would all fall silent in the following years, mirroring the near-total decline of Mauritanian film and cinema.

Taking the metaphorical baton from Med Hondo, Kiffa-born **Abderrahmane Sissako** has emerged as Mauritania's most celebrated director of the 21st century. While his early films of *Heremakono* (*Waiting For Happiness*, 2002) and *Bamako* (2006) were well regarded and won several awards (including the Étalon de Yennenga for *Heremakono*), he exploded on to the global scene with *Timbuktu* in 2014. The dramatic film portrayed the jihadist takeover of Mali's famed desert city, but was in fact filmed in Oualata as Timbuktu remained too insecure. It won seven César Awards (including Best Film and Best Director), two awards at Cannes, and was nominated for the Academy Award for Best Foreign Language Film – Mauritania's first. Sissako returned ten years later in 2024 with *Black Tea*, which screened at the 29th edition of FESPACO in 2025.

There are a few other independent filmmakers active in Mauritania, including **Mariem mint Beyrouk**, who is the country's first female director. Her 2009 short film *Les chercheuses de pierres* (*Women in Search of Stones*) follows a co-operative of women in Zouérate who travel the desert in search of semi-precious stones to process into jewellery (page 214). More recently, **Khalifa Sy**'s *Kafia* won the jury prize at the 2021 Hope Film Festival in Stockholm, and brothers **Sidi Mohamed Tolba** and **Tayib Tolba** have been touring a number of festivals with their 2024 short film *The Father, Probably*.

Nouakchott also hosts a couple of annual film festivals (page 121), though their regularity is dependent on available funding and other factors, so it's not always clear whether a subsequent edition is likely to be held or not. The Maison des Cinéastes in Nouakchott wasn't functional at the time of writing, but if interested, you can try to find some further information in the Facebook group f Amis du Cinéma de la Mauritanie.

There are, of course, also a number of films featuring Mauritania (either in subject or setting) by non-Mauritanian directors, most famous perhaps being Alain Corneau's 1984 drama *Fort Sarganne*, origin of the famously ahistorical fort (page 190). Mauritania had a moment in the Anglophone mainstream recently, as famous TV-motoring trio Jeremy Clarkson, Richard Hammond and James May filmed the penultimate episode of their *The Grand Tour* series in Mauritania in 2024.

Some notable documentaries include Pierre-Yves Vandeweerd's *Le cercle des noyés* (*Drowned in Oblivion*, 2007), about political prisoners held in Oualata, and Senegalese female director Katy Léna N'diaye's *En attendant les hommes* (*Waiting for Men*, 2007), which delves into the lives of the city's women and their artwork. There are also some French-language documentaries on 'The Events' of 1989 (page 262). Ditte Haarløv Johnsen's 2013 *Under den samme himmel* (*Days of Hope*) follows the migrant trail from Nouadhibou to Copenhagen, and Augustin Viatte's 2024 *Mauritanie, à la rencontre des femmes du désert* accompanies French travel writer Blanche de Richemont as she seeks to learn about the lives of Mauritanian women. Surf fans should look out for Laurent Meillan's 2024 *Pumping Swell in the Sahel* (page 57). And for another type of immersion, Christian Vium and Med Lemine Rajel's 2024 multimedia installation *Tales of a Nomadic City* features Mauritania's first virtual reality experience, taking the wearer from anywhere in the world to a typical tea session on the outskirts of Nouakchott.

Finally, despite its name, little of Kevin Macdonald's 2021 *The Mauritanian* is set in Mauritania (for obvious reasons); those interested in a follow-up on Mohamedou Ould Slahi's life after his liberation and return to Mauritania should seek out Laurence Topham's 2020 BAFTA-nominated short *My Brother's Keeper*, which profiles the unlikely friendship between Ould Slahi and one of his former guards at Guantánamo Bay who ultimately visits him in Nouakchott.

ART AND HANDICRAFTS Though not as renowned as its neighbours to the north or south, Mauritania also boasts a refined artistic tradition, primarily in the applied arts. Here, a corpus of traditional handicrafts and decorative items crafted for nomadic livelihoods still survives, having evolved over centuries to meet the needs and rigours of desert life. Today these sit somewhere between practical need and cultural totem, depending on the item. There are several traditional métiers still practised, including cloth dyeing, leatherwork, metalwork, woodcarving, pottery, weaving and mat making. Dedicated fans of craft and traditional art should seek out a copy of Odette du Puigaudeau's canonical *Arts et coutumes des maures*, which, though only available in French, contains dozens of highly refined drawings detailing all aspects of Moorish material culture, from tent pegs to tobacco pipes.

In keeping with Mauritanian society's nomadic roots, these traditional designs tend to be to a greater or lesser extent portable, which for the visitor means it's quite possible to take home some exquisite items without needing to think about shipping! Even large *tasufra* cushions are no problem – you just take the shell and find a filling of your choice when you get home.

And while it's possible to find traditional crafts more or less throughout the country, Nouakchott is the only place where you'll find anything that could be recognised as a gallery (page 125). But Nouakchott is far from the cultural desert it's sometimes painted as being, and here in the capital there is an increasingly diverse and dynamic visual arts scene concentrated on a handful of these cultural centres and galleries. Formed in the late 1990s, the Union des Artistes Peintres Mauritaniens (UAPM) is Mauritania's oldest artists' association, but their headquarters was locked up tight when we checked in, so a stop into the Institut Français, any of the galleries, or the recently opened Institut National des Arts may be a better way to get connected to the arts scene. Arts de Mauritanie (f Artsdemauritanie) also posts about upcoming events of various kinds.

MOURIDE ICONOGRAPHY

The Mouride order is one of the Sufi brotherhoods especially popular among Wolof Mauritanians, and represents a significant religious and political force in neighbouring Senegal, where they are based. So while they're not nearly as ubiquitous in Mauritania, keep your eyes out for Mouride brotherhood founder Sheikh Ahmadou Bamba (1853–1927) painted on shops, cars, walls and anywhere else there's room, especially in Nouakchott and the south. With his face half-obscured in a white shawl, this beloved and endlessly reproduced visage is based on the only extant photo of Ahmadou Bamba and has become an icon for Mourides everywhere.

But the Mourides' distinctive visual signature is not limited to Ahmadou Bamba's mysterious portrait. His first disciple, Sheikh Ibrahima Fall (1855–1930) – also known as Lamp Fall, as he is considered the 'light' of Mouridism – also has only one known photograph; this too is a recurring image, where he is seen giving a serene half-smile in his trademark dark robes.

Ibrahima Fall was also the founder of the Baye Fall movement, a mystical Mouride sect whose members eschew material possessions and practise a heterodox form of Islam in which devotion is expressed through manual labour and hours-long, trance-inducing chants. They often wear long dreadlocks and wildly coloured chequerboard robes known as *ndiakhass*, along with a stack of chunky wooden prayer beads and gris-gris amulets around their necks. They may or may not also have a calabash full of coins in hand, collecting alms for their marabout (not unlike the talibé at Quranic school).

The two figures of Bamba and Fall are often pictured together, sometimes alongside the 87m central minaret found on the grand mosque of Touba, Senegal's Mouride 'capital city'. The minaret itself is also referred to as Lamp Fall and makes up another key component of Mouride iconography, seen wherever Wolofs and/or Senegalese gather – for example at the Port de Pêche in Nouakchott.

In terms of visual arts, painting is the most popular discipline, and there are a number of Mauritanian practitioners, most of whom live in Nouakchott (or sometimes abroad). Many of these painters work in more than one discipline, including sculpture and design. Some notable names, many of whom have exhibited internationally, include Oumar Ball (oumar_ballartist), Saleh Lo (saleh_lo_lo), Mamadou Anne (f), Béchir Malum (bechir_malum), Mohamed Sidi, Abass Souleymane Sow (f abasssouleymane.sow), Gabar Diop (f Galerienkc), Mael Aînine Nema Cherif (maelaininenema) and Mokhtar Sidi Mohammed 'Mokhis' (mokhis_art), who was one of Mauritania's first painters, getting his start way back in the 1970s! (Mamadou Anne has also been active for nearly as long.) Women are also well represented among Mauritania's visual artists (as well as among the gallery curators), and their ranks include Amy Sow (amysowartistevisuelle), Zeinab Chiaa (zeyneb_chiaa), Marita (marita_officiel_) and Zeina Cheikh (zeicm). In addition to the social media profiles listed, examples of work from several of the above (including those without social media) can be found at the exemplary Zeinart gallery's blog (w art-zein.blogspot.com).

There are also a handful of creative photographers working in Mauritania today, notably including Daouda Corera (dcoreraphotography), Malika Diagana (malika_diagana) and Amadou Mbow (vmvdoumbow), as well as travel creators Ahmed Chadhily (ahmedchadhily) and Snackx (snackx.1). The newly unearthed works of Amadou Fall are especially fascinating, as he was Nouadhibou's first professional photographer, documenting life in this hardscrabble city in the 1960s and 1970s; his son Yagfal picked up after him, and their collection of some 20,000 historic negatives had only just begun to be digitised and shared with a larger audience at the end of 2024 (studio.grandfall).

Finally, Mauritanian fashion doesn't simply stop at *sbagha* (dyeing) the daraa and melhfa. There is also a small but stylish scene of couturiers in Nouakchott, where local labels Yak Lebass (w yak-lebass.com; yak_lebass) and Rafet Xol (rafet_xol.officielle) make youth fashion gear with Mauritanian themes, Aziza Made in Mauritania (azizamadeinmauritania) and Bana Korel (f) produce a variety of elegant women's styles, and Danko Bera (dankobera) makes desert-inspired jewellery with a modern Mauritanian twist.

SPORTS AND GAMES

SPORTS Though it's not a country traditionally known for its sporting prowess, **football** still has no trouble getting Mauritanian hearts beating, and most villages will have a well-worn football pitch (mostly) cleared of rocks and getting enthusiastic daily use by a throng of kids with a patched-up ball; along the coast, matches quite naturally take place directly on the sand. The whole of Mauritania swelled with pride when the national team, Les Mourabitounes, first qualified for the Africa Cup of Nations (AFCON) in 2019. Here, they were eliminated in the group stage, but not before the population went wild for the team, who managed draws against Angola and Tunisia. They were again eliminated in the group stage at AFCON 2021, but their best performance to date came at AFCON 2023 in Côte d'Ivoire, when they advanced to the knockout stage after defeating neighbouring Algeria. They went home in the Round of 16, however, after a loss to their other neighbours, Cabo Verde. Mauritania failed to qualify for AFCON 2025.

The country was ranked 109th by FIFA at the start of 2025, but despite this low ranking, Mauritanian football did make a bit of international splash in 2015: during the Super Cup match between FC Tevragh Zeïna and ACS Ksar, play was unexpectedly stopped in the 63rd minute, and the game went straight to penalties! Why? Apparently it was at the behest of former president Abdel Aziz, who was in attendance and seemingly getting bored of the 1–1 match. The football federation denied the pared-down play was political, rather cryptically blaming 'organisational issues' and the encroaching sunset in Nouadhibou's then unlit stadium for the mysterious curtailment. (Whatever the case, FC Tevragh Zeïna ultimately took home the cup with five penalties to Ksar's four, and everyone presumably beat the traffic home.)

The Fédération de Football de la Mauritanie (45 24 18 60; w ffrim.org; f) is the national governing body, which rather unusually also runs its own restaurant in Nouakchott (page 118). The Mauritanian Super D1 League consists of 14 teams, the large majority of whom are based in Nouakchott. There are now 16 teams in the league, however, as since 2024, top Sudanese sides Al Hilal and Al Merrikh (who between them have won all but four of the 50-plus championships in Sudanese history) have also been playing in Mauritania. This was arranged with the Sudan Football Association to keep Sudanese football alive during the war in that country. And they've been off to a flying start: Al Hilal topped the Super D1 League in 2024–25 (while Al Merrikh came in sixth), but though the Sudanese teams are allowed to compete, the official champion (and therefore delegate to the CAF Champions League) must be a Mauritanian side – in this case FC Nouadhibou, who came in second.

A handful of players from Mauritania, or with Mauritanian roots, have made appearances (or careers) in Europe's first-division leagues, including Aly Abeid, Adama Ba, Djeidi Gassama, Ousmane Dembélé, Souleymane Karamoko, Aboubakar Kamara, Sally Sarr, Pape Ibnou Ba, Beyatt Lekweiry and El Mami Tetah.

Off the football pitch, there are a number of other sports with significant followings in Mauritania. With roots in Senegal (specifically the traditional ceremonies of that country's Serer, Diola and Lebou populations), **traditional wrestling**, or la lutte as it's known in French (and làmb in Wolof), is beloved in Mauritania (and Senegal's national sport). With the wild theatrics and outlandish characters of pro wrestling, but minus the made-for-TV fakery of its North American counterpart, la lutte's combat style remains fiercely traditional and a typical match doesn't last more than a few minutes. To start with, the two competitors, typically dressed in nothing but loincloths and a normal person's weight in gris-gris amulets, are daubed with protective powders, lotions and other trade secrets, all designed to confer strength and protection in the ring. More modern fights allow the competitors to strike one another with their hands, but in its most traditional form you've got to pin or throw your opponent by grappling and throwing alone; in either form, if any part of your body except your hands or feet touches the ground, you're out. It's governed by the Fédération Mauritanienne de Lutte (m 22 32 07 83; e federation.rim.lutte2022@gmail.com; f), and there are bespoke facilities for competition in both Nouakchott and Nouadhibou.

Somewhat unexpectedly, Mauritania also excels at **pétanque** (boules), and this may in fact represent their most successful international sporting event. The national team took bronze in the 2010 Pétanque World Championships, and the men's triplette team was ranked fifth globally as of 2024. The Fédération Mauritanienne des Jeux de Boules (m 46 73 90 91, 46 56 15 76; f fmjb.mr) governs the sport, and there are pétanque pitches or boulodromes in Nouakchott and several of the larger cities; they're hugely popular as the evening cool settles in.

Cycling is not as widely practised, but the Fédération Mauritanienne de Cyclisme (f profile.php?id=100063752295621) has been organising the five-stage Tour

SURF MAURITANIA

Unlike its southern neighbour Senegal, Mauritania did not feature in the seminal 1966 surf documentary *The Endless Summer*. But as of very recently, it's been the subject of a surf film of its own, director Laurent Meillan's *Pumping Swell in the Sahel*. Released in 2024, it profiles Mauritania's tiny but passionate surf community, and a number of the spots they frequent, including a rare excursion over the border to La Güera/Lagouira (page 150), where a legendary but forbidden wave awaits. It's worth watching in full, and features the following spots, among others:

Cap Blanc ⊕ 20.7719, -17.0439. Tubular wave south of Nouadhibou at the Cap Blanc beach.

Le Wharf ⊕ 18.0345, -16.0262. Fast right break south of the disused jetty in Nouakchott.

PK60 ⊕ 18.6271, -16.1221. Long westerly swells 60km north of Nouakchott.

Sancho ⊕ 18.2017, -16.0339. Long rollers north of Bahamas Beach restaurant, about 12km north of Nouakchott.

For a full list of known surf spots and live conditions, consult w wisuki.com/country/mr/mauritania; and for surf organisations in Nouakchott, see page 128.

du Sahel since 2018. The stages take in a combination of the flatlands around Nouakchott and Inchiri regions, as well as the many climbs and mountain passes of the Adrar.

There are also small scenes for other common sports, including **tennis** and **basketball**. Both the Féderation Mauritanienne de Tennis (m 46 70 96 61; e fmt.mauritanie@gmail.com) and the Fédération Mauritanienne de Basket-Ball (m 46 95 13 99; w fbbrim.com) put on events and competitions in Nouakchott.

Unsurprisingly, Mauritanians particularly love desert sports, including **marksmanship**, and there are more than 100 shooting clubs active in the country. Target shooting with rifles is considered as much a traditional cultural activity as it is a sporting one, and it's not uncommon to set up a rifle and a can for target practice on trips out in the desert. The Fédération mauritanienne de Tir sportif (m 22 10 60 02; e mauritaniefmt@gmail.com) focuses on modern competitive shooting, while the Union Mauritanienne de Tir à la cible Traditionnelle supports traditional target shooting, organising competitions between shooting clubs, often on culturally significant dates like independence day or during the guetna date harvest.

Camel racing is another culturally significant sport, and the Fédération Nationale de course de Chameaux (m 33 47 17 10, 36 60 43 35; e federationrimcouresse@gmail.com; f coursduchameaux) organises periodic races, especially at the new racecourse north of Nouakchott (page 134). **Horseriding** and races can also be found, starting at the Fédération Mauritanienne du sport Équestre (m 37 27 27 27; f) near the beach in Nouakchott.

But of course Mauritania is an oceanic nation as well as a desert one, and though watersports are a fairly niche pursuit here, there are a few possibilities for **surfing** and **kitesurfing**. Many of the prevailing conditions that have turned nearby Dakhla into a kitesurfers' haven also exist in Nouadhibou, but suffice it to say that the city hasn't caught on like Dakhla has. Still, at least one establishment offers gear and lessons (page 144). For more general information, try Kite Surfing Mauritania (m +34 646

21 00 05; e kitesurfingmauritania@gmail.com; f kitesurfingmauritania). There are a handful of known surf spots in the country, most of which are featured in the 2024 surf film *Pumping Swell in the Sahel* (page 57). There are a couple of parked domains related to surfing in Mauritania (surfmauritania or mauritaniasurf), but no publicly active surf-oriented organisations at the time of writing. Finally, sport **fishing** is also popular, especially around Nouadhibou, and both shore-casting and boat-based fishing is possible, with a long list of potential catches including thiof (white grouper), capitaine (giant African threadfin), Carangue crevalle (Crevalle jack), tuna, swordfish, and more. The Fédération Mauritanienne de pêche sportive (m 26 20 04 00; e anpsndb@gmail.com; f) organises events.

Mauritania has sent athletes to every Summer Olympic Games since 1984, but has yet to win a medal. Presumably the Comité National Olympique et Sportif Mauritanien (w cnosm.mr; f) will be crossing their fingers for Los Angeles and Brisbane!

And if all that wasn't enough for you, Rimsport (w rimsport.net) has got you covered with up-to-date coverage on Mauritanian sports of all kinds (in French).

GAMES Games are also very popular in Mauritania, with several beloved desert pastimes still equally enjoyed by city dwellers of all ages. **Dhamet** (also known as *srand* or *zamma*) is considered the national game. Related to draughts and alquerque, this ancient amusement features a playing field that is more often a grid traced in sand than a physical board, 80 game pieces (half sticks and half stones – or pieces of camel dung!) and mechanics which will be at least vaguely familiar to a draughts player. Unlike draughts, however, a dhamet match inevitably draws a crowd – look out for older men playing in the evening cool – who are there as much for a vigorous discussion of strategy (or lack thereof) as they are for the game itself.

And just as the men crowd around to play and comment on a game of dhamet, so too do the women for a round of **seig** (or essig). Game pieces are again typically twigs, shells, and – you guessed it – camel dung, but the game board, called a lebrah, is no ordinary set of holes in the sand, but a three-dimensional construction evoking the back of an animal. Typically 70cm long and 10cm high, the lebrah looks like a miniature sand dune and is lined with four rows of 12 holes, one on each side of the 'dune', and two at its summit. Eight sticks with differing sides are thrown to determine movement of the pieces, and if you'd like to know more about the (rather complex!) gameplay, there's an excellent explanation of the mechanics here: w globaltimoto.com/africa/mauritania/games/seig.

Finally, **krur** rounds out the trifecta of Mauritania's most popular traditional games. It's a mancala-style 'sowing' game of a sort found around the world, but may be especially familiar if you've spent time travelling in Africa, where variants on the theme are popular from here to Mozambique. Krur is also typically played in the sand, here consisting of two rows of holes from which you count and capture seeds, stones, or again, camel dung, and aim to collect the largest number to win.

Though dhamet, seig and krur are often played in sand, game boards from wood and other materials do exist, and these are often crafted in highly stylised and attractive versions, which make for a popular souvenir.

Finally, **chess** also has a following in this gaming nation, and the Fédération mauritanienne des jeux d'échecs (m 41 50 00 00; w mauritaniachess.com) organises monthly tournaments at Nouakchott Hotel (page 116) in Nouakchott.

2

Practical Information

WHEN TO VISIT

Tourism in Mauritania is highly seasonal, with November to March representing the core travel season. This is essentially a function of the weather, which is fiendishly hot at other times of year, when inland temperatures can crack 50°C during the day and only dip to about 30°C by night. But in the northern winter, the weather remains (relatively) cool and dry, offering hot but not unbearable days and reliably cool nights. The northern winter is also the ideal time for birders, as all the European migrants are in town.

Indeed, you'll be glad to have your sweater, particularly on the coast. Consistent oceanic breezes throughout the year moderate temperatures here significantly, and the average low during the tourist season in Nouakchott is 15–20°C, with daytime highs around 30–35°C. Nouadhibou is similar but cooler still, with the high temperatures generally keeping under 30°C.

Temperatures rise through the springtime and into early summer (April–June) until the rains arrive to cool things off a bit – where it rains at all, that is. The rainiest months are July–September, though what *rainy* means varies dramatically throughout the country. In the north, September is the rainiest month, but this doesn't mean much: Nouadhibou sees barely 5mm of precipitation, while Zouérate gets just 20mm. Further south, August is wetter, and Nouakchott gets 80mm to Kiffa's 120mm. In the far south, Sélibaby is decisively Mauritania's rainiest city, getting 160mm on average in August, with 200mm or more not unheard of. The rains also begin earlier and end later here. Depending on where you are, temperatures may rise again in October as the rains dissipate, before the mercury definitively begins to fall with the arrival of winter. Humidity levels correlate across the country with the prevalence of rain, as you might expect, and the inland south can be mighty humid indeed.

Road conditions were traditionally another factor dictating travel schedules, but with the rapid expansion of Mauritania's surfaced road network, getting around the country is easier than ever, regardless of season. So if you're brave enough to attempt the temperatures and don't mind the occasional rainstorm, Mauritania will be here to receive you. Note that many tourist-facing businesses may be closed for the season, so you'll have to be flexible in your plans. As a reward, though, you could even catch the annual guetna date harvest, usually held around August – it's traditionally a locals-only affair, mostly thanks to the weather scaring all the tourists away!

HIGHLIGHTS

BANC D'ARGUIN NATIONAL PARK This wind-blasted coastline, once home to a Portuguese trading post, is a true study in desolation. The jagged coastline hides an assortment of cerulean lagoons and bays, best appreciated from the deck of a traditional lancha sailboat. Page 152:

BEN AMIRA The world's second-largest monolith (after only Uluru in Australia) towers high over the surrounding desert, with only its neighbouring monolith, Aïcha, for company. An unexpected gallery of modern art hides at its base. Page 188.

CHINGUETTI The town that once gave Mauritania its name may be disappearing into the sands, but its importance to national identity remains undimmed; the city's five-pointed minaret remains Mauritania's most iconic symbol, and its libraries are equally legendary. Page 191.

CROCODILES In a truly unexpected twist, Mauritania is home to dozens of perennial pools where reptilian relics of a much wetter time continue to eke out a living in the middle of the Sahara. Some of the pools are quite remote, while others are easily visited. Page 13.

DIAWLING NATIONAL PARK With mangrove-lined creeks, wide expanses of water and tens of thousands of migratory birds, this national park in southernmost Mauritania will widen your perspectives of this (mostly!) desert country. Page 232.

IRON ORE TRAIN The size and scale of this engineering marvel never fails to impress as it rumbles by, and a ride on one of the longest, heaviest – and certainly dustiest – trains in the world is not one you'll soon forget. Page 218.

NOUAKCHOTT Don't let the naysayers put you off – Nouakchott has its charms if you know where to look! Get into the gentle groove of this nomadic metropolis, which is the largest in the Sahara and certainly among Africa's most unusual capital cities. Page 105.

OUADANE Built at the head of two wadis, this was a critical stop on caravan routes for centuries, and a wealth of stone architecture stands witness to this long-lost past. Along the now-silent Road of 40 Scholars the imagination quickly comes to life. Page 199.

OUALATA The red-and-white bas-reliefs distinguish this painted oasis from its stone-built siblings, but there are no short cuts to Mauritania's furthest corner. The reward for your efforts is sweet, though, and not just the local specialty of date-stuffed pigeon. Page 297.

SENEGAL RIVER As untouristed as it gets, this 1,000km river is the lifeblood of southern Mauritania, and its shores are lined with hundreds of farming and herding villages where life moves to the rhythm of the annual flood, the springtime grass, and the call to prayer. Page 242.

TERJIT The palm trees crane their necks to catch the sun above this sheltered gorge, where pure water runs down the mossy walls and refreshing wading pools full of foot-nibbling pedicure fish line the bottom. Page 179.

TICHITT The smallest and most isolated of Mauritania's ancient ksour, this grey-stone outpost still lives from traditional means, and you may even see the occasional camel train, heavily laden with product cut from the salt pans outside town. Page 282.

SUGGESTED ITINERARIES

The following itineraries are structured on the assumption of having access to a vehicle. Should you be travelling on public transport, the length of time required to cover all destinations indicated will be considerably longer, and some of the off-road destinations will be impossible to access.

ONE WEEK Assuming you start off in Nouakchott, you'll spend your first night there, so try and drop in for colourful scenes at the Port de Pêche, a bit of history at the National Museum (page 130), and a few sniffs at one of the city's livestock markets (page 125), where hundreds of camels congregate. From here, you'll head inland to the Adrar, where a one-week circuit among the ancient ksour and oases is more or less the 'classic' Mauritanian itinerary.

Spend your first night camping under the enormous dune at Azoueiga (page 183), before continuing off-road through the high walls of the Vallée Blanche (page 184) and arriving at the spectacularly hidden oasis of Terjit (page 179), where you can take a dip in the natural springs. You can overnight here or at the neighbouring oasis of Mhaïreth (page 181), where thousands of date palms line the valley.

From here, continue on to the ancient city of Chinguetti (page 191) where libraries of treasured Arabic manuscripts await, and take in an unforgettable sunset in the dunes overlooking town. Continue to Ouadane (page 199) via the tiny oasis of Tanouchert (page 198) and spend the afternoon marvelling at the ruins of this once-great city.

Take in the extraordinary geology of the Richat Structure (page 204) before returning west towards Atar via the Passe d'Amogjar (page 189), stopping to take in the views at Agrour (page 190) and Fort Sarganne (page 190). From Atar, begin the return journey to Nouakchott for your outbound flight.

Alternatively, if you are on one of the weekly charter flights from Paris direct to Atar, you can avoid the transit to and from Nouakchott and use the time saved to take a camel safari (easily arranged from most auberges in the region), drop in on some of the Adrar's other isolated oases like Berbara (page 185) or El Beyedh (page 205), and spend another night or two under the desert stars.

TWO WEEKS A full two weeks allows you to do the classic Adrar itinerary indicated above, plus a chance to either explore the Tagant and Banc d'Arguin National Park, or pick one of the two and take the opportunity for a couple of nights in the desert, as on page 170.

Again starting in Nouakchott, head inland and either break your journey in Aleg (page 267) or continue the extra 65km to Boghé (page 247) if you'd like to have a peek at the Senegal River. Continue northeast into the Tagant region, where a short diversion off-road brings you to the thoroughly unexpected Matmata crocodile pool (page 278); another (longer) diversion nearby brings you to the little-visited ruins of Ksar el Barka (page 277). After the diversion(s), carry on to the regional capital of Tidjikja (page 278), where you can decide whether or not you want to brave the rough track to Mauritania's most isolated ancient ksar of Tichitt (page 282).

At 230km one-way from Tidjikja, it's a real investment to get to Tichitt, and as such barely a couple of handfuls of travellers do so every year. From Tidjikja, take the new road into the Adrar, taking a peek at the scenic town of Rachid (page 281) en route. Stop for the night in Terjit and from here carry on to Chinguetti, Ouadane and Atar as on page 189.

From Atar, instead of returning to Nouakchott, head north towards Ben Amira (page 188) and spend the afternoon marvelling at the world's second-largest monolith and the rock art hidden nearby. After a night camping at the base of the rock, you follow the route of the Iron Ore Train (page 218) to Mauritania's second city of Nouadhibou (page 138) and its extraordinarily busy fishing harbour.

Finally, celebrate your return to the coast with a swing through the Banc d'Arguin National Park (page 152), where you can take a traditional sailboat trip or simply marvel at the shockingly, beautifully austere coastline and its extraordinarily hardy inhabitants. From here, it's only a few hours back to Nouakchott – you could even go straight to the airport.

THREE WEEKS OR MORE With at least three weeks, you can do all of the above plus dip your feet into Sahelian southern Mauritania along the river and get out to Oualata, Mauritania's farthest-flung ksar.

Again starting from Nouakchott, head south towards the coastal lagoons of Diawling National Park (page 232), where many thousands of migrant birds take advantage of the fresh water after crossing the Sahara. From here, start your long sojourn inland along the river road, taking in the lime-green rice paddies and melon fields of Mauritania's greenest corner, known to the Halpulaar locals as the chehama. Overnight in Boghé or Kaédi and continue east into the savannahs of Mauritania's Soninké heartlands, spending the night in Sélibaby (page 258), Kankossa (page 276), or Kiffa (page 271) as your time and ambition allows.

Continuing east from Kiffa along the Route de l'Espoir, it's still a very long push to Oualata, so break your journey in one of the several towns en route, or at Néma (page 293) where the tarmac road ends. (Also be sure to consult locally on the current security situation in this distant corner of the country before setting out.) Arriving in Oualata (page 297), you can give yourself a big pat on the back as you explore the thick-walled homes of this famously remote and famously adorned red-and-white ksar.

From here, it's a two-day (minimum) desert crossing along the base of the Dhar Tichitt escarpment to reach the eponymous ancient ksar and its abandoned counterpart of Akhreijit (page 286), where you rejoin the itinerary listed above. En route, there's water at the Aratane wells (page 303) and scores of evocative rock formations – but none more so than the elephant rock, Al Makhrougat (page 303).

From Tichitt, follow the itineraries on page 61 from Tagant into the Adrar, taking advantage of your unhurried schedule to extend your stay in the most tempting of oases, and returning to Nouakchott via Ben Amira, Nouadhibou and the Banc d'Arguin.

TOURIST INFORMATION AND TOUR OPERATORS

The state tourism bureau, **Office Nationale du Tourisme Mauritanien** (ONTM; Lot 008 ZGE, Ksar, Nouakchott; ☎ 45 29 90 90; w visitmauritania.com; f), handles mostly destination marketing, and given that national park entry and other practicalities are all handled at the individual sites, for the casual visitor there's usually not a compelling need to contact them, though there's some good background information on their website.

Many of the tour operators offering tours to Mauritania are France-based, but the firms listed here would be a better starting point for anglophones. Most run scheduled trips as well as tailor-made tours. Some of the trips listed include a ride on the Iron Ore Train.

International tour operators

Against The Compass ☎ +34 6 13 09 84 94; e hello@againstthecompass.com; w againstthecompass.com. Runs 8-day group trips in Mauritania.

Lupine Travel ☎ +44 1942 366555; e info@lupinetravel.co.uk; w lupinetravel.co.uk. Runs 8- & 12-day trips in Mauritania, some of which conclude in Dakhla.

Native Eye ☎ +44 1473 328546; e info@nativeeyetravel.com; w nativeeyetravel.com. Runs 10- & 21-day small group tours to Mauritania, as well as overland trips from Marrakech.

Overlanding West Africa ☎ +44 1728 862247; e info@overlandingwestafrica.com; w overlandingwestafrica.com. Independent operator with overland trips between Marrakech & Dakar via Mauritania, as well as other destinations in North & West Africa.

Palace Travel ☎ +1 80 06 83 77 31; e info@palacetravel.com; w palacetravel.com. Offers week-long trips in Mauritania.

Penguin Travel ☎ +45 89 88 36 84; e info@penguintravel.com; w penguintravel.com. Runs 7- & 11-day small group trips in Mauritania, some of which begin in Laâyoune (El Aaiún).

Point-Afrique ☎ +33 4 75 53 23 83; e contact@point-afrique.com; w point-afrique.com. This French agency is responsible for ticket sales on the Paris–Atar flight, which can be purchased independent of an accompanying (French-language) tour.

Responsible Travel ☎ +44 1273 823700; e rosy@responsibletravel.com; w responsibletravel.com. Offers 10- & 21-day holidays in Mauritania with a focus on small groups.

Rocky Road Travel ☎ +353 8 76 83 31 11; e info@rockyroadtravel.com; w rockyroadtravel.com. Runs 8-day group trips in Mauritania.

Untamed Borders ☎ +44 1304 262002; e info@untamedborders.com; w untamedborders.com. Runs 13-day group trips in Mauritania.

Young Pioneer Tours m +971 5 85 98 29 17; e tours@youngpioneertours.com; w youngpioneertours.com. Runs 5-day tours in Mauritania.

Mauritania- and West Africa-based tour operators

All of the following agencies are based in Nouakchott unless otherwise noted, & can arrange itineraries throughout the country, including train rides, camel safaris, camping & more. All have English-speaking guides if needed.

Amatlich Tours m 43 55 43 37; e info@amatlichtours.mr; w amatlichtours.mr; f; Instagram

Atar Voyages m 46 57 67 61, (+33) 6 56 70 39 94; e atarvoyage@gmail.com; w atarvoyages.com; f; Instagram

Désert Mauritanie m 46 44 24 21; e info@desertmauritanie.com; w desertmauritanie.com; f

Inimi Tours m 27 55 45 37, 47 55 45 37; e camping.inimi@yahoo.fr; w inimitoursdesertmauritania.com; f; Instagram

Levrigue Agence m 46 40 75 30; e dahid2@yahoo.fr; f

Maham Voyages m 46 63 35 25; e mahamvoyages@gmail.com; f; Instagram

Mauritania Desert Voyages m 36 77 73 33; e mauritaniadesertvoyages@gmail.com; w mauritaniadesertvoyages.com; f; Instagram

Mauritanian Best Tours m 27 27 27 59, 22 33 85 22; e contact@mauritanian-best-tours.com; w mauritanian-best-tours.com; Instagram

Mauritanides m 49 00 59 98, +34 6 31 51 92 97; e info@mauritanides.net; w mauritanides.net; Instagram

Sahel Découverte ☎ +221 3 39 61 56 89; e resa@saheldecouverte.com; w saheldecouverte.com; f; Instagram. This Saint-Louis (Senegal) based agency offers week-long trips along the Senegal–Mauritania border on the vintage 52m *Bou el Mogdad* boat.

Scoot West Africa m +223 70 32 03 44, +221 77 3 87 80 46; e philandmatt@scootwestafrica.com; w scootwestafrica.com; f; Instagram. This Senegal-based agency offers 8-day tours to Mauritania, as well as group & customisable tours (on or off scooters) in the region.

Sidi Tours m 22 23 23 01; e booking@tourmauritania.com; w tourmauritania.com; f; Instagram

Time For Mauritania m 48 17 55 53; e timeformauritania@yahoo.com; w timeformauritania.com; f; Instagram

T'Ore Mauritania m 37 78 75 28; e babaceo@toremauritania.com; w toremauritania.com; ;

Trarza Tour m 46 43 25 59; e sidi202000@yahoo.fr; w trarza-tour.odoo.com; ;

RED TAPE

The Mauritanian government introduced a new **e-visa requirement** in January 2025, cancelling the previous Visa On Arrival (VOA) programme entirely. The new visa process is administered through the Agence Nationale du Registre des Populations et des Titres Sécurisés (National Agency for the Population Register and Secure Titles), and applications must be made at w anrpts.gov.mren/visa/requestvisa.

At the time of writing the system was still frustratingly full of kinks, so a few precautions are in order as you make your application. Firstly, the size requirements for your photo and passport scan are exact. Use a photo-editing/resizing app to adjust your images to the exact dimensions requested, or the uploads will be refused. Secondly, save the case number given when you have submitted your application, as you must log in to check the visa status – *you will not receive an email when the visa is ready, you must check yourself!* Finally, when your e-visa is approved you must download and *print out the approval*. Bring this hard copy with you to the border; mobile copies are not accepted. Visas are generally approved within a couple of days, but many travellers have reported longer waits if their indicated arrival date was far in the future, and there have unfortunately also been reports of visas not being approved in time at all. If you need further assistance or your departure is urgently approaching, you can make enquiries via WhatsApp (m +222 46 19 00 22) or email (e contact@anrpts.gov.mr).

The visa fee is still paid on arrival, and costs €55 in cash (or 2,500UM, should you already have some ouguiya). Authorities strongly prefer payment in euros, but you *may* get them to begrudgingly accept USD, Moroccan dirhams (arriving from Dakhla), Algerian dinar (arriving from Tindouf), or West African CFA (arriving from Senegal or Mali). If accepted, other currencies will be charged at a disadvantageous rate – we were quoted 45,000 CFA at Diama, which converts to nearly €70.

At the border, you will no longer receive a sticker visa but an entry stamp. The e-visa is available for 30/90 days (€55/95), and multiple entries are now available (this was not possible with the previous VOA scheme). On arrival with the e-visa your biometric data will be taken, which unfortunately is only available at larger border crossings, restricting travellers to the following entry points: the airports at Nouakchott, Nouadhibou and Atar, the land border crossings at Rosso (Senegal), Diama (Senegal), Goguï (Mali), PK55 (Morocco-administered Western Sahara) and Hassi 75 (Algeria).

Also note that importing **alcohol** is forbidden. This is generally more of a problem for travellers with vehicles than those on foot, but officials will often search vehicles (or occasionally bags) for alcohol, and will levy fines if alcohol is found.

EMBASSIES

Mauritania has embassies in London (w mauritania-embassy.uk) and Washington (w mauritaniaembassyus.org), but note that the London embassy does not issue visas and refers applicants to the Mauritanian embassies in Paris (w ambarimparis.fr) and Madrid (e ambarim@embajadamauritania.es) instead. A full list of

Mauritanian representation abroad can be found at w diplomatie.gov.mr/fr/ambassades or w embassypages.com/mauritania.

In Mauritania, all neighbouring states have embassies in Nouakchott, including Morocco, Algeria, The Gambia, Mali, Senegal and Guinea-Bissau. There are also a few consulates in Nouadhibou, including for Morocco, Algeria, The Gambia and Guinea-Bissau.

GETTING THERE AND AWAY

BY AIR Opened in 2016, Nouakchott–Oumtounsy International Airport (w aeroport-nouakchott.com) is (almost) Mauritania's only international airport, and sits 35km north of central Nouakchott along the N2 towards Nouadhibou. It's privately managed by Emirati firm Afroport (w afroport.com), while Mauritania's other airports are under the authority of the Société des Aéroports de Mauritanie (w sam.mr). The only other airports in Mauritania with international connections are Nouadhibou (to Las Palmas) and Atar (seasonally to Paris).

Nouakchott is served by a handful of strategic routes for travellers, though isn't overly well connected and coming from anywhere outside of Europe and Africa will require a change of planes, likely in Paris, Casablanca or Istanbul. Arriving from the Canary Islands makes for an unexpected itinerary, and one where you can enjoy a bit of beach indulgence before or after your sojourn in the desert.

Air Algérie w airalgerie.dz. Flights to Algiers.
Air France w airfrance.com. Flights to Paris.
Air Senegal w flyairsenegal.com. Flights to Dakar.
ASKY w flyasky.com. Flights to Lomé via Conakry.
Binter Canarias w bintercanarias.com. Flights to Las Palmas.
Mauritania Airlines w mauritaniaairlines.mr. National carrier since 2010, offering flights to several cities in West & North Africa, including Abidjan, Bamako, Brazzaville, Casablanca, Conakry, Cotonou, Dakar, Las Palmas, Libreville, Pointe Noire and Tunis.
Royal Air Maroc w royalairmaroc.com. Flights to Casablanca.
Tunisair w tunisair.com. Flights to Tunis.
Turkish Airlines w turkishairlines.com. Flights to Istanbul via Banjul.

OVERLAND Officially speaking, Mauritania has four neighbours – Senegal, Mali, Algeria and Western Sahara. But the de facto partition of Western Sahara means that in practice there are five neighbours, as the two sides of Western Sahara operate under completely different administrations.

Crossings to Senegal The 742km border with Senegal is formed by the Senegal River. The most popular crossing by far is that of Rosso, where vehicle ferries (page 85) ply back and forth throughout the day, but a new bridge is scheduled to open by the end of 2026. Rosso, however, has a somewhat justified reputation for hassle and corruption, so many travellers opt for the much more relaxed Diama border to the west instead.

Coming from Nouakchott, the turn-off to Diama is at the junction village of Aouyevia (Awevia), where past reports indicate some people might tell you either the border or Diawling National Park is closed and that you therefore have to go to Rosso. Though the unsurfaced road through Diawling does flood on occasion, the Diama border operates throughout the year and is open to travellers with and without their own vehicles. The river crossing itself utilises the Diama Dam as a bridge, and deposits you only 30km from the Senegalese city of Saint-Louis.

Other than Rosso and Diama, the only crossing currently set up to accommodate vehicles is at Kaédi, where a small vehicle ferry has been present since 2023. Otherwise, there are numerous border posts along the river where pedestrians can cross in a pirogue, including (from west to east) Lexeïba II, Boghé, Kaédi, Toufunde Civé and Gouraye.

Crossings to Mali Mauritania's 2,236km border with Mali is far and away the country's longest, cutting an overwhelmingly linear path through desert and scrubland on the south and east sides of the country. Almost all of the many possible crossings face towards the south, as the areas on either side of the north–south section of border are very sparsely inhabited.

Unfortunately, prolonged insecurity in Mali means that overland travel into the country from Mauritania was not advised as of 2025. In light of this insecurity (as well as other political factors), the Malian embassy in Nouakchott was not issuing tourist visas as of 2025.

Regardless, the most significant crossing point is at Goguï, 125km south of Aïoun el Atrouss and linked by tarmac road on both sides of the frontier. Other border posts that might form part of a cross-border itinerary in more peaceful times include those at Ghabou, Ould Yengé, Hamoud, Tenaha, Adel Bagrou, Fassalé and N'Beiket Lahouach.

Crossings to Algeria Whichever side you approach from, the 460km Mauritania–Algeria border is wildly remote, and the first official border crossing between Mauritania and Algeria only opened in 2024 (page 217). At the time of writing, the route between Zouérate and Tindouf was nearly all off-piste and took some 24 hours to cross, but construction was already underway on 800km of tarmac to facilitate this newly opened connection.

Note that Algerian visa procedures are notoriously tricky, and it's unlikely you'll be given one as a non-resident in Nouakchott, so plan ahead if you'd like to take this route.

Crossings to Morocco-controlled Western Sahara The 80% or so of Western Sahara west of the berm is controlled by Morocco, which claims this territory as its Southern Provinces (page 164). From a visitor's perspective, Moroccan administration of the territory is little different than that of 'mainland' Morocco, and the one official border crossing at Guerguerat functions as any other Moroccan port of entry.

There are no major security concerns on the Morocco-administered side of the berm, though the territory is heavily militarised. Few travellers stray inland from the main coastal road, so you may be subject to questioning at checkpoints should you decide to explore the interior. A new 85km Moroccan road between the Morocco-administered city of Smara and the Mauritanian border north of Bir Moghreïn was completed in 2025; there was not yet any border infrastructure here at the time of writing, but it seems likely enough that it might appear during the lifespan of this edition (see page 216 for details).

Crossings to Sahrawi-controlled Western Sahara The 20% or so of Western Sahara east of the berm is controlled by the Polisario Front, which claims this territory as the Sahrawi Arab Democratic Republic (page 222). Though there are no official border crossings, it was previously possible to visit the handful of villages and military bases here or camp out in the countryside, and most vehicles running

DAKAR DUPLICATES

Though the legendary **Dakar Rally** (w dakar.com) was relocated in 2008 and now takes place in Saudi Arabia, rally racing has returned to Mauritania in the form of the **Africa Eco Race** (w africarace.com), which is a traditional motorsport rally raid in the spirit of the original Dakar Rally. The **Budapest–Bamako** (w budapestbamako.org) is another competitive rally but, with several categories of vehicle, route and competition available, it is open to curious adventurers, as well as professional drivers. Another rally developed in the wake of Dakar's departure, **The Real Way to Dakar** (w realwaytodakar.com) was cancelled indefinitely in 2025.

between Zouérate and Tindouf in Algeria would pass through here. With no official visa or entry procedure as such, depending on who you encountered you might be welcomed with tea and biscuits or escorted back to Mauritanian land.

But Polisario declared an end to the 29-year ceasefire with Morocco in November 2020, and since then the Sahrawi-controlled region has played host to a low-intensity conflict of tit-for-tat attacks, making travel here dangerous. (Though it denies responsibility, many attribute a spate of drone attacks in the territory to Morocco, and a November 2021 strike killed three Algerian truckers near the town of Bir Lehlou.) As such, most Mauritania–Algeria traffic now avoids the Polisario-controlled zone, and many of the area's residents have fled to the Polisario-managed refugee camps in Algeria.

As such, it was unadvisable to attempt to visit the Sahrawi-controlled Western Sahara/Sahrawi Arab Democratic Republic as of 2025. (Note that this is distinct from visiting the Polisario-administered refugee camps in Algeria, which is still possible.)

The Polisario Front has several representative offices around the world (w embassypages.com/sahrawi), and enquiries about the possibilities of travel can be directed to these. As a former Spanish colony, its delegations are especially active in Spain (w frentepolisario.es).

BY BOAT Despite the country's 754km coastline and two significant ports, there is no commercial passenger boat service to or from Mauritania, and most yachties seem to pass right by en route to Dakar. So if you're hoping to score a lift to Cabo Verde or elsewhere, you're likely to have better luck in Senegal; try at the Cercle de la Voile de Dakar (CVD; Dakar Sailing Club; +221 33 832 0720; e cvdkr@orange.sn; cvd.dakar).

HEALTH *with Dr Daniel Campion*

Despite all the hazards listed – it should be emphasised that – as in much of Africa – road traffic accidents present the greatest risk to life and limb you're likely to face in Mauritania. Medical care in regional capitals is basic, so for serious health conditions Nouakchott is the only place to be, and if more complex medical care is necessary, evacuation to Las Palmas, Casablanca, Dakar or Europe is recommended. As with everything in Mauritania, Arabic and French are the operating languages, but some doctors may have a smattering of English as well. Doctor's visits, lab fees, malaria tests and treatment are all inexpensive – don't hesitate to get checked out on account of cost. The US Embassy in Nouakchott maintains an updated list of doctors and clinics at w mr.usembassy.gov/doctors-in-mauritania.

PREPARATIONS Sensible preparation will go a long way to ensuring your trip goes smoothly. Particularly for first-time visitors to Africa, this includes a visit to a travel clinic to discuss matters such as vaccinations and malaria prevention. The following points are worth emphasising:

- Don't travel without comprehensive **medical travel insurance** that will fly you home (or to the nearest high-quality health facility) in an emergency. Travellers should be aware that many standard insurance policies exclude coverage for destinations where government bodies, such as the UK's Foreign, Commonwealth and Development Office (FCDO), advise against travel. This includes several parts of Mauritania – check official websites for the latest recommendations. Given these advisories, obtaining appropriate coverage requires specialised insurance providers that offer policies for high-risk areas.
- Make sure all your **immunisations** are up to date. A yellow fever vaccination is advised to protect against the disease, and you will need to show proof of immunisation upon entry if you are entering Mauritania from another yellow fever endemic area. Since July 2016 all countries have to accept that the yellow fever vaccination lasts for life and travellers do not need to be revaccinated unless they were immune suppressed at the time of vaccination through disease, medication or pregnancy or were under the age of two, in which case they would need to be vaccinated again after ten years. If the vaccine is not suitable for you, then you would be wise not to travel: West Africa has the highest prevalence of yellow fever and there is up to a 50% mortality rate. It is also unwise to travel in the tropics without being up to date on tetanus, polio and diphtheria (usually given as an all-in-one vaccine), hepatitis A and typhoid. If you are at higher risk, be up to date with vaccines against Covid-19 and influenza. Immunisation against rabies, meningitis, hepatitis B, cholera, dengue and possibly tuberculosis (TB) may also be recommended.
- The biggest infectious disease threat is **malaria**. There is no malaria vaccine available to travellers, but a variety of preventative drugs can be used, including mefloquine, atovaquone/proguanil (Malarone) and the antibiotic doxycycline. Malarone and doxycycline need to be started only two days before entering Mauritania, but mefloquine should be started two to three weeks before. Doxycycline and mefloquine need to be taken for four weeks after the trip and atovaquone/proguanil for seven days. *It is as important to complete the course as it is to take it before and during the trip.* The most suitable choice of drug varies depending on the individual and the country they are visiting, so visit your GP or a specialist travel clinic for medical advice. If you will be spending a long time in Africa, and expect to visit remote areas, be aware that no preventative drug is 100% effective, so you may want to carry a treatment kit. It is also worth noting that no homeopathic prophylactic for malaria exists, nor can any traveller acquire effective natural immunity to malaria. Those who don't make use of preventative drugs are risking their lives unnecessarily.
- Though recommended for most travellers, a pre-exposure course of **rabies** vaccination, involving three doses over 21 days, is particularly important if you intend to have contact with animals, or are likely to be 24 hours away from medical help. If you have not had this, then exercise serious caution around stray animals, as you'll need to head for Nouakchott immediately and possibly evacuate for the necessary treatment. See page 129 for more information.
- Anybody travelling away from major centres should carry a personal **first-aid kit**. Contents might include a good drying antiseptic (eg: iodine or potassium

permanganate), plasters (Band-Aids), sunscreen, insect repellent, aspirin or paracetamol, antifungal cream (eg: clotrimazole), loperamide and rehydration salts for diarrhoea, antibiotic eye drops, tweezers, condoms or femidoms, a digital thermometer and a needle-and-syringe kit with accompanying letter from a health-care professional. Those travelling remotely or who are at high medical risk may be prescribed antibiotics for self-treatment of severe diarrhoea.

- Bring any drugs or devices relating to **known medical conditions** with you. That applies both to those who are on medication prior to departure, and those who are, for instance, allergic to bee stings or are prone to asthma attacks. Always check with the country website to identify any restricted medications. Carry a copy of your prescription and a letter from your GP explaining why you need the medication.
- Prolonged immobility on long-haul flights can result in **deep-vein thrombosis (DVT)**, which can be dangerous if the clot travels to the lungs to cause pulmonary embolus. The risk increases with age, and is higher in obese or pregnant travellers, heavy smokers, those taller than 6ft/1.8m, and anybody with a history of clots, recent major operation or varicose veins surgery, cancer, a stroke or heart disease. If any of these criteria apply, consult a doctor before you travel.

TRAVEL CLINICS AND HEALTH INFORMATION A list of current travel clinic websites worldwide is available on w istm.org. For other journey preparation information, consult w travelhealthpro.org.uk (UK) or w wwwnc.cdc.gov/travel (USA). All advice found online should be used in conjunction with expert advice received prior to or during travel.

POTENTIAL MEDICAL PROBLEMS

Malaria This potentially fatal disease is widespread in low-lying tropical parts of Africa, a category that includes central and southern Mauritania throughout the year. In northern provinces (Adrar, Trarza, Inchiri and Dakhlet Nouadhibou), the risk is highest during the rainy season and prophylaxis is recommended between July and October. In addition to prophylactic medication, you should take all reasonable precautions against being bitten by the nocturnal *Anopheles* mosquitoes that transmit the disease (page 70). Malaria usually manifests within two weeks of transmission, but it can be as little as seven days and anything up to a year. Any fever occurring after seven days should be considered as malaria until proven otherwise. Symptoms typically include a rapid rise in temperature (over 38°C), and any combination of a headache, flu-like aches and pains, a general sense of disorientation, and possibly even nausea and diarrhoea. The earlier malaria is detected, the better it usually responds to treatment. So, if you display possible symptoms, get to a doctor or clinic immediately (in the UK, go to accident and emergency and say that you have been to Africa). A simple test, available at even the most rural clinic in Africa, is usually adequate to determine whether you have malaria. You need three negative tests to be sure it is not the disease. And while experts differ on the question of self-diagnosis and self-treatment, the reality is that if you think you have malaria and are not within easy reach of a doctor, it would be wisest to start treatment – typically a course of artemether/lumefantrine.

Dengue This virus is spread by aggressive day-biting *Aedes* mosquitoes. In Mauritania, **dengue** had traditionally been rare, but the first officially reported outbreak took place in 2014, and the World Health Organization indicates that the disease remained present as recently as 2024. Symptoms include headaches, rashes, excruciating joint and muscle pains, and high fever. The illness usually lasts about a week and is not usually fatal. Complete rest and paracetamol are the usual treatments; plenty of fluids also help. Avoid aspirin, ibuprofen or similar drugs: they can worsen the virus's effect on blood clotting. Some patients are given an intravenous drip to keep them from dehydrating. It is especially important to protect yourself if you have had dengue fever before, since a second infection with a different strain can result in the potentially fatal dengue haemorrhagic fever. A vaccine is now available in the UK and Europe and is generally recommended for people who have had dengue once, to prevent a more severe second infection. If you are unlucky enough to have dengue fever in Mauritania, keep a copy of your test results, as this will make vaccination before your next trip easier.

A related virus, **Zika**, has not yet been detected in Mauritania, despite the presence of carrier *Aedes* mosquitoes.

Other insect-borne diseases Although malaria is the insect-borne disease that attracts the most attention in Africa, and rightly so, there are others, most too uncommon to be a significant concern to short-stay travellers. **Chikungunya** is another virus carried by *Aedes* mosquitoes. It occurs in periodic outbreaks and the symptoms overlap with dengue, although joint pain is predominant and some patients may develop ongoing and sometimes disabling joint inflammation.

AVOIDING MOSQUITO AND INSECT BITES

The *Anopheles* mosquitoes that spread malaria are active at dusk and after dark. Using a **mosquito net** over your bed and **covering up** exposed skin (by wearing long-sleeved shirts and tucking trousers into socks) in the evening are the most effective steps towards preventing bites. Bed-net treatment kits are available from travel clinics; these prevent mosquitoes biting through a net if you roll against it in your sleep, and can also improve protection from old and damaged nets. Mosquito coils and chemical insect repellents will help reduce your chances of being bitten, as will sleeping under a fan.

Mosquito repellent must be applied to all exposed skin. DEET (diethyltoluamide) is the active ingredient in many repellents, and has the most evidence to support its use: the optimum concentration is 50%. Icaridin at 20% is an effective alternative. Eucalyptus citriodora oil (or PMD) is the only 'natural' repellent with some evidence of effectiveness against mosquitoes, but it needs to be applied more frequently. Other remedies, such as eating garlic or taking vitamin B, are not evidence-based: never substitute these for an effective repellent. Bear in mind, too, that most flying insects are attracted to light: leaving a lamp standing near a tent opening or a light on in a poorly screened hotel room will greatly increase the insect presence in your sleeping quarters.

It is also advisable to think about avoiding bites when walking in the countryside **by day**, especially in wetland habitats, which often teem with diurnal mosquitoes. Wear long, loose clothes, preferably 100% cotton, as well as proper walking or hiking shoes with heavy socks (the ankle is particularly vulnerable to bites), and apply a DEET-based insect repellent to any exposed skin. You can also treat natural-fibre clothing with clothing sprays that contain permethrin. The insecticide will kill mosquitoes on contact with the fabric; the clothes will survive a few washes and will still be effective.

Vaccination may be recommended for high-risk travellers and during outbreaks: two chikungunya vaccines are now licensed in the UK. **Rift Valley fever** is a viral disease of cattle which occasionally causes outbreaks in humans; it is transmitted by mosquito bites or the consumption of raw milk. Tiny sandflies can transmit **leishmaniasis** at night: seek medical advice if you develop a febrile illness or a non-healing skin lesion. Other potential insect-borne threats include sleeping sickness (transmitted by tsetse flies) and river blindness (blackflies). It is clearly sensible, and makes for a more pleasant trip, to avoid insect bites as far as possible (see opposite). Two nasty (though ultimately relatively harmless) flesh-eating insects associated with tropical Africa are tumbu or putsi flies, which lay eggs, often on drying laundry, that hatch and bury themselves under the skin when they come into contact with humans; and jiggers, which latch on to bare feet and set up home, usually at the side of a toenail, where they cause a painful boil-like swelling. Drying laundry indoors and wearing shoes are the best ways to deter this pair of flesh-eaters.

Tick bites Ticks may spread African tick bite fever and Crimean-Congo haemorrhagic fever along with a few other dangerous rarities. Ticks should ideally be removed intact, and as soon as possible, to reduce the chance of infection. You can use special tick tweezers, which can be bought in good travel shops; or failing this, with your fingernails, grasp the tick as close to your body as possible, and pull it away steadily and firmly at right angles to your skin without jerking or twisting. Applying irritants (eg: Olbas oil) or lit cigarettes is to be discouraged as a means of removal since they can cause the ticks to regurgitate and therefore increase the risk of disease. Once the tick is removed, if possible douse the wound with alcohol (any spirit will do), soap and water, or iodine. If you are travelling with small children, remember to check their heads, and particularly behind the ears, for ticks. Spreading redness around the bite and/or fever and/or aching joints after a tick bite imply that you have an infection that requires antibiotic treatment. In this case seek medical advice.

Travellers' diarrhoea Many visitors to unfamiliar destinations suffer a dose of travellers' diarrhoea, usually as a result of consuming contaminated food or water. Rule one in avoiding diarrhoea and other sanitation-related diseases is to wash your hands regularly, particularly before snacks and meals. As for what food you can safely eat, a useful maxim is: PEEL IT, BOIL IT, COOK IT OR FORGET IT. This means that fruit you have washed and peeled yourself should be safe, as should hot cooked foods. However, raw foods, cold cooked foods, salads, fruit salads prepared by others, ice cream and ice are all risky. It is rarer to get sick from drinking contaminated water, but it happens. Stick to bottled or filtered water which is widely available. If you suffer a bout of diarrhoea, it is dehydration that makes you feel awful, so drink lots of water and other clear fluids. These can be infused with sachets of oral rehydration salts, though any dilute mixture of sugar and salt in water will help, for instance a bottled soda with a pinch of salt. If diarrhoea persists beyond a couple of days, it may be a symptom of a more serious gastrointestinal illness (cholera, dysentery, worms, etc), so see a doctor. If the diarrhoea is greasy and bulky, and is accompanied by sulphurous (eggy) burps, one likely cause is the parasite *Giardia*, which can cause persistent symptoms but is treatable. Again, seek medical advice if you suspect this.

Cholera Cholera is a bacterial infection that can cause severe diarrhoea and dehydration, spreading through contaminated water and food. The disease is most prevalent in rural areas and refugee camps, where access to medical care and sanitation infrastructure is limited.

To minimise the risk of contracting cholera, it is important to take basic food and water hygiene precautions as listed on page 71. If cholera is contracted, symptoms such as severe watery diarrhoea, vomiting and rapid dehydration can develop quickly. Seeking medical help as soon as possible is crucial, as untreated cholera can be fatal. Immediate rehydration is essential. In severe cases, antibiotics may be prescribed by a health-care professional to shorten the duration of the illness.

Most travellers are at low risk, but oral cholera vaccines are available for those heading to known outbreak areas or who are undertaking high-risk activities such as humanitarian aid work.

Bilharzia Also known as schistosomiasis, bilharzia is an unpleasant parasitic disease transmitted by freshwater snails most often associated with reedy shores where water weeds are abundant. It cannot be caught in hotel swimming pools or the ocean, but should be assumed to be present in any freshwater river pond, lake or similar habitat, even those advertised as 'bilharzia free'. The highest-risk areas will be within 200m of villages or other places where infected people use water, wash clothes, etc. Drying off vigorously with a towel after an accidental brief water exposure may help to prevent the *Schistosoma* parasite from penetrating the skin, but should not be relied upon. Ideally you should avoid swimming in any fresh water other than an artificial pool. Bilharzia is often asymptomatic in its early stages, but some people experience an intense immune reaction, including fever, cough, abdominal pain and an itching rash, around four to six weeks after infection. Later symptoms vary but often include a general feeling of tiredness and lethargy. If you may have been exposed, you can be tested or screened at specialist travel or tropical medicine clinics, ideally at least six weeks after exposure. Fortunately, bilharzia is easy to treat at present, typically with two doses of praziquantel.

Meningitis This nasty bacterial infection can kill within hours of the appearance of initial symptoms, typically a combination of a blinding headache (light sensitivity), blotchy rash and high fever. Outbreaks tend to be localised and are usually reported in local media. Fortunately, immunisation with meningitis ACWY vaccine protects against the most serious bacterial form of meningitis. Nevertheless, other less serious forms exist which are usually viral, but any severe headache and fever – possibly also symptomatic of typhoid or malaria – should be sufficient cause to visit a doctor immediately.

Rabies This deadly disease can be carried by any mammal and is usually transmitted to humans via a bite or a scratch that breaks the skin. In particular, beware of village dogs and monkeys habituated to people, but assume that any mammal that bites or scratches you might be rabid even if it looks healthy. First, scrub the wound with soap under a running tap for a good 10–15 minutes, or while pouring water from a jug, then pour on a strong iodine or alcohol solution, which will guard against infections and might reduce the risk of the rabies virus entering the body. Whether or not you underwent pre-exposure vaccination, it is vital to obtain post-exposure prophylaxis as soon as possible after the incident. You should head immediately for the *Institut National de Recherches en Santé Publique* at the *Centre Hospitalier National* in Nouakchott (page 129); they will advise you if they can provide the appropriate post-exposure treatment (supplies have been known to run out) or if you'll have to evacuate straight away. Having the rabies vaccine before travel reduces the amount of post-exposure treatment needed and in most cases removes the need for rabies immunoglobulin (RIG), which is in global short supply, and therefore makes the treatment more available in country. Treatment may differ if your immune system is weakened, eg: if you take immunosuppressant medication. Do take this disease seriously: death from rabies is probably one of the worst ways to go, and once you show symptoms it is too late to do anything – the mortality rate is 100%.

Tetanus Tetanus is caught through deep dirty wounds, including animal bites, so ensure that such wounds are thoroughly cleaned. Immunisation protects for ten years, provided that you don't have an overwhelming number of tetanus bacteria on board. If you haven't had a tetanus shot in ten years, or you are unsure, get a booster dose as soon as possible after the injury.

HIV The prevalence of HIV infection in Mauritania is low compared to other parts of sub-Saharan Africa. The infection is concentrated in cities and among marginalised groups such as sex workers and men who have sex with men. Consistent use of barrier contraception helps reduce the risk of transmission.

Skin infections Any mosquito bite or small nick is an opportunity for a skin infection in warm humid climates, so clean and cover the slightest wound in a good drying antiseptic such as dilute iodine, potassium permanganate or crystal (or gentian) violet. Prickly heat, most likely to be contracted at the humid coast, is a fine pimply rash that can be alleviated by cool showers, dabbing (not rubbing) dry and talc, and sleeping naked under a fan or in an air-conditioned room. Fungal infections also get a hold easily in hot moist climates, so wear 100%-cotton socks and underwear, and shower frequently.

Eye problems Bacterial conjunctivitis (pink eye) is a common infection in Africa, particularly for contact-lens wearers. Symptoms are sore, gritty eyelids that often stick closed in the morning. They will need treatment with antibiotic drops or ointment. Lesser eye irritation should settle with bathing in salt water and keeping the eyes shaded. If an insect flies into your eye, extract it with great care, ensuring you do not crush or damage it, otherwise you may get a nastily inflamed eye from secreted toxins.

Heat illness and dehydration Heat exhaustion and heatstroke can be caused both by hot, dry weather and by humid conditions. Avoiding heatstroke is best achieved by observing how local people behave. Seek shade and stay out of direct sunlight, especially in the middle of the day; cover up with long, loose clothes; wear a hat or headscarf; and drink plenty of water. In hot conditions, you should be drinking at least two to three litres of water, or an equivalent liquid, a day. The glare and the dust can be hard on the eyes, so bring UV-protecting sunglasses.

Symptoms of heat exhaustion include dizziness, tiredness, nausea and headache. Use rehydration salts mixed with water to replenish fluids and salts and find somewhere cool and shady to recover. Some cases may progress to heatstroke, a more severe breakdown of temperature control. This can lead to reduced or absent sweating, flushed skin and disorientation leading to unconsciousness. Cool the body down quickly (cold showers are particularly effective), place the casualty under a fan and seek urgent medical treatment.

Snake and other bites Snakes are very secretive and bites are a genuine rarity, but certain spiders and scorpions (such as the Arabian fat-tailed and yellow fat-tailed scorpion) can also deliver venomous bites or stings. In all cases, the risk is minimised by wearing closed shoes and trousers when walking in the bush, and watching where you put your hands and feet, especially in rocky areas or when gathering firewood. Only a small fraction of snake bites deliver enough venom to be life-threatening, but it is important to keep the victim calm. Immobilise the affected limb (eg: with a splint) and seek urgent medical attention.

SAFETY

The period between 2005 and 2011 saw several ideologically inspired **terrorist attacks** on military and civilian targets in Mauritania, notably including the murder of four French tourists near Aleg in December 2007. This led to the relocation of the 2008 Dakar Rally, and the cancellation of the Paris–Atar charter flights that had been the lifeblood of local tourism since 1996. 2009 saw the abduction of three Spanish aid workers and two Italian tourists (all ultimately released), and the murder of an American teacher. Alongside similar unrest in the rest of the West African Sahara and Sahel, tourism quite understandably disappeared.

The Mauritanian state, however, launched a significant military and socio-political campaign to uproot jihadist activity from the country, and there has not been a terrorist attack on Mauritanian soil since December 2011. But in the meantime, the Quai d'Orsay, British FCO and other foreign ministries around the world had naturally redlined the country.

It wasn't until 2017 that the French foreign ministry revised its maps to reflect the improving security situation in Mauritania, prompting the revival of charter flights to Atar which, Covid disruption excepted, have been going strong ever since. The British FCO also followed suit, and as of 2025, only areas east of Zouérate, Tichitt, Kiffa and Sélibaby remained in the red, and most of the attractions covered in this guide are now in the green zone ('normal safety precautions'). A 2023 prison riot in which four jihadis escaped threatened to puncture this calm, but all the escapees were captured or 'neutralised' within a week.

The French and British maps can be consulted online (w diplomatie.gouv.fr/fr/conseils-aux-voyageurs/conseils-par-pays-destination/mauritanie; w gov.uk/foreign-travel-advice/mauritania), and for more information about travel in eastern Mauritania, see page 285.

Therefore, travel in Mauritania is likely the safest it's been in two decades, and your biggest concern should be to take the **weather** and climatic conditions here seriously. The Mauritanian desert is no joke, and without taking the adequate precautions and supplies, you put yourself in significant danger. Only go into the desert if you are familiar with desert bushcraft or with a trusted guide, and always ensure that you have adequate supplies of food and water, appropriate clothing for hot *and* cold weather, first aid materials and basic emergency equipment like a mirror to signal for help before setting out.

Finally, opportunistic **crime** does exist, but Mauritanian cities are on the whole fairly safe, and outside of the larger cities you are especially unlikely to encounter any issues in this regard – Mauritanians are even sometimes known to brag about how your valuables will be unmolested regardless of where you leave them. (A nice idea, though we wouldn't necessarily test it out!) Therefore the usual precautions about crowded areas like markets and bus stations being hotspots for pickpocketing and the like still apply, but violent crime and robberies remain rare. For more information on safety in Nouakchott, see page 105.

The relevant **emergency numbers** are as follows: SAMU (ambulance) ☎ 101; Sapeurs Pompiers (fire service) ☎ 18; Police Secours (emergency police) ☎ 17; Gendarmerie nationale (gendarmes) ☎ 116.

WOMEN TRAVELLERS *Lucie de Beauchamp*

Mauritania remains an often misunderstood country, and this may raise unnecessary alarms for women wanting to travel the land. However, Mauritania proves to be very hospitable for travellers, including women, as long as some effort is made to understand and adapt to local culture.

Indeed, Mauritania is a devout Muslim-majority country. In practice, this means that decency plays an important role in the interactions between men and women outside of the family circle. While Mauritanians do not expect foreign and non-Muslim visitors to follow the exact same set of rules, it is important for female travellers to understand this. In addition, as in many other parts of the world, customs vary greatly between large cities and more rural areas. Overall, Mauritanians are extremely welcoming, but do appreciate when visitors show respect for their culture. In return, by following standard and basic safety rules, women (including solo travellers) will be able to travel safely throughout the country.

In practice, dressing a little more modestly than what they may be used to is an important way for women to adapt to the Mauritanian way of life. Wearing long trousers, skirts or dresses, as well as T-shirts (to cover shoulders) is usually seen as appropriate. While there is absolutely no need to cover your hair day-to-day, a headscarf is mandatory to visit mosques. As temperatures can rise easily, especially as you progress inland, long clothes in breathable fabric can also be a precious ally against the scorching sun. In addition, Mauritanian women often take public transport, and there is no issue for foreign women wanting to do the same.

In general, Mauritanian men tend to be very respectful of women in public spaces. Some curious staring is to be expected, especially if you venture into slightly less-visited areas, however, catcalling is extremely rare and Mauritanian men will very rarely try to strike up a conversation with women in the street. That being said, as standard advice, it is recommended to avoid walking alone at night, especially in larger cities. In addition, for women travelling alone, if you are engaged in conversation with a man, it is rather common to get questions regarding marital status, to receive unwanted compliments, and even to get semi-serious marriage proposals. For the vast majority, gently and firmly explaining that you are not interested will be more than enough to get your interlocutor to back off. If a situation starts to feel uncomfortable, do not hesitate to call on locals present around you for support.

Importantly, hospitality is an integral part of Mauritanian culture, and invitations for a cup (or three) of tea or a meal are common. While these invitations are completely genuine the vast majority of the time, women travelling alone will decide for themselves whether they choose to accept them or not.

Lastly, it may be more difficult for travellers to interact with local women than men. There are two reasons for this: women tend to be less present in the tourism industry and in public spaces, and on average women tend to speak fewer foreign languages than men. That being said, Mauritanian women are also extremely warm and welcoming.

TRAVELLING WITH A DISABILITY

The UK's **gov.uk** website (w gov.uk/government/publications/disabled-travellers/disability-and-travel-abroad) has a downloadable guide giving general advice and practical information for travellers with a disability (and their companions) preparing for overseas travel. The **Society for Accessible Travel and Hospitality** (w sath.org) also provides some general information. The website **Wheelmap** (w wheelmap.org) has an interactive global map showing accessible and partially accessible properties, including museums, hotels and restaurants.

It must be said, however, that the prevalence of accessible accommodation options in Mauritania is next to nil. As such, Mauritanians with disabilities are often reliant on the help of their communities and fellow travellers, which is freely given but naturally limited in scope; visitors can expect the same.

LGBTQIA+ TRAVELLERS

In a word, no. Mauritania is one of a handful of countries with the death penalty on the books for same-sex sexual activity. The country has had a moratorium on the death penalty since 1987, but still occasionally arrests and jails people it 'suspects' of homosexuality. Eight men were arrested after a video falsely labelled as a 'gay marriage' was leaked in 2020. In reality, the video was of people singing and dancing at a birthday party, but the men were ultimately convicted of 'indecent acts' and 'inciting debauchery' just the same and received two-year jail sentences.

Despite this actively repressive climate, there are Mauritanian men known as *gordiguène* (or *gordigan*, *gordjigen*), which roughly translates to either homosexual or transsexual, who have paradoxically been called 'an inseparable part of Moorish urban culture'. They play the role of entertainers and are invited to weddings and other events to sing and dance. This is not without risk, however, and many of those arrested men may have been *gordiguène* entertainers.

Despite these contradictions, there's little need to belabour the point further – employ maximum discretion.

TRAVELLING WITH KIDS

Though Mauritanians love children and your kid will certainly be making friends left and right anywhere in the country, it must be said that creature comforts are few and far between anywhere outside of Nouakchott, and facilities or accommodations oriented specifically to children are nearly non-existent. Therefore, the difficulties of travel with children here will generally come down to discomfort, not danger (though medical care can often be some distance away). With a child who is sociable, flexible and enjoys camping and the outdoors, Mauritania's welcoming people and wide-open spaces could be the recipe for a dream trip. But with one expecting comfortable digs and reliable Wi-Fi…your days in the desert could feel long and hot indeed.

There are a couple of children's parks and funfairs to be found in Nouakchott and Nouadhibou, however, including Dream Land Ocean (m 44 34 97 16; f) on the way to Nouakchott's airport, and a number of the resort-style complexes catering to Mauritanian families will have their own playgrounds (of varying quality) as well.

WHAT TO TAKE

Generally speaking, Mauritania is reasonably well stocked with all of the little necessities a traveller might require, but this varies greatly depending on where in the country you are. In Nouakchott you'll find almost anything your traveller's heart could desire, from T-shirts to tampons. Most of the brands are French but, unless your needs are quite specific, any clothing, toiletries, food, batteries or other basic goods you might need will be readily available in Nouakchott and likely

Nouadhibou as well. Outside of these cities, availability of just about everything drops off considerably.

Pharmacies are also typically reasonably stocked (again, particularly in Nouakchott), but you should plan to bring a supply of any personal medications needed for the duration of your trip. It's also advisable to carry sunscreen, as you'll have a hard time finding it outside of the largest Nouakchott supermarkets, where it's sold at a significant mark-up. Camping and trekking equipment is not easy to find anywhere in the country. Electricity is 220v at 50Hz, and plugs are European style, with two round pins.

CARRYING YOUR LUGGAGE If you're planning on hiring a vehicle, taking a guided tour, or otherwise not lugging your bags for considerable distances, you shouldn't have any problem with an average suitcase, though take care that it's a durable one so it's ready for off-road bumps and overeager baggage handlers. A bag that can be padlocked can always still be slashed or otherwise broken into, but it will go a considerable way towards deterring opportunistic theft, which is far and away the most common form of thievery you're likely to encounter.

If you'll be getting around on public transport, a backpack is greatly preferable, as weaving your way through a sand-pit bus station with a rolling suitcase is nobody's idea of a good time. As with the suitcase, the ability to lock your bag is ideal, but keeping valuables (camera, phone, etc) in a daypack that stays with you when your larger bag is stowed is also a workable solution. Plus, the daypack will come in handy for any day trips or hikes you intend to go on.

CLOTHES Protecting yourself from the sun is a significant consideration in Mauritania, particularly if you're fair-skinned. Therefore, a comfortable hat, a light long-sleeved shirt, and light long trousers/skirts will all be key items in your pack. (A headwrap purchased in Mauritania will also work well!) At the minimum, you should have one, probably two pairs of trousers/skirts, three shirts, a light pullover, a medium-thickness sweater or jacket, and no less than five days' worth of socks and underwear. On your feet you'll want one decent pair of walking shoes or light hiking boots and one pair of flip-flops or sandals.

Jeans and their suitability for African travel are a topic of some debate. On the negative side, they are bulky and hot, but at least they dry quickly in the Mauritanian climate. On the upside, they're durable, protect against the evening chill and take a good long time before looking dirty (of particular value if you're getting around on public transport). Light cotton trousers or skirts have a significant advantage over jeans in breathability and less space in your pack, but their dirt-hiding abilities are considerably less impressive.

Having a pullover/jacket on hand is a lifesaver in the evenings. In breezy Nouakchott, the average low temperature doesn't crack 20°C for five months of the year; you'll find similar oceanic chills on much of the coast from November to April. Shirts with a buttoning front pocket can be handy for cash as they're nigh on impossible for a pickpocket to get to without attracting your attention.

This might seem to go without saying, but socks and underwear are perhaps the most crucial item in your wardrobe. They're small and light, so bring lots, and bring only ones made from cotton or other natural fabrics. Re-wearing socks and undies can encourage athlete's foot with the former, or prickly heat with the latter (and in a neighbourhood where you'd typically be loath to have anything prickly). You can of course buy more of these locally if you run short, but you'll have to shop around carefully to avoid polyester and other synthetic materials.

It's also important to bear in mind that Mauritania is an Islamic Republic and social mores surrounding fashion will likely be considerably more conservative than what you're used to – for both men and women. It's therefore worth taking note of a few considerations when planning your outfits. As a rule, long shirts and long trousers are ideal. Women shouldn't wear skirts or shorts above the knee, and shirts that cover your upper arms are a good idea as well. It's not necessary for foreign women to wear a hijab/shawl, but you would only ingratiate yourself with the locals by doing so. For men, knee-length shorts are fine in the countryside, but long trousers are a better choice in town – religious considerations aside, shorts are seen as an outfit for schoolboys, not grown men.

OTHER USEFUL ITEMS Whether or not you plan to camp, if you're going the budget route it can be nice to have a sleeping bag (or better yet a sleeping-bag liner/silk sleep sack) in case you wind up staying in a room with not exactly clean bedding, which, on the lowest end of the price spectrum, is indeed possible. Depending on

MAURITANIAN DRESS

No-one arriving in Mauritania can fail to notice the strikingly unique style of its residents. This is one of a shrinking number of countries where traditional styles are still very much everyday dress, and Western fashion still runs a distant second in popularity.

Dress styles differ somewhat between the Moorish and Black African populations, but if there's one iconic piece that's symbolic of the country as a whole, it must be the Moorish men's **daraa** (also sometimes called a boubou). This dramatic billowing tunic is daily wear for men around the country, and styles can range significantly from very simple to very elaborate (for formal occasions), with the latter made from a variety of elegant brocade or damask fabrics. The only rule seems to be that they come in either pure white or one of 50 possible shades of blue – from the faintest of sky blues to a deep rich royal indigo – and spill over and down one's sides, requiring the wearer to repeatedly collect up the extra cloth to drape over their shoulders.

They also come with a greater or lesser amount of embroidered embellishments (depending on how fancy the garment), which are usually done in golden-orange thread. A large front pocket reminiscent of a kangaroo's pouch completes the look, and provides a spot for men to stash their phone, cigarettes, car keys and more. Under the daraa, baggy trousers known as **sarouel** are worn, usually in the same colour as the daraa and typically accompanied by a long dangling leather belt (tijikrit). The accompanying undershirt is often a Western-style button or T-shirt (or occasionally a matching traditional shirt), and it's all topped off with a long (3.5m!) turban known as a **haouli** (or *chèche*, *litham*) wrapped around the head and face.

Moorish women's outfits are no less striking, and the drab, dark abayas often associated with conservative Islam are far from the norm here. Indeed, the women's **melhfa** is quite the opposite, coming in all the colours of the rainbow – and sometimes all at once. Essentially one long piece of fabric that is knotted around the shoulders and then wrapped around the entire body, they measure roughly 4.5m long and 1.5m high and come in a wide variety of patterns. Mauritania is home to a significant tradition of *teinture* (dyeing) that's often associated with the city of Kaédi, so many of these tie-dyed patterns are produced by female where in the country you are, a mosquito net can also be useful to have for cheap accommodation or nights in a khaïma tent; out in the desert it's much less critical than down in the river valley and thereabouts. These can also be good to have if you wind up staying with a local family, which is also quite possible.

Aside from the obvious toiletries of soap, shampoo, toothbrush and toothpaste that you'll clearly want to have, your own stash of loo paper should be added to that list. Most Mauritanians clean themselves after using the toilet using a sort of low-tech bidet system involving a scoop or kettle (known as a *maghrej* or *satalla*) full of water and, while this works just fine once you're used to it, most travellers will be very happy to have something a bit more familiar in the form of a roll of two-ply at the ready in their backpacks. It's available for purchase in many shops, but only kept stocked in the toilet at the fanciest of places. Men might want a razor unless it's Movember or they're working on their hipster beard, while women will definitely want to have at least a period's worth of tampons or pads available in case you find yourself far from a major city.

teinturières living along the river (as well as in Nouakchott). These artisans stitch and tie the fabric into intricate patterns to expose and protect different parts of the cloth from the dye, and the more elaborate patterns can require literally thousands of knots for one garment. (There are also cheaper machine-printed versions that seek to replicate this effect.)

Men from Mauritania's Black African ethnic groups wear styles similar to those seen in Senegal and Mali, with slimmer **boubou** tunics (either knee or ankle length) and matching trousers worn in a range of colours and typically made from bazin cloth that's been beaten to a luminous shine. For a hat, you might have a squarish kufi cap, or even a zig-zag woolly hat called 'Cabral' after the Bissau-Guinean leader who popularised it in the region. There is also a daraa equivalent called a **grand boubou**, differing from the Moorish version primarily in colour – here, the sky (blue) is no longer the limit, and a wide selection of colours are worn. Also, unlike the daraa, this is typically worn as one's 'Sunday best' to Friday prayers, special occasions and the like.

Black African Mauritanian women's dress is more varied than their Moorish compatriots, but similar in its ardour for colour. Women will typically wear either an ankle-length **kaftan** with embroidery embellishments around the neckline or a three-piece set known as a **complet**, comprising a matching bodice, skirt and headwrap. This can be made of colourful bazin fabric, or the vividly patterned and archetypically African wax-print cloth called **pagne**. Long, ankle-length dresses in similar fabrics are also not uncommon.

Another couple of striking items you're likely to see are associated with the Halpulaar, who live primarily in the south. For women, there are beautifully crafted **kwottenai** spiral hoop earrings in gold; these range from the tiny to the enormous – all the better to show off at special occasions with. And for men, a much more workaday but no less striking garment is the **tengade**: a conical straw hat trimmed in leather and perfect for long days spent out in the sun tending the flocks.

If you're going shopping, keep in mind that a high-end grand boubou, mhelfa or daraa can cost well upwards of €150, but basic versions can be had for as low as €10.

For the bespectacled, make sure to have either your prescription (so that you can get a new pair made up) or a spare pair of glasses along with you. Contact lens fluid is available at some shops in Nouakchott, but don't count on finding it anywhere else in the country, and be aware that the dust and intense sunlight can be irritating for contact lens wearers. For other various aches, pains, sprains, rashes, itches, cramps, grumbles (but probably not hangovers), be sure to have a basic medical kit on hand.

Other bits and bobs you might like to have along include a pocketknife, torch (flashlight), pack of cards or other games, and maybe a washbasin plug for doing some sink laundry. If your luggage is capable of locking it would be worthwhile to take advantage of this and bring a padlock to deter opportunistic thieves. Of course an unlocked mobile phone is useful both for making calls and as an alarm clock for the inevitable early morning starts – by bus or camel.

MONEY AND BUDGETING

The official currency in Mauritania is the ouguiya (أوقية), which is at least nominally divided into five khoums (خمس) – making it one of only two currencies in the world that are non-decimal, alongside the Malagasy ariary. The ouguiya was introduced in 1973 when Mauritania left the CFA franc zone, and gets its name from a historical Arabic measure equivalent to the ounce. (And khoums, in turn, means 'one fifth'.)

The ouguiya (UM) was redenominated in January 2018, dropping one zero in a counter-inflationary currency reform. An entirely new set of corresponding polymer notes and coins was issued alongside (see opposite): the new ouguiya comes in notes of 1,000, 500, 200, 100, 50 and 20 ouguiya, and coins of 20, 10, 5, 2 and 1 ouguiya, and 1 khoum.

The old notes and coins are no longer legal tender, but **it is *very* common for traders to still quote prices in the old currency rather than the new** – so if something seems unexpectedly pricey, try dividing it by ten!

ORGANISING YOUR FINANCES In short: bring euros and a Visa card. Credit card payments are really only accepted in a few places in Nouakchott and Nouadhibou, so cash remains king in this corner of the Sahara. Though euros are the most widely recognised hard currency by far, you will still manage to change US dollars – British pound sterling and other less-popular currencies are another story.

Getting cash is generally not a major problem in Nouakchott or Nouadhibou, but other regional capitals may only have one or two ATMs (known locally as *guichets automatiques bancaires* or GABs), so you are at the mercy of their often-uncertain reliability. Therefore, it's best to stock up on the coast before heading inland if possible.

As elsewhere in West Africa, Visa card is preferable, with several banks accepting their use, including the Banque Mauritanienne pour le Commerce International (BMCI; w bmci.mr), Attijari Bank (w attijariwafabank.com) and Banque Populaire de Mauritanie (BPM; w bpm.mr). Only one, however, currently accepts Mastercard as well: Société Générale (w societegenerale.mr). BMCI has the widest network of ATMs and is often the only option for withdrawing money upcountry.

CHANGING MONEY It's possible to change money inside bank branches, but in practice it's often quicker and easier to do so in a shop, as any general shop or supermarket over a certain size will generally be happy to buy your euros in exchange for ouguiya. If you've got currency from the neighbouring countries, keep in mind that the further away you get from the border, the harder this will be to exchange.

MOSQUE MONEY

The new(ish) ouguiya banknotes issued to correspond with the 2018 currency reform are colourful and fetchingly designed, showcasing Mauritanian nature and architecture. The designs all feature one of the country's many historic mosques, and make for a satisfying catalogue of Mauritania's ancient heritage – right in your pocket.

20UM	Gattaga Mosque (Kaédi) and Guelb er Richât (Eye of the Sahara).
50UM	Ibn Abbas mosque (Nouakchott) and teapot, instruments including *tidnit* (men's lute), *ardin* (women's harp) and *neifara* (flute). There is also a newer version of this banknote issued in 2023 to commemorate 50 years of the ouguiya, featuring the central bank building in Nouakchott.
100UM	Oualata mosque and a farm field with wheat and livestock including cattle, sheep and goats.
200UM	Ouadane mosque and camels and goats with sand dunes and date palm.
500UM	Tichitt mosque and industrial and artisanal fishing boats with spotted seabass (*Dicentrarchus punctatus*, to be precise).
1,000UM	Chinguetti mosque and the Iron Ore Train with electricity pylons.

There are generally a handful of moneychangers to be found at border crossings like Rosso and PK55, and while we haven't heard or experienced anything particularly negative in this regard, it's always wise to be on your guard against the overeager and quick-handed. Local shops may again be a calmer and safer option than availing yourself of moneychanger services on the street, and there are a few official exchange offices in Rosso offering reasonable rates. Either way, be sure to educate yourself about the going rates ahead of time (w xe.com is a good website to do this).

Finally, mobile money is very popular in Mauritania, with Bankily (w bankily.mr) among the most popular options for sending money around the country.

BUDGETING Because so much of Mauritania's charm lies in getting off the road network and out into the isolation and serenity of the desert, many travellers will employ a tour provider for much, or at least part of, their time in-country. If so, it's likely that the various components of your trip – accommodation, transport, activities, etc – will be sold as a package, so you'll be able to get a good sense for the costs you're dealing with before setting out. Be sure to check what is and isn't included in your package (which meals, drinks, etc) so as to avoid any nasty surprises when the bill is due. For a fully catered desert trip including transport, camels, etc, bank on roughly 2,000UM (€50) per person per day.

Budget travellers will find Mauritania to be reasonable value when it comes to costs, and especially compared to the rest of West Africa – a region where you'll often find yourself paying lots for very little – value for money here is actually fairly good. One way to cut costs immediately is to travel in a pair or small group; dorm accommodation is fleetingly rare, and most hotels in Mauritania charge by room and not occupancy, so a double room will typically be the same price whether you're alone or with a companion.

In most cases, accommodation will be your number one cost. Outside of the few tourist hotspots, the hospitality sector is chronically underdeveloped (page 86), and many people will only avail themselves of a hotel room if they really have no family (no matter how extended) or friends in the area. Therefore, in a number of towns the cheapest (official) rooms on offer are about €25 (dbl), though these will almost always be en suite with air conditioning. Some gentle bargaining may get this closer to €20, but use your discretion.

In the tourist hotspots of the Adrar and surrounds, options are wider, and you can often get a (double) room in a basic hut or *tikit* using shared ablutions for closer to €15. Your cheapest option, where available, is to stay in a shared khaïma tent, which is generally about €7 per person. Somewhat unusually, it's also possible to find a decent selection of budget-friendly accommodation in the capital, and most of the country's very few dorm beds are located here. Otherwise, an en-suite double room in Nouakchott starts around €30.

As for the gustatory basics, at a local joint a bottled soft drink will run you about 25UM, and there's no beer to buy, so you're already saving there! A street snack or sandwich can be had on roadsides throughout the country for 50UM. A simple sit-down (or lay-down) meal, plat du jour or shawarmas at a cheap and cheerful local place will be in the 100–200UM range, while plates at more upmarket or tourist-oriented restaurants start around 300UM.

Public transport is also easy enough on the pocket, with minibus trips averaging 150UM per 100km.

Thus, scrimpers and savers should plan on spending about €25 daily (slightly less for couples), while €60–80 per day is a more likely range if you require a few more creature comforts like air-conditioned hotels and restaurant meals. These estimates don't factor in one-off excursions like camel safaris, boat trips, national park fees, etc.

GETTING AROUND

BY AIR There are airports in most major centres, but only a handful of them have scheduled flights as of 2025. National carrier Mauritania Airlines (w mauritaniaairlines.mr) is the only domestic operator and serves Nouadhibou, Zouérate and Néma, plus occasional flights to Kiffa.

BY CAR Though it's possible to hire a car for **self-drive** in Mauritania, this is not a popular choice, as unless you're an experienced off-road desert driver, you will be quite limited in how widely you are able to explore. (Some experienced drivers do bring their own vehicles down from Europe, however.) Therefore, most visitors arrange their vehicles with driver as part of a tour package, allowing you to get way out into the desert – presumably a big part of why you're here! But if you are driving yourself, note that it's generally easier to find diesel (gasoil) than petrol (essence). Prices were around 50UM/litre at the time of writing.

Back on the beaten track, there are four routes nationales (national roads) in Mauritania, all of which begin in Nouakchott. All are reasonably well surfaced, with the RN4 probably in the worst shape of the bunch, where a fair few pot-holes decorate this truck-heavy route. The **RN1** runs northwest towards Atar and Zouérate (with an extension to Algeria under construction) and the **RN2** runs south to Rosso. The **RN3** is better known as the Route de l'Espoir (or Tariq al-Amal in Arabic, occasionally the Transmauritanienne) and runs nearly the entire length of the country east towards Kiffa and Néma; the **RN4** runs north to Nouadhibou.

Though they are not considered national roads, there are several other significant surfaced roads in the country, notably the southern **river route** leading between Rosso and Sélibaby, and the **Adrar-Tagant route** connecting Atar and Tidjikja, which was completed in 2017. The Établissement des Travaux d'Entretien Routier (ETER; w eter.mr; f eter222) is responsible for road development and maintenance, and there are several new tarmac routes under development which will open up some interesting travel possibilities, including Tidjikja to Kiffa and Kiffa to Sélibaby.

Mauritania's low population density means that outside of a couple of major centres, traffic tends to be light. After a look at the jam-packed roads of the capital, however, it's hard to imagine that there were less than 1,000 private vehicles (992 to be exact) in the whole Mauritanian territory as of 1956. And by the looks of it, a few of those may still be prowling the streets of Nouakchott, where the roads are a regular catwalk of catastrophically clapped-out vehicles fit to rival the wrecks found anywhere in the world. The most common vehicle on Mauritanian roads is the seemingly indestructible Mercedes 190D, as well as a fair few old Renault 19s and 21s.

TRAVELLING DURING RAMADAN

The Muslim holy month of Ramadan will fall during the main tourist season for the lifespan of this edition (see dates on page 93), so there's a decent chance you'll be here during the holy month and you should be prepared to make a few adjustments. For the duration of the 30-day holiday, healthy adult Muslims are forbidden from eating, drinking, smoking and any sexual activity during daylight hours. Exemptions exist for the sick and the travelling, and while no-one will expect you to fast, quoting the exemption for travellers is a good answer if someone asks, and your knowledge of Islam will earn you a few halal brownie points to boot.

For the (non-fasting) traveller, Ramadan can often mean that otherwise simple activities like getting a bite to eat can wind up being a bit more complicated. Unless you fancy waking up before sunrise for suhoor, the pre-dawn meal taken to gird fasters' stomachs for the long day ahead, it can occasionally be tricky to get meals on a normal schedule during the day. (This will of course not apply if you are on an organised tour where meals are provided.) Most restaurants change their hours to reflect the diminished clientele, and lots of street food sellers will also simply pack up shop during the day. Still, with a bit of persistence and poking around you'll generally be able to find something, but also expect a wait while it's prepared, since most places won't be keeping ready food on hand during daylight hours.

Also be ready for frayed tempers and lackadaisical service as the afternoon wears on – hangry reaches epidemic proportions in the hours just before sundown, and quite understandably so; the fast is an impressive feat of endurance by any measure. On the plus side, the country comes to life at sundown for the iftar meal – the fast is usually broken with a few dates wherever you are when the clock strikes, followed by enormous family feasts which more often than not stretch late into the night. If you're hiring a driver or a guide, it's imperative you allow time in your schedule for them to break their fast, and it's a good opportunity to share a meal. And while socialising goes on into the wee hours and many businesses stay open late, most live music venues scale back their schedules for the month, so it's not a great time to visit if you're here for the concerts.

Besides the aforementioned pot-holes and jalopies, drivers are faced with an array of hazards on Mauritanian roads which you should be aware of before setting out. Firstly, even when you seem to be in open desert, you'll be surprised as to how many little settlements arise from the roadside sands – and with these comes a cadre of carts, children, livestock and any number of other people and things that seem prone to dart into the street without notice. There's little else to say about minimising this risk than simply to take caution and slow down. If you forget this advice, there's no shortage of speed bumps to assist you in heeding it, so be on the lookout for these as well. Outside of a few mountain passes, roads tend to be straight and visibility good, but keep an eye out for speed demons and dangerous overtaking, particularly on some of the newly tarmacked routes.

As in most African countries, driving at night is not recommended. Almost none of the roads are illuminated, not all of your fellow drivers will have working headlights (others will happily show you nothing but their high beams), and the same cast of people and animals is still on the roadside, only considerably more difficult to see when they enter the roadway. Also note that intercity travel is restricted from about midnight until first prayers. This is patchily enforced, but either way, you should not plan to drive through the night.

And finally, when it comes to driving off-road, be very sure you are amply prepared in both skills and supplies and *never* underestimate the desert. Without adequate preparation, a situation here can turn from simply solved to a matter of survival very quickly.

BY PUBLIC TRANSPORT Mauritania is reasonably well served by intercity public transport, and though the improving road network means that travel times have shrunk, remember that Mauritania is still the tenth-largest country in Africa and the distances involved are long indeed. There are no central bus stations in Mauritania. Rather, intercity transport providers tend to operate out of private offices clustered together on the outskirts of town in the direction of travel. Expect to pay roughly 150UM per 100km travelled.

Most transport providers now operate reasonably modern minibuses, often even with air conditioning, though smaller routes are still often served by shared saloon cars, which, to put it mildly, do not have air conditioning. It's also not uncommon for private travellers to sell vacant seats in their vehicles before setting out towards their destination; you will usually find them in a dedicated spot somewhere not too far from the commercial transport providers. Along the Route de l'Espoir, larger coach buses are also common. You will also find 4x4s and pick-up trucks ferrying goods and people between villages and communities located off the main roads. Within the villages (particularly in the south), horse and donkey carts known as *charrettes* are a common sight.

BY RIDE-HAILING SERVICES While none of the major international ridesharing companies are active in Mauritania, there are now a couple of homegrown alternatives available in the form of Sehdini (w sehdini.com) and CarApp (w carapp-africa.net). These apps are available on both Android and iOS, and have the distinct advantage of telling you the price of your journey in advance. So even if you don't use it to get a ride, it can be a useful way to get a sense for the approximate price of a given trip.

BY BOAT The only options for boat travel in Mauritania (beyond simple pirogue or sightseeing trips) involve crossing the Senegal River, which forms the border with Senegal to the south. Ferries on the river are managed by the Société des Bacs de Mauritanie (SBM; w sbm.mr; f). As of 2025, it administers two ferries at the Rosso crossing, and a smaller one suitable for light vehicles between Kaédi and Gourel Oumar Ly (Mollé Walo) in Senegal. Ferries at Rosso run back and forth more or less continually 09.00–13.00 and 15.00–18.00; the crossing costs 500UM per vehicle and is free for pedestrians. (The official fare chart actually lists pedestrians as 4UM, but it seems this €0.10 fee has been waived or isn't considered worth the effort of collecting. On the other hand, cows cross for 10UM and sheep for just 6UM.)

At crossings where there are no ferries (for example Boghé to Démèt), wooden pirogues shuttle goods and passengers between the river's two banks, but it's not possible to bring a vehicle bigger than a motorcycle. SBM has publicised plans to implement ferry services for at least three other locations along the river, namely Jedr El Mohguene (to Dagana), Lexeïba II (to Podor) and Toufunde Civé (to Matam), but it's impossible to say if and when these crossings might (or might not) be equipped, so it's best to assume they will remain pedestrian-only crossings via pirogue for the near term at least. On the bright side, the same piroguiers who punt you across the border will also be willing to take you on a short river cruise for a negotiable fee.

Finally, the opening of the Rosso bridge during the lifetime of this edition will mean SBM is relieved of what is by far its most significant duty. Ideally, this could mean increased resources become available for crossings upriver. Once the bridge

CATCHING A FICHE

If you spend any time on the road in Mauritania at all, you'll be stopped at a checkpoint before too long. There are several state organs responsible for these, including gendarmerie, police, douane (customs) and Groupement Général de la Sécurité des Routes (GGSR; road safety). Unlike in some countries in the region, there's little in the way of baksheesh going on here, at least when it comes to tourists, but rather the authorities are keeping a close eye on people's movements around the country.

So before you get frustrated with the delay, keep in mind Mauritania's difficult neighbourhood and porous borders – the fact that you can explore the country in relative security and freedom today is at least in part facilitated by these many checkpoints, and the people staffing them are by and large just out to do their jobs.

And one of their jobs is to record your details, often by hand. Therefore, you can fast forward this process by showing up armed with a 'fiche', which is just a printout of your basic information. If you'd like to prepare these before you arrive in Mauritania, a simple photocopy of your passport generally works fine; if working with a driver you can add their name, phone number and the vehicle's registration number on the same sheet. Out of many dozens of checkpoints, our entry stamp/visa was only checked once or twice; you can add this information if you wish. If you'd rather make your fiches on arrival, all larger towns have copy shops.

Copies in hand, you will generally be able to hand these over at each checkpoint and continue on your way without further delay. If you plan on travelling extensively within Mauritania, it would not be overkill to make 50 such copies!

is open, SBM has also proposed converting its Rosso facility into a hotel, and one of the former ferries into a floating museum. As to how likely any of that is to happen – *Allahu a'alam!* (God knows best!)

MAPS As with anything, travellers are increasingly relying on online rather than paper maps. For that purpose, Open Street Maps (OSM; w openstreetmaps.org) and the Maps.me (w maps.me) offline mapping app (which uses OSM data) are often more accurate than Google Maps in Mauritania.

Also online, Wikiloc (w wikiloc.com) has many GPS traces of interesting circuits in Mauritania uploaded by drivers, hikers and others. iOverlander (w ioverlander.com) is a useful resource for finding and confirming the status of various services through crowd-sourced reports.

On paper, the most recent map is ITMB's 1:2 200 000 Mauritania & Mali from 2019. Bab Sahara in Atar (page 173) also produces its own hand-drawn map of the Adrar region, which is quite detailed.

Finally, the French Institut Géographique National produced a comprehensive set of 1:200 000 colour maps covering Mauritania in the early independence period, and these have been collected and can be downloaded here: w jemecasseausoleil.blogspot.com/2013/04/cartes-de-la-mauritanie.html.

Roads and similar infrastructure are of course increasingly out of date on these, but they remain unparalleled for the country's natural landscapes.

ACCOMMODATION

The hospitality sector in Mauritania has long been acutely underdeveloped, with only the most basic accommodation available in many places, or sometimes even none at all. At first this might seem ironic for such an avowedly hospitable people, but it's precisely this hospitality that has stunted the growth of a hotel industry. Author Peter Hudson learned of this back in 1990, talking to a Mauritanian friend in his book *Travels in Mauritania*:

> 'Before,' [Ismael] said, 'there were no strangers in the desert and today it is much the same. There are no hotels or restaurants – hospitality is the way of desert men and of Islam. Even if there were these places, nobody would go to them because if they did it would imply that they were bad men, men shunned by society, men who could find no hospitality.'

A consultant's report two decades later observes the same, noting the 'absence of a tradition of staying in hotels' among Mauritanians, because 'it is in fact practically impossible for a Mauritanian to travel within the country without being hosted by a relative or friend'. And in this respect, another 15 years has done little to diminish the age-old ways of the desert and the sacred obligation Mauritanians feel in providing hospitality to one another.

But what does this mean for a newcomer with no relatives or friends? Assuming you don't wind up hosted by a Mauritanian regardless – which does still happen – your choice of accommodation remains rather rudimentary. It must be said that recent years have seen a number of new hotel developments opening around the country, though these are largely aimed at the business or delegation market and are in many cases indifferently managed and middling value. That being said, Nouakchott and Nouadhibou are home to a number of very comfortable options, and there is a growing selection of good mid-range options upcountry as well.

ACCOMMODATION PRICE CODES	
Based on a standard double room or equivalent.	
$$$$$	Over 5,000UM
$$$$	3,000–5,000UM
$$$	2,000–3,000UM
$$	1,000–2,000UM
$	Less than 1,000UM

To start with, most hotels charge on a double room basis, ie: the price is the same whether there is one guest or two, so single travellers pay a penalty. As such, most price listings in this guide are for double rooms, but single-occupancy prices have been noted where they exist. B&B is rare outside of upmarket places.

But along with its unique hospitality culture, Mauritania also offers a fairly unique set of accommodation and architectural options, some of which may merit a short explanation. The most basic auberges often utilise traditional architectural styles. Firstly and most basic, overnighting in a traditional *khaïma* tent is not only cheap, but also a window into the way of life that has sustained Mauritanian society for centuries. You'll usually be given a *matla* (mattress/mat) and a blanket; having a sleeping bag liner or a sleeping bag of your own might be welcome. It should also be said that there's not a whole lot in the way of formal camping infrastructure in Mauritania, but it's nothing if not a nation of campers so if you've got your own tent you'll fit right in and in most cases be happily received.

Next up in the solidity stakes are the *tikit* and *mbar*, both one-room structures of differing types. A tikit can take many forms, ranging from a dome-shaped grass hut to a thatch-roofed rondavel or a square concrete structure with pyramidal roof (and often an ornamental finial on top). An mbar is an open-sided pavilion, often with walls made from wire mesh (sometimes covered in fabric), simultaneously allowing for protection from the sun and exposure to cooling breezes.

Entering the realm of multi-room buildings, many places offer accommodation in a *majlis*, which is essentially a sitting room, generally with little furniture other than mats and cushions lining the walls. (After a joint application from several Gulf countries, the *majlis* has in fact been recognised on UNESCO's List of Intangible Cultural Heritage since 2015.) Hoteliers don't tend to be very fussy about how many people sleep in a *majlis* (and there are plenty of *matlas* to go around), so they can be a good pick for families, though they often use shared ablutions.

From here, options begin to look a lot more familiar. A standard budget or mid-range room in a Mauritanian town will have en-suite ablutions and air conditioning, with the price point mostly determined by the upkeep and quality of the room rather than any other features or perks the hotel might have, which are rare. Only the most upmarket/luxurious options will have a swimming pool or other facilities like spa and fitness, and these are practically non-existent outside of Nouakchott and Nouadhibou.

EATING AND DRINKING

FOOD As with so much in Mauritania, its cuisine has its feet in two worlds, with dishes hewing between North African and West African flavours depending on where in the country you are. This is a blessing for adventurous eaters – you can easily have camel on your plate one day and fresh-caught fish the next. Historically speaking, fish did not factor into the Moorish diet, with these men and women of the desert preferring the meat and milk of their animals on terra firma to the slippery creatures of the sea. But today their fish-fanatic compatriots from the south have more or less convinced them, to the extent that ***thiéboudiène*** is widely considered to be Mauritania's national dish (as well as Senegal's). And it's no wonder – this is a meal so good it was recognised on UNESCO's List of Intangible Cultural Heritage in 2021.

Thiéboudiène (from '*ceebu jën*' in Wolof, called '*marou elhout*' in Hassaniya) literally means rice (*ceeb*, *marou*) and fish (*jën*, *elhout*). It starts with a base of rice cooked in a tomato sauce (akin to the jollof rice found throughout West Africa, all descendants of thiéboudiène) served with stewed cabbage, carrots, cassava, squash, okra, tomato, *jaxatu* (bitter tomato), tamarind sauce, fish (often white grouper, known as *thiof*) stuffed with rof, a parsley-garlic-onion-pepper paste, and finally a sprinkling of savoury burnt rice from the bottom of the pan known as *khogn*. Like most Mauritanian meals, it's served communally in a big metal bowl, and there will usually be a couple of whole habanero peppers on top as well – add spice by giving them a good squeeze on to your section of the bowl. Though you won't see them quite as often, thiéboudiène also has a few cousins that operate along similar lines, namely *thiébou yapp*, which comes with lamb or goat, and *thiébou ginaar*, which is served with chicken.

Other south Mauritanian dishes you're likely to encounter include ***mafé***, which traces its origins to present-day Mali. This richly spiced and creamy peanut-butter-based stew is typically made with beef or lamb/goat and served over rice and is popular throughout West Africa. ***Yassa*** originates in southern Senegal's Casamance region, and this zingy caramelised onion and lemon sauce is usually served with grilled chicken or fish. ***Mbakhal*** is a risotto of sorts, a saucy dish of rice simmered with peanut butter, okra, and fish or meat. Other rice dishes are often simply called '*marou* [*blank*]', ie: *marou viande* (rice and meat), *marou boulette* (rice and meatballs), etc.

As you go north, the popularity of rice gradually gives way towards **couscous** (though both are common across the country), which comes in several varieties, made from millet, sorghum, barley or semolina (wheat). Broadly speaking, barley and wheat couscous is more popular in the north, while millet and sorghum predominate in the south, and the semolina variety is commonly imported from Morocco.

Couscous goes by many names in Mauritania, often depending on the composition, grain size, and more, but you won't go wrong asking for *lacciri* (Pulaar), *thiéré* (Wolof), *futo* (Soninké) or *kuskus* (Hassaniya). As with thiéboudiène, the 'knowledge, know-how and practices pertaining to the production and consumption of couscous' was also placed on UNESCO's List of Intangible Cultural Heritage, after a successful 2020 bid alongside Maghrebi neighbours Morocco, Algeria and Tunisia.

Mauritania's most famous couscous dish originates with the Moors. Known as ***ngommou***, it is typically made with a large-grained, dark couscous that has been seasoned with powdered leafy greens (typically jute, moringa or baobab), and then served with a stew of meat (lamb/goat, camel) and veg (tomato, onion, cabbage, carrots, peppers, etc) on top.

Aside from ngommou, couscous is eaten with a variety of other meat and vegetable sauces, including one from stewed leafy greens (from sweet potatoes, cassava, hibiscus, baobab, jute or moringa) known as *haako*. Millet couscous can also be mixed with sour milk (*lait caillé*) as part of a sweet dish called ***lakh*** or *ngalakh*, popular among the Halpulaar. *Karawo* is a similar porridge-style dish. Couscous can also be served alongside meat and vegetable **tagine** dishes that will be broadly familiar to anyone who has travelled in Morocco.

Mauritania is also home to several local styles of bread. In the cities, you're likely to find rather uninspired machine-baked baguettes (*mbourou courah*), but in smaller towns the handmade ***mbourou lehtab*** (or *tapalapa*) – also baguette-shaped, but denser, more flavourful and often wood-fired – is prevalent. More unusually, and a sure crowd-pleaser and desert favourite, is ***kesra*** (or *tagela*), which is a round bread baked in the sand and embers beneath a campfire. If you spend any nights out in the desert, you'll likely get to give this a try. After the fire gets sufficiently hot, the uncooked dough is placed directly into the sand beneath, which is so hot that it sears the wet dough and forms a toasted crust that separates from the sand. Therefore, once fully baked it's dug up, dusted off and is, believe it or not, generally sand-free!

Several dishes are typically served with kesra, including ***mreifisa***, which has Sahrawi roots and is a lamb/camel stew served over torn-up chunks of kesra. Mauritanians also cure meat (and for the Imraguen, fish) into a jerky called ***tishtar***, which can be eaten as is or cooked and rehydrated into a stew called ***tidkit***, also served with kesra. Finally, ***leksour*** refers to a thin crêpe made with millet and wheat flour and served with a lamb or camel stew on top.

Other starches used in Mauritanian cooking include potatoes, notably used in ***bonava***, a spud-heavy lamb/camel stew, and porridges from a variety of grains. ***Al aïsh*** is a stiff porridge (usually from wheat and millet or sorghum flour) similar to *fufu*, served with an accompanying stew that often features shredded meat, leaf powder and okra.

The embers of a campfire can also be used to cook a favourite shared by all Mauritanians, ***méchoui***. Also known as *dibiterie* or *afra*, this is essentially barbecue, typically with lamb or goat meat and commonly associated with Hausa immigrants from Nigeria or Niger. With a variety of cuts grilled or roasted on a wood fire and wrapped in ersatz butcher paper – usually a repurposed cement bag – méchoui is about as no-frills as it gets, and the theatrics of the grillmaster chopping up your meal with a hatchet or a machete are worth the price of admission alone. You'll often even be able to choose your preferred cut from the goat carcass hung next to the grill. It is served either over rice or with some grilled onions, mustard, salt and a few dashes of Maggi sauce – and no silverware in sight.

Finally, there are a few localised specialties found on opposite sides of the country, including Imraguen fish preparations like the rare mullet bottarga (salted and cured roe pouch), which is prized as a delicacy across the Mediterranean. Down the coast, the Taghrédient who live around Diawling National Park make yet another variety of couscous, this time from water lilies (couscous de *nénuphar*). And all the way inland, *pigeon farci aux dattes* (date-stuffed baked pigeon) is an Oualata specialty.

More familiar options include **shawarmas** and **French tacos** (a sort of burrito–panini hybrid stuffed with meat, fries, cheese and sauce), which are widely available from fast food joints in major cities; these also often serve pizzas and the like (of decidedly varying quality). Street sellers often have ***fataya***, which are basically fried dough pies (much like an empanada or samosa) that can be stuffed with anything, including mince, veggies, fish paste and even French fries (though not all at the same time, thankfully). And as in much of Africa, **fried dough balls** à la Nigerian puff-puff are another common sight, along with savoury **accara** fritters made from a black-eyed pea batter.

For dessert, **dates** are the sweet treat of choice, though these are perhaps more often eaten as an appetiser, dipped in cream or butter. Also keep your eyes out for ***btana***, a paste of pitted dates tightly sewn into a goatskin for preservation. Other favourites include ***thiakry***, which is made from sweetened millet couscous with milk or yoghurt and spiced with cinnamon and vanilla or coconut. Lots of boutiques carry pre-packaged thiakry and sweetened *kossam* (*lait caillé*, sour milk), usually sold chilled or frozen in plastic sachets. Fresh fruit is perhaps the most common dessert, though if you're in Nouakchott, the growing roster of patisseries and gelaterias should manage to keep even the sweetest of teeth happy.

Vegetarians Given that the traditional Mauritanian diet revolves almost entirely around meat and milk, vegetarians and vegans may struggle somewhat. But there are still a few options to lean on, including dates, which are a fantastic source of sustained energy that have been nourishing Mauritanians across the desert for centuries. Main towns will have a decent selection of other fruits and nuts to stock up on, but choices may be limited otherwise. Though common, dairy is easily avoided, as it's generally taken on its own rather than as an element in sauces or stews.

In Nouakchott, choices are unsurprisingly much wider, including Indian and Lebanese restaurants with vegetarian options available, as well as numerous places serving pizzas, pastas, etc. Otherwise, the sauces in the breakfast sandwiches mentioned below are typically meatless, as are the couscous porridges lakh and thiakry. Sweet and savoury fried dough snacks are another common option.

Traditional dishes like mafé or ngommou can also be made without meat, but only on request – those served as a dish of the day or similar will almost always have been cooked with meat inside. If you eat fish, you'll have an easier time, as it's the most common protein in thiéboudiène (marou elhout), which is perhaps Mauritania's most common dish.

Finally, if you're taking any sort of guided tour, the guides and cooks are usually familiar with vegetarian requirements (vegans may have to be more specific) and will be able to make up a number of stews and salads without meat, usually made from a combination of fresh and canned vegetables accompanied by pasta or another starch. Tuna is a common addition for pescatarians.

EATING OUT Hotels usually (assuming they do it at all) do breakfast in the French style, with an assortment of pastries, breads, butter, jam, fruit, coffee and tea, though depending on where you're staying, the spread can range from the miserly to the lavish, and the price is rarely included in the room. For breakfast on the road, keep a lookout for a woman sitting behind a pile of stainless-steel bowls arranged around her like a drum set. Inside these lurks a variety of savoury sauces, including green

RESTAURANT PRICE CODES

Based on a main dish for one.

$$$$$	Over 700UM
$$$$	500–700UM
$$$	300–500UM
$$	150–300UM
$	Less than 150UM

EATING TOGETHER

Katherine Baird

Our professors also instructed us on another vital feature of Mauritanian life: the social graces of communal eating. Mid-day we squatted in small circles around a large bowl. Someone would quietly bless the food, then we would dig into fish-flavored oily rice. With your right hand, you form compact balls of rice mixed with whatever was piled in the bowl's center: fish, cabbage, carrots, goat, or peanut sauce. While eating you engage in steady conversation with those around you, stopping only to quickly plop a well-formed ball into your mouth, or toss a particularly plump morsel on your side of the bowl to someone else. Then you return your hand to the bowl for more rice, all repeated until the bowl runs dry, and someone wanders off to find hot coals for tea.

From Growing Mangos in the Desert *(Apprentice House Press, 2022)*

peas (*petits pois*), black-eyed peas (*niébé*), spaghetti (yes, for a spaghetti sandwich) and some hot sauce (*sosu kaani*) on the side. They'll often have some coals or a gas cooker on which to fry up omelettes as well, and the whole affair comes wrapped in an old Tunisian newspaper and won't run you more than 50UM. Other mealtimes in Mauritania tend to align with the French custom, with lunch from 12.00 to 14.00 and dinner starting from about 19.30. Thus, if you get caught out looking for a bite between these times, it can sometimes be tricky to find a sit-down meal, but you can always pick up a bag of locally baked *sarkela* biscuits or nuts, often served alongside a round of atay.

In Nouakchott, restaurants look much like you might expect, but once you head upcountry it can be hard finding a 'sit-down' restaurant at all, as most are rather 'lay-down' restaurants instead, with food served in an open-sided mbar hut and seating on long cushions lining the floor. Mauritanian men and women will generally sit separately, but this is not a concern for tourists. You must take off your shoes before entering the mbar, and you will be presented with a washbasin and soap to clean your hands before your meal. Eat only with your right hand. After eating, you can order a round of atay which will be brought around glass-by-glass; you're expected to return your glass directly after each of the three rounds, as these will be rinsed and making the rounds to other customers in the interim.

Occasionally restaurants will burn an incense known as *lembarka* made from the resin of the African myrrh (*Commiphora africana*). Also very common in private homes, this is valued equally for its ability to freshen a room after mealtimes as it is to ward off evil spirits.

DRINK When it comes to Mauritania's favourite beverage, there can be only one drink that reigns supreme: ***atay***. This gunpowder green tea is the hub around which Mauritanian social life turns, as jam-packed with social and cultural significance as it is sugar. Sipped scaldingly hot and eye-wateringly sweet from the daintiest of little glasses, it is prepared on a small charcoal brazier (*fourneau*) or gas bottle hob in a carefully choreographed ceremony that's replicated several times a day by all of Mauritania's diverse peoples and in all corners of this expansive land. Many Mauritanians even carry their own tea kits around with them – not unlike Argentinians with their yerba maté gear – and the various accoutrements required for atay even feature on Mauritanian postage stamps. Atay is prepared with fresh

ON CAMEL MILK *Nancy Jones Abeiderrahmane*

Camel milk is thin and snow white, with a clean, delicate flavour and cappuccino-like froth when fresh; it has less fat and sugar than cow milk, indeed it can taste salty depending on the camel's food. The protein and fatty acid composition is unique, closer to human chemistry than cow's (for instance camel milk lowers blood glucose and for some reason helps autism patients). It has lactose but is better tolerated than cow milk lactose. Camel milk contains more minerals and bacteria-fighting enzymes than other milks.

More in-depth research is needed on this valuable gift.

A Hadith says: 'We have given you two wonderful things: the palm tree and the she-camel.'

From Camel Cheese – Seemed Like a Good Idea *(2013)*

mint alongside the green tea, and you'll see vendors selling single-serving sprigs of mint all over the country.

And if it wasn't clear already, atay is not simply a drink, but a social occasion, and the traditional three cups, famously referred to around the Maghreb as 'bitter as life, sweet as love and gentle as death', really do come as a package. Therefore an invitation to tea means three glasses, each poured carefully back and forth from increasingly towering heights to build a bubble-bath foam before serving to each drinker in turn. There's no rushing this process (or desire to), and it's a real faux pas to leave in the middle – better to not accept at all if you've only got time for one glass. Indeed, Mauritanians have their own poetic tercet for the ingredients necessary for a fully realised tea ceremony: *Jemaa*, *Jmar* and *Jarr* – good company, good coals and a good amount of time.

Otherwise, ***zrig*** must be second on the list of emblematic Mauritanian beverages. Served in a carved wooden bowl called a *gued'ha*, zrig is a mixture of camel milk (fermented or fresh), water and sugar, which is served cold and presented to guests either on arrival, or passed around as an appetiser before mealtime.

On the other side of the spectrum, **alcohol** is forbidden in Mauritania (being an Islamic Republic and all), and you may be subject to a fine if your bags are checked trying to import it. It's true, though, that there are a (very) few restaurants in Nouakchott and Nouadhibou that *do* sell beer and wine on the downlow – we haven't specifically publicised these as it could jeopardise their businesses, but as you might expect, foreign-run places represent your best chance. If you do find a tipple, don't be surprised when it's 600UM for a can of beer – it's very much a seller's market, after all.

But in truth, Mauritania is a great place to try your hand at teetotalism, and there's a delightfully tropical selection of juices to be had. The intensely beetroot-coloured ***bissap*** is made from the hibiscus flower (like the Mexican *agua de Jamaica*), and is probably the most popular juice available, followed by the creamy off-white ***tejmakht*** (or *bouyé*), made from the fruits of the baobab tree, and ***gingembre***, a spicy-sweet ginger-based drink. These three are typically sold by women at markets or along roadsides, catering to thirsty shoppers and passers-by. More conventional tropical juices like tamarind, mango and papaya are also around, and the usual varieties of soft drinks (Coke, Fanta and local brand La Gazelle) are bottled in Nouakchott by the Société des Boissons de Mauritanie (SOBOMA) and cheaply available almost everywhere.

And though Mauritanians may only have eyes for *atay*, you might also be offered a glass of ***douté***, or *kinkeliba* tea, made from the boiled leaves of the *Combretum micranthum* bush. This is a drink held in particularly high esteem by the Senegal-based Mouride Islamic fraternity as their founder Ahmadou Bamba was known to espouse its curative properties. Today it's drunk both as an all-around health tonic and as treatment for everything from liver ailments to diabetes to migraines. Bamba was a proponent of at least one other hot beverage in his time, namely the pungent ***café touba***, whose intensely distinctive flavour comes from the ground grains of selim that are added to the coffee before it's brewed. Much like atay, café touba is sipped from small cups with plenty of sugar, but it lacks the rigmarole of atay preparation and can be bought by the cup from hawkers in larger cities, where it's infinitely preferable to their Nescafé-brewing competitors – generally speaking your only other option for **coffee**.

Tap **water** is regarded as unsafe to drink, so most travellers understandably opt for bottled water. The sachet bags of water common elsewhere in West Africa are uncommon here, but bottled water is cheap and readily available. Tayba, Es-Savi and Tirjit are popular brands.

PUBLIC HOLIDAYS AND FESTIVALS

As a Muslim-majority republic, Mauritanian public holidays are primarily religious in nature. These are based on the lunar Hijri calendar, and usually shift by about 11 days annually when compared with the Gregorian calendar. This can move around by a day or two depending on when the moon officially kicking off the holiday is sighted, so all the dates here are predictions.

Mauritania also celebrates several secular holidays with fixed dates, namely New Year's Day (1 January), Labour Day (1 May), Africa Day (24 May) and Independence/National Day (28 November). Government offices and most businesses will be closed on both these and the Islamic holidays listed here (and sometimes the day after as well). Note that Eid al-Fitr (Korité) marks the end of the month-long observance of Ramadan.

Mauritania is also host to a number of annual festivals, which are listed in their relevant chapters.

ISLAMIC HOLIDAYS IN MAURITANIA Note that all of the following holidays are determined according to the Hijri lunar calendar, and so the dates may vary by a day or two.

	2026	**2027**	**2028**	**2029**
Eid al-Fitr (Korité)	19 March	9 March	26 February	14 February
Eid al-Adha (Tabaski)	26 May	16 May	4 May	23 April
1st Mouharram (Islamic New Year)	16 June	6 June	26 May	15 May
Mawlid (Maouloud)	25 August	14 August	2 August	23 July

SHOPPING

Nouakchott and Nouadhibou are by far your best options for shopping, but most basic goods (toiletries, medicines, batteries, etc) can be purchased at smaller supermarkets or pharmacies in towns throughout the country. In Nouakchott, pharmacies stay open all night for emergencies in a rotational system of *pharmacies*

EID FESTIVITIES *Katherine Baird*

The transition from the final flicker of Koorka's [Ramadan's] moon to the glimpse of a new one was just jolting. *Juulde Koorka – Eid Al Fitr* in Arabic – started piously with the village men gathering on the dry sandy river bottom, joined at a respectful distance behind by the women elders. I stood in my backyard some fifty yards above the still river and praying villagers, observing the rites, and watching as a herd of goats wandered amongst them. Looking across to the flat stretch of Senegal beyond, I could see the smoky air promised yet another stifling hot day.

For an hour, Civé's religious leader, the revered Imam Thierno Ly, led the crowd in prayer. Finally, the rhythmic praying and hum-like chanting ended, and in good cheer all headed up the banks. At that exact moment, all hell broke loose. Sheep and goat were slaughtered while women and girls converted their water buckets and pots into drums to accompany the festive music now blaring from fully charged radios.

Straightaway, women and men emerged from their homes to stroll about dressed in their finest. The women's skin glowed from shea butter, and, in an astonishing display of wealth, their bodies shone with more gold than I'd ever seen. Along with cattle, gold was how Pulars held wealth, and on this day out it all came from locked trunks. The elders among them wore necklaces anchored by a large plum-sized gold rock with earrings to match. Many also had feet stained black from manioc-infused henna, and almost all the women elders had covered their heads with new gauze veils, lending a conservative touch to the day's otherwise celebratory air.

Meanwhile, girls paraded by with hands stamped with intricate bright orange geometric motifs. To achieve this, the day before they had designed patterns on their hands with thin decorative tape, slathered henna paste over it, then using socks as mittens, had sat immobilized for half the day. The results were hands stunningly tattooed orange. Other girls showed off tightly braided cornrows, and on rare occasion, a spot of lipstick or a coat of bright red nail polish.

Not to be outdone, the older men bore new elegant bou-bous, some of which were trimmed with rich thick gold embroidered patterns. Younger men sported colorful two-piece baggy outfits that looked all the world to me like pajamas. Mid-day while myself parading the lanes, I halted speechless as two young men in such new digs passed by; one with an outfit made of fabric stamped with large 100-dollar bills, the other loudly projecting portraits of President Mobutu of Zaire, complete with his leopard skin hat. In one way or another, everything contributed to the day's celebratory and bewildering air.

From Growing Mangos in the Desert *(Apprentice House Press, 2022)*

de garde. If you show up at one that's closed, look for a posted notice which will indicate the nearest all-night pharmacy, or better yet, check the current schedule at w ami.mr/fr/pharmacies-de-garde.

As art and handicrafts go, Mauritania is home to many talented artisans working in a variety of mediums, whom we've tried to highlight when their workshops or galleries merit special mention. As with other things, Nouakchott has by far the largest selection. An excellent first stop is Nouakchott's Marché de l'Industrie Traditionnelle (page 126), where you'll find a good variety of wood and metalwork, jewellery, textiles, leather, *hseyra* reed mats, and more. The Foire National de Nouakchott will (inshallah!) likely become the country's largest artisanal market when it reopens. And the commendable Zeinart gallery (page 125) has a beautifully curated selection of higher-end items. If you've got a specific interest, you may wish to contact the **Association pour la sauvegarde de l'artisanat en Mauritanie** (m +33 6 79 47 40 17; e asammauritanie2012@gmail.com; f), headed by Mohamed Salem Sidi Bowba.

Mauritania's musical tradition is unfortunately poorly represented on the market today, and Mohamed Vall's Saphir d'Or music shop, which attracted some amount of media attention in the 2010s, is no longer. There are still plenty of stalls (known as *standards*) selling USB sticks full of Mauritanian music, however, and they can also fill up a memory stick of your own. If you're interested in purchasing a musical instrument, the Musée Ardine (page 130) might be a good place to start. And of course there is quite clearly no shortage of bright blue boubous and rainbow-hued melhfas to buy, nor one of tailors to get you measured up for the proper fit.

ARTS AND ENTERTAINMENT

Though home to a grand and immensely sophisticated musical tradition, conservative Mauritania is not exactly teeming with nightspots, and most musical performances happen at weddings, in private homes or under a khaïma in the desert. That said, there are a few venues in Nouakchott and Nouadhibou where you can reasonably reliably go to catch some live music without an invitation. This includes dedicated nightspots like the creatively named NKC Night and NDB Night, or some of Nouakchott's hotels, restaurants and galleries like Maison Jeloua, Les Sultanes or D'art, all of which put on occasional soirées musicales. There's also a new museum dedicated to the women's harp, the Musée Ardine.

As for the visual arts, the gallery scene in Nouakchott is impressively vibrant, and Mauritania's many artists and artisans have maybe a half-dozen galleries and cultural spaces in which to show their works around the city. (As with so many things in Mauritania, nearly all the action in this regard is taking place in the capital.) These include Zeinart, D'art, Art Gallé, Galerie Sinaa and the Institut Français, all of which will put on the occasional vernissage or event and have a regular stock of works on display and/or sale.

Outside of the capital, there are not really dedicated galleries or concert venues as such, but there's no shortage of artisans or musicians plying their trades. If you keep your ears open, it's not unlikely to hear a bit of music in the evenings – follow the drums and you're likely to be welcomed in to join. (And if it's truly private or men/women only, that will be made clear without fuss or embarrassment.) As for visual pursuits, head for the central markets, where workshops full of artisans still hammer, saw, cut, sew and mould all sorts of traditional products, including all the equipment requisite for nomadic life, refined to perfection over the generations.

OPENING TIMES

Business and banking hours are roughly 08.00–16.00 Monday–Thursday (possibly with a break for lunch) and 09.00–noon Friday and Saturday. Supermarkets, small boutiques and the like will typically stay open into the evening. Mauritania switched from the Islamic Friday–Saturday weekend to the European-style Saturday–Sunday weekend in 2014, but most things still close for the Jum'ah congregational prayers on Friday afternoons, so don't expect to get anything official done after noon on Friday. Hours are also curtailed during Ramadan. Restaurant hours are often somewhat ad hoc (and rarely publicised), but mealtimes tend to follow the French custom, with lunch between noon and 14.00 and dinner starting from about 19.30, but often eaten much later in the evening.

MEDIA AND COMMUNICATIONS

Today, the Mauritanian press operates largely free from governmental interference, and Mauritania has recently become a markedly successful example of a liberalised media environment. Namely, Mauritania came in at first place anywhere in Africa or the Arab world in the 2024 Reporters Without Borders Press Freedom Index. At 33rd place out of 180 countries ranked, not only does Mauritania now outrank its Arab and African neighbours, but also Australia, the US and ten EU countries to boot! These changes have been a rapid and radical shift: in 2023 Mauritania languished in 86th place, and in 2022 they came in at 97th.

A number of legal changes have supported this freer and more transparent climate. Press offences were decriminalised in Mauritania in 2011, but this did not stop bloggers and journalists from being jailed on other charges based on their written works – for example apostasy, for which blogger Mohamed Cheikh Ould Mkhaitir was famously jailed 2014–19. President Ghazouani has pushed forward a number of legislative reforms on journalism and the press since he took office in 2019, though sensitivities remain surrounding issues of religion, caste, slavery, defamation, and more. Matters pertaining to the press are administered under La Haute Autorité de la Presse et de l'Audiovisuel (HAPA; w hapa.mr/fr).

NEWSPAPERS Several Arabic-language newspapers are produced and sold inexpensively in Nouakchott and, as elsewhere, increasingly published and read online. A few of these also produce French-language editions, including *Alakhbar* (w fr.alakhbar.info; f Alakhbar Fr), *Le Calame* (w lecalame.info), *Le Quotidien* (w lequotidien.mr), *Saharamedias* (w fr.saharamedias.net) and *CRIDEM* (w cridem.org). The national news agency, Agence Mauritanienne d'information (w ami.mr/fr), also produces a weekly paper called *Horizons*.

RADIO AND TELEVISION Radio Mauritanie (w radiomauritanie.mr) is the national broadcaster and has branches throughout the country, while Télévision de Mauritanie (w tvm.mr) does the same with TV. There are numerous private radio and TV channels as well, broadcasting primarily in Hassaniya.

If a hotel offers satellite TV, it will typically be with the French Canal+/Canalsat satellite bouquet, which, not surprisingly, offers nearly all programming in French, though you'll occasionally be able to get BBC, CNN or France24 in English.

POST The Mauritanian Postal Service, Mauripost (w mauripost.post), is reasonably reliable and has dozens of agencies around the country, though valuables would be better off with a courier service like DHL. Postcards cost about 50UM to Europe or North America and take a few weeks.

TELEPHONE As in much of the world, landline phones (where they existed) are disappearing, and mobile network access and uptake is expanding. The international country code is +222; there are no area codes, and all numbers (land or mobile) have eight digits. The main providers are Chinguitel (w chinguitel.mr), Mattel

WHATSAPP IN MAURITANIA

This messaging app is enormously popular in Mauritania, and is strongly recommended if you will be moving around the country independently and making your own arrangements with hotels, service providers, guides, etc. It allows you to call, text and send multimedia messages to others who have the app installed, using the data connection on your mobile. Many businesses now rely on it heavily for bookings. It is also the easiest way to reach Mauritania from abroad, and practically free.

To see if a number has WhatsApp, open the app, click the '+' in the top-right corner, and select 'new contact'. Input the number **with the correct country selected**, in this case Mauritania, and it will supply the correct country code (+222). Then input the eight-digit Mauritanian number. If your would-be interlocutor is on the app, you will see a tick confirming this, after which you can save their name in your contacts and send them a message immediately. If they are not, you will be given an option to 'invite' them by SMS, but in practice you will be better off checking another number. Many Mauritanians have several numbers (one for each service provider), but usually only one of these will be linked to WhatsApp.

While WhatsApp-equipped numbers are not systematically indicated in this guide, they will be listed first when we are aware of them.

(w mattel.mr) and Moov Mauritel (w mauritel.mr), all of which have service centres in all major towns. Moov Mauritel has the widest network around the country.

The first numeral in any eight-digit number will tell you the identity of the provider: Chinguitel (2), Mattel (3), and Moov Mauritel (4). Any number in which the *second* numeral is 5 is a landline.

If you bring an unlocked mobile with you, a local **SIM card** with airtime and/or a data bundle is the easiest way to stay connected. Note, however, that in response to the 2023 jailbreak (page 184) there has been a crackdown on SIM card registrations and subsequent confusion about whether or not foreigners are entitled to register Mauritanian SIM cards.

This means you will procure your SIM card in one of three ways: 1) go to an official service centre with passport in hand and they may do it for you; 2) moneychangers at borders and market traders dealing in phones will often also sell pre-registered SIM cards – always be sure to test these before completing your purchase; 3) should you have a guide, ask them to help you register a card. A SIM from the official service centres will retail for something like 200UM, while those in the market are more like 600UM.

As of 2025, **eSIM** provider Airalo (w airalo.com) only offered coverage in Mauritania as part of an Africa-wide package which cost €26 for 1GB of data.

INTERNET Other than auberges in the countryside, most hotels now at least nominally offer Wi-Fi, though this often seems to be in a primarily theoretical capacity. Connections in Nouakchott and Nouadhibou are usually reasonable enough, with quality deteriorating as you travel upcountry, where you'll want to come armed with a mobile data connection if you need to get online.

You can get a local SIM card and data bundle with one of the mobile providers mentioned opposite. Getting online using mobile data is typically reliable enough and the network is surprisingly widespread, though note that there is often no signal along the roads until you reach a settlement. Upcountry and in smaller communities the connection is often limited to 3G reception only and can be frustratingly slow. There is also now at least one co-working space in Nouakchott: Le Bureau Club (m 41 74 08 08; w lebureauclub.com; f).

A note on websites Mauritanian websites have a habit of coming on and offline intermittently, depending on whether the host is operating (or has been paid) – it's often worth checking back another time if you find a page out of service.

ELECTRICITY SUPPLY The national power grid is administered by the Société Mauritanienne d'Electricité (SOMELEC; w somelec.mr). In addition to the country's massive offshore gas reserves (page 31), Mauritania has immense potential in solar and wind energy in particular; SOMELEC reported that these already accounted for nearly 15% of Mauritania's energy mix in 2022, with this number poised to grow. Something like 25% of the energy mix comes from hydroelectric power generated at the Félou, Manantali and Gouina dams in neighbouring Mali, and about 50% from thermal plants in Mauritania.

Nonetheless, power outages do happen periodically, particularly upcountry, and smaller communities may not be connected to the national grid at all.

CULTURAL ETIQUETTE

It should come as no surprise that Mauritania is a conservative, religious society, so bear in mind that behaviour that would go completely unnoticed in Europe or North America will often be inappropriate here. Skimpy outfits and public displays of affection (for opposite- and certainly same-sex couples) are definitely unwelcome, and if the conversation should turn to religion (assuming you are not Muslim), you may find it easier to categorise yourself as Christian rather than atheist or agnostic, whatever your beliefs may be. As for asking personal questions yourself, though issues of language and ethnicity have a fraught history in Mauritania, this is a multi-ethnic country at heart and most people will be perfectly happy to tell you about their background if you respectfully enquire. Mauritanian names usually involve a patronymic, *ould* for men and *mint* for women. These are the Hassaniya terms for 'son of' and 'daughter of', equivalent to the standard Arabic *ibn* or *bint*.

Welcoming guests is considered a sacred duty here, so don't be surprised when you're invited to eat and drink with total strangers, and offered more rounds of tea than you could possibly drink in a day. This is one of the true pleasures of travel in Mauritania, and you should feel free to accept offers that seem genuinely made, but be sure you've got the time to spare: when it comes to tea, if you're in for one glass, you're in for three – it's considered impolite to leave in the middle of this famously tripartite tea ceremony. It's of course equally acceptable to politely decline, should you rather continue on your way.

Greetings are also hugely important, and just launching into conversation or asking someone questions without first taking the time to say hello and ask about their wellbeing (better still, the wellbeing of their mother, father, sister, brother, cousin, aunt, uncle and neighbour as well!) is considered rude. This rule applies everywhere, including in shops, restaurants and on the street, and will usually take the form of a quick succession of enquiries and assurances that the people in question are fine. It's quite possible you'll meet someone who chooses not to shake hands with members of the opposite sex; a hand on your heart and nod of the head does the job nicely in these situations.

Though a certain cultural reserve means that the attention you get as a conspicuous foreigner in Mauritania is considerably less than you're likely to receive in either Morocco or Senegal, you'll probably still have a chance to get familiar with the terms used for those perceived as foreigners and/or Europeans while here – often when meeting with a gaggle of gaping kids. These are *naçrani* in Hassaniya (which comes from the Nazarenes, ie: followers of Jesus of Nazareth), and *tuubaako/tubaabu/toubab* in Pulaar/Soninké/Wolof, which you're sure to hear plenty more times if you're headed south from Mauritania.

Despite the religious nature of the state, there is no morality police or other such enforcement in Mauritania, and no-one is expecting you to dress in fully local or Islamic clothing while here – to make a good faith effort to show courtesy and be respectful of local tradition and mores is enough. If you are travelling upcountry and outside of densely settled areas, feel free to let your hair down a bit; your tour guide (should you have one) is used to the different rules that visitors live by, and it's fine for men and women to swim together on an unpopulated beach or at Terjit, for example. For more information on appropriate dress, see page 78.

PHOTOGRAPHY Mauritania is a spectacular destination for photographers, but local attitudes can be quite conservative, so it pays to bear in mind at least a couple of tips. Attitudes towards photography are somewhat more relaxed in regions of the country that see a lot of tourists, for example in the Adrar, but regardless of where in the country you are, you should always ask your subject's permission. This is especially true in less-visited areas of the country, where tourists and tourism are still very much unfamiliar concepts. Some areas have perhaps suffered the opposite fate, having seen one too many tour groups breezing through and sticking their long lenses where they don't belong – the Port du Pêche in Nouakchott comes to mind, where the boat crews are notoriously camera-averse and asking permission is essential. A little discretion also pays when capturing street or market scenes with large crowds. Mauritanian women are generally speaking more camera-shy than

GREAT GREETINGS *Katherine Baird*

Since greetings are an essential feature of Mauritanian life, I began rehearsing mine. I'm not sure why Mauritanians spend so much time greeting one another. Some historical artifact, no doubt, perhaps dating to an era when encounters among the region's once-roaming residents provided an occasion to learn about forage, ferocious animals, or foes. Or maybe greetings gave information on one's position in the social pecking order, one historically nearly as rigid as feudal Europe's. Or perhaps you could trace their endless greetings to longstanding conflict over the region's few resources, where prolonged ritual-like greetings evolved as a type of diplomacy. Think of the movie *Lawrence of Arabia*, when Omar Sharif's character Ali, and Lawrence of Arabia's guide, chanced upon one another at a watering hole. Maybe if that encounter had first involved long warm handshakes and extended greetings rather than pointed guns, Lawrence of Arabia's guide would have survived that scene. Well, maybe. I know I always felt warmer toward someone after holding their hand while inquiring into their health and wakefulness, learning their name, and hearing them praise each member of my family.

From Growing Mangos in the Desert *(Apprentice House Press, 2022)*

men. Finally, do not take photographs of any government or military facilities, lest you get a stern talking-to from an unamused official in uniform.

TRAVELLING POSITIVELY

Whether or not your aim in travelling is to participate in charitable work, your presence in Mauritania is already a net benefit for the economy and, with some intentionality behind how you spend your money, your visit can be of value to people here long after you leave. As much as possible, try to direct your spending to locally owned businesses – this could mean anything from hotels and restaurants to guides and transport. When you give your guide a fair tip, hire someone to take you on an excursion or eat at a local restaurant, you're providing much-needed employment and income; if people can make a living from legitimate employment in tourism, it encourages the further development of the sector and mitigates against some of the negatives that it often engenders, thus encouraging positive attitudes towards tourism overall.

If you'd like to get involved further, or perhaps even dedicate some of your time in Mauritania as a volunteer, there are a few possibilities. A small handful of local *organisations non-gouvernementales* (ONGs/NGOs) may accept the assistance of short-term international volunteers. These include **Enfants du Désert** (w lesenfantsdudesert.com;) and **SOS Éducation et la Santé Enfants du Désert et au Sahel** (m 44 71 54 50; e contactsoseseds@gmail.com;) in Atar, and **ONG NAD** (Nourricerie Aichetou Diallo; m 26 17 45 71, 34 34 80 08; w ongnad.org; ;) and **AEPN Mauretanienhilfe** (Association pour l'Aide à l'Enfance et aux Parents Necessiteux; w aepn.de;), both in Nouadhibou.

There are a number of NGOs working towards environmental protection and climate change adaptation active in Mauritania, including **Association Mauritanienne de Protection de l'Environnement** (m 46 42 10 84; w natmau.org), **ONG Protection de l'Environnement et le Bien Être des Communautés** (e ong.pebec@gmail.com;), **Ensemble - Environnement Mauritanie** (), **Association Naforé** (w nafore.org;), **ONG BiodiverCités** (w biodivercites.co;) and **Association Mauritanienne pour l'Environnement** (w ame.pro.mr), which is led by filmmaker Abderrahmane Sissako (page 52). For further information on Mauritanian environmental issues, consult the **Ministère de l'Environnement et du Développement Durable** (w environnement.gov.mr; Ministere.Environnement.Mauritanie).

Would-be volunteers can also check the **Workaway** (w workaway.info) portal, which offers volunteering opportunities in a variety of spheres. American volunteers from the **Peace Corps** (w peacecorps.gov) were present in Mauritania from 1967 to 2009, when the programme was closed due to insecurity. It's not clear whether it intends to return in light of the improved security situation.

Finally, the ripple effect of your trip doesn't just continue in Mauritania after you've left, but back in your home country as well. Even if you've just been in Mauritania for a week, you can do great good by simply talking openly and honestly with friends at home about your trip. Misconceptions and stereotypes about Africa abound, and you can help challenge these! Sharing stories about the beauty you encountered and the welcome you received – and even the problems you had – is one of the most powerful ways of changing the dominant narrative that so often misrepresents the reality of life in Africa. You don't have to paint a perfect picture, only an honest one, and your friends may be the next ones booking a trip.

Scheduled guaranteed departures to W. Sahara, Mauritania, Senegal, The Gambia, Guinea-Bissau, and others.

To check all adventures, visit **www.penguintravel.com**

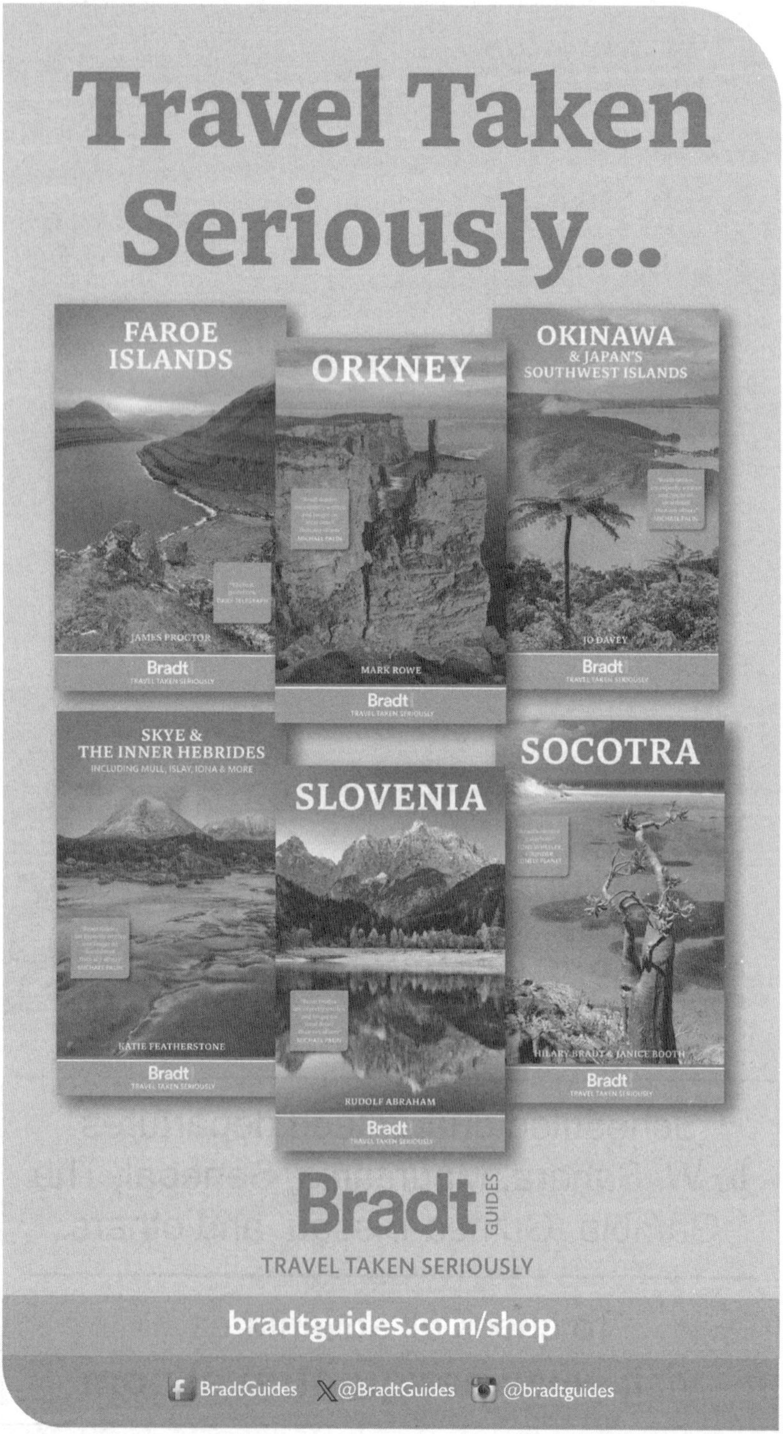
Travel Taken Seriously...
FAROE ISLANDS
JAMES PROCTOR
Bradt
TRAVEL TAKEN SERIOUSLY
ORKNEY
MARK ROWE
Bradt
TRAVEL TAKEN SERIOUSLY
OKINAWA & JAPAN'S SOUTHWEST ISLANDS
JO DAVEY
Bradt
TRAVEL TAKEN SERIOUSLY
SKYE & THE INNER HEBRIDES
INCLUDING MULL, ISLAY, IONA & MORE
KATIE FEATHERSTONE
Bradt
TRAVEL TAKEN SERIOUSLY
SLOVENIA
RUDOLF ABRAHAM
Bradt
TRAVEL TAKEN SERIOUSLY
SOCOTRA
HILARY BRADT & JANICE BOOTH
Bradt
TRAVEL TAKEN SERIOUSLY
Bradt GUIDES
TRAVEL TAKEN SERIOUSLY
bradtguides.com/shop
BradtGuides
@BradtGuides
@bradtguides

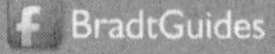

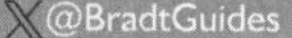

Part Two

THE GUIDE

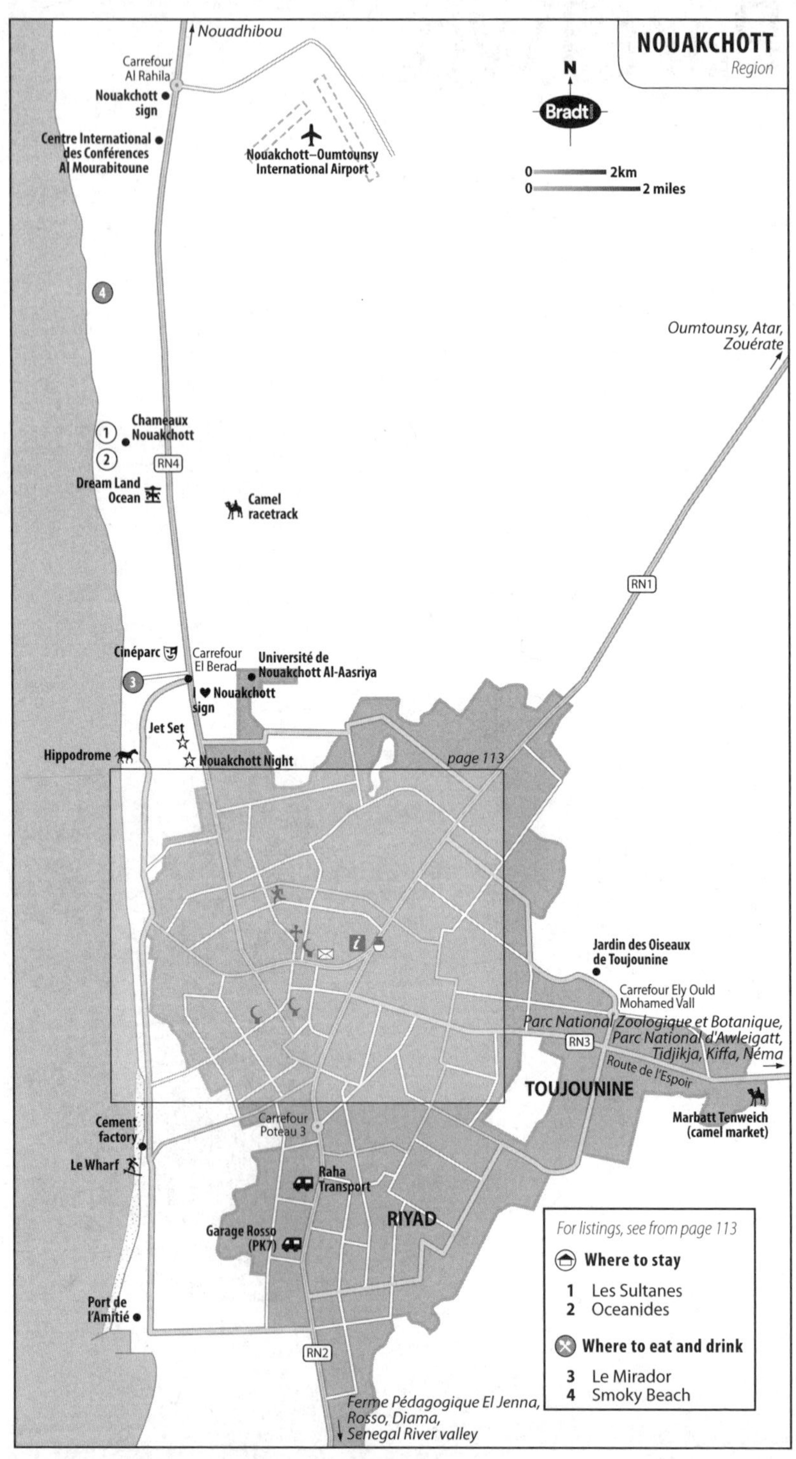
NOUAKCHOTT
Region
N
Bradt
0 2km
0 2 miles
Nouadhibou
Carrefour Al Rahila
Nouakchott sign
Centre International des Conférences Al Mourabitoune
Nouakchott–Oumtounsy International Airport
4
Oumtounsy, Atar, Zouérate
Chameaux Nouakchott
1
2
RN4
Dream Land Ocean
Camel racetrack
RN1
Cinéparc
Carrefour El Berad
Université de Nouakchott Al-Aasriya
3
I ♥ Nouakchott sign
Jet Set
Hippodrome
Nouakchott Night
page 113
Jardin des Oiseaux de Toujounine
Carrefour Ely Ould Mohamed Vall
Parc National Zoologique et Botanique, Parc National d'Awleigatt, Tidjikja, Kiffa, Néma
RN3
Route de l'Espoir
TOUJOUNINE
Marbatt Tenweich (camel market)
Cement factory
Carrefour Poteau 3
Le Wharf
Raha Transport
RIYAD
Garage Rosso (PK7)
Port de l'Amitié
RN2
Ferme Pédagogique El Jenna, Rosso, Diama, Senegal River valley
For listings, see from page 113
Where to stay
1 Les Sultanes
2 Oceanides
Where to eat and drink
3 Le Mirador
4 Smoky Beach

3

Nouakchott and Surrounds

Despite its young age, the city of Nouakchott (نواكشوط) has already lived many lives. The first when it was an isolated and unremarkable set of wells, where nomads filled their *shekwa* goatskins and French soldiers slowly lost their minds. The second as a model city – a proud new capital for a proud new nation, laid out by French architects and planned according to the cutting-edge precepts of the time. And the third as an escape, a last-resort retreat for the thousands upon thousands of nomads who saw their age-old livelihoods wither and die in a series of catastrophic droughts. And today, as those former nomads settled in and put down roots alongside their tent pegs, one of the Sahara's largest and most significant cities.

And indeed, Nouakchott feels just as unusual as its history. Splayed disinterestedly across a plain of former salt pan and scrubland, there's something amorphous about the place – frankly, it can be hard to put a finger on what pulls this low-rise city together. Because Nouakchott is, at its core, a city of nomads, it occasionally feels as if it was built by people who would, given the option, much rather be in the countryside.

But as with the rest of Mauritania, Nouakchott is a place of divergent identities – it really does contain multitudes. It's both one of the most important fishing ports in the region, while at the same time a city you could forget was near the ocean at all. It's a national capital, though with the dusty, low-slung vibe of a provincial market town. It's a city of camels and caravans, but also pirogues and *poisson*, mechanics and middlemen, cafés and khaïmas. But no matter who you are, life in Nouakchott stops and starts for the things that unite all Mauritanians: the call to prayer, when it's time for tea – and when a herd of animals needs to pass. So while it may not have turned out as its designers intended, when it comes to their goal of creating a space for all Mauritanians to meet, it's clearly been a smashing success.

Originally set several kilometres inland, the city has inched towards the ocean over the years, slowly filling in the no-man's land that once separated it from its oceanfront with unsentimental blocks of identikit apartments and shops. But just

SAFETY AND SECURITY

Broadly speaking, Nouakchott is quite safe for a city of its size. The working-class districts of Sebkha (5ème) and El Mina (6ème) and the areas around the main markets are probably a somewhat higher risk for things like pickpocketing, but violent crime and robberies remain rare. It's also worth keeping a close eye on your things in the hubbub around the Port du Pêche. We received reports of a tourist being robbed at knifepoint walking alone on the beach between here and the Plage Al Ahmady to the south in 2024, but this is thankfully an unusual occurrence.

as much as the architecture here can be functional and unadorned, the people's style is flowing and fanciful, and the city's pavements are a catwalk of styles that could only come together here.

Men and women representing all corners of this multi-ethnic nation decorate the dust-blown cityscape. Moorish men channel all the radiance of the sky in their bolt-blue *boubous*, while Peul ladies dazzle in golden earrings and colourful beads. Wolof fellows sport zig-zag Cabral caps and stiff *bazin* tunics in a crayon-box worth of colours, while Soninkés wrap up in cloth of such deep indigo it rubs off on the skin. Herders from the countryside hide their faces in *haoulis* and sunglasses, revealing nothing but the stick of *miswak* between their lips. And made-up Moorish ladies breeze past in metres-long *melhfas*, trailing behind them like a perfume.

And while it's true that Nouakchott rarely reveals its charms overnight, resist the temptation to dismiss the city as a rest stop and nothing more. As much as the desert represents Mauritania, so too do the contrasts of Nouakchott, and whether your day starts with croissants or camel hump, both are key to getting to know this wild, unwieldy country. So slow down and get a taste of this grand, unusual city which is slowly but surely coming into its own – perhaps not according to plan, but as the Mauritanians would certainly say, according to God's will – *Alhamdulillah*.

HISTORY

The fact that Mauritania's colonial-era 'capital' was in fact located extraterritorially, inside the neighbouring territory of Senegal, presented Mauritanian authorities with an unusual problem to solve during the lead-up to independence in 1960. In fact, prior to its baptism as the new nation's capital-to-be in 1958, Nouakchott was nothing more than a cluster of wells and a military outpost. Even the first president, Mokhtar Ould Daddah, who was a major force in choosing the city's ultimate location, referred to it as 'a dune where there are only a few stunted shrubs buried under the fine sand'.

There were two French military posts built here, in 1903 and 1929 (both long since demolished), but unlike Port-Étienne (Nouadhibou) to the north and Saint-Louis to the south, Nouakchott was not a regular stop on the famous Aéropostale airmail route between Casablanca and Dakar and saw visitors only irregularly or in the case of emergency.

One such emergency in the late 1920s sent famed Aéropostale pilot Antoine de Saint-Exupéry to land with a blown crankshaft near the then-fort of Nouakchott:

> This small post in Mauritania was then as isolated from all life as an island lost at sea. An old sergeant lived there locked up with his fifteen Senegalese. He received us as if we were sent from heaven… He cried. 'For the last six months, you have been the first [visitors]. I get resupplied every six months.'

The overwhelmed sergeant quickly offered the stranded pilots a wine (which, admittedly, is more than you're likely to get today), and they set about leaving as soon as they possibly could. French author Joseph Kessel passed through around the same time, where he met the same lonely Corsican sergeant as Saint-Exupéry and decried Nouakchott in even more caustic terms:

> The worst place on the coast. Halfway from [Port-Étienne] to Saint-Louis there is a tiny fort and the sun above it. A backwater worse than anything. [Cap] Juby is a capital city by compare! There are fifteen Senegalese riflemen and a Corsican sergeant there. Full stop, that's all.

So how on earth did the new nation's capital city end up here? Especially in a country that, despite being largely nomadic, *did* in fact have a centuries-old urban tradition in the form of Chinguetti and the other *ksour* of the interior? In short, because of its lack of baggage. The 'ex-nihilo' development of a new city represented a neutral position on Mauritania's central social-geographical fault line: it lies neither in the Moor-dominated north, nor the Black African dominated south, and it overlooks the coast where it was envisioned that a port facility might one day take shape.

And so it was decided, this desolate outpost of a few hundred souls was to become among the world's least-likely national capitals. The foundation stone was laid on 5 March 1958, and the planned city, originally designed by French architect André Leconte, began to rise out of the sand. But beyond the first few years, almost nothing in Nouakchott went to plan. The city was expected to have 8,000 residents by 1970 – instead it had 70,000.

Though in the first years of independence the city actually had a hard time attracting new residents, to the extent it was giving away parcels of land, the series of cataclysmic droughts of the late 1960s and 1970s saw the population explode as people fled destitution in the countryside in hopes of finding some support in the city. The population hit 140,000 by 1980, and another wave of droughts saw the rural exodus continue: Nouakchott counted more than 400,000 residents by 1990 – an almost unfathomable 66,000% increase in population in 30 years.

This explosive population growth ensured that outside the initial centre, the city quickly became a landscape of tents and *baraques* (shacks), surrounding the planned city with a haphazard ring of slum settlements known as *kebbes* or *gazras*. This anarchic urbanisation was the order of the day for many years, but has slowed down over time, and many of these informal neighbourhoods have urbanised over time and now represent the different neighbourhoods of the city.

And though the city is no longer growing at the rates it once did, today nearly 1.5 million people call Nouakchott home, making it one of the largest settlements anywhere in the Sahara. City authorities are finally beginning to catch up on the extraordinary infrastructural demands presented by these decades of chaotic growth, and President of the Nouakchott Regional Council Fatimatou Abdel Malick was elected as the first woman to hold the position in 2018 – she was re-elected again in 2023.

GETTING THERE AND AWAY

BY AIR Nouakchott–Oumtounsy International Airport sits 35km north of central Nouakchott along the N2 towards Nouadhibou. Taxis are available, or most hotels also offer airport transfers for around 1,200UM (€30). Until 2016, Nouakchott's airport was in the Dar Naïm neighbourhood immediately east of the city centre, but this has since been shut down and gridded out with roads for development – the former runway of course being the largest among them!

Airlines A handful of airlines have offices in central Nouakchott.

Air Algérie Av Gamal Abdel Nasser; 45 29 09 92; w airalgerie.dz
Air France Av Kennedy; 45 25 18 08; w airfrance.com
Mauritania Airlines Immeuble Damane, Av Gamal Abdel Nasser; 45 25 67 47; e mai.nouakchott@mauritaniaairlines.mr; w mauritaniaairlines.mr
Royal Air Maroc Av Général Charles de Gaulle; 45 25 35 64; w royalairmaroc.com
Tunisair Immeuble Jawda, Av Kennedy; 45 25 87 62; w tunisair.com

Turkish Airlines Av Général Charles de Gaulle; ☎ 45 24 20 12; **w** turkishairlines.com

BY ROAD All roads lead to Nouakchott, and today the city is connected to surfaced roads in all directions. Nouakchott does not have a central bus station, and transport providers tend to be – though are not always – clustered on the outskirts of town in the direction of travel. Most transporters operate minibuses (or sometimes shared saloon or estate cars), with the exception of along the Route de l'Espoir, where larger coaches are also common.

To Rosso and southern Mauritania For destinations along the Senegal River valley, there are a few different places to pick up vehicles. To **Rosso**, there are two possibilities, either just south of Carrefour Nancy, where Salama Transports (**m** 26 33 25 00, 46 57 25 00) runs vehicles roughly four times daily (07.00, 09.00, noon, 15.00) for 300UM (3hrs), or further south at PK7 where there are several more operators present at Garage Rosso. R'Kiz and Mederdra are also served from either of the above.

To **Diama** (for Diawling National Park or onwards to **Senegal** via the Diama border), numerous providers run minibuses from **Garage Diama** in the Sebkha (5ème) neighbourhood. These generally depart daily in either the early morning (around 07.00); or a couple of agencies (ie: Bolil Transport **m** 49 03 56 07, 46 10 20 15) offer evening departures around 21.00 as well. These stop off at the border for a few hours before continuing when the offices open in the morning. Prices vary whether you cross the border in the same vehicle or change at the border: Diama (700UM; 4hrs), Saint-Louis (1,000UM; 5–6hrs), Dakar (1,500/3,000UM with change/same vehicle). Direct vehicles take about 10 hours to Dakar. Another provider, simply (and rather confusingly) calling themselves Garage Senegal (**m** 47 48 47 42, 22 48 51 47), is a few blocks away, running in either direction twice weekly at 06.00 on Sundays and Tuesdays.

For destinations further up the **Senegal River valley**, such as Lexeïba II, Boghé, Kaédi and Sélibaby, aim for Garage Kaédi [114 D4]. Here, minibuses and estate cars depart when full for Lexeïba II (500UM; 5hrs), Boghé (500UM; 5hrs), Kaédi (600UM; 6hrs) and Sélibaby (900UM; 10hrs) between about 07.00–noon. SONEF (**m** 22 11 43 25) also runs a once-daily coach along the valley to Boghé, Kaédi and Sélibaby, departing at 07.00 from its stop in the El Mina (6ème) neighbourhood.

To Nouadhibou and points north Vehicles for **Nouadhibou** depart from Garage Nouadhibou [114 A2] near Carrefour Sabah, where several companies including Salima Voyages (**m** 47 64 87 89) run vehicles along the 475km road to Nouadhibou via Chami in the mornings and afternoons (700UM; 7hrs). SONEF (**m** 22 11 43 25) also runs a once-daily coach to Nouadhibou at 07.00 from its stop in the El Mina (6ème) neighbourhood (page 105).

To continue into Moroccan-controlled Western Sahara, El Moussavir Plus [114 A1] (☎ 45 25 75 75; **m** 47 72 34 54) has an office about 1km to the north; its early morning departure from Nouakchott meets its Dakhla-bound vehicle from Nouadhibou at the turn-off to the border before reaching Nouadhibou, allowing you to continue directly to the border from Nouakchott.

To Atar and the northeast **Garage Atar** serves all points northeast of the capital, including Akjoujt, **Atar**, Choum and Zouérate. The garage is about 600m past the new flyover at Carrefour Hay Saken on the way out of town towards Atar. Here, numerous companies run minibuses to Akjoujt (300UM; 3hrs), Atar (500UM; 6hrs), Choum (600UM; 7hrs) and Zouérate (800UM; 10hrs), with departures usually around 08.00–09.00 and 16.00 (but only in the mornings to Zouérate). For other destinations in the Adrar (ie: Chinguetti etc), you will change vehicles in Atar. One company, Tiriss Transport (m 43 30 30 25) runs vehicles all the way to Tindouf (Algeria) via the new Mauritania–Algeria border crossing (page 216).

Route de l'Espoir and the east Reaching destinations to the east is a touch more complicated than in other directions, as the companies serving towns along the **Route de l'Espoir** are a bit more scattered than the others, with departures from two sets of locations. The first are splayed out along the road east of Carrefour Madrid [115 E3]. Most offices are located within about 750m on either side of Carrefour 24, and there are at least a dozen companies running either minibuses or coaches to all destinations along the 1,300km route, from Boutilimit (250UM; 2hrs) to Bassikounou (1,400UM; 22+hrs). Not all departures will run the entire route (many stop or change vehicles in Kiffa, for example), but stops include **Aleg** (400UM; 5hrs), **Kiffa** (800UM; 10hrs), **Aïoun El Atrouss** (1,100UM; 15hrs) and **Néma** (1,300UM; 20+hrs).

Companies here include Tayba Transport (m 28 22 67 00/01), Tilemsi Transport (m 42 51 51 68), Tewviq Transport (m 20 59 98 34) and Mecque El Moucarrama Transport (m 46 69 82 10/11). Most departures are between 07.00 and 08.00, but there is usually at least one afternoon departure going as far as Kiffa around 16.00.

The second set of offices are found in the El Mina (6ème) neighbourhood, south of the main market area. Some companies are represented in both locations. In El Mina, you'll find Nour Transport Voyageurs (m 48 30 83 10, 36 81 12 31) and SONEF (m 22 11 43 25, 42 46 43 22, 44 46 43 22) near Carrefour Touré, and another Tilemsi Transport (m 42 51 51 68) a few hundred metres to the southwest, near Carrefour Yéro Sarr. Some SONEF buses also continue to Bamako, but this route was not recommended at the time of writing due to insecurity on the Mali side of the border.

Minibuses to **Tidjikja** and the Tagant region depart from a handful of offices about 500m south of Carrefour Madrid, near the south end of the new flyover. Tagant Transport (m 22 45 36 37, 47 50 58 26; ⊕ 18.0739, -15.9665), El Khalifa Transport (m 44 37 00 86, 48 10 42 91; ⊕ 18.0734, -15.9641) and El Wahatt Transport (m 43 00 03 10) all run daily minibuses to Tidjikja (800UM; 10hrs) departing around 07.00.

BY BOAT Despite being a coastal capital, there are no scheduled boat services to or from Nouakchott, and most yachties heading south from the Canary Islands are making for Dakar or Cabo Verde rather than stopping here. Cargo ships do operate between Nouakchott and the Canary Islands, but we've got no insight on if and how you might get aboard one. The Port Autonome de Nouakchott (Port de l'Amitié; PANPA; w port-nouakchott.com) sits at the far southwestern edge of Nouakchott.

GETTING AROUND

BY BUS There is a public bus network run by Société de Transport Public (STP; m 32 97 83 82; w stp.mr), which has some two dozen lines serving much of the city (but unfortunately not the airport). It runs a combination of full-sized urban buses (lines beginning with L) and 30-seater minibuses similar to a Toyota Coaster (lines beginning with R). Fares are just a few ouguiyas and can be paid on board. (Or there's even an app: 'E-Ticket – STP'.)

In mid-2025, STP inaugurated Nouakchott's first bus rapid transit lines, known locally as *bus à haut niveau de service* (BHNS). These have their own dedicated lanes to avoid traffic, and tickets cost 15UM. The Nouakchott Mobilité 2026 project envisions a considerable expansion and harmonisation of Nouakchott's public transport network in the coming years, so watch this space.

BY TAXI Sehdini (w sehdini.com) and CarApp (w carapp-africa.net) are the local Uber equivalents and offer vehicles in considerably better nick than the shambles on wheels usually found on Nouakchott streets.

Otherwise, shared taxis are the rule. Unless you request a 'course', or private hire, taxis (both marked and unmarked) ply between the city's main junctions for something like 20UM for a short trip. The routes these follow are not random, but there is no signage, so your best bet is to name the next junction or landmark you're headed towards and the driver will indicate if they're going that way. (And if they divert from your intended route, it's easy to hop out and try again!)

It's also possible to hail the many tuk-tuks around town for private hire, though the city government has attempted to ban these from several important axes in the city centre in an effort to reduce traffic chaos.

BY CAR Given how spread out Nouakchott is, driving here is not as awful as it might be in more densely populated cities, but the roads are full of flash new 4x4s jockeying for position with what might be the most clapped-out collection of cars anywhere on the African continent.

A FEW USEFUL BUS ROUTES

The Société de Transport Public publishes a somewhat useful route map here: w stp.mr/wp-content/uploads/RESEAU-URBAIN-STP-10-2023.png

It's unfortunately not scalable, however, and therefore the information contained therein can still be rather difficult to parse.

Most visitors don't spend enough time in Nouakchott to fully sort out the public transport system anyway, but there are a handful of lines that could be useful to reach outlying attractions or transport parks:

BHNS1 runs from Carrefour Madrid south to Carrefour Bamako, stopping at Garage Rosso en route.

BHNS2 runs from Polyclinique to Toujounine via Carrefour Madrid. (Conventional bus **L01** serves a similar route). In combination with bus **L15** (Toujounine to Tenweich), this can take you to Marbatt Tenweich (camel market) at the far eastern edge of Nouakchott. It is also useful for the bus offices along the Route de l'Espoir should you not feel like walking from Carrefour Madrid.

BHNS3 runs from Carrefour Madrid to the Université de Nouakchott Al-Aasriya via Carrefour BMD and Garage Nouadhibou/Carrefour Sabah. **R60** serves a similar route, from Big Market in Tevragh Zeïna to Carrefour Lekbeid just east of Carrefour Madrid.

L62 runs west from Carrefour BMD to the Port du Pêche.

NOUAKCHOTT'S CREATIVE CARREFOURS

For a city somewhat lacking in iconic landmarks, Nouakchott's city planners have made sure that the artwork at the centre of the city's many traffic roundabouts does its very best to make up for it.

There are more of these than we can name here, but a few favourites worthy of mention include the giant *gued'ha* bowl of camel milk (Carrefour Poteau 3), the *ardin* harp (Carrefour Nancy), the scales of justice (Carrefour Foire), several dolphins (Carrefour El Houtat/des Poissons), a miniature Dome of the Rock (Carrefour Al-Quds), a teapot and cups for drinking *atay* (Carrefour El Berad), and finally a sizeable camel saddle at Carrefour Al Rahla, just as you enter/exit the airport.

A couple of these art pieces have been sacrificed to progress in recent years: Carrefour Madrid, for years a famously congested choke point for getting through Nouakchott, got a new flyover in 2025 – the Pont de l'Amitié Mauritano-Chinoise – and lost its stack of books. Carrefour Bamako on the southern edge of the city also received a flyover, Pont Taazour, in 2024.

Carrefour Nancy actually takes its name from British entrepreneur Nancy Jones Abeiderrahmane, who founded the Laitière de Mauritanie, now known as Tiviski (w tiviski.com) in 1989, producing Africa's first fresh pasteurised camel milk. She also published a memoir in 2013: *Camel Cheese – Seemed Like a Good Idea.* For more on Nancy and Mauritanian dairy, see page 120.

But of course the newest and the oldest cars both wait in the same snarled traffic, usually around key junctions like Carrefour Madrid (though here the new flyover should help somewhat at least). Pedestrians on two legs and four regularly dart into the road, and rules on signalling are predictably lax.

Car hire If you want to get off-piste, which most visitors to Mauritania do, visitors generally hire a car with driver through one of the tour agencies as part of a tour package. There are a number of local agencies doing only car hire clustered around Carrefour BMD, though they are unlikely to have much experience working with foreign tourists. So far as we can tell, **Europcar** (m 47 39 39 39, 22 30 32 41; e europcarmauritanie@gmail.com) is the only international car hire chain represented in Nouakchott, with offices at the Azalaï Hotel Marhaba [114 D3].

TOURIST INFORMATION AND TOUR OPERATORS

The **Office National du Tourisme** [115 F1] (ONT; 45 29 90 90; w visitmauritania.com; VisitMauritania & ONTMauritania.corporate) has an office in the airport where it can give you some pamphlets should your flight land during business hours. Its main office is on Avenue Bourguiba in the Ksar neighbourhood. In practice, it's probably easier to just consult your guesthouse: most of the tourist-oriented accommodation in Nouakchott can reliably connect you with guides and vehicles for all upcountry excursions.

MAPS AND GUIDES At risk of tooting our own horn, the book you're currently holding is where you can find the most comprehensive map of Nouakchott's points of interest. But of course paper maps in this size have certain limitations and you may wish to zoom in on some of Nouakchott's many densely populated neighbourhoods. The third edition fold-out Mauritania & Mali map from ITMB (2019) contains an inset focused on Nouakchott, but this is limited to the older districts of Ksar and La Capitale.

Online, Google Maps is reasonably accurate for navigating around Nouakchott, but many location pins are somewhat whimsically placed in the general area, rather than atop the exact site. OpenStreetMap (w openstreetmap.org; and/or the Maps.me app) is also quite good in Nouakchott, particularly when it comes to street names (though aside from the largest avenues, these are neither known nor used locally).

Though it's aimed primarily at expat Francophones, **Nouakchott Accueil** (e nouakchottaccueil@yahoo.fr; w nouakchottaccueil.blogspot.com; f) puts on occasional visits to sites of interest and events aimed at helping new Nouakchottois get to know their city better.

TOUR OPERATORS As Mauritania is a country where many of the destinations are somewhat remote, it pays off more here to hire a guide than it does in some other countries where attractions are more easily accessible independently. As a result, there are a good crop of tourism operators in the country, most of which are based in Nouakchott. All the operators listed below are knowledgeable and able to provide any relevant information, and they are of course in the business of selling tours. Many also work in partnership with accommodation popular with tourists, acting as their go-to agencies when guests want to set up trips. All of the following can arrange short trips near Nouakchott or along the coast, as well as customisable excursions to all corners of the country.

Atar Voyages m 46 57 67 61; e atarvoyage@gmail.com; w atarvoyages.com; f
Mauritania Desert Voyages m 36 77 73 33; e mauritaniadesertvoyages@gmail.com; w mauritaniadesertvoyages.com; f
Sidi Tours m 22 23 23 01; e booking@tourmauritania.com; w tourmauritania.com; f
Time For Mauritania m 48 17 55 53; e timeformauritania@yahoo.com; w timeformauritania.com; f
T'Ore Mauritania m 37 78 75 28; e babaceo@toremauritania.com; w toremauritania.com; f

ORIENTATION

Nouakchott's low-rise sprawl seems to spill in every direction, but it's not overly difficult to get to grips with the city's layout. From above, the city looks more or less grid-like, though the sets of grids defining different neighbourhoods often intersect at unexpected angles, leaving the map somewhat warped, as if it was (appropriately enough) left out in the sun too long and melted here and there.

Politically, Nouakchott consists of three regions: Nouakchott-Nord, Nouakchott-Ouest and Nouakchott-Sud. These regions are further divided into nine communes, namely Dar Naïm, Teyarett and Toujounine (Nord); Ksar, Sebkha and Tevragh Zeïna (Ouest); and Arafat, El Mina and Riyad (Sud). The city's districts used to be numbered, but today the names are typically used, with the exception of Sebkha, which is also commonly known as the cinquième/5ème, and El Mina, the sixième/6ème. (So Sebkha's market could be equally called Marché Sebkha or Marché 5ème.) The lion's share of accommodation, restaurants and other infrastructure for visitors is concentrated in Tevragh Zeïna, while transport infrastructure is scattered throughout several other districts of the city.

Navigation is often done based on travelling towards the nearest known carrefour (crossroads) and then refining from there. These junctions and roundabouts are

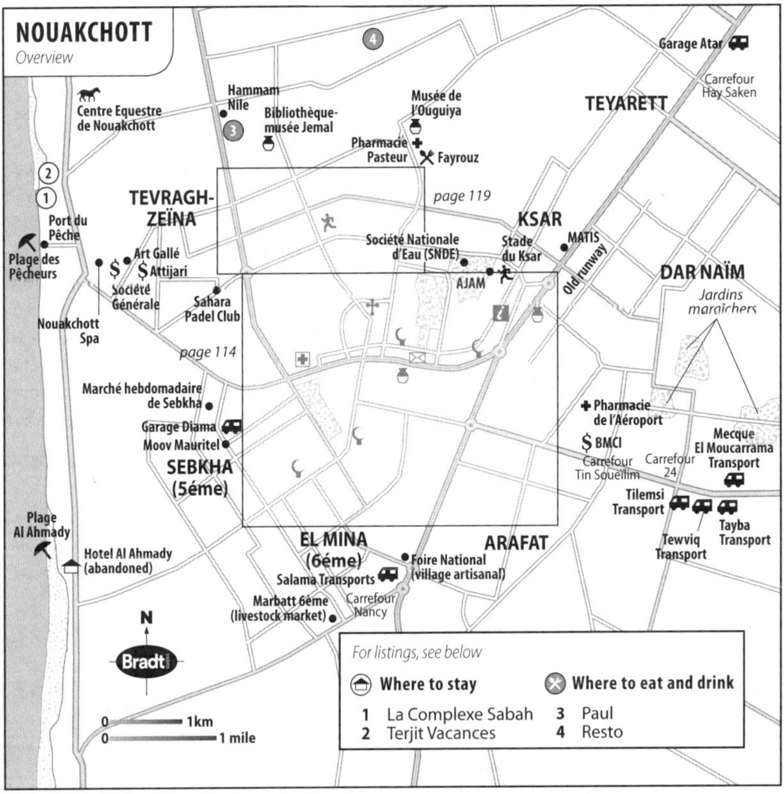

NOUAKCHOTT
Overview

TEVRAGH-ZEÏNA
KSAR
TEYARETT
DAR NAÏM
SEBKHA (5éme)
EL MINA (6éme)
ARAFAT

page 119
page 114

For listings, see below

Where to stay
1 La Complexe Sabah
2 Terjit Vacances

Where to eat and drink
3 Paul
4 Resto

often decorated with large works of art (page 111), and as such are easily memorable. We have marked the most significant of these on the city maps; their names are widely known among Nouakchottois, so you can use them to direct a taxi towards your destination.

The city centre is bisected east–west by Avenue Gamal Abdel Nasser. Nouakchott's main market district, known as Médina, lies directly to the south, while the administrative and business district of La Capitale lies to the north. Here in front of the Marché de la Capitale you'll find arguably the city's central point and busiest junction where avenues Nasser and John F Kennedy meet (though the two leaders never did in real life). Known as Carrefour BMD (after the now-defunct Banque Mauritanienne de Développement), it's perennially jam-packed with shoppers, traders and vehicles, and represents the nucleus of all public transport in Nouakchott. (Carrefour Madrid to the east, now home to the new Pont de l'Amitié Mauritano-Chinoise flyover, is perhaps even busier, but slightly less central.)

WHERE TO STAY

As a rule, clientele at any of the options in the luxury category (**$$$$$**) slants heavily towards those here on business, but accommodation would be equally suited to well-heeled travellers seeking the highest level of comfort. Some offer swimming pools and spa facilities, though these are less common than you might expect, for cultural reasons.

All accommodation in the upmarket (**$$$$**) range will be en suite with air conditioning. Much of it is aimed at business travellers, and will usually accept credit cards as payment.

Many of the hotels in the moderate (**$$$**) category continue to be business-oriented, but there is a greater focus on the tourist market at this price, and many of Nouakchott's nicest boutique hotels fall into this range. These hotels generally have air conditioning and en-suite facilities, and most (though not necessarily all) will accept credit cards.

Some of the best-value accommodation in Nouakchott straddles the moderate-to-budget (**$$**) slice of the market, with several very pleasant owner-operated guesthouses offering a variety of carefully tended rooms in this range.

Finally, there are a couple of places offering shoestring (**$**) accommodation in dorms alongside their private room options, including Auberge Samiraa and Par Quatre Chemins (page 117). Most do not accept credit cards, though some can arrange this through online platforms. Euros are generally accepted if needed.

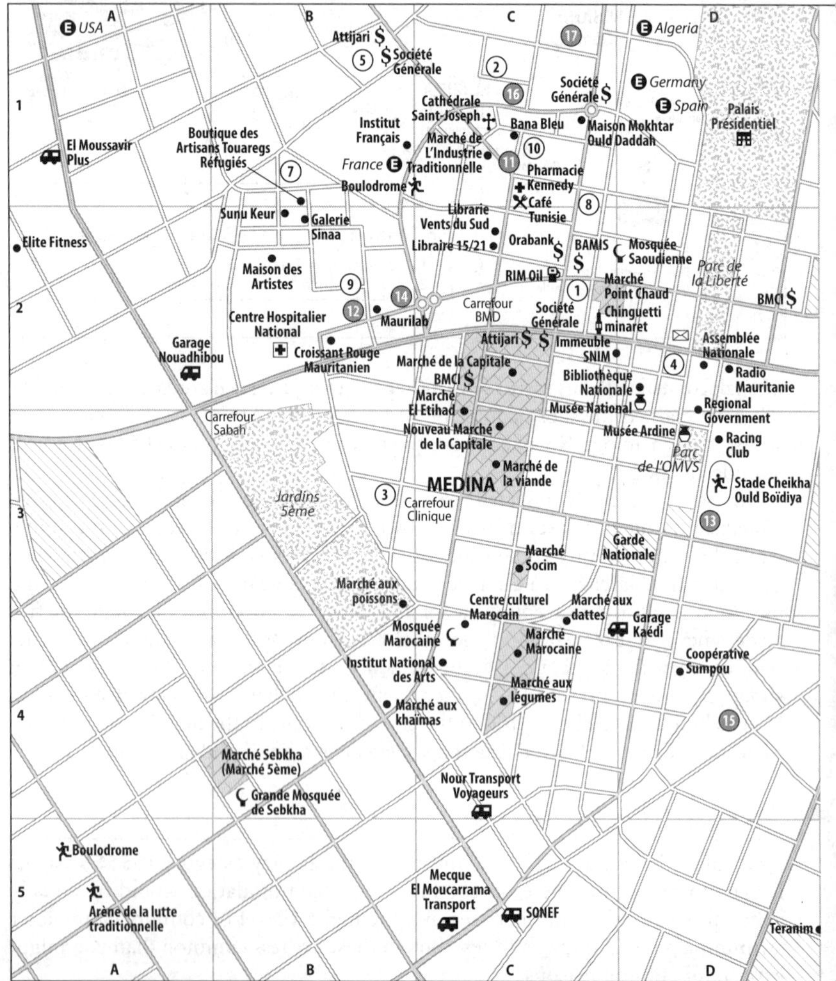

Just about all accommodation in Nouakchott has Wi-Fi by now. Whether it works or not may be a different story, but you shouldn't have *too* much trouble getting connected in the capital.

LUXURY AND UPMARKET

Azalaï Hotel Marhaba [114 D2] Av Gamal Abdel Nasser; ☎ 45 29 50 51; e reservationahm@azalaihotels.com; w azalaihotels.com. This venerable address was one of Nouakchott's first-ever hotels. It was fully remodelled & reopened under new management in 2016, & boasts a very comfortable restaurant-lounge alongside the large swimming pool & stylish rooms. *6,600UM dbl B&B.* **$$$$$**

Fasq Hotel [119 D2] Av Mokhtar Ould Daddah; ☎ 25 00 11 01; m 46 06 60 93; e reservations@fasqhotels.com; w fasqhotels.com. Opened at the end of 2023, this is vying to be the top hotel in town – though the Sheraton makes for stiff competition. The rooms are comfortable & handsomely appointed, the staff are capable & engaged, & there's an indoor swimming pool & spa, 3 restaurants, & a fitness centre. *From 10,000UM dbl.* **$$$$$**

Hotel Monotel Dar El Barka [114 B1] Rte des Ambassades; ☎ 45 24 23 33/4; e contact@monotel-mr.com; w monotel-mr.com. Though its days as *the* luxury hotel in town have long passed, this sprawling stalwart still offers a decent level of services. Some wings have been recently & convincingly modernised, others very much less so. *5,150/7,150UM standard/deluxe dbl B&B.* **$$$$$**

Les Sultanes [map, page 104] Beachfront; m 44 33 22 53; f lessultanes2; lessultanes_plagecheznicolas. Also known as Chez Nicolas after its long-time proprietor, this popular local getaway sits smack on the beachfront about 15km north of central Nouakchott. Mostly known as a restaurant (**$$$–$$$$**), it's also got 3 newly constructed bungalows, which are not cheap but handsomely appointed & right on the sand. *5,000UM dbl B&B.* **$$$$$**

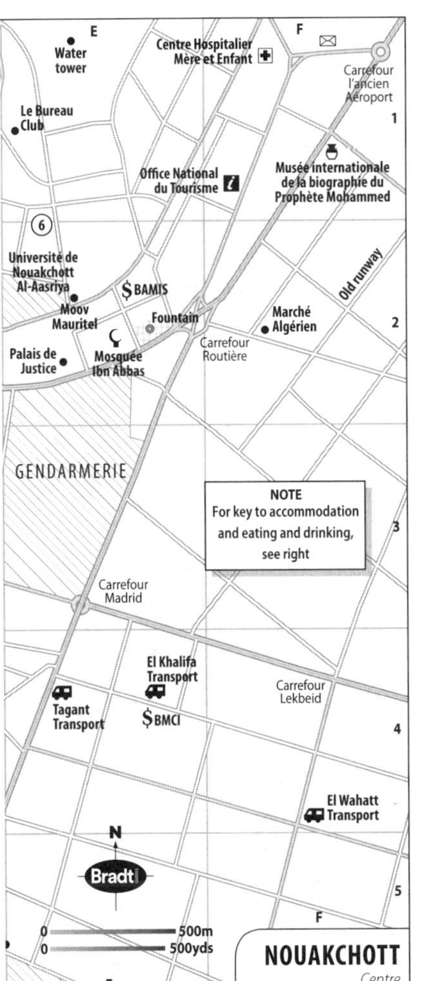

NOUAKCHOTT *Centre*
For listings, see from page 113

Where to stay

1 Al Khaima City Centre......C2
2 Auberge Diaguili......C1
3 Auberge El Assima......B3
4 Azalaï Hotel Marhaba......D2
5 Hotel Monotel Dar El Barka......B1
6 La Palma......E2
7 Le K......B1
8 Maison d'Hôtes La Bienvenue......C1
9 Par Quatre Chemins......B2
10 Semiramis Hotel City Center......C1

Where to eat and drink

11 Boulangerie-Patisserie des Princes......C1
12 Crêperie Iloca 10002......B2
13 FFRIM Café & Restaurant......D3
14 La Palmeraie......B2
15 Restaurant Malien Amandine......D4
16 Resto YoYo......C1
17 Youpi Café......C1

Sheraton Nouakchott Hotel [119 D1] Av Mokhtar Ould Daddah; ☎ 45 41 07 06; w sheraton.com. Nouakchott's first internationally branded hotel opened here at the end of 2025. Situated in a purpose-built 7-storey building, it immediately became the most luxurious address in town, with 167 rooms & 34 suites – including (naturally) an opulent presidential suite – plus several restaurants, swimming pool, fitness centre, & all the expected accoutrements. **$$$$$**

Al Khaima City Center [114 C2] Rue Mamadou Konate; ☎ 45 24 43 95, 45 24 00 12; e hotel@alkhaimacitycenter.com; w alkhaimacitycenter.com. Occupying the top half of what was the country's tallest building until the nearby Immeuble SNIM opened, this business hotel offers very comfortable rooms with all the expected amenities, though not much in the way of atmosphere. The views from the top-floor restaurant are the best in the city, though. *From 4,000UM dbl*. **$$$$**

Hotel Ziwanya [119 F2] Rue Ahmed Ould Mohamed Salem; m 44 31 27 40; e hotelziwanya@ziwanya.com; w ziwanya.com. This multi-storey hotel is aimed squarely at business travellers, & the switched-on management can help with any requests. The en-suite rooms are decisively modern & diligently kept. It only serves b/fast, but there are plenty of restaurants in the area. *3,000UM dbl B&B*. **$$$$**

Nouakchott Hotel [119 D2] Av Mokhtar Ould Daddah; ☎ 25 00 00 30/31/32; m 22 51 77 71; e contact@nouakchotthotel.com; w nouakchotthotel.com. Just across the street from the new Sheraton, the comfortable & modern rooms here aren't as luxurious as those across the street, but they're still among the nicest in town, & there's a small swimming pool at the centre of the complex. *4,500/5,300UM dbl/twin*. **$$$$**

Semiramis Hotel City Center [114 C1] Rue Sidi Mohamed Diagana; ☎ 45 24 00 38; e reservations.cv@semiramishotels.com; w semiramishotels.com. This is a stylish & centrally located option, with very modern rooms that are colourful & carefully appointed, plus a reliable restaurant. *3,800/4,200UM sgl/dbl B&B*. **$$$$**

MID-RANGE

Auberge Diaguili [114 C1] Rue Tripoli; m 46 46 00 03. Hidden away behind door number 458, this boutique guesthouse is set in a very appealing courtyard villa, with ochre walls reminiscent of Oualata. The rooms are carefully appointed, with mosaic floors & modern décor. Good meals available for guests. *2,200UM dbl B&B*. **$$$**

La Complexe Sabah [map, page 113] Beachfront; m 38 82 13 13; e contact@sabah.mr; w sabah.mr. This large oceanside complex sits just north of the Port de Pêche, but it's far enough from the boats & bustle for you to relax. The modern rooms are set in a row of cottages which don't take any advantage of the view, but the restaurant does, so you can have pizza, pasta & Mauritanian plates overlooking the water. *2,800UM dbl*. **$$$**

Le K [114 B1] Rue Seck Mame Diack; m 36 22 87 89; f le.k.nouakchott. The large rooms, leafy gardens, & stylish wax-print décor make this a charming & relaxed address in the city. The restaurant only serves b/fast, but there's a kitchen for guests' use if you'd like to cook. *2,000/2,500UM standard/deluxe dbl B&B*. **$$$**

✷ **Maison Jeloua** [119 B3] Rue Oumar Ben Abdel Aziz; m 36 36 94 50, 37 17 68 85; e maison.jeloua@gmail.com; f. This beautifully appointed guesthouse is among the prettiest in Nouakchott, & the bright en-suite rooms are carefully kept & well equipped. The roof terrace offers cool breezes & views over the neighbourhood, plus an excellent restaurant ($$$) & juice bar hosting events like dance classes & cultural performances. *2,000UM dbl/twin*. **$$$**

✷ **Maison d'Hôtes La Bienvenue** [114 C1] Av Général Charles de Gaulle; ☎ 45 25 14 21; m 46 47 60 68; e labienvenuenkc@gmail.com; f. Set in a charming older house with mosaic floors, the rooms at this centrally located guesthouse are simple, stylish & meticulously kept. The relaxed garden restaurant does a short menu of grills ($$$) & there's a large French-language library in the living room. *1,400/1,600UM standard/deluxe dbl*. **$$**

BUDGET

Africa Escale [119 B3] Rue Hassen Ben Youssef El Alaoui; m 27 26 99 89. This old-school auberge is a little more basic & timeworn than the other stalwarts listed opposite, but clean & pleasant nonetheless. They've been welcoming travellers for years & it's got all the essentials, including hot showers, an attached restaurant & space for overlanders. The characterful courtyard lounge is done up in all kinds of Mauritanian textiles, along with a great old hand-painted map of the country. *1,200UM dbl/twin*. **$$**

Auberge El Assima [114 B3] Rue Ely Ould M'Haimid; m 27 83 86 89, 46 32 52 03, 37 45 41 51. If you'd like to stay in the middle of the market action, the tidy 1st-floor rooms at this unassuming auberge could be just the ticket. **$$**

✷ **Auberge Triskell** [119 B3] Rue Cheikh Mohamed Adel Haye Ould Sabbar el-Mejlissi; m 41 57 59 83. This has long been one of the absolute go-to addresses for travellers in Nouakchott, & with good reason. The rooms come in a variety of configurations, from en-suite dbl to rooftop cabin or khaïma tent. The excellent Restaurant Nakhletein ($$$) is also on site, offering a sophisticated menu of European & African dishes, including several vegetarian choices. Owner Sébastien is a treasure trove of information on Mauritania & can advise on travel to all parts of the country. *€20 dbl khaïma; €20–35 dbl cabin; €35 dbl, €45 deluxe dbl, €55 family room (sleeps 4)*. **$$**

La Palma Hotel [115 E2] Rue Moulaye El Hacen Ould Moctar El Hacen; m 33 33 26 26. This businessy budget option behind the presidential palace is entirely bereft of character, but the management is unfailingly friendly & facilities are good for the price, including TV, AC, mini-fridge & hot showers in large bathrooms. *1,200UM dbl*. **$$**

Oceanides [map, page 104] Beachfront; m 22 91 91 52, 47 19 26 29; e oceanidesmau@gmail.com. The blue-&-white rooms at this well-managed beachfront retreat just south of Les Sultanes look a little scruffy from the outside, but are tidy & well kept on the interior. The restaurant serves a long list of fish & seafood from 400UM. *1,400/1,800UM standard/deluxe dbl*. **$$**

Par Quatre Chemins [114 B2] Rue Dieng Boubou Farba; m 47 00 77 11; e memoire.continent@yahoo.fr; w p4ch.com; f P4chemins. Opened in 2024, this new address from the owners of Auberge Triskell (see left) is located alongside their Crêperie Iloca 10002 (page 118). Accommodation is in rooftop cabins similar to those found at Triskell, coming in 2-, 3- & 4-bed configurations, all with fans & mozzie nets. *650UM pp B&B*. **$$**

Terjit Vacances [map, page 113] Beachfront; m 26 26 25 26, 36 30 62 10; e booknow@terjitvacances.com; w terjitvacances.com; f. One of the original tourism operators in Nouakchott & a long-term favourite for overlanders, this well-managed & family-owned setup offers bright & modern newly built rooms with Netflix & mini-fridges for an excellent price. The beachfront restaurant is also worth a stop. *1,500/1,800UM sgl/dbl*. **$$**

Auberge Samiraa [119 A3] Rue Amourj; m 41 71 82 42, 37 60 70 76; e aubergesamira@gmail.com; f. With rooms in 2-, 3- & 4-bed configurations, as well as a small dormitory, this has been a go-to spot for backpackers in Nouakchott for some years now, & it's well-loved by travellers as a place to hang out & swap stories over atay on the terrace. *1,200UM AC dbl, 900UM fan dbl, 320UM dorm bed*. **$$–$**

WHERE TO EAT AND DRINK

Though there's nowhere that officially serves alcohol, one or two places have been known to do so with a wink and a nudge. Either way, most restaurants will do a good range of fresh juice that goes some way towards slaking your thirst.

Most hotels also serve food, but several of the places listed under accommodation should be particularly noted for their kitchens, including Auberge Triskell, Maison Jeloua and Les Sultanes.

Le Mirador [map, page 104] Beachfront; m 41 84 34 34; f lemirador.mr. Though the surrounding housing development of Ribat al Bahr (originally planned to cover 680ha & have 50,000 residents) has been shelved, Le Mirador remains a popular hangout for well-to-do Nouakchottois enjoying brunch or a leisurely evening meal overlooking the ocean. The menu skews continental with a focus on seafood, & there's occasional live music at w/ends. $$$$

Tafarit Sun House [119 D3] Av Al Quds; t 45 25 46 73. Nouakchottois in the know will point you straight here for grilled fish & seafood, & it's easy to see why. There's a long menu of aquatic delicacies, even including fresh oysters, & the décor is suitably nautical, but not overdone. $$$$

Paul [119 D2] Av Mokhtar Ould Daddah; m 43 05 77 77; w boulangeries-paul.com; . The famous French chain of boulangeries-pâtisseries has arrived in Nouakchott, & is well patronised by the city's upper crust for their coffee, pastries, pasta, sandwiches & other light meals. A second location [map, page 113] opened in Tevragh Zeïna on Av Cheikh Zayed in late 2025. $$$$–$$$

A Casa Portuguesa [119 G4] Rue Ahmed Ould El Aghel; m 36 34 79 86; noon–15.00 & 19.00–22.30 Mon–Sat. This family-run restaurant serves a rotating variety of European cuisine & drinks in a charming little house with shady garden seating. The menu is written out by hand every day & it's a long-time favourite for expats based in Nouakchott. $$$

Al Fantasia [119 F2] Av Mokhtar Ould Daddah; 45 25 13 13; m 47 60 13 13. This long-serving Moroccan address is a solid bet for couscous & tajines, but it also does pizzas, pastas & grills. The inside is comfortable enough, but the rooftop seating is ideal on a breezy night. $$$

Chicago Restaurant-Café [119 G4] Av Général Charles de Gaulle; m 46 27 76 25. Large & comfortable place with outdoor seating & a long menu specialising in seafood, plus a choice of continental meat & pasta dishes, & a few Lebanese options for good measure. $$$

FFRIM Café & Restaurant [114 D3] Rue Mohamed Lamine Sakho; m 41 43 54 54. Run by the Fédération de Football de la République Islamique de Mauritanie (hence the name), this modern café sits next to the Stade Cheikha Ould Boïdiya & serves a continentally inspired range of fish, meat & pasta dishes, as well as paella, tagines & a 3-course daily menu for 350UM. As you might expect, it's also a good place to watch football on TV. $$$

La Maison du Terroir [119 C2] Av Mokhtar Ould Daddah; m 49 67 52 11; lamaisonduterroir.mr; 09.00–23.00 Tue–Sun. Gorgeous new coffee shop & boutique specialising in locally made Mauritanian products, including everything from soaps to seasonings, honeys & hair products (like from nabtacosmetics). $$$

Resto Kamal [map, page 113] Rue Mohamed Vall; m 37 50 03 04, 33 60 73 73. For a taste of the countryside without leaving the city, head out to this spot at the edge of town for Moorish cuisine served under Mauritanian khaïmas or Moroccan-style *caïdale* tents. The menu is strictly traditional, with big platters of méchoui BBQ meats, rice & tagines from 300UM. Traiteur Karim & Frères just across the road is very similar. $$$

Smoky Beach [map, page 104] Beachfront; ; 17.00–midnight Mon–Fri, 09.00–02.00 Sat–Sun; m 20 06 06 92, 38 23 30 01. On the beachfront about 20km north of central Nouakchott, this is the newest of a growing list of beachfront restaurant-resorts north of the city, serving burgers, brochettes, seafood & salads on the sand. Though it's far from town, it's only about 5km south of the airport turn-off, so could make for a good pre-flight stopover. $$$

La Palmeraie [114 B2] Rue Ahmed Ould Mohamed; 45 25 73 44; ; 06.00–midnight daily. This is a rather unusual pairing of café-patisserie & sushi restaurant, but there's nothing to complain about with either the food or the leafy garden setting. The café side is a popular spot for a casual office workers' lunch, & the pastries & cakes may be the best in Nouakchott. $$$–$$

Youpi Café [114 C1] Rue Sidy Yahya Al Kebir; m 49 04 04 66. This is a relaxed spot with shady garden seating on upcycled furniture built from pallets. It's a popular spot to watch the football with a fresh juice, & there's a good selection of grills, burgers & the like on the menu. $$$–$$

Crêperie Iloca 10002 [114 B2] Rue Mohamed Ben Brahim Boukharouba; m 41 57 59 83; ; ; 07.00–22.00 Mon–Thu, 07.00–15.00 Fri, 07.00–11.00 Sat–Sun. Under the same ownership

NOUAKCHOTT *Tevragh Zeïna*

For listings, see from page 113

Where to stay

1	Africa Escale	B3
2	Auberge Samiraa	A3
3	Auberge Triskell	B3
4	Fasq	D2
5	Hotel Ziwanya	F2
6	Maison Jeloua	B3
7	Nouakchott	D2
8	Sheraton Nouakchott	D1

Where to eat and drink

9	A Casa Portuguesa	G4
10	Al Fantasia	F2
11	Chicago Restaurant-Café	G4
12	Delizia	A3
13	La Maison du Terroir	C2
14	Paul	D2
15	Tafarit Sun House	D3

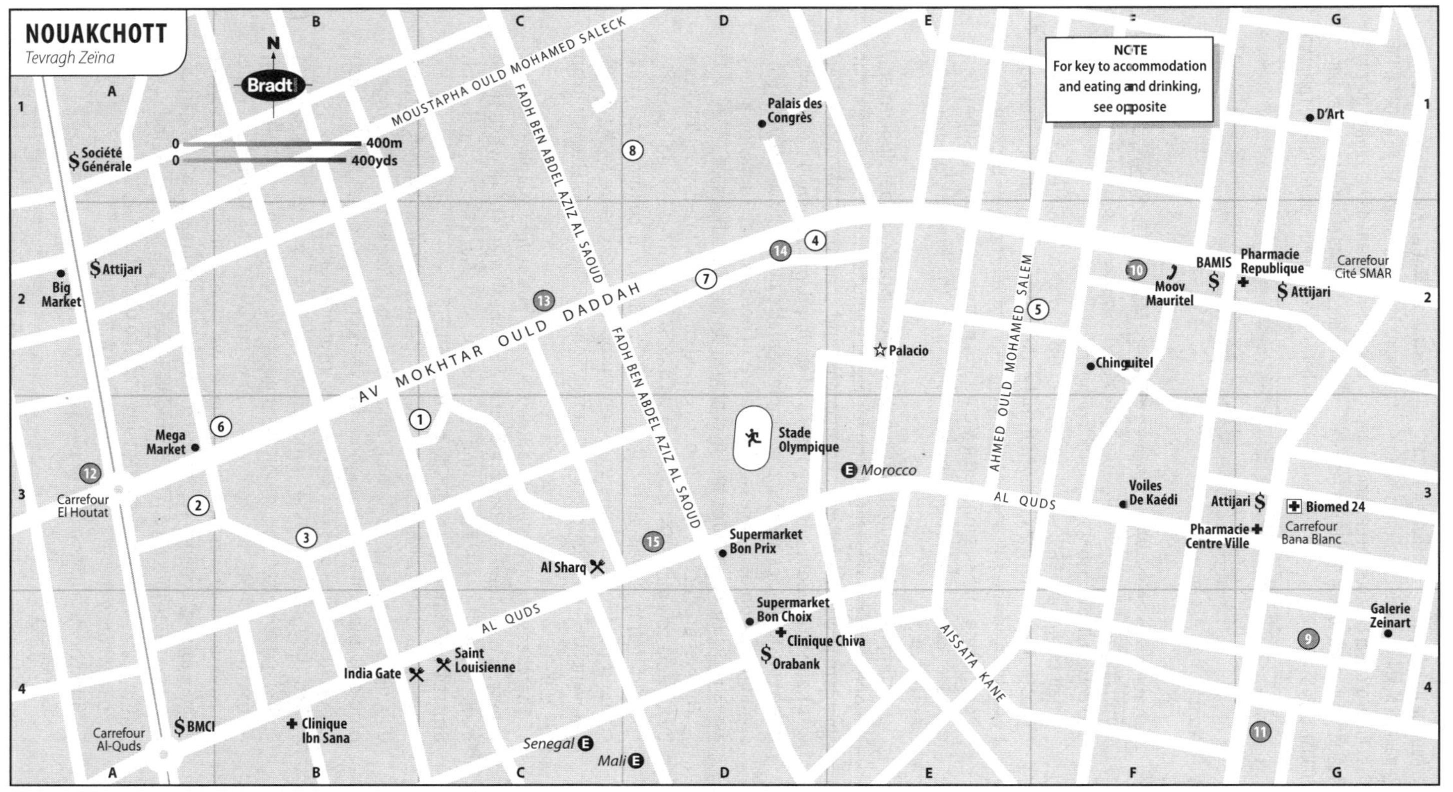
NOUAKCHOTT
Tevragh Zeïna
N
Bradt
0 400m
0 400yds
NOTE
For key to accommodation and eating and drinking, see opposite
MOUSTAPHA OULD MOHAMED SALECK
FADH BEN ABDEL AZIZ AL SAOUD
AV MOKHTAR OULD DADDAH
AHMED OULD MOHAMED SALEM
AL QUDS
AISSATA KANE
Société Générale
Attijari
Big Market
Mega Market
Carrefour El Houtat
Carrefour Al-Quds
BMCI
Clinique Ibn Sana
India Gate
Saint Louisienne
Al Sharq
Senegal
Mali
Palais des Congrès
Stade Olympique
Morocco
Palacio
Supermarket Bon Prix
Supermarket Bon Choix
Clinique Chiva
Orabank
Chinguitel
Voiles De Kaédi
Moov Mauritel
BAMIS
Pharmacie Republique
Attijari
Carrefour Cité SMAR
D'Art
Attijari
Pharmacie Centre Ville
Biomed 24
Carrefour Bana Blanc
Galerie Zeinart
A B C D E F G
1 2 3 4

as Auberge Triskell (page 117) & their excellent Restaurant Nakhletein, this casual café serves a short menu of sweet & savoury crepes, sandwiches & salads, plus a hard-to-beat plat du jour for 100UM. $$–$

Restaurant Malien Amandine [114 D4] Rue Macina Mamadou Lamine; m 46 06 04 54. This long-serving Malian address south of the city centre does a range of fast-food choices, but better to come for the grilled fish, fried plantains

CARREFOUR NANCY AND MAURITANIA'S MODERN MILK

Nancy Jones Abeiderrahmane

Compared to other West African countries, Mauritanian shops display a surprising number of locally made fresh dairy products: pasteurised camel and cow milk in cartons, yoghurts, crème fraîche…

It all began in 1989, when we started up a small all-stainless dairy plant to pasteurise camel milk bought from herders and sell it in cartons. Though I was born in the UK, the idea actually harked all the way back to 1970 when, having met and married a Mauritanian student in France, I submitted the idea as my graduation project – not quite the Nuclear Engineering I was studying!

Starting with a $200,000 loan from the Agence française de développement, the operation ran on a shoestring for years, trying to convince herders that selling milk was not miserly and shameful, and consumers that pasteurised was better than both untreated raw and sterilised imported milks. Gradually these constituencies grew, and we implemented a raw milk collection system spanning hundreds of miles and hundreds of herders, each supplying a daily average of just 10–20 litres, and available in up to 2,000 shops.

The first product was Tiviski (pasteurised camel milk in a carton) followed by El Badia cow milk, then L'Oasis crème fraîche and semi-skimmed cow milk. Yoghurt, fromage frais with dates, plain and flavoured cultured cow milk, cultured goat milk, and the so far only proper camel cheese in the world, Caravane. UHT milk followed, and butter. Some ice cream was attempted on the way.

The cheese project earned a Rolex Award, but as few Mauritanians eat cheese, it was ultimately designed for the European market. But while Tiviski made cheese, the EU was making regulations, and after 15 years' tussle with Brussels our export hopes had to be dropped.

However, once Tiviski looked viable, competitors set in and things became difficult as this split up a relatively small market and herder pool. The range of problems encountered throughout the years amounts to a saga, but cheap imported dairy remains one of the most insurmountable.

And though today Tiviski production is on hold, one of the odder but enduring spin-offs is the unofficial name of the roundabout near the dairy. Across Nouakchott, it's known as Carrefour Nancy or Carrefour Tiviski, because, as there was no city drainage, we piped the dairy's wastewater (from washing, cooling, etc) to the roundabout and created a lush garden, with a concrete milk carton in the middle covering the water tank. Today the carton is gone, but the name remains – and so does the milk.

In how many countries can you hear the following –

'Bring home a carton of milk please!'

'Camel, cow or goat?'

& variety of West African stews like mafé, soupou kandja, & more. $$–$

Resto YoYo [114 C1] Rue Abdallhi Ould Oubeid; m 41 04 07 03, 31 56 70 02; f; ⏲ noon–midnight daily. This low-key Ivorian hangout is a Nouakchott institution, & provides a welcome dose of tropical flavours for anyone whose had one dish of mutton too many out in the desert. You won't go wrong ith an Ivorian-style poisson grillé with alloco (fried plantain) or attiéké (cassava couscous). $$–$

Boulangerie-Patisserie des Princes [114 C1] Rue Monotel; m 32 58 51 10. Hugely popular local bakery (take-away only) serving sandwiches & savoury snacks as well as pastries & cakes. $

Delizia [119 A3] Carrefour El Houtat; m 30 39 19 04; ⏲ 15.00–02.00 daily. This new gelateria connected to the Canarian-owned Hotel Aloe Emira is an icy oasis for anyone back in the capital after some time upcountry. It does sweet crepes, coffees, milkshakes & gelato. $

ENTERTAINMENT AND NIGHTLIFE

NIGHTLIFE AND LIVE MUSIC Though they're not exactly 'nightclubs' in the sense you might be used to, there are a number of nightspots in Nouakchott where you can hang out until the wee hours over big platters of food, mocktails and desserts, and typically shisha pipes as well. These generally look something like an outdoor courtyard ringed with private booths which are open towards the centre, where there's often live music or other entertainment.

There are several hangouts like these on the road to the airport, including **Nouakchott Night** (Rte de Nouadhibou; m 42 42 84 42; f; ig; ⏲ 17.00–02.00 daily) which has a stage and a swimming pool, and **Jet Set** (Rte de Nouadhibou; m 36 95 08 08; ⏲ from 18.00) which has the same, but with a multi-floor set of opera boxes ringing the courtyard. Closer to the centre in Tevragh Zeïna, **Palacio** [119 E2] (m 37 37 02 02; ⏲ 07.30–02.00 daily) is known for its rooftop lounge.

It doesn't stay open as late as the above, but the **Institut Français** [114 B1] (☎ 45 29 96 36; w institutfrancais-mauritanie.com) has the most consistent cultural calendar in town, offering a regular rotation of live music, art exhibitions, cinema nights and more. There is also often live music on weekends at Le Mirador (page 117), as well as at some of the gallery spaces like D'Art (page 126) and the beach clubs north of the city like Les Sultanes (page 115).

Also, though definitively not a nightclub, **Sunu Keur** (m 44 55 07 06) is the home base for the Association El Vajer (e elvajervajer@gmail.com; f), which promotes musical and artistic training for Nouakchott youth. It also organises a variety of concerts and performances, including the Nouakchott Jazz and Nouakchott Reggae festivals (in their tenth and sixth editions, respectively), as well as local participation in the international Fête de la Musique. You'll often find association president Papis Koné and his Walfadjiri band practising or playing here.

CINEMA The second edition of the **Festival International du Film de Nouakchott** (m 33 33 11 14; e fifnrim@gmail.com; w fifn.org; f) was held in Nouakchott's Parc de l'OMVS [114 D2] (opposite the National Museum) in October 2024, with participants from 18 Arab and African countries. Yemeni filmmaker Amr Gamal took first prize with his 2023 film *The Burdened*. The Maison des Cinéastes [114 C2] (House of Filmmakers; m 36 10 80 08; e maisondescineastes@gmail.com; f maisoncineastes) is no longer fully functional. They used to put on the Nouakshort Film Festival (f nouakshort), but it hasn't been held in a few years. The third editon of the Festival national O'Meme du cinema et droits humains (f festivalomeme) was held in July 2025.

Nouakchott's last cinemas closed sometime in the 1980s, but the capital's first cinema in decades opened in mid-2025. Set northwest of the centre at the entrance to the mothballed Ribat al Bahr housing development, **Cinéparc** (Carrefour El Berad; m 36 80 28 28; 18.00–02.00 daily) is rather unexpectedly not a conventional cinema, but a drive-in theatre – which makes a fair bit of sense when you consider how enthusiastic about cars the average Mauritanian seems to be! There's also a restaurant and café ($$$) with fresh juices and coffees, as well as burgers, pizzas and shisha pipes.

FESTIVALS The **Centre Teranim pour les Arts Populaires Traditionnels** (m 46 52 81 78; e teranimpopulaires@gmail.com; w teranim.org; f teranimpopulaires; 18.0679, -15.9676) puts on the **Leyali El Medh** fest every Ramadan. Teranim is an organisation that promotes arts and music unique to the Haratin community, and the festival is a celebration of Haratin praise singing. They also released an album, *Eski*, in 2019.

Musician Aïcha Mint Chighaly puts on the **Ardine Festival** (w ardines.org) every year, also focused on traditional music and particularly the women's ardine harp. She also administers the newly opened Musée Ardine (page 130). The festival's seventh edition was held in November 2024 in Nouakchott's Parc de l'OMVS.

And for even more traditional Mauritanian sounds, the first **Festival de la Musique Traditionnelle** took place in November 2024 at the Stade Olympique in Nouakchott. Organised by the Ministry of Culture, Arts and Communication (w culture.gov.mr; f culture.gov.mr), the festival takes place over three days, with concerts of tidnit, ardin, t'bol and neifara (flute), along with traditional dancing, poetry and discussions. There are plans to hold it again every November, but hosting will rotate between Nouakchott and the regional capitals. For something more modern, the **Assalamalekoum Festival** (f) puts on concerts with local pop stars in June/July, also held at the Stade Olympique.

Montreal-based Mauritanian restaurateur Atigh Ould puts on the **Festival Nomade** (f RestoLaKhaima), which is generally a one-day celebration of Mauritanian nomadic life held in late January every year at the Hippodrome northwest of the city.

The first edition of the **Journées nationales de l'artisanat mauritanien** (National Mauritanian Crafts Days) took place in November 2023 at the Olympic Stadium complex, with artisans from all of Mauritania's wilayas and a handful of regional countries represented. Organised by the Ministère du Commerce, de l'Industrie, de l'Artisanat et du Tourisme, it will hopefully become an annual affair.

For film festivals, see page 121.

SHOPPING

There are plenty of well-stocked **supermarkets** around the city with a wide range of products, many of which are imported from France and Spain. As you might expect, the ritzier side of town in Tevragh Zeïna is home to the supermarkets with the widest selection of imported products. These include Bana Bleu, Big Market, Mega Market, Bon Choix and Bon Prix.

BOOKSHOPS Conveniently set right next to each other, **Librairie Vents du Sud** [114 C2] (m 32 07 24 24; e lvs.mauritanie@yahoo.fr; f) and **Librairie 15/21** [114 C2] (m 36 32 62 48; e Ideuxsiecles@gmail.com; f) on Avenue Kennedy are the most comprehensive bookshops in town. Though both are Francophone-focused, there are a few English-language books to be found as well.

MARKETS Throughout West Africa, Mauritanians are known as avid traders with a shrewd eye for business, and Mauritanian-run boutiques selling batteries, baguettes and bicycle tyres dot the cities, towns and villages of the region, from here all the way to Congo and Angola. So it's no surprise that Nouakchott is full of markets big and small, befitting its status as capital of a trading nation.

The original **Marché de la Capitale** [114 C2] is the city's first and still its largest market, now stretching to include several multi-storey buildings south of Avenue Gamal Abdel Nasser, including the **Nouveau Marché de la Capitale** [114 C3], inaugurated in 2017, and the **Marché El Etihad** [114 C2] across the road. Though the core of the markets is inside these halls, in truth it's hard to know where the market ends and the neighbourhood outside begins, and a cacophonous cavalcade of bikes, barrows, baskets, blankets and boxes stacked with everything from pumps to pastries lines the streets in all directions. So take a deep breath and plunge inside for a window into what makes Mauritania tick – and some bargains while you're at it. There are numerous clothing boutiques here as well, so it's a fine place to shop for colourful *melhfas*, sky-blue *daraas* and supple *haoulis*, should you wish to get fitted with a local look – just don't forget, *tieb-tieb* (bargaining) is the rule of the game!

If you're after electronics, pop across Avenue Gamal Abdel Nasser to the north, where **Marché Point Chaud** ('Hotspot Market') [114 C2] has a head-spinning array of phones and electronics, many sporting brand names that you may have *almost* heard of. Otherwise, make your way south from the Marché de la Capitale, where the **Marché Socim** [114 C3] forms something of a link, soon spilling into the **Marché Marocaine** [114 C4], which itself sprawls over several blocks to the east of the Moroccan mosque. As with the Marché de la Capitale, it's hard to say exactly where the market starts and ends, but within this warren of frenetic blocks there are sections for meat (**Marché de la viande** [114 C3]), fish (**Marché aux poissons** [114 B3]), fruits and veg (**Marché aux légumes** [114 C4]), and even dates (**Marché aux dattes** [114 C4]). To the west of the main market area, you'll find the roadside

MARCHÉ SEBKHA (MARCHÉ 5ÈME)

Peter Hudson

The Cinquième Market is a test of endurance. Its size and intensity – the heat and smell, the crush of people, the vast array of colors and sights – can easily give rise to a sense of claustrophobia. But I like it. The intensity draws me out of myself. I now no longer feel ill. I move, as though swimming, through the close-packed crowds. Sweat pours down my face. We come to the market, which is indistinguishable at first from the surrounding streets. I have no idea what area it covers, but inside there is an infinity of alleyways and covered passageways, each lined with stalls, each of which is piled high with merchandise: 5,000 plastic sandals; 200 meters of juju items; an alleyway of butchers' tables, their strings of blackened offal alive with flies.

Mousa Djeng's stall is in a wide, uncovered passageway. Down the middle of the passageway sit two rows of vegetable sellers: women in multi-colored dresses behind piles of okra and yams, cabbage and mushed onion balls. Down the sides are small boutiques, the turbaned owners of which hover in doorways with dusters in their hands, flicking stacks of suitcases or piles of shiny kitchen items. And in between each boutique, pressed up against a small patch of wall, are the undergarment sellers. One of these is Mousa Djeng. Like the others, his stall is tiny, consisting of only a small table on which are displayed his wares: underpants, handkerchiefs, vests, bras.

From Under an African Sky *(New Internationalist, 2014)*

Marché aux khaïmas [114 B4], where women sell handmade Mauritanian tents, which are sure to be the absolute envy of music festivals and garden parties back home. The khaïmas are sold in a few sizes, including 3x3m (1,500UM), 4x4m (2,500UM) and 5x5m (3,000UM), and believe it or not, they actually fit fairly reasonably within a suitcase.

If you've still got the grit for another go-round, you can keep playing market hopscotch and head another 600m or so to **Marché Sebkha** [114 B4] (also known as Marché 5ème), which is another of the largest markets in the city, and one that's especially popular with vendors and shoppers from the south of Mauritania. Also taking inspiration from travelling markets popular in Senegal and West Africa south of here, the Sebkha municipality recently set up a regular *loumo*, meaning weekly market in Pulaar. The **Marché hebdomadaire de Sebkha** was inaugurated in 2024 and takes place on Sundays (at a different location than the main market). These popular markets are known to attract business from around the region, with traders often travelling long distances to be present at the largest loumos.

Also dealing with long distances, the **Marché Algérien** [115 F2] is another new market in the city, set on the grounds of the former airport just east of Carrefour Routière. The market owes its existence to the newly opened border crossing in Mauritania's far northeast corner, connecting to the southern Algerian city of Tindouf. Both governments have declared their ambition to build a tar road and increase bilateral trade, so the offerings at this informal market are likely to expand significantly in the years to come. There are a handful of shops and stalls, but the rest feels a bit like a car boot sale, with vendors hawking straight out of the lorries just in from Tindouf, almost 1,700km away. The sellers here are especially known for their high-quality Algerian dates – you'll find more here than you can shake a palm frond at.

ON CAMELS

Nancy Jones Abeiderrahmane

Nouakchott is surrounded by small 'peri-urban' camel dairy herds, which have gradually developed to sell raw milk. In some cases the camels are part of a family herd, in other instances they are carefully selected and bought already with calf, to be milked and fattened for a year and then sold, usually for slaughter, as a purely commercial venture. This business has a macro-economic dark side: the number may be small compared to the overall camel population, but in the long run the negative selection is bound to impair the country's gene pool.

Although well-fed camels can yield up to two litres several times a day, traditionally they are only milked at dawn and late in the evening. Besides being fed concentrate, peri-urban camels browse on salty bushes near the sea or *Euphorbia balsamifera* on the dunes, because 'a camel's strength is in its legs'.

Camels are fastidious, and sensitive to insect bites and pests such as mange; herders hold that, unlike cows that 'like to live in their muck', camels need a clean resting place. They are largely disease-free if they are kept clean, and their droppings are small, round and so dry and odourless that they are used to play [traditional game] 'dhamet', but their concentrated urine surrounds herds – and herders – with a pungent aura.

From Camel Cheese – Seemed Like a Good Idea *(2013)*

Carrefour Routière is also the site of the proposed 65m **Monument de la Nation** [115 E2], which, according to the design specs, is eventually meant to house a restaurant, museum and viewpoint – and will look a bit like a rocket ship with Chinguetti's minaret pasted on top. The Ordre Mauritanien des Architectes (Mauritanian Order of Architects; f) was so incensed by the design, they published a letter of protest in 2025, condemning it as 'lack[ing] coherence' and 'creating a strong impression of immaturity unworthy of a national monument'. Whose vision will win out, however, remains to be seen.

Finally, and fully befitting the capital of a nation of pastoralists, there are several **livestock markets** (*marchés de bétail*, or *marbatt* in Hassaniya) around the city, most notably including **Marbatt 6ème** (⊕ 18.0533, -15.9835), 1km southwest of Carrefour Nancy, and **Marbatt Tenweich** (⊕ 18.0567, -15.8508), on the eastern fringes of town at PK12. Both are home to hundreds or thousands, depending on the day, of goats, camels and cows grunting, spitting and chewing their way through the day, along with their gimlet-eyed owners, here to wheel and deal for the capital's most beautiful beasts at the best possible prices. According to at least one source, Marbatt Tenweich may be the second-largest camel market in the world.

Note that, while it's good practice on the whole, it's especially important to ask permission and be discreet with photography in Nouakchott's markets – not everyone here is keen to have their photo taken, and they won't hesitate to let you know if that's the case. That being said, a small purchase and a smile often go quite a long way towards converting the camera-shy!

For Nouakchott's artisanal markets selling primarily crafts and souvenirs, see page 126, and for the fish market at the Port de Pêche, see page 133.

GALLERIES AND WORKSHOPS The Mauritanian craft tradition has grown out of the rigours and requirements of nomadic life, for which household items were honed to perfection over centuries of desert survival. As such, there is much impressive artisanship in wood, leather, metal and textile to be found in Nouakchott (and much of it, by its nomadic nature, is fairly portable!), alongside a younger tradition of painting and other visual arts.

The country's first art school was founded in 2020, and the **Institut National des Arts** [114 C4] (45 25 66 21; e ina.mauritanie@gmail.com; f) trains students in a variety of disciplines, including cinema, theatre, music and visual arts. It doesn't have a gallery per se, but you're welcome to drop by the institute, where you can meet the students at work. Some of the students are organised in art collectives which occasionally exhibit around town, including **Créativ'art** (Jeunes Artistes Mauritaniens; f; creativ_art222) or the **Association des Jeunes Artistes Plasticiens Mauritaniens** (AJAM; Association of Young Mauritanian Visual Artists; m 49 55 55 68; e ajam.mr1960@gmail.com; f AJAM.mr). The latter has its 'maison de la créativité' in the Ksar neighbourhood, where there is a regular calendar of classes for and exhibits by young artists. The **Institut Français** (page 121) also hosts regular exhibitions of Mauritanian art in a variety of mediums.

In Tevragh Zeïna, **Galerie Zeinart** [119 G4] (Rue Mohamed Lemine Ould Tlamid; m 46 51 74 65; e zein.artdesign@gmail.com; w art-zein.blogspot.com;) is probably the best-known gallery in Nouakchott, and with good reason. The extraordinarily fluffy chickens roaming the gardens in front of owner Isabel Fiadeiro's collections add to the homey vibe, and the art, jewellery, textiles and books inside are carefully curated and represent some of the finest offerings in Mauritanian art. Zeinart also puts on a **Marché des Producteurs** (f Marchejardinzeinart) farmers' market on Saturday mornings, where you can buy locally made cosmetics, crafts and produce of various kinds, including the delicious harvests of some of the gardens mentioned on page 133.

About a kilometre to the north, **D'Art** [119 G1] (Rue de Doha; m 41 50 02 02; f dartespacedescreations) was founded in 2021 by photographer Malika Diagana and visual artist Saleh Lo. Billing itself as an 'espace des créations' (creation space), it's a bright and active address, hosting a regular schedule of concerts, painting classes and social events in its green gardens surrounded by flamboyant murals.

On the west side of town, **Art Gallé** (Cité Plage; m 46 44 83 35, 46 52 54 22; e amiart2005@yahoo.fr; f artgallerieresidartisteartcaf) was founded by painter Amy Sow in 2017, and occupies one of Nouakchott's most unusual buildings, built largely of scavenged wood and other unorthodox construction materials. There's a simple café serving hot drinks and juices (where workshops and concerts are sometimes held), and the floors above showcase works from Sow and others, along with some jewellery and other crafts. They also put on their own Festival Art Gallé in late January.

Back towards the city centre, **Galerie Sinaa** [114 B2] (Rue Cheikhna Ould Mohamed Laghdaf; m 36 68 82 39; w galeriesinaa.com;) sells a stylish variety of cloth, jewellery, housewares and art from artisans in Mauritania and other West African countries, including sous-verre artwork from Senegal, and more.

Just a block from here, the **Boutique des Artisans Touaregs Réfugiés** [114 B1] (m 27 09 20 73; e alfaky.artisant@yahoo.com; f) is a very unique address. Though inextricably linked with the Sahara in the popular imagination and famous for their work in metal and leather, few Touareg people actually live in Mauritania. Historically speaking, the Majâbat al-Koubrâ, or empty quarter, in Mauritania's east has separated the traditional lands of the Moors and the Touaregs, but today many have fled the grinding conflict in neighbouring Mali and taken up residence in eastern Mauritania. Most still live in the remote Mbera camp, but some have relocated to Nouakchott seeking opportunities and opened this shop, where Touareg craftsmanship in silver and leather is on full display in their selection of boxes, bags and jewellery. Also nearby, the **Maison des Artistes** [114 B2] (Rue El Mechtabe Ould Mohamed Vall) was once headquarters for the Union des Artistes Peintres Mauritaniens, but the site was non-functional when we checked in.

Again continuing back towards the city centre, the **Marché de l'Industrie Traditionnelle** [114 B1] is Nouakchott's biggest market for artisanal products and souvenirs. Consisting of maybe 15 or so shops on either side of Rue Monotel, it offers a variety of artisanal products, ranging from rather chintzy photo frames full of mass-printed images of Mauritanian life (framed bowl of camel milk, anyone?) to finely crafted jewellery and silverwork, including gorgeous boxes in leather or wood with silver inlay, all manner of rings, bracelets and necklaces, and a selection of melhfas and other textiles. (Remember to be a *tieb-tiaba* – a bargainer – here!) For melhfas and cloth, Hawa Tandia and Coopérative Fatima (m 46 43 43 17, 46 93 35 20) is the best shop on the street, selling Kaédi-style melhfas in a rainbow of colours. About 1.5km to the north in Tevragh Zeïna, **Voiles De Kaédi** [119 F3] (m 33 23 32 94, 47 78 11 94; f) is another good address for these.

And if you're still foraging for fabric, the **Croissant Rouge Mauritanien** [114 B2] (Mauritanian Red Crescent; 45 25 12 49, 45 25 47 84; e croissantrougem@gmail.com, sn_crm@yahoo.fr; f) works with local women expert in **cloth dyeing** as part of its income-generating activities, producing melhfas and other tie-dyed cloths at its headquarters next to the Centre Hospitalier National. Note, however, that these talented *teinturières* don't necessarily work every day, so give it a call or drop by to ask when you might catch them in action.

THE GREATEST EVENT

Around the time of the ribbon-cutting at the Foire Nationale de Nouakchott, and perhaps in connection with the North Korean entertainment provided, Kim Il Sung, first president (and now Eternal President) of the Democratic People's Republic of Korea, visited Nouakchott in 1975. After the visit – according to the predictably understated North Korean newsreel, anyway – Mauritanian President Mokhtar Ould Daddah (who himself visited North Korea in 1967) called Kim's visit 'the greatest event in the history of Mauritania'.

Mauritania would soon cut relations with North Korea, however, after that country's 1976 recognition of the Polisario Front and its Sahrawi Republic – with whom Mauritania was at war at the time.

For a different type of textile, **Mauritanienne de Tissage** (MATIS; Av des Forces des Forces Armées; ☎ 45 25 50 83; m 33 47 60 52, 49 18 28 52; e matis@mauritel.mr, matis@yahoo.fr) in Ksar is a weaving co-operative that has been active for more than 30 years, making hand-knotted rugs from either sheep or camel wool (some of it spun on site) in a variety of local and exotic motifs. Today it has three master weavers and 40-some trainees on site, and they're happy to give you a short tour around the looms and processing facilities.

In addition to the carpets made here in Nouakchott, MATIS also works with more than 2,000 women in over 200 co-operatives around the country, producing carpets and *hseyra* mats from reed and palm fibres, woven together in geometric designs with strips of leather. All this handiwork is on sale, but it doesn't come cheap: rugs can go for €1,000+, while the mats are generally €250–500. It might seem dear at first, but remember that some of these works have up to 100,000 knots per square metre and can take up to three months to complete! There are some smaller, less costly items for sale as well.

Finally, south of the city on the Route de Rosso (300m before Carrefour Nancy), the **Foire Nationale de Nouakchott** (Nouakchott National Exposition) was inaugurated in 1975 under the Ould Daddah administration, with the opening celebrations reportedly even supported by North Korean entertainment (see above). It featured exhibitions on Mauritanian artisanal and industrial products, but eventually fell into disrepair and was ultimately demolished. In June 2022, however, President Ghazouani laid the foundation stone for a large new **artisanal village** here, which is set to have two large exhibition halls, 150 workshops, two restaurants, and more. It was slated for completion in 2024, but a serious fire in May 2023 set the project back for an unknown period. Still, it should hopefully open within the lifespan of this edition.

SPORTS AND ACTIVITIES

CHESS The Fédération Mauritanienne des jeux d'échecs (m 41 50 00 00; w mauritaniachess.com) organises monthly tournaments at the Nouakchott Hotel (page 116).

FITNESS There are a few places to train in the city. **Racing Club** [114 D3] has a fitness centre & also offers karate & other martial arts lessons. **NKT CrossFit** [119 D3] (Stade Olympique; m 32 80 08 00; w nktcrossfit.com) is the local outpost for the international training regimen. **Elite Fitness** [114 A2] (Rue Mohamed Maouloud Ould Daddah; m 47 00 72 82; w elitefitnessnkc.com; f) puts on a competition for Mauritania's strongest woman & man with a 10,000UM prize.

FOOTBALL The 8,000-capacity **Stade Cheikha Ould Boïdiya** [114 D3] (previously & still better known as Stade de la Capitale) opened in 1969 & the 10,000-capacity Stade Olympique in 1983. Both were recently renovated for Mauritania's hosting of the 2021 Africa Cup of Nations for under 20s, & the former is also home to a new FIFA-sponsored training facility including several practice pitches & workout facilities.

There are also many private football pitches around the city. These are smaller than a standard pitch & open late into the evenings – they're easy to spot by the ball-catching netting poking high above the perimeter walls.

HORSERIDING The Fédération Mauritanienne du sport Équestre (m 37 27 27 27; f) manages the beachfront **hippodrome** on the northwest side of town, where it organises occasional horse races. It has plans to develop the surrounding site into an eco-tourism complex, but there was no sign of this (other than a sign board) at the time of writing. The **Centre Equestre de Nouakchott** (m 36 62 51 70; f; 📷; 🕘 16.00–19.30 Tue–Fri, 09.00–13.00 & 16.00–19.30 Sat, 09.00–13.00 Sun) has no signboard, but has stables for 50-some horses 1.5km south of here. It offers guided beachfront horseriding from 700UM/1hr (or 6,000UM for 10hrs). For camel rides, see page 134.

PADEL The **Sahara Padel Club** (f; 📷) opened in 2022, making it the country's first facility for padel (paddle tennis).

PÉTANQUE There are a handful of **boulodromes** or **espaces de pétanque** (pétanque pitches) around the city, & boules is a popular pastime in the evening hours after the heat has broken, or on w/end mornings – but be warned, Mauritanians are killer boulistes & competition is serious (during peak hours at least).

SWIMMING Some of the top-end hotels with swimming pools will allow non-guests to swim for a fee, including the Azalaï Hotel Marhaba (300UM; page 115). Alternatively, the Racing Club [114 D3] has a pool for 200UM/hr.

TENNIS Courts are available at the Racing Club [114 D3] for 200UM/hr, plus negotiable informal racket rental.

WATERSPORTS Nouakchott has a couple of **surf** & **kiting** spots, listed on page 57. There's no surf outfitter as such, but interested surfers can get in touch with **Le Wharf Surf Club Nouakchott** (📷) or **Kite Surfing Mauritania** (e kitesurfingmauritania@gmail.com; f; 📷). Mauritania's only **scuba-diving** agency (w adivingmrt.com) does underwater salvage & propeller polishing rather than scuba safaris.

WRESTLING **Traditional wrestling**, or *la lutte* (also commonly known by its Wolof name, *làmb*), is popular in Mauritania, & a new wrestling arena opened in the Sebkha neighbourhood in 2020. Known variously as L'arène de l'amitié or the Arène de la lutte traditionnelle (⊕ 18.0690, -15.9948), it's managed by the Fédération Mauritanienne de Lutte (m 46 53 01 67, 22 32 07 83; f). Check its Facebook page for upcoming events.

OTHER PRACTICALITIES

The **Bibliothèque Nationale** [114 D2] (National Library; w bnm.gov.mr) is in the same building as the National Museum. In the next building north, the **Centre Culturel de la Région de Nouakchott** [114 D2] (f) has a small theatre space, but tends to put on mostly seminars and the like. Nouakchott's main university, the **Université de Nouakchott Al-Aasriya** (w una.mr), has two campuses: one in the city centre [115 E2], and one on the far northwest side of town.

COMMUNICATIONS

Post The **main post office** [114 D2] (w mauripost.mr; 🕘 08.00–15.00 Mon–Thu, 08.00–noon Fri) is in the city centre on Avenue Gamal Abdel Nasser, just opposite the Azalaï Hotel Marhaba. Postcards can be sent for about 50UM and stamps are available (ours had camel saddles on them) for all your favourite philatelists. The latter may also wish to visit the Musée de l'Ouguiya (page 131).

Internet and telephone Nearly all hotels listed offer Wi-Fi (though this can occasionally be unreliable), and an increasing number of restaurants offer it as well. Getting your phone set up with mobile data is relatively painless and provides basic internet access in Nouakchott and most population centres throughout the country. There are several service providers (Moov Mauritel, Mattel and Chinguitel), but Moov Mauritel is widely regarded as having the most extensive network should you be travelling upcountry.

To purchase a local SIM card for your unlocked mobile, you have to bring your passport to the service provider's office, where they will register your data alongside the new number. These cost 100–200UM at most with the service provider; they can also be purchased from street vendors around Marché Point Chaud for 600–800UM. This is effectively a convenience fee for not needing to go through the registration process, but do test the SIM before concluding your transaction should you go this route. All providers offer voice, SMS and mobile data services on a prepaid basis, and your account can be topped up at most corner boutiques around the country.

Digital nomads should check out Le Bureau Club [115 E1] (Rue Ahmed Ould Bouceif; 45 25 37 18; m 41 74 08 08; f), which offers modern and well equipped co-working space for short or long term.

MEDICAL FACILITIES The **Centre Hospitalier National** [114 B2] (45 25 21 35) is the largest facility in the country, though the private Clinique Chiva [119 D4] (m 22 34 24 29) and Clinique Ibn Sana [119 B4] (m 36 34 14 48) also offer 24-hour emergency reception.

If you need an all-night pharmacy, the Agence Mauritanienne d'Information maintains an updated list of the current *pharmacies de garde*, which rotate throughout the year (w ami.mr/fr/pharmacies-de-garde). If you need lab tests done, Maurilab [114 B2] (45 24 00 79; e info@maurilab.mr; w maurilab.mr) is open every day and does not require an appointment. Biomed 24 [119 G3] (45 24 42 44; e biomed24@biomed24mr.com; w biomed24mr.com) is another option.

Embassies for the US [114 A1] (w mr.usembassy.gov/u-s-citizen-services/local-resources-of-u-s-citizens/doctors-in-mauritania) and France [114 B1] (w mr.ambafrance.org/Sante-1754) maintain lists of clinics, doctors and their specialisations.

MOSQUE VISITS

Generally speaking, mosques in Mauritania are not officially open for visitors, so it's impossible to say for sure whether or not an interested (non-Muslim) visitor will be shown around. In some cases, like the old mosque in Chinguetti, visitors are never allowed. In others, it seems to be down to whom you encounter on the day, and we've had reports of travellers successfully visiting several of the mosques in Nouakchott.

If you'd like to try, be sure to show up outside of prayer times and dressed appropriately. If a caretaker doesn't find you first, you can ask around for the imam or simply 'le responsable' and see what they say. It's possible they'll show you around, but there's an equal or greater chance you'll be sent away.

MONEY Unlike elsewhere in the country, getting cash is generally not a problem in Nouakchott. The banking network is reasonably well developed, with **ATMs** in all areas of town, including at Nouakchott–Oumtounsy International Airport and in the lobbies of several upmarket hotels including the Azalaï Hotel Marhaba, Monotel Dar El Barka, Hotel Fasq, Al Khaima City Center and the Sheraton. You can draw ouguiya against Visa at BMCI, BAMIS, Attijari Bank, Orabank and Société Générale, while for Mastercard/Maestro, Société Générale seems to be the only option. Machines will occasionally be out of service or quite simply out of cash.

If you're arriving with **hard currency**, bank branches will change money at reasonable rates and there are a few private bureaux de change, but it's often easiest to simply ask in a supermarket or other shop – even small boutiques are often happy to change ouguiya for euros, while dollars are much less widely welcomed, and pounds sterling not at all. Check the latest exchange rate before doing so at w xe.com.

WELLNESS AND BEAUTY If you're back in Nouakchott but still finding sand in places you probably shouldn't, there are a few places in town offering spa treatments. **Nouakchott Spa** (Cité Plage; m 20 90 31 31, 20 90 33 00; nouakchott_spa) offers hammam (from 250UM), massage (from 1,500UM) and beauty treatments for women and men. **Hammam Nile** (Av Cheikh Zayed; m 44 30 00 10; hammam.nile.1) also offers hammam baths for men and women, as well as beauty treatments including henna and hair braiding. Mama Sage (Ilot K; m 42 83 76 97, +33 7 83 48 15 36; massage.abhyanga) offers a menu of wellness treatments, including massage and meditation with Reiki and Ayurveda techniques.

WHAT TO SEE AND DO

The conventional wisdom among travellers says there's not much in the way of sightseeing in Nouakchott, though these sweeping pronouncements seem to most often come from those who breezed through for a couple of hours or days en route to the Senegal border. And while it's true that Nouakchott does not reveal its charms as immediately as, say, its sister city Madrid, approached with an attitude of exploration, there's plenty to see here if you know where to look.

MUSEUMS AND HISTORIC BUILDINGS To start with, a visit to the **Musée National** [114 D2] (45 25 18 62; 08.00–16.00 Sun–Thu, 08.00–13.00 Fri, 08.00–15.00 Sat; 50UM) is a rather retro affair, with two floors of dated but nonetheless interesting exhibits. The first floor covers a lot of historical ground, from Mauritania's extensive archaeological wealth to its independence-era politics, while the ethnographic second floor is dedicated to the traditional customs, livelihoods and skills that underpinned Mauritanian life until just a generation or two ago, including information on dyeing, weaving and leatherwork, fishing and pastoralism, and date palm cultivation (phœniciculture). Note, though, that most of the information is in French and Arabic only.

A block from here lies the **Parc de l'OMVS** [114 D3], catchily named for the Organisation pour la mise en valeur du fleuve Sénégal (Senegal River Basin Development Authority), which is often used to host festivals and events, including the film festival (page 121) and Ardine festival (page 122), among others. At the west end of the park, the **Musée Ardine** [114 D3] (m 22 28 00 32, 46 41 11 88) opened at the end of 2024. This new music-minded museum dedicated to the traditional women's harp is the brainchild of famed singer and ardin player Aïcha

Mint Chighaly (who is also behind the Festival Ardine), and features several rooms of exhibits on Mauritanian traditional music, instruments, photos and the Mauritanian iggawen (griot) tradition.

A block north of here, the flashy three-storey **Assemblée Nationale** [114 D2] is quite new, only inaugurated in 2021. The linear **Parc de la Liberté** [114 D2] extends for a few blocks north of here and is rather shadeless during the day, but makes a popular place for an evening stroll.

Across the park, the twin-turreted **Palais Présidentiel** [114 D1] sits in the city's most extensive gardens, but these are mostly hidden away behind high walls and out of public view. Built with Chinese assistance in the early 2000s, the grey marble palace is centred around a large glass-fronted entrance foyer overlooking the gardens, and the complex features its own mosque, reception halls, fountains, and even the **first assemblée nationale**, where Mauritanian independence was officially declared in 1960. A few steps away, also in the palace grounds, lies the city's **foundation stone** (⊕ 18.0936, -15.9716), laid on 5 March 1958. But perhaps befitting Mauritania's characteristically unsentimental attitude towards its built heritage, today the stone sits marooned in the middle of a parking lot (though granted, a presidential one).

A few blocks west of the palace lies **Maison Mokhtar Ould Daddah** [114 C1], the historic home of Mauritania's first president, who led the country from independence until he was overthrown in 1978. Today it's mostly obscured by high trees and a wall; it was not open to the public at the time of writing, but there have been talks for years about turning it into some sort of museum, so this could change one day. (In the meantime, fans of presidential memorabilia and minutiae can check out Ould Daddah's desk at the Musée National.)

Mauritania's tallest building, the 16-floor **Immeuble SNIM** [114 C2] has towered over the nearby minarets since its completion in 2017. But the wedge-shaped tower is all office space, so if you want to get a panoramic view of the city, you're better off heading to the nearby Al Khaima City Center (page 116), which has a restaurant with viewing balcony on the hotel's top (10th) floor.

To the north in Tevragh Zeïna, historian and lifelong collector Ahmed Mahmoud Jemal Ahmedou hosts a private **library-museum** (m 47 65 76 45; ⊕ 18.1147, -15.9924) containing over 10,000 volumes – one of the most important collections of Mauritanian historical and cultural documentation anywhere. Jemal (as he is universally known) is a true scholar and connoisseur, and warmly welcomes interested visitors with advance notice. Researchers may also wish to make note of the Fondation Vergnol (w mauritanie.org; f fondationvergnol) and its private archive-museum, but this is typically not opened for casual visitors.

Another private museum nearby, the **Musée de l'Ouguiya** (m 36 34 39 69; f museelouguiya; ⊕ 18.1163, -15.9725) is also known as the Musée Levghih after its passionate curator Levghih Mbeïrick. Named for the Mauritanian currency introduced in 1973, the museum covers the numismatic and philatelic development of the country (Levghih is also head of the Club Mauritanien de Philatélie et Numismatique; f club.cmpn), but also a wide range of history beyond, including an eclectic variety of historical goods and artefacts emblematic of Mauritanian life in both the historical and modern eras.

Heading west from the city centre, the original building of the Hôpital National is an attractive modernist structure, which boasted 120 beds when it opened in 1966. The facility, now known as the **Centre Hospitalier National** [114 B2], has since expanded, but the central buildings, designed by the French Atelier de Montrouge, still stand, with long balconies shaded by breeze blocks and an angular set of canopies protruding from the roofline. New buildings have slowly eaten away at the greenery of the hospital campus over the decades, but there are still some well-maintained gardens and terraces on the grounds.

RELIGIOUS BUILDINGS Unsurprisingly in this Islamic Republic, in addition to the president's private one, there are several iconic mosques in Nouakchott's city centre. The oldest among them is the **Mosquée Ibn Abbas** [115 E2] (or Mosquée Ould Abbas, 'ould' being the Hassaniya word for the standard Arabic 'ibn', both meaning 'son of'). Dating to 1963, it's the capital's oldest mosque, and the 15 green domes atop the whitewashed main hall evoke the forts and fortresses built around the Sahara during the colonial era, whose multi-domed roofs allowed somewhere for the heat of the day to escape. (Have a look at the modernist **Palais de Justice** [115 E2] next door for even more roof domes.)

However, Nouakchott's most iconic landmark is not the oldest, but rather the tallest (though no-one seems to know exactly *how* tall): these are the twin minarets of the **Mosquée Saoudienne** [114 D2], which is officially named for former Saudi king Faisal bin Abdulaziz, but universally known as the Saudi mosque. Built in 1976, the dun-coloured house of prayer isn't overly opulent, but is accented with attractive geometric motifs and crenellations, and was recently kitted out with luxurious new carpets in the 6,600m^2 prayer area in 2023 – so be sure to look down if you are taken inside (see page 129)!

To the south, Mosquée Hassan II [114 C4] (better known as **Mosquée Marocaine** thanks to its funding) was built in the early 1980s and renovated in 2021. It's done in a suitably Moroccan style, and quite reminiscent of Dakar's grand mosque (which shares a similar provenance but is a couple of decades older), with a green and white geometric filigree over the whole of the tall minaret, and green tiled roofs across the compound, which is also home to the **Centre culturel Marocain** [114 C4] (Moroccan Cultural Centre). If you'd like to see inside, head to the cultural centre first and ask there. The nearby **Grande Mosquée de Sebkha** [114 B4] is less architecturally interesting, but undeniably large.

Nouakchott's newest religious destination, however, is not a mosque but a museum: the Saudi-sponsored **Musée internationale de la biographie du Prophète Mohammed** [115 F1] (100UM), opened near the old airport in 2025, contains a variety of high-tech exhibits on the life and doings of the Prophet Muhammad.

And if you just can't get enough sacred architecture, Mauritania – despite being officially an Islamic Republic – is also home to the Catholic Diocese of Nouakchott, and the **Cathédrale Saint-Joseph** [114 C1] was consecrated down the street from the French embassy in Tevragh Zeïna in 1968. The parishioners mostly hail from all over West and Central Africa, rather than from Mauritania itself, but there's a larger community than you might expect at first glance.

AROUND THE PORT Towards the water at the westernmost edge of town, you'll find Nouakchott's most colourful corner: the **Port de Pêche** (also referred to as the Plage des Pêcheurs), where more than 1,000 pirogues line the seafront, either beached on the sand or bobbing offshore. This riot of brashly coloured wooden boats is a small city unto itself and one of the most significant artisanal fishing ports in West Africa. (The fishermen's association says more than 3,000 boats operate out of Nouakchott alone.) Here, legions of fishermen spend their days following the rhythms of this ancient trade, heaving their technicolour pirogues into the water and hauling in their catches hours or days later, where an army of fishmongers waits to receive them onshore, where sorting, gutting and selling the catch begins right on the sand.

The majority of fishermen here are Wolof, hailing from either Mauritania's far south around N'Diago, or from Senegal itself. Though Moors are not traditionally fisherfolk, the Wolof domination of artisanal fishing in Mauritania is not without some controversy. The government passed a law demanding the 'Mauritanisation' of the sector and forbidding foreigners from the trade in 2017, and though this has been unevenly enforced, it led to fishers' strikes in 2019 and 2020 and remains the source of some tension.

When visiting, note that the Mauritanian coastguard maintains a checkpoint at its entrance where you may be asked to show ID (though cars are often just waved through). The road dead-ends at the main market hall, the **Marché aux poissons**, but the market activities spill well out of the building on to the street in front and the

NOUAKCHOTT'S GREEN GARDENS

Believe it or not, Nouakchott has something approaching a central park, though unlike its counterpart in New York City, the **Jardins 5ème** [114 B3] (or Jardins de Sebkha) are used to grow vegetables. These 20ha of *jardins maraîchers* (market gardens) just southwest of the city centre were part of the original city plan and remain, somewhat miraculously, more or less intact 65 years later. And while there has been persistent nibbling at the edges of this green oasis by developers and the like, it's still just about possible to take a relaxed wander through the palms and leave the city ever so slightly behind. The land here is only becoming more valuable, however, so as with so much of the plans behind Nouakchott, this oasis may soon become a thing of the past.

Thankfully, however, there are a number of other market gardens in Nouakchott, notably in the eastern neighbourhoods of Zaatar (⊕ 18.0810, -15.9384 & 18.0865, -15.9338), Bouhdida (⊕ 18.0789, -15.9227) and Toujounine (⊕ 18.0767, -15.9036). The gardens in Zaatar are closest to the city centre, and the particularly eagle-eyed may even spot several extraordinarily colourful houses painted by Seb Toussaint (w sebtoussaint.com;) around the neighbourhood here. The gardens are crisscrossed by a series of footpaths, and the deep greenery of the fields here is a moving testament to the diligence and dedication of their proprietors – it's no easy task to coax this kind of verdure out of the soils of Nouakchott.

Crops vary from season to season, but the farmers here generally grow a mix including carrots, potatoes, cabbage, onions, lettuce, mint, tomatoes, dates, and even the occasional chilli pepper (the latter being prized in Mauritania's south, and largely ignored in the north).

While the gardens mentioned above are primarily worked by smallholders, there are a couple of somewhat larger farms around the city as well, which work to promote and disseminate ecological and agronomic knowledge on successful agricultural techniques and potential crops suited to the local climate. The **Jardin des Oiseaux de Toujounine** (m 36 33 27 15; ⊕ 18.0835, -15.8969) is home to numerous ducks, turkeys, ostriches, chickens and peacocks, as well as crops of fruits, vegetables, and herbs like coriander and rosemary. South of the city at PK17, the **Ferme Pédagogique El Jenna** (m 41 76 50 73, 37 76 50 73; ⊕ 17.9393, -15.9784) raises chickens and produces moringa, bissap (hibiscus), chillies, eggplants, okra and more in its *espace-test agricole* (agricultural test area).

beach behind. Be sure to take a quick glance up from the hubbub to check out the wavy modernist roof of the hall built in co-operation with Japan in 1996.

From here, the beach is dense with pirogues for almost 800m in either direction, so pick a direction and stroll away. In addition to the fishermen and fishmongers, the boat builders responsible for keeping everything afloat sand, scrape and paint away throughout the day, patching up leaky hulls in need of attention and building replacements for the battered vessels which have made their last trips out to sea. The whole affair is a sensory feast (including some very vivid scents!), but do be discreet with your camera and ask permission before taking photos of people – this is emphatically not a tourism-oriented setup, and people here have been known to quite freely express their annoyance with impolite photographers.

About 4.5km to the south, the abandoned Hotel Al Ahmady overlooks an empty beach of the same name, and another 3km brings you to an old rusting wharf, which was Nouakchott's first port. And while the derelict wharf and dusty cement factory just behind aren't exactly the stuff of *Endless Summer*, surf-flick fantasy (page 57), this unlikely setting may in fact be Nouakchott's best **surf spot**, and is a regular haunt for the city's tiny coterie of board riders. Nouakchott's current port, the Chinese-built Port de l'Amitié, lies a further 4km to the south and was opened here in 1986.
Back up at the Port de Pêche, if the beachside bedlam leaves you feeling like one of the unlucky fish gasping for fresh air, head a few hundred metres north up the sand to Terjit Vacances (page 117) or Complexe Sabah (page 116) for a cold drink and a breather from the feverish fishery below.

Camel rides A bit further up the beach, and fully befitting a desert nation par excellence like Mauritania, if you want to find your inner chamelier or chamelière, you barely have to leave the capital to do so. Based near Les Sultanes, about a dozen kilometres north of the Port de Pêche, the commendable **Chameaux Nouakchott** (m 43 61 71 34; e chameauxnouakchott@gmail.com) offers a variety of customisable camelback excursions across the beaches, dunes and backcountry north of the city, with a particular focus on animal welfare. The camel rides here are intended not simply as a hop-on, hop-off photo-op, but as a way to get to know the animals and associated cameline culture and skills more holistically, with trips including tuition on camel care, instruction, kit, riding and more.

The standard trips begin around 09.00 and run until either noon (2,000UM pp) or sunset (4,000UM pp). The full-day trip includes a lunch break (for both you and the dromedaries!) at either a beachside restaurant or by cooking a meal together in the dunes. Bespoke multi-day trips for individuals and groups can also be arranged, with a variety of possible itineraries, nights under the stars, and plenty of time to bond with your new camel confrère.

And for a different kind of camel adventure entirely, there's a new **camel racetrack** (⊕ 18.2073, -15.9979) way out in the scrubland north of town. Built in partnership with the UAE and inaugurated in 2024, it's about 2km east of the main road; take the turn-off at the sign for the Fédération Nationale de course de Chameaux (National Camel Racing Federation; m 33 47 17 10, 36 60 43 35; e federationrimcouresse@gmail.com; f coursduchameaux) and follow the tracks. Call or check its Facebook for upcoming events.

Beaches Despite its oceanfront location, Nouakchott can hardly be considered a beach destination. There are a few reasons for this, among them cultural factors relating to modesty and swimming etiquette, but also the simple fact that Mauritania's long, unprotected coastline lends itself to rough surf conditions – a fact taken good advantage of by a handful of surfers (see opposite), but one that also means any would-be swimmers must take very good care in the water.

In town, the Port de Pêche is obviously not the place for a dip, but you may find some people splashing their feet along the shores to the north, in front of Terjit Vacances and Complexe Sabah. If you'd like a more relaxed, less crowded time on the sand, you should head to the handful of small resorts north of the city, like Les Sultanes and Oceanides. Here, you can hire a cabana to shelter from the sun and wind in between your forays into the water. Kitesurfers sometimes hang out here as well, but there was no formal equipment rental at the time of writing.

AROUND NOUAKCHOTT

PARC NATIONAL ZOOLOGIQUE ET BOTANIQUE East of town at PK19 on the Route de l'Espoir, the Parc National Zoologique et Botanique can unfortunately not be recommended. Despite being managed by the ONG Pour la Protection et la Sensibilisation sur Conservation de la Faune et de la Flore en Mauritanie (m 22 74 98 93, 48 37 04 17; e opscffm@yahoo.fr; 100UM), it visibly does not have the resources to provide the animals a good standard of living. The unlucky residents include a couple of baboons, western red colobus, side-striped jackals, peacocks, geese, turkeys, warthogs and snakes. Even if it wasn't literally right next door to an abattoir – which, in a couldn't-make-it-up-if-you-tried twist, it actually is – animal lovers would be sure to walk away depressed.

PARC NATIONAL D'AWLEIGATT About 60km east of Nouakchott along the Route de l'Espoir, this new national park (45 25 54 66; parcnationaldawleigatt) seems set to be a more hopeful destination than the zoo. Gazetted in 2016, it covers 1,600ha divided between a large fenced wilderness sanctuary and a smaller zoo area. It was only open for school groups and official delegations at the time of writing, but this should change during the lifespan of this edition, and there are plans for tourist accommodation here as well.

The entrance gate (17.8887, -15.5091) sits at the end of a tarmac feeder road about 7km south of the Route de l'Espoir. Take the right-hand turn-off at Idini village and continue past the China-built Centre de Démonstrations des Technologies de Élevage (Livestock Technology Demonstration Centre) on your left.

In terms of the fauna, the species represented here are a mix of exotics and endemics, with a particular focus on antelopes. Species currently resident in the park include rhim gazelle (*Gazella leptoceros*), blackbuck (*Antilope cervicapra*), common ostrich (*Struthio camelus*), common eland (*Taurotragus oryx*), Arabian oryx (*Oryx leucoryx*), blue wildebeest (*Connochaetes taurinus*), impala (*Aepyceros melampus*), sable antelope (*Hippotragus niger*), plains zebra (*Equus quagga*), greater kudu (*Tragelaphus strepsiceros*), springbok (*Antidorcas marsupialis*), gemsbok (*Oryx gazella*) and nyala (*Tragelaphus angasii*).

The park also aims to provide habitat for a number of threatened species, including the critically endangered Nubian giraffe (*Giraffa camelopardalis*), the near-threatened defassa waterbuck (*Kobus ellipsiprymnus defassa*), the near-threatened Barbary sheep (*Ammotragus lervia*) and the vulnerable dorcas gazelle (*Gazella dorcas*). Rarer still, the scimitar-horned oryx (*Oryx dammah*) is also present; these were downlisted from 'extinct in the wild' to 'endangered' at the end of 2023, after a successful reintroduction programme in Chad, where there is now a wild population of more than 600 individuals. Finally, the park is also home to nearly 30 critically endangered addax (*Addax nasomaculatus*), which were translocated from the UAE at the end of 2023.

THE LOST PORT OF PORTENDICK

The **Port de Tanit** (w port-tanit.com) sits about 60km north of Nouakchott, very near to the one-time Dutch trading post of Portendick. Today the port largely serves fishing vessels, but it has been an important export hub off and on since the earliest days of European contact in Mauritania. It was developed by the Dutch as a gum-arabic entrepôt in 1721, but previously visited by the Portuguese (the name is thought to derive from Porto d'Addi or Portudaddi, after Haddi ould Ahmad ould Daman, Emir of the Trarza Emirate). The Dutch outpost proved to be a short-lived enterprise, however, as intense jockeying for position between the French and Dutch on the Mauritanian coast saw the French destroy the Dutch positions in Portendick in 1724.

The area continued to be used for trade with the Trarza Emirate, however, though relations between the Trarzas and the various European powers who would visit seeking their precious gum-arabic could fluctuate a great deal. France attempted to impose several naval blockades of the settlement in the 19th century, and French writer Étienne Tréfeu described the settlement as 'a small seaside town belonging to one of the most turbulent Moorish tribes, the Trarzas'.

Today the Port de Tanit is a modern construction, and little, if anything remains of the former Portendick. But the wild, undeveloped coast on either side of this small port looks much the same as it might have done centuries ago; it's no struggle to imagine the khaïmas and caravelas lined up on sand and sea, eyeing each other warily, each waiting for the others' next move.

OUMTOUNSY MONUMENT Built as a memorial to the soldiers fighting on the French side of the 1932 Battle of Oumtounsy (or Oum Tounsi), this half-forgotten colonial-era monument sits just off the road to Atar about 80km northeast of Nouakchott. The battle saw nomads from Boutilimit and French troops, including Tirailleurs Sénégalais and Goumiers Marocains, ambushed in a razzia (raid) at the wells of Oumtounsy by Oulad Delim warriors from over the border in Spanish Sahara.

Some three-dozen troops were killed on the French side, including Lieutenant Patrick de Mac Mahon, and two dozen of the Oulad Delim. The monument was originally raised as a memorial to Mac Mahon's death, but evolved into a nationalist symbol. Its legacy is today somewhat contested, prompting debate in Mauritanian society as to whether the battle was an example of anti-colonial resistance or simply an inter-tribal quarrel. The former interpretation is the official line, at least – hence the name given to Nouakchott's new airport in 2016.

The monument itself lost its plaque naming the dead sometime in the early 2010s, and is today covered in graffiti, but the lonesome whitewashed arches of the 5m tower still make for an evocative sight, surrounded by nothing but dunes 450m northwest of the tarmac road.

4

Nouadhibou and the Northwest

Even by Mauritanian standards, the country's northwest is sparsely populated, with vast tracts of empty land between the handful of population centres, including the country's second-largest city, Nouadhibou (نواذيبو), and several other minor urban centres including Akjoujt and Chami.

Even before the droughts of the 1970s sent thousands fleeing the countryside into urban centres, northwestern Mauritania was considered a 'large, entirely desert and almost uninhabited district'. And while Nouadhibou has grown by leaps and bounds in the decades since, the description still holds broadly true for Dakhlet Nouadhibou and Inchiri regions as a whole, with the rural settlements of herders so common elsewhere in Mauritania few and far between. This is in part because the area here is a true desert; Nouadhibou records an average of only 20mm rain in an entire year.

While the hinterlands have traditionally been populated, insomuch as they are populated at all, by Moorish herders, the cities are quite cosmopolitan, with both

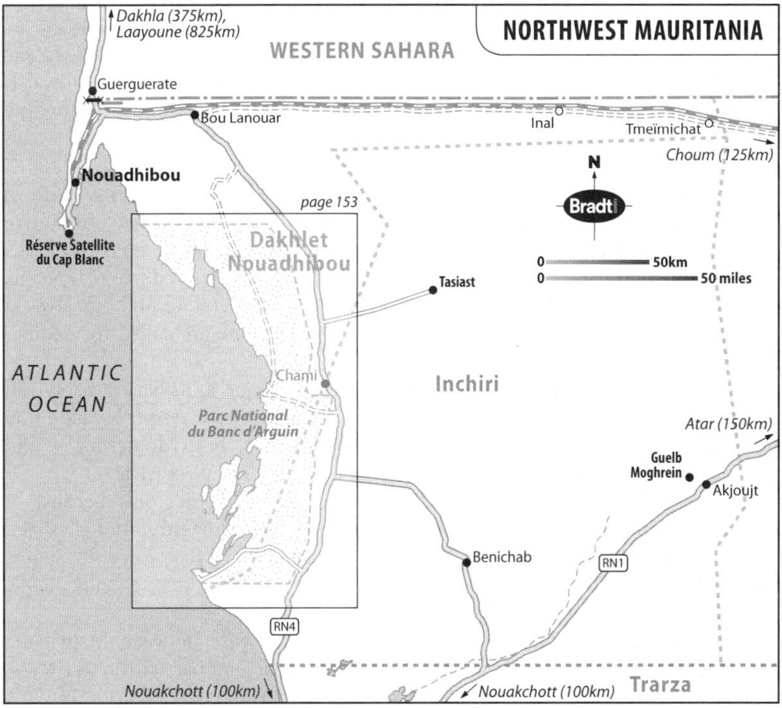

Nouadhibou and Chami attracting residents from all over the country and West Africa as a whole. In Nouadhibou, most are here for either trade or migration (Nouadhibou has long been a jumping-off point for irregular crossings to the Canary Islands), while in Chami, gold is the only game in town.

The lands along the coast, most of which today fall within the Banc d'Arguin National Park, are the traditional home of the Imraguen, a tribe of fisherfolk living in a series of tiny villages on the coast, who are related to the Moors. Their blink-and-you'll-miss-them villages are the only real population centres along the several hundreds of kilometres of coast between here and Nouakchott. And though you're unlikely to see it, they have become the stuff of travel legend for their supposedly co-operative mullet fishing tradition in which friendly dolphins help them drive the fish into their nets.

Inland, Akjoujt is in fact the capital and largest city of Inchiri region, but as the city sits along the Nouakchott–Atar road and the vast majority of visitors passing this way will be en route to the tourist sights of the Adrar, Akjoujt is included in the Adrar chapter on page 168.

The landscapes here, especially as you get nearer to the coast, have a bright, washed-out, bleached brilliance to them – the shades of earth and sand somehow feeling desaturated compared to the rich oranges, browns and ochres of the interior. Taking this into account, the name given by European explorers to the peninsula on which Nouadhibou sits, Cap Blanc, gains a degree of logic. This headland, and the Baie du Lévrier behind it, represent the only naturally sheltered harbour on the Mauritanian coast. Cap Blanc was also named as a counterpart to Cap Vert, the peninsula on which Dakar sits 700km to the south.

NOUADHIBOU AND SURROUNDS

Set in Mauritania's far northwestern corner, this windblown waterfront town sits atop the sandstone Ras Nouadhibou (Cap Blanc) peninsula, facing east towards Dakhlet Nouadhibou bay (also known as the Baie du Lévrier). The shoreline alternates between beach and cliffs, and the city is hemmed in by two smaller bays to its north and south, the Baie de l'Étoile and Baie de Cansado.

Nouadhibou (*noo-AH-dee-boo*) is Mauritania's second-largest city, with a population of 173,525 *Stéphanois,* as its residents are known. This unintuitive appellation originated in the colonial era, when the city was known as Port-Étienne, after a French minister of colonies. As the name Étienne is derived from Stéphane, which in turn originates with the Greek *Stéphanos* – we therefore find ourselves at *Stéphanois.* (Residents of the French town of Saint-Étienne are called the same – somebody ring the sister cities people!)

The city is often called Mauritania's 'capitale économique' as its fisheries and iron ore export have long dominated the national economy. As a result, Nouadhibou has steadily attracted a flow of job-seeking migrants, both domestically and internationally, and is home to residents from all corners of West Africa.

The town therefore has quite a multi-cultural presence, not only because of the significant business opportunities, but also because it has traditionally been a popular jumping-off point for West African migrants trying to reach Spain's Canary Islands. Authorities have clamped down on this over time, so many people got stuck here, and some simply decided to stay.

The peninsula is politically divided in half lengthwise between Mauritania and Western Sahara, which is uninhabited here, but *de jure* part of the territories administered by the Polisario Front, and *de facto* administered by Mauritania. Only a few itinerant fisherfolk live west of this border, in the ghost town of La Agüera (page 150). This unusual political and physical geography means Nouadhibou has taken on a long, linear form, stretching some 12km north to south, but is only 2km east to west at its widest point. The railway line acts as the de facto western border, with only open desert and a few gardens found beyond. The city also serves as a 'neutral' meeting point for Sahrawis living on either side of the divided Western Sahara (or in Algeria) to meet, which can be difficult for them otherwise.

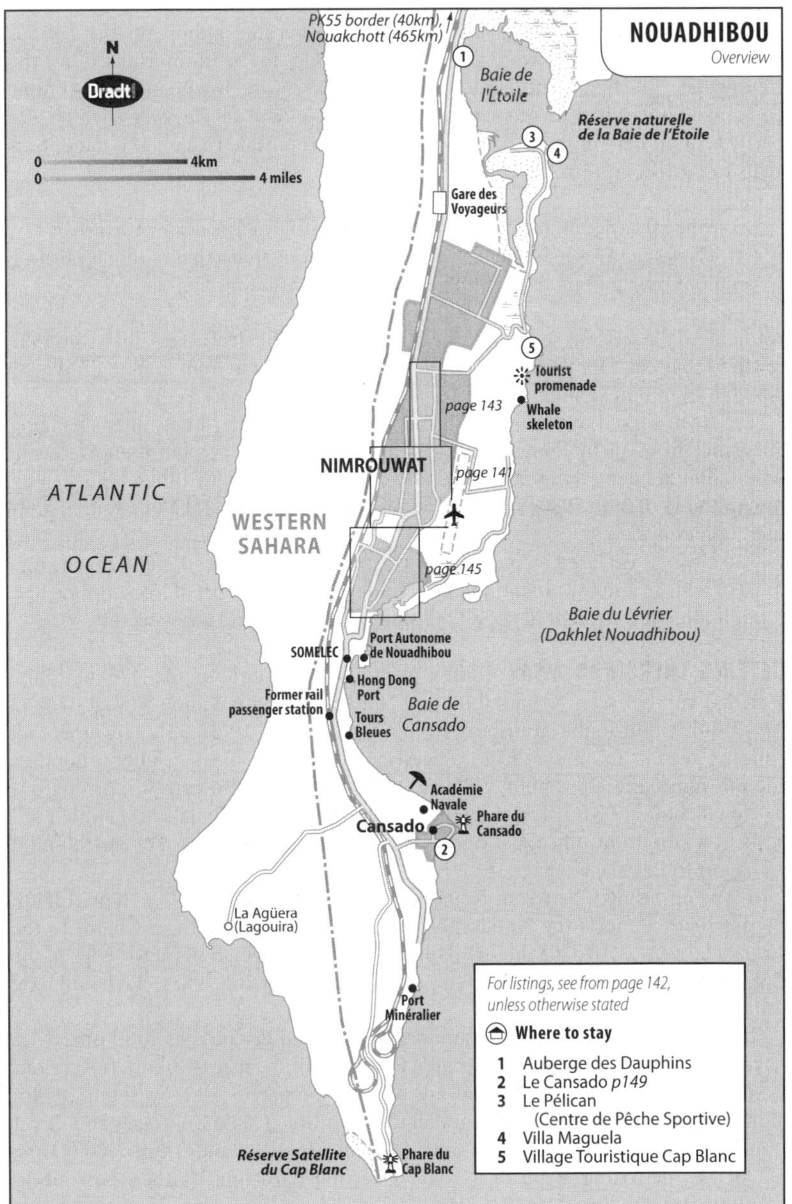

HISTORY Thanks to its position along the Canary Current, the fishing grounds around Nouadhibou have always been rich (page 132), and the site had been visited by Canarian and Imraguen fishers for years. The modern settlement of Nouadhibou, however, was founded by colonial edict in 1907 as Port-Étienne, after a French study urged the country to get involved in the fish trade here. The following years saw a fort, pier, lighthouse and radio station built on this dry and desolate peninsula, and several fishery companies settling on the peninsula. The most significant, the Société Industrielle de la Grande Pêche (SIGP), was founded here in 1919.

An airstrip soon followed, and Port-Étienne became a stop on the famous Latécoère Casablanca–Dakar airmail route, soon to be immortalised as the Aéropostale. The first flights landed here in June 1925, and legendary pilot Antoine de Saint-Exupéry had this to say in his 1939 book *Terre des Hommes* – which was partly written here in town at the Maison de l'Aéropostale (page 147) – about his visits to Port-Étienne in the 1920s:

> Located on the edge of the rebellious territories, Port-Étienne is not a city. There is a fort, a hangar and a wooden hut for our crews. The desert around it is so absolute that, despite its weak military resources, Port-Étienne is almost invincible.

And indeed the area was so dry, and the hinterland so difficult of access, that from 1923 to 1955 fresh water for the settlement was literally shipped in from France. (Today it's piped in from Bou Lanouar, after reserves were discovered here in the 1960s.)

The town served as a base for British Sunderland flying boats after changing allegiance from Vichy France during World War II (page 24), but there were still only 2,500 residents here at independence in 1960. As with other Mauritanian towns, the 1970s and 1980s saw huge waves of urbanisation, and Nouadhibou grew many times over.

The city was declared a *Zone Franche* (Economic Free Zone; w ndbfreezone.mr) in 2013 with an aim towards stimulating trade through the Port of Nouadhibou and foreign direct investment in the city's fishing, industrial, and other sectors.

GETTING THERE AND AWAY There's plenty of transport on the 475km (7hrs; 700UM) run between Nouadhibou and **Nouakchott**, with Salima Voyages (m 43 43 43 30), Ghourtouba Transport (m 27 29 20 20, 27 19 33 33), and others all running regular minibuses from offices in the 6ème Robinet neighbourhood in the mornings and afternoons. SONEF (m 42 46 43 14) also runs a morning bus to Nouakchott at 08.00. There are also private vehicles to Nouakchott, which sell seats at a storefront office just north of Carrefour al-Atihadiya. For northbound transport to **Dakhla**, see page 165.

If you're headed between Nouadhibou and **Atar** (725km), a new 135km bypass road connects the Nouakchott–Nouadhibou road south of Chami to the Nouakchott–Atar road via the small town of Benichab, which sits at the edge of the Erg Akchar dune field and is known primarily for its spring, where Tayba mineral water is bottled.

This bypass saves a significant amount of time and distance, as you'd otherwise have to go via Nouakchott if you wanted to stay on the tarmac (910km). (Of course, if you have your own vehicle and are off-piste prepared, it's only about 540km along the desert tracks running parallel to the railway.) Salima Voyages run direct minibuses between Nouadhibou and Atar on Mondays and Thursdays (11hrs; 1,200UM), departing at 06.00. (If you're feeling hardcore, it's then possible to continue straight from Atar to Zouérate.)

Nouadhibou's **airport** is right in the city, and Mauritania Airlines flies three times weekly to Nouakchott, twice weekly to Zouérate, and once weekly to Gran Canaria. You can buy tickets at the Mauritania Airlines (☎ 45 74 42 91; e agencendb@gmail.com; w mauritaniaairlines.mr) ticket office in town.

The **Iron Ore Train** stops at the Gare de voyageurs (passenger rail station; ⊕ 21.0073, -17.0318) north of the city, which is more than a little dilapidated (though renovations were scheduled for 2025). For more information on taking the Iron Ore Train, see page 218.

GETTING AROUND Given its long, linear nature, Nouadhibou is fairly easy to navigate, as shared taxis (both marked and unmarked) trundle north and south along the city's main axes, charging something like 20UM depending on the length of the ride. Otherwise, it's also possible to request a 'course', or private taxi; this costs about 250UM to/from the Gare des voyageurs and less within town. Local ride-hailing app Sehdini (w sehdini.com) is active in Nouadhibou as well.

ORIENTATION Arriving in town from the north on the RN2, you pass the Baie de l'Étoile about 10km north of town, before the city really begins around Carrefour al-Atihadiya. From this crossroads, a left-hand turn brings you to the growing Les Cabanons neighbourhood, where a mushrooming assortment of luxury houses and flats border the Baie du Lévrier.

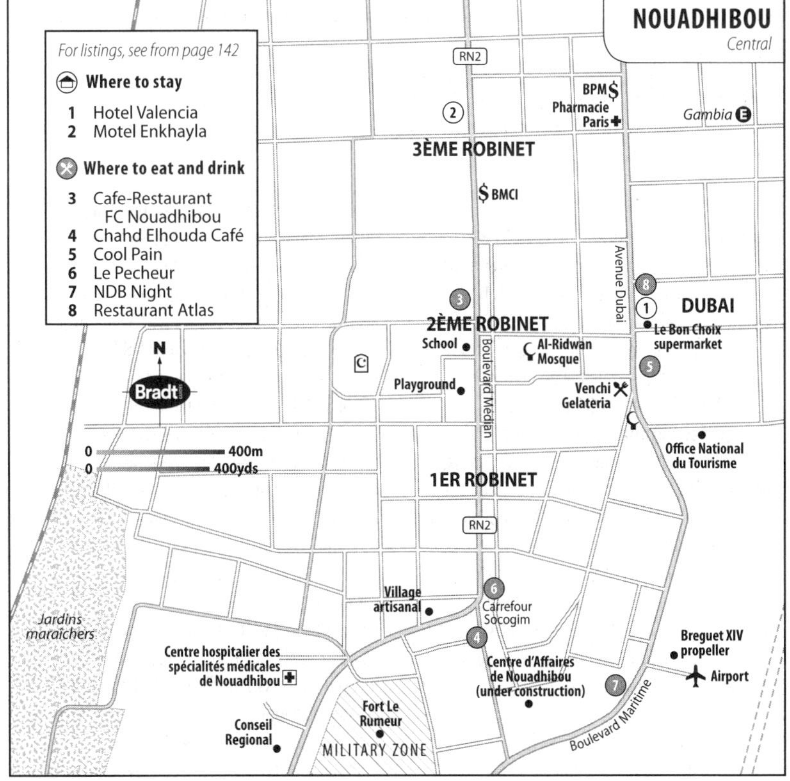

Continuing straight south, you are in the newest part of the city known as Nimrouwat, meaning 'the numbers'. Commercial life in Nouadhibou is essentially organised along two parallel axes: to the west there's the Boulevard Médian, which is the main RN2 road leading into and out of town, and to the east there's a parallel road known as Avenue Dubai until roughly the airport, south of which it proceeds towards the port area and is known as Boulevard Maritime.

The Boulevard Médian proceeds through a numbered set of neighbourhoods named after the areas' original water taps (*robinets*), starting at Carrefour al-Atihadiya with the sixth, 6ème Robinet, and continuing south counting down to the 1er Robinet, which is just north of the Carrefour Socogim. This axis accounts for much of the trade and transportation activity in the city, with transport companies largely found around the 6ème Robinet, and the city's main market at the 4ème Robinet.

The parallel road, Avenue Dubai, is newer and more upmarket (hence the name), and home to many hotels, restaurants and supermarkets, and a wealthier residential quarter to the east, also known as Dubai.

The two roads continue south in parallel, passing west of the airport and artisanal port and entering the older quarter of Ghairane. Here the two roads border Nouadhibou's administrative quarter on either side, where several banks, the city and regional governments, and the Place de l'Indépendance are found. The two roads finally meet at the south end of town, forming a junction at the old SIGP buildings. The Boulevard Médian continues south from here towards the main commercial port, eventually leading to Cansado and Cap Blanc.

A new coastal road/bypass running east of the airport was under construction as of 2025, but the city's development plan for this area was not yet clear at the time of writing.

WHERE TO STAY *Map, page 145, unless otherwise stated*

The Time4Mauritania tour agency (page 63) also has a simple apartment in Nouadhibou which is available to rent.

Upmarket and mid-range

Hotel Tasiast Bd Maritime; 45 74 51 07; e reservation@hoteltasiast.com; w hoteltasiast.com. The upmarket rooms at this newish hotel are aimed at the business market, & handsomely appointed in black stone & modern décor. No restaurant, but meals available on demand. *2,900/4,100UM sgl/dbl.* **$$$$**

Auberge des Dauphins [map, page 139] RN2; m 49 66 37 37; e laubergedesdauphins@gmail.com; f kitemauritanie1. Set about 10km north of central Nouadhibou on the Bou Lanouar road, the octagonal chalets here face directly out on to the Baie de l'Étoile, where kitesurfers take advantage of the peninsula's legendary winds. They have a sister property up the coast in Dakhla, the Auberge des Nomades. Gear rental & instruction can be arranged. *1,800UM pp FB.* **$$$**

Hotel Delphin Bd Maritime; 45 74 38 48; m 33 93 10 00; e info@delphin-hotel.com; w delphin-hotel.com. This new hotel near the airport & Alliance Française has excellent facilities by any standard, & makes a fine choice if you're after some comfort after long days in the desert. It also has a rooftop restaurant with views over the city. *From 2,500/2,800UM sgl/dbl.* **$$$**

Hotel Sahel Bd Maritime; 45 74 38 57, 45 74 38 58; e reservation@hotel-sahel.com. Decorated in bright yellows & trimmed out in wood, this feels like a Mediterranean holiday hotel that's been inexplicably transplanted to Nouadhibou – the Spanish management may be a clue as to why. Rooms are rigorously kept & organised around a central staircase. *2,500/2,700 sgl/dbl or twin.* **$$$**

Hotel Valencia [map, page 141] Av Dubai; m 42 88 88 88; w hotelvalenciandb.com. This business-focused address in the Dubai neighbourhood is a reliable pick for its central location & comfortable facilities. Next door on either side, the Hotel Bon Choix & Hotel Free Zone are equally serviceable options, should Valencia be full. *From 2,500UM dbl.* **$$$**

Village Touristique Cap Blanc [map, page 139] Les Cabanons; m 46 64 12 33; e villagetouristiquendb@gmail.com; f. This huge new whitewashed waterfront complex in the Les Cabanons neighbourhood was built in 2023 & seems aimed towards workshops & wealthy families. As is common in Mauritania, the décor can be a bit sparse, but the rooms are undeniably done to a high standard. There are 2 indoor pools (sex-segregated) & an outdoor pool under construction, alongside a restaurant serving meals for 300–500UM. *From 2,300/2,800UM dbl/twin.* **$$$**

Le Pélican (Centre de Pêche Sportive) [map, page 139] Les Cabanons; t 25 01 80 05; m 41 28 75 05, 44 40 01 60. Set on a headland overlooking the mouth of the Baie de l'Étoile, this long-serving sport & activities centre has been the go-to for sport fishing in Nouadhibou for many years. The rooms are a bit dated, but decently kept & were getting a fresh coat of whitewash when we checked in. Can arrange scenic boat trips (from 1,000UM), fishing excursions (from 6,000UM ½ day), & surf fishing from shore. *1,200UM dbl.* **$$**

Budget and shoestring

Auberge Sahara Off Bd Médian; m 48 19 79 13, 47 90 49 81; w aubergesaharandb.wordpress.com. It doesn't look like much from the outside, & is undeniably simple, but this popular shoestring option is kept absolutely spotless, offering first-floor rooms with fan & a breezy roof terrace. The shared baths have hot water – a blessing when the oceanic chill blows in. Proprietress Fanta can arrange fine meals at friendly prices. *300UM pp.* **$**

Camping Baie du Lévrier Bd Médian; m 46 50 43 56; e alylevriers2003@yahoo.fr. Basic but clean & central, this has been a go-to address for overlanders for many years, with plenty of space to park inside the compound. All rooms use shared ablutions with hot water. *500/800UM sgl/dbl.* **$**

Motel Enkhayla [map, page 141] Bd Médian; m 47 31 76 81. Though the location in the centre of the market area won't be to everyone's tastes, the rooms here are surprisingly well kept & reasonably priced. *400UM room using shared bath, 600/800UM en-suite sgl/dbl.* **$**

Nouadhibou Guest House Off Bd Maritime; m 32 74 11 57, 31 07 29 66. There are just a few rooms at this new Australian-owned address, but

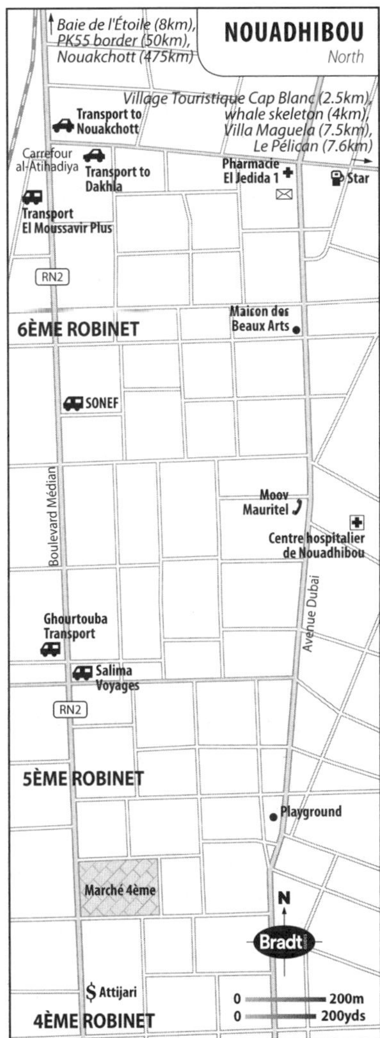

they're all perfectly tidy & recently modernised. This has quickly become a popular choice in Nouadhibou, & rightfully so. *850UM dbl, 1,300UM large dbl with kitchenette.* **$**

✷ **Villa Maguela** [map, page 139] Les Cabanons; m 41 56 54 90; e stdowmr@gmail.com. Home-cooked dinners (500UM) are taken communally at the long living room table at this attractive traveller's haunt at the edge of the Baie de l'Étoile. The handful of simple sea-facing rooms are a mix of en suite & those using shared facilities, & it's a popular address for overlanders as well. Owner Victor often goes out on boat trips where guests are welcome to tag along, otherwise you can arrange an excursion on your own schedule for 200UM pp (min 4). Scooter rental also available. *600/800UM sgl/dbl.* **$**

WHERE TO EAT AND DRINK *Map, page 141, unless otherwise stated*

Restaurant Galloufa [map, opposite] Bd Maritime; m 42 16 87 70. This Spanish-run hangout is a firm favourite among expats in Nouadhibou, & not just because of its unusual drink selection. The menu (mains from 300UM) ranges from poisson to paella (ring in advance), & the management aims to please. $$$$–$$$

NDB Night Bd Maritime; m 20 11 65 65. Nightspot with live Mauritanian music & traditional seating around a large courtyard, serving up big platters of couscous & grilled meats, & even mugs of chilled *zrig*. $$$

✱ **Le Pecheur** Carrefour Socogim; m 48 50 48 89. With long hours & a long menu, this is a Nouadhibou stalwart where everyone is sure to find something to their tastes, from grilled fish to fast foods, & the chatty Tunisian owner will make sure you're well taken care of. $$$–$$

Restaurant Atlas Av Dubai; m 46 28 17 18; ⏲ 08.00–01.00. Serving a long menu of Turkish favourites including manty, pide & more, this is a comfortable pick in the Dubai area, with a plat du jour for 250UM. $$$–$$

Restaurant Merou [map, opposite] Bd Médian; m 47 42 92 58. Popular with Nouadhibou's large Chinese contingent when craving a taste of home, this low-key address is a fine stop if you're also craving some variety in your diet. Serves a satisfying selection of Chinese dishes & drinks from 150UM. $$$–$$

Café-Restaurant FC Nouadhibou Bd Médian; m 48 06 37 35. Come support the local side at this football-themed café serving a good selection of seafood & continental dishes alongside pizzas & other fast-food options. $$

Chahd Elhouda Café Carrefour Socogim; m 36 54 36 36. This is a cheap & cheerful Moroccan café serving pizzas, pastries, juices & espresso overlooking Carrefour Socogim. Wi-Fi. $$–$

Restaurant Marocaine [map, opposite] Carrefour SIGP; m 46 42 79 92. Though it's got all the ambience of a mechanic's workshop, the stews, tagines & baked goods here are a treat (& easy on the wallet). $$–$

Cool Pain Av Dubai. There's nothing painful about the croissants & sweet pastries churned out by this popular patisserie. $

SPORTS AND ACTIVITIES You can catch a **football** match at the Stade Municipal (Municipal Stadium), where FC Nouadhibou (f FCNouadhibou) often plays its rivals from down the road in Cansado (page 149). The stadium was totally renovated when Mauritania hosted the Africa Cup of Nations for Under-20s in 2021. The Marathon International de Nouadhibou (f marathon.nouadhibou) is held every April.

Though not nearly as popular as Dakhla up the coast, Nouadhibou is a noted **kitesurfing** destination, with enthusiasts often surfing the Baie de l'Étoile. The bayside Auberge des Dauphins (page 142) can arrange gear and lessons. **Surfing** is also possible, though uncommon; the quest for local breaks was even made into a film in 2024, called *Pumping Swell in the Sahel* – see page 57 for more.

Despite its coastal location, Nouadhibou is not exactly a **swimmer's** paradise. There are a few options, however. In the Baie de l'Étoile, the Plage des Dauphins (just in front of the Auberge des Dauphins mentioned on page 142) and its neighbour directly to the south, the Plage de Kellami are both fairly protected; it's also possible to swim near Villa Maguela or Le Pélican, or near the abandoned resort and whale skeleton in Les Cabanons.

It's also possible to see traditional **wrestling** or *la lutte* (commonly known in Mauritania by its Wolof name, *làmb*) at a new traditional wrestling complex (⊛ 20.9130, -17.0549) built by the SNIM Foundation in 2024.

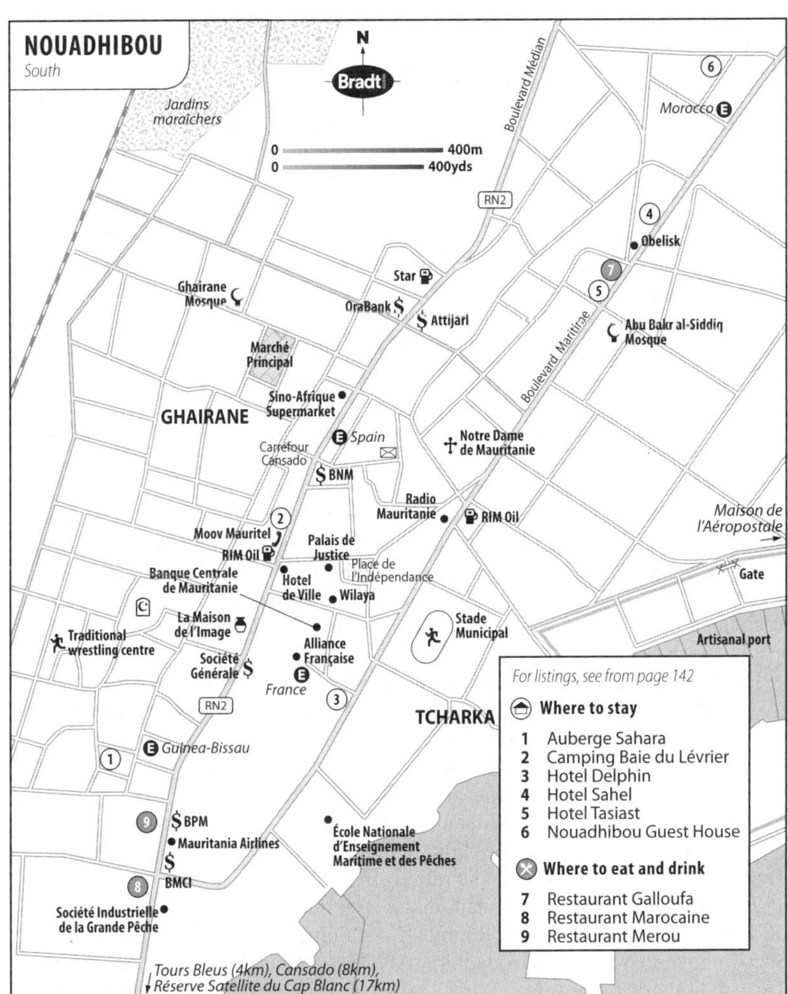

OTHER PRACTICALITIES All of Mauritania's major **banks** are represented in Nouadhibou with ATMs, including BMCI, Attijari Bank, BPM and Société Générale (with the latter accepting Mastercard). There are plenty of **supermarkets** around – Nouadhibou is indeed a city of traders – including Le Bon Choix, underneath the hotel of the same name (which also has a café attached), or the Sino-Afrique Supermarket which, as the name implies, carries a variety of Asian imports.

There are a few **consulates** in town, including Morocco (45 74 50 84), Algeria (45 74 83 37), Guinea-Bissau (m 36 62 88 08), The Gambia (45 74 00 24; m 36 36 89 10), Spain (45 74 53 71) and France (m 36 37 11 47).

There are two **hospitals** in Nouadhibou, the Centre hospitalier de Nouadhibou, and the Centre hospitalier des spécialités médicales de Nouadhibou, which was inaugurated in 2017 and has Cuban doctors on staff.

Deep tissue, Thai **massage** and other spa treatments are available at Chez Marriame (m 31 69 33 61; f).

WHAT TO SEE AND DO There's only one way in and out of this long, linear city (by land, at least), so the sights and activities described below are listed in a broadly north-to-south order, as that's the direction from which you will enter the city.

The **Baie de l'Étoile** north of town also happens to be Mauritania's newest protected area, only gazetted in mid 2024. The **Réserve naturelle de la Baie de l'Étoile** covers about 12km², and offers the opportunity for boat excursions to several tidal beaches and sandbanks around the bay. The timings for these are (obviously) dictated by the tides, but also the winds, which are a force to be reckoned with in Nouadhibou and should not be underestimated. The bay is also a destination for sport fishing (see Le Pélican, page 143) and kitesurfing (see Auberge des Dauphins, page 142). Boat trips exploring the bay and to the sandbank **beaches** are easily arranged through Villa Maguela or Le Pélican (page 143). The sebkha (floodplain) north of the bay is still used for salt extraction (along with an area near the airport).

The east side of Nouadhibou sits directly south of the Baie de l'Étoile and is known as **Les Cabanons**. Partially separated from the mainland by a marshy tidal river dominated by cordgrass (now also part of the protected area), it's home to a growing neighbourhood of upmarket housing and several guesthouses and resorts, including the large Village Touristique Cap Blanc (page 143). Just south of here, a brand new **tourist promenade** and viewpoint signals further development of the area to come. Continuing south for another 1.5km, the Cabanons road dead-ends at an abandoned resort, where there's a massive **whale skeleton** you can check out just inside the grounds.

Heading into the central city, you can go south on either Boulevard Médian or Avenue Dubai. Along Boulevard Médian you'll find the **Marché 4ème**, which is the city's largest market, selling everything you might imagine and then some. While a few blocks to the east on Avenue Dubai, you pass through a more upmarket district, with numerous hotels, restaurants and larger shops, as well as the city hospital and **Maison des Beaux Arts de Nouadhibou** (f), where you'll find local artists at work. You may also see information online about a museum, the Musée Bagodine des Arts et Traditions, but this closed down definitively in 2022.

The **Al-Ridwan Mosque** is Nouadhibou's largest and most impressive, set a block off Boulevard Médian in 2ème Robinet. Continuing south, bear right at Carrefour Socogim, where you'll find Nouadhibou's **Village artisanal** 100m past the junction. This small market has a dozen or so rather dusty shops selling an assortment of leatherwork, figurines, jewellery and carvings, plus there are a couple of artisans tinkering away.

From here, you'll pass between the new hospital and **Fort Le Rumeur**, which sits atop a hill and behind high walls. Other than the late-colonial church (see opposite), it's probably the most obvious historical building in town, though, as with so many of its contemporaries throughout Mauritania, it still serves a military purpose and is therefore not open for visitors.

Straight west of here, there is a series of **jardins maraîchers**, which is a welcome oasis in this relentlessly windy, sandy city. You can go have a mooch around in the greenery, where the gardeners coax an impressive variety of vegetables out of what are – it feels like a glaring understatement to call – challenging climatic and soil conditions.

Boulevard Médian continues past the fort into the Ghairan quarter, which is the city's oldest residential neighbourhood and administrative district. Here you'll find the city's oldest market, **Marché Principal**, which is a dense warren of workshops and traders and worth diving into. A few blocks northwest of here, the 1960 **Ghairane Mosque** was the oldest in the city, but it had fallen into disrepair and was rebuilt from scratch in 2022, making it more a Mosque of Theseus than a historical site in itself.

Just to the south, between Boulevard Médian and Boulevard Maritime, lies the administrative quarter, where the Palais de Justice, regional and city governments, and the Place de l'Indépendance are found. Near here on Boulevard Médian, **La Maison de l'Image** (m 20 50 21 02, 33 02 11 72; w saheldev.org; f lamaisondelimage. mauritanie; ⏲ closed Mon) has a small exhibit of historical and modern photos, including Mauritanian historical figures and Nouadhibou over the years; there are also some traditional instruments on display and the curators are enthusiastic about international visitors.

Turning our focus back to Avenue Dubai/Boulevard Maritime, there are several sights along the road south of the airport. (If you fly here, look out for a **propeller** as you deplane and enter the terminal; this is from a Breguet XIV, the first plane to land here in 1925.) Also in the airport grounds, the **Maison de l'Aéropostale** (⊕ 20.9207, -17.0289) sits on a clifftop on the far side of the runway overlooking the Baie du Repos. It's not publicly accessible, but the new road running east of the airport passes just in front. It dates to the 1920s and was the guesthouse where pilots Antoine de Saint-Exupéry, Jean Mermoz and others stayed during the Latécoère–Aéropostale era.

About 1.5km south of the airport, a left turn off Boulevard Maritime brings you to the Tcharka neighbourhood and its astonishingly large **artisanal fishing port**. The port itself is walled off, with only a few points of entry and exit. Ask at the main gate (⊕ 20.9149, -17.0397) if you can have a look around and you'll most likely be waved through after a cursory inspection.

Inside the gates is effectively an entire parallel town, solely dedicated to servicing the enormous fleet of small fishing boats docked here: shops, restaurants, mosques, workshops, and any other kind of personal or piscatory need you could imagine. If you don't make it inside, have a look on satellite imagery to get a sense of the enormous scale of the place and the sheer number of boats – there are at least several thousand splaying out in all directions, with crafts parked double-, triple- and quadruple-deep from the piers.

Back on Boulevard Maritime, look out for a mysterious **obelisk**, which is fastidiously whitewashed and roped off but entirely unmarked. The road then passes the large Abu Bakr al-Siddiq Mosque, followed by the **Notre Dame de Mauritanie** church (w evechenkc.org). Consecrated in 1958 by Marcel Lefebvre, archbishop of Dakar, the church is totally unique, built atop a small hill in what was colloquially referred to at the time as a *nichon* – a boob – for reasons that will be obvious once you see it. Popular in the late-colonial era, there used to be a number of these boob-buildings around the city, but this breasty basilica may be the last example remaining. There is a small **cemetery** in the same compound.

Continuing south 300m, you'll have the Place de l'Indépendance on your right and the newly renovated **Stade Municipal** (Municipal Stadium) on your left. This modern stadium is home to FC Nouadhibou (page 144). The **Alliance Française** (m 20 16 71 47; e admbb.ndb@gmail.com; f afndb) is just south of here on the right side of the road. It's an older building with a charming garden, and supposedly there used to be a tunnel between here and Fort Le Rumeur. (Unless it was just a rumour…)

Heading south again for 700m, the persistently parallel Boulevard Maritime and Boulevard Médian finally meet just north of the former **Société Industrielle de la Grande Pêche** (SIGP; ⊕ 20.9069, -17.0526) headquarters, founded in 1919.

NORTHWEST MAURITANIA'S FAMOUS FISHING GROUNDS

Let us remark, however, before we go any further, that, notwithstanding the sterility of this part of the coast, it is not without importance, on account of the rich produce of the sea which bathes it. The *agriculture of the waters* as a celebrated naturalist has said, offers too many advantages, for the places that are adapted to it, to pass unobserved: this part of the sea, known by the name of the Gulph of Arguin, is especially remarkable for the immense quantity of fish which visit it, at different seasons, or which continually frequent these shores. This gulph, included between Capes Blanco and Merick [Cap Timiris], and the coast of Zaara [Sahara], on which, besides the isle of Arguin which was formerly occupied, there are several others at the mouth of what is called the river St John [Baie de Saint-Jean/Dakhlet Acheïl], is as it were closed towards the west, in its whole extent, by the bank which bears its name. This bank, by breaking the fury of the waves, raised by the winds of the ocean, contributes by securing the usual tranquillity of its waters, to render it a retreat for the fish, at the same time that it also favours the fishermen. In fact, it is from this gulph, that all the fish are procured which are salted by the inhabitants of the Canaries, and which constitute their principal food. They come hither every spring in vessels of about 100 tons burden, manned by 30 or 40 men, and they complete their operations with such rapidity, that they seldom employ more than a month.

From Alexandre Correard and J B Henry Savigny's
Narrative of a voyage to Senegal in 1816

Its century-old buildings stand inside a walled compound and are increasingly derelict, but if you ask nicely, the watchman may allow you to have a look around. In addition to still lending its name to the junction (Carrefour SIGP), SIGP's importance to Nouadhibou's history can hardly be overstated; colonial Port-Étienne was little more than a SIGP company town for many years. The company even minted its own token-currency in its heyday; these rare coins are now sought out by numismatists online, fetching upwards of €100 each.

South of here, the town gives way to the main commercial port, the Port Autonome de Nouadhibou, and the Chinese-managed Hong Dong Port and fish-processing facility. Passing these, you'll find Fort la Batterie 4km south of the SIGP junction, which isn't so much a fort, but best known for the **Tours Bleues**, or Blue Towers. These faded lapis lookouts and a surrounding network of tunnels were built in the lead-up to World War II to protect the harbour and SIGP facilities against the rising fascist threat, including against Francoist Spanish forces, which were just a few kilometres away in La Agüera (page 150). In the end, neither the towers nor the massive anti-naval gun emplacements (still visible today) saw combat, as Mauritania fell under Vichy control until the successful Allied invasion of French North Africa in Operation Torch triggered a change of allegiance at the end of 1942. The area subsequently became an anti-submarine surveillance base used by British Sunderland flying boats until the end of the war.

The site is still operated by the military, but is unfenced and the towers themselves are no longer in use. The stairs have been removed so you can't climb them, but having a look around is generally tolerated, but be prepared to identify yourself and perhaps end your visit early if requested.

The **ship graveyard** in the Baie de Cansado that became famous online in the 2000s is long gone; a clean-up effort in the late 2010s saw all of the hundreds of ships once illicitly scrapped here dismantled and removed.

CANSADO AND THE RÉSERVE SATELLITE DU CAP BLANC

At the southern end of the peninsula lies the unusual company town of **Cansado**. Something of a coastal cousin to Zouérate, it was built in the early 1960s by the Société Anonyme des Mines de Fer de Mauritanie (MIFERMA) as it prepared for the railway to come online in 1963 and iron ore exportation to begin in earnest. MIFERMA was nationalised and became SNIM in 1974, which still administers the town and most of its facilities today. Though it remains essentially a quiet company town and suburban bedroom community for Nouadhibou, it's of interest for the sheer contrast between here and the buzzing streets of Nouadhibou just up the road. Here, tidy rows of workers' cottages line the streets, adorned with neatly trimmed hedges and freshly painted kerbs, and the handful of shops and restaurants cluster around the sleepy taxi stand in the town centre.

Past the railway settlement of Cansado, at the very southernmost tip of the Cap Blanc (Ras Nouadhibou) peninsula, the **Réserve Satellite du Cap Blanc** protects a roughly 5km stretch of shoreline. Administratively connected to Banc d'Arguin National Park, the reserve was gazetted in 1986 because of the Mediterranean monk seals (*Monachus monachus*) that live here. The peninsula's tip offers extraordinary clifftop views over the ocean, but is otherwise an impossibly harsh and weather-beaten place, battered by constant winds whipping in from the Atlantic. The monk seals don't find it quite so harsh, however: it's home to the world's largest colony, estimated at 360 individuals in 2019, which shelter and breed in eroded caves at the base of the sandstone cliffs forming the peninsula.

These seals are actually part of a rare conservation success story, with their conservation status progressively up from Critically Endangered in 2015 to Vulnerable today. The global population was estimated at 450–600 as of 2024, with the greatest population increases seen in Greece and the eastern Mediterranean.

GETTING THERE AND AWAY Shared taxis run between Nouadhibou's Carrefour Ghairane and Cansado throughout the day for 20UM/seat, but there's no public transportation to Cap Blanc, so you'll have to either charter a taxi (roughly 1,800UM including waiting time), or arrange the trip through your accommodation (eg: Villa Maguela; page 143), which may even work out cheaper.

WHERE TO STAY AND EAT *Map, page 139*

There is no accommodation at Cap Blanc, but SNIM's tourism arm, Somasert, administers the hotel in Cansado and there are a couple of small restaurants in the town centre.

Le Cansado City centre; t 45 74 27 00; m 44 90 66 45; e lecansado.hotel@snim.com; w somasertsa.com. This surprisingly nice waterfront hotel is clearly used to business guests & not tourists, but the vintage facilities are kept in decent nick & the carefully kept gardens are a shockingly green oasis in this coastal desert. If you plan to stay a couple of days, it may also be possible for you to use some of the company's sports facilities (tennis etc) in town; ask reception how best to arrange. *2,150/2,650UM sgl/dbl.* **$$$**

OTHER PRACTICALITIES BMCI and Société Générale both have ATMs in Cansado.

WHAT TO SEE AND DO There's not much in the way of sights in Cansado, but the impressively large anchor and train wheels greeting you at the town entrance give a good inkling of what keeps this blue-and-beige industrial settlement (painted in the same colour scheme as the locomotives on the Iron Ore Train) afloat. The city is home to a small 8m **lighthouse** at the Pointe de Cansado, shorter and younger than its counterpart at Cap Blanc (page 152). You'll often spot some fishermen casting from the cliffs near here. And while most of the oceanfront in Cansado is

THE LOST CITY OF LA AGÜERA

Situated on the west side of the Ras Nouadhibou (Cap Blanc) peninsula about 10km southwest of Nouadhibou and across the international border, the settlement of La Agüera was officially founded as a Spanish outpost in 1920. This frontier settlement, primarily occupied by fishermen and soldiers staking out the Spanish claim, was described as 'a very minor Spanish counterpart to Port-Étienne' in 1962. Though it counted barely 1,500 residents at its peak in 1974, it was home to a fishmeal factory and was by some accounts the most important fishing port anywhere in the Spanish Sahara.

Though originally derived from an old Spanish word for an irrigation ditch, the settlement's name has shifted over time, and varies depending on who you speak to. Today the Polisario know it as La Güera, while for the Moroccans it's Lagouira. But whatever you call it, today the town has no residents at all – save for a few Imraguen fishermen – though plenty of people talk about it just the same! Indeed, if you've come down from the north, you'd be justified in thinking you were headed to quite a major settlement, as just about every road sign from Laayoune (El Aaiún) on down dutifully offers you the distance to Lagouira. Yet odder still for this town with no residents and many road signs, the road doesn't actually go here either! It's on all these signs because Morocco regards it as its southernmost point, and it's known throughout that country as the far end of a cartographical axiom describing the kingdom's expanse – '*de Tanger à Lagouira*'.

But the reality of this little corner of the Sahara is not so clear-cut as the schoolbook slogan might imply. In fact, in the vexatious political history of the Western Sahara, perhaps no spot is more confused than right here. When the Spanish withdrew in November 1975, independence-minded Polisario forces immediately took over the town. But as Mauritania was intent on annexing Western Sahara's southern third at the time (page 26), their soldiers were soon marching in from Nouadhibou, and the Mauritanians took over La Güera after a ten-day battle with the Polisario. After the Mauritanian withdrawal from the war in 1979, Morocco also sought to hold the town, but its location made it a difficult spot for them to defend.

Fighting between Moroccan and Polisario forces on the doorstep of Mauritania's economic capital also posed real difficulties for Mauritanian authorities, and they proposed to control La Güera and the surrounding territory pending a final resolution of its status. For the Polisario, Mauritania's 1984 recognition of their independence as the Sahrawi Arab Democratic Republic meant they were not particularly afraid of Mauritanian annexation, even if Nouakchott were to temporarily control – but not develop – the territory. For the Moroccans, it meant they could redirect resources away from holding this isolated, hard-to-defend outpost, and pursue their war aims more effectively elsewhere – and presumably take over from Mauritania after the Polisario were decisively vanquished. And for the Mauritanians, it bought peace in and around Nouadhibou for the price of a few military patrols.

With this seeming confluence of interests from all sides, Mauritania's offer to take this particular piece off the Western Saharan chessboard was broadly low cliffs, there's a **beach** slightly north of town where you can get your feet in the water, opposite the Académie Navale. On the northwest side of town, ASC SNIM (f ASCSNIM) plays football at the stadium, often against its rivals in Nouadhibou (page 144). There's also the **Arrahma Mosque**, which having been built in 1960 actually makes it the oldest in the area.

accepted, to the extent that when Morocco finished the final phase of its 'mur des sables' (wall of sand) in 1987, they left Lagouira outside of it, and today the Moroccan wall (and therefore Moroccan control) ends at the seashore nearly 60km north of this geopolitical ghost town.

At the time of writing, La Güera/Lagouira is still, some 40 years later, *de facto* administered, but not claimed, by Mauritania. It remains *de jure* within the Polisario-administered Western Sahara (since the 1991 ceasefire), though as with the entire territory, is claimed by both Morocco and the SADR. And so not unlike 100 years ago, there are still just a handful of soldiers and fishermen who might consider the place home.

GETTING THERE – OR NOT Given all of the above, it should perhaps come as little surprise that La Agüera also remains difficult to access. Firstly, do not attempt to get here on your own – not only because there's an administrative prohibition on unaccompanied visitors, but because there are also a significant number of landmines left behind from the conflict. But getting approval for a casual visit is not easy, and the authorities have little incentive to grant such a request (and indeed are sometimes rather suspicious of those making them), so unless you're particularly well connected, persistent and have time to spare, you're unlikely to manage it. If you insist on trying, a tour guide and/or the gendarmerie in Nouadhibou would likely be a good place to start.

All that being said, with the right connections (and the right directions!) people *very* occasionally do manage to go. Though everything is crumbling in the endless wind, you'll find an old crenellated lighthouse and fort, at least one Francoist mosaic coat of arms still visible, and the remains of the *correos* (post office), *banco* (bank), dome-roofed hospital and the 1965 Iglesia de la Inmaculada (Church of the Immaculate), with a striking compass rose mosaic still visible on the back. There's even a rarely surfed break here, known as one of the area's best waves (page 57).

But since you're unlikely to get a glimpse of the town yourself, you can console yourself with a few interesting photo essays and films produced in the last decade or so: travellers Angus MacKinnon (w cargocollective.com/angusmackinnon/La-Guera) and Kolja Spöri (w luxuryrogue.wordpress.com/2024/06/02/la-guera-the-war-torn-ghost-town-in-west-sahara) have both published short pieces, and directors Fiorella Bendoni and Gilberto Mastromatteo produced a 30-minute film in 2015. You can watch the English-language trailer to *La Güera, My Forgotten Land* at w vimeo.com/113060068.

Both the Moroccans and the Polisario make periodic statements about taking back control of the town and reviving its silent streets with new residents, developments and all the trappings of modern life. But at the time of writing this ghost town's Gordian knot remained decidedly uncut – so it seems the fishermen and soldiers of La Güera/Lagouira will have the silence and sunsets of the west coast all to themselves for a while longer yet.

A further 10km down the peninsula at the 210ha **Réserve Satellite du Cap Blanc**, the 42 terrestrial hectares of the reserve sit at the peninsula's southernmost point, atop the chalky sandstone cliffs that guard the entrance to the Baie du Lévrier, Mauritania's only natural harbour. The reserve is home to a roughly marked 1.5km walking trail which forms a loop between several viewpoints and a small **museum** that contains a series of informational panels and dioramas of monk seals in their habitat. And that habitat sits effectively just below you, with the seals typically hanging out in the eroded caves at the base of the west-facing cliffs – which, unfortunately, makes them rather tricky to see from the top of the same cliffs! If you're lucky you may spot a few little grey heads bobbing around in the waters offshore. About 500m east of the museum, it becomes easier to get near the water, though, as the peninsula slopes down to a beachy area popular with fishermen where the seals will occasionally gather. The beach here was also once home to the shipwreck of the *United Malika* refrigerated cargo ship, which ran aground and sat photogenically rusting away until it was scrapped in the mid 2010s.

Between the cliffs and the beach, there's also a 20m historical **lighthouse** here, which was originally built in 1910. The lighthouse keeper has been known to show visitors around and take them up the black-and-white striped tower for a small tip, though this is not guaranteed. There's also theoretically a 200UM charge to visit the reserve, but it's possible there will be no-one around to collect it.

BANC D'ARGUIN NATIONAL PARK

(45 25 85 42; e secretariat.pnba@yahoo.fr; w pnba.mr; f; 200UM pp per night) The Parc National du Banc d'Arguin covers some 12,000km², nearly a third of Mauritania's coastline, between Cap Timiris in the south and Pointe Minou in the north. The park was gazetted by the Mauritanian government in 1976, listed as a Ramsar Wetland of International Importance in 1982, and recognised as a UNESCO World Heritage Site in 1989. It protects the largest winter concentration of wading birds anywhere in the world, and can see upwards of 2.25 million migratory waders and shorebirds overwintering here. As such, it's quite obviously also been awarded Important Bird Area status, and while it's true that many of the travellers coming here are avowed aviphiles here to work on their checklists, the sheer numbers and concentration of birds here makes for an awesome display that even the most avi-gnostic among us would struggle to say no to.

The astonishingly barren desert interior, predominantly comprised of endlessly flat sebkhas cut through by rolling dunes, has its opposite number in an exceptionally rich and biodiverse seascape offshore, where a combination of shallow waters, nutrient-dense Saharan sediment, and a cool oceanic upwelling contribute to an extraordinarily fruitful marine environment and high plankton production. Here, the presence of more than 400km² of offshore seagrass meadows, essentially underwater prairies, provide habitat and sustenance for a dizzying array of aquatic and avian fauna. These tidal shallows can extend up to 40km offshore, and host populations of dolphin, shark, sea turtle, whales, rays and more.

Beyond its outstanding land- and seascapes, the park is also historically significant. Though there are no remaining sights as such, several world-changing historical movements are intimately linked to the Banc d'Arguin. Firstly, the 11th-century Almoravid movement, which would go on to conquer and convert everywhere between Mauritania and Lisbon, is thought to have coalesced here, in a fortified redoubt on the park's largest island, Tidra. Several centuries later, the pendulum swung the other way, and Portuguese raiders established an outpost

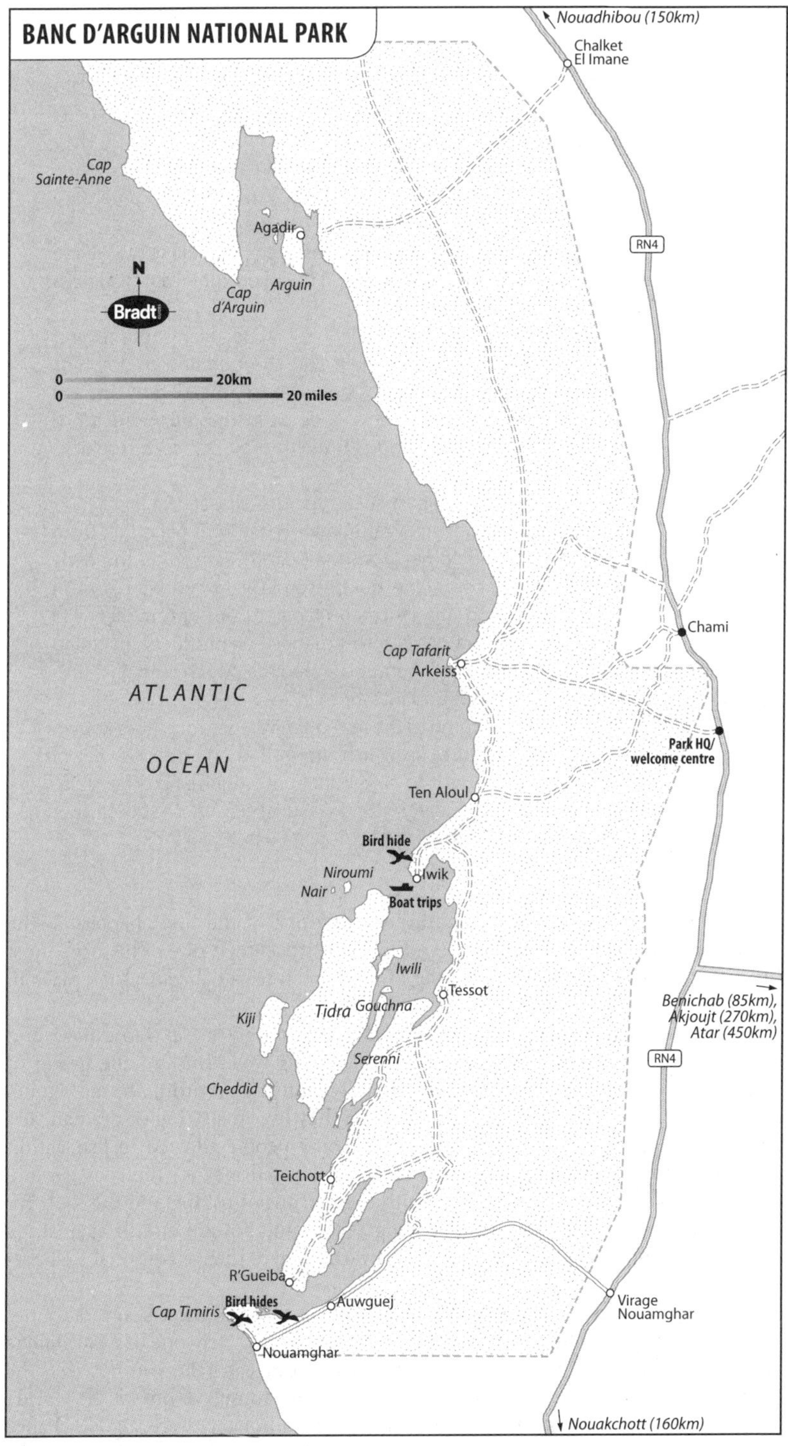
BANC D'ARGUIN NATIONAL PARK
Nouadhibou (150km)
Chalket
El Imane
Cap
Sainte-Anne
Agadir
RN4
N
Bradt
Cap
d'Arguin
Arguin
0
20km
0
20 miles
Chami
Cap Tafarit
Arkeiss
ATLANTIC
OCEAN
Park HQ/
welcome centre
Ten Aloul
Bird hide
Niroumi
Iwik
Nair
Boat trips
Iwili
Tessot
Tidra
Gouchna
Kiji
Benichab (85km),
Akjoujt (270km),
Atar (450km)
RN4
Serenni
Cheddid
Teichott
R'Gueiba
Bird hides
Auwguej
Cap Timiris
Virage
Nouamghar
Nouamghar
Nouakchott (160km)

THE IMRAGUEN

Numbering no more than a couple of thousand people, the Imraguen are the Banc d'Arguin's first, and still largely only, residents. Today they speak Hassaniya, but they come from a mixed ethnic background (page 40). They have been fishing in the area for centuries, but until the early 20th century, they hardly used boats at all, fishing either on foot or using only rudimentary rafts. This is at least in part a function of the area's marine topography: the Banc d'Arguin's shallows extend many kilometres offshore, making it possible to haul in a satisfactory catch without needing to cover significant distances by boat.

In fact, the Imraguen became legendary for a peculiar shore-fishing technique that seemingly solicited the help and co-operation of dolphins to herd schools of yellow mullet (also known as flathead grey mullet; *Mugil cephalus*) into their nets. This seems to be an increasingly rare, if not vanishing, practice, but tales of collaboration with their cetacean sidekicks still circulate (page 158).

Today, most Imraguen utilise a particular type of sailboat, the *lanche*, for fishing. These boats arrived on the Mauritanian coast with fisherfolk from the Canary Islands (the name comes from the Spanish *lancha*) in the early 20th century, and have become the quintessentially Imraguen vessel in the century since. The men primarily catch tilapia, turbot and mullet, and Imraguen women process the catch into a variety of products including *tishtar* (dried fish), *moka* (fishmeal), *bottarga* (cured roe pouch) and *dhin* (fish oil made from boiling the heads and intestines in seawater).

In the wintertime, people come to the Imraguen villages for what's known as the *cure de poissons* (fish cure), in which they're fed an intensive diet of *tishtar* and *dhin*, which is thought to cure lumbago, fatigue and other cold-season illnesses. This coincides neatly with the tourist season, so should your lumbago start acting up, the fish oil will be flowing when you arrive.

on another island in the park, Arguin, opening one of the first chapters in the centuries-long Atlantic slave trade. And in the 19th century, one of history's most infamous shipwrecks, the 1816 sinking of the French frigate *Méduse*, took place in the notorious shallows offshore.

Today, the Banc d'Arguin remains home to not only an extraordinary and unusual array of wildlife, but an ancient people as well. This unique group of fisherfolk is known as the Imraguen, and has been living according to the rigours of this unforgiving landscape for generations. They live in a string of dramatically isolated villages along the coast, and are the only people allowed to fish within the park boundaries – and only using non-mechanised means. Their villages are utilitarian, ramshackle affairs, dotted with the detritus of fishing and the tools for a life at sea. Barracks built of wood, corrugated tin and flotsam huddle against the furious elements on land, looking ever seawards, where their traditional sailboats bob offshore.

This elemental and contradictory world, where sebkhas meet seagrass, dunes meet dolphins and mangroves meet monk seals, is collectively one of Mauritania's wildest and most unique corners, where a single day can take you between the perfect emptiness of the desert and the cacophonous tumult of one of the world's largest gathering of birds. Throw in a fascinating traditional culture, a good chance of dolphin sightings and a grilled fish dinner at one of the park's tented camps, and you'll wonder why it seems so empty out here at all.

HISTORY Portuguese navigator Nuno Tristão captained the first European ship to reach the Banc d'Arguin in 1443, where he encountered a settlement on the Île d'Arguin. Not content with the shiploads of monk seal skins and lard procured in the area, he set about raiding the village and returned to Portugal with more than a dozen captives. This triggered a rush of would-be enslavers who returned to ransack the area in the years following, and the Portuguese set up a more permanent trading post on the island in 1444. Despite the area's low population density, ten years later the port at Arguin was sending some 800 enslaved people to Portugal every year It's therefore little exaggeration to say that the Atlantic slave trade that would go on to devastate much of Africa and profoundly reshape the world at large began right here in the Banc d'Arguin.

A stone-built fort was completed here in 1461, and Arguin remained a Portuguese outpost dealing in gum arabic, enslaved people and gold until it was conquered by the Dutch in 1633 during the Dutch–Portuguese War. The three ships of the Dutch West India Company – the *Jager*, the *Noortsterre* and the *Regenboog* – had no trouble overpowering the 14 Portuguese soldiers inside and, other than a few months of English occupation in 1665 as part of the Second Anglo-Dutch War, Arguin remained Dutch until the French swooped in during the Franco-Dutch War in 1678. They did not occupy the island, however, but instead simply knocked down the fortress and abandoned it.

Imperialists abhor a vacuum, though, and the Margraviate of Brandenburg (later Brandenburg–Prussia) occupied the abandoned island in 1685. Arriving on the *Rother Löwe* frigate, Captain Cornelis Reers set up a post here trading in salt, fish and ostrich feathers, but which primarily existed to support slaving between Fort Fredericksburg in the Brandenburger Gold Coast (now Ghana) and Saint Thomas in the Caribbean. Arguin changed hands yet again in 1721, as part of a decade of Dutch–French rivalry in the area. This ended when the fortifications were once again destroyed, and the island was definitively abandoned by Europeans in 1728. They would not return until around 1880, with the arrival of a Marseillaise fishing concern (page 163).

WILDLIFE

Birds Avibase (w avibase.bsc-eoc.org) counts 170 bird species present in the Banc d'Arguin, and the park is not only the most significant site anywhere in the world for Palearctic migrants, it's also host to the largest winter concentration of wading birds anywhere in the world, the most important wintering site for waders along the East Atlantic Flyway, and arguably the most important water bird breeding site in West Africa as well, boasting up to 56,000 nesting pairs. These significant numbers of nesting bird come from 15 species, including greater flamingo (*Phoenicopterus roseus*), long-tailed (*Microcarbo africanus*) and great cormorant (*Phalacrocorax carbo*), Eurasian spoonbill (*Platalea leucorodia*), great white pelican (*Pelecanus onocrotalus*), slender-billed gull (*Chroicocephalus genei*) and several species of heron and tern. There are also localised subspecies of spoonbill (*P. l. balsaci*, nests on Zira and Arel) and grey heron (*A. c. monicae*, nests on Kiaone and Arel) found here.

Annual bird surveys, however, regularly record that upwards of 90% of all birds in the park are waders, and the staggering counts of 2 million-plus migratory waders and shorebirds overwintering here each year are what brought the park to global attention. During the season, the skies here dance in great murmurations of plovers, sandpipers and godwits, and the daily tidal expansion and contraction of the area's islands leads to incredible concentrations of these birds, seen at this density nowhere else in the world. Some species even see a majority of their global populations arrive here during the season, including more than two thirds of all bar-tailed godwits (*Limosa lapponica*) and nearly half of all red knots (*Calidris canutus*). There are 16 species of plover represented, and other waders like dunlin (*Calidris alpina*), curlew sandpiper (*Calidris ferruginea*) and sanderling (*Calidris alba*) are all present in the tens or even hundreds of thousands. Finally, there are a handful of birds of prey also present, including lanner falcon (*Falco biarmicus*) and spotted eagle owl (*Bubo africanus*).

The park has also produced its own dedicated bird guide, 2006's *Les Oiseaux du Banc d'Arguin* by Paul Isenmann, though copies of this are scarce.

Marine wildlife A variety of **cetaceans** live in the waters offshore, including six species of dolphin and 15 species of shark. This includes hammerhead (*Sphyrnidae*) and tiger sharks (*Galeocerdo cuvier*), and the Atlantic bottlenose dolphin (*Tursiops truncatus*), which is closely associated with the Imraguen's fishing tradition (page 158). It's also possible to spot Atlantic humpback dolphin (*Sousa teuszii*), common dolphin (*Delphinus delphis*), striped dolphin (*Stenella coeruleoalba*), spinner dolphin (*Stenella longirostris*) and Atlantic spotted dolphin (*Stenella frontalis*), along with harbour porpoise (*Phocoena phocoena*). Several whale species are present, including both short-finned (*Globicephala macrorhynchus*) and long-finned pilot whale (*Globicephala melas*) and occasionally even orca (*Orcinus orca*).

Sea turtles also live in these waters, particularly the green sea turtle (*Chelonia mydas*). Other species, including loggerhead (*Caretta caretta*) and leatherback (*Dermochelys coriacea*) also come here to graze. Nesting is fairly uncommon but not unheard of, though nests are often subject to predation by jackals and the occasional fisherman.

Ichthyological fauna extends to more than 250 species of **fish**, including the Imraguen's mainstay of yellow mullet (*Mugil cephalus*), plus barracuda, grouper, hogfish, guitarfish and more than a dozen species of skates and rays. The Baie d'Arguin is also thought to be the mouth of the ancient Tamanrasset palaeoriver, which flowed here over 5,000 years ago, leaving behind certain estuarine species like the blackchin tilapia (*Sarotherodon melanotheron*). Offshore, Cymodocea and Zostera seagrasses predominate in the park's famous tidal shallows, and many thousands of fiddler crabs (*Ocypodidae*) will march out on to the flats to feast on zostera during particularly low tides.

The Reserve Satellite du Cap Blanc (page 149) and its world-beating population of monk seals (*Monachus monachus*) sits just across the Baie du Lévrier from here and is considered an exclave of the Banc d'Arguin National Park, though the seals themselves are typically spotted on the other side of the bay.

Terrestrial animals Life on land is limited when compared to the park's riches in air and water, but there are still several noteworthy species present. Perhaps the most unexpected mammal to be found is the Dorcas gazelle (*Gazella dorcas*), which clings on in a relict population of several dozen (recent surveys have counted between 30 and 80) on Tidra island after being extirpated on the mainland. At low tide, these can sometimes be seen on the mudflats grazing on *spartina* cordgrasses and mangrove leaves. On the mainland, canids like the side-striped jackal (*Lupulella adusta*) and African golden wolf (*Canis lupaster*) hunt rodents and scavenge around the villages, along with the notorious striped hyena (*Hyaena hyaena*). Lesser predators like fennec fox (*Vulpes zerda*) and Rüppell's fox (*Vulpes rueppellii*), as well as African wildcat (*Felis lybica*) and sand cat (*Felis margarita*), are present as well, though all are fairly reclusive and difficult to spot. Cape hare (*Lepus capensis*) and African savannah hare (*Lepus victoriae*) also live in the park, along with rodents including lesser jerboa (*Jaculus jaculus*) and lesser Egyptian gerbil (*Gerbillus gerbillus*).

There are also 21 **reptile** species present, including the sizeable desert monitor (*Varanus griseus*), plus desert agama (*Trapelus mutabilis*) and a handful of other skinks, geckoes and lizards like the dune gecko (*Stenodactylus petrii*) and golden fringe-fingered lizard (*Acanthodactylus aureus*).

For land **flora**, the low dunes fringing the coast are dusted with vegetation consisting largely of spurge and sea purslanes, but otherwise the vegetation here can be remarkably sparse, save for occasional stands of tamarisk and acacia in the dried up oueds criss-crossing the terrain.

Studies have been conducted as to whether and how certain species formerly present in the park, such as ostrich (*Struthio camelus*), dama gazelle (*Nanger dama*) and addax (*Addax nasomaculatus*), might be reintroduced in the future, though this seems likely to be some way off.

GETTING THERE AND AWAY Without your own vehicle, accessing Banc d'Arguin independently is tricky, but not entirely impossible, though once you're in the park, there is no transport of any kind, so your movements will be severely limited. Most agencies based in Nouakchott can easily set up a two- or three-day Banc d'Arguin itinerary, which will allow you to get out and take in the extraordinary scenery found in the park in ways impossible without a vehicle, so this is an instance in which splashing out on an organised excursion may be money well spent.

Independently, any vehicle running between Nouakchott and Nouadhibou can drop you at the park's various access points, including Nouamghar Virage (⊕ 19.4037, -16.0537, from where it's 57km to Nouamghar), the park's welcome centre (⊕ 20.0427, -15.9188) south of Chami, or Chami itself.

From Chami or the welcome centre, tracks lead 35–40km to Arkeiss, or 50–55km to Iwik. You can arrange a local vehicle to carry you to either village, but it's expensive: we were quoted 3,000UM. In the park's far north, there's also the turn-off for the 45km track to the Île d'Arguin at Chalket El Imane (⊕ 20.8115, -16.1207).

WHERE TO STAY AND EAT From south to north, there are three villages with accommodation in the park: **Nouamghar**, **Iwik** and **Arkeiss**. Another guesthouse at Tessot was inactive at the time of writing. Outside of the park, the nearest accommodation is in Chami (page 163). There are no restaurants inside the park, and only the most basic of shops. The accommodation providers can all arrange meals, but it's a good idea to arrive with extra provisions regardless. Wild camping in the park is officially forbidden; how that's enforced in the park's enormous expanses is another question altogether.

News reports showed the government approved the construction of a five-star resort just south of the park boundary near Nouamghar in 2023, but no-one in town had heard of the project when we dropped by, so don't count on luxury digs any time soon.

Auberge Nouamghar Nouamghar; m 42 33 31 58; ⊕ 19.3694, -16.5273. Set in a lonely spot 2km from town where the mangroves begin, the cabanas here got some refurbishments in 2021, so it's in pretty good shape despite being (like all the options in the area) fairly basic. Shared ablutions. Ask at the PNBA office in Nouamghar (⊕ 19.3577, -16.5088) to set up your stay. *1,000UM dbl.* **$$**

FISHING WITH THE IMRAGUEN

Peter Hudson

My luck must have been in…the man who had called out was pointing to a piece of what looked to me like flat, undisturbed sea but suddenly all the people on the beach jumped up, threw off their boubous and, taking the poles with the fishing nets on them on to their shoulders, walked out into the sea in two long lines. There were boys as young as ten or eleven carrying the nets as well as old men; one old man I noticed was blind and had to be led. Some of the nets were so long that they hung on one pole on someone's shoulder, then looped back to another pole on someone else's, and the two men went out in convoy.

The two lines of men waded out until those in the front were just bobbing heads. Cautiously, the two lines came round until they had encircled a large patch of sea, then quickly the fishermen slipped the nets off their poles and drew them out until the patch was encircled with nets hung from cork floats and weighted at the bottom by pieces of lead. Immediately the sea erupted, hundreds of fish leaping out of the water like missiles, attempting to jump the nets. The water boiled with grey flesh and fins and soon the fishermen could hardly be seen in the turmoil and frenzy. And then suddenly I saw, circling the ring of fishermen and nets, the arching backs of dolphins, skimming and surfing, twisting and turning after the mullet that had managed to escape. It was an orgy of feasting and catching and it lasted about ten minutes, gradually lessening towards the end. The dolphins disappeared as quickly as they had appeared and the fishermen began to thread their nets back on to their poles, dragging them to shallower water where they put them on their shoulders, took up the strain and rose up to run quickly up the beach, muscles bulging and veins throbbing under the weight of fifteen or twenty large grey fish hanging in the nets by their broken necks. Far out to sea I saw the skimming backs of a school of fifteen to twenty dolphins.

From Travels in Mauritania *by Peter Hudson (Flamingo, 1990)*

Camping Arkeiss Arkeiss; m 46 46 76 77, 26 27 86 56; ⊕ 20.1256, -16.2558. Set a 10min walk from Cap Tafarit, this campsite sits on an endless sweep of beach, offering accommodation in either khaïma or Moroccan-style *caïdale* tents – the name of the latter derives from *qāid*, the Arabic for leader, so these are a fair bit fancier, & pricier, than the khaïmas, & come with private (but separate) bathrooms. The kitchen does good meals for 400UM/plate, & manager Alassane is a helpful presence. *1,000/1,500UM for 2/4 people in a khaïma, 2,500UM larger caïdale tent*. **$$**

Community Camp (Blue Cabanas) Iwik; m 38 58 51 50; ⊕ 19.8848, -16.3064. With 20 cabanas set around a sandy courtyard, this unsignposted compound is a fair bit larger than the Iwik Vacance Camp nearby – though you're still fairly likely to have the place to yourself. The cabanas have en-suite ablutions & manager Ahmed Medou is a well-known fixer around town. *1,000UM dbl, meals 300UM pp*. **$$**

Iwik Vacance Camp (White Cabanas) Iwik; m 36 36 40 44; ⊕ 19.8867, -16.2991. Also unsignposted, here you'll find 3 standing cabanas, with khaïma tents also available. Manager Sokeina cooks good meals, but if she's out of town you may have to make arrangements elsewhere. *1,000UM dbl*. **$$**

WHAT TO SEE AND DO Though they are not official designations, the park can be roughly divided into northern, central and southern sections. Though the majority of activity takes place in the central sector surrounding Arkeiss and Iwik, in the interests of continuity and geography, this section is ordered from south to north, assuming an approach from Nouakchott. Though the terrestrial portion of the park stretches several dozen kilometres inland, most of the attractions inside the park are coastal.

Southern sector The southern sector of the park is centred around **Nouamghar** (or Mamghar), which is the largest settlement within the park boundaries – though this isn't saying much. From the south, Nouamghar is approached along a tarmac feeder road branching off the RN2 at Nouamghar Virage. This road cuts west through the scorching plains until reaching the shores of the Baie de Saint-Jean and following them southwest to Nouamghar and Cap Timiris.

If the tides are right, it's also possible to approach Nouamghar along the beach, and this was the main route between Nouakchott and Nouadhibou before the road was completed in 2005! This stretch of coast is almost entirely uninhabited, with just a handful of fishing hamlets between here and Nouakchott, 150km to the south. Here, dunes fall directly into the sea, and the fishing boats change from the sail-driven Imgraguen lanches to the multi-coloured West African pirogues seen across the region. You'll also notice a separate fishing settlement about 2km south of Nouamghar, a community of non-Imraguen fisherfolk exploiting the waters just outside the boundary. North of here, inside the park boundary, only Imraguen people are allowed to fish.

As the biggest Imraguen settlement, it's worth a quick look around to see the local fishing economy at work, but Nouamghar itself probably isn't why you're here. (Though do check out the giant whale skeleton at the park office.) **Cap Timiris**, however, is less than 5km west of town, and this scenic peninsula hemming in the southwestern edge of the Baie de Saint-Jean breaks up into a cluster of mangrove creeks and mudflats on its east and west coasts. There are a number of little spits of land jutting into the tidal lagoons from here, offering spectacular views. As you approach the peninsula (less than 500m from the auberge), there's a bird hide (⊕ 19.3721, -16.5305) overlooking the scene. It had a big chunk of its floor missing when we dropped in, meaning it's probably just about serviceable if you're agile, but unlikely to be suitable for hours of viewing unless it undergoes some repairs.

There's an alternative, however. The mangroves along the eastern side of Cap Timiris at the entry to Baie de Saint-Jean, in an area known as Eïzzenâyya, may be even more extensive than those west of Nouamghar – and the bird hide here (⊕ 19.3705, -16.4746) even has an intact floor. The hide is about 4km northeast of town, so it makes a good stop if you're continuing towards the central section of the park.

Central sector The main Nouamghar road follows the Baie de Saint-Jean northeast for some 25km out of town until it turns inland towards the RN2. Here, we depart the tarmac and continue north along the east coast of the bay, rounding its northern end and eventually reaching the village of **Tessot** after 33km.

If you've got the time, a scenic detour would round the top of the bay and head west towards the similarly named **Teichott** village instead, where you'll find a 100m floating pier and a sprinkling of pretty launches bobbing offshore. This is the closest jumping-off point to the islands of Cheddid, Touffat and Kiji, as well as the largest island, Île Tidra.

Going via Teichott just about doubles the mileage, but allows you to continue north along the coast rather than through the interior. It's also possible to take a detour 16km south from Teichott to **Rgueïba**, which sits opposite Nouamghar at the mouth of the Baie de Saint-Jean, but note that deep sand on the peninsula makes for challenging driving (and you'll have to double back). Rgueïba is home to a boat-building and repair facility for the Imraguen lanches, which may explain the above-average number of wrecks on its cluttered shoreline.

Back in Teichott and continuing north along the coast, the Île Tidra comes into view to the northwest before being blocked by the nearer tidal island of Serenni. The narrow bay that (sometimes) divides Serenni from the mainland is a spectacular sight, where a horizon of shimmering water and dunes will quickly leave you struggling to tell mirage from reality.

It's 30km from Teichott to Tessot, where you round the north end of Serenni and the îles Tidra, Gouchna and Iwili pull into view. The village is home to a set of tourist bungalows identical to the ones at Nouamghar, but these are unfortunately defunct (seemingly for want of a manager, as they at least appear to be in mostly decent nick).

From Tessot, it's 25km north and west around the Baie d'Aouatil to the village of **Iwik** (or Iouîk), where most of the park's tourist infrastructure is found. Set on a headland just 4km across the water from Île Tidra, Iwik is a small Imraguen village much like the others in the park, but this is the most common jumping-off point for **boat trips** to the islands. (In concept it would probably be possible to arrange informal boat trips at most of the villages in the park, but in practice they are most prepared to arrange this in Iwik.) Iwik is also positioned just opposite the most extensive tidal banks and seagrass beds in the park, making it a hotspot for the park's extraordinary avian and aquatic life.

The boat trips are taken in traditional sail-driven Imraguen launches (which feel very much like an Indian Ocean dhow, despite their Canarian origins), and typically approach some combination of the islands of Zira, Niroumi, Nair and Tidra; the diminutive Arel lies some 10km further out. Though completely uninhabited, the 196km^2 Île Tidra is noteworthy for both cultural and conservational reasons. Firstly, it's thought to be the place where the Almoravids spent several years consolidating their movement before their lightning attack across the Maghreb and Mediterranean (page 177), though this is the subject of some debate and there's currently no visible evidence of their stay on the island. Secondly, the island is today a redoubt of another kind, and home to the park's (and possibly Mauritania's) last wild population of dorcas gazelle (*Gazella dorcas*), with at least several dozen individuals present.

Trips in the launches are best done at high tide (which comes twice in 24 hours), as the rising waters not only allow the boat to navigate the Banc d'Arguin's notorious shallows, but also serve to concentrate the birdlife on to the reduced land area, making for some extraordinary displays, with tens of thousands of individuals jockeying for position on the ever-shrinking sands. Nair and Niroumi, islets at the north end of Île Tidra, are especially good places to see this phenomenon in action. At low tide, the birds spread out, pecking and poking along the seagrass meadows and tidal flats – where Tidra's gazelles are known to come out and forage at low tide too. And while the Imraguen's legendary dolphin-assisted fishing may be largely a thing of the past, the dolphins still like to come and follow the boats.

These excursions last at least several hours or until you're ready to head home, but the pricing structure is fixed at 3,500UM per trip, for a maximum of seven passengers. (It's possible to carry up to nine for an additional 200UM per person.) Disappointingly, they don't make any accommodations for small groups or solo travellers, who are subject to the same 3,500UM fee. If that's a bit steep for you, there's still plenty of birding to be had on the mainland: head to the seafront bird hide (⊕ 19.8927, -16.3109) about 1.5km northwest of Iwik. The park offices in Iwik and Nouamghar can sometimes also provide birding guides, charging 1,000UM for a roughly half-day excursion.

Continuing north from Iwik, it's about 33km to Arkeiss, passing through the hamlet of Ten Alloul halfway along. Looking seaward as you pass Ten Alloul, keep your eyes out for the islets of Ichekcher, Grand Kiaone and Petit Kiaone floating in the Fata Morgana haze several kilometres offshore. The weatherbeaten pair of Kiaone islands are an unexpectedly notable nesting site for flamingos, who have taken up residence here despite their generally preferring a gentler lagoonside landscape.

Arkeiss itself sits just below the high, rugged headland of Cap Tafarit. In the village below, there's a charming stone-built mosque that's worth a snapshot, but otherwise it's the tourist camp that really steals the show. Here, there's a photogenic line of khaïma tents arranged directly on the beachfront, and it's less than a kilometre (mostly uphill) from here to the dramatic cliff-edge drop-off of Cap Tafarit. In a straight line from the cape, the next landfall is 6,000km away at Cabo Maisí in Cuba, and this lunar stretch of coast feels like the end of the world indeed. Arkeiss is also known as a hotspot for sport fishing, but unfortunately you've got to come prepared, as there was no equipment for rent at the time of writing. But other than the sport fishers, no-one is catching or processing fish near the camp, so the beach here makes for a good place to get in the water for a (potentially chilly) dip.

Many itineraries will exit the park from here, as Chami (page 163) lies directly east of Arkeiss, only 30km away. Back on the RN2 road (or on your way here), be sure to stop at the fish-shaped(!) **park HQ** and Centre d'Interprétation Environnementale (Environmental Interpretation Centre; ⊕ 20.0427, -15.9188), which sits east of the main road some 15km south of Chami. It was inaugurated in 2009 with Spanish support and features exhibits on the flora, fauna and traditional culture of the park.

Northern sector North of Arkeiss, the park becomes remoter still. There are absolutely no accommodation or other facilities here, and only one settlement: the village of **Agadir**, which is not on the mainland at all, but rather sits offshore on the Île d'Arguin, inside a bay of the same name. The island is known as the site of one of the earliest European outposts in West Africa, chosen for its sheltered position in the Baie d'Arguin (Dakhlet Agadir).

Getting to the island from Arkeiss involves about 75km of driving across some impressively, even disorientingly, featureless flats, and the same is true if you come in from the RN2 junction at Chalket El Imane. Either way, you arrive at the same *débarcadère* on a small tidal inlet, from where boats make the 2km crossing to the island. There are a couple of huts and khaïmas at the débarcadère for shelter, but precious little else, and as you might imagine the boatmen don't exactly work to a strict schedule. Expect to pay a few hundred ouguiya for the crossing, less if you can

ARGUIN'S ANCIENT ORIGINS

Whence comes the name of Arguin? Who gave it to this gulph? If we consider the heat of the sun which is experienced here, and the sparkling of the sandy downs which compose the coast, we cannot help remarking that *Arguia* in Phenician means what is *luminous* and *brilliant*, and that in Celtic, *Guin* signifies *ardent*. If this name comes from the Carthaginians, who may have frequented these coasts, they must have been particularly struck with their resemblance to the famous Syrtes [dangerous sandbanks north of Libya] in their own neighbourhood, which mariners took so much care to avoid.

From Alexandre Corréard and J B Henry Savigny's *Narrative of a Voyage to Senegal* (1818)

hop in a boat that's already going. Should you have to wait, it's a tempting spot for a swim, but be very cautious as the tidal current filling and draining the inlet is fierce!

Boats drop anchor at the village of Agadir, which is today little more than a diminutive fishing hamlet, but with an extraordinary historical pedigree. A Portuguese-built stone fort stood here from 1461 to the early 1700s, when it was knocked down by the French. As such, there are no longer any visible traces of the fort, other than perhaps some low foundation outlines of indeterminate origin.

THE SHIPWRECK OF THE *MEDUSA*

At the time one of the world's most notorious shipwrecks ('a 19th-century version of the *Titanic*', according to one scholar), the French frigate *Méduse* ran aground in the Banc d'Arguin in 1816. The ship was en route to Senegal as part of a four-vessel convoy sent to take Saint-Louis from the English, as agreed during the 1815 Congress of Vienna at the conclusion of the Napoleonic wars. Its captain, Hugues Duroy de Chaumareys, was appointed by King Louis XVIII as thanks for his support during the Bourbon Restoration, but he had little navigational experience – a fact that would soon bear dramatic consequences.

A series of navigational mistakes and miscalculations separated the *Méduse* from its convoy and revealed Captain Chaumareys as hopelessly out of his depth. On 2 July 1816, the *Méduse* and her 400-odd passengers were irreparably beached on the Banc d'Arguin's notorious shallows. Three days later, the decision was made to abandon ship, but there were not nearly enough lifeboats for all aboard.

As such, they fashioned a crude raft, on which an astonishing 150 people set off into the raging surf, towed by their compatriots in the lifeboats. But the raft made navigation for the lifeboats difficult, and they soon cut the tow ropes and abandoned the raft to its fate.

These unlucky souls would spend 13 days adrift in circumstances that can only be described as bedlam. The raft threatened to break up, the weak were pushed into the sea, fights and killings erupted over access to the limited reserves of wine (the water had gone with the lifeboats), some committed suicide, and the dead who remained on board were eaten for survival. When the convoy's brig *Argus* pulled into view – by happenstance, no less – just 15 survivors remained.

When word of the shipwreck reached France, it triggered a massive scandal over the series of corrupt and incompetent decisions that allowed such a human catastrophe and national embarrassment to unfold. Captain Chaumareys (who had survived, as did most passengers on the lifeboats) was court-martialled and imprisoned, and two of the raft's survivors, Alexandre Corréard and J B Henry Savigny, wrote a tell-all exposé, the *Narrative of a voyage to Senegal*, in 1818, which the French government took great pains to suppress.

The apocalyptic circumstances of the raft's passengers was immortalised in *Le Radeau de la Méduse* (The Raft of the Medusa), painted by the 27-year-old Théodore Géricault. Unveiled in 1819 and measuring an enormous 4.9m by 7.2m, this monumental painting has gone on to be the defining image of the shipwreck, and a quintessential avatar of the French Romantic period. It is on display today in the Louvre.

A newer building, now also ruined, occupies the same site. This dates to 1880, when a Marseillaise fishing company, La Marée des Deux Mondes, set up shop here. The richness of the Banc d'Arguin's fishing stocks had been known by Canarian and other fishers for years (page 154), but after several years of operation here the company decamped to the growing fishing settlement of Port-Étienne (Nouadhibou). Today the roofless stone building remains, along with at least two sets of long, regular rows of stones in the ground – their drying racks.

The island settlement's long history is only partly explained by its protected anchorage: there's one more critical factor present in the form of a well (⊕ 20.6135, -16.4546), which is one of the very, very few freshwater sources to be found anywhere on the Mauritanian coast. Set about 750m inland from the village, you'll also find another astonishing sight here: a solitary tree.

Should you want to try and contract your boatman for a longer journey, there are also significant shallows and seagrass beds in the bay north and west of the island, particularly around the islets of Ardent, Marguerite and the Île aux Flamands.

Finally, at the extreme northwestern end of the park some 30–40km beyond Agadir, there's another set of seagrass beds and tidal lagoons near Cap Saint-Anne (Khechem Bellâ'a). This uninhabited area sees very few (human) visitors, though the Île des Pélicans just offshore is certainly popular with its namesake bird. Exiting the north end of the park, it's possible to continue on towards Nouadhibou via desert tracks, but these are infrequently used, so be sure you've got emergency supplies, and that you (or your driver) know very well what you're doing.

CHAMI

This new city sits equidistant between Nouadhibou and Nouakchott along the main road between the two. Intentionally developed by the Mauritanian government as part of a policy known as *regroupement*, which seeks to systematise the sometimes-chaotic urbanisation that characterises so many Mauritanian towns and to strategically settle certain sparsely inhabited corners of the country, Chami's foundation stone was laid in 2012 by former president Mohamed Ould Abdel Aziz. And it really was starting from nothing: the 2013 census counted a grand total of 51 residents here. Ten years later, there were 4,214 – a modest 8,162% increase! The years to come seem set for more of the same, making the French term *ville-champignon*, or mushroom town, perfectly apropos for Mauritania's newest would-be metropolis.

Chami's growth has also been spurred by a boom in artisanal gold mining, which turned the city into a Klondike overnight in 2016, when a nearby gold find spurred thousands of would-be miners to descend on the city. The government sought to channel and keep this growth in Chami, setting up processing and purchasing infrastructure in the city. Today the hinterlands around Chami are still home to dozens of wildcat mining operations, and the dense warren of processing outfits in the industrial park south of town have no shortage of work.

Known as 'Grillage' (⊕ 20.1457, -15.9634), this area is a cacophony of improvised millwheels, diesel generators and toxic dust, where truckloads of rock are crushed down into a wet slurry. Mercury is then added, as it forms an amalgam with the gold in the soil, after which it is burned off with blowtorches (hence *grillage*), leaving the gold – and an environmental and health catastrophe – behind.

This is unfortunately a common story across the continent, where mercury contamination and artisanal mining go hand in hand, but Chami's proximity to the Banc d'Arguin National Park does not augur well for the future of the fauna – or residents – of the park, much less Chami itself. The remaining mercury-treated sand is then purchased by other actors who repeat the process with more sophisticated equipment and extract further gold – some estimate that the artisanal methods practised here only net 40% or less of the soil's actual gold content.

The richness of the earth here is not entirely a surprise, however; the enormous open-pit Tasiast Gold Mine sits in a remote stretch of desert about 65km northeast of town, straddling the uninhabited borderlands between Dakhlet Nouadhibou and Inchiri regions. Here, Tasiast Mauritania, a subsidiary of the Canadian Kinross Gold Corporation, has been mining since 2010, extracting something like 11.5 million tons of gold every year.

And while most Mauritanians now know Chami as the 'gold capital', the city is also, as previously mentioned, a gateway to the Banc d'Arguin National Park (page 152), whose boundary sits just 5km south and west of town. The park's welcome centre (page 157) sits 15km south of Chami towards Nouakchott.

WHERE TO STAY

Hotel Ghouffa RN4; m 36 29 29 08, 33 23 10 00, 44 22 02 14. Chami's first hotel opened its doors in 2019, & its AC rooms are still the most modern & upmarket in town. *1,500UM dbl.* **$$**

Auberge l'or du Sahara RN4, opposite Hotel Iwik; m 46 77 39 94. The tikit-style rooms here are cheaper than either of the other options, but also considerably more basic & run-down. *From 600UM dbl.* **$**

Hotel Iwik RN4; m 36 83 77 77; e lokassarl41@gmail.com. Reasonably modern & well-kept en-suite rooms at the north end of Chami. *From 800UM dbl.* **$**

OTHER PRACTICALITIES BMCI and Attijari Bank are both represented with ATMs on the main road through town. There are several fuel stations and small supermarkets.

CROSSING TO/FROM MOROCCAN-CONTROLLED WESTERN SAHARA (SOUTHERN PROVINCES)

Perhaps no border crossing in Africa has had as much ink spilled about it, at least in traveller circles, as that of Guerguerat to the north of Nouadhibou. All kinds of rumours of lawlessness (overstated, at least these days) to landmines (very much present) swirl around this politically complex but practically straightforward crossing, and its nicknames of *Al Hufra* (the hole) or Kandahar probably don't help in the reputational stakes.

The complexity surrounding this crossing has its roots in the Western Sahara conflict, specifically relating to the so-called 'berm' or 'sand wall' that the Moroccans built through the desert in stages throughout the 1980s to fend off Polisario attacks. Each stage of this wall progressively brought more of the contested territory under Moroccan control. The sixth and so far final stage of that wall surrounded Guerguerat in 1987. Everything west of this wall is administered by Morocco; to the east, by the Frente Polisario/Sahrawi Arab Democratic Republic (SADR; page 222).

This arrangement was codified in the ceasefire signed between Morocco and the Frente Polisario under UN auspices in 1991. The Guerguerat crossing was first opened in 2001, and has been a periodic source of conflict since, as it passes through several kilometres of what is, according to the official ceasefire agreement, Polisario-governed territory subject to military use restrictions within 5km of the wall.

This narrow slice of territory has always been difficult for the Polisario to effect control in, but the conflict over Guerguerat snapped into focus when Moroccan forces crossed the sand wall to dismantle a blockade that Polisario forces had been intermittently enforcing in the 3.5km between the Moroccan and Mauritanian border posts in 2020. This is the area that travellers often refer to as 'No Man's Land'.

As part of this operation, the Moroccans also surfaced some of the road in between before they were stopped. Today, 2.3km is surfaced, and only 1.2km is still rough track. The 'Kandahar' camp of Polisario-backed protesters and general smugglers has been evicted and was inactive at the time of writing.

GETTING THERE AND AWAY What's important to remember is this: at the time of writing (and for the foreseeable future), the crossing operates as a direct border crossing between Mauritania and Morocco, and entry procedures are as they would be at any other entry point to each country.

Mauritanian control ends at **PK55** (Point kilométrique 55, as it is 55km from Nouadhibou; ⊕ 21.3337, -16.9471), and Moroccan control begins 3.5km later at the **Guerguerat** border post (⊕ 21.3618, -16.9606). There are a handful of clapped-out taxis that will shuttle you between the respective gates, or it's even possible to walk, *but stay on the vehicle tracks – the threat of landmines here is real!*

El Moussavir Plus (m 46 09 19 98, 43 66 66 44; f) and Supratours (m +212 (0) 6 61 40 05 94, +212 (0) 5 28 93 10 13; w supratours.ma) connect Nouadhibou with Dakhla daily. (Depending on the day, the Moroccan bus may also be operated by CTM; w ctm.ma) Buses depart in either direction around 09.00–10.00.

In either direction, you purchase one ticket (1,300UM/290 dirham; 435km; 9–10hrs), but you have to change vehicles at the border. El Moussavir Plus provides a minibus directly to the Moroccan gate, after which you walk through Moroccan border formalities and board a coach waiting on the other side; they also operate this connection from Nouakchott (2,000UM/470 dirham).

If you miss the morning departure, there are also private cars that sell seats between Dakhla and Nouadhibou, which run a few times daily with departures into the afternoon. These charge 1,600UM and leave from an unmarked storefront garage (⊕ 20.9644, -17.0387) 100m east of Carrefour al-Atihadiya, just around the corner from El Moussavir Plus.

WHERE TO STAY AND EAT There are a few guesthouses and cafés on both the Mauritanian and Moroccan sides of the border, so if you get stuck for whatever reason, there are options. On the Mauritanian side, things are more basic, with **Auberge Porte d'Afrique** (m 46 41 50 03, 22 41 50 03) and **Traveller's Rest Hotel** (Arabic-only signboard; m 41 01 02 21, 47 20 37 38) both offering simple rooms on the right-hand side of the road just before you enter the border complex. There's also good Senegalese food available at **Restaurant Mina La Rose** next door.

On the Morocco side, there are budget rooms on the first floor at **Hotel Guarguarat** (m +212 (0) 6 48 58 30 02, +212 (0) 6 23 28 71 49 (Morocco); e bfgmaroc@gmail.com), on the left next to the border complex, or much nicer rooms at **Hotel Al Shmokh** (m +212 (0) 5 28 95 06 31; w hotelalshmokh.com; from €40 dbl), on the right 250m north of the crossing. There's also good food here, or there are a few cafés just next to the border complex, including **Ouled Salek**.

Heading north, it's 85km to the first real settlement at **Bir Gandouz**, where the appealing **Hotel Barbas** (m +212 (0) 5 28 81 96 99; from €30 dbl) is a must-stop for overlanders, with good en-suite rooms and a restaurant serving quality pizzas, tajines and other dishes in a high, covered atrium. There's also a small supermarket at which you should be able to change dollars/euros into dirhams (though ouguiya are less welcome; better to change these to dirham at the border).

WESTERN SAHARA – WHAT IS IT EXACTLY?

Sharing more than 1,500km of border with Mauritania, Western Sahara is larger than the UK; but with only 650,000 residents, it is among the most sparsely populated (and least-understood) territories on the planet. Spain claimed the area in 1885 and began to exert control over Saguia el-Hamra and Río de Oro, later becoming known as Spanish Sahara. Agitation for independence accelerated in the 1960s, and in 1973, the territory's primary independence movement was founded: the Frente Popular de Liberación de Saguía el Hamra y Río de Oro, or Polisario Front. International pressure, Polisario guerilla attacks, and the decline of dictator Franco saw Spain concede to demands for a self-determination referendum in 1974. But Mauritania and Morocco both claimed the territory and brought the case to the International Court of Justice. The court, however, ruled that neither country's historical ties overrode the residents' right to self-determination. Undeterred, in November 1975, Morocco launched the Green March, a mass demonstration pressuring Spain into handing over the Spanish Sahara. Weeks later, Spain, Morocco and Mauritania signed an agreement splitting the territory between the two neighbours. Tens of thousands of refugees began to flee for Algeria. Spain withdrew on 26 February 1976, and the Sahrawi Arab Democratic Republic (SADR) declared its independence. But the war continued. Mauritania was forced to withdraw and sue for peace with the Polisario in 1979, and SADR joined the AU-predecessor OAU in 1982. Morocco fought on, building defensive walls through the desert. Hostilities continued until a 1991 ceasefire and UN deployment, mandated to finally administer the long-promised referendum. But disagreements over voter eligibility and a seeming lack of political pressure saw the process increasingly bogged down. Morocco consolidated its control to the west of its walls, and Polisario administered the east and its refugee camps in Tindouf. A stalemate crystallised, and despite the ceasefire's 2020 collapse, Western Sahara remains defined by this division, with resolution or reunification a seemingly distant prospect.

OTHER PRACTICALITIES There's an ATM dispensing Moroccan dirham at Al Barid bank on the Moroccan side, opposite Hotel Al Shmokh. The nearest Mauritanian ATM is in Nouadhibou, but there is no shortage of moneychangers, particularly on the Mauritanian side. You may need their services, so have an idea of the going rates before you arrive.

BOU LANOUAR

Leaving Nouadhibou, the road is lined with electricity-generating windmills and a new pipeline providing water to the city. Set some 80km from Nouadhibou where the road turns towards the south, the only settlement of any significance between here and Chami is Bou Lanouar (population 3,369). This thoroughly desolate small town is a common first stop in Mauritania for trucks arriving from over the Moroccan border, and has all the charm you might expect of such a settlement. It's also the point where the road and railway part ways, the latter beginning its long western trajectory towards Choum and Zouérate. If needed, there are better-than-expected rooms at the newish **Hotel El Iza Raha** (m 36 23 88 87; 1,000UM dbl), set about 1.5km south of town. They can arrange food at request, and there's also a small shop attached.

5

Adrar and the Northeast

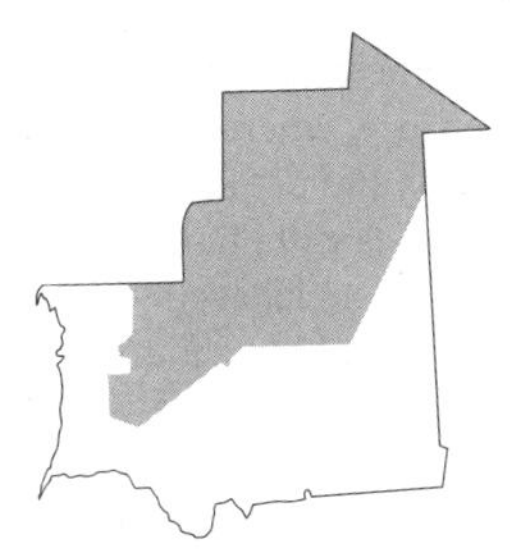

Taking its name from the Amazigh for 'mountain', the Adrar (ولاية أدرار) is where the Sahara's great, numinous, awe-inspiring power stretches out and reveals itself in its extraordinary fullness. A grand rocky plateau stretching up to 500m high and cut through by innumerable valleys, canyons and oases, the Adrar is Mauritania's travel heartland sans pareil, and with very good reason. On first glance, the high plateau is an unforgiving expanse of oxidised black-and-orange stone baking in the sun, seemingly devoid of, or outright incapable of, supporting much life at all – let alone that of humans. But in each and every nook, cranny, crack and crevasse where life is just about possible, it has, as the saying goes, found a way, and a legion of hardy plants has found and colonised these havens, no matter how small or tenuous.

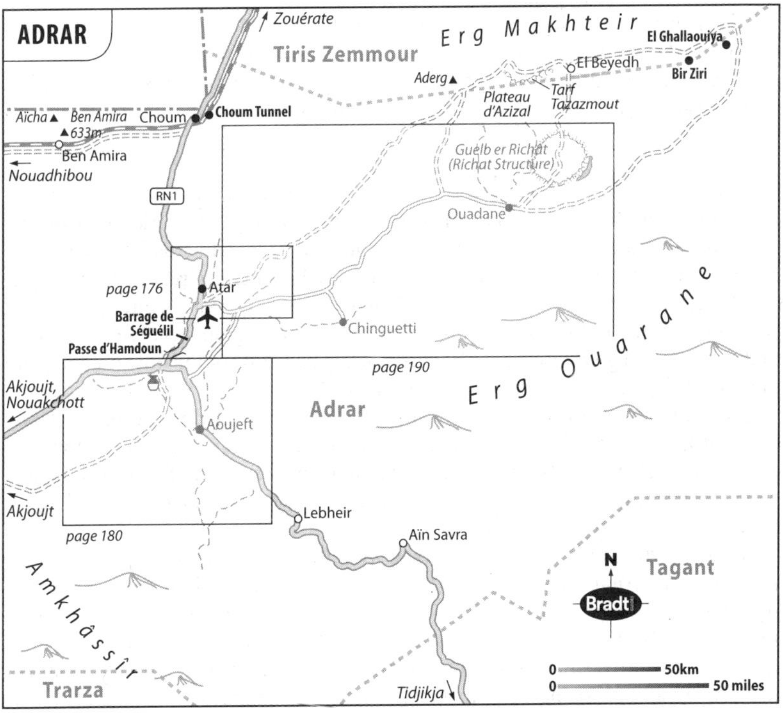

And where plants go, so too do people: though the Adrar is Mauritania's second-largest region by area (just a hair smaller than the UK) with Mauritania's second-smallest population (just 71,623 Adrarois), the region is by no means empty. Rather, it's liberally sprinkled with diminutive oasis villages alongside these pockets of verdure, where Moorish families in stone-built houses still make a living from the herds and the dates, as has been done here for time immemorial. Many Nouakchott families still maintain houses in these villages, just so they can be here for the year's largest social event – the annual date harvest.

A lot of Mauritanian itineraries spend the vast majority of their time in the Adrar, and it's easy to see why. Between the priceless calligraphy of Chinguetti, the lost-world oasis of Terjit, and the staggering dunes of Azoueiga, the region is home to a surfeit of cultural and natural riches that can fill not just one visit, but many. Indeed, more than a few visitors have found themselves fully bewitched by the Adrar's scenery and serenity, returning many times to wander the trails, camp under the stars, and sip sweet tea with friends and nomads in a landscape of immense human and natural beauty. Spend a few days here, and there's a fair chance you might – *Inshallah* – become one of them.

To the north, Mauritania's Tiris Zemmour region is larger still (just a hair larger than the UK, but with 79,129 residents), though here the landscape is considerably emptier, with flat, stony *reg* desert often extending to the horizons in all directions. Also unlike the pinprick oases of the Adrar, the vast majority of the population here is concentrated in the urban centres surrounding the mining operations at Kedia d'Idjil mountain, the country's highest at 915m, and made of nearly pure iron ore.

But no matter the endless baking plains – a large percentage of the visitors in Tiris Zemmour have got one thing and one thing only on their minds: Mauritania's world-famous Iron Ore Train. Checking in at up to 3km long, this is one of the world's largest and heaviest trains, and it carts hundreds of wagons of dug-up and ground-up Kedia d'Idjil over 700km to the coast at Nouadhibou a couple of times per day, every day, all year long. And unlike any other train of its kind, you can actually ride it. Other than the train, travel up this way used to be a bit of a cul-de-sac, but with new road projects underway to the Moroccan and Algerian borders, the region will soon form part of a newly opened route between North and West Africa, ready and waiting for the first few adventurers to give it a try.

AKJOUJT AND THE ROUTE TO ATAR

Formerly known as Fort-Repoux, the small copper-mining city of Akjoujt (أكجوجت) sits roughly midway between Nouakchott and Atar. It is not actually in the Adrar region at all, but rather the capital of the desolate Inchiri region (population 29,500), Mauritania's least populous. Akjoujt is the only major settlement you'll encounter on the route from Nouakchott to the Adrar region, because in addition to its copper and gold reserves, it has historically been one of the only points along this route with an even more valuable resource – water.

The Nouakchott–Atar road cuts a straight line northeast through the flatlands of Inchiri, which are largely uninhabited, covered in endless fields of stony *reg* and occasional dunes. The first real topography arrives in the form of the black rock Tammagout mountain, which stands alone on the left side of the road 40km before Akjoujt.

As befits the country's most sparsely populated region, Akjoujt is also the smallest of Mauritania's regional capitals (population 18,138). In recent years, some Akjoujtois complained that funding is being redirected from here to Inchiri's other settlements like the new town of Chami (page 163) and Benichab (known primarily for its water source where Tayba mineral water is bottled), where the government has laid out a large road grid in an effort to spur further growth.

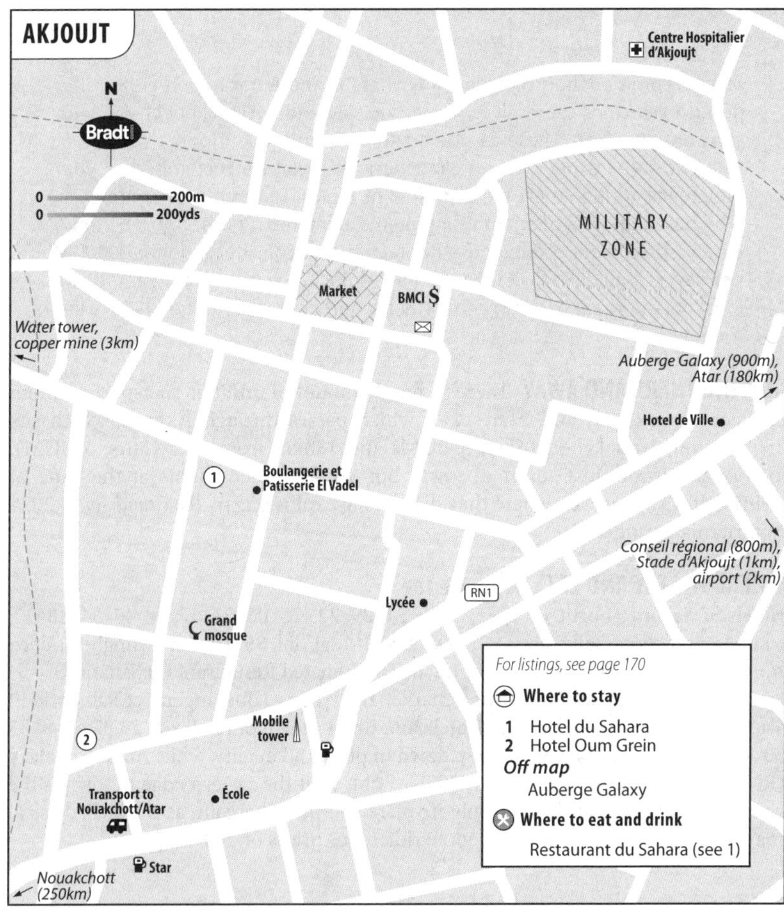

But Akjoujt isn't purely a modern creation: though contemporary copper prospecting began here as early as 1945, sites nearby have been linked to ancient forms of metallurgy taking place as early as the 8th century BCE. And these first forgers have a decidedly modern descendant: about 4km west of town, the Guelb Moghrein Mine started production in 1970. Though a series of price and energy shocks in the following decades mean that production has fluctuated considerably and the mine even closed down altogether for a number of years, today the enormous open pits produce 13,400 tonnes of copper annually (along with lesser amounts of gold) for Mauritanian Copper Mines, owned by the Canadian First Quantum Minerals.

Akjoujt has the usual amenities one would expect in a regional capital, including an ATM, hospital, supermarkets, accommodation and fuel, but is otherwise of limited interest to tourists other than as a jumping-off point towards the Erg Amatlich and Azoueiga (page 183). As far as we could ascertain, it's not possible to tour the mine as a casual visitor. On the southeast side of town, the Stade d'Akjoujt was inaugurated in 2019 and has a capacity of 1,000 (more than 5% of the town), so there's plenty of room to drop in and see FC Akjoujt thrash the competition. Outside of town to the east, Akjoujt is ringed by a half-circle of rock mountains which are known for their avian life (page 170).

DESERT EXCURSIONS

Most accommodation providers anywhere in the Adrar region either offer desert excursions themselves, or can quickly and easily connect you with someone who can. These can be anything from a day trip in a saloon car to a two-week expedition on camelback, and can be customised to your preference, though there are a number of 'typical' routes most outfitters will offer based on local geography and points of interest. Prices vary depending on the size of your group and other factors, but consider roughly 2,000UM per day as a guide, or 5,000UM with a 4x4 (inclusive of fuel, food and gear). Most operators are based in either Nouakchott or Atar; see page 112 for a list.

GETTING THERE AND AWAY There's a good amount of minibus transport running between Nouakchott and Atar, all of which passes through Akjoujt, which sits 250km from Nouakchott (4hrs; 350UM) and 180km from Atar (3hrs; 300UM). There's an airport just south of town, but no scheduled flights at the time of writing. It was, however, where they did the big explosions in *The Grand Tour*'s 2024 Mauritania episode.

WHERE TO STAY AND EAT *Map, page 169*

Hotel du Sahara (north of RN1; ☎ 45 21 29 22, 25 06 53 67; m 46 54 88 22; e hotelsahara06@gmail.com; f; 1,500/1,800UM sgl/dbl; **$$**) has surprisingly modern rooms that are certainly the best in town. The affiliated Restaurant du Sahara ($$–$) is right next door, alongside a supermarket and bakery (Boulangerie et Patisserie El Vadel). A couple of blocks away, **Hotel Oum Grein** (north of RN1; ☎ 45 23 05 76; m 33 33 12 12; 1,000UM dbl; **$$**) is a step down in price and quality, while **Auberge Galaxy** (RN1; m 49 22 11 98, 42 92 21 81; 800UM dbl; **$**) at the eastern edge of town is the cheapest (and grubbiest) – but only if you're willing to bargain, as the lackadaisical management has been known to quote ridiculous prices on first enquiry.

ENTERING THE ADRAR REGION

Departing Akjoujt, the landscape of rocky *reg* plains and dunes begins to shift. A series of imposing black mountains rise on the horizon, making a dramatic backdrop for the hardy scrub and grasses eking out their living on the plain below. This area, known as **Arâguîb el Jahfa**, straddles the road about 10km east of Akjoujt, and has been recognised as an Important Bird Area since 2001, with populations of African collared-dove (*Streptopelia roseogrisea*), pale rock martin (*Ptyonoprogne obsoleta*) and white-crowned wheatear (*Oenanthe leucopyga*), among others.

The dunes of **Erg Amatlich** (page 183) are soon also visible to the south, with multiple tracks departing the road as you leave the rocks of Arâguîb el Jahfa behind. Continuing east, the Adrar massif's westernmost extension soon rises up between you and the dunes, cutting them off from the road. These cliffs, known as **Ibi El Akhdar** (Ibi Noir) and **Ibi El Abiod** (Ibi Blanc), are also recognised as an Important Bird Area, where small springs and gueltas in the rock attract populations of crowned sandgrouse (*Pterocles coronatus*), Nubian bustard (*Neotis nuba*), Pharaoh eagle-owl (*Bubo ascalaphus*) and more. The cliffs pull progressively closer to the road as you approach the village of **Aïn Ehel Taya**, where the road first ascends to the mesas and valleys of the Adrar. From here, the regional capital of Atar sits just under 40km to the northeast.

ATAR

Situated at the heart of the Adrar, Atar (أطار; population 35,170) is not only the regional capital, but also the most important crossroads and transport hub anywhere in northern Mauritania (inland of the coast, at least). Though today it doesn't even crack Mauritania's top ten largest cities, Atar has long been the cradle of Moorish power in the north, and served as the capital of the Adrar Emirate, which refused negotiations with the colonialists and was the last of Mauritania's traditional emirates to fall under French control in 1909. It then became an important military and administrative base for the French, and even became host to Mauritania's first airport in 1925.

Situated at the meeting point of several oueds, the city sits at around 230m of altitude – higher than the plains to the west, but lower than the Adrar highlands surrounding it. As such, access to Atar is via mountain passes in all directions, so no matter where you're approaching from, the drive will be spectacular. Most would say the city itself is somewhat less of a stunner, however, and it's true that Atar rather lacks the evocative atmosphere and historical sights found in the ancient ksour and oases nearby. But this workaday regional hub and market town remains one of Mauritania's most important centres for Moorish culture – and has a fine museum dedicated to just that, along with a small historical quarter and a teeming modern town to explore.

So while most people tend to use Atar as a logistical base for excursions into the surrounding desert – and for that it's an excellent choice – the buzzing market, surprisingly compelling museum and a couple of colonial relics dotted around the city make it a worthwhile stopover in its own right as well, if only for a glimpse of modern life in a Moorish metropolis, warts and all.

HISTORY Adrar was founded by a group of religious dissidents from Chinguetti in the 17th century. The schism which separated this tribal grouping, known as the Smacides, from their neighbours in Chinguetti arose over doctrinal matters regarding the conduct of prayer, and they decamped to what is now Atar, founding the first mosque here in 1674. The town grew into a stopover for trans-Saharan trade, as well as a centre for agriculture and date-palm cultivation utilising the several oueds that traverse the surroundings.

Atar then became capital of the Adrar Emirate after its founding c1732. The Adrar Emirate was the last of Mauritania's traditional emirates to be founded, and famously resisted the French political advances, refusing to submit to outside control as their contemporaries in Trarza, Brakna and Tagant had done. Instead, the Adrarois, led by Cheikh Ma El Ainin, famously fought the French invaders until overrun by Colonel Henri Gouraud and his invading colonne de l'Adrar (Adrar Column) in 1909. The city quickly became one of France's most significant centres in Mauritania, though sporadic raids against French interests would continue until the surrender of the dissident Rgueibat tribal leadership in 1933.

Upon independence, Atar was among the country's most important cities (it was the first to be electrified in the 1950s), and a strong candidate to be the new nation's capital. It was ultimately passed over in favour of Nouakchott for a variety of reasons, not least among them that this northern city was too inextricably linked to the Bidhani Moor population to credibly administer and unite as large and fractious nation as the new Mauritania.

The years of post-independence drought that ravaged Mauritania hit Atar particularly hard, and the 1970s saw the city shrink as many residents, newly

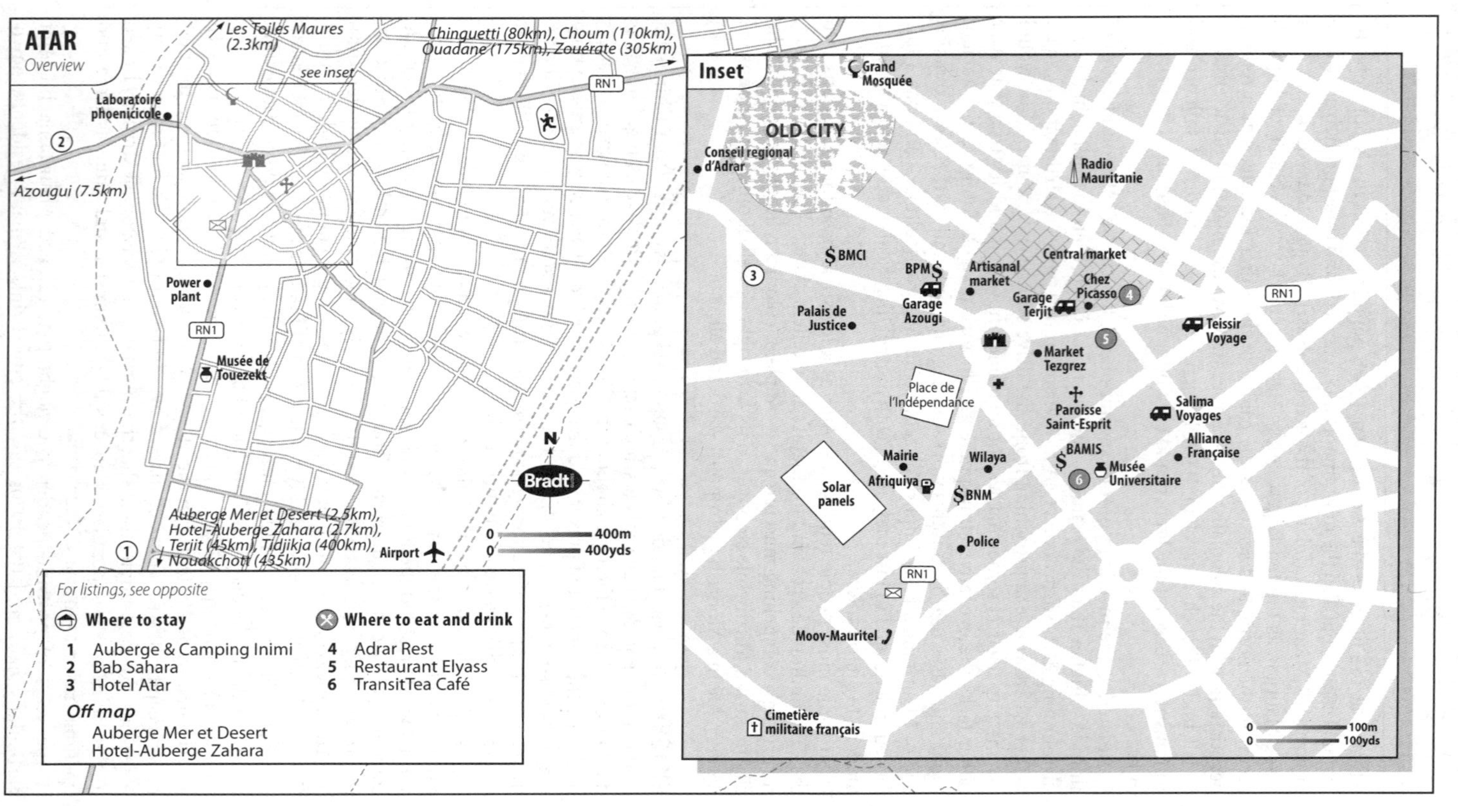
ATAR
Overview
Les Toiles Maures (2.3km)
Chinguetti (80km), Choum (110km), Ouadane (175km), Zouérate (305km)
see inset
RN1
Laboratoire phoenicicole
Azougui (7.5km)
Power plant
Musée de Touezekt
Auberge Mer et Desert (2.5km), Hotel-Auberge Zahara (2.7km), Terjit (45km), Tidjikja (400km), Nouakchott (435km)
Airport
N
Bradt
0 400m
0 400yds
For listings, see opposite
Where to stay
1 Auberge & Camping Inimi
2 Bab Sahara
3 Hotel Atar
Off map
Auberge Mer et Desert
Hotel-Auberge Zahara
Where to eat and drink
4 Adrar Rest
5 Restaurant Elyass
6 TransitTea Café
Inset
Grand Mosquée
OLD CITY
Conseil regional d'Adrar
Radio Mauritanie
BMCI
BPM
Artisanal market
Central market
Chez Picasso
Garage Terjit
Garage Azougi
Palais de Justice
Teissir Voyage
Market Tezgrez
Place de l'Indépendance
Paroisse Saint-Esprit
Salima Voyages
Alliance Française
BAMIS
Musée Universitaire
Mairie
Wilaya
Afriquiya
BNM
Solar panels
Police
Moov-Mauritel
Cimetière militaire français
0 100m
0 100yds

pauperised by the losses of their herds and farms, fled to the growing capital city. Another blow arrived in 1984, when catastrophic floods destroyed up to two-thirds of the entire city. Significant rebuilding has taken place since then, but much of Atar's historical architecture was lost forever.

The first charter flights to Atar landed in 1996, kicking off formalised tourism in the region, and it seems that Atar has at least somewhat turned a corner in the 21st century: the city's population is no longer declining, and in fact grew by almost 50% between the year 2000 and today.

GETTING THERE AND AWAY

By air Atar's **airport** is at the south end of the city, and though there were no domestic flights at the time of writing, it's possible to fly here directly from France! Point-Afrique (w point-afrique.com/vols-atar) run weekly charter flights from Paris between October and March. Tickets cost around €350 each way, but there are sometimes significant discounts at the edges of the season. The airport has a foreign exchange desk, as well as an information kiosk from the Office National de Tourisme.

By road Atar is the most important route junction in northern Mauritania, and as such has a large selection of direct bus connections. Multiple companies run minibuses to **Nouakchott** (7hrs; 500UM) in the mornings and afternoons daily. It's also possible to go directly to **Nouadhibou** with Salima Voyages (m 43 43 43 61), which run direct minibuses in either direction on Mondays and Thursdays (11hrs; 1,200UM), departing at 06.00 for the 725km journey via Benichab. Atar is also well connected to **Zouérate** (5hrs; 500UM) with minibuses departing every morning and afternoon, including with Salima Voyages (m 43 43 43 61), Eljewda Voyage (m 48 83 82 80) and Tiriss Voyage (m 49 40 81 53, 36 40 57 57). Zouérate-bound vehicles can also drop you in **Choum** (2hrs; 250UM).

Several companies also connect south on the new tarmac road to **Tidjikja** (6hrs; 400km; 700UM) daily, including Jreiv Voyage (m 44 44 62 67, 33 44 62 67) and Tagant Transport (m 47 50 58 26), departing mid-morning around 09.00–10.00.

For local destinations like **Ouadane** (4hrs; 500UM), **Chinguetti** (1½hrs; 250UM) or **Terjit** (1hr; 200UM) there are shared taxis which depart on an ad hoc basis. Note that if you wish to visit both Ouadane and Chinguetti, *go to Ouadane first* (there is usually a vehicle departing Atar around 14.00), as it is much easier to find a vehicle from Ouadane to Chinguetti than it is the other way around.

WHERE TO STAY *Map, opposite, unless otherwise stated*

Note that there are also several options 8km northwest of the city in Azougui (page 177).

Hotel Atar Azougui road; m 32 03 75 75; e hotelatar@gmail.com; w hotelatar.com. Inaugurated at the end of 2023, these are certainly the most upmarket rooms in town, built with an eye towards the various ministers & other dignitaries on official business in Atar. It's not cheap, but fully modern. *3,000UM dbl, 4,000UM suite, all rates B&B.* **$$$$**

✷ **Bab Sahara** Azougui road; m 47 81 31 47, 41 50 54 23, (+31) 610 545 839 (Netherlands); e info@bab-sahara.com; w bab-sahara.com; f. Set in a shady grove on the west side of town, this has been the go-to address for travellers in Atar for many years. The 2024 death of founder Justus Buma threw its future into question, but his partner Leonie has stepped ably into the breach & it remains a haven for travellers & overlanders, with plenty of parking, cosy rooms with local character, & good meals available. *1,300/1,450UM en-suite dbl with fan/AC; 1,000/1,150UM dbl* *using shared bath & fan/AC; 300UM bed in shared khaïma.* **$$**

Hotel-Auberge Zahara Azougui road; m 43 34 34 34, 26 38 30 20. Though it's a bit out of the way at the southern edge of town, the new rooms here are centred around a green courtyard & very trim; all come with en-suite hot water. *1,500UM dbl.* **$$**

Les Toiles Maures [map, page 176] Azougui back road; m 46 55 35 35; e lestoilesmaures@gmail.com; w lestoilesmaures.net; f. This is a well-loved rural escape in a quiet spot 2.5km north of the city, with mountain views & even a plunge pool. The recently renovated en-suite rooms are modern & comfortable, & there's plenty of shade in the palm-filled garden. *1,500UM dbl B&B.* **$$**

Auberge & Camping Inimi Akjoujt road (RN1); m 27 55 45 37, 47 55 45 37; e camping.inimi@yahoo.fr; w campinginimi.blogspot.com; f. Headquarters of the tour agency of the same name & operating here since 2007, this is a fine pick for budget travellers looking to arrange regional tours. The facilities are basic but clean & orderly, though they lack the charm of Mer & Desert (see below). All rooms use shared ablutions & there's plenty of parking for overlanders. *700UM dbl or trpl.* **$**

✷ **Auberge Mer & Desert** Akjoujt road (RN1); m 22 37 79 89. This pleasant & rural-feeling compound on the south side of town is run by the lively & accommodating Aisha, who is happy to help with anything she can. The rooms come in a variety of configurations, but all are done up in an appealing & eclectic desert style, & the prices are hard to beat. *700/900UM en-suite dbl/trpl with AC.* **$**

WHERE TO EAT AND DRINK *Map, page 172*

Though Atar has numerous good options for accommodation, restaurants are much slimmer pickings. There are a couple of simple & decent local eateries to the east of the main roundabout, including **Adrar Rest** (m 30 40 22 25; $) and **Restaurant Elyass** (m 26 42 20 02; $), both of which do a rotating selection of Mauritanian favourites like thiéboudiène, couscous or méchoui barbecue. The new **TransitTea Café** (m 48 17 55 53, 30 60 27 34; $) in the city centre is also worth a mention, as it's under the same ownership as the Time For Mauritania tour agency (page 112) and is a pleasant place to catch the football over a coffee, juice or shawarma. They also have Wi-Fi.

OTHER PRACTICALITIES There are several **banks** with ATMs accepting visa represented in Atar, including BMCI and BAMIS; it's also possible to change money here. To stock up for trips into the desert, the Market Tezgrez **supermarket** on the main roundabout is impressively well stocked. For **medicines**, the Depot Pharmacie Melanine (m 22 45 29 95) sits just on the main roundabout. Atar is also home to a new **hospital**, the Centre hospitalier d'Atar, which was inaugurated in 2023 and sits on the Nouakchott road 5.5km south of the main roundabout.

It has also traditionally been possible to extend your **visa** at the Atar airport if you went to see the immigration officers before the Point-Afrique flight from Paris arrived, but it's not clear how the January 2025 introduction of the e-visa has affected this process.

WHAT TO SEE AND DO While most people use Atar as little more than a logistical base for excursions further afield in the Adrar, there are a few sights in this Moorish metropolis worthy of attention before you slip off into the desert.

Any exploration of Atar would do well to start out at the **Musée de Touezekt** (Akjoujt Rd, RN1; m 36 61 35 79, 44 28 44 55; e museetouezekt@gmail.com; f), which is home to one of the most important historical collections in Mauritania. Curator El Khalil Ould Dah N'Tahah is a passionate historian who took it upon himself to begin collecting artefacts in 2002 and opened the Touezekt Museum in the process. Today it's the only institution of its kind in Atar, counting more than 6,000 objects in its collection, which range from ancient Neolithic arrowheads to medieval Islamic manuscripts and colonial-era rifles, plus traditional leatherwork and implements of nomadic life. There's technically another museum in town, the **Musée Universitaire**, and though it's officially connected to the Université de Nouakchott Al-Aasriya, it seemed to be inactive on last inspection. Down the block, the **Alliance Française** (m 22 80 69 80; e afm.atar@gmail.com) mostly focuses on French classes and the like.

As in other Mauritanian cities, few colonial relics survive, and those that do are frequently still in use by either the military or other state organs (and as such not open to the public), but Atar is in fact home to at least one significant colonial relic in the form of the **Cimetière militaire français** (French Military Cemetery; Akjoujt Rd, RN1). The tidy rows of whitewashed markers here in fact commemorate more Africans than Frenchmen, with 176 of the 252 tombs honouring African soldiers who fought in service of France. The graves of 44 hold the remains of French soldiers, with the remaining 32 honouring predominantly military wives and children. In contrast to some other historical gravesites in Mauritania (such as that of Coppolani in Tidjikja or the mysterious memorials of Boghé), the multi-confessional cemetery here is kept scrupulously neat and benefited from a full restoration in 2004. It's usually locked, but easy enough to peek over the wall. Not far away, the **Paroisse Saint-Esprit** (w evechenkc.org) Catholic mission represents another unexpected French legacy in town, though it occupies a modern building (but built in traditional local stone). Despite the near-total lack of a local congregation, it's been operating here continuously since 1955. On the western side of town next to the Laboratoire phoenicicole (date-palm cultivation laboratory), the arcaded **Conseil régional d'Adrar** (Adrar Regional Council; Akjoujt Rd/RN1) also dates to the colonial era, and originally served as the city's first hotel and bar, managed by a famously strong-willed proprietress named Lilette. In a satisfying historical echo, Atar's newest hotel now happens to sit just opposite, though one suspects the bar may be a bit less lively than in Lilette's day!

Atar, of course, also has a long pre-colonial history before the French ever came sniffing around, but much of the city's historic architecture was destroyed in a set of catastrophic floods that took place in 1984. These destroyed some two-thirds of the entire city, taking much of Atar's historic **quartier ksar** with it. And though many of Atar's historic buildings continue to fall victim to damage or redevelopment, the old quarter's alleyways are still worth a quick wander. The **grand mosque** at its centre, though claiming a pedigree dating back to 1674, has clearly been remodelled however many times in the intervening centuries; today it looks decidedly non-ancient, but is nonetheless worth a look for its aesthetic angular style.

The central roundabout is home to an attractive **archway** built in local stone and ever-so-slightly giving off the feel of an Adraroise Arc de Triomphe. On one side of this roundabout, you'll find the city's **Place de l'Indépendance** where important official ceremonies are held, while on the other is the **marché artisanal** (artisanal market). Here, a handful of sellers under tents sell objects in stone, metal and leather, along with haouli shawls, wood carvings, and assorted jewellery and nomadic bits and bobs. This sits just in front of the **main market hall**, where vendors hawk everything an Atar resident could wish for, from tea sets to T-shirts and dates to daraas. The market spills out of the main hall and continues for several blocks to the east, where the streets remain chock-a-block with the comings and goings of commerce large and small. Here you'll also find **Chez Picasso** (m 26 40 24 03) just east of the roundabout, where the friendly proprietor has a small selection of souvenirs including carvings, cloth, jewellery and clothes.

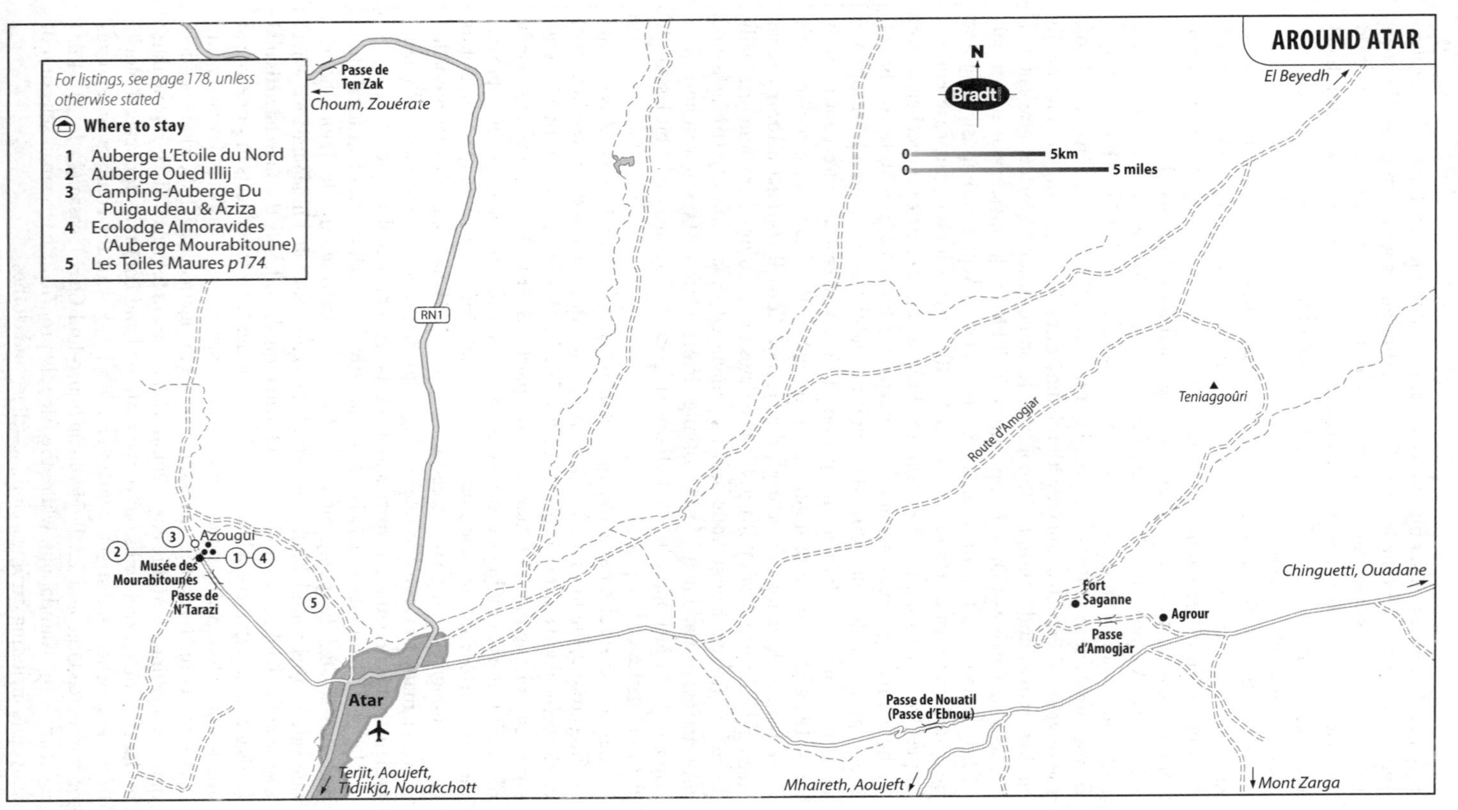
AROUND ATAR
El Beyedh
N
Bradt
0
5km
0
5 miles
For listings, see page 178, unless otherwise stated
Where to stay
1 Auberge L'Etoile du Nord
2 Auberge Oued Illij
3 Camping-Auberge Du Puigaudeau & Aziza
4 Ecolodge Almoravides (Auberge Mourabitoune)
5 Les Toiles Maures p174
Passe de Ten Zak
Choum, Zouérate
RN1
Route d'Amogjar
Teniaggoûri
Azougui
Musée des Mourabitounes
Passe de N'Tarazi
Atar
Fort Saganne
Agrour
Passe d'Amogjar
Chinguetti, Ouadane
Passe de Nouatil (Passe d'Ebnou)
Terjit, Aoujeft, Tidjikja, Nouakchott
Mhaireth, Aoujeft
Mont Zarga

A few steps to the east, a large stone **mosque** was built here during the colonial period, but was rejected by the local population as a foreign-imposed fake. It was torn down and replaced after independence, and while its concrete replacement Mosquée Enour may have appeased the pious, few architects would be likely to agree. Just over 1km east of here, the **stadium** is home to local squad FC Teïssir d'Atar, and the **livestock market** (marbatt) sits about 100m beyond, on the south side of the road.

West of the city centre, the Oued d'Atar is dotted with **market gardens** and **palm orchards** running the length of the city, and makes for a fine place to walk in the mornings or evenings, outside the heat of the day. The well-known Bab Sahara auberge (page 173) sits just across the oued in the village-feeling Edebay neighbourhood on the other side.

AZOUGUI

Set in a long, steep-walled valley 3km across and just under 10km northwest from Atar, the small town of Azougui (آزوكي) sits at the foot of the **Passe de N'Tarazi** (N'Tarazi Pass) and stretches north up the valley bottom along the west side of the Oued d'Atar. The views from the pass are certainly impressive, but Azougui is best known for its historical pedigree rather than its dramatic landscapes – though it's got no shortage of either. The village sits alongside a massive palmeraie, dramatically sandwiched between the oued and the high, rocky cliffs behind, and makes a fine base to drop your bags (or rest your camels) for a couple of days.

Azougui earned its historical bona fides as the first major base for the **Almoravids**, an 11th-century politico-religious movement that grew out of the Berber Sanhadja Confederacy, which conquered the wider region and monopolised much of the caravan trade in the western Sahara nearly overnight. It was a short-lived prosperity, however, and today Azougui is a fair bit sleepier than all that historical conquering and trading might imply. The relics of this history are there in plain sight, however, and the ruins of the Almoravid Fort bear witness to the long-lost moment nearly 1,000 years ago when this unassuming oasis town was, however briefly, the most important centre of political power between the Senegal River and Marrakesh.

HISTORY Led by theologian Abdallah ibn Yasin, the Almoravids, primarily composed of Lamtuna Berber warriors (one of the three tribes making up the Sanhadja Confederacy), launched a lightning campaign in the 1040s that would quickly see them take control of much of the western Sahara and Maghreb. They were therefore able to control and profit handsomely from the most important trans-Saharan caravan routes, and by the 1050s Azougui had become one of their most significant outposts. Not all the Sanhadja were pleased with the Almoravid ascendancy, however, and the 1056 Battle of Tabfarilla which occurred near Azougui saw Lamtuna Almoravid forces defeated by Sanhadja armies from the Gadala tribe.

Nonetheless, the Almoravids continued to consolidate their control and the 11th-century Andalusian geographer Al-Bakri describes Azougui as the 'Almoravid capital', adding that it was home to not only military functions, but a qadi (judge) and 20,000 palms in the surrounding oasis as well. Historian Al-Idrisi claimed that Azougui was the first major caravan stop in the Sahara at the time, taking just 13 days from Sijilmasa (apparently his camels were quick!).

Though the Almoravids moved their capital to Marrakesh in 1062, Almoravid leader Abu Bakr ibn Umar (Abdallah ibn Yasin was killed in 1059) would nonetheless utilise Azougui as their southern base until his own death in 1087. The Almoravid entity would continue to rule for several decades beyond, but it ultimately ceased to exist nearly as quickly as it arose, and had all but disappeared by the mid-1100s. The capital city of Azougui would soon be overtaken in importance by the growing settlements of Chinguetti and others, becoming again one desert oasis among many in the Adrar.

WHERE TO STAY AND EAT *Map, page 176*

Azougui has a larger-than-expected selection of accommodation for its size, with several comfortable options that would make a fine alternative if you'd rather stay outside of Atar. All of those listed are within 500m of the Passe de N'Tarazi except the Camping-Auberge Du Puigaudeau & Aziza, which is a further 1.25km north. There are no bespoke restaurants in Azougui that we could find, so most accommodation can arrange meals without trouble.

Auberge L'Etoile du Nord m 48 66 11 11, 36 30 39 96; e aubergeetoiledunord@gmail.com. This is a neat, orderly & new(ish) address offering trim modern rooms in concrete tikit-style houses with AC, fridge, TV & en-suite hot water. They were only serving b/fast at the time of writing. *1,200UM dbl.* **$$**

Auberge Oued Illij m 26 26 56 83; f. They went a bit heavy with the paving stones between the winding paths at this mid-sized resort, but the modern en-suite rooms & round houses are pleasant & well equipped – hard to quibble with. *1,200/1,500UM dbl round house/room.* **$$**

✷ **Camping-Auberge Du Puigaudeau & Aziza** m 46 45 49 16; e o.puigaudeau@gmail.com; w auberge-puigaudeau-aziza.dromy.co; f. The extraordinarily friendly & knowledgeable owner Mamine is reason enough to stay at this family-run auberge, but the tidy rooms & khaïmas, pétanque pitch & plunge pool seal the deal. It's nothing fancy, but run with heart & Mamine can arrange all excursions in the area. *800/1,000UM dbl (sleeps up to 4) with/without AC.* **$**

Ecolodge Almoravides (Auberge Mourabitoune) m 42 57 19 45; e almoravidesland@gmail.com; f. The first compound at the bottom of the pass, with a palm-lined drive & combination of thatched tikit huts & rooms in either bedroom or majlis salon style. It's also home to the Musée Almoravides (see below), which is worth a stop. Plunge pool, though may be out of service. *800UM dbl (sleeps up to 4) using shared bath.* **$**

WHAT TO SEE AND DO Considering the town's legacy, most people's first stop in Azougui is at the former **Almoravid Fort** (sometimes also referred to as the Almoravid citadel), which is right in the centre of town. It dates at least in part to the 11th-century Almoravid period during which Azougui served briefly as the capital of a region stretching from today's Morocco to Senegal, but you'd be hard-pressed to see the resemblance today. Set inside a fenced-off 1ha parcel, the low walls of the fort's remains, all but destroyed and partially overgrown with tamarisk, require a bit of an archaeologist's imagination to get much out of (particularly if the man with the gate key isn't around). That being said, a new excavation – the first in 25 years – was announced in 2025, and a collaborative team from the University of Nouakchott and the French Centre national de la recherche scientifique (CNRS) had just broken ground at the time of writing. A short walk to the northwest lies the unadorned **tomb** (or cenotaph, depending on which side of a byzantine theological debate you fall on) of noted 11th-century theologian Imam al-Hadrami, who was the Almoravid qadi in Azougui until his death in 1095.

Despite the promise of the new round of excavations, to really get a sense for the Almoravid history of the town, your best bet today is to aim for the **Musée Almoravides** (on the main road; ⌚ 10.00–14.00 & 16.00–20.00 daily; 100UM) inside the guesthouse of the same name. This unexpected collection features an array of ethnographic artefacts on Mauritanian traditional life, as well as a thorough set of informational panels detailing the Almoravid movement and its history in Azougui and beyond – but note they're in French and Arabic only.

The **palmeraie**, a delicious layer of bright green nestled between the beige of the valley floor and the brown of the rocks behind, stretches some 8km along the Oued d'Atar between Azougui and the neighbouring village of Teyarett to the north and makes for an appealingly shady walk between the carefully tended plots. It's also possible to just keep going north up the valley from Azougui; the shade mostly runs out north of Teyarett, but you'll reach the main Atar–Choum road at the bottom of the Passe de Ten Zak (page 186) after about 18km.

On the west side of the valley directly facing Azougui and Teyarett, you'll also find a couple of perennial **gueltas** in the two oueds that cut west into the valley wall, Oumm Lemhar (⊕ 20.5870, -13.1462) and Oued Illij (⊕ 20.6338, -13.1410). These seasonal watercourses narrow significantly into dramatic **canyon** formations after 1.5–2.5km; it's possible to hike out here, though you may quickly find your way blocked by cliffs or water unless you bring a local guide along.

SOUTH OF ATAR

Heading south from Atar, you reach the turn-off for **Barrage de Séguélil** (Séguélil Dam) at the **Passe d'Hamdoun**, 25km south of the city. Here, a rock engraving commemorates the second Compagnie de Pionniers de Mauritanie, who built the first road up the pass here in 1942–43. The 19-million-m³ capacity dam was first filled in 2019, and sits at the end of a 3km tarmac spur road. You can walk out on to it and take in the views over the flooded valley, where depending on the season palm trunks still poke above the waterline.

Back on the main road and continuing south, it's 9km further to the junction where the roads to Nouakchott and Tidjikja split. Unsurfaced tracks leading into the Vallée Blanche also branch off to the south from here. Following the road to Nouakchott, you pass the **Musée Amatil** (m 22 01 91 18; f; ⊕ 20.2590, -13.2155; 50UM) after 4km on your left. The rather dusty museum (you may have to go hunting around for the keyholder) is a regular photo opportunity for government dignitaries and the like, as it commemorates one of the last resistance battles in the colonial takeover of Mauritania. Here at Amatil, Adrar warriors led by Ma El Ainin fought against French forces led by Colonel (later General) Henri Gouraud (for whom F'Dérick was once named) in a December 1908 battle that was among the largest in the 1908–09 campaign to 'pacify' the Adrar. The French would take final control later in 1909 after occupying most of the Adrar's palmeraies. The exhibits include a selection of historical photos, colonial-era weapons and some nomadic implements of the time. The Amatil oasis (⊕ 20.2315, -13.2075), from which the museum takes its name, sits about 3.5km to the south along a rough track.

Just 1km west from the museum and down the escarpment you reach the village of **Aïn Ehel Taya**, gateway to the Adrar. West of here, you are quickly back on the burning plains.

TERJIT Perhaps the most spectacular desert oasis anywhere in the country, Terjit is truly the stuff of storybook desert fantasy. Surrounded by barren, flat-topped mesas at the bottom of a high and progressively narrowing valley, this picturesque village is, like so many across the Adrar, a tiny community still reliant on the rhythms of the herds and the seasons of the date palm. But thanks to its astonishing setting, it's also become one of the must-see stopovers on any tourist circuit of the Adrar. Arriving from the south, the fantastical **Passe de N'Tourvine** is another must-stop,

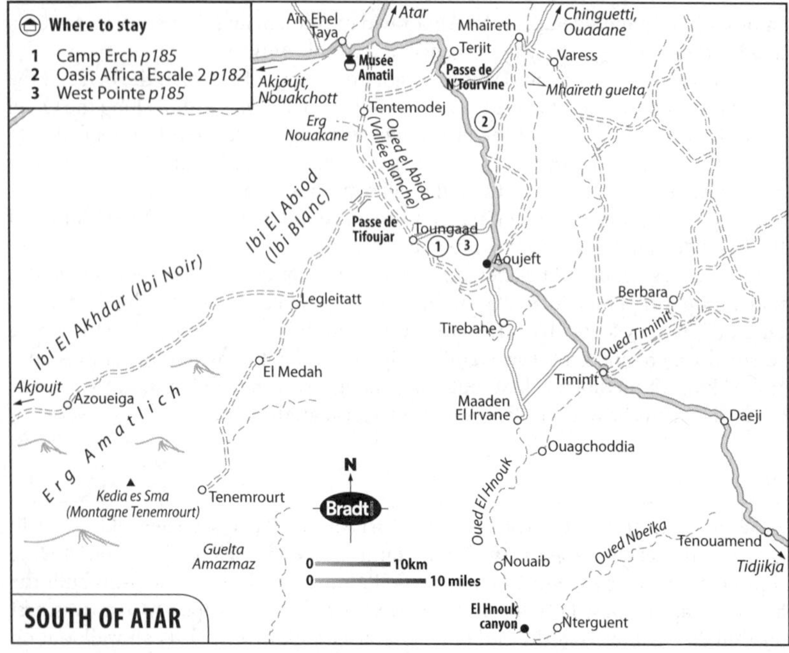

offering some of the Adrar's most expansive views just over 2km south of the Terjit turn-off; arriving from the north, the bird's-eye overview of this dramatic corner is emphatically worth the detour if you can.

Terjit village itself sits alongside a long palmeraie on the valley floor, which grows denser and denser as you continue through the settlement towards the end of the valley. Here, rather than facing a dead end, you instead plunge into a narrow canyon so dense with palms they blot out the sky – where all memory of the baking desert outside is forgotten in an instant. The palm trees crane skywards, shaggy crowns peaking near the lip of the narrowing canyon. A small stream zig-zags along the valley floor, and further along, a moss-covered rock face drips with cool, filtered water; multi-coloured plastic buckets just below collect and overflow with this precious bounty. Further still, a natural wading pool beckons, populated with a school of tiny fish ready to nibble the calluses off your dry desert feet.

Getting there and away Terjit is 45km south of Atar, and just 1km off the main surfaced Atar–Tidjikja road. Shared taxis connect to and from Atar (200UM) irregularly, typically a few times throughout the day.

Where to stay All of the accommodation in Terjit is basic, but some of it is very pleasant just the same. Still, don't expect AC, Wi-Fi or charging sockets in the rooms.

Auberge Caravane du Désert On the main road; m 44 30 45 11, 22 30 45 11, 33 30 45 11; e agencecaravanemauritanie@gmail.com. The blue-and-white round houses here are as simple as it gets but very neatly kept, & there are a couple of larger 3-person rooms as well. The bougainvillea-draped gardens are a shady retreat, & the management can arrange all meals & excursions. *600UM dbl.* **$**

Auberge Sahara On the main road; m 46 45 25 94, 37 13 08 16. The stone huts here are undeniably cheap, but they're also looking rather tired, making the other options in town better value. *500UM dbl.* **$**

✷ **Chez Jemal** On the main road; m 36 12 91 84, 46 47 18 36; e jemalterjit@gmail.com. Set in a garden on a small rise inside the valley, accommodation at this friendly address is all in khaïma tents, & there are fabulous views across the valley. The switched-on management is happy to arrange all manner of excursions in the region, including trips by camel, 4x4 & foot. They've got their own little plunge pool, which even had water in it when we dropped by! *250UM pp per night; 150UM b/fast; 250UM lunch/dinner.* **$**

Terjit Oasis m 37 13 08 16, 36 35 86 49; e terjitoasis@gmail.com; . These are the khaïma tents right inside the canyon, & the cool & atmospheric setting here is equally popular for picnicking day-trippers & other visitors. So while it might not be the top choice for privacy, it's a lovely spot & comes with good bath facilities in a newly renovated toilet & shower block. *750UM pp FB, cheaper for bed only.* **$**

What to see and do Following the path from the parking lot and souvenir stand at the entry to the oasis (200UM), you'll walk through the date-palm grove for a few minutes before emerging at a small clearing bordered to the right by a mossy rock wall dripping water. Here, there are a few khaïma tents where you can lounge away the day (or even spend the night, see above), and you're sure to be invited to tea by any Mauritanians here doing the same.

Continuing along, there are two **pools** where you can swim. The first one you'll encounter is a knee-deep natural pool just past the tents. Here, you can bask in the warm water and let the pedicure fish take care of your cuticles, or rather continue along to the second pool for a slightly more bracing (and less fishy) experience. Set more or less at the end of the canyon, the second pool is a shoulder-deep concrete-built box filled directly from the spring, meaning it's very cold indeed! Note also that the oasis's Edenic qualities seem to apply to social mores as well, and while you should by no means try on your *costume d'Adam* or *Eve*, it's perfectly acceptable to don a Western-standard bathing suit for your swim here.

Also here at the second pool, you'll see a concrete staircase leading up a small outcrop, but with the bottom half of the stairs broken off, necessitating the use of an attached rope to scale the rise. Assuming you're reasonably fit, it's not nearly as intimidating as it looks from the bottom, and once you're past the few steps which utilise the rope, it's only a couple of minutes' walk on a not especially steep trail until you emerge from the palms on to the rocks above, from where there are worth-the-effort views over the treetops densely packed into the oasis canyon below.

MHAÏRETH About 9km east of Terjit as the Arabian bustard flies, the fantastically scenic oasis village of Mhaïreth sprawls breezily along the west side of the Oued Aoujeft under a long set of cliffs and dunes running along either side of the valley. Stretching along the oued for more than 6km, there's little separation between the stone-built homes and the numerous palm groves tended by the families here, and a tangle of sandy lanes stretches up and down the valley connecting homes and gardens. The occasional ageless Mercedes trundles its way through the village, but the outside world is otherwise quickly eclipsed by Mhaïreth's oasean charm.

And it's little surprise one finds it so easy to get lost in the arboreal allure: Mhaïreth's palmeraie is among the largest in the Adrar. According to a 2015 survey, there were more than 290,000 palms here, and though a 2021 fire destroyed dozens of homes and hundreds of palms in the village, the oasis remains impressively lush today.

Arriving from the west (ie: from the Atar–Tidjikja road), there's a worthwhile viewpoint about 900m before reaching Mhaïreth at the valley bottom. Look out for a mobile phone mast with some souvenir-seller stalls beneath it on the right side of the road; there are fabulous views over the oasis from just behind the shop stalls here (and a few interesting souvenirs to boot, should you be in the market). Following the road through the village and climbing back up on to the plateau on the east side of the oued (towards Chinguetti/Ouadane), there are equally expansive views over Mhaïreth and the extensive patchwork of palm groves below.

Getting there and away Whether approached from the Atar–Tidjikja or Atar–Ouadane roads, Mhaïreth lies 65km distant from Atar by road. From the turn-off on the surfaced Atar–Tidjikja road, it's a further 13km on a well-graded road to Mhaïreth. Following the Ouadane route, the Mhaïreth turn-off is east of the Passe d'Amogjar near the Agrour rock art site, from where Mhaïreth village is 35km to the south on a graded road.

Shared taxis connect to and from Atar (250UM) irregularly, typically a few times throughout the day. There's no public transport between Terjit and Mhaïreth, but you could walk (or camel) between the two: it's about 20km following the oueds.

Where to stay and eat In addition to the accommodation on offer in Mhaïreth itself (listed here), there's also the **Oasis Africa Escale 2** [map, page 180] (⊕ 20.1778, -13.0461), which is in an isolated spot along the Tidjikja road, 8.5km south of the Mhaïreth turn-off (and a further 2km down a signposted turn-off to the east). Sometimes also called Oasis Teneguev, it's under the same management as the eponymous auberge in Nouakchott and offers stone-built tikit huts and as of 2025 was even seeking volunteers via Workaway (w workaway.info).

Auberge Tembehgit m 47 70 45 10. Follow the road south 2km from Auberge Toul & the main junction. Here you'll find thatched tikit huts in the upper half of the compound, & khaïmas in the palm grove across the road & down below. It's not quite as charming as Auberge Toul, but closer to the gueltas & similarly priced. **$**

Auberge Toul m 47 91 84 73, 46 73 00 22. Once you descend into the valley, this is 1.5km south at Mhaïreth's main junction (this is something of a generous description) where you turn off to cross the oued. It's in a charming leafy compound offering very simple but very photogenic accommodation in large palm-built tikit huts with mattresses & mozzie nets. *400UM pp bed only, 800UM pp FB.* **$**

What to see and do Down in the valley itself, Mhaïreth's vast palmeraie and oued invite relaxed walking and appreciation, and you could easily spend a couple of hours just wandering between gardens and taking in this desert Arcadia. As elsewhere in Mauritania, morning and evening are the liveliest times; most afternoons you'll find the villagers sheltering from the heat. (Not to mention these are also the prime photographic hours to capture such a naturally photogenic village!)

There are also two particularly scenic **gueltas** (perennial pools) along the oued just south of Mhaïreth. The closer (⊕ 20.2368, -13.00394) of the two is 1.3km past Auberge Tembehgit, situated at the confluence of a side channel branching east and the main north–south course of the oued. The further (⊕ 20.2238, -12.9996) sits astride a narrow canyon that rises after another 1.5km south along the oued. Both are easily accessed on foot from the village.

From the first guelta, it's also possible to walk to the neighbouring village of **Varess** (or Farès; ⊕ 20.2451, -12.9628), by following the small side channel in which the pool sits. Continuing east along this oued for 4km, you arrive in the midst of

The smallest and most isolated of Mauritania's ancient *ksour*, Tichitt still lives from traditional means; those who venture this far may spot a camel train passing by PAGE 282

above (SC)

While Atar may lack the atmosphere and sights of the country's historic settlements, it is one of Mauritania's most important centres for Moorish culture PAGE 171

below (EVG/S)

above (SC) Around Es Sba, stone pillars and pinnacles protrude from the sands creating an otherworldly landscape PAGE 303

left (SS) The paintings inside the rock shelters of Agrour are believed to be between 3,000 and 5,000 years old PAGE 190

below (RN/S) Ben Amira is the world's second largest monolith (after Uluru in Australia) PAGE 188

Enjoy spectacular views from the Passe d'Amogjar, east of Atar PAGE 189

above (SS)

The origins of the Richat Structure – 'Eye of the Sahara' – on the Adrar Plateau have been debated since it was first spotted in aerial photos of the early 20th century PAGE 204

right (GM/S)

Terjit (*below left*) is among the Adrar's most popular oases, while Berbara (*below right*) is among its most hidden, but both make for an idyllic desert retreat PAGES 179 & 185

below (both SC)

left (S73/S) The coastline of Banc d'Arguin National Park is best appreciated from the deck of a traditional sailboat PAGE 159

below (SC) Southern Mauritania can be surprisingly steamy, like here along the Sekan River, a marshy tributary of the Senegal PAGE 243

bottom (AK/D) Banc d'Arguin National Park is arguably the most important water bird breeding site in West Africa PAGE 152

The Senegal River is the lifeblood of southern Mauritania, and its shores are lined with hundreds of farming and herding villages PAGE 247

right (SS)

Nomads water their camels along the impossibly remote back route between Tichitt and Oualata PAGE 302

below (RM)

The Imraguen are renowned for their unusual mullet-fishing methods PAGE 40

bottom (SS)

above left (SC) The drinking of *atay* – a type of green tea – is an integral part of daily life for all Mauritanians PAGE 91

above right (RM) Made from sweetened and diluted camel or goat milk, *zrig* is traditionally served as an appetiser or to welcome guests PAGE 92

below (SS) In Oualata, homes are decorated with intricate and beautiful frescoes, inside and out – these are traditionally painted by women PAGE 298

In the south of the country especially, donkey carts known as *charrettes* are a common sight above (SS)

The female stonecutters of Zouérate forage their own semi-precious stones before working them into unique beads and accessories PAGE 214 below left (SC)

Colourful and intricately decorated wooden bedframes (*khabta*) for sale in Kiffa PAGE 274 below right (SC)

Livestock is never far away in this nation of herders, and will occasionally try for a cheeky nibble inside when no one is looking (SC)

THE GUETNA *Peter Hudson*

Having passed the afternoon [drinking tea] I stepped outside the tikit. I walked up to one end of the village [Mhaïreth] and looked at its well-constructed houses; small mud-brick and cement boxes with no windows and firmly shut doors. There was nobody about, so I climbed up the steep side of the valley. The evening view from where I sat down was obscured in the dusty atmosphere, but I could see the sweep of sand on the valley floor, dotted here and there with tikits looking like pieces of flotsam. Soon I saw that the young man who had made the tea was climbing up to me. When he reached me he introduced himself as Ibrahima. He had a round, cheery face, quite shiny with good health. We lit cigarettes that burned like firecrackers in the strong wind, and I asked him why the Ksar was so deserted.

'Oh, there's nobody in the Ksars at this time of year,' he replied.

'You've come at the wrong time. All you'll find are old people and children and servants.'

'What are you doing here, then?' I asked.

'I'm a student in Nouakchott. I'm just here for a short holiday.

The best time of year to be in the Ksars is the *guetna*, the date harvest. Then you wouldn't believe it. All the houses are full and the desert around is full of nomads' camps. There is great merriment and many marriages and arguments and divorces,' he laughed.

'Everyone comes together and exchanges their news of the year. It is a good time, the *guetna*, it's our time to forget our worries and enjoy ourselves.'

From Travels in Mauritania *(Flamingo, 1990)*

Varess's palmeraie, which, though not as large as the one in Mhaïreth, straddles the oued for about 2.5km.

ERG AMATLICH AND SURROUNDS The Erg Amatlich sand sea rises in western Mauritania near Oum Tounsi and runs nearly 300km towards the mountains of the Adrar, cutting a massive beige brushstroke across the landscape more than a dozen kilometres wide. The erg runs mostly parallel to the RN1, with the most common approach from the west departing the tarmac 25km after Akjoujt at Laeraguib.

From here, it's about 50km until the **Ibi El Akhdar** mountain, where the **Ibi El Akhdar** (Ibi Noir) and **Ibi El Abiod** (Ibi Blanc; page 170) rise along the erg's northern shore; a series of sand tracks and stone-built date-palm villages stretch out along an oued tracing the course between mountain and dune. Among these villages is **Azoueiga** (⊕ 19.8735, -13.5533), where one of the tallest dunes in the Erg Amatlich sand sea is found 2km to the southwest (⊕ 19.8563, -13.5607). Azoueiga's palmeraie continues up a narrow valley for a couple of kilometres northeast; if you've got the time and energy to hike into the hills a bit, a few kilometres further will land you at the delightfully hidden Enikel (or Tenchela) palmeraie (⊕ 19.9059, -13.5455), a cloistered clutch of trees and water secreted away at the confluence of two narrow valleys. There's also a set of brilliant white dunes about 5km to the west (⊕ 19.8441, -13.6022), which make a striking contrast with the erg's generally golden hue. Erg Amatlich continues east another 30-odd kilometres until its blowing sands are finally hemmed in by the rising mountains of the Adrar at the village and palmeraie of **Legleitatt** (⊕ 19.9848, -13.2874).

Some 7km southwest of here on the south side of the erg, **El Medah** (⊕ 19.9228, -13.3238) supposedly has one of the largest palm groves in the country, more than double the size of the one at Legleitatt. South past El Medah, the villages start to thin out. About 20km past you reach Tenemrourt, which faces **Kedia es Sma**, or **Montagne Tenemrourt**. Another 20km brings you to the Adrar's very western edge and the wildly remote **Guelta Amazmaz** (⊕ 19.7041, -13.3824) where there's a permanent pool and some engravings. The area surrounding Tenemrourt and Amazmaz is so remote that it was in the mountains south of here where a group of jihadis who had broken out of prison in Nouakchott were discovered hiding out in 2023 after a nationwide manhunt. The Mauritanian authorities 'neutralised' them at the time.

But most travellers head east from Legleitatt, where after 15km or so the **Passe de Tifoujar** (⊕ 20.0941, -13.2041) descends a spectacular sandy pass to the Oued el Abiod or Vallée Blanche (see below), one of the most beloved sights in all the Adrar.

VALLÉE BLANCHE The Vallée Blanche (White Valley) is a long north–south valley following the course of the **Oued el Abiod** between Aïn Ehel Taya and Aoujeft. The landscape here is a microcosm of everything that makes the Adrar so special – towering dunes, imposing rock faces, vertiginous mountain passes, timeless villages and tranquil palmeraies, all seemingly neatly lined up for your enjoyment along the steadily narrowing valley. It's a favourite on visitor circuits in the Adrar, and most tours in the region will pass through here at least once, but there's little sign of this popularity on the ground, and there's no tourist development here: the valley remains home to a clutch of traditional palm-growing and herding villages, and little else.

There are also no roads in the valley, so the soft bottom of the oued serves as the trunk road, with stony tracks branching off here and there to connect the various villages and palmeraies. As elsewhere in Mauritania, don't be surprised to see an ageless Mercedes 190 incongruously picking its way through this otherworldly setting. (And you can ask in Atar for vehicles going to Toungaad for a ride in one of them.) All told, from departing the tarmac near Aïn Ehel Taya to returning to it at Aoujeft is about 45km, depending on which tracks and detours you take.

Heading into the Vallée Blanche from Aïn Ehel Taya and the plains to the north, the valley soon begins to narrow, and after about 8km you reach the first village, Tentemodej (or Te-n-Tamdej), and its associated **Palmeraie de Lemeillah** next door. Just to the south behind this large palmeraie, the impressive dunes of the **Erg Nouakane** rise up on the west side of the valley, pushed up against the high rock walls forming the plateau behind, and leading south for 7 or 8km along the valley's western edge.

This western wall soon opens up on to the **Passe de Tifoujar** (⊕ 20.0942, -13.2041), a spectacular, sand-choked pass leading west to the Erg Amatlich and its surrounding villages like Azoueiga (page 183). Here even the indefatigable Mercedes have to call it quits, and the climb is best appreciated on foot (and watching any 4x4s struggle valiantly alongside). Depending on the day, you may even find a souvenir seller camped out here brewing a pot of atay at the viewpoint.

Another 8 or 9km south along the valley past the Tifoujar turn-off, you reach **Toungaad** village, which is the largest settlement in the valley. Sprawling for several kilometres between the twin mountains of Châtou el Kbîr (to the north) and Châtou eç Çghîr (to the south), the settlement surrounds the magnificent **Palmeraie de Toungaad**. One of the largest in the area, it gives the impression of being quite a bit denser than many of its contemporaries, and is all the more impressive for it. Here, you can dive right in and enjoy the paradisiacal shade and tranquillity, or head for the upper part of Toungaad where there's an expansive viewpoint (⊕ 20.0604, -13.1300) over the palms and up the valley towards Châtou el Kbîr. There are minimal services available in Toungaad, but at the southernmost fringes of town you'll find **Camp Erch** [map, page 180] (⊕ 20.0454, -13.1137; m 41 80 26 99; **$**), an Italian-Mauritanian household offering basic accommodation in a few tents or simple rooms. It's quite an informal affair, so they don't do fixed prices – just discuss what you're after when you get there and you'll make a fair deal. There's also a rather stifling room available above the village shop, **Complexe Toungaad** (⊕ 20.0546, -13.1215; m 46 56 71 08, 33 56 71 08; **$**).

From Toungaad, there's a rocky track leading east over the plateau for 6–7km to **Loudey** village, where there's accommodation at West Pointe (see below), 1km south of the village. Otherwise, keep following the valley south, and after another 8km or so you'll reach the confluence with the Oued Aoujeft; from here you're less than 4km from Aoujeft town (see below) and the tarmac road.

Should you rather keep going south, the valley briefly narrows before opening up on to a plain south of the Oued Aoujeft near the scenic village of **Tenial** (or Tignal; ⊕ 19.9419, -13.0447), overlooking a dune-filled oued and larger settlement at **Tirebane**, 8–10km past the Aoujeft turn-off. Though the Vallée Blanche is now over, it's possible to continue south from Tirebane without doubling back to Aoujeft or the tarmac road by following tracks south out of Tirebane, from where it's just 15km to Oued Timinit and the Sufi village of Maaden El Irvane (page 186).

AOUJEFT AND SOUTHERN ADRAR The Vallée Blanche is eventually joined from the east by the Oued Aoujeft, which leads northeast from the confluence for about 5km to the town of **Aoujeft** (population 5,362). Approached from the road, Aoujeft sits 75km south of Atar, and it's the Adrar region's largest town after the capital. Though it has a large and attractive palmeraie along either side of the oued about 1.5km southeast of the town centre and a small stone-built ksar quarter dating to the 19th century, it's mostly known as a useful stopover for provisioning. Basic services including food, fuel and medicines are available here, but there are no banks with ATM.

There are also a couple of transport agencies, including Emine Pour le Transport (m 42 90 40 08) which runs minibuses between here and Atar, or even direct to Nouakchott, should you not wish to backtrack. There's basic accommodation in town at **Auberge Egunu** (m 30 75 75 35; **$**), but it's nicer to head the 4km or so northwest of the centre to the newly built **West Pointe** [map, page 180] (m 43 72 74 70, 38 37 40 40; w westpointe-mauritania.com; **$$**) if you can, where there's a nice garden, swimming pool (really!), khaïma tents and a handful of rooms.

Continuing south from Aoujeft on the Tidjikja road, you descend into the **Oued Timinit** (⊕ 19.9083, -12.9077) after about 22km, where there are fabulous views over the large dune field running down the riverbed in either direction. The oued leads about 17km east to **Berbara** oasis (⊕ 19.9862, -12.8230), where you'll find an extraordinarily well-hidden permanent guelta. Approached from above, it's almost indistinguishable from the rock-strewn horizon – you could practically drive straight into it, like an unexpected sinkhole. But looking down over the edge is like peering into a parallel, miniature world, where life has been happily going on quite separately from the happenings on the plateau above. The green-blue guelta – even with a small, moss-covered falls – and dozens of palms and grasses make for a stunning, paradisiacal scene.

It's possible to approach Berbara from above via a very stony track running north of the Oued Timinit which takes about 45 minutes from the tar road, or from below via the oued, where you'll ascend the plateau opposite the village of Timagazine (⊕ 19.9740, -12.7916) and continue about 6km until you reach Berbara village. Here you may find a few people, or just as likely not a soul – the diminutive village is only reliably inhabited during the guetna date harvest. From here it's a very steep climb down into and up out of the oasis, but this should take under 15 minutes each way for the sure-footed (who can reward themselves with a swim at the bottom).

If you were to return to the road and instead follow the oued southwest, after 13km or so you'd arrive at the unique village of **Maaden El Irvane** (⊕ 19.8573, -13.0167), whose name means 'the crucible of knowledge' in Hassaniya. Unlike its neighbours, Maaden El Irvane was founded as an intentional community, when Cheikh Mohammed Lemine Sidina settled here in 1975 and sought to found a village according to Tijjânya Sufi precepts, with a focus on solidarity, equality and hospitality. Today some 800 people live here, and the village has become a model in not just social relations, but sustainable agriculture as well. Cheikh Sidina died in 2003 at the age of 95, and his mausoleum in the village remains a destination for pilgrims. His son Taha Sidina carries the torch today as village imam. French agroecologist Pierre Rabhi was involved with the village from 2017 until his death in 2021, and alongside Maurice Freund of Point-Afrique, worked to support it in becoming a model agroecological community; today the village's market gardens produce fruits and vegetables sold in Nouakchott and beyond. There are no guesthouses as such here, but there is always accommodation for visitors – ask to be shown to the *hidra*.

Crossing the oued to the south, the village of **Ouagchoddia** sits atop a rocky outcrop 5km from Maaden El Irvane; from here it's about 19km to the oasis village of **Nouaib** (Nweib, N'Oueibe; ⊕ 19.6932, -13.0436) where there is an impressively dense palmeraie along the Oued El Hnouk, or 'Oued of the Jaws' in Hassaniya. Continuing 8km further south, the name begins to become clear, as the riverbed narrows and narrows as you approach the sheer, imposing rock walls of **El Hnouk** (⊕ 19.6302, -13.0174), where the oued shrinks to just a couple of hundred metres wide. Here, perfectly sheer walls stretch up to 80m high on either side, compressing you through the 2–3km-long canyon and depositing you on the far side where the oued opens up once again. Here, the Oued El Hnouk meets the Oued Nbeïka near the village of **Nterguent** (⊕ 19.6110, -12.9672); the Tidjikja road is roughly 40km northeast of here along the Oued Nbeïka, but the topography here is challenging, so be sure you've got a good navigator if you plan to go this way.

The main road south towards Tidjikja is sparsely populated after this, with the village of **Aïn Savra (Aïn Çefra)** offering the last accommodation before Rachid in the Tagant region (120km further along) at **Auberge Oasis de Desert** (m 37 33 00 66, 48 52 98 36; **$**). From here, the road cuts through a remote stretch of desert studded with barchan dunes. These mobile dunes need regular ploughing to keep them off the roads – which needless to say makes for a fantastic photo opportunity.

CHOUM

Approaching Choum (population 2,168) from the south, you first come down the **Passe de Ten Zak** 30km outside of Atar. (*The Grand Tour* came down this one too, just not using the road.) Continuing northwards and parallel to the plateau to your east, 65km further along you'll find **Aggi** (⊕ 21.1788, -13.1170), where a fort-resthouse once monitored and catered to traffic along the colonial-era Piste Impériale N°1. Today the structure is abandoned and filling with sand, but the adjacent wells are still in use and there are good views from the rooftop.

Arriving in Choum itself, it's hard not to feel a sense of Wild-West desolation as this low-slung town of breezeblock and earth sprawls out before you. Stretched across a baking, treeless plain and bisected by the railway tracks, Choum has none of the oasean charm of its neighbours secreted away on the plateau to its south. Indeed, the town is a modern creation, especially compared to the palm-growing and herding settlements around the plateau, and its raison d'être has been the same since day one: the Iron Ore Train. Choum is home to a large SNIM maintenance and administration base, and represents what is effectively the only stop on the train's 700km journey between Zouérate and Nouadhibou.

There's now an auberge here, which has been a godsend for travellers getting on and off the train, as services here are otherwise quite limited, running to the basics of food, fuel and onward transport, and not much beyond.

WHERE TO STAY

Auberge du Choum West of the centre; m 49 48 10 67, 48 17 55 53. The only game in town, & thankfully it's a good one! Under the same ownership as the Time For Mauritania tour agency & TransitTea Café in Atar, they provide accommodation in a variety of configurations, from standard en-suite rooms to tikit-style thatched huts (with en-suite bathrooms behind) & khaïma tents. Meals can be arranged at request. Note their services may be somewhat limited since the change in rules surrounding riding the train. *300UM pp in a khaïma tent; from 800UM/1,200UM sgl/dbl room.* **$$**

WHAT TO SEE AND DO Most people come to Choum to hop on the train and that's about it. If you're looking for some kind of vintage stationhouse sign saying 'Choum' for a photo op (we did!), there isn't one. The SNIM 'Base de Choum' archway just inside the maintenance yard could do for a photo instead – just be aware you might have to answer the guards' questions first.

Otherwise, there's not much to keep you here, but there are a couple of interesting sites within striking distance of the town. Most easily accessible is the **Choum Tunnel** (⊕ 21.3286, -13.0037), which lies 8km to the northeast and has been dubbed among the finest 'monument[s] to European stupidity in Africa' found anywhere on the continent. Construction of this nearly 2km-long railway tunnel began just prior to Mauritanian independence, and it opened shortly after, in 1962.

Unluckily for the French, an escarpment rises just at the border's right-angle corner (another victim of European mapping from afar) beneath which they had hoped to route the train tracks – but to do this and stay on the plains meant straying into the Spanish-controlled Sahara, however briefly. The Spaniards and French couldn't come to an agreement, so the French decided that it would be cheaper and easier to blast through 2km of pure rock than accept the terms proposed by Spain.

And blast they did, for several years. But despite the blood, treasure and sheer stubbornness involved in completing it, the tunnel was ultimately in use for less than 30 years. The tracks were rerouted in 1991, cutting the very corner that so much effort was spent trying to bypass, and today the train tracks, road and electrical wires connecting Choum to Zouérate all follow the plains instead of going through the mountain. This means that all road and rail traffic technically passes through several kilometres of SADR territory – it seems the Mauritanians and Sahrawis were able to find an agreement where the French and Spanish could not. There are no signboards or any other indicators of crossing the border, however, and it is functionally identical to the rest of the journey.

The tunnel therefore sees no traffic, and is in fact even possible to drive through. This was used to some comedic effect in *The Grand Tour*'s Mauritania episode, though they took more than a little creative licence in implying that it spits you out into a Western Saharan minefield. In reality, you're still very much in Mauritania on the other side – and of course you are, as that's the whole reason the tunnel exists in the first place! Above the tunnel, the troublesome border marker (⊕ 21.3336, -12.9998) and a ventilation shaft into the tunnel are still visible and accessible by a rough 4x4 track.

Unfortunately, Choum is a small place indeed and if you don't have your own wheels it can be tricky to find a vehicle to take you to the tunnel. The Auberge du Choum doesn't have its own vehicle; it's possible, but not guaranteed that they may be able to refer you to someone who does. (The same is true for accessing the nearby Ben Amira Monolith.)

MONOLITHE DE BEN AMIRA

In the opposite direction, 62km to the west of Choum, looms the Monolithe de Ben Amira (Ben Amira monolith; ⊕ 21.2305, -13.6621). Though sources vary on how high it actually is (some say 633m, though 560m may be more accurate), it's in any case the world's second-largest monolith, after only Uluru in Australia. An enormous grey granite inselberg rising straight out of the desert plain, Ben Amira is by far the largest of a wide scattering of rock mountains pockmarking the desert plains on either side of the Mauritania–Western Sahara border, which lies less than 10km to the north. The mountain's surface alternates between enormous fields of smooth rock face, burnished by generations of blowing sand, and jagged, chaotic boulder seas, the midden heaps for millennia of rockslides and erosion sloughed off the mountain's face. Unlike Uluru, climbing Ben Amira is allowed – so long as you're sufficiently motivated – and you're guaranteed to have the mountain just about all to yourself.

Some 7km northwest of here lies **Aïcha**, Ben Amira's 'wife' in monolithic matrimony – she is smaller than Ben Amira, but if you take a spin over to the west side of the rock, it's pretty easy to see why the desert dwellers of old decided that Aïcha was the 'female' of the two. (Guides today have occasionally dubbed it *L'Origine du monde*, in a nod to Courbet's famously explicit painting.) Aïcha's east side is also home to an exhibition of sorts, namely an open-air **rock art gallery**. But unlike most of the rock art found around the Sahara, these works date to the turn of *our* millennium, rather than those previous. Curated by Burkinabé artist Siriki Ky and convened by French tour agent Point-Afrique and SNIM, the Symposium de Ben Amira took place over December–January 1999–2000, and brought more than 15 sculptors here to carve works into the rocks around Aïcha's base. The artists hailed from countries around the world, including China, Colombia, Canada and Côte d'Ivoire, and a wander through the boulders here reveals an extraordinary collection of both abstract and naturalistic forms etched into the landscape. A third inselberg (and/or third wheel?), **Haddad** sits 5km to the northeast of Ben Amira (and 8km southeast of Aïcha).

Since 2020, a number of **bolted climbing routes** have been established up all three inselbergs, and a handful of local mountain guides have now been trained as well. There are now 15 bolted routes up Ben Amira, eight up Aïcha, and four up Haddad, with more likely in the works. Jean-Louis Lauféron and Anne de Bélinay opened the first technical routes here alongside a team of French climbers and doctors, and they have since gone on to create the Médecine et Montagnes du Monde (MMM; w escalademauritanie.com) organisation, which encourages the development of climbing activities on and around Ben Amira. Jean-Louis Lauféron and Philippe Craplet have written a climbing guidebook to the mountain, *Escalades en Mauritanie*, available through the MMM, and the organisation works towards ensuring that the area's development as a climbing tourism destination provides meaningful material and health benefits to the population in nearby villages. There's an interesting photo essay on climbing one of the bolted routes here: w wildmanlife.com/climbing-ben-amera-second-tallest-monolith-sahara.

It's also possible to **hike** the summits by traditional, non-technical routes, but these can reach a 45-degree gradient in parts, so you still have to have good shoes and be sure-footed. Assuming you're prepared, it's also possible to spend an unforgettable night bivouacking at the top! You can reach the summit of Ben Amira via a challenging but non-technical route in less than 2 hours, and can reach the top of Aïcha in less than an hour. See online for information on the hiking routes up Ben Amira (w escalademauritanie.com/ben-amira-voie-normale-450-m-1-heure) and Aïcha (w escalademauritanie.com/ben-aicha-voie-normale-400m-45-minutes). Though comfortable climbers may be able to follow these routes on their own, taking a guide is recommendable, and keep in mind you are several hours from medical assistance at minimum. Another good reason to employ a guide is that officially speaking a permit is required to summit Ben Amira; this may be checked by the gendarmerie in Ben Amira village, and your guide will be able to solicit the required permissions. Finally, for those who'd like to stay a little more earthbound, it's about a 6km walk around the perimeter of Ben Amira, and about 3km around the base of Aïcha.

WHERE TO STAY AND EAT To sleep, there's a beautifully located **camp** (⊕ 21.2380, -13.6664) of khaïma tents on the north side of Ben Amira, which is managed by tour agency Mauritanides Voyages (m 49 00 59 98; e kadimehdi93@gmail.com, kadi@mauritanides.com; w mauritanides.com). Assuming it's not already occupied by a group, individual travellers are welcome with advance notice (€30/40 sgl/dbl in a khaïma, €10 pp b/fast, €20 pp lunch or dinner).

OTHER PRACTICALITIES For water and other (very) basic provisions, there's a **shop** in Ben Amira village (⊕ 21.1985, -13.6779) along the railway tracks 3km south of the mountain. Mauritanides Voyages is also the best point of contact to arrange climbing permissions, gear, guidance and other assistance. If you don't have your own transport, it's better to arrange a visit to Ben Amira from Atar rather than Choum, where despite its nearby location, options to find a vehicle/driver are slim.

EAST OF ATAR

Leaving Atar towards Ouadane and Chinguetti, there are two passes allowing access to the plateau: the **Passe de Nouatil (Passe d'Ebnou)** and the **Passe d'Amogjar**. Surfaced in the year 2000, the Passe de Nouatil is now the primary route to Chinguetti and Ouadane. Former Chinguetti mayor Ould Ebnou financed its construction, so the route has since taken on his name as the Passe d'Ebnou. It's 110km between Atar and Chinguetti via the Passe d'Amogjar, but only 80km via the Passe de Nouatil/Ebnou. And while there are spectacular views to be had on either route, if you've got the time and the transport, it's absolutely worth the detour to the Passe d'Amogjar. (Some of the roughest stretches were surfaced in 2023, making for a slightly more comfortable journey as well.)

The Passe d'Amogjar is a 50km trip from when you leave the main Atar–Ouadane road at a turning 10km east of Atar to when you return to it 32km east of Atar. The

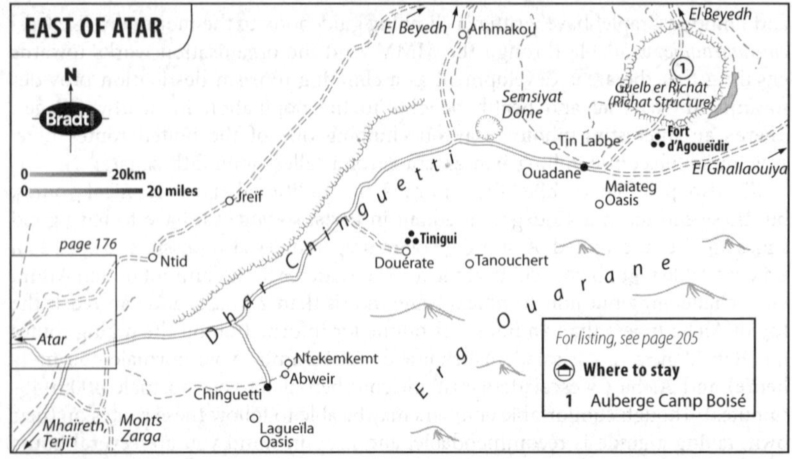

unsurfaced route draws close to the massif as you head northeast out of Atar, taking a long loop around a northeastern promontory of the plateau before looping back on itself, plunging southwest into the valley of the Oued Amogjar. Here, you're driving beneath **Teniaggoûri**, the highest point in the Adrar and second highest in all of Mauritania (which is somewhere between 786m and 820m high, depending on who you ask). The track continues down a valley strewn with boulders and acacias, eventually emerging from the tight-walled valley floor to a series of hairpin bends and expansive viewpoints as you climb the plateau. These expansive views are as strategic as they are impressive, and you'll see a number of ruined lookout posts along the way, where Mauritanian soldiers kept watch for Polisario arriving from the north in the 1970s.

Nearing the top, a 700m side track leads to one of the Adrar's oddest attractions, **Fort Saganne** (w fort-saganne.com; f). Though looking every bit the historical relic, this stone-built fortress dates back only to the prehistoric 1980s, when it was built as part of the set for Alain Corneau's 1984 film *Fort Saganne* – a tale of war and romance in the Sahara that was France's biggest-budget film production ever at the time. And so this unlikely fortress has only seen combat on the silver screen, but still makes a strangely compelling stopover, and is undoubtedly an evocative backdrop for a round of tea or lunch while enjoying the panorama. As you might expect for a movie set, it wasn't necessarily built with longevity in mind, but there's a group of supporters who have organised to sponsor some renovation works. There's often a guardian there, who may or may not charge you a 50UM entry fee, but would regardless appreciate a tip for what is undoubtedly a very lonely job.

Continuing along 2km from the Fort Saganne turn-off and reaching the top of the pass (from which there are incredible views), the track approaches the rock shelters of **Agrour** (m 38 27 07 97, 37 33 98 66). These are home to some of the most intriguing and easily accessible rock art in Mauritania, thought to be between 3,000 and 5,000 years old. The walls here are decorated with ancient ruminants, hunters and herders, and even a giraffe inscribed into the overhang reflecting the great climatic changes the area has seen. The artworks sit behind a locked gate, at which the guardian will collect the 80UM entry fee (or you can ring him if no-one is around). From here, the main Atar–Ouadane road is just 1.5km beyond.

The turn-off to **Monts Zarga** (Zarga Mountains) is just 1km west of here, after which the northern end of the mountains lies just under 25km to the south along a track that starts out decent and deteriorates. Zarga itself is a small, snake-like massif, a narrow, shattered ridgeline with multiple peaks stretching some 20km long and topping out at more than 750m. The mountain is swamped with sand at various points and known for its dramatic contrast between black rock and blonde sand. The dunes and rocks compete for superiority in height, making it possible to climb a section of dune only to find yourself atop a mountain of rock. From here, it's possible to return via the Mhaïreth road, which is about 22km away to the northwest and accessible via desert tracks.

Finally, some 15km south of Monts Zarga, the **Cratère d'Aouelloul** (Gleib Aouelloul; ⊕ 20.2412, -12.6747) is the product of an ancient meteorite strike. Measuring roughly 350m across, this shallow crater sees few visitors, but meteoric remains like kamacite have been found here.

CHINGUETTI The largest and most famous – but also the youngest – of Mauritania's ancient desert ksour, the grey-orange stone city of Chinguetti (شنقيط) was once so influential that the western reaches of the Sahara as a whole were known as *Bilâd ash-Shinguît*, the land of Chinguetti. Frequently invoked as the seventh-holiest city in Islam, it was a storied destination for scholarship and trade that attracted thousands of pilgrims from far and wide, and historians report camel trains more than 10,000 strong departing the city for Mali, Morocco and even Mecca.

But the stone-walled city you visit today, supported with beams and lintels in palm and acacia and built along the shores of an oued 300m wide, is not Chinguetti's first iteration. As ancient as Chinguetti may feel, today's old city was built when the city's original site, a few kilometres up the oued, began to be swallowed up by the dunes of the Erg Ouarane. This enormous sea of sand still looms on the horizon, nibbling at homes on the outskirts, providing for incredible sunset views, and yet again threatening this historic settlement with its even more ancient power.

This 'new' Chinguetti was built in the 13th century and would go on to be a critical stopover for trans-Saharan caravans, boasting more than 20,000 residents during its 17th-century heyday – while today's population is just a quarter of that number, and much of the old city is in a ruinous, semi-abandoned state. But despite the fact the last census counted only 4,844 Chinguettiens, the city's reputation holds fast, retaining an outsized importance in the Mauritanian psyche that belies its much-diminished size. The city's famed five-pointed minaret, built in the late 1200s, remains Mauritania's most iconic symbol: it features on the 1,000 ouguiya note, and there's even a replica in downtown Nouakchott (with another potentially on the way).

But for outsiders, the city's libraries are perhaps Chinguetti's best-known calling card, and the dozen or so families that maintain their traditional libraries here guard them fiercely – much to some conservationists' and curators' chagrin, as they fret about the conditions of these priceless folios. There are a few libraries now open to visitors, managed by hereditary archivists who are undeniably passionate about their patrimony. And while you may not be able to understand the text, there's an undeniable thrill in witnessing these centuries-old repositories of religious, scientific and geographical lore in their birthplace, at home here in this beguiling city of the desert, Mauritania's crucible and crown jewel.

History Depending on your perspective, Chinguetti (whose name comes from the Soninké *sí-n-gèdé*, or 'horse well/spring') began its life as a city in either the 700s or the 1200s. The city's first iteration, Abweir, was founded in the 8th century – some sources say the event took place in the year 777CE, though this may be more a nod to auspicious numerology than hard historical fact – but Abweir was several

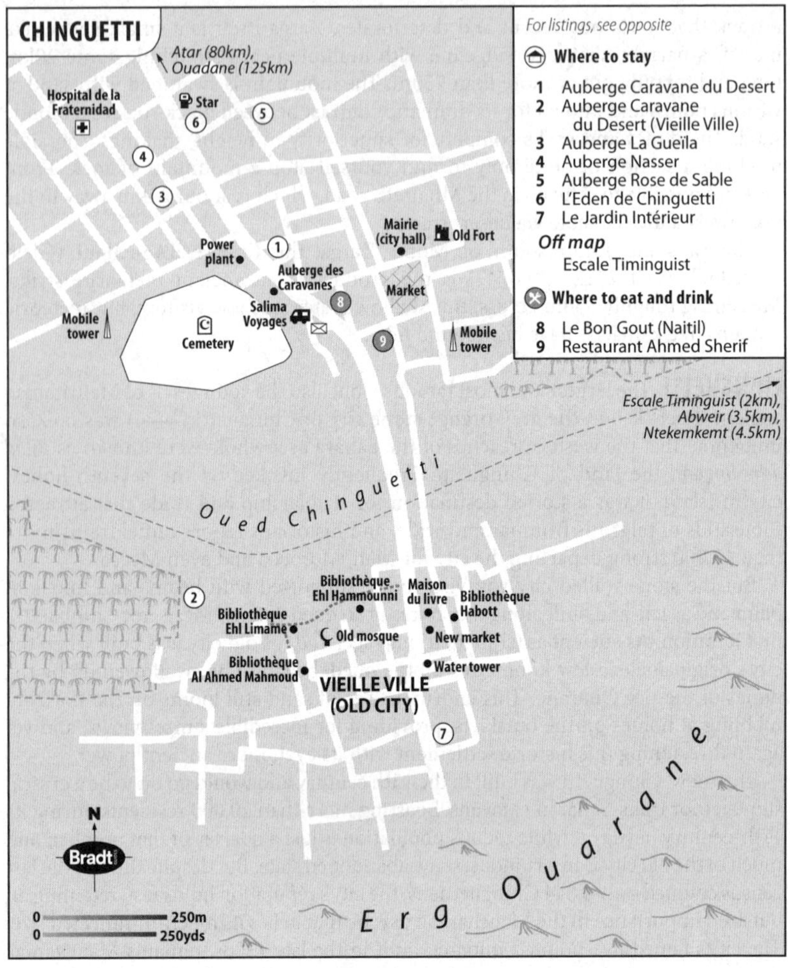

kilometres away from what we now know as Chinguetti. The shifting sands of the Erg Ouarane made Abweir increasingly unliveable, and most residents decamped towards Chinguetti, which decisively superseded Abweir in the 1200s when Chinguetti's famous mosque was first constructed.

Chinguetti was not mentioned by the renowned Arab travellers and geographers of the time like Ibn Battuta, but in fact first enters the historical record by virtue of the Portuguese, with the 1507 Valentim Fernandes Manuscript mentioning it as one of four cities in the 'mountains of the Baffour', named after the pre-Berber group known to inhabit Mauritania (page 18), and now known as the Adrar. In the 16th, 17th and 18th centuries, Chinguetti would become a key stopover on the caravan routes from Sijilmasa to the cities of the south, trading in salt (particularly from the Idjil saltworks near F'Dérick, page 208), wheat, dates and copper from the north for gold, ivory and enslaved people from the south. This was Chinguetti's economic and cultural golden age, and many scholars and traders took up residence in the burgeoning city.

The accelerating reorientation of trade routes away from the Sahara and towards the Atlantic that first began with the arrival of the Portuguese on the Mauritanian coast at the end of the 1400s would ultimately cost Chinguetti its prosperity, and the city entered a decline by the late 19th century from which it has never fully recovered.

The colonial era saw the city become a military centre for French authorities, but it nonetheless remained an isolated outpost through much of the 20th century. Along with Mauritania's three other ancient ksour, Chinguetti was inscribed as a UNESCO World Heritage Site in 1996, and tourism has provided a new source of income in this city that had long outgrown its raison d'etre. The construction of a new road on the Passe de Nouatil (Passe d'Ebnou) in 2000 began to alleviate the city's isolation, and the remaining kilometres to Chinguetti should be surfaced within the lifespan of this edition, connecting this ancient crossroads to a modern highway for the first time. What it all will mean for this stubbornly ancient town in a decidedly modern world *Allahu a'alam!* (God knows best!)

Getting there and away Construction works were underway to surface the 80km between Atar and Chinguetti as of 2025. Until this is done, the road is graded but prone to washboarding. There are a few daily vehicles making the run between Atar and Chinguetti (1½hrs; 250UM), departing when full. It's common for guesthouses in Chinguetti to ring and reserve a seat for you on the next morning's departure to Atar, and they may even pick you up – just ask.

Note that if you wish to visit both Ouadane and Chinguetti and you are approaching via public transport from Atar, go to Ouadane first, as it is much easier to find a vehicle from Ouadane to Chinguetti than it is the other way around.

Alternatively, it's still possible to hitch up a camel and set out into the sands – it's a one-week trip between the two towns by camel, via the isolated oasis of Tanouchert (page 198).

Where to stay and eat *Map, opposite*

There are few bespoke eateries in Chinguetti, so most visitors generally end up eating at their accommodation, where meals generally cost 300–600UM. Exceptions include **Le Bon Gout (Naitil)** (m 37 87 24 04) near the post office and **Restaurant Ahmed Sherif** (m 32 33 35 39) in the old city. The **Lodge du Maure Bleu** (m 20 58 69 07; e lodgemaurebleu@gmail.com; f) was once among the nicest options in town, but closed in 2020; it's possible they will reopen during the lifespan of this edition. There's also accommodation in the dunes south of town at Campement de Chinguitty (Abeir Silence; page 199).

✷ **Auberge La Gueïla** Atar road; m 26 16 49 77, 46 48 25 26; e info@lagueila.com; w lagueila.com. Looking every bit the fortress from the exterior, this gorgeous stone-built courtyard building has a library, lounge, roof terrace & shady interior garden, & the tastefully decorated rooms are perhaps the nicest in town. Uniquely for the area, they also offer massages & wellness treatments, alongside the usual array of trips into the desert, etc. *1,300/1,600UM sgl/dbl B&B.* **$$**

L'Eden de Chinguetti Atar road; m 46 46 25 96, 36 46 25 96; e mahmoudeden@yahoo.fr; w eden-chinguetti-hotel.com. With clean & comfortable rooms decorated in a minimalist Mauritanian style, this is a charming & good value option built around a central courtyard. Owner Mahmoud Ould Beija is a legend in Chinguetti hospitality, and has been working in tourism for more than 30 years. He also owns the **Escale Timinguist**, 2km up the oued east of town, which is built to a similar standard and a fine choice if you're after an even more tranquil desert escape. *1,000UM dbl/twin.* **$$**

Le Jardin Intérieur Vieille Ville; m 47 46 70 66; e leminbahan@gmail.com. In a renovated traditional house on the old side of town, this traveller-recommended address has simple & comfortable whitewashed rooms set around a welcoming garden courtyard. *850/1,700UM sgl/dbl.* **$$**

THE MYSTERIOUS CHINGUETTI METEORITE

Meteor strikes are not necessarily an unusual occurrence in the Mauritanian desert, and their remains – more easily spotted and preserved here in the desert than elsewhere – are often located by nomads and sold. Historically speaking, most strikes and finds have been small, with a few exceptions, such as the strike that formed the Cratère d'Aouelloul (page 191).

But the biggest exception of all was, maybe, the Chinguetti Meteorite. Reportedly measuring some 40m tall by 100m long, French colonial Captain Gaston Ripert recorded the presence of this gargantuan space rock in 1916, touching off more than a century of searching and speculation which remains active to the present day. If found, Ripert's enormous meteor would easily dwarf Namibia's 60-tonne Hoba meteorite, today the largest ever reliably recorded.

But the uncertainty of Ripert's notes – a meteor mountain larger than any known, but seen only by night, under the guidance of nomads some 10 hours by camel outside of Chinguetti – lent themselves to all manner of speculation and treasure-hunting. The 4kg specimen Ripert returned with was enough proof for many, and the reporting of ductile rock needles, which were at the time unknown to science, gave further credibility to his tale.

But the mysterious mountain stubbornly refused to appear! Sent at the behest of the Muséum d'Histoire Naturelle in Paris, explorer Théodore Monod became involved in 1934, searching the deserts around Chinguetti without success for this massive missing mountain, supposedly somewhere less than 45km from the ancient town. He even offered a 1,000-franc reward if someone could lead him to the site.

One might think that would have been the end of the affair; but the unique terrain around Chinguetti, the enormous shifting, living dune sea of the

Auberge Caravane du Desert Atar road; m 44 30 45 11. A bit confusing on first glance, there are in fact 3 locations in Chinguetti associated with this auberge: firstly the large & clearly signposted facility which is no longer functional (other than as space for overlander parking), secondly the unsignposted new building just across the road where there are tidy & comfortable traditional rooms, & thirdly the old city (*vieille ville*) address, which has rooms that are large & comfortable, if somewhat sparsely furnished. *1,200UM dbl.* **$**

Auberge Nasser Atar rd; m 47 46 67 66. With a handful of khaïmas & thatched tikit huts in a sandy compound on the north side of town, this welcoming address isn't long on creature comforts, but it's clearly cared for & the prices are no mirage. *250UM pp.* **$**

Auberge Rose de Sable Atar road; m 27 46 67 63, 47 46 67 63; e amarc9670@gmail.com. The facilities are a little timeworn at this long-serving address, but it's well priced, & friendly owner Cheikh makes up for any shortcomings. As elsewhere, he can arrange all manner of desert activities around town & beyond. *800/1,500UM fan/AC dbl, 1,200UM twin with fan, 400UM dorm bed, 900UM trpl.* **$**

What to see and do As with so many Mauritanian towns, Chinguetti straddles both sides of a wide oued. The old city sits along its southern shore, while the north side is where most of the modern conveniences – those that exist, anyway – can be found, as well as a few colonial-era relics. It's a hot, sandy slog for the 300m crossing, so plan to explore each side of town fully before crossing (back) over.

Starting on the south side of the oued, much of the **vieille ville** (old city) is in a semi-abandoned state, with the centuries-old dry-stone masonry giving up the ghost inch by inch, sometimes slowly and sometimes dramatically collapsing in

Erg Ouarane, meant that it was very much not. Could the dunes have swallowed up Ripert's mountain? They are certainly large enough. For his own part, Ripert continued to swear to its existence, even in later communications with Monod.

The following decades would see scientists from France and the USA mount searches for the missing meteor mountain, but all to no avail. Visual searches, magnetometer readings, all came up empty handed. Monod picked up the task periodically throughout his life, even conducting searches in the early 1990s, when he himself was approaching 90 years old. It was then he finally concluded the meteor could not have been real, writing that:

> The existence of a giant meteorite in the Adrar of Mauritania, largely accepted since 1924, must now be abandoned. There was a mistake on the nature of the rock of a butte that is entirely sedimentary with no trace of metal.

He published a book on the decades-long quest, *Le fer de Dieu: histoire de la météorite de Chinguetti*, alongside Birgitte Zanda in 1992.

Another blow to the story came with a 2001 radionuclide analysis that concluded Ripert's 4kg sample could not have come from an original piece larger than 1.6m. But even today, the mystery lingers and not everyone has these conclusions. Improvements in geo-sensing technology and magnetometry mean that some scholars think now is the time the mystery can be definitively solved. The most recent significant paper on the topic, 'New evidence on the lost giant Chinguetti meteorite', was just published in 2024, and calls for a partnership with the Ministry of Petroleum Energy and Mines to solve the mystery once and for all.

upon itself – so be careful if stepping on roofs and the like! Chinguetti's iconic **vieille mosquée** (old mosque) is the heart of the city, and in many ways, Mauritania as a whole. Built in the late 13th century, the five-pointed minaret towers over old Chinguetti, topped with five clay ostrich eggs meant to symbolise purity and fertility.

These unusual ovoid embellishments make an elegant reminder of how Chinguetti and its sister cities throughout the Sahara were never just isolated outposts, but rather parts of a closely connected system: ostrich eggs also adorn the mosque at Ouadane (page 202), as well as some of the famed earthen mosques along the Niger River, over 1,100km away. Though the old mosque is closed to non-Muslims, it's still possible to get some nice photos from the entry gate. There are often people praying and resting in the courtyard just inside the gate – it's fine to take photos, but do be respectful.

Chinguetti's other claim to fame is certainly its **libraries**, home to a range of medieval Arabic manuscripts on topics from Arabic grammar to astronomy and agriculture – though the majority are religious in nature (page 196). Held by various families, there were once about 30 of these private libraries, but today that number is perhaps a bit more than a dozen, holding some 4,000–6,000 manuscripts (estimates vary depending on your source). A small handful of these bibliothèques are open to visiting tourists or scholars, with the two most visited (and those that are most likely to be ready to receive you without prior notice) being **Bibliothèque Habott** (m 47 47 85 05, 46 41 08 01; e habott4@yahoo.fr; f) and **Bibliothèque Al Ahmed Mahmoud** (m 33 15 80 29), both in the vieille ville.

LIBRARIES AND MANUSCRIPTS

Mauritania's desert manuscripts, known in Hassaniya as *makhtoutat*, are many centuries old and, despite the fact that few tourists can make head nor tail of them in any meaningful sense, have nonetheless become famous around the world and retain the undeniable power to enthral even those – like myself – fully illiterate in Arabic. Product of countless hours of exacting labour and written out on paper that was once a rare and costly luxury good, these manuscripts have been the pride of their families for generations, and are considered as among the most precious heirlooms one can have. They lie at the heart of Mauritanian culture as a whole, and are guarded with a jealousy that reveals their profound importance.

According to one study, there are more than 33,000 of these priceless volumes in the country, kept between 675 different libraries, the vast majority of which are privately held by families. More than 70% of the manuscripts are religious text and analysis, covering multiple disciplines of Islam including Fiqh (jurisprudence), Tasawwuf (Sufism/mysticism), Tawhid (monotheism), Sunnah and Hadith (the ways of the Prophet), Ibadah (worship) and Tafsir (interpretation), as well as copies of the Quran itself. The remaining manuscripts range widely, including texts on politics, medicine, astronomy, philosophy, geography, agriculture, arithmetic, geometry, logic, rhetoric, history, literature and grammar.

Known to outsiders since at least the time of Théodore Monod's early research, there have been numerous initiatives to catalogue and preserve these documents over the years, though most of these schemes have been a mixed success at best. As part of one preservationist initiative, all four of the UNESCO-recognised ancient cities had a 'maison du livre' built in them – and all four of these sit empty today, including Chinguetti's, which has overlooked the main square in the old city since 2003.

But as hallowed as these texts might be, the realities of centuries stored in trunks and saddlebags are clearly visible, and many of the volumes are undeniably tattered – even if they are today handled with white gloves. Therefore, the best approach to the long-term preservation of these heirlooms remains a matter of quite some debate between academics, the state and the traditional librarians, which seems unlikely to be resolved any time soon. But as scholar Jean-Marie Arnoult observed in 2010, the scrapes and scars of the books' long history is today part of what makes them such fascinating artefacts:

> Besides their intellectual content, these documents are also interesting as archaeological objects, as they harbour amazing wealth in terms of knowledge about the materials they are made of, their history, bygone-day techniques, and economic and commercial history. Also fortunately and singularly, these documents still have visible and palpable traces from their travels through time and space.

A visit to one of the libraries (entry/suggested donation 100UM) will generally involve an explanatory speech (a bit of French is handy here!) and a showcase of other historical and cultural items. These might include the *azàyyâr* stick, used to pinch and coerce girls into eating during the gavage (page 38), or a demonstration of the ingenious traditional wooden door locks historically used in Chinguetti. But of course, you are ultimately here to see the books. Today they're often stored in an incongruous mix of weather-beaten wooden trunks and factory-made filing cabinets, but the moment your guide unveils the cracked leather binding and fragile calligraphic pages of these texts – either hand-scribed in these very sands or carried from abroad on camelback centuries ago – is not soon forgotten. It is also perhaps emblematic of a trip to Mauritania on the whole – the beauty and wisdom of this desert civilisation is here for those who care to seek it, and offered with open hearts – but without patience, care, and even a bit of reverence, you'll go home having found little in these unforgiving sands.

Visitors to Al Ahmed Mahmoud are first greeted with a sign, '*Le savoir est une fortune qui n'appauvrit pas celui qui en offre*' (Knowledge is a fortune that does not impoverish the one who offers it), and the librarian, Saif al Islam al Ahmed Mahmoud – who graces the cover of this book – is a natural-born storyteller and real raconteur. With more than 1,000 volumes in its collections, Bibliothèque Habott is the larger of the two libraries, and librarian Abdullah Habott is also a compelling host and exceedingly dedicated to his calling. There are a cluster of smaller libraries just north of the old mosque, including **Bibliothèque Ehl Hammounni** (m 46 91 57 16) and **Bibliothèque Ehl Limame** (m 46 81 79 78), though these might need a bit of notice before being able to receive you.

Continuing in the old city, the narrow lanes invite aimless wandering and photography, and since so many of the houses are semi-abandoned, it's easy to disappear between the city's high stone walls and feel like you've got the place all to yourself. The high walls and low doorframes tell of a tumultuous history, but goats make light work of it all, hopping effortlessly between crumbling walls in search of any scrap of vegetable matter that dares show itself in these untended alleys.

But during the annual guetna **date harvest**, usually held in August, many of the homes that you might have assumed to be abandoned are again full of life for several weeks, as families from Nouakchott and beyond descend on the city for this beloved festival. The city also comes alive for the **Festival des Cités du Patrimoine** (sometimes called Mada'in Tourath or the Madain Heritage Festival), the 13th edition of which was held here in December 2024 (page 204).

At other times of year, a stroll among sand, stone and silence is the best way to absorb the essence of this ancient city – until the **souvenir sellers** spot you, that is. Chinguetti's hawkers are known for putting on a hard sell, and the reputation has some merit, with itinerant vendors in the old city often a fair bit more insistent than those you've encountered elsewhere in the country. In an attempt to counter what had ultimately become recognised as a nuisance, the city government moved these itinerant sellers to a dedicated **market** at the centre of old Chinguetti in 2025 – but only the sands of time will tell if this ultimately sticks. There are also a few simple souvenir shops set around the mosque and libraries, many with cheeky names or slogans like '*moins cher que gratuit*' (cheaper than free), '*c'est Mamout qui écrase les prix*' (it's Mamout who crushes the prices) and '*la Fnac*' (after the French media giant).

South and east of the old city, the enormous **Erg Ouarane** sand sea dominates the horizon, a constant reminder of the fate of its ancestor, Abweir (page 198), up the oued. Just southeast of the old city at the edge of the dunes there are a number of artisanal **mines** where banco clay is extracted by hand. Miners are lowered into the pits, which conceal hand-dug underground caverns, by a shadoof, as if descending into a well. (You may also be able to descend yourself, should you be feeling brave!)

And while the buildings out here at the edge of town with sand up to their fanlights are an eerie, vaguely apocalyptic sight, the heights of the erg itself offer

TINY TANOUCHERT

If you take the back way between Chinguetti and Ouadane, you'll pass through the isolated oasis of **Tanouchert** (⊕ 20.7175, -11.8824) roughly midway between the two ancient ksour. And while it lacks the obvious historical pedigree of its neighbours, this is a true oasis community, with a handful of residents eking out a living from their gardens fastidiously fenced in from the ever-encroaching dunes (and ever-hungry goats).

About 15km northwest of here lies another small village, **Douérate**, which is the modern counterpart to the ruined settlement of **Tinigui** (⊕ 20.7387, -12.0041) that it shares a site with. Tinigui, though it sees just a fraction of the visitors that Chinguetti might, is in fact the elder of the two settlements, though the ancient city here is more comprehensively ruined and more of an archaeological site than an 'old city' like those found in Chinguetti or Ouadane.

Tanouchert is a common stop for tours between the two ancient cities, whether by camel or 4x4; most people carry on after lunch or a glass of tea, but it's also quite possible to spend the night. There's no phone signal in the village, but ask for Chigaly and he will arrange a place for you.

heartening views over the whole of Chinguetti and far beyond. There's a huge dune about 2km east of town (⊕ 20.4676, -12.3428) that's a popular spot for watching the sunset. And as you look out over the city, take a moment to remember the world of dunes behind you carries on uninterrupted for hundreds of kilometres. Timbuktu is 1,000km to the southeast across this empty desert – only 45 days away by camel.

On the north side of the oued, the **new city** still looks every bit the desert outpost, with banco-built buildings and a few colonial-era historical sites like the **Vieux Fort** (Old Fort). Originally known as Fort Claudel when it was built in 1919, it has fallen into disuse over time, but was restored in the early 1980s so that it could serve as a shooting location for French film *Fort Saganne* (page 190); it has since largely fallen into disuse again. The city's usually sleepy **main market** is also worth a look, and Chinguetti's palmeraies sit along either side of the city and opposite banks of the oued: one on the southwest edge of town, and the other on the northeast. Music fans might be able to set up an evening soirée with a talented **tidnit** player living in Chinguetti, Ahmed Sidi Bella (m 47 46 68 97).

Leaving the city behind and following the oued's southern shore to the east for about 4km you arrive at the hamlet of **Abweir** (or Abeïr; ⊕ 20.4743, -12.3318), which is believed to be the site of Chinguetti's first iteration, founded in or around the year 777CE. The historical city has long since been lost beneath the sands of the Erg Ouarane, but a few herders and date-palm growers still live here, and the picturesque Mosquée d'Abweir sits at the edge of the dunes. Its precise origins are poorly documented, but the structure here today is a relatively modern reconstruction of Abweir's ancient mosque, standing in as an homage to the lost Chinguetti underneath. Across the oued, the larger village of **Ntekemkemt** has a beautiful palmeraie, the largest in the area and very much worth a stroll if you're out here.

Finally, about 9km southwest of Chinguetti, **Lagueïla Oasis** (⊕ 20.3760, -12.4001) is a popular destination for excursions on camelback, and this little patch of green lost in the sometimes-orange, sometimes-white dunes of the Erg Ouarane is plucked straight out of a desert adventurer's storybook. There's also a khaïma camp 5km east of here (and 7.5km south of town): the **Campement de Chinguitty (Abeir Silence)** (m 36 43 82 24, 22 43 82 24; e abeirsilence.voyage@gmail.com; w abeirsilence-voyage.com; f; ⊕ 20.3871, -12.3512), which makes a fine base to experience the absolute peace and stillness (other than a handful of 'singing' dunes) of this expansive and extraordinary landscape.

OUADANE Beyond Chinguetti, at the end of the (bumpy) road and halfway along the Adrar highlands' easternmost protrusion, lies the city of Ouadane (وادان) – one of Mauritania's four UNESCO-recognised ancient ksour, and also the Adrar's easternmost major settlement. With nothing but desert and a few semi-nomadic hamlets beyond, the 3,833 hardy Ouadaniens have gotten used to life at what feels like the edge of the earth. If you've been travelling in Mauritania for a while, though, you may have noticed that the desert is rarely quite as empty as it seems, and a few nomads and their camels have a way of popping up in the most unlikely seeming places. But head east out of Ouadane, and you really are on your own – this is where the Majâbat al-Koubrâ (page 206), or 'great crossing' begins, and the next settlements of any size heading east are a full 1,300km away in Mali and Algeria.

And so, here at the ragged end of the road we find not a Fata Morgana or pot of gold, but one of Mauritania's most tantalising prizes of all – a true hilltop casbah lost in the deepest desert, and today falling to rack and ruin in the most scenic way possible. Founded in the 12th century, Ouadane sits on a stone escarpment above the confluence of two oueds, from where it derives its name, meaning, quite appropriately, 'the two oueds'. It's said that these are symbolic, referring to the oued of knowledge (for the city's significant scholarly tradition) and the oued of dates (as it's reputed to be among the first places the date palm grew in Mauritania), but it also sits between two literal wadis as well: the Oued Aferzi and Oued Chouk, which run underneath the urbanised escarpment above.

Once a critical stopover for trans-Saharan trade, there were more than 3,000 stone-built houses standing in the old city during Ouadane's heyday, and laying

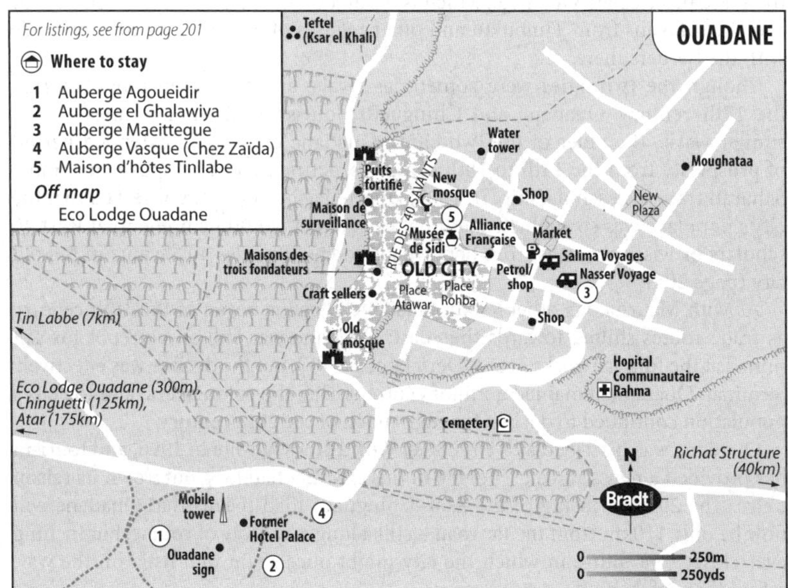

eyes on the city you are reminded quite vividly of the fact that the word ksour originates with the Latin *castrum*, or castle. But the re-routing of trade networks and implacability of the harsh Mauritanian environment have left this desert castle in dire shape, as famed desert explorer Théodore Monod observed arriving in 1934, finding Ouadane 'a black cliff, scaled by a vertiginous heap of ruins, emerging from a verdant river of date palms: stuck to the rock to which it is now restoring the rubble it had borrowed…an overripe fruit that bursts in the sun, a gigantic flow of rubble…broken terraces, a veritable labyrinth of stairs, corridors, dead ends.'

And so Ouadane is a place, even in its diminished state, that quite simply looks more legendary than real, and a visit here rightly ranks among the highlights of any trip to Mauritania. Throw in the fact that it's also the jumping-off point for the geologically famous Richat Structure (page 204), and you'll find there are plenty of reasons indeed to carry on all the way to the end of the road.

History Archaeological findings point to several thousand years of human settlement in the Adrar Plateau area, but the Ouadane of today – somewhat like Chinguetti – traces its history to a cluster of largely disappeared 8th-century settlements thought to be populated by Black Africans (including Teftel, which is still visible a few hundred metres northwest of Ouadane; page 202), only to enter a period of decline and be 're-founded' several centuries later.

In the case of Ouadane, there are three legendary hajis from the Amazigh Idaou el-Hadj tribe who founded the city in 1142, and whose houses can still be seen in the old city today (page 202).

As with Chinguetti, Ouadane was not mentioned by the renowned Arab travellers and geographers of the time like Ibn Battuta, but also first enters the historical record through the Portuguese, who had begun to explore the interior from their island fort at Arguin (page 162), and may have even had a hand in constructing the mysterious Fort d'Agoueïdir (page 205) just outside of Ouadane. An observation attributed to Nuno Tristão in the late 15th century noted that 'behind Cape Blanco there is a place called Ouadane, which is located inland at a distance of six days by camel…caravans from Timbuktu and other regions of blacks arrive there to trade with the Berbers there.'

Though the two cities were sometimes rivals, and they even fought during the 17th century, Ouadane and Chinguetti flourished at similar times and in similar ways. The older of the two cities, Ouadane enjoyed an extended period of prosperity from the 14th to 18th centuries, acting as a key stopover for trans-Saharan trade and scholarship. In 1507, Duarte Pacheco Pereira observed that the city's populace was so sophisticated that each street would be home to at least 40 scholars or wise men; it is from here we get today's Rue des 40 Savants in the old city (page 202).

As with Mauritania's other ksour, Ouadane's decline began in the 19th century as trade routes shifted towards the coast; Ouadane was still an entrepôt for salt mined at the Idjil saltworks near F'Dérick (page 208), but the decline was effectively terminal. Ouadane remained a minor centre during the colonial era, and the city's population continued to decline through much of the 20th century.

Ouadane was inscribed as a UNESCO World Heritage Site in 1996, and tourism has provided a new source of income in this city that had long outgrown its raison d'etre. The 2025 surfacing of the Atar–Chinguetti road means that Ouadane will now be only 110km from the tar road – still a long way away of course, but inching ever closer to a future in which the city might once again find itself on the way, rather than left behind.

Getting there and away From Atar, a daily minibus departs around 14.00 (4hrs; 500UM) for the 180km trip to Ouadane, and perhaps another vehicle or two on an ad hoc basis. The first 65km or so before the Chinguetti turn-off will benefit from 2025 surfacing works, but otherwise the road here is graded but prone to (sometimes severe) washboarding.

Note that if you wish to visit both Ouadane and Chinguetti, *go to Ouadane first*, as it is much easier to find a vehicle from Ouadane to Chinguetti than it is the other way around. When in Ouadane, ask your accommodation to find out about any vehicles towards Chinguetti that you might be able to hitch a lift on. Otherwise, Chinguetti sits 16km from a turn-off (Virage Chinguetti) on the Atar–Ouadane road, but there are no facilities and no shade at the crossroads, and traffic volumes are low – so do not underestimate the conditions if you're thinking to try and hitch!

Where to stay and eat *Map, page 199*

There are few bespoke eateries in Ouadane, so visitors generally end up eating at their accommodation, where lunch/dinner generally costs 300–600UM.

Eco Lodge Ouadane Atar road; e viaggimauritania@gmail.com; w viaggimauritania.com. Connected to an Italian tour agency, this new lodge is now the most upmarket accommodation in Ouadane. Set on the southwestern edge of town, the solar-powered en-suite rooms are cool & clean, & it's all built out of local stone. *2,850/3,350/4,000UM sgl/dbl/trpl.* **$$$$**

Auberge Agoueidir South of the oeud; m 46 49 10 10, 31 29 12 12, 46 49 11 11; e aubergeagoueidir@gmail.com; f. Just beneath the small hill with the Ouadane sign on the southwestern edge of town, this is another good address with carefully kept en-suite rooms with AC in a variety of configurations set around a large garden courtyard. *1,000UM dbl.* **$$**

Auberge el Ghalawiya South of the oeud; m 44 44 59 55; e aubergeelghalawiya@gmail.com; f. With a good location on the rise south of town, the simple tiled rooms here are rather short on character but comfortable enough, & the enthusiastic welcome from owner Salam makes up for any shortcomings. *1,000UM dbl.* **$$**

✷ **Auberge Vasque (Chez Zaïda)** South of the oeud; m 47 68 96 66; e zaidabilalnza@gmail.com; f. Run by the charismatic Zaïda Bilal, this has long been a traveller's go-to in Ouadane, & it's not hard to see why. The meals are top-notch, & she can arrange all local excursions, including to a women's farming co-operative she sponsors, or trips to the Richat Structure & beyond (page 204). The rooms come in a variety of shapes & sizes (all with AC & hot water), so have a look at a couple before you choose. It's also possible to sleep in a khaïma. *1,200UM dbl.* **$$**

✷ **Maison d'hôtes Tinllabe** North of the oeud; m 36 32 58 57, 47 53 54 55; e agence-isselmou@yahoo.fr. Right on the edge of the old city, the tidy rooms with hot water, AC & TV here are already appealing, but the unexpectedly delightful palmeraie in the back seals the deal. *1,200UM dbl.* **$$**

Auberge Maeittegue North of the oeud; m 46 99 14 39; e aubergefatmamaeittegue@gmail.com. This is a very basic affair run by a kind family offering small rooms with domed ceilings and mats ('matlas') on the floor, plus a couple of other larger majlis-style salons. All use shared ablutions. *700UM dbl; meals for 300UM.* **$**

What to see and do Ouadane's main draw is its UNESCO-recognised **vieille ville** (old city; 200UM), which spills down the west side of the escarpment on which the city sits. Though on the whole the old town is more comprehensively ruined than the one in Chinguetti, it may nonetheless be even more impressive, thanks to the spectacular hillside location, offering a grand overview on what is a genuinely epic sweep of rubble cascading down the hillside into the palms and tamarisk of the oued below.

You will usually find yourself here with a guide, either provided by your accommodation or who will simply find you, as it's not that big of a place. They're not pushy and can really enrich your experience (and navigation!) of the old town, though you'll struggle to find one that speaks English. After paying the entry fee and spending some time with the guide (if desired), you're free to wander the old town as you please. A number of projects initiated between the Fondation Nationale pour la Sauvegarde des Villes anciennes (National Foundation for the Preservation of Ancient Cities) and several foreign development programmes have supported the restoration of many of the old city's landmarks over the last 25-plus years, including rebuilding more than 1.5km of wall surrounding the city, and several of the significant buildings and plazas inside.

From the south and west, the old city can be entered from a handful of gates in the city wall. Starting from the southernmost gate into the old city, you'll immediately come upon the **ancienne mosquée** (old mosque), which is by far Ouadane's most iconic building. It dates to the city's 12th-century founding, and unlike most other sacred architecture in the country, you are free to explore, and in this case even climb the minaret! (This is because it's no longer used for prayer.) The rows of roofless arcades at the base of the minaret make for a deliciously symmetrical photo opportunity, and it goes without saying that there are fine views from atop the rather stout minaret (it was safe to climb at the time of writing, but obviously use your judgement and watch your step!).

Continuing north, you are walking along the **Rue des 40 Savants** ('Charii Al Arbaiine'; Street of 40 Scholars), which is the main drag, cutting north–south through the whole of the old city. After about 180m, you'll reach a clutch of restored buildings that host a handful of **craft sellers**; unlike in Chinguetti, there's little hard selling going on here, so you can browse at your leisure.

About 50m further along, the **maisons des trois fondateurs** (homes of the three founders) sit side by side, where the three legendary hajis who are credited with founding the city – Ali, Ethman and Yacoub – once lived. You can still recognise some of the household features inside, including ablutions, storage and living spaces. From here, the Rue des 40 Savants carries on straight north, but you should branch northwest for some 80m to have a look at the **puits fortifié** (fortified well), which draws its water from the oued below. Obviously a critical bit of infrastructure, the city planners built a long extension of the town's fortifications to keep the well inside the city walls. This walled peninsula sticks out some 25m from the rest of the city walls, and is flanked by two **maisons de surveillance** (guardhouses) at its base.

From here, there are several good spots along the city's western edge to enjoy the views: looking out to the northwest, the ruins of **Teftel** (Ksar el Khali; ⊕ 20.937278, -11.6249) are visible 400m across the oued, and to the south the decidedly more modern ruins of the domed former **Hotel Palace**, perched on a hilltop near the mobile phone mast and giant **'Ouadane' sign** at the south end of town.

The **nouvelle mosquée** (new mosque) sits about 150m inland of the guardhouses as the crow flies, and is embellished with a similarly struthious ostrich-egg crown as the mosque in Chinguetti. It was built after inter-clan fighting destroyed the older mosque to the south around the year 1450. And if you didn't follow any of the directions above, don't worry – part of the fun of exploring Ouadane is getting lost in the labyrinthine alleyways, so don't be afraid to explore. Just wear good shoes and be very mindful of loose stones, as there are about a million of them to trip on! This ruined part of the old city is also a good place to spot a **rock hyrax**, as they love the jagged, rocky slopes.

The **nouvelle ville** (new city) to the east blends more or less seamlessly into the old, and as you wander 'inland' from the cliff-edge western border of the ruined city, you'll suddenly start to notice signs of life – sturdier stone walls, renovated wooden doors, and eventually even a little corner boutique or two. But the history remains as well: look closely and you may even find board games carved into the stone (for more on Mauritanian games, see page 58). As you continue east away from the old town, things become progressively more modern. There's a sleepy **central market** and petrol pump, as well as several auberges, a few governance buildings and plazas, and a hospital.

Back at the fringes of the old city, the **Musée de Sidi**, informally named after its founder Sidi Mohamed Ould Abidine Sidi, is less a museum than it is an Aladdin's cave collection of historical knick-knacks, scattered haphazardly across the building and its courtyard. Sidi wasn't living in Ouadane at the time of writing, however, so it may not be possible to visit; ask locally for the latest. There is also a government-sponsored **Maison de la culture** just north of the old city, but as in the other ksour, local families have been reluctant to place their treasured artefacts in the care of the state, and it has not fulfilled its intended purpose. The **Alliance Française** (m 47 68 96 66, 34 61 80 49) also has a small outpost here, primarily offering French instruction.

And though Ouadane is less renowned for its manuscripts as neighbouring Chinguetti, there are still at least 800-some volumes stored in over a dozen family **libraries** here, and the oldest manuscript ever found in Mauritania came from here (though this is now in Nouakchott); ask your accommodation to call and arrange a visit to the **Bibliothèque Mohamed Lemine Kettab** or **Bibliothèque Abidin Sidi** (this is the same Sidi as above, so he may be unavailable).

Down off the escarpment, Ouadane's **palmeraie** follows the oued south of the city centre. Across it you'll find a couple of auberges and the attractive city signboard (think Hollywood letters) on the hillside.

Outside the city but not too far away, **Tin Labbe** is a scenic valley village set 7km northwest of Ouadane up the Oued Aferzi. Here there is a large palmeraie, along with some mysterious **caves** (⊕ approx 20.9639, -11.6722) known for inscriptions in Arabic and Tifinagh (Amazigh). If you keep following the oued past Tin Labbe, after 10km you'll find the **Foum al-Maï** guelta (⊕ 21.0041, -11.7327), where the oued's high southern wall shelters a perennial pool.

On the other side of Ouadane, camel safaris typically aim for the wooded **Maiateg Oasis** (⊕ 20.8430, -11.5610), 11km southeast of town. This remote haven sits between dunes, *reg* (stone desert) and a salt-encrusted sebkha, and it's possible to spend the night. Be mindful that there are no facilities, however, so you'll need to be fully self-sufficient.

Festivals There are a couple of festivals held in Ouadane, including the **Caravane Ouadane** (w caravaneouadane.weebly.com; f; ◎), which is affiliated with the admirable Zeinart Gallery in Nouakchott (page 125). Held annually, it brings a host of international artists, musicians and more to the city for a series of concerts, workshops and discussions every November. Envisioned and implemented as a creative collaboration and conversation between Ouadane locals and artists from outside, it's a fascinating few days to be in town.

In August, the Club Al-Nasser culturel et sportif (m 44 44 68 41) puts on a **cultural festival** timed around the traditional guetna **date harvest** celebration. The festival is a celebration of traditional life, with evenings of music and poetry alongside showcases of nomadic crafts, regional dishes, games, dances and athletic performances.

FESTIVAL DES CITÉS DU PATRIMOINE (HERITAGE CITIES FESTIVAL)

Since 2011, the **Festival des Cités du Patrimoine** (Heritage Cities Festival; also sometimes known as the 'Medayine' festival or the Festival des Villes Anciennes) has been held in December–January every year, with the host city rotating annually between the four UNESCO-recognised ksour of Chinguetti, Ouadane, Oualata and Tichitt. While the performances may follow a familiar format of Quranic recitals, poetry, music, dance, and traditional nomadic crafts, games and the like, the president often attends at least a part of the proceedings, so this is a slightly larger and bigger-budget affair than some of the other cultural festivals you might encounter periodically in towns throughout the country.

The most recent 13th edition was held in Chinguetti in 2024.

RICHAT STRUCTURE AND ADRAR PLATEAU East of Atar, the Adrar Plateau forms a highland 'peninsula' jutting east, separating two enormous dune seas for nearly 300km, with the Erg Makhteir to the north, and the Erg Ouarane to the south. Along the southern edge of the outcrop, the two ancient ksour of Chinguetti and Ouadane sit facing the Erg Ouarane, while to the north the division is much starker, fronted by a long unbroken cliff (tarf) stretching from Passe d'Ebnou in the west to El Ghallaouiya in the east. Mauritania's most talked about geological feature, the Richat Structure, sits smack in the middle of this outcrop, only 20-some km northeast of Ouadane as the Arabian bustard flies.

Richat Structure Also known as the Guelb er Richât (قلب الريشات) or more poetically, the 'Eye of the Sahara', the **Richat Structure** has been the subject of enormous interest, and an equal amount of speculation, since it was first spotted in aerial photos from the early 20th century (its full form is rather tougher to appreciate from eye level). Was it formed from a meteor strike? A volcano? Is it – and stay with us now – the remains of the fabled lost city of Atlantis? All of these theories and more have been proposed about this massive landform, and many are still out there on various internet forums proselytising about the veracity of the last one.

But the geologists have come to a rather more prosaic conclusion, namely that the Richat Structure is what's known as a geologic 'dome': a round area in which the earth's layers, normally horizontal beneath your feet, have been ruptured in a process known as tectonic uplift. This uplift creates a protrusion above the earth's surface, which, if eroded or cut away, reveals a pattern of concentric rings – the original stratigraphic layers of earth – that are youngest at the outermost and increasingly ancient as you approach the centre.

But the prosaic reality of its creation does nothing at all to take away from its spectacular nature, and the concentric bullseye rings stretch 45km across in a formation essentially unique in the world. It's true that, much as the early residents of Mauritania and the latter-day Saharan explorers experienced, it can be hard to get fully to grips with the scale of the structure from ground level, but it's a spectacular desert landscape nonetheless, with expansive views from the various ridgelines, and an exciting drive up repeatedly climbing and descending the rings as you approach the centre.

Inside the structure, the views are generally the main event, but you can also stop at a lonely tree where Théodore Monod's wife, Olga Pickova, spent her time when accompanying her husband on research, which has now been commemorated as the Arbre de Madame Monod (1972–74), or it's also worth dropping in on the family at Camp Boisé (see below) at the very centre of the structure for a bit of shade and a cup of tea.

On the way here from Ouadane, you can also stop at the **Fort d'Agoueïdir** (⊕ 20.9982, -11.4399), a highly degraded ruin that is somewhat controversially thought to be a Portuguese fort dating to the late 15th century, likely between 1485–90 – thus representing some of their earliest forays on the continent, and entirely unique in its position so far into the interior of the African landmass. And while it's ultimately somewhat difficult to parse fact from legend on the matter, the fort makes for a mildly diverting stopover, though the structures today are quite eroded, including some seemingly more recent reconstructions of the fort's corner turrets. You can buy an assortment of polished stones and other trinkets here, which are endearingly sold on an honesty basis – just put an appropriate amount of money into the tin at the (usually) unattended display you purchase from.

The nearby **Semsiyat Dome** (⊕ 21.0166, -11.8320) 45km southwest is thought to have arisen from similar geological forces, though is much smaller (only about 5km across) and of much shallower relief.

Getting there and away There's (unsurprisingly) no transport to reach here, but Chez Zaïda and the other auberges in Ouadane can arrange day trips in a 4x4 for around 2,500UM (up to four passengers). Longer circuits via **El Beyedh** (see below) can also be arranged.

Where to stay and eat *Map, page 190*

Surprisingly enough, however, there *is* a place to sleep, should you be so inclined. The **Auberge Camp Boisé** (m 26 40 51 70; ⊕ 21.1256, -11.3989) sits smack in the bullseye centre of the structure, and can set you up in a khaïma for 300UM per person. Meals are also available at 200/300UM for breakfast/dinner, but obviously be aware that their inventory may be limited.

Beyond Richat Heading north out of the Richat Structure you climb back up on to the plateau via an incredibly rocky track, arriving to a plain area called **Azizal**, which was once the preserve of addax and dorcas gazelle. Today these are a vanishingly rare sight, however. The plateau narrows as you continue north, pursing in to an end-of-the world cliff edge at the **Tarf Tazazmout** (Tazazmout Cliff), from which there are expansive views over stands of acacia and nomad encampments at the base of the cliff, and to the endless dunes of Erg Makhteir stretching to the northern horizon and beyond. Some 30km to the west, the 647m **Aderg** inselberg sits just inside the dune fields, making for a dramatic contrast against the endless waves of ochre and beige unspooling themselves beyond. Some 25km south of Aderg, the tiny village of Arhmakou (Aghmakem) sits near the mouth of an enormous deep-walled oued of the same name.

Coming down off the plateau to the north, the hamlet of **El Beyedh** (27km east of Tarf Tazazmout; ⊕ 21.4878, -11.3325) sits at the northern outflow of the **Oued Enchegdane**, a long high-walled wadi stretching some 15km to the south which is home to numerous rock carvings. This perhaps explains in part why El Beyedh is the (very) unlikely home of a small **archaeological museum** (sometimes called the Musée de la Préhistoire or Musée du Désert) run by local resident and long-time curator Yeslem. The museum is really more of an mbar shed full of artefacts, but the impulse and execution of such a collection in such a remote locale is impressive just the same. Yeslem will also lead you up and around the oued to some rock carvings nearby depicting cows, antelopes, and even some inscriptions in ancient Tifinagh. As of recently, Yeslem's daughters Dija and Lihdia run the **Auberge du Musée de la Préhistoire** (m 48 65 28 37, 34 44 90 60; **$**), where you can be hosted and fed in khaïma tents.

East along the base of the escarpment, the abandoned **Bir Ziri** fort (⊕ 21.5556, -10.7731) lies about 60km east of El Beyedh as the crow flies. From here it's a further 18km east to the very end of the escarpment, and the Adrar Plateau more generally, at **El Ghallaouiya** (⊕ 21.5937, -10.6017). This is more a fort and military outpost than anything else, but also an Important Bird Area and by some accounts also home to the biggest collection of rock carvings in Mauritania, with depictions of cows and herders, as well as wild fauna like ostriches, giraffes, gazelle, elephant and even rhinoceros found in the valleys surrounding the base. Beyond this, the Erg Makhteir and Erg Ouarane sand seas end their long separation and combine into one of the least hospitable and least touched regions anywhere in the Sahara.

Beyond El Ghallaouiya Eastern Mauritania is dominated by the **Majâbat al-Koubrâ**, which literally translates to 'the great crossing'. Nearly totally devoid of even traces of humanity since at least the Neolithic period, and almost entirely lacking in water points or other essentials of survival, desert explorer and academic Théodore Monod called this area the 'desert of deserts'. He made four traverses of the region in the 1950s and 60s, trekking between Ouadane or El Ghallaouiya and the Puits d'Aratane east of Tichitt (page 303) or Araouane in Mali – crossings of between 600 and 800km each!

Others also know the region as El Djouf or the 'empty quarter'. But in a hint of irony for a place with so many names, today's maps of it have no names themselves, as there are so few landmarks after which one might title them. Instead they are simply coded – NE-29-XXII, NE-29-XXIII, NE-29-XXIV, and so on. These 1:200,000 sheets take on the appearance of contemporary art – not the familiar visual vocabulary of roads, borders, oceans and lakes, but rather abstract exercises in beige pastels and shading.

Somewhere out in this wilderness of many and no names also lies the answer to the mystery of the lost caravan, **Ma'den Ijafen**. Discovered by hunters, this bona fide haul of desert treasure was spotted somewhere south of a (now seemingly also vanished) shallow well known as El Mrayyer in 1962 and eventually brought to Monod's attention, who organised an expedition to track it down. Monod and his guide, antelope hunter Salek ould Guejmoul, did ultimately find the cache, though it took two separate missions to do so.

On inspection, they determined it was likely left behind by an 11th-century caravan headed to Tichitt or Oualata that ran into problems and had to offload goods to be picked up later. The cache contained over 2,000 brass bars and a plethora of cowrie shells, thought to have been traded here from as far away as the Maldives. (According to Ibn Battuta, these would have traded at 350 times the value they had back in the Maldives.) But some 900 years later, this precious cargo remained lost in the sands, a silent witness to whatever unknown misfortune kept these ancient traders from returning.

But in an uncanny echo of the caravan that was never to return, the Ma'den Ijafen cache is lost again, never spotted since the time of Monod and Guejmoul's mission. At the time, Monod said it would be impossible to find without the assistance of his guides, and despite the efforts of a variety of academics and would-be sleuths, time has very much proven him right – so far.

TIRIS ZEMMOUR REGION

Covering 252,900km^2, Tiris Zemmour (ولاية تيرس زمور) is Mauritania's largest region by area – just a bit larger than the whole of the United Kingdom – but also its third-least populous, with only 79,129 inhabitants (compared against the UK's slightly larger 68 million). The region's only two population centres of any significance, F'Dérick and Zouérate, sit just 25km apart on either side of the Kedia d'Idjil mountain.

This massive black outcrop of nearly pure iron ore tops out around 915m, making it the highest peak in all of Mauritania. Given its composition, it also represents a towering peak in the Mauritanian economy, and the primary raison d'être for the existence of both towns – particularly Zouérate. Much like Nouakchott, Zouérate was constructed from nothing in the early 1960s, in this case to support the rapidly developing mine. F'Dérick is much older, having served as a French military post in the colonial era, but today is very much the junior partner. The only other town of any size is the frontier settlement of Bir Moghreïn, an isolated outpost some 300km to the north.

The area north and east of Zouérate and F'Dérick is studded with numerous similar but smaller peaks (known as *guelbs*), rising dramatically from the otherwise fairly flat desert scrub characterising the region. These outcrops are in many cases equally packed with precious ore, and the area will likely be a mainstay of the Mauritanian economy for many years to come.

Thanks to the walled partition of Western Sahara to the west and the enormous uninhabited expanses of desert to the east, the region has long been something of a dead end in travel terms, but 2024 brought significant changes with the opening of an official border crossing with Algeria – the two countries' first since

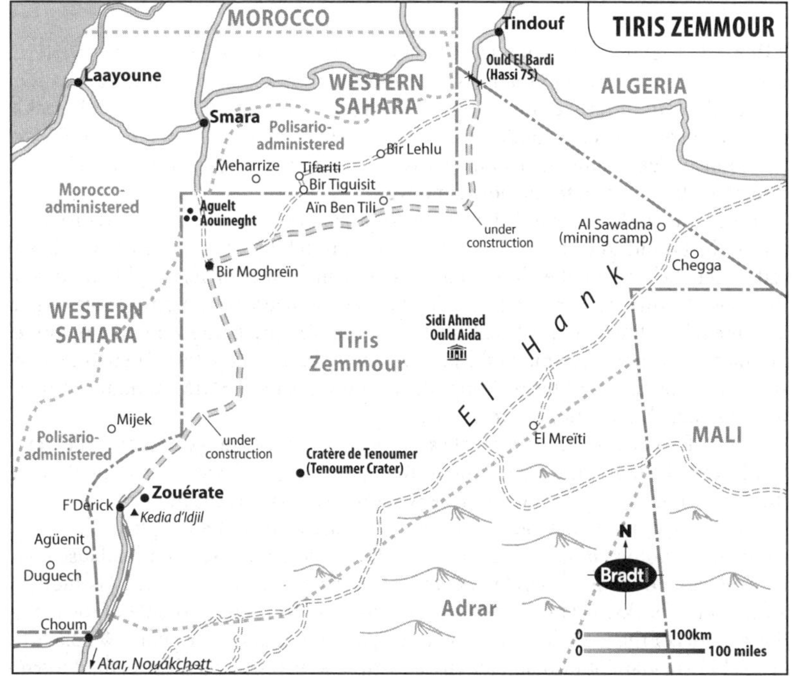

THE LOST GUELTA OF OUM LEHBAL

Approaching from the south, about 10–20km before reaching F'Dérick, a number of tracks break east towards the remote southern face of Kedia d'Idjil. In sharp contrast to the mountain's industrialised northern slopes, even by Mauritanian standards there's next to nothing out here, save for one or two herders' hamlets and some SNIM infrastructure in the southeast. But there is one very unexpected sight hidden away in this bleak, black mountain landscape – a large guelta, known as **Oum Lehbal** (or Oum El Habel; ⊕ 22.6164, -12.5554). Set about 16km east of the Choum–F'Dérick road as the crow flies, it's hard to imagine a less likely spot for this isolated pocket of water, cradled in the barren rock and divided into a smaller upper and larger lower pool. Unlike at many other gueltas, little grows here, but after the rains, a small dam south of the perennial pool holds back an ephemeral lake that can even cover several hectares. There is at least one other isolated pool in the area (⊕ 22.6318, -12.5734), up a parallel valley from Oum Lehbal, about 2.5km to the northwest.

independence! An 800km road link from Zouérate to the border was announced at the same time, and construction is already ongoing. Tiris Zemmour is therefore already transitioning from dead-end street to significant trans-Saharan artery, with talk of a dry port in Zouérate and other significant infrastructure to come.

The far northeast has also become the site of Mauritania's second gold boom after that in Chami (page 163), and this traditionally uninhabited region – much of which has long been a closed-off military zone – has seen a massive influx of wildcat mining operations working in some of the furthest-flung corners of the country.

F'DÉRICK The small town of F'Dérick (افديرك; population 11,623) sits at the western end of the Kedia d'Idjil mountain, whose imposing black mass pulls into view as you approach town, utterly dominating the skyline to the east and making F'Dérick's grid of dusty, low-slung buildings feel quite small indeed. Lesser outcrops like the conical Guelb Atomaï, also intensely black and thoroughly infused with iron, punctuate the horizon to the north and west.

Though F'Dérick is first in line when approaching from the rest of Mauritania (all traffic bound to or from Zouérate passes through here), it has otherwise been rather left behind in the development stakes in favour of its neighbour down the road. Known as Fort Gouraud during the colonial era, the settlement began as a French military outpost built in 1933, therefore predating Zouérate by three decades, but is now very much the junior partner between the two. There is a mine site here, though it had been sitting idle for 40 years until SNIM announced they would relaunch operations here in 2023.

Most of what limited action takes place in F'Dérick happens along the very Wild-West-feeling main drag through town, and while services are limited here, there are a couple of places worth a peek should you have the time.

The eponymous Fort Gouraud is gone, but there are still a couple of decaying colonial-era domed buildings in town. The larger sits along the main road just after it turns east towards Zouérate and the smaller (⊕ 22.6806, -12.7121) is hidden away on the backstreets west of the main road. Also on the west side of town are the remains of the French airstrip, with the guidance marker for pilots (⊕ 22.6741, -12.7277) – a giant 50m-diameter circle reading 'IDJIL' still visible. North of town, a small and seasonal water reservoir helps a handful of doggedly determined gardeners coax a few crops out of this all but Martian landscape, and about 28km to the northwest, there is an enormous sebkha salt pan where traditional salt production has taken place for centuries (⊕ 22.8821, -12.8206). This sebkha and the neighbouring Kedia d'Idjil mountain have also been recognised together as an Important Bird Area.

As you head out of town towards Zouérate, 2km after passing the SNIM control building where you board the train (page 223), there's an old **railcar graveyard** (⊕ 22.6923, -12.6631) where dozens of ruined wagons and locomotives are piled up to decay under the relentless desert sun. It's fine to poke around (watch your step), but probably best practice to go and greet the caretakers should you see them around before or while doing so.

Where to stay and eat There is no official accommodation in F'Dérick. If you'd like to overnight here, the friendly woman running Restaurant Atak Al Khair (Arabic-only signboard; m 44 65 61 66) on the main road may be able to help you find a room/tent.

ZOUÉRATE The largest city (population 62,380) and capital of the Tiris Zemmour region (population 79,129) both literally and figuratively sits in the shadow of the Kedia d'Idjil mountain, owing its existence almost entirely to this massive outcrop of impressively pure iron ore. The city began its life as the Cité d'Idjil, laid out as a company town for the Société des mines de fer de Mauritanie (MIFERMA) in 1961. Unlike its purpose-built counterpart of Cansado on the coast, Zouérate (الزويرات) has grown far beyond initial expectations, with thousands of people flocking to the city over the years seeking employment in the mine or its supporting industries. Today it's the fifth-largest city in the country.

Approaching from the south, the industrial landscape already begins in F'Dérick, and the drive into town reveals a scene worthy of an L S Lowry painting. Enormous machinery trundles about, barrelling down rough roads blasted into the jet-black mountainside, traincars line up along the roadside to be loaded with ore, and all manner of diggers, loaders, hoppers, conveyors and a host of hard-to-identify steel-scaffolded contraptions litter the dust-dark landscape, dwarfing the cars and people passing by in their shadow.

Arriving in Zouérate, the low-rise city sprawls across a plain, with the original town plan – European management north of the main road, African labour to the south – still visible in the sizes of the houses and tidy street layout, but otherwise long since swamped by the unplanned urbanisation that characterises so many Mauritanian towns. The city's grid system still just about remains, though, and even if it could hardly be called a tourist hotspot, Zouérate thrums with the commercial and entrepreneurial energy often found in these sorts of settlements populated by strivers who've arrived from far afield to seek their fortune.

Getting there and away

By air There's an **airport** just north of town, and Mauritania Airlines run a twice-weekly flight between Nouakchott–Nouadhibou–Zouérate on Mondays and Wednesdays. The ticket office (📞 45 44 15 98; m 44 48 26 43; e mai.zoueirat@mauritaniaairlines.mr; w mauritaniaairlines.mr) sits along the road to the airport.

By road Most transport leaves from a string of private offices along the main road, where there are plenty of **minibuses** going to Atar (4hrs; 500UM) every morning,

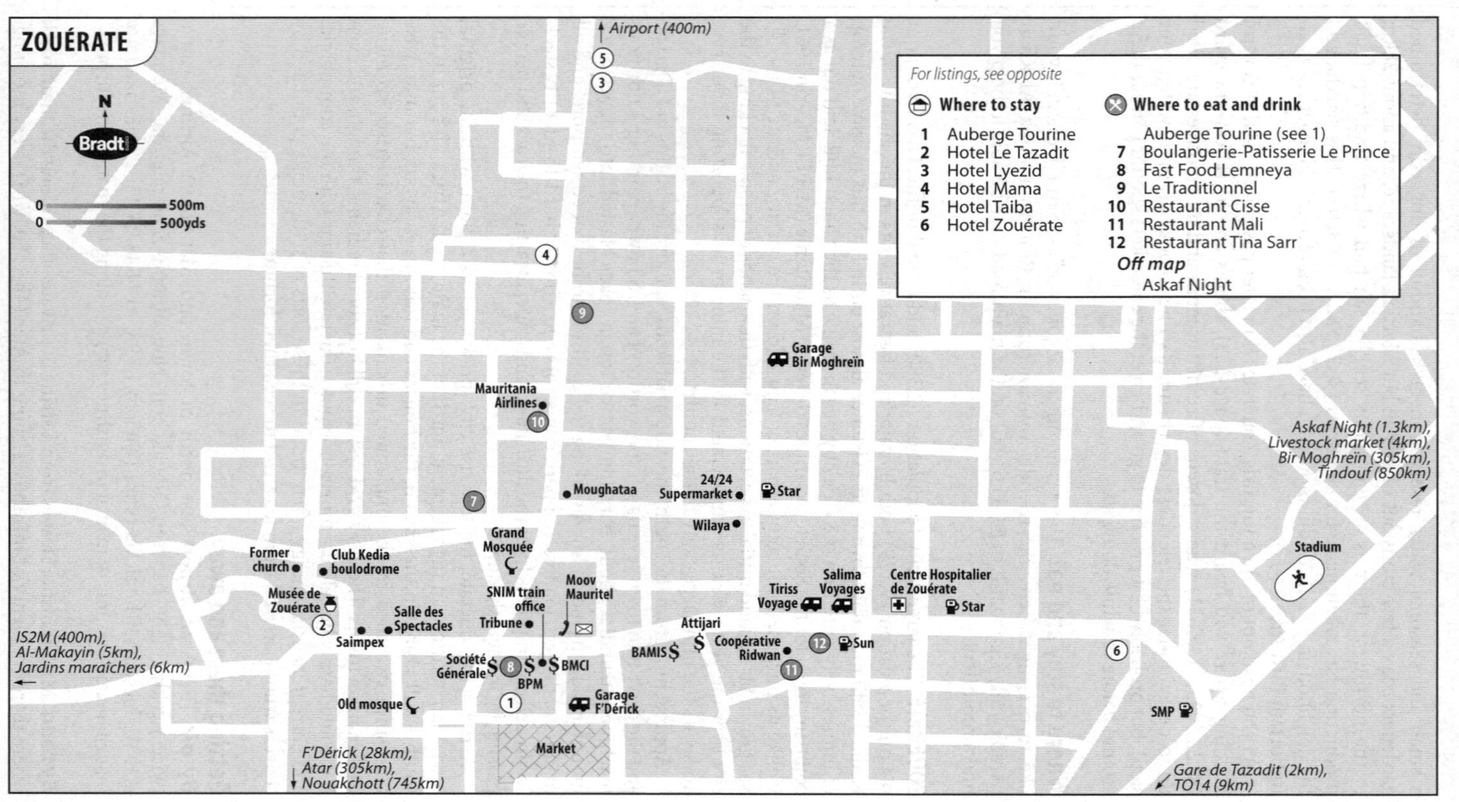
ZOUÉRATE
N
Bradt
0 500m
0 500yds
Airport (400m)
For listings, see opposite
Where to stay
1 Auberge Tourine
2 Hotel Le Tazadit
3 Hotel Lyezid
4 Hotel Mama
5 Hotel Taiba
6 Hotel Zouérate
Where to eat and drink
Auberge Tourine (see 1)
7 Boulangerie-Patisserie Le Prince
8 Fast Food Lemneya
9 Le Traditionnel
10 Restaurant Cisse
11 Restaurant Mali
12 Restaurant Tina Sarr
Off map
Askaf Night
Garage Bir Moghreïn
Mauritania Airlines
Askaf Night (1.3km), Livestock market (4km), Bir Moghreïn (305km), Tindouf (850km)
Moughataa
24/24 Supermarket
Star
Wilaya
Grand Mosquée
Former church
Club Kedia boulodrome
Stadium
Musée de Zouérate
SNIM train office
Moov Mauritel
Salima Voyages
Tiriss Voyage
Centre Hospitalier de Zouérate
Star
Salle des Spectacles
Tribune
Attijari
IS2M (400m), Al-Makayin (5km), Jardins maraîchers (6km)
Saimpex
BAMIS
Coopérative Ridwan
Sun
Société Générale
BPM
BMCI
Old mosque
Garage F'Dérick
SMP
Market
F'Dérick (28km), Atar (305km), Nouakchott (745km)
Gare de Tazadit (2km), TO14 (9km)

including with Salima Voyages (m 43 43 43 61), Eljewda Voyage (m 48 83 82 80) and Tiriss Voyage (m 49 40 81 53, 36 40 57 57). Some of these minibuses will continue all the way to Nouakchott (1,000UM).

Local **taxis** (painted green) serving F'Dérick (70UM shared, 300UM private 'course' taxi) leave from a crowded station just north of the central market. 4x4s to Bir Moghreïn (305km; 6hrs) leave from the gare routière north of here, where you'll also find private cars running to Tindouf/Rabouni in Algeria and the gold mining areas to the east.

For more information on transport to the new border crossing and **Algeria**, see page 215.

By train See page 221.

Where to stay *Map, opposite*

Hotel Le Tazadit Cité Cadres; 45 44 64 63; m 44 90 66 46; e hotel.tazadit@snim.com; w somasertsa.com. Formerly known as L'Oasian, this is 1 of 2 hotels owned & operated by Somasert, SNIM's tourism arm, & is unfortunately not nearly as nice as its sister hotel in Cansado. The rooms are very much showing their age, making it poor value at the price. *2,100/2,600UM sgl/dbl.* **$$$**

Hotel Lyezid m 46 25 37 85, 22 44 35 33; e hotellyezid@gmail.com. At the north end of town just a few hundred metres from the airport, the rooms at this conscientiously managed address are kept to a high standard, & come with the expected amenities. The friendly English-speaking owner is a great help & can arrange anything needed in the area, including car hire. *2,500UM dbl.* **$$$**

Hotel Taiba m 33 60 39 19. Next door to Hotel Lyezid, this is also a carefully managed place, offering well-kept rooms of a similar standard aimed at business travellers. *From 2,200UM dbl.* **$$$**

Hotel Zouérate Main road; m 26 67 60 60. Opened in late 2023, this is Zouérate's newest hotel, with appropriately modern rooms at the east end of town. *2,500UM dbl.* **$$$**

Hotel Mama m 31 15 80 95, 49 34 20 80. This is a clean & quiet option along the Airport Road, with homey (read: frilly) en-suite rooms set around a large interior lounge. The pick if you're after a bit more comfort than the below without stretching the budget too far. *1,500UM dbl.* **$$**

Auberge Tourine m 46 99 32 38, 38 75 96 84. With 1st-floor rooms between the market & main road, this certainly isn't the quietest spot in town, but it's likely to be the cheapest. The rooms are clean & decently kept, & there's even en-suite hot water. There's a good & affordable restaurant on the 1st floor. *From 850UM dbl.* **$**

Where to eat and drink *Map, opposite*

There are a good number of restaurants scattered around the city, mostly of the cheap and cheerful variety, including a number of addresses aimed at labourers from around the region. These include the Senegalese **Restaurant Tina Sarr** (m 26 25 20 30; $) on the main drag and **Restaurant Mali** (m 41 39 05 97; $) near Coopérative Ridwan. There's also Mauritanian food at **Le Traditionnel** (Arabic-only signboard; m 49 00 80 80; $$) on Airport Road, which has seating in private booths open towards a central courtyard. Nearby, **Restaurant Cisse** (m 20 39 58 12; $) does grills and fast-food options like shawarma. **Fast Food Lemneya** (m 33 10 83 04; $) on the main road has a similar menu, while the restaurant at **Auberge Tourine** (see above) has a plat du jour for only 60UM. **Boulangerie-Patisserie Le Prince** ($) has a range of baked goods, and there are a handful of decently stocked supermarkets as well, most notably Saimpex on the main road.

The newly opened **Askaf Night** ($$) on the eastern edge of town is a restaurant and nightspot in the style of the evening hangouts found in Nouakchott and Nouadhibou, where you can find grilled meats, shisha pipes and occasional live music.

Other practicalities Several banks are represented in Zouérate with ATMs, including BMCI, BAMIS, BPM, Attijari Bank and Société Générale. The Centre Hospitalier de Zouérate is on the main road.

What to see and do Though it's true that if Zouérate weren't the terminus for Mauritania's gargantuan train, few tourists would make it here, there are still some

CLIMBING MAURITANIA'S HIGHEST PEAK – KEDIA D'IDJIL

Eric Gilbertson (w countryhighpoints.com; twinstothetops)

My brother Matthew and I are attempting to climb the high points of every country in the world, and Mauritania's, **Kedia d'Idjil**, sounded potentially challenging. The mountain is made mostly of iron and is owned by the Société Nationale Industrielle et Minière (SNIM). Because of this, permission is required to climb to the summit. This is not a peak that is climbed often, and I'm only aware of two (other) foreigners who have done so.

I tried emailing SNIM but didn't get any response, so I started messaging SNIM employees on LinkedIn to see if they knew whom I could ask for permission. I also messaged a professor at the new SNIM-affiliated university, IS2M, in hopes that maybe since I was also a professor and mechanical engineer they might be interested to help out.

Everyone I messaged was extremely helpful. The professor at IS2M said they would contact SNIM on our behalf and invited us to meet at the university. A SNIM employee connected me with Mohammed, their administrative attaché for exploitation. After explaining our plan, Mohammed invited us to meet in Zouérate and discuss the details.

This all sounded promising. Arriving in Mauritania, we arranged transport to Zouérate with Mohamed at Mauritania Best Tours (page 63), as well as a translator, Cheikh (m 46 80 60 31; e aakr734@gmail.com), as we figured we'd need to do quite a bit of talking with SNIM representatives and our French is kind of rusty.

For the intended route we didn't really have any beta on the exact route other climbers had taken, but satellite images showed a long valley northeast of the summit that might be a good access point, along with a faint road going into the valley. There were no active mining operations or buildings, so we figured it might work.

The next morning we had breakfast with some professors from IS2M and drove over to SNIM headquarters at 09.00. We brought some fancy clothes along for a more professional look.

Mohamed soon met up with us and said the magic words – 'no problem'. Both Mohamed and SNIM were very interested in our project, and even arranged for some local journalists to accompany us as we set out. We would need to start hiking at 15.00, with a plan to camp on the summit and return the next morning.

We packed up and drove to the starting point, where the journalists started interviewing us and taking pictures. We then *all* started walking up the road. This was definitely not how I expected to be climbing Kedia d'Idjil! The road soon got washed out, and we continued up a talus creek bed with intermittent signs of an old road.

On the east side of the road we saw mining trucks at the top of the hill dumping rocks down the hillside. I think they do 24/7 operations up there. One journalist worthwhile stops to make while you're in town. To start with, the Cité Cadres neighbourhood is the heart of the original planned city of Zouérate, and the trim villas here were previously home to many of MIFERMA's expatriate staff. Just behind Hotel Le Tazadit, the **Musée de Zouérate** is a rather dated affair, but worth a spin through the rooms on prehistory, contemporary artefacts, and of course the mine itself. Across the road, the Club Kédia **boulodrome** (pétanque pitch) is where

told us the west side of the valley was mined decades ago, but is not currently being exploited.

The canyon walls were steep cliffs and I was a bit nervous we wouldn't be able to find a way out. The journalists were surprised we knew where we were going, having never been there before; we didn't exactly know, but acted confident that it would work out.

After a few kilometres I saw a low-angle exit at the head of the canyon, and breathed a sigh of relief. The old roadbed ended, and the crew joining us decided to turn back here. I was surprised they had joined us so far – I hope they had fun hiking!

We waved goodbye and picked up the pace a bit. There was actually a faint trail leading up out of the canyon, and it appears locals, perhaps goat herders, occasionally take it.

We crested the col at the head of the valley and then the terrain got much easier. The ridge to our right was smaller rocks and travel was fast. Based on my research I thought there might be some uncertainty on the true location of the highpoint, so I brought a surveyor's sight level to definitively measure.

With sunset approaching, we jogged a bit on the ridge to the northern summit. There was no cairn and it seemed obviously shorter than the southern summit. We then proceeded south, jogging on the easy sections, and by 18.30 reached a cairn on the southern summit.

I took out my sight level and measured: the northern peak was 17m shorter and the others shorter still. So we were definitely on the highpoint of Mauritania, known as **Galb Selaya** (915m).

We still had plenty of time to admire the views. Interestingly, we were far enough from the mine that we couldn't see any signs of civilisation in any direction. Just rolling black hills and desert in the distance. There was a small thorny bush near the summit but otherwise essentially no signs of life.

We soon got to work picking out a campsite. We only had bivvy sacks instead of a tent and the top was a bit windy, but there was a small flat col nearby. We made a wind break, carefully piling up rocks into a knee-high 10ft-long rock wall, which actually worked pretty well.

We went to bed around sunset. A lone mosquito somehow managed to join us, but it won't be bothering anyone anymore! I'm not sure how it survived in the desert so far from any water.

We got up around 04.30 and started down by headlamp. We took a more direct route, dropping down a fun scrambly canyon and then back up a gentle slope to the col at the head of our entrance canyon. We then hiked back down as the sun rose, and met Cheikh and Mokhtar at the end of the dirt road.

We threw our bags in the truck and started back to Nouakchott. Everything had gone as well as could be expected, and we were very satisfied with our ascent. We made the local, and maybe even national, news!

the local boulistes – some of whom have competed internationally – practise in the evenings.

Exiting the pitch and heading a few steps to the north, the former Sainte-Barbe de Zouérate **church** was built to accommodate the neighbourhood's French expatriates, but as this population steadily decreased over the years, the Catholics eventually wrapped things up here in 2013. After handing the keys back to SNIM, the building was converted into a mosque, now known as Mosquée El Ihsan.

Back on the main road, the **Salle des Spectacles** is a unique open-topped cinema dating to the city's early days, though you're more likely to catch an organisational meeting than a film here these days. East of here behind the **tribune** used for festivals and other events, Zouérate's sizeable new **grand mosque** was inaugurated in 2023. With room for 4,000 faithful Zouératois over its 5,000m^2, it dwarfs the city's **original mosque**, which is south of the main road in the worker's district and dates to Zouérate's founding.

About 250m to the east of the old mosque is Zouérate's **Marché central**, which spills across several densely packed blocks, where melhfas, mobile phones and mining equipment are all ready and waiting for the sharp-eyed buyer, along with any cushions, blankets or extra layers one might wish to take on the train.

Back on the main road and heading east, the street is lined with pharmacies, banks, bus companies and other essential services. A block south of the main drag, the **Coopérative Ridwan** (m 46 46 74 25, 46 72 14 76) is a women's stonecutters co-operative, where a dozen or more members work cutting, scraping, carving and polishing a variety of semi-precious stones into beads, keychains, jewellery and more. Most of what they work with they've foraged in the area themselves, and they coax an impressive palette of colours from their findings, plucking hues of turquoise, lapis, coral and more out of the city's barren-seeming surrounds.

On the west side of town, Zouérate has since 2018 been home to a new vocational school, the **Institut Supérieur des Métiers de la Mine de Zouérate** (Higher Institute of Mining Professions, IS2M; w is2m.mr). The modern campus is worth a peek as the whole set of buildings are organised into the shape of SNIM's striking logo (that to this author's eye looks plucked straight out of a sci-fi film).

Past the institute and continuing to the west, there's a large artisanal **gold processing site** known as al-Makayin (the machines; ⊕ 22.7323, -12.5260), not dissimilar from the one found at Chami (page 163). It can be found about 5km outside of town to the west and 2.5km north of the road to F'Dérick. Some 3km north of here is a large lot of **jardins maraîchers** (market gardens; ⊕ 22.7552, -12.5370) where palms and more are grown, impressive if for nothing else than their tenacity.

In the opposite direction, the local **football** squad, ASC Kédia, plays at the 2016 Stade de Zouérate on the east end of town. Passing the stadium and continuing about 4km northeast of the city, Zouérate's **livestock market** ('marbatt'; ⊕ 22.7652, -12.4340) is home to thousands of hooved animals, many of whom will soon fill the bowls of hungry workers clocking out of a sweaty, dusty shift.

Finally, it's also possible to **tour the mine**, though it takes a bit of arranging and approval from SNIM higher-ups. Tours visit the TO14 deposit (⊕ 22.6584, -12.4371) about 9km south of Zouérate, taking in the enormous open pits and equipment, but not the indoor facilities. SNIM management doesn't generally wish to deal directly with tourists, so you typically have to find an agency to chase the permission on your behalf (ask your guide if you have one already). If you'd like to try and arrange it yourself, contact Bechir (m 36 43 82 18) on WhatsApp, who can act as a go-between and facilitate requests to management for a reasonable fee.

Requests are not always approved to get in as a solo traveller, but in season, groups taking the Train du Désert (page 221) generally tour the mine on Mondays, and it's also possible you will be allowed to tag along with one of these groups with advance notice. Contact either Bechir or Kadi Medhi of Mauritanides Voyages (m 49 00 59 98; e kadimehdi93@gmail.com, kadi@mauritanides.com; w mauritanides.com;) to enquire, and expect to pay perhaps €50 to get the permission and €50 for the tour.

A few travellers have also managed to climb **Kedia d'Idjil**, which is wholly owned by SNIM and also requires special permissions – see page 212 for details.

Festivals **La fête des mineurs** (Miners' Day) is celebrated on 4 December (the feast day of Saint Barbara, patron saint of miners – for whom Zouérate's erstwhile church was once named) every year, and the city brightens up with a number of sport and cultural activities in the days leading up to the holiday. Many of these are organised by ASC Kédia (Association sportive et culturelle de Kédia; m 44 90 59 40), which puts on a variety of activities, from *medh* praise singing concerts, poetry recitations and board game tournaments to cycling, shooting and traditional wrestling competitions.

Also in December, a new addition to the Zouérate cultural calendar, the first **Festival des villes minières** (Mining Towns Festival; f EXPOvilleminieres) was held in Zouérate over 20–22 December 2024, with a series of concerts and other cultural events. Sponsored by most of the major mining companies working in Mauritania, it may rotate through some of the country's other important mining centres in the years to come.

BIR MOGHREÏN AND THE ROUTE TO ALGERIA Marooned in a roadless expanse some 300km north of Zouérate, and hemmed in by the SADR border to the north and west, there's a convincing argument to be made for **Bir Moghreïn** (بئر مغرين) as Mauritania's most isolated town. Known as Fort Trinquet during the colonial era, Bir Moghreïn (population 5,126) is still effectively a garrison town. The south of the city is dominated by a walled military base almost as large as the town itself, inside which are the ruins of the original Fort Trinquet, dating to the 1930s, are inside, but inaccessible. With the air of a frontier town and all that comes with it, the city's economy revolves around trade (both licit and illicit) with Sahrawi across the border, and increasingly the gold boom that has entirely upturned labour and employment in northeastern Mauritania. As if to put a cherry on top of the city's desert-fortress vibe, it's also long been home to one of Mauritania's maximum security prisons (though many of the convicts here were moved to a newer facility in N'Beïka in 2021).

Approaching the city from Zouérate, you cross 300km of roadless plains and sebkhas (crossing the Tropic of Cancer after 100km), eventually pulling close to a cluster of jagged rock formations and broken mountains that dot the plain surrounding Bir Moghreïn (6hrs; 700UM). There are no ATMs here, but fuel, food and lodging (Auberge Lyezid; **$**) are all available. If you've made it all the way here, you're likely on the way to Algeria or are – security allowing – planning to visit the SADR side of the Western Sahara (page 222). There are also reportedly some rarely visited rock carvings around **Aguelt Aouineght**, 50km to the north. It's possible to find transport to Tindouf that originates here in Bir Moghreïn, but note that depending on the security situation, some vehicles cut the corner and pass through SADR territory via the Sahrawi towns of Tifariti, Bir Lehlu or Bir Tiguisit. This knocks about 100km off the 800km journey, but this was not considered safe at the time of writing due primarily to the risk of indiscriminate Moroccan drone strikes.

Therefore, it may be easier to take a vehicle directly from Zouérate to Algeria, unless you have a particular urge to overnight in Bir Moghreïn. From Zouérate, Tiriss Voyage (m 49 40 81 53, 36 40 57 57) run vehicles to **Tindouf** three times weekly (2,000UM), departing Zouérate at noon on Sundays, Tuesdays and Thursdays. Bear in mind the 800km journey takes something like 24 hours, with a rest stop overnight at Aïn Ben Tili, and you *must* have your Algerian visa arranged ahead of time. At the time of writing, Tiriss Voyage follows the route that stays fully within Mauritania.

In the colonial era, rather ostentatiously named Piste Impériale No 1 connected Tindouf and Mauritania, and while this was never more than a series of desert tracks, a new 840km tarmac road is already under construction as you read this, and will link Zouérate, Bir Moghreïn and Tindouf in Algeria, supposedly by the end of 2026 or in 2027.

The new road will go through an extraordinarily remote stretch of desert in which Bir Moghreïn is the only settlement of any size, and even the herders' hamlets so common throughout Mauritania all but disappear. But as the gold rush has also reached this part of Mauritania, extensive dig sites are popping up at breakneck speed (for example at ⊕ 26.1856, -8.64144), meaning the route is more populated than it has been in the past, though this is relative indeed. If you're headed this way, you'll pass through the southern stretches of the **Tamreïkat Massif**, which is the last major relief you'll see for many hundreds of miles. Set some 60km northeast of Bir Moghreïn, this isolated chain stretches 75km to the northwest and was recognised as an Important Bird Area in 2001.

Given this remoteness, it's worth noting that there's at least one phone tower between Zouérate and Bir Moghreïn at Rich Enajim (⊕ 24.2914, -11.8822) and another between Bir Moghreïn and Aïn Ben Tili at Hassi Loughar (⊕ 25.4054, -10.7521). That being said, this is all set to change considerably with the arrival

MOROCCAN CONNECTION

News reports in 2025 covered the completion of a new Moroccan road connection between the Morocco-controlled Western Saharan city of Smara and Bir Moghreïn in Mauritania, running between the two halves of the Polisario-controlled Western Sahara and emerging from behind the Moroccan wall where it meets Mauritanian territory directly. The Dakar Rally has run this way in years past, though until now no crossings had been allowed for a number of years.

It is only about 180km between Smara and Bir Moghreïn, and as of 2025, the 85km in Morocco-controlled Western Sahara is now fully surfaced, while the remaining 95km in Mauritania is still desert tracks. Despite the road's partial completion, at the time of writing, border infrastructure had yet to be established, so the practicalities of the crossing remain somewhat unclear. This seems likely to change during the lifespan of this edition, with significant implications for travel possibilities and logistics in the region.

A new border crossing here would be the second official crossing between Morocco and Mauritania, and would allow travellers in northeastern Mauritania to join the Moroccan road network and reach Laayoune and its airport within a day's travel from Bir Moghreïn (390km). Royal Air Maroc also used to run direct flights between Smara and Casablanca, though this route was inactive at the time of writing.

of the new road, especially as the Algerian Naftal company has been awarded the concession to develop and manage a number of service stations along the route.

As it stands, most traffic passes via or rests overnight at the outpost at **Aïn Ben Tili**, a fabulously isolated military outpost smack on the Sahara border, which was originally built by the French in 1934. Polisario forces occupied it in 1976, and it took two years and Moroccan assistance for Mauritania to eventually reclaim it.

The new road is slated to run about 20km to the south of Aïn Ben Tili, and from here it will continue parallelling the Saharan border at a similar distance all the way to the border crossing with Algeria. This crossing, which was only officially opened to all traffic in February 2024, goes by a surprisingly long list of sobriquets, and you may see it referred to as PK75 (as it's 75km from Tindouf), Hassi 75 or Puits 75 (meaning 'wells' in Arabic or French), as well as Mustapha Ben Boulaïd (after a martyr in the Algerian revolution) and Ould El Bardi (after a 20th-century Rgueibat sheikh who tussled with the French).

Once at the border post (whatever you call it), it's a further 75km on new tar to Tindouf; Algerian authorities may send you with a police escort. This route is possible (or perhaps would even be easier) heading south into Mauritania as well as heading north into Algeria, as Mauritanian authorities *are* able to process e-visas on arrival at this crossing. Tiriss Voyage's contact number in Tindouf is m (+213) 656 78 44 44.

CHEGGA AND THE FAR EAST For many years a closed military zone, the enormous desert expanses of northeastern Mauritania are effectively devoid of population, save for a small handful of military outposts and an increasing number of wildcat gold-mining operations. The terrain is open and flat, defined by plains cut through with dry oueds and barren expanses of sebkha salt pan, with the occasional rocky outcrop rising to a few hundred metres for punctuation.

Heading east from Zouérate, the **Cratère de Tenoumer** (Tenoumer Crater; ⊕ 22.9183, -10.4058) is one such bit of topography, rising from the plain after 215km in a perfect circle 2km across. It's thought to date to a meteor strike more than 1.5 million years ago. Nearly 200km northeast of here, the **tomb** of the last Adrar emir, Sidi Ahmed Ould Aida, has got to rank among the world's most isolated graves (⊕ 23.7751, -8.8066); he died out here in 1932 after leaving the Adrar as part of a dispute with the French colonialists.

Having paid your respects, turn southeast for 100km and you'll reach the El Hank escarpment, which rises to the south and divides Tiris Zemmour from the Adrar region. Here lies the astonishingly remote outpost of **El Mreïti** (or Lemgheity; ⊕ 23.4760, -7.8607), which is home to a permanent set of wells, an airstrip and a military base. Though it's been recognised as an Important Bird Area since 2001, it's unfortunately best known as the site of the first attack against Mauritanian interests during the modern Islamist insurgency in the Sahel, when the Algerian Groupe Salafiste pour la Prédication et le Combat ambushed the base in June 2005, killing 15 soldiers.

From here, the escarpment runs northeast for another 300km until reaching the exaggeratedly isolated fort of **Chegga**, near where the borders with Algeria and Mali come to a tripoint. The fort here dates to the 1930s, in the same era as those in Bir Moghreïn and Aïn Ben Tili, but the rock carvings and small spring on the site attest to a human history countless years older than the final colonial penetration of the country.

Today, though Chegga (also recognised as an Important Bird Area) has long been almost impossible to access due to a combination of remoteness, insecurity, bureaucracy and more, this is changing quickly, as the region surrounding the fort has seen an unprecedented influx of wildcat gold miners from around the region setting up camp in the backcountry surrounding Chegga after gold was found in the region around 2019. They have kept plenty busy since then carving enormous trenches into the earth that are easily visible from satellite imagery (eg: ⊕ 24.7984, -6.6865). As in Chami and near Zouérate, the state has given its blessing (and taken its cut), and a clutch of increasingly sophisticated settlements like Al Sawadna (⊕ 25.6359, -6.1709) are taking on a few rudimentary trappings of permanency, with mobile provider Chinguitel even setting up a mobile antenna in one of the largest camps near Gleib N'Dour.

But it's not only artisanal miners with a large and growing interest in the region. Very near the encampments around Gleib N'Dour (or Gleïb en Ndour), the Tiris Uranium Project and its Australian backer, Aura Energy, received government approval and plan to mine and export uranium here starting in 2026, claiming there are world-class deposits both here and at another site near Aïn Ben Tili.

It's impossible to explore this remote region without your own transport and guide, but if you've got those, you *might* be able to make it as far as El Mreïti without too much trouble if you're determined. Beyond here, you're likely to be turned back unless you've got an official (documented) reason to be headed for Chegga or surrounds – and don't forget the Mauritanian soldiers out here asking for your papers 100 times are also the reason you're able to safely travel around here today.

But since you won't make it to Chegga, do the next best thing and have a look at this fascinating collection of 1970s photographs from a geologist who was once based at the site: **w** heinandwil.net/CANWebpages/Chegga.htm.

THE IRON ORE TRAIN

Long a favourite topic of West African backpacker lore, Mauritania's famous Iron Ore Train (known locally as the **train minéralier** or mineral train) runs between the iron ore mines around Kedia d'Idjil to the coast near Nouadhibou, where this critical material is loaded into ships and sent to countries around the world for processing into steel. The parastatal Société nationale Industrielle et Minière (National Industrial and Mining Company), better known as SNIM, administers both the mine and the train, and as such controls a hefty slice of the Mauritanian economy.

In 2022, the train transported 12.79 million tonnes of ore and SNIM counted more than 6,600 employees on their payroll. The company's activities accounted for just under 10% of Mauritanian GDP, representing 22% of state revenue and 32% of all exports. Just over half of the exported ore goes to China, with Algeria (10%), Italy (8%) and Australia (7%) next in the queue. About 3% goes to the UK. SNIM also has more than a dozen subsidiaries operating in different fields, including tourism (page 221).

The single-track standard-gauge railway runs 650km east from the mineral port south of Nouadhibou at Cansado to Zouérate, and a further 50km to the very end of the line at the Guelb El Rhein mine site. (A 42km extension to the new mine sites at El Aouj and Atomaï was also planned in 2025.) There are 17 sidings along the route where trains can pass one another, and maintenance bases along the way at Choum and Tmeïmichat.

But unlike most pieces of mining infrastructure which do not become world famous, the train minéralier has grown to have something of a global reputation, and is widely referred to as the longest train in the world, checking in at up to 3km long and consisting of 200-plus wagons. While this accolade may not be strictly correct today – there are a handful of similarly long ore and coal trains around the world now – it's undoubtedly among a very small handful of trains of this length worldwide, and almost certainly the only one you can ride as a passenger. It also sits comfortably among the world's heaviest, weighing up to 20,000 tonnes depending on the day's load. The General Motors locomotives pulling it along (it uses either two or four) have up to a colossal 4,500 horsepower each.

Mauritanians needing to travel or trade have been hopping the train between the two cities for decades, either in the passenger car guard's van, or atop/inside the ore wagons, depending on the direction of travel. Since its inception, the train has been the quickest and easiest way to get between Nouadhibou and Zouérate (even today the road link still involves a long detour), as well as an efficient way for traders to move a fair amount of cargo for minimal cost. Over time, a trickle of adventure-seeking backpackers also showed up on the train alongside them, particularly after the 2001 opening of the Guerguerat border crossing made overland travel from Morocco possible, and it carried on this way for many years.

But the last decade or so has seen the train ride explode in popularity among tourists, and the train became not only an Instagrammer's and YouTuber's delight, but an increasingly large draw for adventurous tour groups. But alongside the epic photo and video content, reports of travellers behaving recklessly on the train – jumping between cars, balancing on the edges, etc – began to seep out as well.

As such, the train, or train ride rather, seems to have become a victim of its own popularity. SNIM, weary of a growing headache surrounding travellers and presumably loathe to find itself implicated in the injury or death of one, announced an official prohibition on riding in the ore carts in December 2024. The announcement reminded travellers that there is indeed a passenger car on the train, which they are welcome to take. The advice contained on page 220 is therefore written with this new reality in mind.

HISTORY The enormous iron ore deposits at Kedia d'Idjil were first identified in 1934, but commercial exploitation did not begin until decades later. When the French ultimately began to eye up the deposit for development in the 1950s, there were two routings considered for the railway line needed to export the ore to the coast. The first would have headed directly west towards Villa Cisneros (now Dakhla) in the then Spanish Sahara, only 400km away. But negotiations between the French and Spanish broke down, and in 1960 construction began on what would become the Mauritania Railway, running entirely within Mauritanian territory to a purpose-built mineral export port at the also purpose-built town of Cansado. French–Spanish negotiations failed so completely that the railway was not allowed to transit even a few kilometres of Spanish territory to avoid an escarpment at Choum, but instead a tunnel was blasted through 1.5km of rock, keeping the alignment within Mauritanian land (page 187).

Mining at Zouérate began in the early 1960s under the private Société des mines de fer de Mauritanie (MIFERMA), and the first ore trains started rolling in April 1963. By the late 1960s, iron ore exports accounted for an overwhelming 80% of Mauritania's foreign earnings. But much of the wealth went offshore to European investors and expatriate employees, a persistent source of resentment among Mauritanian workers. Troops put down a strike here in May 1968, shooting nine demonstrators dead. Though calm ultimately returned to the city, the mine's continuing profitability and an increasingly experienced Mauritanian workforce meant that the mine was eventually able to be nationalised in 1974, under the newly organised Société nationale industrielle et minière (SNIM). Today, the Mauritanian state holds 78% of SNIM's shares, while a handful of Arab and Islamic finance organisations administer the remainder.

But this lifeblood of the Mauritanian economy and state was also a plum target for Polisario rebels when Mauritania set out to annex part of the Western Sahara in 1975. They immediately recognised its value and vulnerability and began to sabotage the line. By 1977, these attacks (including deadly raids on Zouérate and Nouakchott) had paralysed the railway almost entirely, with predictably dire knock-on effects for the Mauritanian economy and development, ultimately leading to the overthrow of first president Mokhtar Ould Daddah in 1978 and the signing of a peace treaty with Polisario in 1979, which recognised their right to the territory Mauritania had previously claimed. The disabled railway was back up and running at the start of the 1980s, and has been hauling ore ever since.

RIDING THE TRAIN Mauritanians who have been riding the ore carts for decades will presumably continue to do so, but reports of travellers being kicked off the train had already been percolating earlier in 2024, and the official announcement means that, despite having ridden the train as part of the research for this book, we now must advise against attempting to do the same.

While individuals or small groups may still be able to get away with it, both railway staff and local police and gendarmes are aware of the prohibition. At the time of writing, a number of tour agencies were still offering group trips atop the train; it's unclear what sort of official or unofficial exemptions they may have solicited to this end.

But as travel in the passenger carriage remains permissible, the advice above remains applicable. Keep in mind that the train is operated exclusively for industrial purposes, with passenger service a complete afterthought. As such, train services run according to the needs of the mine, and may change significantly from day to day, depending on production factors as well as considerations like the weather.

It also means that some trains have the passenger wagon attached, but some do not. There are up to three daily departures, with at least one having the wagon attached (this is the run for which we have attempted to give rough timings below). If so, the train will stop in Choum, but otherwise generally not. If the passenger wagon isn't attached, the train will also bypass the station in Nouadhibou, instead continuing directly to the port area south of Nouadhibou.

It's therefore possible to take either (or both) of the two legs of the journey, between Zouérate and Choum or Choum and Nouadhibou. The train generally makes a 10–15-minute stop at Choum, during which it's possible to embark and disembark. The ride between Zouérate and Choum takes about 4–5 hours, and about 12–14 hours between Choum and Nouadhibou. Assuming it leaves on time, the leg from Zouérate to Choum is the best for desert scenery and sunset over

INFAMOUS INAL

The village of Inal is notorious in Mauritania as the site of a 1990 massacre in which Bidhan troops murdered 28 of their black colleagues on Mauritanian Independence Day, one of the many 'events' that characterised the Mauritanian socio-political crisis of the late 1980s and early 1990s (page 262).

An English-subtitled documentary investigating the Inal massacre can be viewed at: w youtu.be/NmNpzmtHs8k?si=IFTE2ShpN1eGWf-a.

THE TRAIN DU DÉSERT

This sky-blue train is totally distinct from the Iron Ore Train (train minéralier, page 218). The **Train du Désert**, also called the 'petit train bleu', is a three-car train that's been set up exclusively for tourism. It consists of a former Czech compartment car (in considerably better nick than its poor cousin on the train minéralier), locomotive and double-decker lounge car, which is fully decked out in Mauritanian style with rugs and cushions and the lot. The train carries tour groups of about 20 between Zouérate and Ben Amira, making stops for a tour of the mine itself, spending some nights camping near Ben Amira, and taking vehicle excursions to Chinguetti and other sites in the Adrar.

It's managed by SNIM's tourism arm, the Société Mauritanienne de Services et de Tourisme (SOMASERT; 45 74 27 00, 45 74 90 43; w somasertsa.com; f Somasert SA), though in practice it's likely easier to deal with an agency if you'd like to get aboard. Several French agencies offer week-long itineraries utilising the train for around €1,600, including Point-Afrique (w point-afrique.com), Terres d'Aventure (w terdav.com) and Nomade Aventure (w nomade-aventure.com).

Alternatively, you can just contact local agency Mauritanides Voyages (m 49 00 59 98; e kadimehdi93@gmail.com, kadi@mauritanides.com; w mauritanides.com;) directly to enquire. And should you have €14,600 on hand (the price for a group of 20), you can have it all to yourself.

Western Sahara; it will generally be dark by the time you reach Choum until the next morning as you approach Bou Lanouar and Nouadhibou.

The train maxes out at 60km/h, but speeds of 35–45km/h are more typical. Derailments do infrequently occur, with incidents of varying severity recorded in 2015, 2017 and 2023, but fortunately these caused no significant injuries or deaths.

The train passes a handful of tiny villages along the tracks en route, including Ben Amira (page 188), Tmeïmichat (population 1,615) and Inal (population 183; see opposite). It often makes a short stop in Tmeïmichat to refresh staff or pick up or drop off supplies as SNIM has a base here.

If it's not clear by now, this is not a trip that can easily be predicted. In most cases, the easiest way to find out the train's current status is to ask at your accommodation. Most establishments in the area are used to people coming and going on the train, and they've often got someone they can call who's got the inside scoop.

And finally it should go without saying that if you plan to take the train, it's key to allow sufficient wiggle room before any fixed onward travel plans.

From Nouadhibou Trains arrive and depart from the Gare de Voyageurs (Passenger Rail Station; ⊕ 21.0073, -17.0318) north of the city. There are no facilities at the dilapidated station, but Somasert announced renovation plans in 2024, so perhaps it will be a little less shambolic by the time you read this.

Arriving from Zouérate, taxis wait here to meet the arriving trains and bring you into Nouadhibou. The ore wagons are empty when leaving Nouadhibou and trains generally depart towards Zouérate around 14.00–17.00 (Further departures are possible between 19.00–22.00 & 00.00–02.00.).

From Zouérate and F'Dérick As the iron ore is loaded from several deposits around Zouérate depending on the day, there are several spur tracks leading to these different mine sites (including F'Dérick, Rouessa, Tazadit, TO14, Guelb El Rhein and M'Haoudat), and it's not until F'Dérick that all of these tracks converge – meaning train movements can be more unpredictable on the tracks around Zouérate, but *all* trains must pass (and stop at) F'Dérick before heading west.

There is no station at F'Dérick, but the best place to board the train is near a SNIM control building just over 4km east of town (⊕ 22.6829, -12.6806). This is a

SITES IN THE SAHRAWI-CONTROLLED WESTERN SAHARA (SAHRAWI ARAB DEMOCRATIC REPUBLIC)

One of the least-understood corners of the map of Africa – or more likely anywhere in the world – is the eastern portion of Western Sahara that sits between the Moroccan-built desert wall and the Mauritanian border. This sparsely populated area, divided into two sectors covering some 20% of the territory's total area, is administered by the Sahrawi independence movement, the Polisario Front, as part of what they call the Sahrawi Arab Democratic Republic (SADR). Since its declaration of independence from Spain on 27 February 1976, the SADR has been recognized by 80-some countries, and is a full member of the African Union.

The area west of the Moroccan wall is administered by Morocco as their Southern Provinces, while the territory east of the wall is administered by Sahrawi/Polisario forces and has traditionally been home to a small handful of settlements, including Tifariti (declared as the SADR's provisional capital), Bir Tiguisit, Bir Lehlu, Meharrize, Agüenit, Duguech, Mijek and Zug. Polisario authorities (who, thanks to the territory's colonial history, use Spanish as their second working language after Arabic) typically refer to this area as the Territorios Liberados (Liberated Territories).

Moroccan authorities instead commonly refer to the area as a 'buffer zone', rather than a territory in its own right. The United Nations, which regards Western Sahara as a whole as a non-self-governing territory, simply refers to 'west of the berm' and 'east of the berm' to maintain a neutral stance between the diametrically opposed claims.

The area near the berm/wall is a heavily militarised zone which is impossible to cross or approach other than at Guerguerat (page 164) and potentially soon near Smara (see opposite). Conversely, there are no controls between the Mauritanian border and the Polisario-controlled portion of Western Sahara. Indeed, Mauritanian road and railway infrastructure crosses this border for several kilometres near Choum.

Polisario forces actively patrol the area, but an uptick in the conflict since 2020 (page 166) means that it's currently dangerous and strongly discouraged to attempt to visit the territory, and many of the area's residents (estimated as between 10,000 and 70,000 people, depending on your source) have fled to the Polisario-administered refugee camps near Tindouf in Algeria to avoid this resurgence in conflict and a real risk of drone strikes. There are, therefore, currently no officially declared visa or entry procedures. Prior to 2020, a handful of travellers attempting the crossing reported either being welcomed with tea and biscuits or escorted back to either the nearest base or the Mauritanian border. To enquire further, contact a Sahrawi mission abroad (page 67).

All that being said, should the situation change, there are a number of potential sites of interest located in the Polisario-controlled zone that are within just a few hours of Mauritania's northern cities (and in effect are only accessible from here). These are mentioned below for a hopeful future reference.

shunting yard where wagons from the different mine sites are collected and hitched before starting the long journey to the coast. A shared taxi between Zouérate and F'Dérick is about 70UM, and a 'course' (private) taxi about 300UM.

If the train is being loaded from the Tazadit/TO14 deposit, you can catch the train from Zouérate from a lay-by about 2.25km south of town (⊕ 22.7079, -12.4642), sometimes rather generously called the Gare de Tazadit

Probably the most famous 'sight' in the region, the SAAF *Avro Shackleton 1716* (⊕ 22.6304, -13.2373) or 'Pelican 16' was a restored old British/South African military plane that crash landed here en route to an air show in the UK in 1994. All 19 of its SAAF crew survived, and today the wreck sits open to the elements along a track some 60km west of F'Dérick and 15km into Sahrawi-controlled territory. Sahrawi authorities have erected a small commemorative plaque here.

About 75km to the west of the *Avro Shackleton* wreck, Leyuad (Lajuad; ⊕ 22.4481, -13.9212) is a scenic cluster of inselbergs, similar to those found 130km to the south at Ben Amira (page 188). These top out at around 600m tall, and host several shelters where ancient rock carvings can be found depicting human, animal and geometric motifs. The area is also sometimes known as the Cuevas/Montes del Diablo (Devil's Caves/Mountains). The nearest Sahrawi settlement to either of the above is at Agüenit (⊕ 22.1838, -13.1392).

Some 350km to the north, the ruin of a colonial-era Spanish fort (⊕ 25.0699, -12.0428) sits along the Uad Tanafed, some 50km southwest of Bir Moghreïn and less than 5km over the border into Sahrawi-controlled territory. Its name seems to be unrecorded – even the official UN documents just refer to it as 'old Spanish fort'. As with much of northern Mauritania, this once-desolate area has become a hive of gold-mining activity over the past several years, with wildcat operations now dotting the landscape.

The Moroccan-built wall then dips into Mauritanian territory northwest of Bir Moghreïn, which is where the proposed border crossing from Smara is likely to be built (page 223). Northeast of here, the Sahrawi settlements of Tifariti (⊕ 26.1588, -10.5591) and Bir Lehlu (⊕ 26.3495, -9.5771) are the area's most significant, and were typical stopovers for transport between Zouérate/Bir Moghreïn and Tindouf until increased instability forced most traffic to stay within Mauritania and route via Aïn Ben Tili instead.

In the past, provisional capital Tifariti was host to the ARTifariti (w artifariti.org) festival, though security concerns mean this international art festival now takes place in the camps near Tindouf. Some of the remains of festivals past still decorate the landscape, however, including the unlikely and enormous Audrey Hepburn-inspired rock art reading 'Breakfast at Tifariti' (⊕ 26.1602, -10.5657), just about legible on satellite imagery for the keen-eyed. Bir Lehlu is about 100km to the east, and famous among Sahrawi as the location from which the SADR was first proclaimed in 1976.

For those interested in a further look at this little-understood region's ancient history, the 2018 book *The Archaeology of Western Sahara*, edited by Joanne Clarke and Nick Brooks, is the most authoritative information available on the region's archaeological patrimony. Nick Brooks also maintains a blog on the region at w sandanddust.wordpress.com.

– despite the conspicuous lack of 'gare' here. There is a small garden next to the tracks, though, inside of which you'll find an entrepreneur and his tiny shop selling snacks and basic provisions for the journey. A private taxi here should only cost 100UM. The SNIM control building for this shunting area sits 1.25km south of here. These trains will also stop in F'Dérick, however, either for a few minutes or a few hours depending on how many wagons need hitching and rearranging. The ultimate departure from here is usually in the afternoon, anywhere between 14.00 and 18.00. (Further departures are possible between 20.00–23.00 & 01.00–04.00.)

There is a SNIM office in Zouérate (⊕ 22.7348, -12.4723) where you can get information on the day's planned departure. There's unfortunately no longer a dedicated phone line, but it's located right on the main drag between the BPM and BMCI banks.

From Choum Choum is home to a maintenance base for SNIM and you can embark or disembark from the train here during the short stop made on the way in either direction. Towards Nouadhibou, trains theoretically pass through between 19.00 and 21.00. It's less popular to board in Choum towards Zouérate, likely because trains will generally pass through between 02.00 and 04.00, but equally possible. The Auberge du Choum (page 187) is a short walk from the tracks, and an excellent resource for all train-related queries and needs.

On the train Since SNIM's December 2024 statement, we must advise against attempting to ride in the ore wagons. Therefore, the passenger car that is appended on to the back of the train is now the prescribed option. Unfortunately, the abject condition of the passenger facilities is one of the reasons people were so keen to hop on the ore in the first place.

To call them catastrophic would be generous. Start with a pre-1990 Czechoslovak railcar and bash it back and forth through the desert every day with no cleaning or cosmetic service for years. These wagons have received nothing more than the most essential mechanical maintenance, and they very much look it – a pure, undiluted distillate of Mauritania's often-Mad Maxian vibe. The wagon is divided into several compartments which would have at one point held seats, but dilapidated wooden benches are all that remain. Neither power nor water functions and the toilets are therefore exactly the disaster you would expect. Remember that the full ride can take 16–20 hours, so you must be self-sufficient in food and water, and temperatures plummet overnight. You'll also be charged 300UM for the privilege.

But perhaps the biggest shame of all is that most of the windows are broken and patched with wood or metal, and those that are not are so dirty and damaged as to be largely opaque. There are also one or two sleeper wagons for SNIM employees and their families – if you can blag your way on to one of these, conditions are ever so slightly nicer; there's still no power or water, but there are some (dirty) mattresses and uncovered portholes through which it's possible to peek at the landscape. In short, our advice is to bring snacks, something soft to sit on, and a serious sense of humour!

Having said all that, the Mauritanians who crowd into this absolute jalopy of a wagon are experts at making themselves comfortable, and you can expect to be bosom buddies with all your carriage mates by the time you reach the end of the line. It perhaps goes without saying that there's no snack trolley passing through, but your fellow passengers are likely to be making tea and even cooking throughout the trip, so in true Mauritanian style you will very likely be invited – perhaps emphatically – to join in.

JOURNEY BOOKS

CONTRACT PUBLISHING FROM BRADT GUIDES

DO YOU HAVE A STORY TO TELL?

- Publish your book with a leading trade publisher
- Expert management of your book by our experienced editors
- Professional layout, cover design and printing
- **Unique** access to trade distribution for print books and ebooks
- Competitive pricing and a range of tailor-made packages
- Aimed at both first-timers and previously published authors

"Unfailingly pleasant"... "Undoubtedly one of the best publishers I have worked with"... "Excellent and incredibly prompt communication"... "Unfailingly courteous"... "Superb"...

For more information – and many more endorsements from our delighted authors – please visit: **bradtguides.com/journeybooks.**

Journey Books is the contract publishing imprint of award-winning travel publisher, Bradt Guides. All subjects are considered for Journey Books, not just travel. Our contract publishing is a complement to our traditional publishing, not a replacement, and we welcome traditional submissions from new and established travel writers. Please visit **bradtguides.com/write-for-us** to find out more.

6

Diawling and the Southwest

The Trarza Emirate, from which the **Trarza region** (ولاية الترارزة) covering southwestern Mauritania takes its name, coalesced around the middle of the 17th century and ultimately controlled much of the trade that reached Saint-Louis. It spent the 19th century either trading or warring with the French, before it was ultimately declared a French protectorate in 1902. (And even then, the French presence remained minimal.)

Saint-Louis continued to be an important part of Trarza's story in the colonial period as well, since, until independence in 1960, Mauritania was officially governed from there. As such, southwestern Mauritania has been an important place of transit and trade for centuries, and one with a particular eye towards its neighbours to the south.

The emirate was a primarily Moorish political construction living off nomadic animal husbandry and trade, but the lower Senegal River has always been a cultural crossroads, where nomadic and settled Wolof and Peul communities lived, straddling both sides of the river; in that respect, little has changed today.

The region today covers 67,800km^2 (a bit smaller than the Republic of Ireland) and is home to about 272,000 people. The interior of the region is largely dominated by an enormous system of longitudinal dunes, some of them dozens of kilometres long – the Erg du Trarza. The area is very sparsely populated other than settlements along the Route de l'Espoir (page 265) and near the Senegal River in the south, though there are a number of tiny and unimaginably hardy pastoralist communities making a living in the long valleys between the dunes. Following the contours of the river, the region tapers to a point in the southwest corner of the country where the waterbird haven of Diawling National Park can be found.

Both of Mauritania's primary border crossings to Senegal are located here and, as in centuries past, huge amounts of trade flow between the two. The region's main city, Rosso, is the epicentre of that trade and not known as a tourist magnet – anything but, in fact – but don't let that stop you from taking in this incongruous corner of Mauritania, where the boundaries between desert and delta, and between the countries on either side, can blur like the best kind of Fata Morgana.

ROSSO *(population 51,000)*

Sharing a name with the smaller Senegalese city just across the water (population 16,000), the two Rossos represent the primary border crossing between Mauritania and Senegal. The town(s) also have an infamous reputation among travellers in West Africa as the home of hassle, corruption, dust, disease, mosquitoes and just about any other pestilence you can come up with – including occasional locusts and floods. And while it's probably not *quite* as bad as you've heard – these sorts of

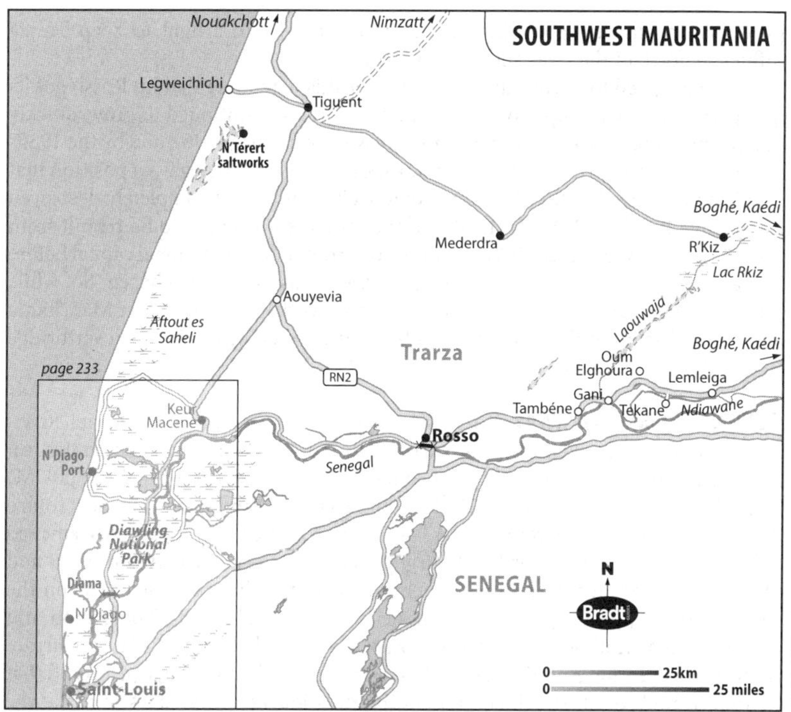

travel tales tend to undergo a bit of sensationalist accretion over time – Mauritania's third-largest city does remain something of a difficult place to love.

Though Rosso began its life as a Wolof village, today it's as multi-ethnic as anywhere in the country, drawing residents from around Mauritania to work in trade and agriculture, since, in addition to being Mauritania's busiest border, it also sits at the heart of the country's rice-growing region. Furthermore, it's a significant garrison town, with seemingly every branch of the Mauritanian security services represented here with a large base. These are, in fact, all lined up in a neat formation (very military-style indeed) along the riverfront, which has the unfortunate side effect of blocking off the river almost entirely, leaving the unfortunate 'Rossossois' with all of the mosquitoes and none of the views.

The one exception here is that of the ferry dock, where – as long as you're ready to fend off any would-be helpers and politely answer any questions the authorities might have – you can actually hang out a bit and watch the riverine bustle. There's usually a good show on, with the rather chaotic loading and unloading of the ferry, traders of all sizes and stripes, and a small flotilla of wooden pirogues vying for passengers too pressed or too impatient to wait for the larger boat.

HISTORY With its origins as a Wolof fishing village founded in the 17th century, Rosso has a long history, but was little more than a village for most of that time. Named for one Ma Rosse Wande who settled here, Rosso's proximity to the growing city of Saint-Louis just downriver meant it became an increasingly important *escale* (stopover) for traders plying the river seeking gold, gum arabic, ivory, people to enslave, and salt, which were exchanged for cloth, sugar, tea and weapons. Thus, Rosso remained a small trading post where the French and Trarza would exchange products or gunfire, depending on the year – mostly in a fight to keep Trarza influence north of the river and French south.

The two agreed to a truce in 1902 and, after this détente settled in, Rosso got its first permanent buildings around 1920. Its importance continued to grow, quickly outstripping the nearby gum-arabic town of Mederdra (page 240), and by the 1930s it was Mauritania's primary trade and transport gateway to Senegal – a position that remains unchanged to this day. The growing city was almost completely destroyed by massive floods in 1952, with 90% of the settlement needing to be rebuilt from scratch. Several years later, Rosso was a serious contender for national capital before Nouakchott – at the time barely even a village – was ultimately chosen. So, while political power may have eluded Rosso, its role as the hinge between Mauritania and Senegal seems only set to grow with the 2026 opening of the first-ever bridge to join the two countries.

GETTING THERE AND AWAY Rosso sits on the north bank of the Senegal River, 200km south of Nouakchott on the surfaced RN2. Several transport companies run minibuses from Carrefour Nancy or Garage Rosso in **Nouakchott** (3–4hrs; 300UM) including Salama Transports (m 22 33 25 00, 22 34 25 00) and Raha Transport (office 3km south of Carrefour Nancy; m 43 48 09 09, 43 34 09 09). It's a well-trafficked route and there are more or less hourly departures every day between 07.00 and 15.00, with fewer departures over lunchtime. Private drivers also sell seats on the route (350UM), picking up passengers near Carrefour Nancy in Nouakchott and the Star fuel station near the port in Rosso; they usually have their last departure in the early evening. And if you're feeling impatient with any of this, just recall that in 1926 it took the first vehicles attempting this journey three days to make the crossing between Rosso and Nouakchott – not 3 hours!

Heading east, clapped-out Mercedes 190s and Renault/Peugeot estate cars cover the 200km-long asphalt road to **Boghé** (3–4hrs; 350UM) from a stop near the Marché des Viandes. There are no direct vehicles to Kaédi, but it's simple enough to change vehicles in Boghé.

There are two routes from Rosso to **Diama** (page 231), but no direct transport between the two.

WHERE TO STAY *Map, opposite*

Online sources may point you to Auberge de la Conseil or Residence du Centre, but neither were functional as of 2025, and the apartments at Mauritour Hotel may have been nice at one stage, but are now quite run-down and the staff like to try it on with the prices. As such, those venues listed here seem to be the best options available.

Hotel Talhaya m 43 58 76 76, 46 78 16 36. On the north edge of town & hidden just behind the defunct Chehama Hotel lies Rosso's nicest accommodation. Though it's very much aimed at conferences & government junkets (& a little sterile in the way that places like this tend to be), the modern AC rooms here are a fine retreat if you need a break from the city outside. *2,500/3,000UM dbl/twin.* **$$$**

Hotel La Case 100m east of the Grand Mosque; m 41 33 09 95, 46 17 97 44; e dableya6@gmail.com. Probably the best option in town if you don't have the budget for the Talhaya or would rather be closer to the city centre; though see if you can get one of the rooms that doesn't look out directly on to a brick wall. *1,200/1,500UM en-suite dbl/twin with AC.* **$$**

Merci Rosso m 37 37 86 59, 46 60 78 33. A block over from La Case, offering similar rooms at similar rates. **$$**

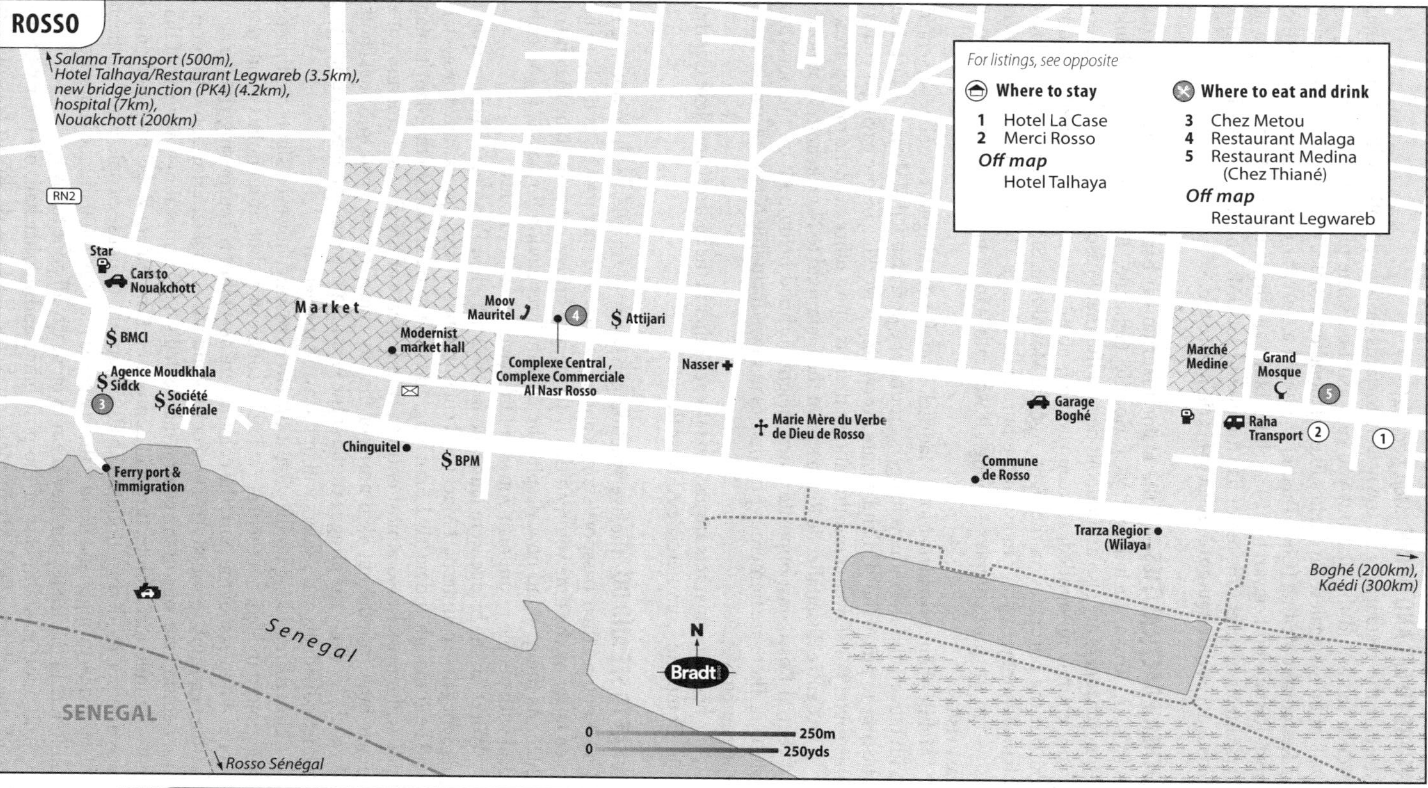
ROSSO
Salama Transport (500m),
Hotel Talhaya/Restaurant Legwareb (3.5km),
new bridge junction (PK4) (4.2km),
hospital (7km),
Nouakchott (200km)
RN2
Star
Cars to Nouakchott
Market
BMCI
Agence Moudkhala Sidck
Société Générale
3
Modernist market hall
Moov Mauritel
4
Attijari
Complexe Central, Complexe Commerciale Al Nasr Rosso
Nasser
Chinguitel
BPM
Ferry port & immigration
Marie Mère du Verbe de Dieu de Rosso
Garage Boghé
Commune de Rosso
Marché Medine
Grand Mosque
5
Raha Transport
2
1
Trarza Regior (Wilaya)
Boghé (200km), Kaédi (300km)
Senegal
SENEGAL
Rosso Sénégal
N
Bradt
0 250m
0 250yds
For listings, see opposite
Where to stay
1 Hotel La Case
2 Merci Rosso
Off map
Hotel Talhaya
Where to eat and drink
3 Chez Metou
4 Restaurant Malaga
5 Restaurant Medina (Chez Thiané)
Off map
Restaurant Legwareb

WHERE TO EAT AND DRINK *Map, page 229*

Most of the restaurants in town lean towards fast-food options like shawarma, French tacos and the like, but you can also find some plates of the day going as well, often Senegalese favourites like thiéboudiène, mafé, yassa, etc. Have a gander at **Restaurant Medina (Chez Thiané)** ($) near La Case, or **Chez Metou** ($) near the port. **Restaurant Legwareb** ($$) at Hotel Talhaya is the fanciest option, serving à la carte meals of meat, chicken or fish for around 250UM. And if you're itching for the Costa del Sol, **Restaurant Malaga** ($) is right here too.

OTHER PRACTICALITIES All the major Mauritanian **banks** are represented with ATMs in Rosso, including BMCI, Société Générale, BPM and Attijari Bank. **Moneychangers** are also around, but be mindful that Rosso's reputation for hustlers is not entirely unfounded, so keep your wits about you. In the first block of shops outside the port gates on the right, Agence Moudkhala Sidck is a decent option to change money, or you can ask at the Bureau de Change Mutualisé de Rosso, which is within the port complex – though it was rather inexplicably out of cash on our last visit.

Mobile phone providers Moov Mauritel, Mattel and Chinguitel are all represented with offices, and the moneychangers around the port also sell **SIM cards** – just take the time to put in the SIM and ensure everything is working before paying if you go this route! For slower communications, there is a **post office** near the market area.

The **Centre Hospitalier de Rosso** sits on the main road to Nouakchott, 7km north of central Rosso, just opposite a new neighbourhood being built on the outskirts of town. There are numerous pharmacies in town, including Nasser pharmacy near the church.

The best **supermarkets** are just next to each other in the centre: Complexe Central and Complexe Commerciale Al Nasr Rosso.

WHAT TO SEE AND DO The overwhelming majority of travellers will do nothing in Rosso but get their passport stamps and move on, and that process is likely to be even faster by the time you read this with the new **bridge**, set to open by the end of 2026. As things stand now, despite the crossing's reputation for hassle, if you only deal with people in uniform you shouldn't have any major issues.

Works on the bridge were launched in late 2021 when President Ghazouani and his Senegalese counterpart Macky Sall cut the ribbon on this long-awaited project. It will be 20m high and nearly 1.5km long, and the approach road on the Mauritanian side will bypass Rosso almost entirely, running east of the city and emerging at a newly built roundabout 4km north of the city centre on the road to Nouakchott. As such, it's likely the **pirogue** traffic at the existing port won't disappear entirely, as some individuals and traders will opt to avoid the detour.

Other than soaking up the vibe at the river crossing, however, sights are thin on the ground indeed, but there are at least a couple of architectural points of interest. About 400m east of the port, the colonial-era **post office** is a surprising vintage gem with a beautiful, rounded Art Deco corner and old-school lettering above the door. Just behind here, one of the central **market halls** has an appealingly wavy roof that fans of modernist architecture will approve of. (The 'Satara Zone' neighbourhood was another modernist initiative in Rosso, meant to house people who had been displaced by drought and flood – there were as many as 1,400 unique 'dome homes' built here in the 1980s, but they seem to be nearly all gone today.)

And another 400m east of the post office and market hall, on the riverfront road, the whitewashed Marie Mère du Verbe de Dieu de Rosso was built in

1957, making it Mauritania's oldest **church**. (Unlike Catholic missions in some countries, they don't offer any rooms or the like, but they're quite friendly.) The **Grand Mosque** sits another 500m further along, one street in from the riverfront near Hotel La Case.

DIAMA

Site of a controversial river dam opened in 1986, the actual town of Diama sits on the Senegal side of the river. There's not much on the Mauritanian side other than a clutch of official buildings on the north side of the dam and a bunch of Hiluxes and minibuses waiting to carry people onwards, usually to Nouakchott. At the time of writing, this was the only fixed crossing between Senegal and Mauritania, but this is soon to change with the expected opening of the Rosso Bridge (page 85).

The nearest settlement is Birette, 3.5km northwest, where you'll find the usual array of village shops, but that's about it. There are no banks or other facilities on the Mauritanian side of the border, but you'll have no trouble finding the moneychangers. The nearest accommodation is 10km to the north in Bouhadjra (page 236), and the nearest ATMs dispensing ouguiya are in Rosso, Tiguent and Nouakchott.

The crossing here is very relaxed, and it's an enjoyable walk across the dam, from where there are expansive views over the Senegal River. There are even some benches here where you can take a load off and enjoy the scenery. The border is open from 08.00 to 18.00.

GETTING THERE AND AWAY Nouakchott is 230km away on the RN2, and it's no trouble to find a vehicle at the border post, even if you might have to wait a bit. In the other direction, vehicles heading from Nouakchott to Senegal via Diama depart from Garage Diama (page 108) in Nouakchott every morning around 07.30 and charge 700UM for a seat to Diama.

ENTERING MAURITANIA FROM SENEGAL

Until January 2025, Mauritania issued visas on arrival for most passports, but this is no longer offered after the introduction of an e-visa programme, and if you turn up without an approved – and printed – e-visa, you will be sent back across the border (see page 64 for full details).

But even with the new e-visa, you will make payment and have your biometrics taken at the border post itself. Because of this, it's only possible to *enter* Mauritania at ports of entry where they have the requisite equipment to take fingerprints, etc. That means that, as of 2025, the **only** border crossings with Senegal where this is possible are at Diama and Rosso. (Note you can still receive an exit stamp and *depart* Mauritania at any official border crossing, ie: Boghé or Kaédi, but you cannot enter here unless you already have a visa in your passport from a Mauritanian embassy abroad.)

The cost for a one-month e-visa is €55. It's also possible to pay in CFA (42,000 francs) or ouguiya (2,500UM), but you get the best rate when paying in euros. It's best to have as close to exact change as possible, but they will usually make small change in ouguiya for you without too much trouble. The crossings are generally open from 08.00 to 18.00, but beware there is often a long midday lunch break when you'll have to wait.

And even though most people come to Diama expressly to *avoid* Rosso, it's worth mentioning that there's a 100km unsurfaced direct route to the city which more or less follows the river if you'd rather try that instead of heading up to Aouyevia (Awevia) and back south again (130km, all tarmac).

On the Senegal side, there are also vehicles waiting to take you the 33km to Saint-Louis. It's about CFA10,000 (€15) for a private taxi, and much cheaper for a shared one.

DIAWLING NATIONAL PARK

(w pnd.mr; f Parc Diawling; see page 235 for entry fees) Taking in 16,000ha of wetland basins, coastal dunes and estuarine mangrove in Mauritania's extreme southwest corner, Diawling National Park and its peripheral zones (covering a further 56,000ha) occupy a narrow tongue of land between the Senegal River and the Atlantic Ocean, following the river's right bank as it flows southwest towards the oceanfront Senegalese city of Saint-Louis.

The park was gazetted by the Mauritanian government in 1991 and listed as a Ramsar Wetland of International Importance in 1994. It is contiguous with the Parc national des oiseaux du Djoudj (gazetted in 1971) just across the river in Senegal, and has also been recognised as part of the UNESCO-sponsored Réserve de Biosphère Transfrontalière du Delta du Fleuve Sénégal (RBTDS) since 2005, incorporating a wide swathe of land on both sides of the border.

These layers of recognition and protection are indicative of the area's massive importance to African and European birdlife, particularly Palearctic migrants. Diawling and Djoudj represent some of the first freshwater sources south of the Sahara, making them a key destination for hundreds of thousands of birds as they depart Europe and cross the Sahara in search of more amenable climes.

Diawling has a rather unusual origin story, however – rather than being gazetted to protect an existing or at-risk ecosystem, it was in fact created to restore an ecosystem that had already collapsed, in which both people and wildlife were no longer able to support themselves. The **Diama Dam** was developed in response to the droughts that devastated the region in the 1970s, in order to limit saline incursion up the Senegal River and enable expanded irrigated agriculture in the valley upriver of the dam.

Completed in 1986, it did enable the significant expansion of wet rice growing above the dam, but at the cost of a total collapse of the estuarine flood cycle downriver. Prior to the building of the dam, the Diawling area would be subject to seasonal flooding between August and November that would inundate all but the Ziré, Birette and côtière (coastal) dunes, creating a major destination for migratory birds and allowing for the maintenance of a centuries-old seasonal economy of herding and fishing. That all ended when the dam was first filled.

As such, a plan was drawn up to attempt to restore this devastated landscape, starting with the gazetting of the park in 1991. The plan revolved around the development of a network of embankments and ouvrages hydrauliques (sluice gates) which would allow the manual replication of the seasonal flooding that had governed these lands since time immemorial. Unlike traditional conservation models, Diawling's founding principles were to safeguard and restore not only the natural patrimony of the area, but also the sustainability of traditional livelihoods as they had been practised in the area for centuries.

The ecological collapse was so total that a 1993 survey recorded a total of just ten waterbirds (from three species), full stop. Another contemporaneous report dismissed the new park as 'a dusty salt desert with a few sickly-looking cows'.

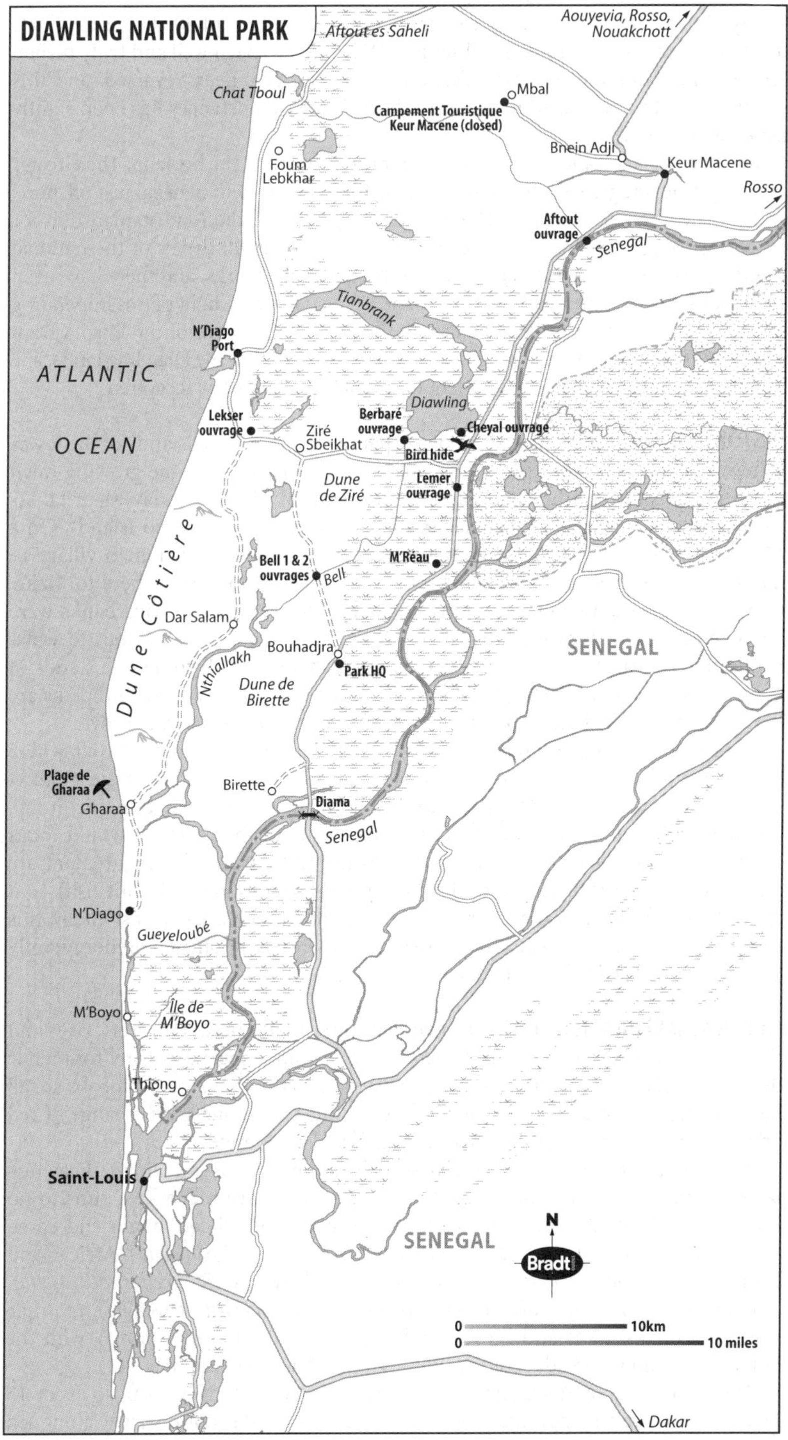
DIAWLING NATIONAL PARK
Aftout es Saheli
Aouyevia, Rosso, Nouakchott
Chat Tboul
Mbal
Campement Touristique Keur Macene (closed)
Bnein Adji
Keur Macene
Rosso
Foum Lebkhar
Aftout ouvrage
Senegal
Tianbrank
N'Diago Port
ATLANTIC OCEAN
Diawling
Lekser ouvrage
Ziré Sbeikhat
Berbaré ouvrage
Cheyal ouvrage
Bird hide
Lemer ouvrage
Dune de Ziré
Dune Côtière
Bell 1 & 2 ouvrages
Bell
M'Réau
Dar Salam
Nthiallakh
Bouhadjra
Park HQ
SENEGAL
Dune de Birette
Plage de Gharaa
Gharaa
Birette
Diama
Senegal
N'Diago
Gueyeloubé
M'Boyo
Île de M'Boyo
Thiong
Saint-Louis
SENEGAL
N
Bradt
0 10km
0 10 miles
Dakar

Today, those same waterbird figures are between 100,000 and 200,000 individuals or more – and the cows look healthier too. Diawling has been well and truly turned around, the dam's most catastrophic consequences have been reversed, and this small national park created in the most difficult of circumstances has been rightly hailed as a success.

But *plus ça change*, another development project lurks on the horizon. The Greater Tortue Ahmeyim gas field straddles the maritime border with Senegal just offshore, and a major new port near N'Diago intends to become the Mauritanian hub for oil and gas development, which is expected to be the main driver of the national economy within the next decade. A tarred road is in the works, and there have even been plans floated for a shipping canal to the Senegal River. In light of this impending transformation, we can only hope that the hard-earned lessons of the Diama Dam will be remembered, and the hard-won successes of bringing the Diawling landscape back to life for the benefit of both people and nature will not be forgotten.

HISTORY Though today they sit in two separate countries, the islands of the lower Senegal Delta were important sources of wood and pasture for the growing town of Saint-Louis during the colonial era. The island of M'Boyo, today Mauritania's southernmost, was even known at the time as 'Île aux Bois' (Wood Island). On a 1757 visit to the village of Thiong (still the southernmost Mauritanian village in the delta), French naturalist Michel Adanson observed that, from here to Maka, near the current dam and something like 25km upriver, the two riverbanks were 'so covered with mangroves' that it was 'impossible for people on foot to walk'. While this is unfortunately no longer the case, there are still some fine stands of mangroves to be found along the river and the creeks of the estuary, and plans are in the works for a reforestation of at least 100ha of red and black mangrove.

The lower Senegal Delta region has long been a cultural crossroads as well, where Wolofs would traditionally fish in the sea and practise smallholder agriculture, both Moors and Peul would trade and raise cattle or camels, and a unique group, the Taghrédient – considered the oldest occupants of the region – would focus on fishing in the river and its many freshwater tributaries. The Taghrédient are connected to, but distinct from, the Moors (who traditionally do not fish), and can still be found practising their traditional trade in the park's basins. Today, this southwestern corner of Mauritania remains a crossroads, populated predominantly by Haratin Moors, Wolof and Peul.

FAUNA AND FLORA It's said that Diawling is a crossroads between desert, river and ocean, and the park's trees speak elegantly to this unique meeting of environments: desertic acacias, flood-loving rônier (borassus) palms and savannah baobabs are all here in varying concentrations depending on the area, along with a fringe of red and black mangroves providing shelter to fish and birds alike.

And though it can sometimes play second fiddle to Senegal's Djoudj, Diawling is also recognised as an Important Bird Area, and its **avian** checklist runs to no less than 225 species. This includes multiple species of pelican, heron and egret, alongside cormorant (*Phalacrocorax lucidus*), black stork (*Ciconia nigra*), African and Eurasian spoonbill (*Platalea leucorodia/alba*), pied avocet (*Recurvirostra avosetta*), African darter (*Anhinga rufa*), black-crowned crane (*Balearica pavonina*), multiple species of ducks, terns and geese, and both greater and lesser flamingo, with the latter's only known breeding site in West Africa occurring here (page 11).

The population of Palearctic migrants peaks around the New Year, so every 15 January park rangers and international ornithologists take a bird survey along ten transects in the park. When taken against the literal ten birds counted here in the early 1990s, Diawling's resurrection has been an almost unbelievable success: in 2022, the survey recorded 251,957 individuals from 116 waterbird species – just slightly more than ten! And while these numbers may be encouraging, they can also vary wildly: the 2023 count recorded a dramatic drop, with only 115,243 individuals (from 110 species) observed. So while Diawling's story is certainly a success, the park still faces significant challenges.

Among these challenges, invasive *Typha* reeds found along much of the lower Senegal River have also colonised much of the Gambar basin and beyond, crowding out waterbirds and their prey, as well as endemic plants. There are efforts underway to clear the weeds and create a use for them by processing them into biofuels etc.

As for the **mammalian** population, it's true that you may see a fair amount more livestock than anything else. As part of the park's mission to develop and restore sustainable traditional livelihoods for local residents, there are thought to be more than 60,000 head of cows, sheep, goats and camels in the park and its peripheral zones, and estimates predict the livestock population will hit nearly 160,000 by 2030.

But as for their wilder cousins, there are still many enjoyable sightings to be had at Diawling. Warthogs (*Phacochoerus africanus*) are almost certainly the easiest to spot, and there are hundreds of them in the park. Side-striped jackal (*Lupulella adusta*) and African golden wolf (*Canis lupaster*) are also present, but much rarer, alongside honey badger (*Mellivora capensis*), African wildcat (*Felis lybica*), pale fox (*Vulpes pallida*) and striped hyena (*Hyaena hyaena*) – all of which have been recorded here, but are not commonly spotted. There are also a number of Patas monkey (*Erythrocebus patas*) around. The last red-fronted gazelle (*Gazella rufifrons*) was seen in 1991, and the last lion shot in 1970.

There are six amphibian and 26 reptile species present in the park, including a stable population of West African **crocodile** (*Crocodylus suchus*) numbering some 40–80 individuals, which like to hang out in the Bell basin between October and March. After this, the basin becomes too dry and they retreat further up the river. Nile monitor (*Varanus niloticus*) are also present, along with plenty of southern long-tailed lizard (*Latastia longicaudata*).

Sea turtles have infrequently been witnessed nesting on the beach in Diawling, particularly the green sea turtle (*Chelonia mydas*). Other species, including loggerhead (*Caretta caretta*), olive ridley (*Lepidochelys olivacea*) and leatherback (*Dermochelys coriacea*) sea turtles have been seen nesting a bit further up the coast, between Tiguent and Nouakchott, and this is about the northernmost limit of their African nesting range. On land, the African spurred tortoise (*Centrochelys sulcata*) is also present in Diawling in low numbers.

Underwater, the West African manatee (*Trichechus senegalensis*) is only present upriver of the Diama Dam. Overall, there are around 65 species of fish recorded in the park, and the most common catches are tilapia, shrimp and catfish, which are dried locally or sold in Nouakchott and Saint-Louis.

Though it doesn't officially cover Mauritania, Diawling is right next door so serious birders will be happy to have a copy of *Birds of Senegal and The Gambia* by Nik Borrow and Ron Demey, the second edition of which was published in 2023. The park has also produced its own dedicated bird guide, which is available online but only in French (w pnd.mr/wp-content/uploads/2021/09/Guide-des-oiseaux-du-PND.pdf).

ENTRY AND FEES There is a 200UM (or €5) park fee (per person, per visit) to enter Diawling National Park and a 50UM road tax (per vehicle) levied by the

N'Diago Municipality. Mauritanian citizens/residents don't pay the park fee, but all foreigners pay, even if just transiting the park to/from Diama.

If you are passing through on the road to and from Diama, you don't need a guide, but it could be very helpful if you'd like to explore beyond this main route (and is in some cases required, though not always enforced). A day's accompaniment costs 400UM. If you don't have a vehicle, there's not exactly one available at all times, but park staff can find out what's around on a given day and negotiate a price depending on what you'd like to do. The checkpoint just north of Bouhadjra is a good place to make arrangements – it took us quite a while to find the person responsible at the offices in Bouhadjra.

GETTING THERE AND AWAY All vehicles headed to or from Diama pass directly in front of the park HQ at Bouhadjra. Coming from Senegal, one seat in a vehicle from the Diama border to the park HQ at Bouhadjra is about 100UM. Coming from Nouakchott, Senegal-bound vehicles depart Garage Diama (page 108) every morning around 07.30 and charge 700UM for a seat to Diama (you can just disembark 10km early in Bouhadjra).

ORIENTATION The core park area covers 16,000ha, primarily over the three main basins of Gambar, Bell and Diawling-Tichilitt, but many of the attractions and activities fall within the 56,000ha *zone peripherique*, which stretches about 60km north to south, from Chat Tboul to Île de M'Boyo and the Senegalese border. Here there are more floodplains and basins attached to the hydrological network, as well as a few dozen Moor (mostly Haratin), Peul and Wolof villages. The main road through the park runs 45km from Keur Macene to Diama along an embankment sometimes called the *digue internationale*, between the park's basins and the river, and a couple of different tracks north of Bouhadjra branch east towards the Ziré villages and the Atlantic coast.

WHERE TO STAY AND EAT

Auberge Maurisert (9 rooms) Bouhadjra; m 41 40 63 32, 20 03 55 62, 49 26 77 77; e maurisert@gmail.com, talebeghaly@yahoo.fr; w pnd.mr. This is the only accommodation in the park (& for quite some distance beyond), & offers good & well-maintained rooms, though you pay a bit extra for the remote location. Still, it's comfortable & the staff are attentive. There are a few standing khaïmas in the compound for those seeking a budget option (or they'll pitch you one at Gharaa; see opposite). Toilets in the shared block are squat-style, but there are Western-style toilets next to reception. Food & drink is also a little pricey (500UM/plate for lunch or dinner, 400UM b/fast) but you may also be able to negotiate meal provision with park staff, who will charge you 250UM pp for both dinner & b/fast. It's also fine to bring your own food. *1,500/2,000UM sgl/dbl using shared bath; 2,000/2,500UM en suite sgl/dbl, 2,500/3,500UM deluxe sgl/dbl. 500UM per vehicle (for car campers), 600UM pp their khaïma.* **$$$–$$**

WHAT TO SEE AND DO In order to imitate the natural flood cycle disrupted by the construction of the dam, the network of *ouvrages hydrauliques* (sluice gates) are opened every 1 July, allowing the park's huge wetland basins to slowly fill over the coming months. The gates are left open until 1 November, after which they are closed and the ponds and wetlands begin to dry out. Peak season for high water and high numbers of waterbirds generally runs from December to February. And though most visitors are here for the spectacular birding, the dazzling landscapes and traditional villages are worth exploring even if you're not a twitcher. (If one *is* a twitcher, however, aim for the **bird hide**

(⊕ 16.4159, -16.3323) overlooking the Diawling-Tichilitt basin just north of the Cheyal ouvrage.)

Not only does Diawling look like nowhere else in Mauritania, there is an impressive diversity of scenery packed into a small area. The marshy lagoons of the core park area are interspersed with great dunes – some sandy, some forested – and wide salt-pan *sebkha* plains, which also occasionally flood. In the south, as the river tapers towards the ocean, the land is cut through by a cluster of creeks and backwaters, breaking up into several small riverine islands, dotted with tiny fishing villages and dusted with a green fringe of mangroves. The park is best explored by a combination of boat and 4x4, but there are also good opportunities for walking near where the Dune de Ziré and Bassin du Bell meet (⊕ 16.3566, -16.4024).

The landscape takes on a dramatically different look between the seasons. The annual flood spreads out in all directions across the lowlands from August, filling the park's basins, sebkhas and seasonal lakes – and even sometimes overtopping the main road (which explains its rough condition). Large tufts of green Sporobolus grasses begin to sprout, soon to be harvested by local women for the production of traditional grass-and-leather mats. The intricately patterned designs can be quite beautiful – ask the park staff if you'd like to see where they're made.

Taghrédient people, considered the park's original inhabitants, live in the Ziré area and can still be found practising their traditional fishing techniques in the park's basins, particularly near the Lemer and Cheyal ouvrages in the Bassin du Bell. Artisanal fishing in the basins begins when the sluice gates are shut on 1 November and continues until they dry out fully, by May at the latest. The Taghrédient also harvest water lilies and lotuses, making them into flour and couscous – ask about *couscous de nénuphar* if you'd like to sample this rare dish.

Not far from where the Taghrédient do their fishing, the park's resident population of West African **crocodile** (*Crocodylus suchus*) can be spotted from the main road near M'Réau (⊕ 16.3448, -16.3479). Some 40–80 individuals typically live here between October and March before they go seeking wetter climes up the river.

Of course, there is also the Atlantic – the Mauritanian coastline tends to be raw, rugged and wind-blasted, and Diawling is no exception – and you'll notice many of the villages in the park are strung out in a single-file line, just behind the coastal dune and taking good advantage of its protection from the battering winds of the coast. This dune runs parallel to the shore for most of the park, reaching its peak at the gorgeous oceanic moonscape (with a few less-lunar palm trees thrown in for good measure) of the **Plage de Gharaa** (Gharaa Beach). Here, though you're only a short distance from the village of Gharaa, the world feels very far away indeed. (As elsewhere in Mauritania, the beach is unprotected and the waves can be rough – would-be swimmers take caution.)

Gharaa is about 38km from the park HQ at Bouhadjra on unimproved tracks passing the Ziré villages and turning south along the Marigot de Nthiallakh (or Tialakht). The ease of getting here can vary significantly with the rains, so ask about conditions if you are unsure. And while Gharaa can easily be visited in a relaxed afternoon from Bouhadjra (or even by pirogue if you prefer), you can also arrange with Auberge Maurisert (see opposite) to put up a khaïma and spend the night here – a simply magical way to start or end a trip in Mauritania.

Pirogue safaris depart from the south end of the park, at the village of Birette. These enter the main channel of the Senegal River and travel south towards the Marigot de Gueyeloubé (or Gueylebou) (Gueyeloubé Creek). Trips are more or less customisable to your preference, but the basic itinerary goes some distance down the Gueyeloubé and returns upriver towards Birette (roughly 25km; 2½hrs). You'll see plenty of waterbirds, and birds of prey like osprey, plus local fishermen at work in the river, casting and pulling their nets.

A longer trip continues down the Gueyeloubé and circumnavigates the Île de M'Boyo before re-entering the main channel of the Senegal River at the park's southernmost point and returning towards Birette. This takes about twice as long, plus a stop for lunch (which should be packed/arranged in advance, as there's nothing to be found en route). The longer itinerary also takes in the largest mangrove forests in the park, found surrounding the Île de M'Boyo.

Note that the park only has one boat (a large metal pirogue that can hold roughly ten passengers), so you may need to ask about combining groups – which can be a good way to save on the 4,000UM cost. (Though we were assured there was no difference in price between the shorter and longer trips!)

CHAT TBOUL Just north of Diawling is the 15,500ha **Réserve naturelle du Chat Tboul** (or Chott Boul; ⊕ 16.6066, -16.4361), which covers the area surrounding a former mouth of the Senegal River and the 1.2km break in the coastal dune it once flowed through. Today it's a landscape of lagoons, mudflats and marshes, and the most important West African site for the black-necked grebe (*Podiceps nigricollis*), with more than 300 individuals. It's also a good site for bustards, with Arabian, Savile's and white-bellied all present. It's recognised as both a Ramsar site and Important Bird Area and effectively functions as an extension of the national park (which is also the best access point; go 25km north from the Lekser *ouvrage* turn-off towards the tiny village of Foum Lebkhar). There are no facilities of any kind here at present, but it's only 15km from the new N'Diago Port, so this could change.

Finally, the **Aftout es Saheli** (⊕ 16.6960, -16.3376) lagoon and depression directly north of Chat Tboul is the only site in West Africa where lesser flamingos (*Phoeniconaias minor*) have been known to nest. Greater flamingos (*Phoenicopterus roseus*) also nest here. Numbers of both fluctuate as the birds are subject to predation from jackals and hyenas among others. A 2011 monitoring project noted 4,800 lesser and 10,200 greater flamingos, plus 14,000 chicks of both species. The Aftout es Saheli depression parallels the coastline all the way up to Nouakchott, and also lends its name to a major public works project pumping water from the Senegal River all the way to the thirsty citizens of Nouakchott.

KEUR MACENE

This small, predominantly Wolof town (population 6,272) is where the tarmac ends on the way to Diama, and has an appropriately Wild-West feel: the dust-blown main street is lined by a workaday selection of services from farriers to fuel and welders to washers (but alas, no saloons). You're unlikely to spend long here, but there are a few basic restaurants, a pharmacy and a very sleepy central market hall – but no auberge.

Shared taxis (50UM/seat) trundle back and forth over the 35km of wooded dunes and shallow valleys leading to Aouyevia (Awevia) on the Nouakchott–Rosso road, where there's accommodation in basic tikit-style huts for 600UM at **Café et Auberge La Routard** (m 46 17 65 85, 48 73 72 09; **$**). Amenities are limited to thin floor mats and mosquito nets, but the management is friendly at least. Transport between Keur Macene and Diama is infrequent (or full), so you may have to hitch.

Some 9km west of Keur Macene, the long-serving **Campement Touristique Keur Macene** (m 22 61 00 02, 42 49 12 12; f; ⊕ 16.5876, -16.3115) was once owned by Air Afrique, until the pan-African airline's 2002 demise. It has recently changed hands again and is now home to Chinese construction crews working on the new road to N'Diago Port. This will likely be the case for some time but, should it open up to tourists again, it's got a fantastic rural location overlooking a verdant floodplain frequented by waterbirds. There is also a private hunting camp in Keur Macene, but they only work with groups who come here to shoot warthogs.

N'DIAGO

Despite lending its name to the development, the new N'Diago Port, soon to be a major oil and gas hub (page 234), is actually 32km up the coast from N'Diago town, and residents here are concerned about being left behind. Sandwiched between ocean and lagoon at the far corner of the country, N'Diago has always been a peripheral place, predominantly Wolof and culturally conjoined to the fishing villages of coastal Saint-Louis, barely 15km away, but across the border in Senegal. Central N'Diago sits atop a small coastal bluff overlooking a beach lined with colourful wooden pirogues; but similar to Saint-Louis, the town has suffered from significant coastal erosion and flooding in recent years and many beachfront buildings now sit abandoned and gap-toothed, with former bedrooms and boutiques staring out into the world like some kind of perverse sitcom set, their fourth walls swallowed by an increasingly unpredictable and destructive sea. The town cemetery, just in from the beach and next to the central 4x4 garage, is an evocative place, with memorials and even an impromptu mosque built out of planks, boards and other bits of boat no longer fit for purpose – a true seafarer's memorial, and a reminder of the risks of this dangerous profession.

Compounding N'Diago's sense of isolation, the new road to the eponymous port will not extend to the town itself, and residents worry that the government has no intention of better connecting them to the potential prosperity the new port might

M'BOYO'S MYSTERIOUS BORDER

At the northern end of the seafront portion of the Senegalese city of Saint-Louis, the city ends abruptly at what appears to be not much more than a line in the sand bisecting the Langue de Barbarie peninsula. The city's northernmost neighbourhood is known as Goxu Mbathie, and there's a Senegalese immigration post here (⊕ 16.0501, -16.5065). Despite its proximity to the tourist hub of Saint-Louis, this post is hardly ever used by travellers, but rather exists to manage flows of cross-border fishermen, which are often a bone of contention in Senegal–Mauritania relations.

There's a checkpoint on the Mauritanian side at M'Boyo (⊕ 16.1056, -16.5087), but it is not equipped to issue visas or anything of the sort (and potentially not even to stamp passports). But if you're feeling adventurous and wanted to *depart* Mauritania this way, it ought to be possible to get your Senegalese entry stamp at Goxu Mbathie (after fielding a few questions, no doubt). It's only 13km between Saint-Louis and N'Diago, but M'Boyo is only reachable at low tide, when 4x4s drive along the beach between here and N'Diago. It's 7km from M'Boyo to the Goxu Mbathie border post – walkable if you can't catch a lift.

bring, while leaving them alone to deal with whatever adverse effects the offshore activities might have on their livelihoods. Other than a few basic boutiques, there are no visitor services to be found here, and the local gendarmes were surprised to see us, despite being only a handful of kilometres beyond the tourist-draw beach at Gharaa (page 237). N'Diago is 45km from Bouhadjra and 65km from Keur Macene, where you may be able to flag down or hop on an occasional 4x4 heading here. Some 4x4s continue down the beach to M'Boyo at low tide, and this could be an adventurous way to enter Senegal (page 239).

If you arrive here by boat, N'Diago is bisected by a seasonal riverbed, the N'Gadad. This backwater reaches just south of town throughout the year, allowing access into the Marigot de Gueyeloubé, and therefore onwards to M'Boyo and the Senegal River.

TIGUENT, MEDERDRA AND R'KIZ

On the main road roughly halfway between Nouakchott and Rosso, **Tiguent** is a small crossroads town where the eastbound road to Mederdra (50km) and R'Kiz (105km) branches off. It's also a popular weekend break destination for Nouakchottois looking to escape the hustle of the city and get in touch with their nomadic roots. This is especially true from July to October during the *hivernage*, or *kharif* (rainy season), when the rains turn the countryside a life-affirming green – and fresh pasture gives the local milk a rich, brisk taste.

Tiguent is also the nearest town to the **N'Térert saltworks** (⊕ 17.1072, -16.1285), which was a great moneymaker for the Trarza Emirate, which controlled production here and would export to colonial Saint-Louis and beyond via the river port at Rosso. The saltworks are astonishingly still in use, though being only about 7km off the tar road, the salt no longer moves by camel caravan – but the baking grey moonscape dotted with pits and peaks is just as otherworldly as it must have been centuries ago. Some 13km to the northwest of here, the tiny fishing settlement of **Legweichichi** (⊕ 17.2019, -16.1944) seems to have more boats than buildings, with more than 100 10m-long pirogues lining the wave-battered beach. It's 17km back to Tiguent from here.

Tiguent's population is said to triple on some weekends in season, so while most visitors bring their own khaïma to chill out and drink endless glasses of *atay* and *zrig* underneath, there's also an unusually large selection of accommodation in town to cater to the weekending crowds. Try the upmarket **Maravilla** (m 20 69 31 31; from 3,000UM; **$$$$**) or **Tiguent Palace** (m 46 66 03 43; **$$$**), or **Hotel Raha Tiguent** (m 41 02 00 00; from 1,300UM; **$$**) for something more affordable. There's an Attijari Bank with ATM on the main road. Any transport between Nouakchott and Rosso can drop you here.

About 50km to the east, **Mederdra** (population 8,800) was founded as a colonial outpost in 1907 when several French military bases were consolidated here after the France–Trarza agreement pacified the area. Equally importantly, it was an ideal place from which to oversee the lucrative gum-arabic trade, as the region's forests of *Acacia senegal* trees were significant sources of the valuable resin. After harvesting, the gum was hauled to Rosso for export, and the river port city quickly overtook Mederdra as Trarza's main seat of power as far back as the 1930s. Mederdra took a further blow to its stature when the 1968–74 drought killed off more than 70% of the acacias, largely ending the local trade. Nowadays the town subsists primarily on herding and agriculture, and though it also has a reputation for quality handicrafts, Mederdra is probably best known today as

PILGRIMAGE TO THE HEART OF THE DESERT

Members of the Fadiliyya branch of the Qadiriyya Sufi order make a pilgrimage to the village of **Nimzatt** (or Nimjatt, ⊕ 17.4086, -15.6897) every year for the Eid al-Fitr holiday (also known as Korité) to pray and pay respects at the mausoleum of holy man and prolific religious writer Cheikh Saad Bouh, who died here in 1917. He was brother to anti-colonial fighter Cheikh Ma El Aïnin, whom he encouraged to end his war against the French. Saad Bouh was hugely influential in spreading the reach of Qadiriyya throughout Mauritania and Senegambia in particular, and his pilgrimage (*ziarra*) attracts thousands of faithful from north and south of the river every year.

Pilgrims reliably outnumber the town's few hundred residents and overwhelm its receptive capacity, so khaïmas spring up all over town, with pilgrims eating, sleeping, cooking, chanting, praying, and playing on every patch of spare ground. The Qadiriyya are known for their devotional songs and chants accompanied by large drums known as tabalas, which are played late into the evening. Nimzatt is reached by an unsurfaced 50km road that branches northeast from the Tiguent–Mederdra road just south of Tiguent. Saad Bouh's whitewashed mausoleum, carefully trimmed out in green, sits in the Salikhina cemetery at the end of town.

the birthplace of legendary songstress Malouma Mint El Meidah, known to all as Malouma.

To the east again, **R'Kiz** (population 17,871) is another agricultural town, perched 55km east of Mederdra and just to the north of its eponymous lake. Like most bodies of water in Mauritania, Lake R'Kiz is highly seasonal, in this case depending on the marshy Laouwaja and Sekan rivers, which provide water from the Senegal River. The lake was recognised as an Important Bird Area in 2001, but recent years have seen the lion's share of the lagoon given over to irrigated agriculture as part of a major development project in the region, funded in part by the Saudi government. This has come with a fair amount of controversy and sparked demonstrations in R'Kiz over the allocation of land and water rights associated with the project.

Of course, this dramatic change in habitat means it may no longer be the avifauna hotspot it once was. Old records show the presence of black-tailed godwit (*Limosa limosa*), spur-winged goose (*Plectropterus gambensis*), and significant numbers of waterbirds, though recent records are hard to find. At the southeastern edge of the lake/rice fields, near the mouth of the Laouwaja, **Jokha** (⊕ 16.8042, -15.2925) is a popular picnic and hangout spot on the banks of a small seasonal lagoon attached to the Louwaja and would probably be a good place to start if you want to get a feel for what birdlife remains (or just enjoy the view).

Salama Transports (m 22 33 25 00, 22 34 25 00) runs two minibuses a day from Carrefour Nancy in Nouakchott to Mederdra and R'Kiz (3–4hrs; 300UM) at 10.00 and 15.00. The tar road runs out at R'Kiz, but if you'd rather not double back, you may find a lift on the 40km piste connecting down to the surfaced river road at Bezoule (⊕ 16.7283, -14.9628) village, not far from the turn-off to Lexeïba II on the Senegal River facing Podor. We're not aware of any formal accommodation in Mederdra or R'Kiz, so this is a time to put that legendary Mauritanian hospitality to the test!

7

Senegal River and the South

Flowing along Mauritania's border with Senegal for 742km, the wide expanse of the Senegal River cuts a startling blue-green bolt through miles of crusty, baking acacia scrub on either side of the border. Like much of Mauritania, the land here can look barren and harsh on first impression, but this is in fact the country's most important agricultural region, and the farmers and herders of this wide river valley have centuries of expertise in coaxing a riot of life and greenery from these sun-baked soils. Though it can sometimes be hard to tell in the seemingly endless Mauritanian landscapes, the Senegal River valley is in fact the most densely populated part of the country, thanks largely to this significant agricultural potential. Fishermen also ply these waters, and major occasions are still marked with spectacular pirogue races, where boats of 20 or 30 rowers thrash their way up the river to beat their rivals.

Broadly speaking, a trip up the river takes you through the traditional lands of the Wolof, who live along the lower river near the coast, the Halpulaar, who are settled along the lion's share of the middle valley, and the Soninké, at home along the upper reaches of the river. Both Bidhan and Haratin Moors live throughout the Mauritanian side of the valley as well, after many of them arrived from the north in the wake of the droughts of the 1970s. And though it serves as the international border, the Senegal River valley is best understood not as a divider between the two countries at all, but as the very heart of a shared cultural space with the river at its core, where the peoples, languages and customs on either side of the water are cut from the same cloth. There's even a saying in Pulaar: *Maayo wonaa keerol* – the river is not a border. Known as the Chemama in Mauritania, the settled area stretches 10–20km on either side of the river, where seasonal agriculture is possible along the riverbanks and in the many marigots (creeks) and seasonal oueds (wadis). As such, settled farming communities have existed here for hundreds of years, living alongside herders who have been running their flocks on either side of the river for just as long.

Across the river in Senegal, the same swathe of land is typically known as the Futa Tooro, after an 18th- and 19th-century Peul kingdom in the area, which was a historical rival to the Brakna and Trarza emirates to the north and stretched along both sides of the river, from just shy of Rosso in the west to Gouraye in the east. But, despite its dense population and long history, from a tourism perspective the river valley is almost totally undeveloped and you're unlikely to run into another tourist while you're here. But you absolutely *will* run into men in mirror-shiny *bazin*-cloth *boubous* (in not just blue, but every colour of the rainbow), women in Mandé-style earrings and bangles, hand-hammered from copper and bronze, and a whole host of warm and welcoming riverside residents who will have plenty of questions as to what exactly landed you here. And just as in the rest of Mauritania, these are best answered over a few cups of tea.

So it's true that here in the valley the TV sets tend to be tuned towards Mali and Senegal, and the Moorish culture and symbolism that Mauritania is often defined around can start to feel quite distant. But if Mauritania is truly the *trait d'union*, or link, connecting North Africa and Black Africa, as first president Mokhtar Ould Daddah famously envisioned, then there is no understanding this massive and mystifying land without taking the time to unfurl its most important artery – to dip your feet and feel how culture and water ebb and flow together along the length of this iconic river.

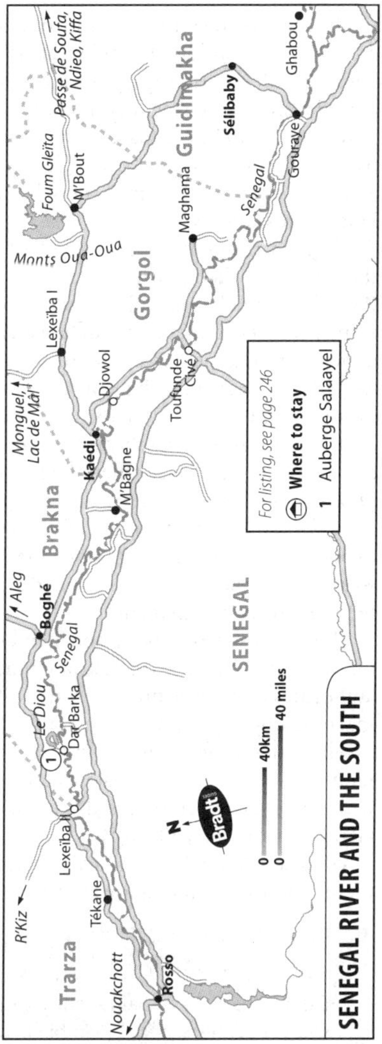

THE RIVER ROUTE TO KAÉDI

Heading east from Rosso, the road loosely follows the Senegal River, with a combination of seasonal and irrigated riverine agriculture dominating the landscape. The floodplain is cut through by tributary creeks and backwaters that twist their way along parallel to the river's main channel, forming small riverine islands and oxbows. Many of these are seasonal oueds (wadis) used for cultivation, but some flow more or less throughout the year, such as the Ndiawane (or Diayane) and Koundi. About 30km east of Rosso, there's the first of several fetching riverside viewpoints, reached from a short bridge at Tambéne village crossing the marshy Sekan River, which connects Lac R'Kiz to the Senegal River. This is a great place to arrange pirogue excursions: follow signs towards **Thiemben Relax** (m 26 21 59 35), which has a campsite (and plans for rooms) at the confluence of the Senegal and Sekan.

Another 11km east through irrigated rice paddies and wide fields of melon, squash and more, the road crosses the Laouwaja River, which also feeds Lac R'Kiz (page 3), just after the village of Gani (where there's an official crossing point to the Senegalese town of Gaé). The road then pulls close to another tributary, the Guidayo, for about 7km before crossing it at Oum Elghoura village. From here, it's a further 5km to the turn-off for the small town of **Tékane**, which sits about 1.5km south of the main road on the south bank of the Ndiawane, connected by a 200m bridge built in 2010. Tékane is a small market town of low mud-brick buildings with a tall, tiled dual-minaret mosque done up in an unexpectedly Greek-feeling blue and white. Near the entrance to town, the Centre de Pêche Artisanal and its large concrete boat landing could be a good place to ask if you'd like to find someone to take you for a little spin on the river.

The main road continues east from here along the north bank of the Ndiawane, crossing the Koundi after 10km at its confluence with the Ndiawane, just after Lemleiga village. The zigzags of the Senegal's main channel sweep back into view periodically, before reaching the turn-off for **Lexeïba II** (also known as Lexeïba du Toro, and not to be confused with Lexeïba I in the Gorgol region; page 256), 35km past the Koundi Bridge at the village of Mbignik. From the junction (where there's a service station), it's 8km to Lexeïba II, facing the historical Senegalese town of Podor across the river.

The French established a trading post in Podor in the mid 18th century, and today the view from the Mauritanian side of the river still makes for an evocative sight: Podor's venerable quayside architecture dates to the late 1700s, and pastel-hued former traders' homes and warehouses line the waterfront, creating a time-warped atmosphere like nowhere else on the river. Podor is also the site of a large fort, which took its current shape in 1854 after it was expanded and reinforced as part of colonial governor Faidherbe's drive to solidify French control over river trade.

If your timing is lucky, the final puzzle piece in this atmospheric and anachronistic scene will fall into place when the historic river ship *Bou el Mogdad* (see opposite) pulls up and docks at Podor's historic quay.

As for the Mauritanian side of the river, 19th-century French explorer Gaspard-Théodore Mollien only mentioned that it occupied the lower of the two banks, and was therefore 'almost always flooded'; today it is still very much the junior partner between the two settlements.

There's no shortage of personal and commercial traffic crossing back and forth on wooden pirogues (pedestrian only) throughout the day, but Mauritanian authorities could not process entry with e-visas at Lexeïba II as of 2025, which makes taking a quick dip in and out of Senegal here a bit complicated. Podor is an excellent option for crossing *into* Senegal, however, as many nationalities do not require a visa and the Senegalese authorities in Podor can give you the entry stamp without problem. There are daily vehicles between Lexeïba II and Nouakchott's Garage Kaédi (5hrs; 500UM).

Unfortunately, all visitor facilities are on the Senegalese side of the river, where there's good accommodation at La Cour du Fleuve or Auberge du Tékrour (Maison

REPORTS FROM THE RIVER

During his time in Saint-Louis, preparing for his journey in search of the sources of the Senegal, Gambia and Niger rivers, French explorer Gaspard-Théodore Mollien (who was also a survivor of the 1816 shipwreck of the *Méduse* frigate in the Banc d'Arguin; page 162) visited several trading posts, or *escales*, along the Senegal River and had this to say:

> An *escale* is a gathering of tents that the Moors usually pitch in a place where the river forms a bend. Wherever they settle, they destroy all traces of vegetation, and sterility reigns in the vicinity of their camps. The lowing of herds can be heard in the distance, and long lines of camels and oxen cross this vast market in all directions. Young girls called *pourognes*, descended from blacks and Moors, carry calabashes full of milk aboard the ships, offering them to the rich merchants, without demanding payment, in order to obtain a higher price, and often granting them more precious favours. At midday, the priests call out the name of Allah and strike the earth with their foreheads.
>
> Gaspard-Théodore Mollien, 1817

BOU EL MOGDAD

The undisputed grande dame of the Senegal River, the 52m *Bou el Mogdad* river cruiser was for decades a lifeline for Senegal River communities as far upriver as Senegal's Matam, until its 40-odd years of service came to a halt in the 1980s. Road transport in the river region has since rendered these once-remote communities on both sides of the river more accessible than ever, but more than 20 years after its premature retirement, the *Bou el Mogdad* was bought and returned to the river by the Saint-Louis family behind Senegalese tour agency Sahel Découverte (w saheldecouverte.com) and Hotel La Résidence (w hoteldelaresidence.com) in Saint-Louis. Today it plies the waters between Senegal and Mauritania once more, this time as a tourist boat, connecting Saint-Louis and Podor on what is without question the region's quintessential boat journey.

It makes the run between Saint-Louis and Podor every two weeks from October to May. The week-long cruises start at €1,056/1,680 for a single/double cabin all-inclusive, and you can embark in Saint-Louis, Podor or any of the stops in between, including Djoudj, Richard Toll, Dagana and others. Bookings are possible through Sahel Découverte or w bouelmogdad.com.

Because Mauritanian e-visas were not being processed at the Lexeïba II (Podor) border crossing as of 2025, this is a better way to *depart* Mauritania than it is to arrive, so get your Senegalese entry stamp at Podor and cruise your way back to the coast in style – an unbelievably sweet reward after a sojourn in the desert. And did we mention there's wine on board?

Guillaume Foy) – and even a (whisper it!) unsignposted little bar just on the water. Podor is also known as musician Baaba Maal's hometown, and it hosts the Blues du Fleuve (w bluesdufleuve.sn) music festival every year, usually in December.

Continuing east on the river road, you'll cross the Koundi River (again) 800m beyond the turn-off for Lexeïba II/Podor, and then pass the junction for the unsurfaced 40km back route to R'Kiz (page 241) at Bezoule village, 1km after the bridge. Not far past here, the road crosses into Brakna region (ولاية البراكنة). Like Trarza to the west, Brakna is named for one of Mauritania's four pre-colonial emirates. French Governor Louis Faidherbe and Brakna Emir Sidi Muhammad wuld Muhammad signed a treaty regulating the gum-arabic trade in 1858 at Podor, but Brakna would not be brought under French control until 1905.

Some 32km further along at the village of Cham (⊕ 16.7511, -14.6872) there is a turn-off to **Dar El Barka**, which sits 8km south of the main road. Though it's also known as the birthplace of Mauritania's first female government minister, Aïssata Touré Kane (appointed in 1975), the village is mostly of interest to visitors for its position at the northern end of a large oxbow lake, known as Le Diou. Formed by a wide meander in the Senegal River, the lake is about 9km long and is still connected to its mother river during the rains, so it never dries out entirely.

At the south end of Le Diou (continue past Dar El Barka until you've nearly reached the Senegal River at Ali Guelel (Wour Aly) village and turn left) is the Forêt communautaire de Loboudou (⊕ 16.6501, -14.7112), an 18ha protected forest between the lake and **Loboudou** (or Loboudou Ibrahima Ly) village. This predominantly Halpulaar settlement was the first village in Mauritania to declare itself an 'eco-village', taking inspiration from several villages across the border in Senegal and joining the Reseau pour l'Emergence et le Développement des

Ecovillages au Sahel (REDES; w redes-ecovillages.org). The community forest is small, but nonetheless impressive, especially considering it was fenced and reforested from nearly barren land over the past two decades. Today warthogs, monkeys and dozens of bird species are once again resident in the area, and fish stocks in Le Diou are improved. The village is keen to welcome tourists, and offers basic rooms at the **Auberge Salaayel** [map, page 243] (m 44 41 29 84; w adcsalaayelloboudou.org; ⊕ 16.6484, -14.7103; **$**), where you can arrange pirogue trips or jaunts around the village on horse and donkey carts (known as *charrettes*) from 400UM for a half day, as well as cultural performances and guided walks in the forest.

The village also hosts periodic **festivals**: REDES (see above) organised the second Festival des Ecovillages au Sahel in February 2025, celebrating the village's ecological and social innovations. The fourth Festival Korel Nomade (;) took place here in November 2023 – check social media for the next edition of this music and fashion fest put on by Mauritanian designer Bana Korel ().

If you instead turn right at the Ali Guelel (Wour Aly) village junction, you'll reach **Sinthiane Diama Alwaly** (⊕ 16.6594, -14.76313) after 5.5km. Here you'll find a 19th-century banco (mud-brick) mosque that is contemporaneous with the string of Sudano-Sahelian mosques found just across the river on Senegal's Île à Morfil, which are famously associated with firebrand anti-colonialist El Hadj Omar Tall (see below). Finally, there's another forested oxbow 5km further west near

ÎLE À MORFIL AND EL HADJ OMAR TALL

Between the Senegal River to the north and its tributary the Doué to the south, the Île à Morfil is the river's largest island, sandwiched between these two waterways and separated from the mainland for nearly 150km. 'Morfil' is an antiquated French term for raw ivory, and the island got its name in the mid 17th century from French colonialists who would come here for, believe it or not, elephant hunting. Once home to not only elephants but also lions and more long-gone big game, the island today is better known for its string of traditional banco-constructed villages predominantly populated by Toucouleur and Peul. Several buildings and mosques here date back to the times of Île à Morfil's most famous resident, El Hadj Omar Tall, who was born in Alwar (or Halwar) village – less than 15km away from Sinthiane Diama (see above) – when the island was part of the Futa Toro Imamate sometime around 1797. These include mosques in Alwar, Guédé and Donaye villages.

A legendary anti-colonial leader and Islamic revivalist, Tall went on to found and lead the Toucouleur Empire around 1850. At its greatest extent, this short-lived empire stretched from the eastern shores of the Senegal River in today's Guidimakha region all the way to Timbuktu and, though he recruited many of his followers from Île à Morfil and the surrounding valley, French expansion along the river meant that his home village of Alwar and the island as a whole would never fall under his rule. In 2019, France repatriated a historical sword attributed to Tall, where it is now kept in Dakar's Musée des Civilisations Noires.

If crossing the border into Senegal at either Lexeïba II (to Podor) or Boghé (to Démèt), you first step ashore on to the island, rather than 'mainland' Senegal. From here, several recently built bridges and surfaced roads now make it easy to cross the Doué and continue south into the rest of the country.

The heart of authenticity

visitmauritania.com contact@ontm.gov.mr

Mesmerizing Landscapes, Where Infinite Desert Meets Majestic Ocean

Vibrant Traditions that Enchant the Senses

Immerse Yourself in an Authentic Cultural Experience

Explore Historical Landmarks Rich in Heritage

Experience Unmatched Hospitality and Warmth

@VISIT_MAURITANIA_

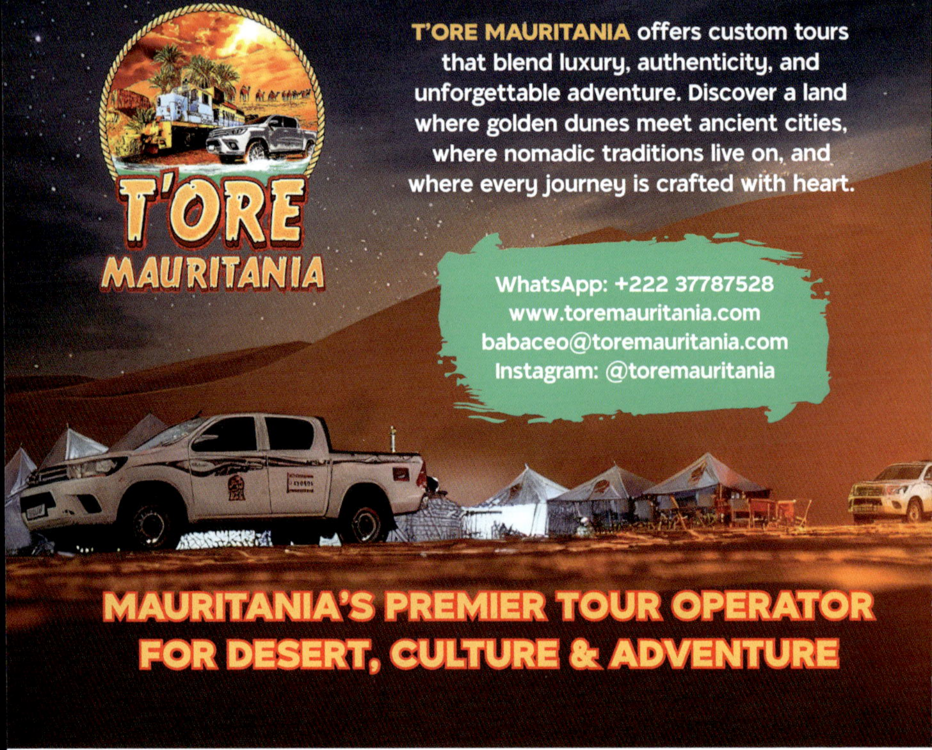

T'ORE MAURITANIA

T'ORE MAURITANIA offers custom tours that blend luxury, authenticity, and unforgettable adventure. Discover a land where golden dunes meet ancient cities, where nomadic traditions live on, and where every journey is crafted with heart.

WhatsApp: +222 37787528
www.toremauritania.com
babaceo@toremauritania.com
Instagram: @toremauritania

MAURITANIA'S PREMIER TOUR OPERATOR FOR DESERT, CULTURE & ADVENTURE

Discover Mauritania with Style

Siditoursmauritania@gmail.com
Sidi@tourmauritania.com
WhatsApp: +222 44 55 13 87
https://tourmauritania.com
Instagram: @tourmauritania.com

SIDI TOURS, in business since 2002, is a renowned local tour operator committed to sharing incredible Mauritanian experiences with the world through the country's breathtaking landscapes, genuine nomad culture, historical and archaeological sites, and premier hospitality. We specialise in individually tailored private all-inclusive tours and group tours in 4x4 vehicles, as well as camel-back riding and trekking. **Let us show you a Mauritania that you never could have imagined!**

Experts in Mauritania since 2014

Discover Mauritania's highlights and hidden corners

Straddling the line between north and west Africa, Mauritania is one of Africa's best kept secrets.

Our group tours and private tailored trips explore the very best of this enigmatic land - from the sublime landscapes of the Adrar region to the incredible birdlife of Banc D'Arguin, and the ancient Saharan cities of Chinguetti and Ouadane. Camping and accommodated trips accompanied by expert guides.

Contact us to plan your trip to Mauritania.

www.nativeeyetravel.com
info@nativeeyetravel.com
+44 1473 328546

MAURITANIA

EXPERIENCE THE MOST EXTREME TRAIN JOURNEY ON THE PLANET

JOIN THE IRON ORE TRAIN

WWW.YPT.SU/MAURITANIA

OUNG
IONEER
OURS

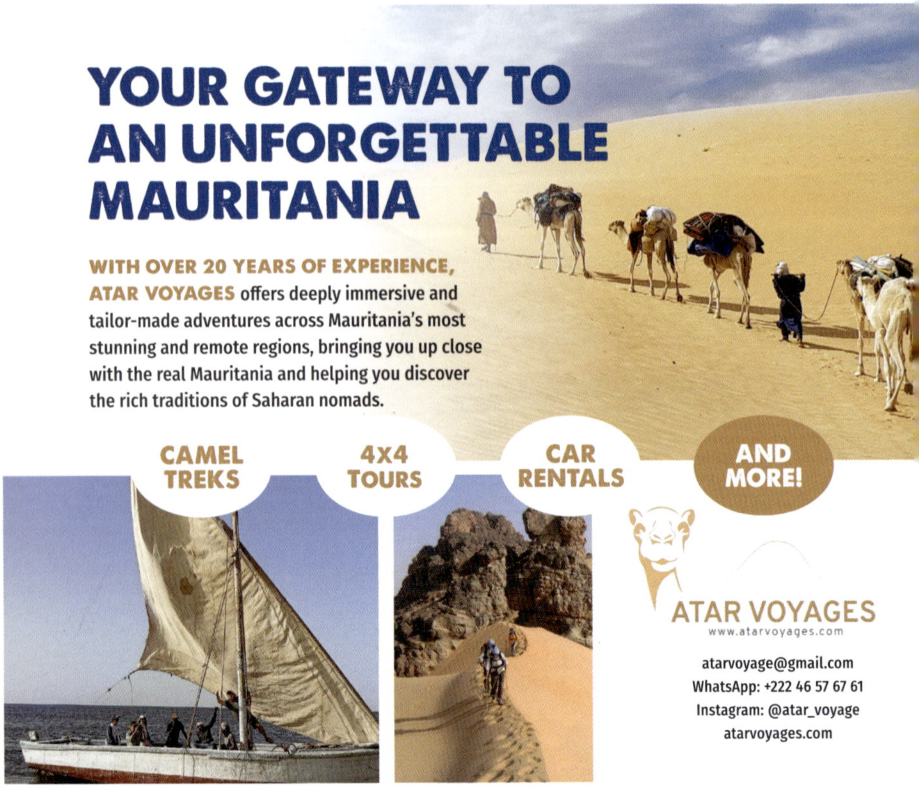

YOUR GATEWAY TO AN UNFORGETTABLE MAURITANIA

WITH OVER 20 YEARS OF EXPERIENCE, ATAR VOYAGES offers deeply immersive and tailor-made adventures across Mauritania's most stunning and remote regions, bringing you up close with the real Mauritania and helping you discover the rich traditions of Saharan nomads.

CAMEL TREKS | **4X4 TOURS** | **CAR RENTALS** | **AND MORE!**

atarvoyage@gmail.com
WhatsApp: +222 46 57 67 61
Instagram: @atar_voyage
atarvoyages.com

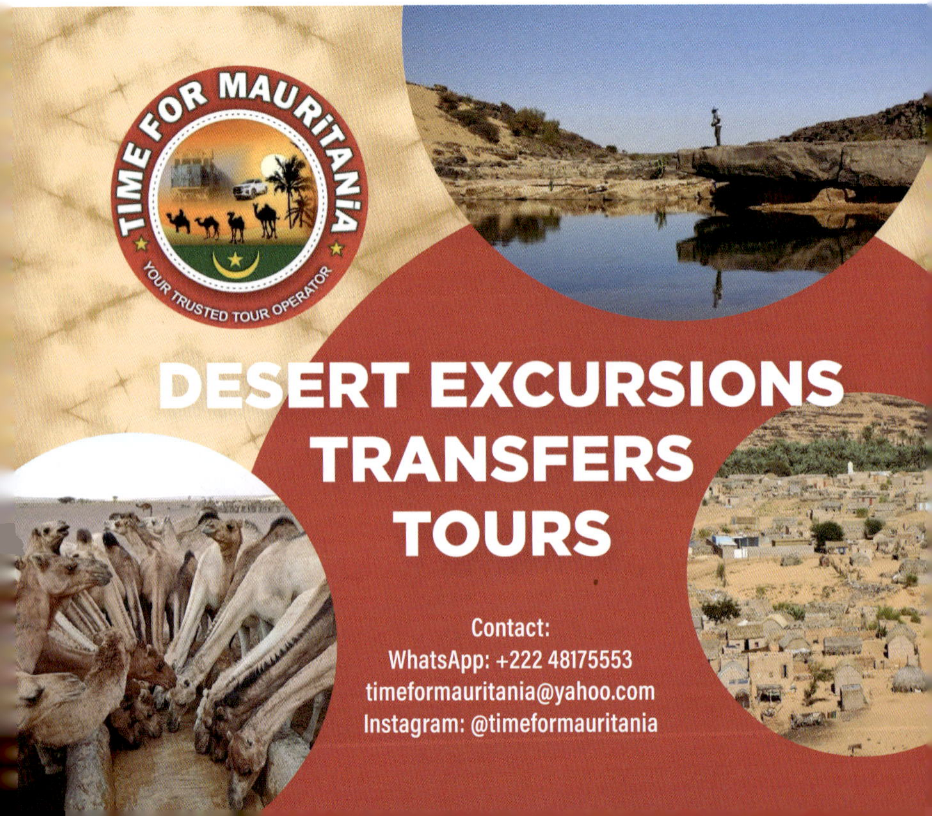

TIME FOR MAURITANIA
YOUR TRUSTED TOUR OPERATOR

DESERT EXCURSIONS TRANSFERS TOURS

Contact:
WhatsApp: +222 48175553
timeformauritania@yahoo.com
Instagram: @timeformauritania

the villages of Féthie and Bangué. Back on the main road at Cham, the tarmac runs along the edge of the *chemama* floodplain (10–15km north of the river's main channel), with dunes to the north of the road and cultivation to the south for the remaining 60km into Boghé.

BOGHÉ Though inland Aleg is the capital, riverside Boghé is the largest town in Brakna region, with just over 50,000 residents. The city's name comes from Pulaar, the language of the city's primarily Peul and Toucouleur residents (known collectively as Halpulaaren, 'those who speak Pulaar'). It was originally called Bokki – simply the word for baobab, which once grew plentifully here, though the city's significant growth means far fewer of these iconic trees are seen in town today.

Like many Mauritanian settlements, Boghé is split in two by a watercourse – here by the seasonal Marigot de Djintou. Entering by road, you arrive in Boghé-Dow, meaning 'Upper Boghé' in Pulaar. Boghé-Dow is where you'll find all the visitor facilities, including accommodation and banking. Its counterpart Boghé-Less (Lower Boghé) sits between the seasonal marigot and the mighty Senegal River, and is largely given over to Boghé's fabulous, frenetic market where the Boghéens do an impressively brisk business selling to shoppers from all corners of the *chemama* and beyond. Boghé-Less is also sometimes known as Boghé-Escale thanks to its origin as a French-built river port, established in 1908. The city is not long on tourist attractions, but it has decent facilities for visitors and remains a significant centre for trade and transport, even if most of it today happens by road rather than river.

Getting there and away

Boghé (بوكي) is the point at which the river road and the Route de l'Espoir come closest to meeting; the Brakna regional capital of Aleg (page 267) is a major stopover on the Route de l'Espoir and sits just 60km north of Boghé. Therefore, coming from the west, Boghé is easily reached from either Nouakchott (310km) or Rosso (200km). Most transport leaves from just east of the main roundabout in upper Boghé, with vehicles for Aleg (1hr; 100UM), Kaédi (2hrs; 150UM), Rosso (3hrs; 350UM) and Nouakchott (5hrs; 450UM). For Kiffa or Sélibaby, you may get lucky, or you'll likely have an easier time changing vehicles in Aleg or Kaédi, respectively. SONEF (m 43 46 43 05) coach buses to Nouakchott (500UM) pass through Boghé two or three times daily, generally mid-morning and mid-afternoon. One or two buses head the other direction towards Sélibaby (600UM) as well.

Boghé also sits along the Senegalese border, and you can get a lift across the river in a wooden pirogue (there is no vehicle ferry). You arrive on to what is actually a river island, the Île à Morfil, in the Senegalese village of Démèt. There's an immigration post here, and it's 60km of surfaced road to the next larger town of Ndioum. Mauritanian immigration was unable to process e-visas at Boghé as of 2025.

To get between Boghé-Dow and Boghé-Less, it's easy to flag down a vehicle running along the one road between the two for just a few ouguiya.

Where to stay

Map, page 248

Hotel Diam Near Lycée de Boghé; m 49 59 31 31, 46 43 88 19; e hoteldiam@gmail.com. Opened in 2023, this is the newest & fanciest option in town. The en-suite rooms come with AC, mini fridge & TV, & meals are available for 100–200UM. It looks a bit foreboding behind its high security walls, but the welcome is warm. *1,600/2,000UM sgl/dbl B&B.* **$$$**

Auberge Ecotourism Kaédi road; m 47 82 32 41. At the eastern edge of town, this is slightly

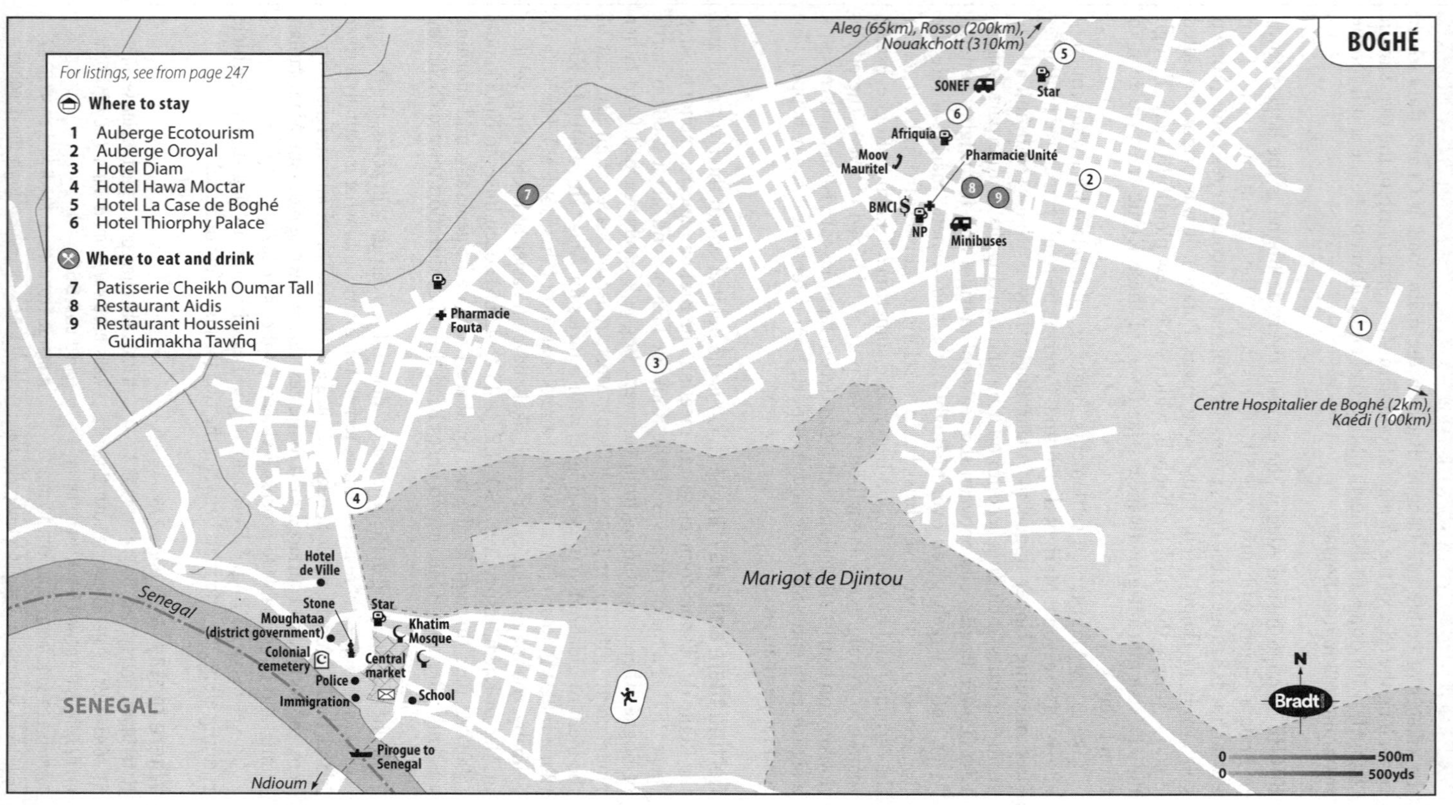
BOGHÉ
For listings, see from page 247
Where to stay
1 Auberge Ecotourism
2 Auberge Oroyal
3 Hotel Diam
4 Hotel Hawa Moctar
5 Hotel La Case de Boghé
6 Hotel Thiorphy Palace
Where to eat and drink
7 Patisserie Cheikh Oumar Tall
8 Restaurant Aidis
9 Restaurant Housseini Guidimakha Tawfiq
Aleg (65km), Rosso (200km), Nouakchott (310km)
SONEF
Star
Afriquia
Moov Mauritel
Pharmacie Unité
BMCI
NP
Minibuses
Pharmacie Fouta
Centre Hospitalier de Boghé (2km), Kaédi (100km)
Marigot de Djintou
Hotel de Ville
Stone
Moughataa (district government)
Colonial cemetery
Police
Immigration
Star
Khatim Mosque
Central market
School
Pirogue to Senegal
Senegal
SENEGAL
Ndioum
N
Bradt
0 500m
0 500yds

cheaper than most of the competition, but dingier as well. They've got the nicest garden of the bunch, though. *1,000/1,200UM dbl/garden rondavel B&B.* **$$**

Auberge Oroyal Off Kaéfi road; m 41 97 51 87, 36 43 76 85. This small guesthouse with AC rooms is a bit wonky but homely; the welcoming owner lives on site & is happy to help with any questions or requests. *1,000UM dbl.* **$$**

Hotel Hawa Moctar m 42 12 90 37. Just up from the dry streambed dividing the town (though not really taking advantage of any view), this feels like a meandering old family house but the rooms are well kept. There's no signboard, but it's the first building at the corner with the solid black gate. *1,000/1,500UM sgl with shared bath/dbl en-suite.* **$$**

Hotel La Case de Boghé m 41 32 48 86, 34 72 31 92, 47 87 87 10. A popular option on the main road into town with simple en-suite AC rooms. There's no kitchen, but it's right next door to a bakery. *1,200UM dbl.* **$$**

Hotel Thiorphy Palace Rosso/Aleg road; m 46 52 54 09. This is a business-minded address which hosts workshops for visiting NGOs & the like with a nice green garden out front. The en-suite AC rooms are well kept & meals are available on demand. *1,500UM dbl B&B.* **$$**

Where to eat and drink *Map, opposite*

Most of the restaurants in town are clustered around the minibus park in upper Boghé, serving primarily grilled meats and rice, with maybe a bowl of couscous or thiéboudiène in the offing if you're lucky. **Restaurant Aidis** (m 20 27 36 21; $) and **Restaurant Housseini Guidimakha Tawfiq** (m 41 23 71 46; $) are two of the busier options. On the way to lower Boghé there are baked goods at **Patisserie Cheikh Oumar Tall** (m 49 70 24 13; $), and in lower Boghé you'll find some very basic eateries catering to market vendors.

Other practicalities There's one **ATM** in Boghé, at the BMCI on the main roundabout in upper Boghé. Moov Mauritel is also represented here. The **Centre Hospitalier de Boghé** is 2km east of the city on the road to Kaédi, and there are several **pharmacies** in town. The **post office** is near the market in lower Boghé.

What to see and do In keeping with its history as a colonial-era *escale* for river trade, lower Boghé has a handful of early-20th-century **colonial buildings** slung along the riverfront, but most of these are either behind high walls, home to various branches of the police and military, or both – be discreet if you're taking photos. A few metres away lies a small and comprehensively ruined colonial **cemetery**. The handful of graves are overwhelmingly destroyed, apparently at least in part desecrated by a truck driver who ran down the stones in the early 2000s. He was arrested, but the only trace of information we could find – either in the cemetery or elsewhere – was a broken stone dated 1926.

But Boghé has no shortage of mysterious **stones** to puzzle over, with another example just across the road at lower Boghé's main junction. Here, a large rock sits atop a short plinth, decorated with a thoroughly uninformative blank spot where the dedication plaque was once affixed. Again, we were unable to find out what was so special about this particular rock, but the goats are quite content with the shade it provides.

Finally, it's definitely worth rolling up your sleeves and taking the plunge into Boghé's **central market**. Perennially busy and ram-jammed with everything from trousers to tweezers and teapots to *tengadês* – the conical leather-trimmed hats worn by the Peul – it's one of the most significant markets on the river and attracts custom from far and wide. Locally fired clay pots with hand-painted designs are also a regional speciality, though unfortunately a bit tricky to lug home as a souvenir. The market sits just inland from the riverfront, so, when you've had enough, head to the banks to cool off and take in the riverine comings and goings, with pirogue traffic aplenty between here and the Senegalese shore.

Just north of the market lies a very unusual mosque, notable not only for its banco-mud construction and its age – it dates back to 1922 – but for its shape as well: it's built into the form of a **khatim**, an eight-pointed star considered in Islamic iconography as the prophetic 'seal of Muhammad'. A much larger mosque sits just a few blocks away; built in 1962, its dual minarets and rectangular shape are attractive but considerably more conventional.

LIVELIHOODS IN THE SOUTHERN VALLEY

Peter Hudson

In the early days of my visits to Lexeïba I, the countryside around the town looked all much the same to me. Parts of it were sandy, parts hard, baked earth, parts dotted with scrub and stunted trees. But it was all dry and of much the same level. It was only as time went on that I began to understand that this was not the case. Indeed, it was fairly flat country, but not entirely so, and it was these small variations in height, I discovered, sometimes as little as a meter, that made all the difference. This is because of the nature of the rainfall. Coming, as it does, in large downpours after a long dry season when the ground has been baked to a concrete hardness, runoff is extremely rapid, quickly filling the dry riverbeds, or *oueds*, that drain into larger rivers, which in turn flow into the Senegal River. The speed with which this all takes place means flooding is inevitable and indeed, in a normal year, vast areas can be inundated. This is not a problem as the inhabitants of the region have situated their villages in places that are above all but the most exceptional floods and have shaped their agricultural practices around this event.

It is the speed with which the water drains from the land that is so significant. Only tiny variations in elevation can mean the difference between land that drains in an hour, land that holds water for a week, and land that dries up over the period of three months. These, in conjunction with soil types, dictate exactly to what use each part of the land can be put. The higher sandy areas, for example, which drain the fastest, are good only for brief pastures. Land with a higher clay content, say in a slight depression, will hold water for a little longer, allowing sufficient water penetration for a quick crop of sorghum to be grown. Land lower still, where the water takes even longer to drain away, can be planted with millet. And the land with the highest clay content at the lowest elevation, even though perhaps still only a few meters below the highest ground, constitutes the primary agricultural area where millet and maize can be grown in abundance in a good year.

The exact annual precipitation and precise level of the preceding floods are therefore vital. A minor reduction in the rainfall and decrease in the floods can leave huge areas that normally produce crops high and dry. Then again, years that have exceptional rainfall can cause havoc, flooding villages, washing away crops and stranding livestock. If one throws in the fact that the densities of livestock in the south have risen hugely in recent years, due to a general migration from the dryer north – livestock that can cause untold damage to unfenced crops – it becomes clear how very marginal and vulnerable life is in the region.

From Under An African Sky *(New Internationalist, 2014)*

Finally, if you're here in July/August, be sure to see if the Image du Fleuve festival (w festivalimagedufleuve.org) is on, during which Boghé hosts a series of expositions, concerts and open-air film screenings on the banks of the Senegal River. Organised by Boghé-born director Djibril Diaw, the fifth edition was held in 2025.

KAÉDI AND GORGOL REGION

The road cuts a more or less straight line on the 100km between Boghé and Kaédi, but the river takes a considerably more relaxed path, meandering 160km between the two cities. Some 33km before reaching Kaédi (and 20km after the pleasingly alliterative agricultural town of Bababé), there's a 16km tarred feeder road leading to the remote river outpost of **M'Bagne**. This market town on the banks of the Senegal sits a short distance upstream of the Senegalese town of Saldé, another trading centre on the opposite shore. Literature fans consider Saldé to be the likely (though officially undefined) setting for Matam-born author Cheikh Hamidou Kane's 1961 novel *Ambiguous Adventure*. Though Senegalese, the experience of traditional life and schooling on the river outlined in Kane's semi-autobiographical work could have easily taken place in either country. Saldé was also a designated escale for the gum-arabic trade between the Brakna Emirate and the French in the late 19th century, where 600kg of gum from Brakna's acacia forests were exchanged for one guinea, containing a quarter-ounce (7g) of gold.

Back on the main route, the road says goodbye to Brakna and enters the Gorgol region (ولاية كوركول) before once again pulling close to the river several kilometres before reaching the region's waterfront capital city of Kaédi. The endless dunes of Trarza and Brakna begin to give way to a landscape of rolling plains and dry grasslands engraved with waterless oueds and punctuated by the occasional rocky outcrop and plateau. The *wilaya* takes its name from the Gorgol River, Mauritania's only permanent watercourse other than the Senegal.

KAÉDI Situated at the confluence of the Senegal and Gorgol rivers, Kaédi (كيهيدي) is the largest (population 62,790) and most important city of the middle Senegal valley. Its position at the meeting of two rivers made it a natural gathering place, and unlike some of the other settlements along the river, its importance well predates the colonial era and the gum-arabic trade. Little of this history survives, however, as Kaédi was largely destroyed in an 1890 French bombardment meant to punish the town for sheltering Alboury Ndiaye, the last independent *bourba* (king) of Djolof (a Wolof kingdom in what is now north-central Senegal), who had gone into exile rather than accede to French demands. As the French ultimately solidified their control over the river valley in the late 19th and early 20th centuries, Kaédi became an important stopover for colonial ships bound between Saint-Louis and Kayes in present-day Mali.

Though still in the Halpulaar heartlands, Kaédiens today come from all backgrounds, and the city is a magnet for trade – look no further than the absolutely heaving central market for proof. Here you'll find heaps upon heaps of the valley's fresh produce, much of it quickly sold and trucked north to the waiting cooking pots of Nouakchott and Nouadhibou, alongside all manner of agricultural tools, fishing tackle and hand-dyed cloth – the city has long been known for its textile-dyeing tradition.

And cementing Kaédi's status as one of Mauritania's main agricultural hubs, Mauritania's oldest agricultural research institute is based here, where they study improved techniques for river valley agriculture in the *walo* (Pulaar for the floodplain farming area) and the *diéri* (rain-fed agricultural lands beyond the river's seasonal flood), as well as phoeniciculture (date palm cultivation) in the country's many oases.

Getting there and away Kaédi is 100km east of Boghé along the river road, and fairly regular vehicles connect the two (2hrs; 150UM). The road between these cities was in rather rough shape as of 2025, but repair works were underway at the time of writing. It's also possible to find direct vehicles to Nouakchott (6hrs; 600UM), Aleg (3hrs; 250UM), Kiffa (via Aleg: 7hrs; 600UM), Sélibaby (3½hrs; 400UM) and Maghama (2hrs; 150UM) from Kaédi's main garage/*gare routière*. For Rosso you will have to change vehicles in Boghé. There are a few SONEF (m 43 46 43 10) coach buses to Nouakchott daily, departing at roughly 07.30, 11.30 and 13.30. SONEF also runs a bus to Sélibaby in the afternoon around 15.30.

Heading east, what we have until now been referring to as the main 'river road' in fact breaks free of its companion at Kaédi, charting a path through the plains towards M'Bout along the north side of the Gorgol River instead.

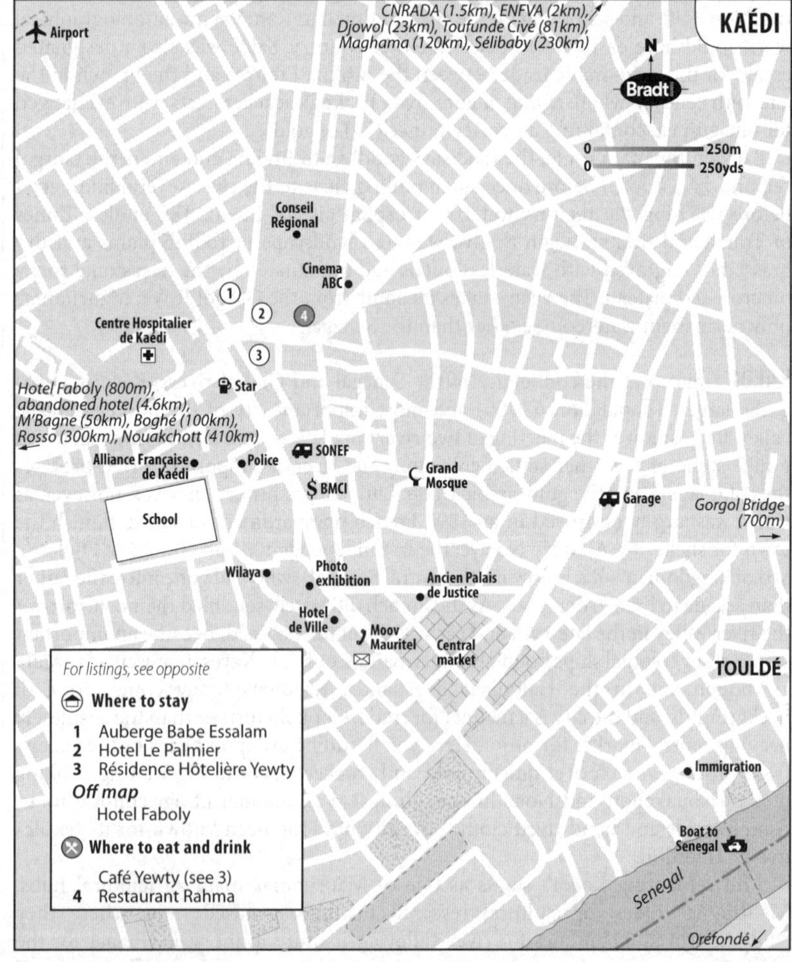

There is, however, another road that continues along the Senegal River, leading 120km surfaced kilometres southeast from Kaédi and roughly following the waterway until the tarmac ends at the town of **Maghama**. This route passes the turn-off to the border village of Toufunde Civé after 75km.

Toufunde Civé sits along the river 7km beyond the junction, and you can take a pirogue (passenger-only) across to the historic Senegalese town of Matam from here. (Immigration posts for both countries are subject to the usual visa caveats.) Similar to the situation between Lexeïba II and Podor, visitor facilities are all on the Senegalese side of the river, where you'll find accommodation in Matam and in Ourossogui, 8km further into Senegal (where there are also ATMs dispensing CFA francs). To stay on the Mauritanian side of the river near here, you might arrange a homestay in **Civé** village (2.5km before the Toufunde Civé turn-off) through Samba Konaté (m +1 614 500 0119), who has experience working with US Peace Corps Volunteers.

From Kaédi's riverfront, **pirogues** shuttle back and forth across the river to the Senegalese village of Mollé Walo (also known as Gourel Oumar Ly) throughout the day, from where it's 34km on unsurfaced roads to Oréfondé town on the main RN2 river road in Senegal. The Société des Bacs de Mauritanie (w sbm.mr) inaugurated a new, locally built vehicle barge/**ferry** here in 2023, so it's now also possible to make the crossing here with light vehicles and trucks (anything seriously heavy will still have to go to Rosso). There were still no biometric facilities for entry with an e-visa at Kaédi as of 2025.

Kaédi also has an airport at the north edge of town, but there were no scheduled flights as of 2025.

Where to stay *Map, opposite*

Auberge Babe Essalam Near Centre Hospitalier; m 47 91 66 66. Assuming the wildly overpriced rates we were quoted here were just the manager trying it on & can therefore be bargained down, it could be a deal. At the quoted rate, it's terrible value compared with the competition. *1,300UM dbl.* **$$**

Hotel Faboly Boghé road; m 44 20 68 04. Once upon a time probably the best option in town, this old stalwart at the western edge of town is looking rather tired these days, but the rooms are decently kept & all come with AC & en-suite bathroom. Meals available on demand. *1,000/1,500UM dbl/suite.* **$$**

Hotel Le Palmier Near Centre Hospitalier; m 46 45 92 05. In a whitewashed 3-storey block, the rooms here come in a variety of configurations but all have AC & en-suite ablutions. It's tidily kept & the management is friendly. The restaurant isn't operational, but Café Yewty (see below) is just across the road. *From 1,000UM dbl.* **$$**

Résidence Hôtelière Yewty Near Centre Hospitalier; 45 33 51 03; m 22 16 30 10, 46 57 03 76; e jikke.tht@gmail.com, ibrahim-diagana@hotmail.com. Trim, tidy, central & with Kaédi's best restaurant attached, this is the glaringly obvious pick. The simple & clean rooms all come with AC & en-suite bathroom. A few plants might brighten up the aggressively angular tiled courtyard, but that's just a minor quibble. *From 1,000UM dbl.* **$$**

Where to eat and drink *Map, opposite*

For a town of its size, Kaédi is rather low on bespoke eateries, but there are several on the road leading east from the hospital, mostly connected to hotels. Your best bet is **Café Yewty** ($$) – under the same ownership as but in a separate building to the Résidence Hôtelière Yewty – where they do an excellent grilled fish for about 200UM. (Across the road, Le Palmier advertises itself as a restaurant but there was no food available when we checked in.) In a newly built shopping centre just before the Cinema ABC, **Restaurant Rahma** (m 36 95 79 19; $) does cheaper fast-food dishes, and there's also a nameless place across the street from here with Mickey Mouse holding a shish kebab skewer painted on the front.

Other practicalities There is an **ATM** at the BMCI bank on the main road. The **Centre Hospitalier de Kaédi** is at the centre of town, and there are several **pharmacies** just opposite. Moov Mauritel and the **post office** are both found near the Hotel de Ville.

Though it's mostly a destination for language classes and their lending library rather than regular cultural events, the **Alliance Française de Kaédi** (m 46 51 23 68; e alliancefrancaisekaedi@gmail.com; f AFKaedi) is a friendly address for Francophones (or aspiring ones).

What to see and do Unfortunately, Kaédi's most notable building (mostly) met the wrecking ball in 2012, when the new and thoroughly uninteresting Centre Hospitalier de Kaédi replaced the 1984 **Kaédi Regional Hospital**, which was built under Italian architect Fabrizio Carola and the Association pour le Développement naturel d'une Architecture et d'un Urbanisme Africain (ADAUA). Built from local brick fired by burning waste from rice production, it won the Aga Khan Award for Architecture in 1995.

There are only a few scraps of the previous hospital's curvaceous corridors and vaults, pointed ogival arches and otherworldly domes left to see, but if you tell the guard at the gate you just want to take a look at the building, they'll usually let you have a poke around. (You can also see some archival photos here: w archidatum.com/projects/kaedi-regional-hospital-association-pour-le-d%C3%A9veloppement-dune-architecture-et-dun-urbanisme-africains) Most of what remains is at the southeast and northwest corners of the campus, including a series of open-sided domes used as waiting rooms – be mindful of the fact that this is an active health facility.

And while most of the hospital's architecture is gone, there is an abandoned, but standing, **hotel** (⊕ 16.1480, -13.5510) built in similar style a bit less than 5km west of town towards Boghé. You can have a look around, but as always in Mauritania, be sure to greet and introduce yourself to any caretaker or others who may be around.

Not far from the hospital, the seemingly abandoned **Cinema ABC** actually still holds the occasional concert or other event – have a look if there are any advertising banners strung up out front. Either way, the dated façade makes for a good photo op.

The **Grand Mosque** in the Gattaga neighbourhood has a newer and older portion, and though its 1947 opening date makes it much younger than its counterparts elsewhere in the region, it's built in a similar Sudano-Sahelian adobe style, with a squat minaret at one end dotted with the protruding support beams so characteristic of the style. Though Gattaga is a crowded neighbourhood, all roads lead to the mosque – it's known as the 'carrefour des 6 chemins', or the crossroads of the six paths. (Or if you still need some help, it's at: ⊕ 16.1482, -13.5014) The mosque was restored in 2012 and has featured on the 20-ouguiya note since 2021. The modern mosque adjacent towers over the old portion, but it is of decidedly less architectural interest.

Kaédi is also known as an important centre for traditional **wrestling**, known as *la lutte* or *làmb* (page 56). There's no dedicated arena in town, but matches are held from time to time in Gattaga's open squares.

A few streets south of here is the **Ancien Palais de Justice**, which dates to the colonial era. It seems to have been out of service for quite some time but can be identified from an inscription just under the point of the roof. The **marché central** spills over several blocks just south of here, so be warned if you're driving – the boxes, barrows, bowls, basins and boubous spilling over the roads here seem very much to have the right of way, and you could be stuck for quite a while!

North of the market towards the city's administrative centre is a very interesting open-air **exhibition**. Mounted on 20-some signboards in front of the Hotel de Ville, it presents a French-language overview of the river's middle and upper valley, with a focus on its three most important cities: '*Bakel, Kayes et Kaédi, des villes en mouvement sur le fleuve Sénégal*' (Cities in Motion on the Senegal River). There's no shade at all, so you can finish up with the online version once you've reached your limit in the sun: w grdr.org/IMG/pdf/mavil_livretexpo_ok_web.pdf.

Kaédi is also known for its **cloth-dyeing** tradition, and in a country where your average woman is wearing nearly 5m of colourful fabric at all times, this is a critical skill indeed! Though the trade is now practised by women of all ethnic groups, Kaédi's dyeing tradition is thought to originate primarily with the Soninké, who even today are known for their striking indigo robes. Most of the dyeing work (known as *gara* in Soninké, *sbagha* in Hassaniya, *gobou* in Pulaar, and *thioub* in Wolof) is done in family compounds, so it's unfortunately somewhat challenging to recommend one specific place to see the process take place. That being said, you can either ask your hotel to help point you in the right direction or ring up Hawa Tandja (m 46 93 35 20, 46 43 43 17), who runs the Coopérative Fatima shop at Nouakchott's craft market (page 126). She's originally from Kaédi and can connect you with family who do dyeing work in the city (which she also sells in her shop). To shop for the cloth in Kaédi, your best bet is to visit the central market, where Coopérative Yambaye, among others, has a shop.

RICE HARVEST ALONG THE RIVER

Katherine Baird

October arrived, and with it the hard work of the rice harvest. By the time the sun was one palm high, men were already squatting beside dry rice stalks. With a small hand sickle, they swung hard once, twice, three times to cut through each handful, each hard swipe accompanied by a grunt and bead of sweat. Meanwhile, all capable of it ferried off bulging eight-foot-wide bundles of the fallen stalks, carting them off to a cleared area just past the perimeter's reach. Women then swept up thick handfuls of the long stalks and began vigorously thrashing them against overturned rusty barrels, *bang-bang-banging*, until the rice lost hold and shattered to the ground. All day long, the deep rumble of those hollow drumbeats filled the air.

'Let's sing,' someone would occasionally call out, and lyrical voices would arise while the random beatings turned into coordinated drumming. If still fresh, a few young girls would even halt their work to add playfully suggestive dancing to the merriment. During harvest, everyone worked, even the youngest. Those not yet waist-high were handed a large tin to scoop paddy rice from the ground into recycled burlap bags. During breaks, men carefully and tightly stitched each bulging sack closed with cloth strips attached to oversized needles. Then donkeys were led in and held steady while sixty-pound sacks of rice were strapped to their backs. Finally, a stick-bearing boy would silently accompany the beast back to the village [Civé]. Then night came, and everyone would lay exhausted but happy, nursing hands sliced raw by the stiff dry stalks. Until daybreak, that is, when all set out with steely cheer for a repeat performance.

From Growing Mangos in the Desert *(Apprentice House Press, 2022)*

On the river at the east side of the city lies **Touldé**, Kaédi's oldest quarter. Though as elsewhere the architecture is increasingly made from concrete blocks, there are still some older mud-brick constructions to be seen on a wander through the neighbourhood's narrow alleyways. About 300m beyond the eastern edge of the city, there's a **bridge** over the Gorgol just up from its confluence with the Senegal (⊕ 16.1489, -13.4891), which makes a great place to watch the earthy brown waters of the Gorgol meet and mingle with the Senegal's great blue-green flow. Across the bridge, rice paddies stretch for miles towards the horizon.

At the eastern edge of town along the road to M'Bout, the Centre National de Recherche Agronomique et de Développement Agricole (CNRADA; National Centre for Agronomic Research and Agricultural Development; ☎ 25 06 82 16; w cnrada.org) and École Nationale de Formation et de Vulgarisation Agricole (ENFVA; National School of Agricultural Training and Extension; m 41 60 11 39; f) sit next to one another, and their appropriately green agricultural campuses are worth a peek.

Some 25km southeast of Kaédi along the road to Maghama, the riverside town of **Djowol** (or Diéwol, Djeol) held the first Festival Culturel De Djowol (f) over several days in March 2023. There was plenty of song, dance, speechifying and pageantry, with President Ghazouani even in attendance, but it wasn't held in 2024, so it's not clear if it's set to become a reliably annual event. Even without the festival, Djowol is a scenic spot, built around a steep outcrop which separates it from the neighbouring village of Gory and offers commanding views of the river.

M'BOUT AND LAC DE FOUM GLEÏTA Continuing east from Kaédi, the road runs north of the Gorgol River, passing **Lexeïba I** (or Lexeïba Gorgol) after about 40km. Lexeïba I is a busy trading town and the junction for Monguel and the Lac de Mâl (page 270), from where you can continue to the Route d'Espoir, 160km to the north. This route was being surfaced as of 2025. Just before entering the town, the Association pour l'Agriculture Durable en Mauritanie (f Admaperda) administers the Green Leaf Farm (f thegreenleaffarm), which got its start as a collaboration between British author Peter Hudson (page 48) and Mauritanian farmer Mohamedou Sall. The farm serves as a demonstration of agro-ecological principles and offers training and agricultural extension services to farmers all along the river valley.

Upriver of Lexeïba I, the Gorgol splits into two tributaries, the Gorgol Blanc and the Gorgol Noir. From Lexeïba I, it's another 55km east to the turn-off for the **Barrage de Foum Gleïta**. This 45m-high dam on the Gorgol Noir blocks a narrow gap in the **Monts Oua-Oua** and was inaugurated in 1984. It can hold up to 500 million cubic metres of water, making it Mauritania's largest dam, and the reservoir covers an area between 50km^2 in the dry season and 100km^2 when the annual floods arrive between July and October.

To reach the dam, continue 25km north from the junction until the road ends. The eponymous town of Foum Gleïta sits halfway along this route, which is surfaced the whole way. There were no restrictions on access when we visited in 2024, though it would be wise to have your passport handy. (In fact, no-one asked us any questions at all – a bit of a shock considering the prickly attitudes many countries in the region take towards visiting or photographing 'critical infrastructure'!)

It's possible to walk out on to the dam and take in one of the most unusual views in Mauritania – water as far as the eye can see! The lakeshore is rocky, but there's a small accessible cove reached by following the track past the dam on foot for about 175m. It's also possible to climb the hill behind this cove for fine views over the surroundings. The reservoir mostly serves to irrigate surrounding rice plantations and market gardens, but there is also a small contingent of artisanal fishermen at work here, who can be seen casting their lines and nets either above or below the dam, depending on fishing conditions.

Back on the main route and continuing towards M'Bout, the road also crosses the Monts Oua-Oua (or Wa-Wa; ⊕ 15.9773, -12.6841) at a pass in this narrow north–south ridge that tops out around 100m. **M'Bout** itself is a small departmental (*moughataa*) capital, largely dedicated to agriculture, thanks to the nearby dam, and offering a handful of basic shops and restaurants, but otherwise few facilities for visitors. (There are rooms above the petrol station at **Appartement Rawahel** (m 20 20 80 13, 47 86 75 75; **$**) if you need to spend the night.) It sits at the junction of the surfaced road south to Sélibaby and the rough track east towards the Kiffa–Kankossa road in Assaba region. The eastbound track reaches tar again after about 140km, passing through the village and **Passe de Soufa** (Soufa Pass; ⊕ 15.9388, -12.0116) en route. If going this way, it's worth the 10km diversion from Soufa to the Soninké village of **Ndieo** (⊕ 15.8653, -12.0422), which has a dramatic location directly beneath the Massif d'Assaba, and its own perennial spring at the base. (You can also continue around the southern end of the escarpment from here via the Passe de Tektaka; page 261.)

SÉLIBABY AND GUIDIMAKHA REGION

Leaving M'Bout and driving towards Sélibaby, you exit Gorgol and enter Guidimakha region after about 40km. Separated from Mali to the east by the Karakoro River and Senegal to the west by the Senegal River, Guidimakha is Mauritania's southernmost region, cupped between its two West African neighbours and more culturally and environmentally similar to either of these than the rest of Mauritania to the north. Here, you're as likely to hear Soninké and Peul as you are Hassaniya, radios are tuned to Dakar and Bamako, and camels have been decisively replaced by cows.

Guidimakha takes its name from the legendary first Soninké settler in the region, Makha Malé Douo Soumaré, and from the Soninké name for the Massif de Assaba, *guidé*, which rises some 400m in the region's northeast. Over the centuries, this morphed into Guidimakha, or 'Makha Mountain', and the region remains Mauritania's Soninké heartland to this day. Though they arrived in Guidimakha more recently, the Soninké claim a lineage going back as far as the Ghana Empire and its ancient capital of Koumbi Saleh (page 291), 500km to the east in today's Hodh Ech Chargui region.

The landscape of rolling plains cut through by oueds here is noticeably greener than the rest of the country, though a bit of perspective may be in order. The climate in nearly all of Mauritania is classified as 'hot desert', while Guidimakha is a refreshing 'hot semi-arid' instead. So, while you could be forgiven for not noticing the change while sweating away in the back of a minibus, the climatic differences are significant for the many Guidimakhankés making their livelihoods from agriculture (primarily Soninké) and herding (largely Peul and Moorish): the annual rainfall here can top 500mm – a full ten times what you are likely to get in Nouakchott – and the region is known as a bread basket for the country, even producing the decidedly non-desert crops of banana and mango.

Soninké also have a decorative tradition of large-scale geometric mural artwork, known as *diabandé*. Originally painted using traditional pigments foraged in the surrounding bush, the style has echoes of the 'painted villages' of Sirigu in Ghana or Tiébélé in Burkina Faso (or even of their compatriots in Oualata), though – and perhaps going some way towards explaining why it's less widely known – diabandé is generally used to decorate the interior, rather than the exterior of buildings.

About 35km south of M'Bout along the border between Gorgol and Guidimakha, the village of **Djajibiné** is home to the Coopérative Féminine de Djajibiné Gandega ('Djida'), who travelled to Barcelona in 2010 to create a piece as part of a multinational exhibition on mural art. As with so many traditional art forms, diabandé is increasingly hard to find, but make a stop in Djajibiné and ask for the collective to learn more. (East of the main road, Ould Mboni Edebay (Oulombomé) (⊕ 15.6958, -12.2969) and Bouanze (⊕ 15.8189, -12.2353) were once known as centres of the practice, but it's not clear how much you'll find there today.)

As you continue south into Guidimakha, the humble architecture of farming and herding communities starts to be interspersed with some unexpectedly big houses and mosques. These incongruously grand constructions tell a story of a newer Soninké tradition: international migration. In fact, Soninké people were among the first sub-Saharan Africans to migrate to Europe in any significant numbers, lured by France's desperate need for labour in the post-war period. In 1968, 85% of all sub-Saharan Africans in France were Soninkés, and in the 1970s, it was estimated that one in every three Soninké men of working age had migrated to France. So these houses and mosques are the product of long hours, days and lives worked in France and elsewhere and represent the fulfilment of so many youthful promises made upon departure to distant and uncertain futures.

Continuing south through the rangelands of Guidimakha, you'll see a number of examples of this phenomenon, but the mosque in **Artémou** (42km past Djajibiné) stands out. With a striking black-and-white colour scheme, cake-frosting crenellations and stripey onion domes – the latter unexpectedly reminiscent of Saint Basil's Cathedral in Moscow – it's by far the most photogenic of the bunch. About 9km further along at Tachott village, the road crosses the large Oued Haouissé, where, depending on the time of your visit, you'll see a mosaic of seasonal farm plots coaxing squash, tomato, okra, black-eyed peas and more out of the dry riverbed.

SÉLIBABY The gendarme who checked our *fiche* on the way into town seemed genuinely perplexed when we informed him that the purpose of our visit was tourism, so if you love the feeling of being the only traveller in town, Sélibaby (سليبابي) may just be the place for you. This little-visited regional capital is also a fine example of how Mauritania straddles two cultural worlds. Though unmistakeably Mauritanian, Sélibaby sways to a West African beat, with significant Senegalese and Malian influence on the culture, music and cuisine in the city. (So get ready to hear Akon as often as you hear an *ardin*.)

Taking its name from the area's first settler, a nomad by the name of Ould Ely Baby, the city is today something of a boomtown. Though Guidimakha is closely associated with the Soninké, Sélibabiens today represent all of Mauritania's ethnic groups, with many migrants from Assaba and Gorgol regions in particular. Having overgrown its location between two wadis, it's now divided roughly into thirds, with newer districts of town growing north and south of the centre on the far sides of the dual oueds that once cradled the settlement.

These wadis are also home to numerous small farms and market gardens, as Sélibaby is Mauritania's wettest regional capital, receiving more than 500mm of rain each year between July and September. Most of the action in terms of services and accommodation is in the northernmost sector, while the main market and transport park sit alongside the city's oldest neighbourhoods in the central part of town. Though certainly somewhat out of the way in Mauritanian travel terms, it's

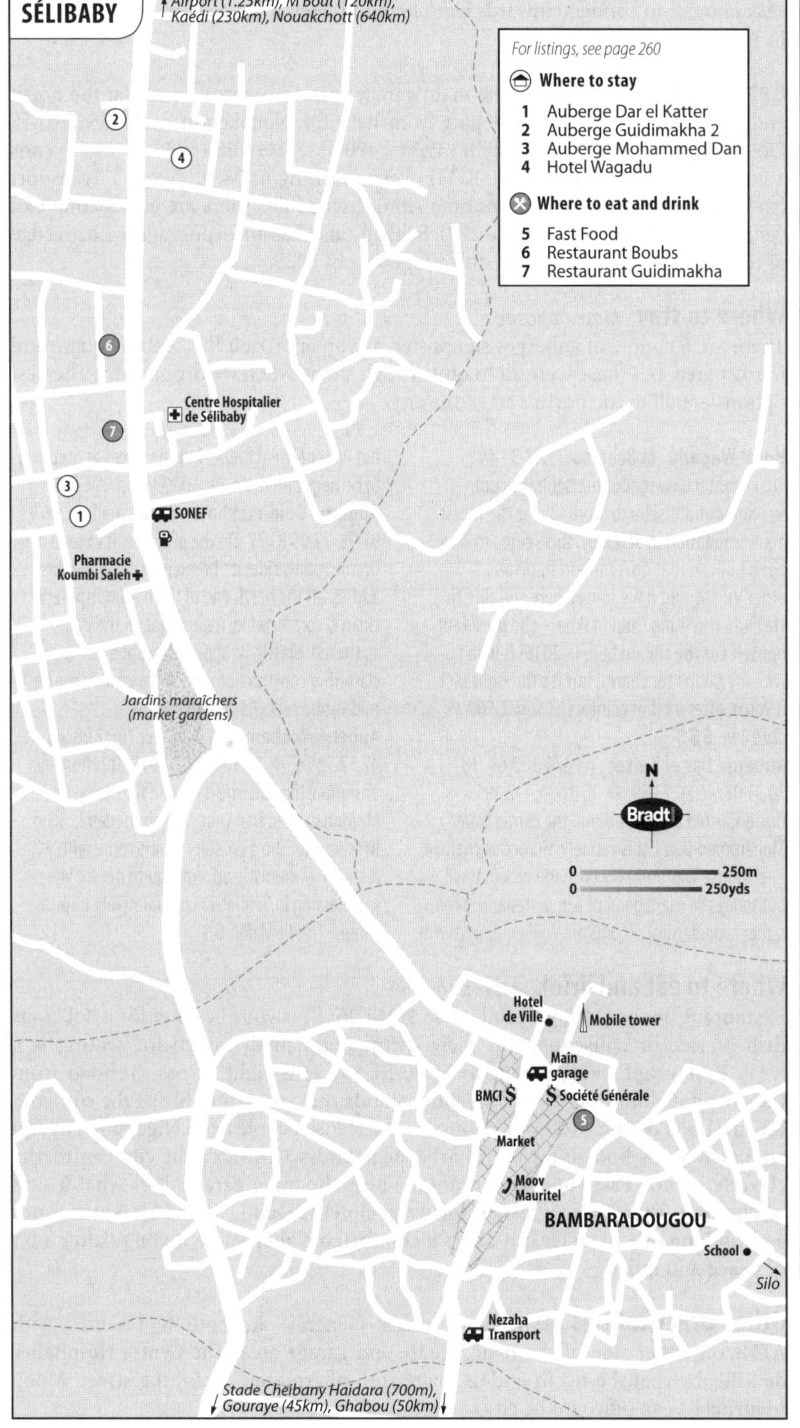
SÉLIBABY
Airport (1.25km), M'Bout (120km), Kaédi (230km), Nouakchott (640km)
For listings, see page 260
Where to stay
1 Auberge Dar el Katter
2 Auberge Guidimakha 2
3 Auberge Mohammed Dan
4 Hotel Wagadu
Where to eat and drink
5 Fast Food
6 Restaurant Boubs
7 Restaurant Guidimakha
Centre Hospitalier de Sélibaby
SONEF
Pharmacie Koumbi Saleh
Jardins maraîchers (market gardens)
N
Bradt
0 250m
0 250yds
Hotel de Ville
Mobile tower
Main garage
BMCI
Société Générale
Market
Moov Mauritel
BAMBARADOUGOU
School
Silo
Nezaha Transport
Stade Cheibany Haidara (700m), Gouraye (45km), Ghabou (50km)

easy enough to connect onwards from here to Bakel in Senegal or even up to Kiffa in Assaba region.

Getting there and away The main garage is in the central square at the north end of the market. Vehicles depart from here for Nouakchott (10hrs; 900UM), Gouraye (1hr; 150UM) and Kaédi (3½hrs; 400UM). SONEF (m 43 46 43 09) runs a coach bus to Nouakchott (900UM) every morning at 08.00; Nezaha Transport (m 41 15 98 38) runs minibuses on a similar schedule. There are also a couple of vehicles to Kiffa every day (page 272). Sélibaby also has an airport at the north edge of town, but there were no scheduled flights as of 2025.

Where to stay *Map, opposite*

There are a couple of auberges signposted as you approach the central square and market area, but these were all in quite rough shape when we dropped by. The best options are all in the north part of the city.

Hotel Wagadu M'Bout road; 45 34 44 18; e contact@wagaduhotelselibaby.com; w wagaduhotelselibaby.com. By far the nicest accommodation in Sélibaby, this seems to have been built so that government ministers & other VIPs would have somewhere suitable to stay when visiting Guidimakha – the president himself cut the ribbon here in 2019! It won't win any points for charm, but it's the right pick if you're after a bit of comfort. *2,500/3,500UM dbl/twin*. **$$$**

Auberge Dar el Katter m 47 72 23 69, 38 70 31 08, 46 80 73 59; ⊕ 15.1684, -12.1911. Unsignposted but just around the corner from Mohammed Dan's, this vaguely Moroccan-themed guesthouse was probably once the pick in town, but today the management & maintenance seems rather lackadaisical. Rooms are well equipped with hot water & mini fridge, but the prices quoted beg to be negotiated. *1,500/2,000UM sgl/dbl*. **$$**

Auberge Guidimakha 2 M'Bout road; m 46 93 97 98, 22 05 83 77. On the plus side, it's brand new. On the minus side, it's brand new. So while this address at the north end of town is undisputedly clean & comfortable, it's also got all the paint-spattered, plastic-wrapped atmosphere of a clattering construction site. Still probably the best mid-range pick. *1,500UM dbl*. **$$**

Auberge Mohammed Dan m 36 32 08 55, 47 52 52 26; ⊕ 15.1687, -12.1915. This homely, unsignposted auberge is named for the owner, Mr Mohammed Dan (not 'Mohammedan'!), who lives on site. The 4 en-suite rooms come with AC & they'll even rustle up a mosquito net for you – a blessing in Sélibaby's comparatively tropical climes. *1,000UM dbl*. **$$**

Where to eat and drink *Map, page 259*

Restaurant Boubs (M'Bout road; m 46 90 44 26; $) is your best bet for a delicious dish of rice or couscous, and their surprisingly shady courtyard seating is a treat. **Restaurant Guidimakha** (m 36 20 51 89; $) is right across the road from the hospital alongside several méchoui stands that spark into life as the sun goes down. (Look out for Méchoui Haoussa – the Hausa people from Niger and Nigeria are particularly known for their barbecue prowess.) Towards the city centre, the cleverly named **Fast Food Restaurant** ($) near the main garage does what it says on the sign. There's also a restaurant at the Hotel Wagadu ($$$–$$), which is not exactly long on character but offers a comfortable alternative if you're after a bit of peace and quiet.

Other practicalities BMCI and Société Générale are both represented with **ATMs** on either side of the main square and garage area. The **Centre Hospitalier de Sélibaby** is at the north end of town, with **pharmacies** across the street. Moov Mauritel has an office in the city centre.

What to see and do Reinforcing the city's multi-ethnic bona fides, Sélibaby's oldest quarter, **Bambaradougou**, is named for one of Mauritania's smallest minorities. Just to the east of the central market and garage, the suffix 'dougou' means 'village', while Bambara, though few in Mauritania, are the largest ethnic group in neighbouring Mali. So here in the Bambara village at the centre of Sélibaby, the labyrinthine streets (once used to confuse potential invaders – now certain to confuse you) are still home to some Bambara speakers, banco mud-brick buildings and Sélibaby's first school, still operating today. As elsewhere, the traditional architecture is quickly being replaced by concrete block and roofing sheets, but it's still worth a wander if you're here.

Next door, the traders in the helter skelter **central market** take good advantage of Sélibaby's triple-border location, and if there's a product available for a better price in Senegal or Mali, you'll be sure to find stacks of it sold here, alongside the usual array of veterinary medicines, vehicle parts and La Vache qui rit (Laughing Cow cheese). If you're after local crafts, contact the Fédération des Coopératives Artisanales du Guidimakha (m 47 77 17 00, 46 84 50 03).

Along the main road heading east from the central square and past Bambaradougou, you'll find '**silo**', a quite tall (and ever so slightly phallic) double-barrelled grain silo dating to colonial times, which lends its name to the neighbourhood and has very charmingly been dubbed the 'Eiffel Tower of Sélibaby'. There is a small colonial cemetery several hundred metres north of here.

On the south side of town, you can catch local football squad ASC Itihad Sélibaby at the Stade Cheibany Haidara. There are also some very attractive *jardins maraîchers* (market gardens) scattered throughout the city along the edges of the

TEKTAKA AND THE ASSABA MASSIF

The Assaba hardly exceeds a hundred metres altitude. Several transverse valleys, cut sharply into the plateaus, serve as passes: Tak-Tak [Tektaka], Sou Galoula, Goussas, Faram. Then comes the Tagant. Sources rise in its foothills. The limpid waters of tarns or gueltas, lying in deep hollows, are peopled with crocodiles and cat-fish. Here water was no longer a problem. Even when the little watercourse were dried up there were always these enormous natural reservoirs, to say nothing of the marigots or lakes of the plain which were never dry.

The most southerly pass, as well as the most frequented, was the Tak-Tak, and it also provided the best means of getting to Kiffa [from Guidimakha]...The car stopped under a baobab tree at the entrance of the Tak-Tak pass. On the left the sculptured mountain thrust forth a hostile snout. On the right were volcanic peaks looking Japanese, whose bases spread wide on to the plain. Rocky bastions flanked by towers and terraces guarded the pass.

But a hundred metres from this severe landscape was a limpid mountain stream coming out of the rock, widening out into a guelta, and then disappearing once more. Through the water we could see the white sandy bottom. It was surrounded by reeds and here and there the water was hardly visible beneath its covering tufts of plants. On the wet banks all the diurnal and nocturnal drinkers of the animal world had left their imprints. Tracks of lions and hyenas and many others mingled with those of birds, and again with those of men and their camels. There were also the huge round footprints of elephants, a herd of which roamed about the Guidimaka.

From *Barefoot through Mauretania* by Odette du Puigaudeau (1936)

wadis, which take good advantage of the city's somewhat milder climate to grow a wider range of crops than what's possible up north.

ONWARDS FROM SÉLIBABY Past Sélibaby, the tar road continues 45km southwest to **Gouraye**, from where you can cross the border to the Senegalese town of Bakel. Though Gouraye is the junior partner between these two towns, there's a brisk trade in cement, cooking oil and other goods, which cross the border on dozens of heavily laden pirogues every day, often taking clever advantage of price differentials between the two countries. There's regular transport between Gouraye and Sélibaby (1hr; 150UM), but as with the other upriver border crossings, Mauritania was not processing e-visas here as of 2025.

Bakel is set in a cluster of hills and home to an impressive French fort dating to the mid 1800s, when the city was one of the most important trading posts on the river. The derelict Pavillon René Caillié is also here, built as a staging post for the renowned French explorer's journey to Timbuktu in the 1820s. The fort still stands guard over a magnificent bend in the blue-green river, but today the long-rusted cannons guarding the gates serve as a drying rack for the local washerwomen. We're not aware of any official accommodation in Gouraye, but there are several options in Bakel, as well as ATMs dispensing CFA francs.

It's also possible to continue east from Sélibaby, to **Kankossa** and Kiffa in Assaba region (page 276). As of 2025, there was no surfaced road between Sélibaby and Kankossa (after which there is a good road to Kiffa), so this route takes in about 110km of pistes via the town of Ould Yengé on the border with Mali. There are plans to surface this section, possibly during the lifespan of this edition, but until then the only vehicles serving this route are 4x4s and pick-up trucks, which depart from Sélibaby's main garage once or twice daily. To Kiffa, it's 700UM for a seat up

'THE EVENTS' OF 1989

Years of increasing social tension spurred by desertification, Mauritanian land tenure reform and the competing interests of those making their livelihoods on and around the river came to a boil along the river in 1989, marking one of the most significant crises in post-independence Mauritanian (and Senegalese) history. Today simply referred to as *les événements* ('the events'), they began on the Senegalese bank just north of Gouraye and Bakel, with a local conflict between Mauritanian herders and Senegalese farmers over grazing rights. It quickly spun out of control, touching off riots, a diplomatic feud and ultimately ethnic pogroms against those perceived to be citizens of the opposing country – typically along racial lines.

Senegalese and Mauritanian interests in Nouakchott and Dakar were torched and hundreds of people were killed on both sides. The border was closed, and diplomatic relations between the two countries were severed. In under two months, an estimated 170,000 Mauritanians and 75,000 Senegalese had fled to their country of origin, and as many as 53,000 Fulbe, Toucouleur and other Mauritanian citizens of black African ethnicities were labelled as foreigners and forced into Senegal. The borders would not reopen again until 1992. Many gave up on the idea of returning and took up permanent residence on the other side of the river, but even today, there are several thousand Mauritanian refugees in Senegal and Mali who have yet to be successfully repatriated despite a stated desire to do so.

front (recommended), or 500UM for one in the back. Call Hussein (m 22 20 57 00) or Momadou (m 46 98 88 82) to reserve a seat, or just show up early.

The public vehicles will go around, but if you've got your own wheels the **Passe de Tektaka** (Tektaka Pass; ⊕ 15.5770, -11.9581; page 261) at the very southern end of the Massif d'Assaba is a worthy diversion along the way to Kankossa. It's not a high pass, but rather follows a wadi through a dramatic valley between the main body of the escarpment and the cluster of isolated mountains trailing off its southern flank.

Another road project promises to continue south out of Sélibaby for the 50km to **Ghabou**, which sits at Mauritania's southernmost point, opposite Mali along the Senegal River. Ghabou is also only about 15km west of the Senegal–Mali–Mauritania triple border, at the confluence of the Senegal and Falémé rivers. Here the Mauritanian village of Diogountourou looks across the river at its counterparts Aroundou (Senegal) and Gouthioubé (Mali). Cross-border trade and relationships are deep here, but there's no official immigration post as far as we are aware.

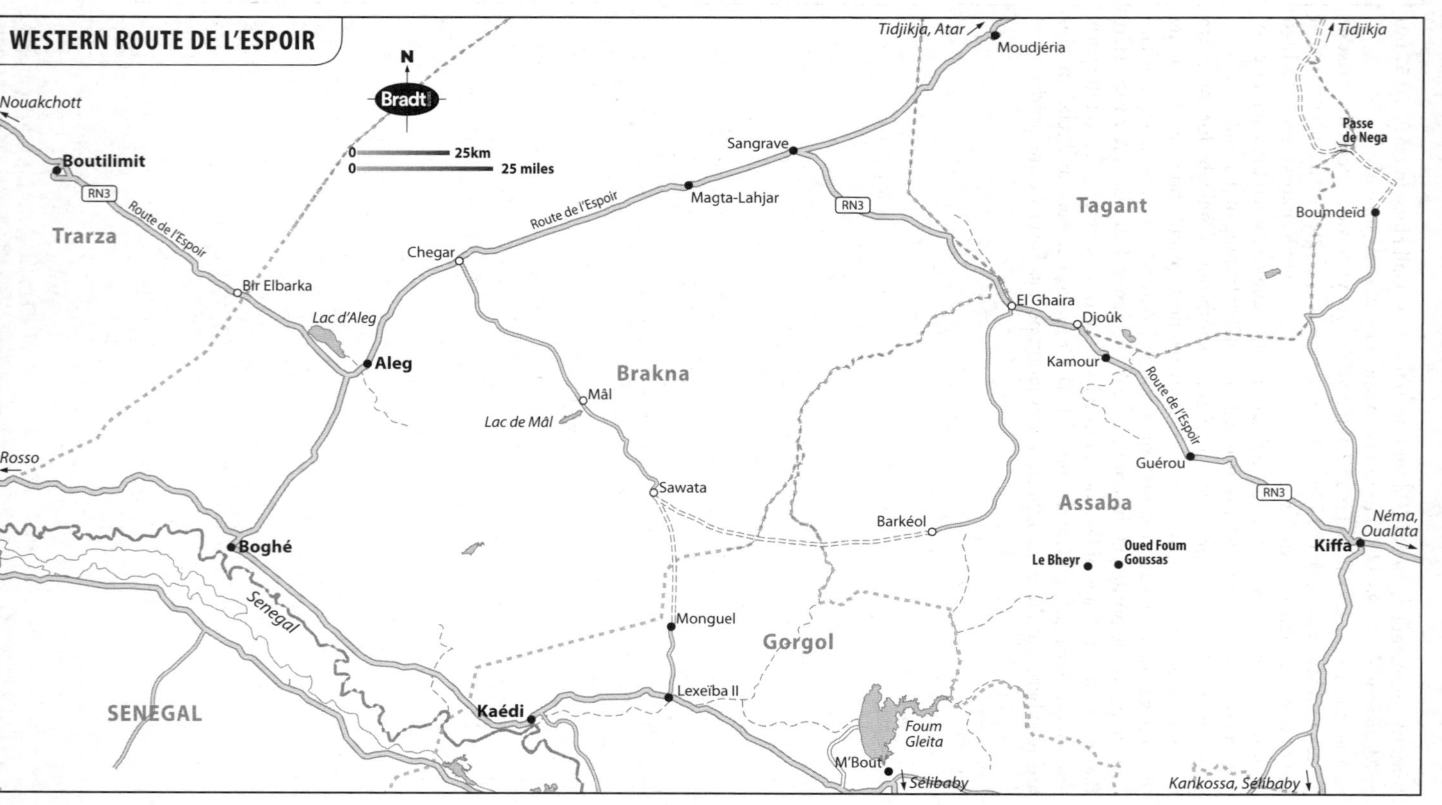
WESTERN ROUTE DE L'ESPOIR
N
Bradt
0 25km
0 25 miles
Nouakchott
Boutilimit
RN3
Route de l'Espoir
Trarza
Bir Elbarka
Lac d'Aleg
Aleg
Chegar
Rosso
Boghé
Senegal
SENEGAL
Sangrave
Magta-Lahjar
Brakna
Mâl
Lac de Mâl
Sawata
Monguel
Lexeïba II
Kaédi
Gorgol
Foum Gleita
M'Bout
Sélibaby
Barkéol
Tidjikja, Atar
Moudjéria
Tagant
El Ghaira
Djoûk
Kamour
Guérou
Assaba
Le Bheyr
Oued Foum Goussas
Tidjikja
Passe de Nega
Boumdeïd
Kiffa
Néma, Oualata
Kankossa, Sélibaby

8

The Route de l'Espoir, Tagant and the East

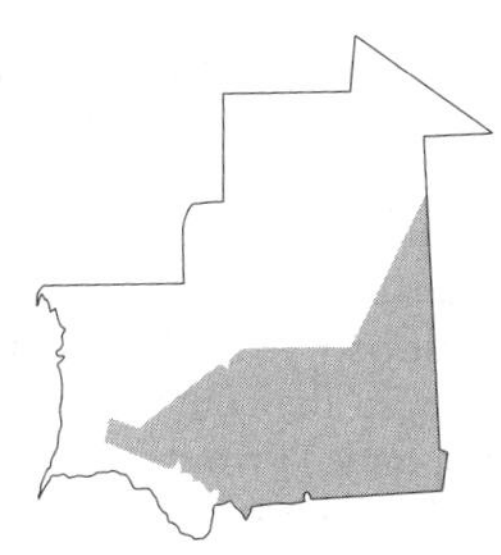

It may seem that this chapter is rather ambitious and covers a lot of territory, but owing to the nature of the Mauritanian road network, most travellers will approach the featured regions and sites in the order listed here. Therefore, the following sections are arranged based on an approach from Nouakchott, ie: first the western section of the Route de l'Espoir, then the Tagant region (reached from a turn-off between Aleg and Kiffa), and then the eastern section of the Route de l'Espoir from Kiffa onwards.

This route takes you clear across the country, more than 1,100km from the wild and windswept dunescapes east of Nouakchott, through until you reach the Tagant and Assaba mountain massifs, where the road snakes just between these two sets of dark, boulder-strewn mountains which bisect the country. Another 200km or so and you're crossing the jagged topography of the Affolé Massif before descending on to the endless plains of the Aoukar Depression, a basin so big that it gives its name to both the Hodh El Gharbi and Hodh Ech Chargui regions, which simply mean 'Western Basin' and 'Eastern Basin' in Hassaniya, and are collectively known as *les Hodhs*.

Two of Mauritania's four UNESCO-recognised *ksour* (fortified towns) are found here, with Tichitt in Tagant and Oualata in Hodh Ech Chargui still many miles from the nearest road and by far the least-visited of the four. Built from local stone and mud, they feel exuberantly far from the homogenising effects of globalisation, every bit the desert outposts of storybook lore and childhood fantasy.

Traditionally, travellers heading along the Route de l'Espoir would have most often been aiming for Mali, but insecurity in that country has seen tourist traffic on this route dry up like an out-of-season wadi. Therefore, 'most' (if one can use such a term) travellers continuing east of Kiffa today have Oualata in mind, though travel warnings and huge distances mean the city still hosts just a handful of intrepid souls every year.

Therefore, travellers without the time or endurance to head all the way to Oualata are likely to branch north from the Route de l'Espoir into the Tagant region, where the stone-grey ksar of Tichitt is found – just 230km from the nearest scrap of road! But even if Tichitt is a bridge too far, the Tagant Plateau is home to a dramatic landscape cut through by dozens of wadis, oases and floodplains, and the remnants of countless clifftop Neolithic settlements overlooking a valley floor that can be as much as 300m below.

The mountain massifs of these regions also hide an unexpected diversity of animal life, with dozens of isolated pools playing host to a fantastically incongruous population of crocodiles (page 13), as well as a steady population of the near-threatened Guinea baboon, with nearly 100 sites confirmed in a 2023 study.

THE WESTERN ROUTE DE L'ESPOIR: BOUTILIMIT TO KIFFA

Built between 1975 and 1982, in part as a response to the horrific droughts that ravaged the country in the 1970s, the Route de l'Espoir or 'Road of Hope' both responded to and facilitated an influx of former nomadic pastoralists who had lost their livelihoods relocating to Nouakchott and Mauritania's other urban centres.

The road leads straight inland from Nouakchott, first creeping through the city's growing eastern sprawl, and then cutting a straight line southeast through rural western Mauritania. To the south, numerous pastoralist villages dot the landscape, where they lie mostly hidden, stretching out along the long valley floors between the fixed dunes that dominate the region. (These interdunal valleys are known as *goûds.*) To the north, the dunescape continues and intensifies, and the area is almost completely uninhabited.

The government was seeking tenders for a new dual carriageway road connecting Nouakchott and Boutilimit at the time of writing. If built, it will run parallel to and probably 5–10km south of the existing Route de l'Espoir.

BOUTILIMIT Some 150km east of Nouakchott, Boutilimit (بوتلميت) is the first major population centre you'll encounter as you set out along the Route de l'Espoir. Decently sized by Mauritanian standards, this town of 32,347 is famous as a centre for religious studies and as the birthplace of Mauritania's first president, Mokhtar Ould Daddah, who was born here on Christmas Day 1924. The settlement was originally founded by Cheikh Sidiya El-Kebir, whose family library is still kept here.

Effectively one large marketplace, Boutilimit serves as an intermediate point where traders from upcountry and from the capital exchange goods. This means the city centre has the hustle, hubbub, hue and cry of a city several times its size – and all the traffic as well. What's left of the 1910 **French fort** (⊕ 17.5482, -14.7033) can be seen atop a dune on the east side of town, near a water tank and some mobile phone masts about 700m from the main road. The **mausoleum** of Cheikh Sidiyya Baba, grandson of Cheikh Sidiya El-Kebir, who worked closely with Xavier Coppolani during the colonial period, is also nearby. Boutilimit is also known for its **libraries**, but none of these are currently organised for casual visits; ask your accommodation or your guide if you'd like to set up a tour.

Unless you've got a late start coming or going from Nouakchott, there's not much to keep you overnight in Boutilimit. If you do stick around, **Hotel Manam** (m 43 00 31 10, 38 26 15 16; **$$–$**) is absolutely the pick. Set on the main road at the western entrance to town, rooms here come in several constellations ranging from an 800UM budget double room to a suite sleeping five for 2,500UM, all with air conditioning and hot water. The Complexe Touristique de Boutilimit (m 46 07 70 37) just across the road is seriously run-down and attempts to charge nearly the same prices – don't bother. There is a BMCI branch in Boutilimit, but no ATM.

Getting there and away The east–west orientation of the Route de l'Espoir is interrupted here, instead running north–south through Boutilimit for about 5km, following the interdunal valley (or *goûd*) in which the town sits. There's a short bypass road that avoids the city centre entirely; most transport without passengers departing or alighting in town will take this route instead.

MAATA MOULANA, THE 'LEARNING VILLAGE'

Down a parallel dune valley about 50km southwest of Boutilimit, the town of **Maata Moulana** (⊕ 17.3133, -15.1459) is an unusual outpost. It was founded in the 1950s by Muhammad al-Michry, a disciple of Senegalese holy man Ibrahima Niasse, and established as a 'learning village' (or *mahdara*), where students of any origin could be hosted and receive Islamic tuition according to the Tijani brotherhood's Sufi precepts. The village continues to maintain close links to Kaolack in Senegal, where Ibrahima Niasse's *zawiya* (religious centre) still operates.

Today the village is led by Muhammad's son, Al-Hajj ould Michry, and functions as something of a state-within-a-state, broadly similar to the semi-autonomous Senegalese communities of Touba (governed by the Mouride order) or Medina Gounass (also Tijani), where religious rules often supersede those of the government. For example, tobacco, quite popular throughout the rest of Mauritania, is banned in Maata Moulana. There are government-run schools, however, and Al-Hajj himself once studied economics in Dakar. Perhaps most uniquely, however, is the fact that Maata Moulana has attracted a steady trickle of students from beyond West or North Africa, and dozens of spirit-seeking disciples from Europe and North America have come here questing after desert solace and Sufi wisdom in the 40-odd Quranic schools here over the years. Al-Hajj is responsible for all visitors, so ask to see him on arrival and you'll be taken care of. The village also has a large garden of medicinal herbs which are sold to traditional healers throughout the country, and the NGO Terre Vivante works here.

Some 30km northeast as the crow flies, the village of **Nabbaghiyya** is another *mahdara* village that attracts students of Arabic and Islamic sciences from around the world. Founded by Sheikh Bah, this remote desert academy may be the first of its kind to offer online courses. See their 'English Mahdara' program (w en.mahdara.org) for more.

There's no shortage of transport in either direction along the Route de l'Espoir (towards Nouakchott or Aleg) throughout the day. Fewer vehicles go to R'Kiz (page 241), which is about 90km southwest of here and is reachable on unimproved desert tracks following the *goûd* dune valleys. The dunes here all run southwest–northeast, and there are numerous villages set in the valleys between them, including Errebine (Rebinett) 65km southwest, where there's surprisingly modern accommodation at **Ruby Town Resort** (m 36 30 56 26; f; ⊕ 17.1194, -15.1054; **$$**).

ALEG Aleg (ألاك; population 27,120) is famous in Mauritanian history for the Congres d'Aleg (Aleg Congress) of 1958, during which leaders of the nascent nationalist movement gathered under khaïma tents to discuss the contours of what an independent Mauritanian state might ultimately look like. It's also the best-serviced town between Nouakchott and Kiffa, with a surprisingly good selection of accommodation and quite a few restaurants (though these are admittedly all of a rather basic standard), so this is the place to stop.

The town has unfortunately become associated with the 2007 murder of four French tourists and their Mauritanian guide, which took place nearby and was the most serious attack against tourists in Mauritanian history, leading to the cancellation of the Paris–Dakar rally and its ultimate relocation from West Africa. Aleg is today as safe as any other town in Mauritania and there are no particular security concerns here.

Getting there and away Aleg is an important junction town, with vehicles heading towards Nouakchott (255km) and Kiffa (345km), but note that many of the vehicles serving Aleg pick up and drop off at the **Carrefour d'Aleg** (Aleg Junction) 5km west of town, where the road towards Boghé (65km) and the Senegal River branches off to the south. For Tidjikja, first aim for Sangrave and change vehicles there. SONEF (m 42 46 43 15) buses pass through Aleg, but it will usually be faster to get one of the frequent minibuses rather than waiting for one of the few passing daily coaches.

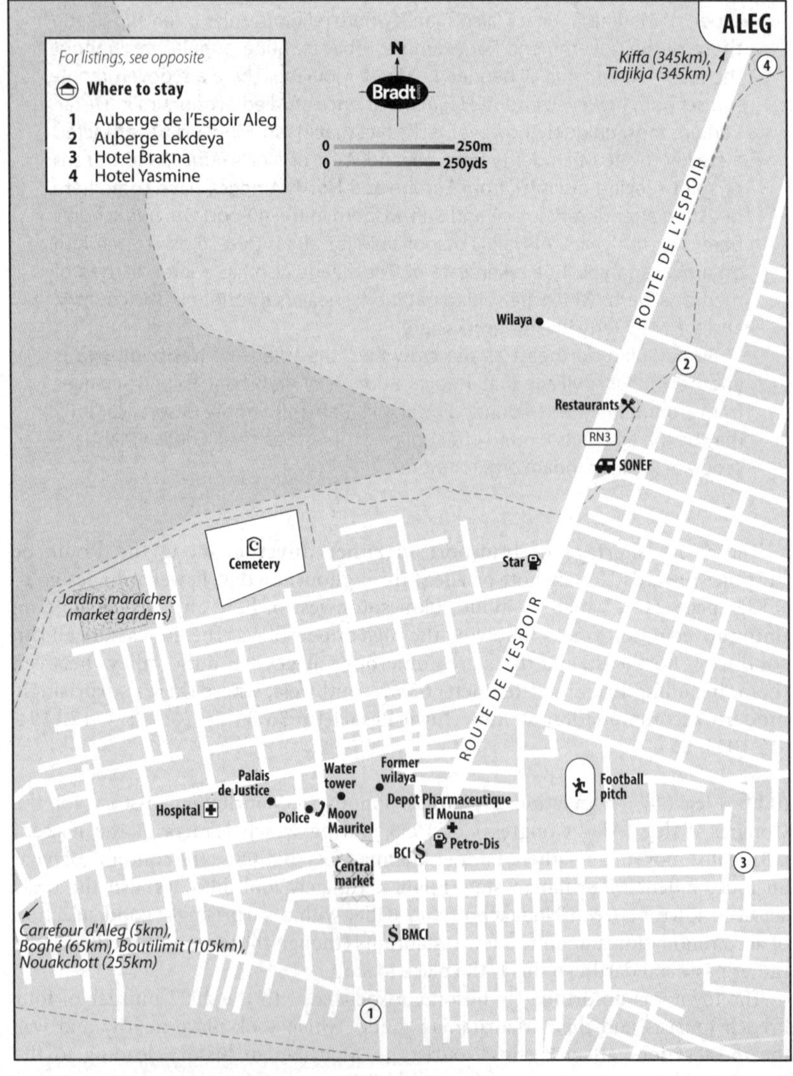

Where to stay *Map, opposite*

There's a surprisingly good choice of accommodation in Aleg, reflecting its status as an important crossroads.

Auberge de l'Espoir Aleg At the southern edge of town; m 47 77 89 11; f. At the edge of town overlooking fields to the south, this is a dated but decent choice, with adequately equipped en-suite rooms in a sprawling compound. *1,000UM dbl.* **$$**

Auberge Lekdeya At the northern edge of town; m 48 54 44 13, 22 93 66 12. The unexpectedly green gardens & neat modern rooms at this guesthouse on the north side of town make this an easy pick. The friendly management can help with any enquiries around town. *1,000UM dbl, 2,000UM suite sleeping up to 5.* **$$**

Hotel Brakna East of the central junction; m 32 88 88 70, 42 61 61 30. Signposted about 750m east of the main road, this is a newer & well-managed option that's quickly become one of the go-to addresses in Aleg. The modern rooms are well equipped & carefully kept. *1,200UM dbl.* **$$**

Hotel Yasmine Northeast on the Route de l'Espoir; m 42 25 25 70; e hotel.yasmine.aleg@gmail.com; f. Set about 1km outside of town along the Route de l'Espoir, this relatively new address is aimed squarely at the conference & government market (check out the *suite ministérielle*), but the modern rooms set in a handful of chalets ringing the property could be a good option if you're after some peace & quiet. Rooms come with AC, hot water, mini-fridge & the like. *1,500/2,000UM dbl/deluxe.* **$$**.

Where to eat and drink

Perhaps thanks to its roadside stopover status, Aleg is known as the méchoui (barbecue) capital of Mauritania, and there is no shortage of casual roadside restaurants serving up grilled meats, alongside a few other popular plates like couscous or thiéboudiène. As is common in upcountry Mauritania, many don't have signboards, and the dining areas consist largely of open-sided mbar huts with plastic floor mats and long cushions around the perimeter. So, follow your nose, pick out a fine-looking lamb shank, and take the opportunity to stretch your own while you wait for the grillmaster's work to be done.

Alternatively, 45km west of Aleg you'll find **Bir Elbarka** (⊕ 17.2368, -14.2500), which is little more than a handful of roadside mbars, tikits, and a mosque, but alongside the chop shops of Aleg, this little settlement is known to all drivers along the Route de l'Espoir as *the* place to stop for a meal.

Other practicalities

Aleg is the most significant stopover between Nouakchott and Kiffa, with a couple of banks (including BMCI with an ATM), a hospital (Centre Hospitalier d'Aleg), several fuel pumps and a Moov Mauritel office on the main road.

What to see and do

Aleg is by and large a workaday town, with no shortage of street life and all the haggling and horse-trading you would expect of a major crossroads, but little in the way of major sights. The main exception here would be the **Lac d'Aleg**, which sits just outside town to the northwest. Recognised as an IBA, this marshy endorheic lake in fact was once a branch of the Senegal River that was long ago cut off by dunes and is now sustained by seasonal rainfall flowing in from the seasonal Oued Katchi.

At maximum flood (generally around October), it's around 20km long and 5km wide, though only a few metres deep. The lake attracts a significant number of herders looking to water their animals. This is especially true in the dry season, as it never dries out completely. The marshy banks are also used for seasonal flood recession agriculture – the surface area of the lake shrinks considerably as the dry season takes its toll, so there's plenty of floodplain to go around. After the rains, the lush greenery sprouting all around the lake attracts picnicking Mauritanian families keen for a day out sipping tea under the khaïma.

The perennial availability of water is also of critical importance to the avifauna, and annual bird surveys at the site regularly turn up 25 to 50 species, including thousands of garganey, spur-winged goose, white-faced whistling duck, black-winged stilt, western swamphen, western cattle egret and fulvous whistling duck.

If you've got no wheels, ask your accommodation to set you up with somebody to take you out for a little spin around the lake; the furthest shore is only about 20km from town.

FROM ALEG TO KIFFA Proceeding east out of Aleg along the Route de l'Espoir, there's a small 2008 cenotaph dedicated to the slain tourists and guide 7km from town; otherwise, it's 40km until the village of Chegar (⊕ 17.3199, -13.6813), from where a new tarmac road leads 60km south to the **Lac de Mâl** (see below). Continuing east on the Route de l'Espoir, you'll pass the busy town of Magta-Lahjar after 70km. From here, it's a further 30km to **Sangrave** (indicated as Çangarâfa on some old maps), which is the junction for Tidjikja and the Tagant region (page 277). Note however, that, despite it being an important crossroads, there's not much in the way of services in Sangrave (the nearest official accommodation is back in Magta-Lahjar at Hotel El Medina; m 26 17 00 00, 42 65 65 46; **$**).

From Sangrave, the Route de l'Espoir turns southeast and reaches **El Ghaira** village after 80km (where it meets the to-be-completed road from the Lac de Mâl; page 272). Here you can visit the perennial *guelta* which is reachable by foot less than 1.5km south of the main road. This is also where you begin to leave behind the

LOOPING AROUND THE LAC DE MÂL

Set to the south of the village of Mâl and 60km from the Route de l'Espoir, the **Lac de Mâl** is a long, shallow lake similar to the Lac d'Aleg (page 269), itself only 60km to the west as the crow flies. As with the Lac d'Aleg, the Lac de Mâl is also recognised as an IBA for its importance to waterbirds and waders.

A trip here offers the opportunity to make a loop off the Route de l'Espoir, should you wish to break up what can be a long slog across the country, or to take a new route to Gorgol in the south. At the time of writing in 2025, the tarmac continued 30km south past the lake until the village of Sawata, but President Ghazouani laid the foundation stone for a new set of roads here at the end of 2023, so it should soon be possible to continue in two directions from here: either south to Gorgol region and the river road or in a loop east back to the Route de l'Espoir.

Heading south, the road will continue another 47km past Sawata to the first Gorgol town of Monguel. From here, it's just over 20km of tarmac to Lexeïba I (also known as Lexeïba Gorgol; page 256), which sits along the main river road between Kaédi and Mbout.

To loop back on to the Route de l'Espoir, the new stretch of road will lead 76km east from Sawata to Barkéol (⊕ 16.6524, -12.4519), where the tarmac resumes, and it's a further 80km until you rejoin the Route de l'Espoir at El Ghaira, where there's a scenic perennial rock pool, the **Guelta El Ghaira** (⊕ 17.1856, -12.2482) just south of town. From here, it's a further 65km to Guérou and 125km to Kiffa.

plains and dunes of western Mauritania, as the road plunges into the gap between the two mountainous plateaus that dominate the region, with the Massif d'Assaba running some 200km to the south from here, and the Plateau du Tagant running some 200km to the north.

Continuing west from El Ghaira, after 15km you reach **Djoûk**, a small oasis village and mountain pass. Here, the valley pulls in close, and there are several casual mbar restaurants where you can arrange a tea break or a plate of food for something like 100UM per person. There's potentially good rambling around Djoûk as well, with several seasonal watercourses spilling off the plateau here (eg: here ⊕ 17.1767, -12.0982; and here ⊕ 17.1402, -12.1204), making for periodic waterfalls after the rains.

There's a checkpoint atop the pass, and then, 15km east of Djoûk, the small town of **Kamour** has a scenic location between the wooded Oued Galangali (Oued Gôlangalli) on one side, and a conical (or breast-like, depending on who you ask) sugarloaf mountain on the other. Topping out just shy of 365m, it's a sweaty climb, but offers phenomenal views over the town and increasingly dramatic escarpment landscapes beyond. There are good camping possibilities along the oued to the south of town.

The road continues southeast through a wide valley, about 10km south of a dramatic chain of inselbergs, representing the last gasps of the Tagant Plateau as it gives way to the wide plains that separate it from the Affolé Massif to the east. After 35km, you arrive in **Guérou** (population 40,315), which has dramatic views of the inselbergs to the north and is home to Assaba region's largest palmeraie, running southwest from town for almost 13km. There's accommodation at the surprisingly nice **Hotel Le Palais** (Route de l'Espoir (RN3); m 46 13 17 70; dbl 1,500UM; **$$**), where the tidy rooms all have air conditioning and hot water.

Leaving Guérou along the remaining 55km approach to Kiffa, the landscape once again opens up on to a wide plain, backed by rocky outcrops in the distance and periodically cut through with dunes.

KIFFA With just under 85,000 Kiffistes living here, Kiffa (كيفة) is Mauritania's third largest city (though technically the Mbera Refugee Camp, where tens of thousands of Malians live, is now larger – a sad reflection of the severity of that crisis). Outside of Mauritania, Kiffa is most famous as the namesake for Kiffa beads, vividly colourful glass beads made using a traditional firing technique, which attract collectors and devotees around the world (page 274). But despite Kiffa's demographic and commercial importance (the market here is massive!), the city remains a minor player when it comes to travel and tourism in the country, and most people will visit here to simply break their journey and move on. The town sprawls for miles around the Oued Khouda, which, when in flood, flows south to the Karakoro River, which ultimately leads to the Senegal.

First used as a French military staging post in the wake of Coppolani's 1905 killing in Tidjikja, Kiffa was converted into a permanent outpost in 1907. Originally governed as part of France's Haut-Sénégal et Niger colony, Kiffa has long been a cultural and commercial crossroads, making it a surprisingly cosmopolitan corner of the country, where residents can trace their roots all over Mauritania, Mali, Senegal and beyond. Its role as the gateway to south-central Mauritania only seems set to grow with planned new roads connecting directly to Tidjikja in the north and Sélibaby in the south.

Getting there and away As befits a major junction town, Kiffa is well connected in all directions. Along the Route de l'Espoir, there are lots of morning minibuses

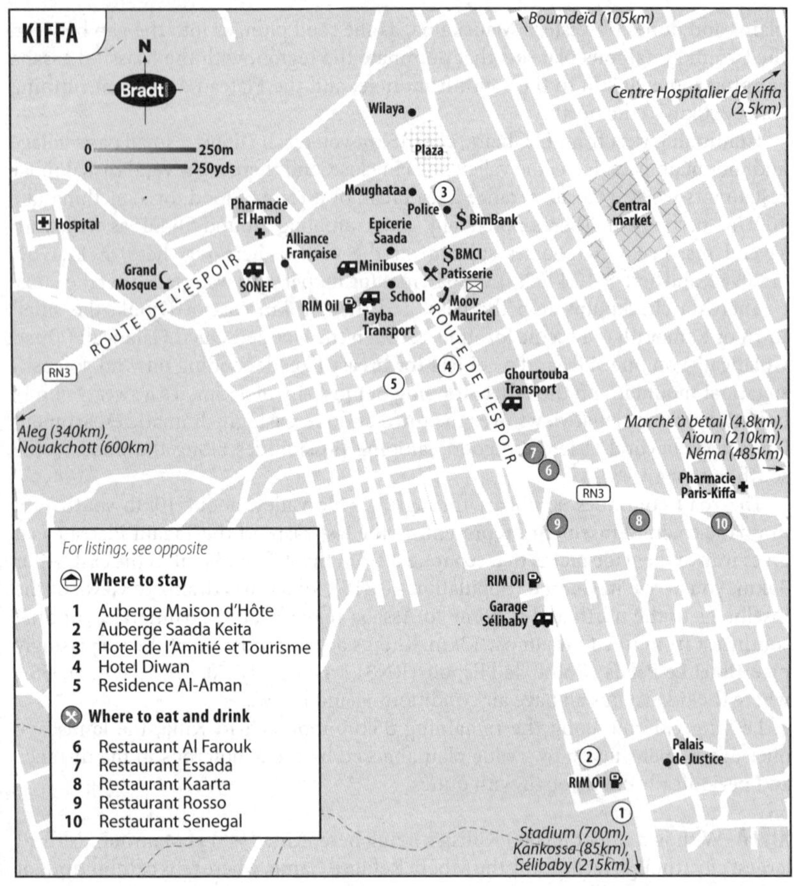

serving Aleg (345km) and Nouakchott to the west, or Aïoun and Néma to the east. SONEF (m 42 46 43 18) runs coach buses in either direction along the Route de l'Espoir, all in the morning. Nouakchott buses (900UM) depart at 05.00, 06.00 and 10.00, while Néma departures (700UM) go at 05.00 and 06.00.

To the south, it's also possible to connect to Sélibaby via Kankossa. The surfaced road ends after 85km in Kankossa, followed by 110km of pistes via the town of Ould Yengé on the Malian border. There are plans to surface this section, possibly during the lifespan of this edition, but until then the only vehicles serving this route are 4x4s and pick-up trucks, which depart from Kiffa once or twice daily. It's 700UM for a seat up front (recommended!), or 500UM for one in the back. Ring Hussein (m 22 20 57 00) or Momadou (m 46 98 88 82) to reserve a seat, or just show up early.

And to the north, the road is surfaced for the 105km to Boumdeïd. Northwards from Boumdeïd, a new road to Tidjikja is in the works; when complete, it will connect to Tidjikja via the **Passe de Nega** (⊕ 17.6335, -11.4151) and the crocodile *guelta* at **El Gheddiya** (⊕ 17.8349, -11.5580), joining the Tidjikja–Sangrave road after about 120km. At the time of writing, however, for Tidjikja you should first aim for Sangrave along the Route de l'Espoir and change vehicles there.

Kiffa's airport is 2km south of town, but there were no scheduled flights as of 2024.

Where to stay *Map, opposite*

Hotel Diwan Route de l'Espoir; m 42 93 15 15, 48 25 83 30. The 4 very modern 1st-floor rooms here aren't particularly cheap, but they're well equipped & a real respite from the chaotic street below. *2,500UM suite.* **$$$**

Auberge Maison d'Hôte Kankossa road; m 27 28 33 83, 44 84 78 62. Confusingly named & unsignposted, this fairly large hotel near the Palais de Justice is among the longest-serving picks in town, & the rooms are in good shape, but a little pricey for what you get. *1,500UM dbl.* **$$**

Auberge Saada Keita Off the Kankossa road; m 46 45 68 35, 22 20 04 02. The frilly rooms here are a little wonky, but they're kept clean & the welcome is reliably warm. Plus it's connected to a local women's co-operative, so you're supporting their worthwhile mission. *1,000UM dbl.* **$$**

Hotel de l'Amitié et Tourisme Next to the police station; m 41 23 09 48. This centrally (perhaps too centrally) located stalwart is very much showing its age, but is still in reasonable enough shape, especially if you can negotiate a couple of hundred ouguiya off the price. *1,200UM en-suite dbl.* **$$**

Residence Al-Aman Off Route de l'Espoir; m 41 56 86 84, 38 25 47 09. This family-run address a few blocks off the Route de l'Espoir is newly built & comfortable, though entirely characterless. *1,200/1,500UM dbl with shared/en-suite bath.* **$$**

Where to eat and drink *Map, opposite*

Kiffa may be rather short on tourist sites, but at least you won't go hungry: the city centre is chock-a-block with hole-in-the-wall restaurants where you can pick up a cheap plate of rice and whatever's going on that day. These are mostly clustered around the turn-off towards Néma, and include **Restaurant Rosso** ($), **Restaurant Essada** ($), **Restaurant Al Farouk** ($), **Restaurant Kaarta** ($) and **Restaurant Senegal** ($). **Epicerie Saada** is a reasonably stocked supermarket.

Other practicalities BMCI has a branch with an ATM near the main market. Moov Mauritel is just around the block. The Centre Hospitalier de Kiffa is just east of town.

What to see and do As befitting a capital of commerce and transport, Kiffa's main draw is the city's heaving **central market**. Though not at all oriented towards tourists, it's not just a good place to pick up camel dewormer, irrigation tubing

KIFFA'S MARKET *Peter Hudson*

The whole of the centre of Kiffa was a market. Every street was a market and every door opened on to a boutique. The streets were filled with boys and their 'chariots', as the donkeys and carts were called, transporting merchandise or merely doing nothing but squabble with each other and bash their donkeys with lengths of steel drainpipe. There were men hauling girders, brick makers, shoe makers, herdsmen with flocks of sheep, the occasional camel, trucks disgorging sacks into boutiques and a general confusion in the streets where they became a part of the workshops and the boutiques became a part of the streets. Every corner had its knot of Moors talking together, and old women set up stalls under pieces of tent in the middle of everything, selling water and milk and sweets and cigarettes to the busy merchants and their workers. The press of business ebbed and rose like a tide drawn not by the moon but by the sun, which at midday cleared the streets of all but the dusty old women dozing like dolls, slumped where they sat.

From Travels in Mauritania *(Flamingo, 1990)*

KIFFA BEADS – MAURITANIA'S ANCIENT ORNAMENTS

Thomas Stricker, Prescott Trading Post and Bead Museum (w tasart.com)

The Mauritanian city of Kiffa lends its name to Kiffa beads, a rare and highly valued type of powder-glass bead named for where they were first documented by French ethnologist R Mauny in 1949. These beads, known locally as *Muraqad*, represent a pinnacle of artistic skill and ingenuity, crafted by women artisans using simple materials and techniques rooted in a blend of African and Islamic influences.

The beads come in various colours – blue, red and polychromatic combinations of yellow, black, white and blue – with specific colour sequences and patterns that are consistent in traditional designs.

HISTORICAL CONTEXT AND ORIGINS Kiffa beads are believed to trace their origins to as early as 1200BCE, potentially inspired by Islamic beads from Fustat, the first Islamic capital of Egypt. Mauritanian bead-making likely also draws from the cultural heritage of the ancient Ghana Empire, with influences from Soninké leather crafts and drawings. Nonetheless, little definitive archaeological evidence has been found to confirm the exact age of this practice.

Kiffa beads utilise recycled materials like pulverised European glass beads, bottle glass, pottery shards and tin cans, combined with binders such as saliva or gum-arabic diluted in water. These materials were shaped without moulds, using basic tools like twigs, steel needles and open fires, showcasing remarkable innovation and creativity despite constrained resources.

TECHNIQUES AND MATERIALS The process of making Kiffa beads is labour-intensive and involves:

1 **Grinding glass** Artisans crush glass into a fine powder, often using a stone, a process that can take an entire day.
2 **Forming beads** The powdered glass is mixed with a binder (saliva or gum-arabic) and hand-rolled into shapes such as triangles, diamonds, spheres, cylinders or cones.
3 **Decoration** A glass slurry is applied with pointed tools, such as steel needles or twigs, to create intricate patterns, including chevrons, eyes or nested triangles.

and lengths of rebar, but also artisanal goods that might be a bit more exciting to a visitor from out of town. Much of the city centre is a buzzing warren of vendors and artisans, and is a fine place for either a few hours or a few minutes of exploration, depending on your tolerance for heat, dust, noise and all the tricky-to-define smells a market can produce.

Though Kiffa beads take their name from the city, visitors in search of them may leave somewhat disappointed, depending on how serious a collector they are. While you'll certainly find a few merchants around the market with beads for sale, you're likely to see more imported plastic bits than you are the authentic *muraqad* beads that have become famous worldwide (see above). If you're on the hunt, our advice is to remember the Hassaniya proverb, 'If you have a tongue, you don't get lost', and ask, ask, ask.

While perusing, also keep an eye out for stacks of wooden bedframes decorated in intricate multi-coloured designs. Known as *khabta* (or *tibirit*/*tshagar* depending on

4 Firing Beads are placed in small containers, often sardine cans, and heated over open fires to fuse the glass, without the use of moulds, resulting in unique, slightly irregular shapes.

CULTURAL SIGNIFICANCE Kiffa beads hold deep cultural and spiritual meaning, believed to possess amuletic properties. Their colours, shapes and patterns carry specific symbolic significance, though many of these meanings have been lost over time. Common beliefs include:

- **Protection** The 'eye' motifs on beads are thought to ward off the evil eye and protect against malice or envy.
- **Fertility** Triangular beads, often worn on bracelets or as hair ornaments, are associated with fertility, possibly mimicking the shape of cowrie shells.
- **Status and adornment** Beads were worn by both men and women, sewn on to leather strips for bracelets or used as hair ornaments, with specific arrangements reflecting traditional aesthetics and family styles.

DECLINE AND REVIVAL By the 1970s, the traditional craft of Kiffa bead-making had nearly vanished, with only a few elderly women continuing the practice. The 1980s and 90s saw a modest revival sparked by interest from foreign collectors, and groups of women resumed production using similar techniques, but often with modern paints and coarser designs. These beads preserve the traditional manufacturing process, but the aesthetic and cultural depth of the originals remains unmatched. Unfortunately, the production of these new beads remains extremely limited, and it will be a challenge for visitors to Mauritania to locate artisans actively engaged in the craft.

CONTEMPORARY LEGACY Today, authentic antique Kiffa beads are rare and highly collectible, displayed in Mauritania's national museum and sought after by collectors worldwide. Kiffa beads remain an elegant and attractive testament to Mauritanian ingenuity, blending African and Islamic artistic traditions into a unique form of wearable art that continues to captivate collectors and cultural enthusiasts globally.

where in the country you are), these have their origins with a traditional collapsible nomadic bed, and have now been adapted for sedentary lifestyles. Despite the fact that some can still be taken apart, it might be a challenge to get one of these home – but there are some more portable goods done up in similarly elaborate designs, like the *sarmiyya* (or *lûssâda*) leather pillows. Just as Mauritania's artisans are organised according to gender (men work in wood and metal while women work in leather), so are some of their products: look out for the 'women's pillow', whose suggestive pinch in the middle alludes to a woman's hips!

Kiffa's new ***marché à bétail*** (livestock market/*marbatt*; ⊕ 16.6137, -11.3528) sits some 3km out of town to the east. Whether or not you'll actually find any animals there, however, is a different question: it's been subject to a running dispute between herders and the government over the appropriateness of the facility.

Once you've had enough of the markets, catch your breath with an evening stroll on the large **plaza** in front of the regional government (*wilaya*) building. If you've got more time in the city, head down the Kankossa road to see local side ASC Entou Kiffa play at the **stadium** on the southwestern outskirts of town. The green-trimmed **grand mosque** near the transport park is also worth a look. And the **Alliance Française** (m 46 92 37 47; e direction.afmkiffa03@gmail.com; f AFKiffa) is active here as well, though mostly in French tuition and the like.

KANKOSSA This pleasant riverfront town 85km south of Kiffa is mostly of note today as the end of the tarmac road towards Sélibaby, but it's also a relaxed place to watch the world go by, where the Sahelian vibes of southern Mauritania once again come to the fore. The passenger pirogues punting back and forth across the sluggish Karakoro River mark time throughout the day, and make for a perfectly West African tableau.

It's also at the north end of an eponymous IBA, which covers 1,500ha of the Karakoro and surrounding wetlands south of town and hosts an array of waterbirds including northern pintail, glossy ibis, fulvous whistling duck, garganey, spur-winged goose, ruff and white-faced whistling duck. The river stays wet much of the year and is an important source of water for both herders and farmers, whose vegetable patches line the banks.

The only accommodation is at the **Auberge Assaba** (m 44 03 03 14; **$**), which was under construction on the main road when we dropped by, but has a selection of simple tikit style rooms around a central courtyard, with air conditioning promised at least. There are a couple of restaurants in the main market area. There's a decent amount of transport to and from Kiffa, but 4x4s headed to Sélibaby may arrive here full from Kiffa, complicating your ability to get a lift.

TAGANT REGION

The Tagant (ولاية تكانت), similar to the Adrar to the north, is centred on an eponymous mountain plateau at the centre of the country, and is cut through with a tangled carving of canyons hiding all manner of oases, palmeraies, floodplains, gueltas and plenty of tiny villages. It was long one of Mauritania's most isolated regions, though this changed with the 2019 opening of the road connecting Atar to

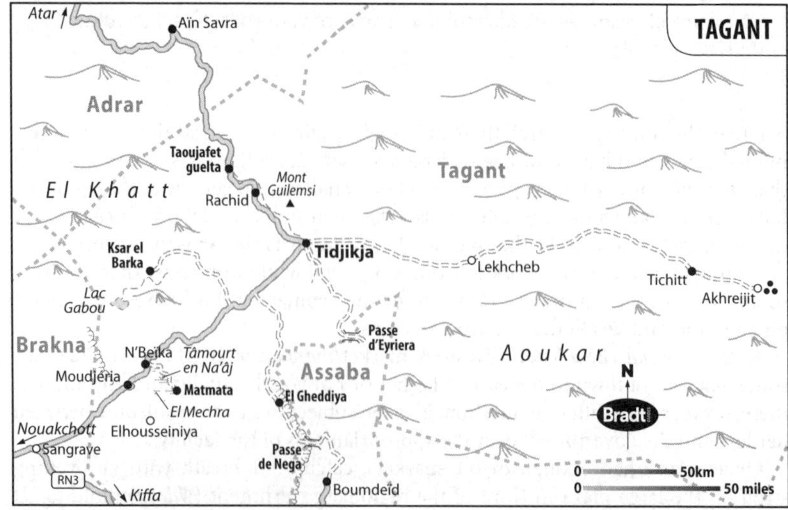

Tidjikja – except the much-vaunted new route was quickly buried under drifting dunes in numerous places and required rebuilding. Today, there are road crews responsible for the regular *désensablement* of the route, and bulldozers and diggers pushing dunes off the road are a common sight (and a great photo opportunity). Much of the region remains quite remote, however, and only a handful of localities have any services geared to travellers, so it's a great place to explore further afield if you're self-sufficient.

Historically, the Tagant was the centre of one of Mauritania's four pre-colonial emirates. Like the contemporaneous Trarza and Brakna emirates to the south, Tagant was brought under French control during the era of so-called colonisation pacifique under Xavier Coppolani in 1905. But the Tagant would prove difficult terrain for the French: Coppolani was killed just months later by a follower of Oualata-born anti-colonial leader Cheikh Ma El Aïnin.

THE ROAD TO TIDJIKJA The road to the Tagant region and its capital Tidjikja branches off the Route de l'Espoir at Sangrave, 140km northeast of Aleg. Though it's a relatively important junction, services in Sangrave are limited to a handful of roadside restaurants and the usual boutiques selling daily necessities. From here, the road sets out to the northeast, entering Tagant after 35km and arriving at the base of the Tagant Plateau in Moudjéria after 65km. There's little in the way of accommodation between Aleg and Tidjikja, so plan accordingly (though the rules of Mauritanian hospitality of course still apply; ask around and you'll certainly be accommodated somewhere).

As with much of the rest of the Tagant region, the area around **Moudjéria** once supported Neolithic settlements (page 14), and the ruins of these ancient villages can still be seen on the cliffs above town, known as Gleib Sid'Ahmed. The modern city of Moudjéria, clustered at the foot of these cliffs marking the start of the Tagant Plateau, traces its origins to Coppolani's pacification campaign in the Tagant, and it was set up as a French garrison and administrative centre in 1905.

Unlike many of its contemporaries, however, the historical structures here are neither completely destroyed nor still in use by the military. (Just up the road in N'Beïka, for example, the old French outpost was retrofitted into a maximum-security prison in 2021.) Therefore, it's possible to have a look at some of these historical structures in a way that's somewhat uncommon in other Mauritanian towns. The former regional government building (⊕ 17.8807, -12.3326) is the best example, and is neither in use nor completely ruined. Dating to the early 20th century, it's worth a stop to take in the heavy stone construction, arched windows and thick, two-storey walls that would have kept the administrators of this remote outpost (relatively) cool during the scorching summer months.

Continuing on from Moudjéria, the road climbs immediately upwards on to the Tagant Plateau, after which it's another 18km to N'Beïka. But before you reach N'Beïka, the turn-off to the **Ksar el Barka** ruins (⊕ 18.4027, -12.2235) beckons. This little-visited ruin is completely abandoned today but was once a significant centre of trade and commerce. Founded in the 17th century, the city is of a similar medieval pedigree as Mauritania's other fortified *ksars*, but after a tumultuous history marked by several rounds of destruction and rebuilding, it was definitively abandoned in the early 20th century. Given its relatively recent abandonment, there are still many standing ruins and the city's urban layout is clear to see; the dozens of standing pillars in the former mosque (see earlier GPS co-ordinate) are particularly evocative. The ruins are 70km north of the road on unimproved tracks, so it's not exactly a short detour, but you're practically guaranteed to have the place to yourself.

En route you'll pass **Lac Gabou** (⊕ 18.2774, -12.3696), which is recognised as both an IBA and RAMSAR wetland (known as Lac Gabou et le réseau hydrographique du Plateau du Tagant). As with all bodies of water in Mauritania, its size varies considerably from season to season, but the lake can cover more than 2,000ha in full flood, providing much-needed water and forage to livestock, but also crucial habitat for Afrotropical and Palearctic waterbirds and waders. Regular sightings include garganey, spur-winged goose and white-faced whistling duck.

There is another IBA across the road to the south, **Tâmourt en Na'âj** (⊕ 17.8845, -12.1875). This 1,000ha site also falls within the RAMSAR wetland, which encompasses a massive 9,500ha on either side of the road between Moudjéria and Tidjikja, and was recognised for its particularly extensive network of seasonal wadis and wetlands that survive at the very edge of the Sahara. Bird species are similar to those found at Lac Gabou, and include the northern pintail, glossy ibis, fulvous whistling duck and ruff. About 20km south of Tâmourt en Na'âj along the Oued Bourâgga, Elhousseiniya (⊕ 17.7377, -12.2439) has an especially scenic location between floodplain, mountain and palmeraie, but no services.

Back on the road you'll soon arrive in **N'Beïka**. This roadside market town serves as the access point for Mauritania's most famous reptiles, the **crocodiles** at Matmata. Some 25km southeast of town on a very rough track, these scaly survivors are relics from a time when Mauritania's climate was significantly wetter. As the area dried out, the crocodiles were pushed further and further into the few remaining permanent water sources, ultimately forming an archipelago of isolated populations scattered across the mountains of south-central Mauritania (page 13).

These groups are the subject of some scientific interest, as researchers seek to understand how these secluded populations manage to survive. Crocodile numbers at Matmata fluctuate, but it's not uncommon to spot between a handful and a dozen crocs sunning themselves along the banks. It's possible to see the crocs from two sides, either approaching from above and looking down on the guelta and its reptilian residents (this viewpoint becomes a waterfall during the rains), or coming up the oued from below, to the end of the canyon where the guelta sits. Be careful when hiking around the cliffs above the guelta – a German tourist fell to his death here in 2025.

Though the **Auberge Matmata** (m 47 42 41 64; ⊕ 17.8926, -12.1238; 300UM pp; **$**) has a fetching location about 5km from the crocs alongside the oued and just outside a couple of nearby palmeraie villages, it looked like it had been quite some time since anybody stayed over when we stopped by in 2024. The four stone huts could be serviceable for backpackers ready to rough it, but be sure to show up prepared with food and drink from town, as there's none on offer here.

Without a vehicle, it would be possible to have a Sangrave–Tidjikja minibus drop you in N'Beïka and then hire someone with a 4x4 to take you to visit the crocs and then back to the road, from where you can pick up onward transport to Tidjikja or back towards the Route de l'Espoir. You could try ringing Auberge Matmata to arrange this, or simply ask around in town and someone will eventually point you in the right direction.

From N'Beïka, it's a further 120 relatively flat kilometres atop the plateau until you reach the regional capital of Tidjikja.

TIDJIKJA Though the earliest evidence of human habitation here dates to the 1st millennium BCE, the modern settlement of Tidjikja (تجكجة) was founded in 1660 by members of the Idaw 'Ali tribe who were fleeing the ructions of the Char Bouba War in the Adrar. The city's medieval quarter is, like so many others in the region, in an advanced state of disrepair, though the architecture that remains points to a settlement of some significance and sophistication. With a current population of just about 20,000 Tidjikjois, 21st-century Tidjikja is a somewhat modest trading centre, and was for many years considered to be perhaps the country's most isolated regional capital.

Today, however, good tar roads connect the city to both the Route de l'Espoir in the south and to Atar and the Adrar region in the north (and a new route to Kiffa is also in the works at the time of writing). This means it's now easier than ever to incorporate the city and its spectacular surroundings in the Tagant into an itinerary without the need for significant doubling back and, perhaps more importantly, allows the stitching together of two halves of the country that were previously somewhat difficult to combine in one trip. All of the expected services are available in town, including food, accommodation, fuel and an ATM, and it's also the jumping-off point for the ancient ksar of Tichitt (page 282), marooned deep in the desert several hundred kilometres to the east.

As with other oases in the region, Tidjikja also celebrates the guetna date harvest every summer, and the city opens up with a series of cultural events and performances, including music, poetry, the preparation of traditional dishes and, of course, the tasting and discussion of who's got the best dates this year. Unfortunately, however, local water shortages mean that phœnicicultural production around Tidjikja has suffered in recent years, so much of the local produce now comes in from smaller oases and villages around the Tagant and Adrar regions – a pity for the Tidjikjois, but delicious for you just the same.

Getting there and away Tidjikja is now connected to both Atar and the Route de l'Espoir by tar road. Both routes are served by public transport, usually minibuses originating in Atar, Sangrave or Nouakchott. From Kiffa, Aleg or other intermediate points, you may have to change vehicles at Sangrave.

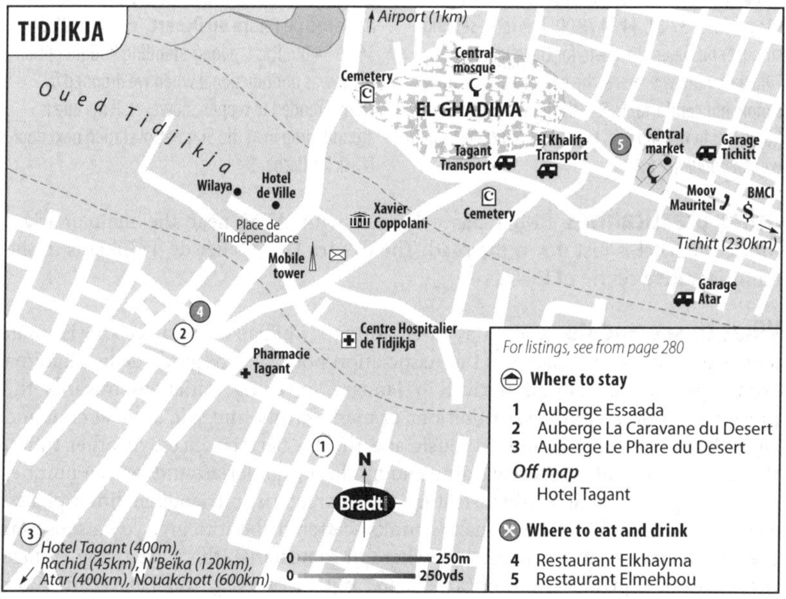

El Khalifa Transport (m 44 37 00 86, 48 10 42 91) and Tagant Transport (m 47 50 58 26, 22 45 36 37) run daily minibuses to Nouakchott (600km; 9hrs; 800UM) at 07.00. Several companies run daily to Atar (400km; 6hrs; 700UM), including Jreiv Voyage (m 44 44 62 67, 33 44 62 67) and Tagant Transport (m 47 50 58 26), departing mid-morning around 09.00 or 10.00. For Tichitt, the **garage** (m 36 81 10 72, 43 55 56 57, 46 81 10 72) is a shopfront with an Arabic-only sign at ⊕ 18.5556, -11.4251. There's usually at least one vehicle weekly (page 284).

To the south, there is a road under construction which will link Tidjikja directly to Kiffa, branching south from the Sangrave road about 45km from Tidjikja. From here, it will proceed roughly 120km south to Boumdeïd, via the village and crocodile *guelta* at **El Gheddiya** (⊕ 17.8349, -11.5580) and the **Passe de Nega** (⊕ 17.6335, -11.4151), where you descend from the Tagant Plateau and enter Assaba region. As of 2025, the tarmac reached as far as Boumdeïd, 105km north of Kiffa.

Tidjikja has an **airport** at the northern edge of town, but there were no scheduled flights as of 2025.

Where to stay and eat *Map, page 279*

All of the accommodation options can arrange food, but there are also are a couple of restaurants around town doing local staples, including **Restaurant Elkhayma** (m 46 95 72 89; $) near the Auberge Caravane du Desert, and **Restaurant Elmehbou** (m 46 50 64 32; $) on the main market square. The accommodations listed below are all south of the oued.

Auberge Essaada m 44 42 21 22. The newest option in town, with surprisingly modern rooms set in a row of tikit-style huts around a pleasant central courtyard. Rooms come with AC, TV & mini fridge, though the surround-sound mosques nearby could be a downside. *1,500UM dbl.* **$$**

Auberge La Caravane du Desert ☎ 45 24 48 91; m 46 42 37 24, 34 34 78 00. This long-serving stopover has been the go-to for travellers to Tidjikja for many years, & the en-suite rooms are simple but comfortable & well kept. There's solar hot water in the showers too. *1,300/1,000UM dbl with/without AC.* **$$**

Hotel Tagant m 49 48 53 45, 36 16 46 86. Ostensibly the most upmarket place in town, the modern en-suite rooms here are somewhat undermined by the rather lackadaisical management. Still, it's a comfortable enough option as long as you keep your expectations in check. *1,500/2,000UM dbl/twin.* **$$**

Auberge Le Phare du Desert m 46 77 75 24, 36 10 34 00. This is a long-standing budget option, but it was not functional when we dropped by. They intended to reopen, however. If no-one is around, drop in at the Star petrol station next door & ask for Batna. **$**

Other practicalities BMCI has a branch with ATM near the main market. Moov Mauritel is just down the road. The Centre Hospitalier de Tidjikja is in the administrative centre of town.

What to see and do Known as El Ghadima, Tidjikja's **old quarter** *ksar* is in an advanced state of disrepair, but the Association pour la sauvegarde de la Ghadima (ASG) puts on a cultural festival in January featuring initiatives towards the preservation of the old city, exhibitions of manuscripts, and sale of local craft and agricultural products, as well as music and theatre performances. At other times, the neighbourhood is still rewarding enough for a wander around, with a number of standing walls visible which feature the characteristic triangular lintel pieces, as well as plenty of roof-beam palm-trunks scattered about to give you a sense for the architecture in its prime. As elsewhere in Mauritania, there are many vintage manuscripts kept in private libraries here, but in practice you'll have an easier time viewing them in one of the four UNESCO-recognised *ksour,* which are better prepared to receive visitors.

Tidjikja's **central market** is low key and friendly enough, and benefits (from a wanderer's perspective, at least) from not being located smack on the main drag through town, as so many others are. Though it's overwhelmingly dedicated to daily necessities, there's some leatherwork and other crafts to be found if you look carefully – and often better prices than in a more touristed locale like Atar or Chinguetti.

Tidjikja's central oued splits in two to form a small **river island** (though of course the oued is dry most of the year), where the Place de l'Indépendance, hospital and most of the administrative buildings can be found. It's worth taking a walk along the backstreets and winding footpaths (with a few dead ends) east of the hospital, where there are many large homes with gardens and palm groves which make for a peaceful, shady wander in the middle of the city. Also on the island is the **grave of Xavier Coppolani**, who was responsible for bringing the Tagant region under French control in 1905. His success here was short-lived, however, as he was killed by a local resistance fighter only months later. There's no longer an inscription on his tomb (⊕ 18.5545, -11.4310), which sits largely forgotten in an alleyway just behind the post office.

Outside of the city, there's a nice canyon at the village of Baghdad, reached by following the oued 10km south of town. Further to the south, the remote **Passe d'Eyriera** (⊕ 18.1015, -11.2027) overlooks a particularly dramatic point at the edge of the Tagant Plateau, where it rises nearly 300m from the Aoukar Depression below. It's 65km south of Tidjikja on desert tracks. The road down the escarpment from here is so rough, somebody has cheekily – and not altogether inaccurately – tagged the route on Google as 'rock climbing'! As elsewhere in the Tagant, the escarpment here, known as **Dhar Tagant**, is peppered with the ruins of Neolithic sites.

FROM TIDJIKJA TO ADRAR REGION A new road makes travel between the Tagant and Adrar regions easier than it's ever been, with the 400km between the regional capitals of Tidjikja and Atar easily covered in a day. After taking the turn-off outside Tidjikja, the first settlement you'll encounter headed towards Atar is the small village of Lehweitat, after about 20km. **Mont Guilemsi** (⊕ 18.7124, -11.5610) sits off the road about 6km north of here. This serpentine sandstone ridge tops out around 70m high and is known for its concentration of painted rock art sites, which can be found predominantly on the southern face of the 11km ridge. None is marked or otherwise developed, however, so they can be difficult to locate without guidance.

Another 20km or so further up the road towards Atar you'll find the small town of **Rachid** (الرشيد). Set between mountain and oued, Rachid has a magnificent location, tumbling down the hillside and into a little valley formed by the meeting of two oueds, with enormous boulders dotting the town. The oldest part of the city sits on the other side of the oued, and its stone-built cityscape dates to the early 18th century. Rachid's founders hailed from the Kounta tribe, who also founded Ksar el Barka nearby (page 277). As with Ksar el Barka, the old city declined in the late 19th and early 20th centuries, thanks to a series of tribal raids followed by French punitive expeditions launched after Xavier Coppolani was killed by a resistance fighter in Tidjikja.

There are a couple of places to stay near Rachid, including the **Auberge de Saguya** (m 41 19 01 15; **$**) in town, and the **Auberge Essagya** (m 36 36 05 82; e yesmey2005@gmail.com; f; **$**), which is signposted on the right, 5km northwest towards Atar.

Leaving Rachid, the **Taoujafet** *guelta* (⊕ 18.8717, -11.8176) sits just left of the road after 23km, where you'll find a permanent pool and even a (usually) dry waterfall, where orange sand cascades off a rock ledge into geometric heaps on the valley floor. From here, the road descends into the dunes of El Khatt, a lowland area between the Tagant and Atar massifs. The dunes pile up almost immediately, swallowing the road in places and keeping the ploughs and diggers busy throughout.

It's a further 40km until you leave Tagant and enter Adrar region. The first settlement of any significance in Adrar is 55km past the regional border at **Aïn Savra** (Ain Çefra), though note that many vehicles take a brief off-road short cut which bypasses Aïn Savra by a few kilometres, so be clear if you need to be dropped off here. There's accommodation in Aïn Savra at **Auberge Oasis de Desert** (m 37 33 00 66, 48 52 98 36; **$**).

TICHITT Arguably Mauritania's most isolated town, and certainly the most *reculé* of the four UNESCO ksours, slate-grey Tichitt (تيشيت; population 3,331) cuts a dramatically lonely figure, poised at the base of the escarpment to which it has given its name, with Dhar Tichitt to the north and the uninhabitable flats and dune seas of the Aoukar Depression to the south. As the crow flies, Tichitt is 200km from both Tidjikja in the west and Aïoun el Atrouss to the south, but access is nearly always via Tidjikja.

The city's provenance, though assuredly ancient, is poorly recorded, but its medieval golden age was built on white gold. Both a supplier of salt itself, as well as a waystation for salt caravans between Idjil (near F'Dérick) and the Sahelian markets to the south, Tichitt in many ways owed its raison d'être to salt. And it even still does: Tichitt's *salines* are still active, and the barren pans are just a short distance outside of town.

The city also grows dates and a few other crops, but Tichitt's isolation affects all aspects of life here, and irregular transport means that bringing any perishable goods to market is often impossible. Tourism is also a challenge, and it seems likely that Tichitt sees the fewest visitors out of Mauritania's four ksours.

While it may be difficult to get here, the rewards are as sweet as the dates. Profoundly isolated, dripping with history and nearly untouched by tourism of any kind, Tichitt is an oasis for those seeking *authenticité*. If you've got the time, come and see why people stay in such a seemingly inhospitable place – you're likely to learn as much about yourself as you are about Tichitt.

History Though the founding of the current settlement of Tichitt is somewhat unclear – some sources say 11th century, others 14th, and others still 8th – what's clear is that the escarpment around Tichitt is one of the oldest inhabited places in the whole of Mauritania. These stone-built settlements are thought to comprise some of the first, if not *the* first, complex societies found in West Africa, and their industrious inhabitants were active along the Dhar Tichitt escarpment (and continuing along the escarpment to the east) at least as far back as 2200BCE.

It's thought that these escarpment settlements were largely occupied by a proto-Soninké group (who were also thought to be among the original inhabitants of much of the Tagant and Adrar), who later migrated south in the face of desertification and eventually competition with Amazigh from the north over trade routes. Tichitt is therefore a predominantly Moorish town today.

The isolated town never enjoyed the status of its peers like Oualata or Chinguetti, but nonetheless enjoyed a heyday from the 15th to 18th centuries, when it served as an important node along the salt route, both producing its own and serving as a waystation for caravans between the salt pans at Idjil (near F'Dérick; page 208) and the Sahelian markets to the south. As with the other ksours, an urban population

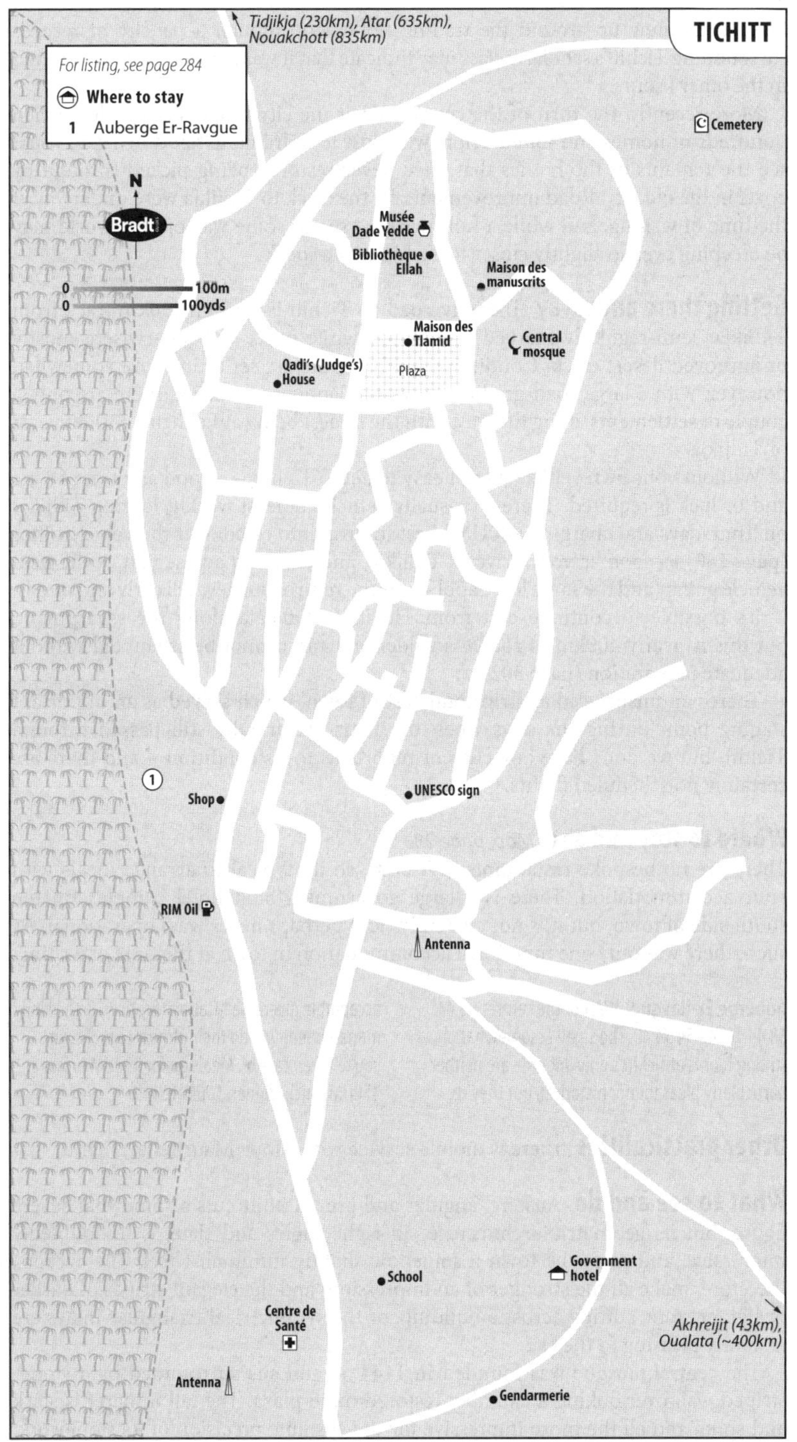
TICHITT
Tidjikja (230km), Atar (635km), Nouakchott (835km)
For listing, see page 284
Where to stay
1 Auberge Er-Ravgue
N
Bradt
0 100m
0 100yds
Cemetery
Musée Dade Yedde
Bibliothèque Ellah
Maison des manuscrits
Maison des Tlamid
Central mosque
Qadi's (Judge's) House
Plaza
1
Shop
UNESCO sign
RIM Oil
Antenna
Government hotel
School
Centre de Santé
Akhreijit (43km), Oualata (~400km)
Antenna
Gendarmerie

of scholars grew up around the trading settlement, though a paucity of records surrounding Tichitt's scholarly class may indicate that it was smaller than those found in the other ksours.

More recently, the turn of the century dealt the city a devastating blow when hundreds of homes and manuscripts were lost to a dramatic flood in 1999; you'll see the remains of the homes that were never restored being picked through by goats in the old city. Road improvements on the track to Tidjikja were underway at the time of writing, and while a full surfacing seems some way off, the world may be creeping ever so slightly closer to Tichitt as we speak.

Getting there and away The only 'road' to Tichitt is a rough 230km track from Tidjikja, semi-regularly marked by red-and-white posts, but otherwise a mostly unimproved desert track. Conditions on this route are set to improve somewhat, however, with a large road-grading operation launched in 2024. There are only a couple of settlements along the way, with the largest being at Lekhcheb, 100km east of Tidjikja.

Without your own vehicle it's not easy to get to Tichitt – a good amount of time and/or luck is required. There are usually vehicles at least weekly, leaving Tidjikja on Thursdays and charging 900UM. Best to drop into or contact the vehicle office (page 280) as soon as you arrive in Tidjikja, and they can advise you of the next vehicle going (and the same logic applies for the return journey; ask early and often).

It's possible to continue east from Tichitt to Oualata along the escarpment, but this is nearly 400km of roadless wilderness and cannot be attempted without adequate preparation (page 302).

There's an unsurfaced airstrip southeast of town, which served as an important staging point during the days when the Paris-Dakar rally still passed through Tichitt, but we don't have any current reports as to its condition – and there are certainly no scheduled flights.

Where to stay and eat *Map, page 283*

There are no bespoke restaurants in Tichitt, so it's typical to arrange meals with your accommodation. There is a large government-built hotel complex on the south side of town, but it is not currently (and perhaps never was) operational. As such, there was only one functional accommodation in town at the time of writing.

Auberge Er-Ravgue West of the centre; m 44 68 44 10, 42 54 54 40. The small & somewhat stifling rooms at Tichitt's only auberge are neither particularly pleasant nor historical, but they're acceptable given the location (& price), & the kind management will do their utmost to make sure you're taken care of. Meals go for 120UM b/fast & 350UM lunch/dinner. *500UM dbl.* **$**

Other practicalities There is mobile service with Moov Mauritel in Tichitt.

What to see and do Austere, angular and grey, Tichitt cuts a somewhat severe figure, but its geometric architecture, all right angles and slate, is undoubtedly impressive, and gives the town a somehow slightly minimalist feel. The accents, therefore, make all the stronger of an impression, and the elegant stripes of darker or lighter stone cutting across a building, or the symmetrical triangular inlays are instantly pleasing to the eye.

The **central mosque** was founded in 1144CE, and sits surrounded by a stone-striped wall overlooking a carefully restored main plaza. The tall minaret is stark and solid, and all the more impressive for the absolute precision of its stonework.

Not far away, the Maison des Tlamid (Student's House) and Qadi's (Judge's) House represent the city's scholarly and juridical tradition, which were well developed at the city's height.

Tichitt's libraries hold nearly 3,500 volumes in more than ten family collections. Just on the main plaza, you'll see the Maison des manuscrits (House of Manuscripts), but it may or may not be operating when you drop by. Therefore, just a few blocks away through the higgledy-piggledy collapsed walls and sandy lanes of the old city, aim for the **Bibliothèque El Vaghih Mhamed Ould Hmah Ellah**, which holds more than 1,000 volumes alone, and is happy to receive visitors and answer questions about their manuscripts. In the same building as the El Vaghih library, the single-room **Musée Dade Yedde**, named for the father of the current curator, is home to an impressively dusty collection of implements and accoutrements of rural and nomadic life. Any visitor to El Vaghih will be shown around here as well.

After visiting the old city, go and see the salt production in the sebkha 3km southeast of town (⊕ 18.4216, -9.4722), where the summer rains on the floodplain dry into a hard-baked sand-and-salt crust known as *amersal*. This is then scraped, broken and packed into 50kg sacks to be loaded four apiece either on massive lorries to Tidjikja, or – yes, still – on to camels which make the ten-day crossing south across the Erg Aoukar towards Aïoun el Atrouss. Here it's sold locally or shipped onwards to Mali, where it's prized for its mineral content and is a mainstay for herders using it as a salt lick to supplement their livestock's diet.

A NOTE ON SECURITY

Primarily due to the region's proximity to the chronic insecurity and ideologically inspired violence across the border in Mali, many European foreign ministries advise against visiting large swathes of eastern Mauritania.

The French foreign ministry advises against all travel to Hodh el Gharbi (except Tamchekett and Aoudaghost), all of Hodh ech Chargui, and the back route between Tichitt and Oualata (in Tagant and Hodh ech Chargui regions).

The French advice is sometimes different than that provided by the British FCO or other foreign ministries, but given the deeper involvement of the French in the region, we consider the advice provided to generally be more nuanced. It is available on w diplomatie.gouv.fr/fr/conseils-aux-voyageurs/conseils-par-pays-destination/mauritanie.

In our 2024 research, we visited the entirety of the Route de l'Espoir until Néma, returning west via Oualata and Tichitt. Broadly speaking, the closer to Mali the higher the risk, so areas south and east of the Route de l'Espoir should be treated with particular caution. Though it used to be an overlander staple, the border crossing to Mali at Gogui was not recommended as of 2025 due to insecurity on the Malian side. There are several other border crossings to Mali south of the Route de l'Espoir, and none were considered safe to use at the time of writing.

All that being said, the Mauritanian military is very active in patrolling the area (page 296), and the last terrorist attack on Mauritanian soil took place in 2011; most Mauritanians you speak to seem to balk at the idea that there is a significant security risk here today. So if you choose to travel here, remember that those innumerable roadside checkpoints are keeping a close eye on you for a reason, always seek and follow local advice, and try not to make your visit higher profile than it needs to be.

Outside of town in the other direction, the city's sparse but beautiful palmeraie runs several kilometres to the west, and would make a fine place to camp, should you have gear and wish to avoid the limited options in town.

If you have time (or are heading this way anyway; page 303), drive 40km east to the ruins of **Akhreijit** (⊕ 18.3614, -9.1511), where a steep stone staircase (bring water!) climbs to a partially restored Neolithic settlement atop the Dhar Tichitt, where more than 180 enclosures cover 20ha of land. Dating back more than 4,000 years, the alleys and lanes between waist-high walls give a surprisingly effective feel for what these ancient settlements may have looked and felt like – and the views from the top are spectacular.

THE EASTERN ROUTE DE L'ESPOIR: KIFFA TO NÉMA AND OUALATA

Continuing east from Kiffa, the wide open landscapes of eastern Mauritania are dotted with umbrella thorn acacia (*Vachellia tortilis*), Egyptian balsam (*Balanites aegyptiaca*) and gum arabic trees (*Vachellia nilotica*). This remote area is home to significant and little-explored Neolithic ruins (Aoudaghost, Koumbi Saleh and the Dhar Tichitt), several hidden crocodile gueltas, and a number of modern cities.

Departing Kiffa, the Route de l'Espoir continues its long sojourn to the east, crossing an open landscape of plains and dunes dotted with multiple floodplains (*tamourts*) and oueds which vary significantly in size throughout the year. Around 25km east of Kiffa, there's a bridge over the Oued Mansour (which eventually connects to the Karakoro) which is rich with greenery after the rains.

Some 40km past here, the road crosses into Hodh el Gharbi region at Fam Lekhedheiratt village, where there's a perennial guelta 5km south of the road (⊕ 16.4798, -10.8276) and the swampy **Tamourt Bougâri** (⊕ 16.5332, -10.7970) 2.5km to the north. The regional border is formed by the Affolé Massif, and the road climbs the escarpment here, rising about 100m above the village. There's a small waterfall next to the road during the rainy season. The **El Metrewgha** (or Metraucha; ⊕ 16.5373, -10.7414) guelta also sits at the base of the escarpment here, less than 5km north of the road. This is one of the several perennial water sources around Mauritania where relict populations of crocodiles can be reliably spotted.

The sandstone Affolé forms a rocky and uneven plateau, and marks the southeastern boundary of the *hodh*. The *hodh*, simply meaning basin, refers to the Aoukar Basin/Depression, a wide, flat and largely uninhabited lowland which stretches more than 400km from east to west, covering a wide swathe of southeastern Mauritania. Hemmed in by the Tagant to the west, Dhar Tichitt to the north, and the dhars Oualata and Néma to the east, it gives its name to both the Hodh el Gharbi ('Western Basin') and Hodh Ech Chargui ('Eastern Basin') regions.

After crossing into Hodh el Gharbi, it's just over 15km to the junction for **Tamchekett** (population 5,000; ⊕ 16.4896, -10.6315). This isolated town was founded as a French outpost in 1927, and a century later still feels every bit the isolated desert redoubt, sitting atop a dune at the very end of a 90km feeder road through the Affolé (but at least that road is now tarmac!). Though a few banco structures dating to the town's early days are still standing, Tamchekett is known primarily for its proximity to **Aoudaghost** (also known as Tegdaoust; ⊕ 17.4231, -10.4101) and **Togba** (⊕ 17.3921, -10.3555), two ruined medieval cities that were once among the northernmost reaches of the Ghana Empire, and a significant conduit for that empire's trans-Saharan trade.

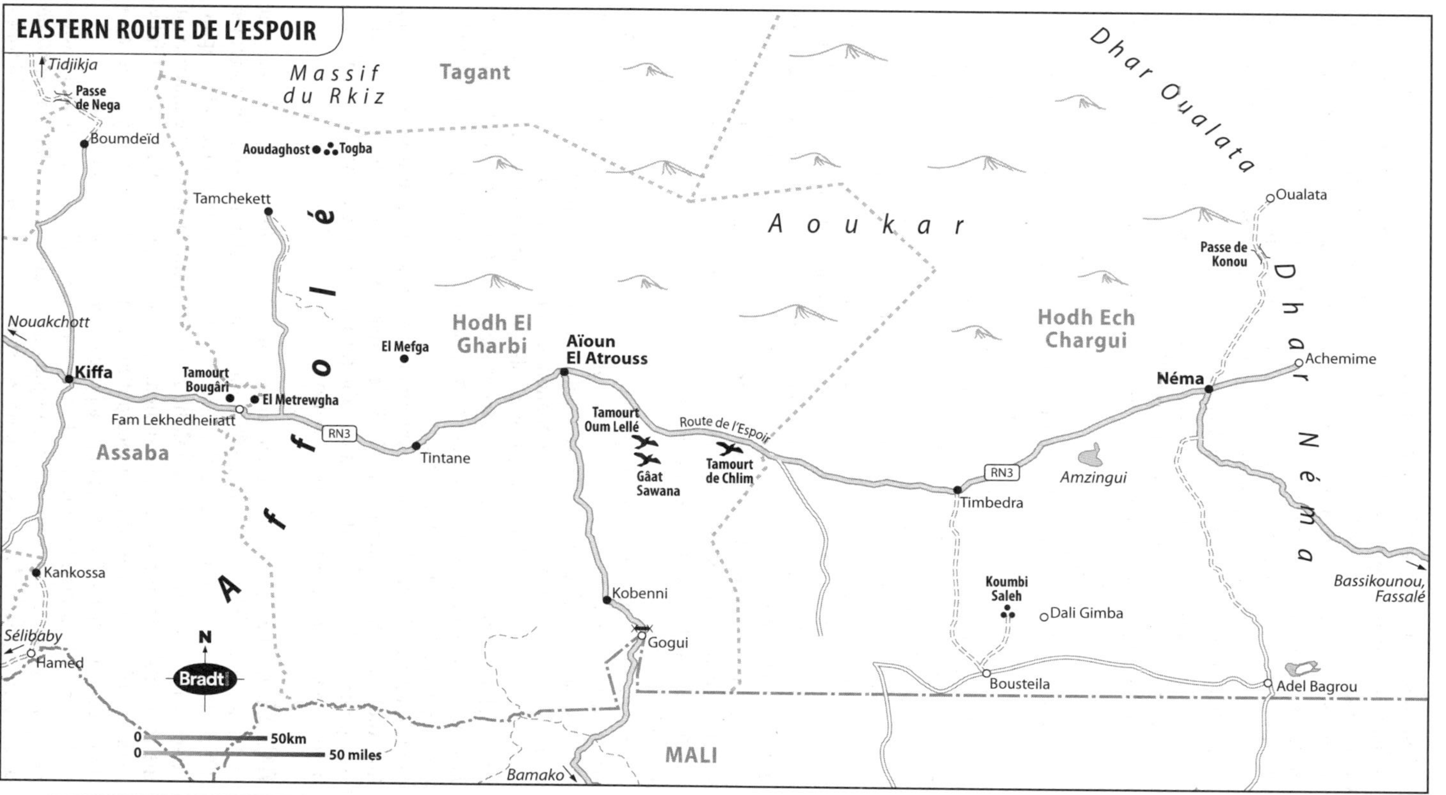
EASTERN ROUTE DE L'ESPOIR
Tidjikja
Passe de Nega
Boumdeïd
Massif du Rkiz
Tagant
Aoudaghost
Togba
Tamchekett
Affolé
Nouakchott
Kiffa
Tamourt Bougâri
El Metrewgha
Fam Lekhedheiratt
Assaba
RN3
Tintane
El Mefga
Hodh El Gharbi
Aïoun El Atrouss
Tamourt Oum Lellé
Gâat Sawana
Tamourt de Chlim
Route de l'Espoir
Aoukar
Kankossa
Sélibaby
Hamed
Bradt
N
0 50km
0 50 miles
Kobenni
Gogui
Bamako
MALI
Hodh Ech Chargui
Timbedra
Amzingui
Koumbi Saleh
Dali Gimba
Bousteila
Adel Bagrou
Néma
Achemime
Dhar Oualata
Oualata
Passe de Konou
Dhar Néma
Bassikounou, Fassalé

Aoudaghost itself originally dates to the 5th century, and before falling into the hands of Ghana, was once the most important centre for the Berber Sanhadja Confederacy, who exercised control over most of the trade routes across the western Sahara. By the end of the 10th century, Ghana sought to control more of this trade and moved in from their capital at Koumbi Saleh (page 291), some ten days by camel to the southeast, to occupy Aoudaghost. Its control was relatively short-lived, however, as the fanatical Almoravids captured the city in 1054 as part of their lightning offensive across the Maghreb.

The aftermath of the Almoravid takeover and increasing desertification meant the town began to decline in the centuries that followed, and Oualata began to overtake Aoudaghost as the preferred southern terminus of the trans-Saharan trade starting in the 11th century.

Aoudaghost is reached by desert tracks running some 35km northeast of Tamchekett, and sits nestled into the isolated rock outcrop of the Massif du Rkiz (not to be confused with the lake and town in Trarza region; page 241). Togba is about 7km further east as the crow flies. These two little-visited sites are completely undeveloped for tourism and have only undergone limited excavation and restoration, largely before 1976. As such, Aoudaghost is covered in many low stone walls in various stages of disrepair, though the rocky topography allows for visitors to get a vantage point from above in which the cityscapes become more obvious. As at Koumbi Saleh (page 291), there is a mosque among the ruins here that counts as among the oldest in the region. The rock shelter at Aguentour El Abiod near Aoudaghost is also home to several much older rock paintings, including cows and what some archaeologists think are meant to be chariots – a rare and unusual sighting this far south! (Photos can be viewed at w prehistoireouestsaharienne.wordpress.com/category/massif-du-rkiz.) Both sites have modern villages about 1km to their south (Noudache and Togba, respectively), but there are no services available at either.

Though little official scholarship is currently taking place at Aoudaghost, armchair travellers can enjoy a couple of good recent blog posts with photos of the site at w wildmanlife.com/aoudaghost-economic-hub-of-the-sahara and w lucaonadventure.com/aoudaghost-economic-center-of-the-sahara.

It's possible to get to Tamchekett by public transportation (if you can't find a direct vehicle from Kiffa, 175km away, try at the Route de l'Espoir junction known as Tamchekett Virage), but you'll have to hire someone to drive you from there to the sites, roughly a 90km round trip.

Back on the Route de l'Espoir, the road continues through a wide valley in the Affolé, roughly following the Kediet el Freïdi escarpment to the north. The escarpment pulls close to the road and the town of Tintane comes into view just beyond, 50km after the Tamchekett turn-off.

TINTANE The first major settlement after Kiffa, there's not much to detain you in Tintane (الطيْنطان; population 35,995), but you'll quickly notice it looks rather different from other towns along the road. This is because it suffered catastrophic flooding in 2007, which rendered much of the city uninhabitable. The majority of the residents were displaced, several died, and the stagnant waters did not fully recede until they were finally pumped out more than a year later. The waters also uprooted more than 1,000 date palms, a huge economic and cultural loss.

A development plan to resurrect the city was eventually drawn up, and a wide new grid of streets has been laid out in the dunes south of the old city, at a safe distance from the wadi. Along these widely spaced new roads, the city still looks oddly empty (a bit like the new city of Chami far off to the west, page 163), but head towards the central market and you'll see there's plenty of life in Tintane yet. All that life means chock-a-block traffic on the direct route through town, however, so take the right-hand bypass when you enter if you'd like to avoid this.

There's not a huge choice of facilities here, but you can stop for lunch at **Restaurant Ch'akirine** (m 48 80 82 84), and though you might not initially consider spending the night here, there's an unexpectedly interesting setup just west of town. **Hotel Vreidy** (m 30 77 08 77, 34 44 46 91; ⊕ 16.3606, -10.2050; **$$**) is 2km west of Tintane along the Route de l'Espoir and offers newly built en-suite rooms with air conditioning. (They also offer simpler accommodation in the city centre at Auberge Vreidy El Waha m 31 77 08 77; **$**.) The affiliated **Vreidy Farm** (e vreidyfarm@gmail.com; f) is off the road about 3km to the southwest of the hotel. Set near the base of a tall boulder-strewn outcrop cut through by a oued, this working farm is a popular relaxation spot for locals who want to chill, grill and sip *atay* in the shade all day. You can overnight in a khaïma tent for 700UM, and they can arrange food and drink.

They even put on a festival here: the International Shepherds' Music Festival (w isf-vt.org; f; intshpfes) was held for the second time in August 2024, and is a three-day celebration of traditional Mauritanian rural life and culture, featuring music, folklore, artisanship and theatre performances. In the other direction, deep into the hills 35km north of town, the **El Mefga** *guelta* (⊕ 16.6873, -10.1921) is home to a family of crocodiles (page 13).

AÏOUN EL ATROUSS The Route de l'Espoir continues northeast from Tintane, running through the plains south of the Affolé Massif until spectacularly rejoining the mountains as you approach Aïoun El Atrouss (عيون العتروس; population 36,517) after 65km. Known as Aïoun, it's a major crossroads town, where the main road to Mali turns south off the Route de l'Espoir. This was once upon a time a popular route for overlanders, but insecurity in Mali means it's currently not recommended. It's still a very popular commercial corridor, however, and the town is built in and around the easternmost outcrop of the Affolé Massif, which makes for some genuinely dramatic scenery around town (look out for the Galb al-Azbul rock formation right on the main road), and good hiking and scrambling opportunities for those with the time to explore them. There are some fantastic eroded archways and caverns at **Guelb Inimech** (⊕ 16.8090, -9.6128), 16km north of the city.

Getting there and away Plenty of vehicles run in either direction along the Route de l'Espoir, to Néma in the east or Kiffa to the west. SONEF (m 42 46 43 20) buses to Nouakchott (1,100UM; 15hrs) pass through Aïoun en route to both Néma and Bamako. Other companies like Nour Transport or Tayba Transport do the same. The turn-off for Gogui (Mali border) is at the centre of town, where the junction is decorated with a Quran in a traditional *rehal* stand. This was once a popular route for travellers, and vehicles covering the 125km stretch to the border are still easy enough to find, but it's not recommended given the insecurity on the Malian side of the border.

Aïoun also has an airport about 7km north of town, but there were no scheduled flights as of 2024.

Where to stay and eat *Map, page 290*

There are a handful of basic eateries along the main road through Aïoun, and the hotels can arrange meals on demand.

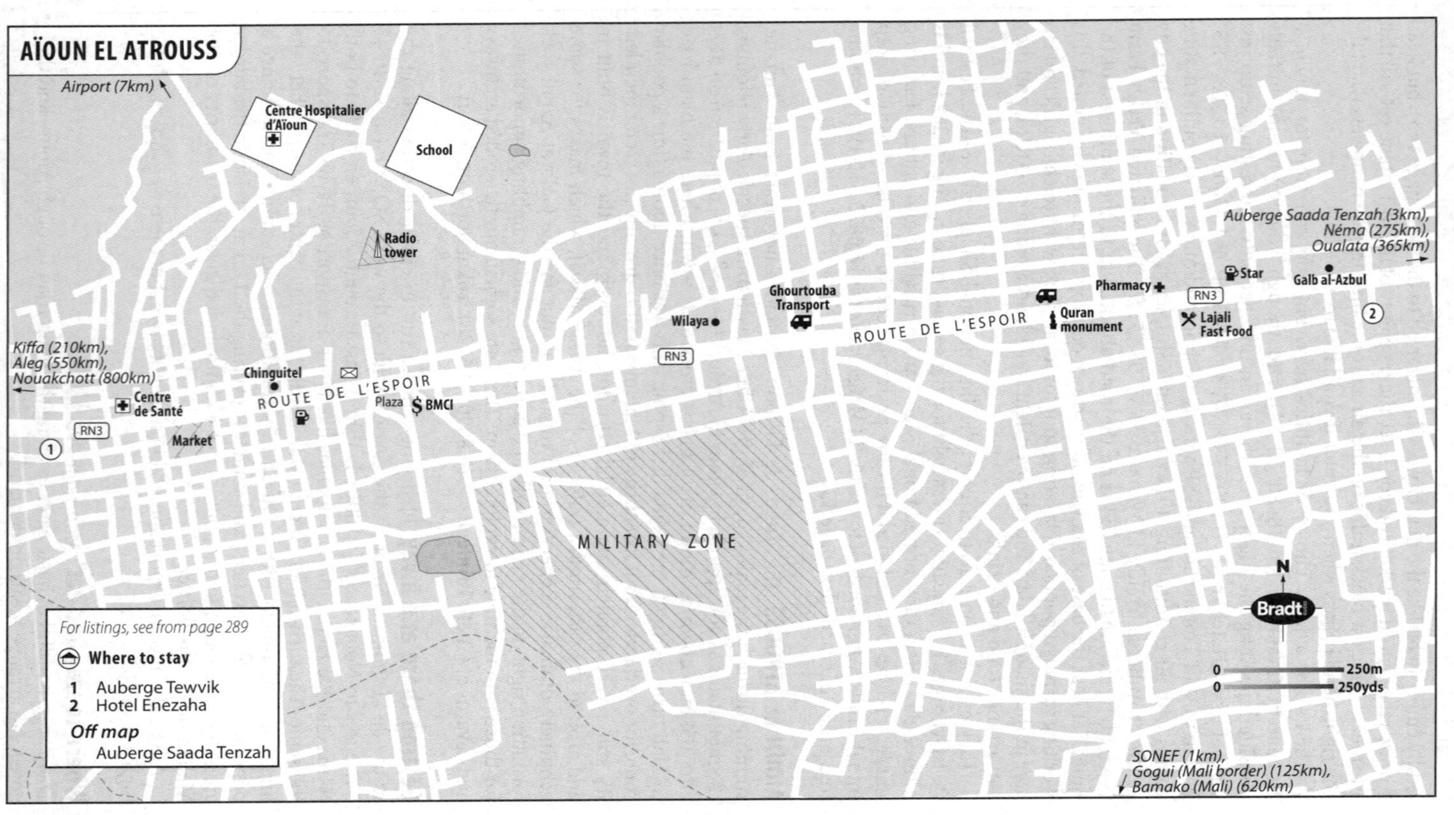

AÏOUN EL ATROUSS
Airport (7km)
Centre Hospitalier d'Aïoun
School
Radio tower
Kiffa (210km), Aleg (550km), Nouakchott (800km)
Centre de Santé
RN3
Market
Chinguitel
ROUTE DE L'ESPOIR
Plaza
BMCI
RN3
Wilaya
Ghourtouba Transport
ROUTE DE L'ESPOIR
Quran monument
Pharmacy
RN3
Star
Lajali Fast Food
Galb al-Azbul
Auberge Saada Tenzah (3km), Néma (275km), Oualata (365km)
1
2
MILITARY ZONE
N
Bradt
0 250m
0 250yds
SONEF (1km), Gogui (Mali border) (125km), Bamako (Mali) (620km)
For listings, see from page 289
Where to stay
1 Auberge Tevvik
2 Hotel Enezaha
Off map
Auberge Saada Tenzah

Auberge Saada Tenzah m 44 00 03 05. At the eastern edge of town, this is a long-serving option with AC rooms & a large courtyard. It used to see a fair bit of overlander traffic before the route to Mali dried up. *1,200UM dbl.* **$$**

Auberge Tewvik m 22 28 89 49. Centrally located a few hundred metres west of the main market & other services, the handful of 1st-floor rooms here are decent value. *1,000UM dbl.* **$$**

Hotel Enezaha Route de l'Espoir (RN3); m 49 22 00 87, 46 52 69 33. The sign might be spelled differently (it was 'Enezahz' when we dropped by, others seem to call it Nezaha) but the facilities are in better order than the orthography. *1,500UM dbl.* **$$**

THE ROUTE DE L'ESPOIR FROM AÏOUN TO NÉMA After Aïoun you leave the Affolé Massif behind, and plunge into the endless plains of the Aoukar. There are two Important Bird Areas (IBAs) set southeast of Aïoun: the combined **Gâat Sawana** (more than 800ha; ⊕ 16.2994, -9.2757) and **Tamourt Oum Lellé** (more than 400ha; ⊕ 16.3887, -9.2984), which sit 16km and 8km south of the Route de l'Espoir respectively, and **Tamourt de Chlim** (500ha; ⊕ 16.4023, -9.0543), which sits further to the east and 4km south of the Route de l'Espoir. The road crosses the regional border between the twin *hodh* regions after 85km, entering Hodh Ech Chargui ('Eastern Basin') at the rather desolate, windblown settlement of Aweinatt Zbil.

From here it's 80km to the next major settlement of **Timbedra** (تمبدغة; population 34,244), which is primarily of note as the turn-off for **Koumbi Saleh** (⊕ 15.7707, -7.9864), former capital of the Ghana Empire. Found in a field about 65km south of Timbedra (and 30km north of the Mali border), the site of Koumbi Saleh is abandoned today, belying entirely the site's epochal significance in West African history. Tracing its origins to at least the 6th century CE, the Soninké-dominated Ghana (also known as Ouagadou/Wagadu), the first of the major West African empires, controlled a significant territory in southeastern Mauritania and western Mali from its capital here at Koumbi Saleh, where the empire's 'ghanas' (kings) were resident from at least the 10th century onwards. For several centuries, Ghana got rich on trade, serving as a middleman between the goldfields of the south and the salt caravans of the north, and Koumbi Saleh became a prosperous city. In his *Book of Roads and Kingdoms,* Al-Bakri described the settlement as having both a royal and a commercial town, separated by several miles, but as yet only one of these has been uncovered.

Indeed, due to its remote and today potentially insecure location, there is no active archaeological scholarship taking place at Koumbi Saleh, and it has been many years since the last significant works were undertaken here. As such, the site remains entirely undeveloped, despite it hosting one of the oldest mosques in West Africa (⊕ 15.7643, -7.9677), and earlier scholars considering the site's 'Column Tomb' to be an 'outstanding building in the history of West Africa, unique both for its size and the nature of its layout, for which no comparable example is known'. There is equally no tourism or other development of any kind at the site, most of which remains unexcavated and difficult to perceive from ground level. The settlement's decline began when it was sacked by the Almoravids in 1076, limping on as an increasingly minor outpost for several centuries thereafter. And while the time and effort spent getting out here may only be worthwhile for the most dedicated history and archaeology buffs, it's certainly still worth a look on satellite imagery, where building foundations and parts of the settlement's urban layout are perceptible to this day.

There are no services near Koumbi Saleh other than the basic goods available in the modern settlement of the same name about 1km south of the archaeological site, but there are a few rooms available in Timbedra should you need. On the Route de l'Espoir there's a first-floor option, where the sign is only in Arabic except 'Apartment 2021' on the first floor (m 22 09 88 78; **$**).

Ten kilometres east of Koumbi Saleh lies **Dali Gimba** (also known as Dali Koumbé or Dalghoumba; ⊕ 15.7785, -7.8794), which is known as the home of an extended clan-family, the Awlād Ummār, with a hereditary predisposition to blindness passed along for more than seven generations. The clan patriarch, who passed away in 2022, was known for his preternatural skills in water divination, and is said to have established more than 1,000 wells across Mauritania in his time. One-third of the 200-strong population of the village are thought to be blind, but rather than a handicap, their blindness is instead considered to be a *karāma*, a source of miraculous inspiration and supernatural abilities, from water divination to extraordinary charisma. The village is the subject of a fascinating 2024 PhD dissertation, *Blindness and Water Divination in the Saharan West* by Saquib Usman (available at w deepblue.lib.umich.edu/handle/2027.42/193347).

In better times, there is a border post south of here at **Bousteila** (⊕ 15.5777, -8.0819) through which you could continue into Mali.

From Timbedra, the Route de l'Espoir continues 105km northeast across the plains to Néma. About 45km before reaching Néma, the **Gâat Mahmoûdé** IBA (⊕ 16.3890, -7.7026) covers 16,200ha, including the 2,500ha perennial lake at Amzingui (also known as the Mare de Mahmouda). The road approaches the mountains of the Dhar Oualata/Dhar Néma escarpment as you reach Néma, and arriving here, you have not only officially crossed the Aoukar, but reached the end of the Route de l'Espoir!

NÉMA Capital of the Hodh Ech Chargui ('Eastern Basin') region, Néma (النعمة; population 35,042) has since 1985 been the endpoint of the Route de l'Espoir, a long black ribbon unspooling all 1,100km west to Nouakchott. And though the tarmac now extends 260km further east, it remains by far the most important commercial centre in the region, serving as the nearest significant market for the hundreds of tiny herding settlements to the south and east – because as much as you might think you've reached the end of Mauritania once you get here, the Malian border is still more than 125km away in any direction! Given its strategic location, it's also a key garrison town with a significant Mauritanian military presence.

If you're here, it's overwhelmingly likely you're one of the determined trickle of tourists headed towards Oualata, and if you spend longer in Néma than it takes to change buses, you'll be part of a much smaller group still. And while it's not for nothing that people make the effort to get to Oualata, you won't regret taking a little swing through Néma. The city has a long pedigree: it was first founded in 1486 by religious leaders fleeing the Songhai sacking of Timbuktu, then

SAFETY AND SECURITY

In the past, at least, the gendarmerie in Néma was known to limit tourists' movements within the town. This is not universally enforced, however, and perhaps less so as the security situation within Mauritania is seen to have improved, so your mileage may vary. On the bright side, they've equally been known to send someone with you to make sure you get to the right place to find the vehicles to Oualata.

Other than the issues outlined in the box on page 285, we are not aware of any specific risks that are greater in Néma town than elsewhere on the eastern Route de l'Espoir, but as always take local advice seriously.

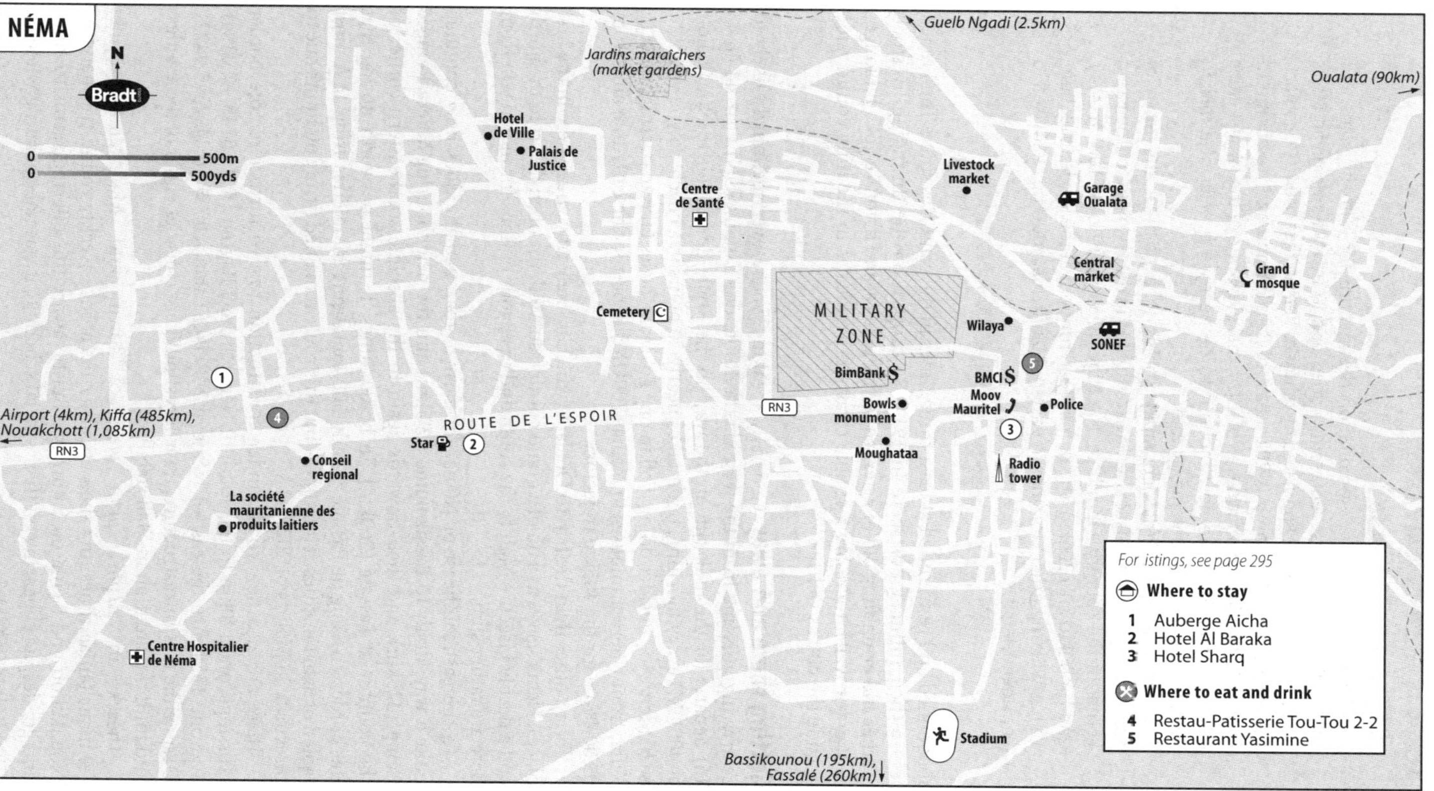
NÉMA
N
Bradt
0 500m
0 500yds
Guelb Ngadi (2.5km)
Jardins maraîchers (market gardens)
Oualata (90km)
Hotel de Ville
Palais de Justice
Centre de Santé
Livestock market
Garage Oualata
Central market
Grand mosque
Cemetery
MILITARY ZONE
Wilaya
SONEF
BimBank
BMCI
Moov Mauritel
Police
Bowls monument
Moughataa
Radio tower
RN3
ROUTE DE L'ESPOIR
Airport (4km), Kiffa (485km), Nouakchott (1,085km)
Star
Conseil regional
La société mauritanienne des produits laitiers
Centre Hospitalier de Néma
Stadium
Bassikounou (195km), Fassalé (260km)
For istings, see page 295
Where to stay
1 Auberge Aicha
2 Hotel Al Baraka
3 Hotel Sharq
Where to eat and drink
4 Restau-Patisserie Tou-Tou 2-2
5 Restaurant Yasimine

BASSIKOUNOU AND MBERA

Bassikounou and Mbera are common destinations for humanitarians and other NGO workers, but represent a dead end in travel terms given Mali's ongoing inaccessibility. Populated by refugees fleeing that country's conflict, the **Mbera Refugee Camp** is 20km east of Bassikounou and was home to about 115,000 Malian refugees as of 2024, making it one of the largest cities in Mauritania. There are now thought to be nearly a quarter of a million Malian refugees in Mauritania, all told.

Mauritania's geometric geography comes to a point at the town of **Fassalé**, 260km southeast of Néma and situated in the absolute southeastern corner of the country. From here, the Niger River is just over 100km away, and Timbuktu only 300km. The tarmac road runs out at the border post here, but as with the other crossings in eastern Mauritania, you'd be ill-advised to consider using it.

abandoned and re-founded at least three times in the centuries since. The French set up their military post here in 1912. So drop in on the thronging livestock market and crumbling old quarter while you're here, and if you've got a bit longer to stay (or wait), there are a couple of attractive locales in the hilly countryside outside the city as well.

Getting there and away Generally speaking, you're overwhelmingly likely to be arriving in Néma from the west via the Route de l'Espoir. SONEF (m 44 46 43 16) departs for the milk run all the way up the Route de l'Espoir to Nouakchott (1,400UM) every morning, but it takes nearly 20 hours in a coach, so you've got to be hardcore to consider doing it all in one go. Many buses take an overnight rest in Kiffa, from where minibuses to Néma (700UM) depart in the early morning from 05.00/06.00 for the 485km trajectory.

Today, other than the trip to Oualata (which is likely why you're here in the first place), Néma serves as a bit of a grand cul-de-sac. With the open desert to the north and a deeply insecure Mali to the south and east, your options for moving on from here are rather slim.

To the east/southeast of Néma, the tarmac road actually does now continue quite a way: firstly to **Bassikounou** (195km) and the neighbouring **Mbera Refugee Camp** (225km), and then onwards again to the absolute southeastern corner of the country at **Fassalé** (260km). In better times, it might be worth noting that the border crossing at Fassalé is only 300 tantalising kilometres from that most fabled of Saharan cities, Timbuktu – but this route remained firmly off limits due to insecurity in Mali as of 2025.

There are also new roads under construction to two further remote border crossings, one 140km to the south of Néma at **Adel Bagrou** (⊕ 15.5248, -7.0394), and one 155km to the east of Néma at **N'Beiket Lahouach** (⊕ 16.8452, -5.9422). Despite the new infrastructure, travellers should not consider either of these unless and until the situation in Mali stabilises.

There's an **airport** 5km west of town, and Mauritania Airlines (w mauritaniaairlines.mr) theoretically runs a once-weekly round trip between Nouakchott and Néma on Saturdays. But be aware this offering seems to come and go: despite appearing on their official schedule, it was not operating when we tried to buy tickets.

Where to stay *Map, page 293*

Many travellers only stay in Néma long enough to change vehicles, but if you miss the connection or simply can't bear the thought of more hours on the road, there are a few decent options in town for a restorative night's kip.

Auberge Aicha Just off the Route de l'Espoir; m 33 69 77 77, 43 46 67 83. A bit simpler than the Al Baraka, but another decent option at the west end of town. *1,000UM dbl.* **$$**
Hotel Al Baraka Route de l'Espoir; m 22 04 57 43, 41 35 66 48; e barakahotel@gmail.com. Probably the nicest pick in town, the en-suite rooms here come with AC & are reasonably kept. The management is friendly & happy to help as best they can. *1,200UM dbl.* **$$**
Hotel Sharq m 26 37 64 18. Centrally located near the police station, the en-suite AC rooms here are the pick if you'd like to be a bit closer to the action. *1,000UM dbl.* **$$**

Where to eat and drink *Map, page 293*

There are a handful of small restaurants dotted around the city serving workaday Mauritanian fare. Try **Restaurant Yasimine** (m 41 32 50 99; $) near the police station, or if you're on the west side of town there's **Restau-Patisserie Tou-Tou 2-2** (m 33 69 77 77; $), which also carries a few baked goods.

Other practicalities The new Centre Hospitalier de Néma is on the southwest side of town, and there's a smaller Centre de Sante (health post) closer to the city centre. BMCI is represented with an ATM in the centre. Mauritel Moov has a central office as well.

What to see and do Néma's old quarter, known as Edelibu, sits northeast of the central oued cutting through the city. Like most of its contemporaries, much of it is crumbling, with many residents abandoning these ancient stone homes for the concrete structures of the modern city that surrounds. Néma's grand mosque still sits at the centre of the neighbourhood, however it's considerably younger than most of the homes and buildings that surround it.

The city's largest roundabout is recognisable by the giant bowls in the centre – known as *gued'ha*, these are the carved wooden bowls traditionally used to serve the sweetened milk drink known as *zrig*. As with so many Mauritanian settlements, Néma is split down the middle by a oued. And while the city's **market** carries a similar array of workaday goods as those found in the others along the Route de l'Espoir, much of Néma's commercial action takes place right on the sands of the dry riverbed (as well as in the streets on either side).

On the west side of town, La société mauritanienne des produits laitiers (SMPL) opened a major UHT milk factory here in 2017, providing an opportunity to preserve the milk produced by pastoralists in this remote corner of the country and sell it elsewhere. The factory has a 25,000 litre/day capacity, though supply issues mean output is often much less. The milk is sold under the brand name Ngadi, which takes its name from an isolated hill to the northwest of town, **Guelb Ngadi** (⊕ 16.6390, -7.2734). The hill is one of Néma's most important symbols and makes for a good short climb with views to the city and surrounding hills and desert; follow the oued northwest for just over 3km, passing a series of impressive *jardins maraîchers* (market gardens) along the way. About 3km northeast of Guelb Ngadi, passing a disused dam en route, Gleitat Elsabe (⊕ 16.6577, -7.2559) is a small but scenic canyon with a high southern wall towering above the wadi bed.

The first Festival de Néma pour la Culture et le Patrimoine (m 49 47 47 00; e nemafestival2024@gmail.com; f Le festival de Néma pour la culture) was held at

MODERN MÉHARISTES: THE CAMEL PATROLS OF EASTERN MAURITANIA

Joost Bastmeijer (w joostbastmeijer.com; joostbastmeijer)

Amid the violence that has spread across the Sahel in recent years, Mauritania has managed to stop jihadism at the border, thanks to a special army unit of *gens de la brousse* – men of the wilderness.

In the courtyard of a sand-coloured fort with four pointed watchtowers, M'Beirik Messoud looks down the polished barrel of his Kalashnikov. The brigadier in the Mauritanian army will spend the next few days in the desert patrolling for jihadists along the border with Mali. The border area he and his men are travelling through is so inhospitable that even the strongest off-road vehicles cannot reach it. Messoud and his men therefore do not brave the sandy plains with four-wheel drive, but on the back of a camel.

They are members of the so-called Méharistes, a special camel brigade of the Mauritanian army. Their camp is located at the end of the road in the small town of Achemime, 35km east of Néma. For the nomadic shepherds who roam this area, the Méharistes and their animals are familiar passers-by. Messoud and his men are soldiers, doctors, policemen, intelligence services and advisers all at once.

The 300-member unit was created by the French in 1912, when Mauritania was still a colony. Its objective has not changed: to guarantee the safety and well-being of the inhabitants of Hodh Ech Chargui, a gigantic province in the east of the country covering more than 180,000km^2. But in recent decades a core task has been added to their charge: preventing jihadism, which is rampant in the rest of the Sahel, from crossing the border into Mauritania.

In the courtyard of the fort, dried goat meat, water, boxes of tea and kilo bags of sugar are laid out. Brigadier Messoud distributes them into his men's saddlebags. The 55-year-old Messoud has a friendly, bespectacled face, with broad cheekbones. 'Easy, easy,' Messoud mumbles to his camel as he climbs into the saddle. The 1,000kg monster stands up, gurgling. 'They are moody animals,' he admits. A smile forms on his grey-bearded face.

There are hardly any paths here. Yet Messoud knows this area like the back of his hand. 'This is my homeland,' he says. 'We navigate by the stars, the wind, the vegetation and the ground colours.'

Here, the State was barely present. 'The nomads live here in such isolation that they lack everything,' says Messoud. That makes them vulnerable to the beautiful promises of jihadists. To turn the tide, Mauritania invested in its Méhariste unit – and successfully. Thanks in part to them, even as their eastern neighbours have succumbed to protracted conflict, there has not been an attack on Mauritanian territory since 2011. 'We are bringing the State to the most remote parts of the country,' says Messoud.

Among the sand dunes on the horizon, the nomadic village of Em Gheizine looms. A man comes running from under an acacia tree and introduces himself as Muheisim Desha, the village elder. He leads the Méharistes' doctor, Famori

the end of December 2023, with traditional game competitions, Quranic recitations, theatrical performances, concerts, and both classical and popular poetry recitations. Preparations were underway for the second edition in December 2025, just as this book went to print.

Keïta, to a multi-coloured tent. Mainly women and children wait there; the men of the settlement travel around with their cattle and are often away from home for weeks.

While the doctor listens to the lungs of a coughing girl, Desha looks on with satisfaction from the corner of the tent. 'We see the Méharistes about once every three months,' he says. This helps with regular check-ups, as 'the nearest clinic is a few days' walk to the west.' Keïta soon finishes his work; he does not charge for his medicines and advice. 'It shows that the Mauritanian government cares about its citizens,' says Desha.

However, the Méhariste unit is largely funded by the EU, which is bankrolling some 250 camels, the fort in Achemime and the training of hundreds of recruits, in the hopes that the Méharistes can help keep jihadists as far away from Europe as possible.

That evening, the soldiers set up their camp on a nearby sandy ridge. They relax and drink *atay*; one listens to some music on his phone while smoking tobacco from a hollowed-out goat bone. Suddenly, a short, muffled scream sends the Méharistes instinctively reaching for their Kalashnikovs, and two figures emerge from the bushes.

But the soldiers quickly relax: the screams were from a goat – a treat from two passing shepherds, 'in gratitude for keeping this area safe'. The youngest soldiers deftly hang the carcass on a thorny acacia branch, before cutting it apart from head to tail.

After a cold night under the stars, the men stretch their stiff limbs and untie the hobbles restricting their camels' movements. Their saddles, which had provided shelter from the desert wind last night, are strapped back on to the beasts and the group resumes its journey.

The secret of the Méharistes, says Hassane Koné, a security specialist at the Institute for Security Studies in Nouakchott, is that 'the Méharistes are recruited in the areas they protect.' Indeed, these *chameliers* are intimately familiar with not just the local area, but the local language and faith. 'We have been going to Quran school since we were four and we know the Sharia laws on which our constitution is based,' explains Koné. 'So when people come with radical ideas, we know what we are opposing.'

How the Méharistes gather intelligence becomes clear when the camel brigade approaches the Malian border. Two riders suddenly dig their bare heels into the flanks of their mounts, leaving the herd at a trot to chat with a shepherd further away. What they discuss is secret, says Messoud. 'The shepherds are our eyes and ears,' he says. 'Their information is crucial to knowing who is moving through the area.'

Messoud takes the passport photos of his four children out of his saddlebag; his family lives to the west in Néma. He does this work for them. 'We defend our homeland,' says Messoud, 'and ensure that our children grow up without war or oppression.'

OUALATA Here, at the end of a long, long journey east from the coast (or south across the desert), lies Oualata (ولاتة). The oldest of Mauritania's ancient UNESCO-recognised ksour, it was first settled by Soninké agriculturalists (who referred to the city as Biru) around the 7th century, and even today residents sometimes proudly refer to the city as the 'older sister' to the world-famous Timbuktu, which lies some 425km to the east. But of Mauritania's four ksour. Oualata stands out not only for its age, but also for its look: rather than the dry-stone masonry found in the other three, Oualata is built from a fiery red banco mud brick, in a style more commonly connected to the Sahel than the Sahara. And while the materials may be Sahelian, the city is Maghrebian in form – a tight hilltop casbah of winding alleyways, expansive courtyards, and ornate wood-and-ironwork doors.

But beyond the simple change in materials, it's what the Oualatiens have done with them that's spectacular. Each home is covered in the most intricate and unexpected frescoes: filigrees frame the windows, intricate emblems bookend the doors, and ornate and organic loops, swirls and finials grow up the walls and columns of the interior. In the golden light of a Saharan sunset, it's a photographer's dream.

And while the Oualatien works of art have no neighbouring traditions either stylistically or geographically, travellers familiar with the region might be reminded of the painted villages of Tiébélé in Burkina Faso or Sirigu in Ghana (or, to a lesser but perhaps closer extent, some of the Soninké decorative traditions in Guidimakha; page 257). And just as in those famously painted towns, here in Oualata it's women who paint the walls, both freehand and by hand, literally applied with the touch of a finger and refreshed after the rainy season each year. The origin and meaning of the motifs is the topic of much academic discussion, but at least some of the designs around the doors are an amuletic form of protection.

Outside of their extraordinary home design, the Oualatiens are also the inheritors of a grand sacred and scholarly tradition (Odette du Puigaudeau called it the 'city of saints and merchants' in 1938) and, like the other ksours, the city's libraries hold hundreds of irreplaceable manuscripts. But as impressive and dynamic as their decorative, scholastic and commercial traditions may be, there is no denying that, also like Mauritania's other ksours, depopulation and desertification are taking their toll on the city. Today the census counts 4,782 residents, though the *moughataa* of Oualata covers an astounding 93,000km^2, almost all of it open desert. And while this enormous administrative division gives you a sense of just how remote the town is, there are still a few people living out in those not-quite empty lands, meaning Oualata itself has not quite as many residents as the census implies, which is easily seen in the empty homes, collapsing walls and fading frescoes of this extraordinary, and extraordinarily isolated city. Yet while Oualata's future feels a touch uncertain, it would seem foolhardy to bet against people who've been figuring out how to survive and thrive here since around 600CE.

History Though first settled centuries earlier, and with Neolithic ruins in the area that predate even that, Oualata first rose to prominence as part of the Ghana Empire and it began to supplant Aoudaghost as the preferred terminus of the trans-Saharan trade from Sijilmasa in the 11th century. Its importance would grow significantly with Ghana's decline and the ascendance of Mali in the 13th century, but just as Oualata had overtaken Aoudaghost as a node for trans-Saharan trade in the 11th century, it began to be overshadowed itself by Timbuktu in the early 14th century.

By the time of Ibn Battuta's 1352 visit, Oualata was a secondary hub to Timbuktu, but this city of Soninké and Amazigh residents would go on to be a significant centre of trade and scholarship through the collapse of Mali (which saw many residents and scholars decamp from Timbuktu to Oualata) and the rise of the Songhai Empire in the 15th century, and through the collapse of that empire at

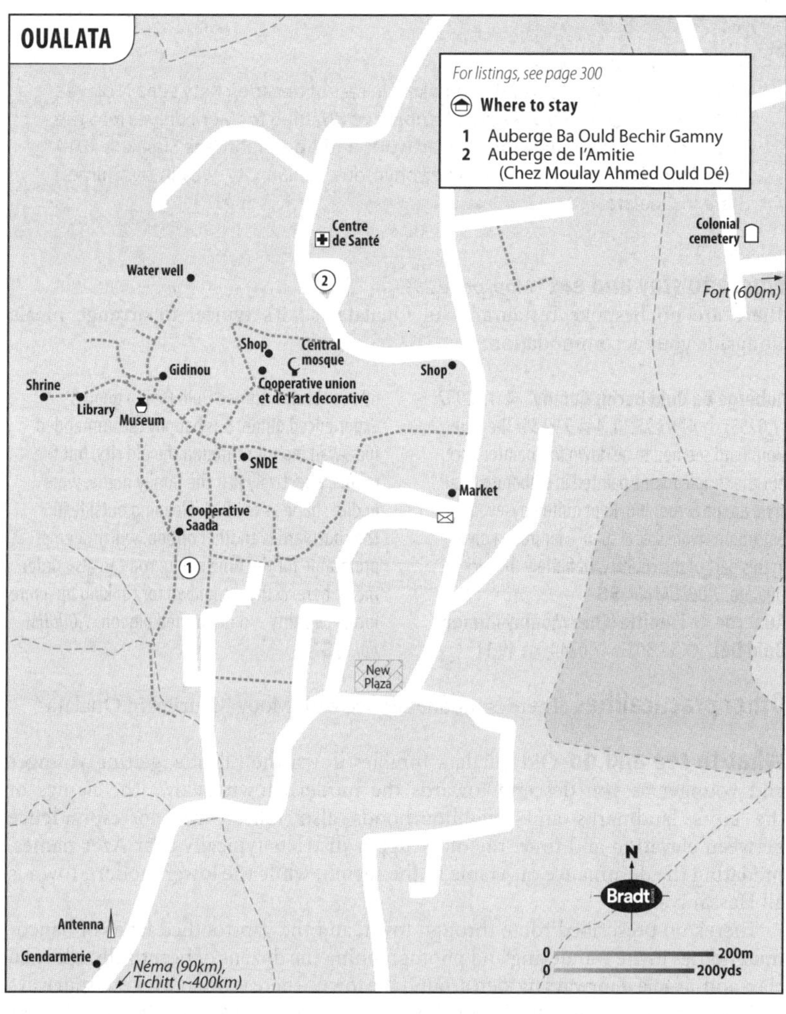

the end of the 16th century as well. From the 17th century (and in the wake of the Char Bouba War) the city was pulled into the Moorish sphere of influence, and its regional importance began to wane. The town's Soninké-Amazigh creole of Azer would soon disappear, giving way to Hassaniya in the intervening years. The French built their fort opposite the city in 1912, and Oualata was witness to yet another empire's rise and fall.

Getting there and away The tarmac road runs out at Néma, after which it's 90km on unimproved desert tracks to Oualata. Though it doesn't seem all that far, allow 3 or 4 hours to get through as the desert route is rudimentary at best. The route comes down the Passe de Konou (⊕ 17.1651, -7.0442) about 15km before reaching the town, from which there are expansive views over the surrounding desert.

There are daily trucks between Néma and Oualata, usually departing for Oualata around 15.00 (400UM). Trucks typically make the return journey to Néma in the early morning; your host will help you arrange a seat the day before.

OUALATA IN FILM

Oualata has inspired several filmmakers in recent decades: Katy Léna N'diaye's 2007 documentary *En attendant les hommes* (Waiting for Men) delves into the lives of the city's women and their artwork, and Abderrahmane Sissako's 2014 film *Timbuktu*, though set in the eponymous Malian city, was in fact filmed here in Oualata.

Where to stay and eat *Map, page 299*

There are no bespoke restaurants in Oualata, so it's typical to arrange meals alongside your accommodation.

Auberge Ba Ould Bechir Gamny ⊕ 17.2982, -7.0255; m 47 43 25 30, 44 75 99 31. The blue signboard seemed to be down for maintenance, but the simple rooms painted in elaborate local style are up & running. Kept quite tidy, even the bathrooms were spic & span – far from a given in this part of the country. Definitely the pick in Oualata. *1,000UM dbl.* **$$**

Auberge de l'Amitie (Chez Moulay Ahmed Ould Dé) ⊕ 17.3012, -7.0240; m 49 11 69 37. Moulay Ahmed Ould Dé is a good & experienced guide, & is happily recommended for a walking tour through the old city, but the rooms, effectively just the family home, were in dire shape as of 2024. Sleeping outside in the courtyard is another option, which seems preferable for the time being. You can also order meals here, & they're known for cooking up a rare local speciality – date-stuffed pigeon. *1,000UM dbl.* **$$**

Other practicalities There is mobile service with Moov Mauritel in Oualata.

What to see and do Old Oualata tumbles down the hillside, getting younger and younger as you descend towards the modern town below. The names of the city's landmarks and neighbourhoods also reflect this correspondence between elevation and time: the older upper districts typically bear Azer names, predating the dominance of Arabic in the region, while the lower modern town is all Hassaniya.

There's no prescribed route through town, and the gap-toothed lanes of banco-mud homes invite wandering and photographing the dozens of beautifully adorned clay-and-acacia **doorways** hidden around the town. There is no shortage of stairways and odd angles in this hillside city, however, so wear good shoes and watch your step well!

As with the other ancient towns of Mauritania, the houses here hide any number of priceless ancient manuscripts, but you'll need a guide to show you the way if you'd like to see any of them. The **museum** and main library were unfortunately in need of renovation and not functional during our visit, but there are still plenty of manuscripts to be seen with the right guidance.

Moulay Ahmed Ould Dé from Auberge de l'Amitie (see above) is a good guide, and will take you around for a half day for 200UM, though he does not speak English. You can wander the city on your own (don't mind any would-be guides who insist that you can't), but hiring a guide will give you access to homes and **courtyards**, many of them also intricately adorned, that would otherwise be nothing more than a closed (albeit pretty) door. It will also give you access to some of the town's private **libraries**, where more than a dozen old Oualata families hold more than 1,500 centuries-old volumes between them. Therefore, even if you don't speak French, it might be worth taking Moulay or another guide on for the additional access alone.

However you choose to explore the city, be sure to make a stop in one of Oualata's most photogenic corners, known as **Gidinou**. There's nothing to indicate it other than a set of particularly nice façades at the top of a small staircase, but this was one of the main centres for scholars active in the city at its height, and the opulent doorways surrounding this intimate block of the city reflect just a hint of this urbane sophistication all the way to present day.

The central **mosque** (as featured on the 100UM note) suffered significant flood damage in mid-2024, collapsing several of the structure's outer walls. President Ghazouani himself visited the site in the aftermath of the flooding, however, and ordered a full reconstruction 'with the care that is worthy of the houses of Allah' – so you can be sure it will be in saintly condition by the time you read this. Many other ancient buildings were also damaged, however, and these are much less likely to be repaired in good time (or at all).

Just opposite the central mosque, Cooperative union et de l'art decorative (m 44 45 67 23) has a selection of crafts and souvenirs for sale, including clay work, which is a local speciality. Artists here and at the Cooperative Saada near Auberge Gamny

OUALATA'S INFAMOUS FORT

The imposing triangular fort on a hilltop just east of Oualata was built in 1912, during the French colonial campaign for control of what is now Mauritania's Hodh region. But it would become infamous only after independence, when it became a dumping ground for political prisoners, a sort of Mauritanian Devil's Island in the desert.

The prison's most famous resident was not Dreyfus, but rather Daddah – Mauritania's first president, Mokhtar Ould Daddah, spent about a year here after he was overthrown in 1978, before being sent into exile in France.

The military regimes that ruled after Daddah kept the prison busy through the 1980s, however, particularly after the 1986 publication of *Le Manifeste du Négro-Mauritanien Opprimé* (Manifesto of the Oppressed Black Mauritanian) by banned opposition group Forces de Libération Africaines de Mauritanie, whose authors were quickly rounded up, handed long jail terms and imprisoned here. The inhumane conditions in the fort saw numerous inmates die, including author and poet Tène Youssouf Gueye.

This period is the subject of former prisoner Alassane Harouna Boye's 1999 memoir, *J'étais à Oualata: Le racisme d'État en Mauritanie*. The travails of these unfortunate prisoners have also been chronicled on film with Pierre-Yves Vandeweerd's 2007 *Le cercle des noyés* (released in English as *Drowned in Oblivion*), which is available in English on YouTube.

Most of these prisoners were released in the early 1990s as the Mauritanian government sought to resolve the border crisis 'events' of 1989 (page 262) and repair the ongoing rupture in relations with Senegal. But the fort remained in use into the new millennium, when it was even rumoured to have been a CIA 'black site' for the Americans under George W Bush – an allegation the Americans and Mauritanians both strenuously deny.

The government announced plans to finally close the notorious prison in 2018, though its reputation as a '*prison-mouroir*' (prison–place to die) will assuredly linger. But with the country's first-ever peaceful transfer of power following in 2019, one hopes the days of this Saharan gulag are well and truly finished.

AN EARLY VISITOR TO OUALATA (1352)

Taken from a description by 14th-century traveller Ibn Battuta

My stay at Iwalatan lasted about fifty days; and I was shown honour and entertained by its inhabitants. It is an excessively hot place, and boasts a few small date-palms, in the shade of which they sow watermelons. Its water comes from underground waterbeds at that point, and there is plenty of mutton to be had. The garments of its inhabitants, most of whom belong to the Massufa tribe, are of fine Egyptian fabrics.

Their women are of surpassing beauty, and are shown more respect than the men. The state of affairs among these people is indeed extraordinary. Their men show no signs of jealousy whatever; no-one claims descent from his father, but on the contrary from his mother's brother. A person's heirs are his sister's sons, not his own sons. This is a thing which I have seen nowhere in the world except among the Indians of Malabar. But those are heathens; these people are Muslims, punctilious in observing the hours of prayer, studying books of law, and memorising the Quran. Yet their women show no bashfulness before men and do not veil themselves, though they are assiduous in attending the prayers. Any man who wishes to marry one of them may do so, but they do not travel with their husbands, and even if one desired to do so her family would not allow her to go.

produce finely decorated works, including incense burners and miniature models of the Oualata houses crafted in clay. These miniature dollhouses are not just some tourist bauble, either: Odette du Puigaudeau saw them on her visits to Oualata in the 1930s.

Visible east across the oued from the main part of town lies the French-built 1912 **fort**. Though no longer used for the purpose, this was the most notorious prison in Mauritania for decades (page 301) and remains a military site today.

The earliest settlements in the area can be seen some 2km west of town (⊕ 17.3016, -7.0447), where Neolithic ruins called Tizert (or Tizzeght) – some say the ruins of Oualata's earliest incarnation – bake silently in the sun.

THE BACK WAY BETWEEN TICHITT AND OUALATA

Though there is nothing even remotely resembling a road between the two, it's possible to cross directly between Tichitt and Oualata (or vice versa) along desert tracks that roughly parallel the base of the Dhar Tichitt and Dhar Oualata escarpments, which form the northern border of the Aoukar Depression.

To start with, ignore the route you see on Google Maps: this is nearly 400km of uninhabited roadless wilderness and takes at least two days to cross. There is no road here, nor any proposal to build one. This crossing cannot be attempted without either a guide or confident desert skills and adequate preparation. The only communities between the two towns are a handful of extremely small hamlets on the outskirts of Tichitt (populated by the last of the Nemadi hunters; page 40) and Oualata, between which you'll find no more than a couple of isolated wells.

The irony of this route's profound remoteness today is that the area used to be a significant population centre, and home to one of West Africa's earliest complex societies. The string of sandstone escarpments ringing the Aoukar Depression (from west to east known as Dhar Tagant, Dhar Tichitt, Dhar Oualata and Dhar Néma) are lined with the remains of hundreds of Neolithic settlements, spread over hundreds of kilometres. Known today as the Tichitt Tradition, there were more than 400 settlements here between 2000BCE and 200BCE, and the thousands of residents lived an agro-pastoral existence in a climate very different than that found today.

When the lakes at the base of the escarpment began to dry up and they could no longer water their cattle here or propagate barley and millet, they began to abandon these villages and move south; many think the refugees from ancient Tichitt and their descendants went on to form the Ghana Empire centuries later. The ruins of their stone-built villages perched atop the escarpment are largely unstudied and undeveloped for visitors, with one exception.

Heading east out of Tichitt, your first stop should be at **Akhreijit** (page 286), which is both a modern village (⊕ 18.350, -9.1886) and a significant ruin (⊕ 18.3628, -9.1526) of the same name on the escarpment above. Uniquely among the region's many Neolithic sites, it has been partially restored and is recognised as a national historical site by the Mauritanian government. This is visible largely in the improved staircase allowing access up the escarpment to the site, and the restoration of many of the nearly 20ha site's dry-stone walls.

Continuing 20km east of Akhreijit, you'll pass Tweijinitt (⊕ 18.3429, -8.9517), the last modern settlement before beginning the great crossing to Oualata in earnest. The largest of the area's Neolithic settlements, **Dakhlet el Atrouss I** (⊕ 18.2663, -8.76983) lies about 22km further beyond, near the eastern end of Dhar Tichitt. This ancient town covers almost 300ha atop a promontory, making it more than three times larger than any of its Tichitt Tradition contemporaries, but the site remains entirely undeveloped and unprotected. More than 1,300 stone-built enclosures still mark the landscape here, and among these enclosures, two large tumuli at the town centre – the largest of which is 30m across at its base – indicate significant burials and are unique in all of Mauritania. Though the site is little studied, archaeologists suspect this to have been the Tichitt capital of the time. (For more information on Dakhlet el Atrouss and photos of the site, see w prehistoireouestsaharienne.wordpress.com/2021/08/30/la-culture-neolithique-de-tichitt-elements-diconographie-3.)

From here, the Dhar Tichitt escarpment fades away and a handful of significant sites mark the open desert crossing before the escarpment rises again as Dhar Oualata some 60km or so to the east. The first of these is also the most spectacular: **Al Makhrougat** (also known as Rochers des éléphants, or Elephant Rocks; ⊕ 18.4009, -8.5740). This massive outcrop, set some 25–30km northeast of Dakhlet el Atrouss I, rises out of the surrounding plain, and is a rock-hewn playground cut through with numerous caves, archways and dunes. Unlike some other creatively named rocks that require more than a pinch of imagination to conjure their namesakes, it's also got an undeniably elephant-shaped nose.

The area's most important wells, the **Puits d'Aratane** (Aratane Wells; ⊕ 18.3819, -8.5208) lie just 6km southeast of here, and are a good place to refill your supplies – you're likely to meet nomads here doing exactly the same. The wells stretch along a straight line for several hundred metres, following the course of an underground river.

A further 7km to the southeast, the Martian landscape around **Es Sba** (*Les doigts*, the fingers; ⊕ 18.3510, -8.4609) requires a bit more imagination to see the titular fingers jutting up from the sand, but the surrealist pillars and pinnacles of stone found here are impressive just the same.

There are also a couple of stone-built aviation markers along the way, which date to the colonial era. These are flat stone circles about 60m in diameter with letters in the centre, meant to be readable from the air and indicating airstrips and waypoints that pilots could use for navigation. There's one of these at Bou Zib (Bou Dhib; ⊕ 18.3528, -8.1444), about 33km east of Es Sba.

From here, the track meets Dhar Oualata about 15km to the south at the rocky plateau of Tinigart (⊕ 18.1985, -8.1143), where a handful of wells (⊕ 18.1689, -8.1313) sit at the confluence of several dry wadis. The equally rocky Enji (⊕ 18.1456, -8.1051) plateau sits just to the south, and both offer spectacular views and difficult driving. Oued Chibe (⊕ 18.1042, -8.0906) is just east of Enji, and makes a good campsite to break the journey; there's another old Neolithic site just above.

Some 23km southeast of the neolithic site at Oued Chibe, the difficult-of-access Guelta de Kédama (⊕ 18.0124, -7.9560) sits more than 2km up a narrow oued and beneath yet another ruined Neolithic settlement. Here, you should find an ever-so-small pool of perennial surface water hidden in the boulders at the valley's edge. There's another aviation marker at Oujaf (⊕ 17.8240, -7.9027) just over 20km to the south, and a set of wells (⊕ 17.8560, -7.9204) near it.

From here, it's roughly 50km further southeast until the first modern settlements resume at the herders' hamlets of Tegourarett (⊕ 17.6601, -7.4876) and Bamoira (⊕ 17.6675, -7.4276), but don't expect any services at either of these outposts. Ploughing on to the southeast, you're now finally about 75km from Oualata – and from the completion of this extraordinary desert crossing.

We have indicated the above route as starting in Tichitt, but it's equally possible to do this trip in either direction. For detailed maps and photos of the Tichitt Tradition Neolithic sites, see: w prehistoireouestsaharienne.wordpress.com/2021/10 (western sites); w prehistoireouestsaharienne.wordpress.com/2023/07/11/cartographie-des-villages-des-dhars-orientaux-aratane-oualata-nema (eastern sites); and w wildmanlife.com/akreijit-and-the-neolithic-society-of-dhar-tichitt (Akhreijit).

Appendix 1

LANGUAGE

Mauritania's most widely spoken language is Hassaniya Arabic, a dialect of Arabic which traces its origins to the Beni Hassan tribes that began to arrive in and occupy Mauritania from the northeast at the end of the 13th century. Hassaniya Arabic is not written according to Hassaniya convention, but rather according to the norms of Fusha, or Modern Standard Arabic.

Outside the Hassanophone population, Pulaar is the second most widely spoken language in Mauritania. Below you will find useful vocabulary for travellers in French, Hassaniya and Pulaar.

Regardless of which language the conversation will take place in, most interactions in Mauritania begin with the traditional Islamic salutation of '*As-salamu alaykum*' ('Peace be upon you'), to which the reply is '*Wa alaykumu s-salam*' ('And upon you be peace'). And one should never skimp on greetings in Mauritania; see page 98 for details.

VOCABULARY

Hassaniya Arabic *Courtesy of Mohamed Ahmedou*

	French	Hassaniya (phonetic)	Hassaniya (حسانية)
Greetings			
Good morning	*Bonjour*	*Sabah annour*	صباح النور
Good evening	*Bonsoir*	*Massaa annour*	مساء النور
		Shkiv Lmerouah	شكيف المرواح
Good night	*Bonne nuit*	*Layla Sa'ida*	ليلة سعيدة
		Tbat ala khair (m)	تبات على خير
		Tbaty ala khair (f)	تباتي على خير
Goodbye	*Au revoir*	*Ila allighaa*	الي اللقاء
		Wadaatak lallah	ودعتك لله
See you later	*À plus tard*	*Neshawvou Baadain*	نشاوفو بعدين
How are you?	*Comment allez-vous (polite)*	*Sh'halak (m)* *Sh'halik (f)*	شحالك
	Ça va (informal)	*Ayak Lebass*	اياك لباس
	Comment tu vas (informal)?	*Sh'tary*	شطاري
I'm fine	*Je vais très bien/ Ça va bien*	*Mouavy/Bikhair*	بخير / معافي
Basics			
yes	*oui*	*Eheh*	اهيه
		Naam	نعم
no	*non*	*Ebde Laa*	ابدي لا
please	*s'il vous plaît*	*Min fadlak*	من فضلك

Appendix 1 LANGUAGE

A1

	French	Hassaniya (phonetic)	Hassaniya (حسانية)
thank you	*merci*	*Shoukran*	شكرا
		Merci	مرسي
thank you very much	*merci beaucoup*	*Shoukran Jazeelan*	شكرا جزيلا
		Merci Hatteh	مرسي حتته
you're welcome	*de rien/je t'en prie*	*L'afou*	العفو
excuse me	*excusez-moi, pardon*	*Afouan*	عفوا
I would like…	*je voudrais…*	*Ndor*	ندور
there	*là*	*Hauck*	هوك
here	*ici*	*Hawn*	هون
stop	*arrêtez*	*Weggev/wegvi*	وقف
		*Ehne**	اهنى
		*Ehnay**	اهناي

*Is used if you want someone to stop something they are doing but the first word Weggev/wegvi is used if you want someone to stop moving or stop while driving.

Help!	*Au sécours!*	*Awenni*	عاوني
		Saa'edni	ساعدني
Do you speak English?	*Parlez-vous anglais?*	*Tetkelem (m) /Tetkelmi (f) bi l'engliziya*	تكلم / تكلمي بالإنجليزية
I don't understand	*Je ne comprends pas*	*Ma vhemtak (m)*	مافهمتك
		Ma vhemtik (f)	
I don't speak French/Arabic	*Je ne parle pas Français/Arabe*	*Ana Ma netkelem b Lvaranciye/L'Arabiye*	انا مانتكل الفرنسية/ العربية
A bit	*un peu*	*Shway*	شوي
Where is…?	*Où est…?*	*Mneynhou (for a male person/animal/thing)*	منينهو, منينهي
		Mneynhi (for a female person/animal/thing)	منين

Health

chemist	*la pharmacie*	*Pharmacy/Saydaliya*	الصيدلية
doctor	*le médecin*	*Edwa*	ادوا
		Eddewaa	الدواء
hospital	*l'hôpital*	*Ettab*	الطب
		Moushteshva	المستشفى
malaria	*le paludisme/le palu*	*Himmet ennamouss*	حمة الناموس
mosquito net	*moustiquaire*	*Lghebba*	القبة
		Ennamoussiye	الناموسية

Accommodation

toilet	*la toilette, le WC*	*Douche*	الدوش
How much is it?	*C'est combien?*	*Dha Se'arou shinhou*	ذا سعرو شنهو
It is too much!	*C'est trop cher!*	*Dha wa'er*	ذا واعر
air conditioning	*climatisé*	*Moukeyev/Climatisé*	مكيف
May I see the room?	*Puis-je voir la chambre?*	*Nged Nshowv*	نقد نشوف البيت
hotel	*l'hôtel (all sorts of accommodation)*	*Autel/Voundough (hotel)*	اوتل فندق/ استيديو

	French	Hassaniya (phonetic)	Hassaniya (حسانية)
auberge	*l'auberge (inexpensive)*	*Auberge*	اوبرج
studio/apartment	*le studio* (small apartment)	*Appartement*	ابرتماه

Food

restaurant	*le restaurant* *le maquis (small, informal eatery)*	*Mat'aam*	مطعم
market	*le marché*	*Lmarsa*	المرصة
bakery	*la boulangerie*	*Foor*	افور
supermarket	*le supermarché*	*Supermarchee*	سوبر مرشى
some food	*de la nourriture/ quelque chose à manger*	*Shi min Et'aam*	شي من الطعام
breakfast	*le petit-déjeuner*	*Esbouh*	اصبوح
lunch	*le déjeuner*	*Leghda*	لغدى
supper	*le diner*	*Li'esha*	لعشى
bread	*le pain*	*Mbourou* *Lkhoubz*	امبورو الخبز
butter	*le beurre*	*Beurre*	ببير
sandwich	*un sandwich*	*Sandouje*	ساندوج
chocolate bread	*pain au chocolat*	*Mbourour shokola*	امبورو شوكولا
vegetables	*les légumes*	*Lkhedra*	الخضرة
meat	*la viande*	*L'ham*	اللحم
beef	*le boeuf*	*L'ham libghar*	لحم لبقر
pork	*le porc*	*Lkhanzir*	لخنزير
chicken	*le poulet*	*Dyouk*	اديوك
fish	*le poisson*	*Lhoutt*	الحوت
grilled meat/fish	*les grillades*	*L'ham/Lhoutt Lmeshoui*	لحم المشوى الحوت المشوى
I don't eat meat/fish	*je ne mange pas de viande/poisson*	*Ana manewkel L'ham/Lhoutt*	انا مانوكل اللحم/الحوت
bush meat	*la viande de brousse*	*L'ham libhaniss*	لحم لبهانيس
only vegetables	*juste des légumes*	*Ela lkhidra*	الا الخضرة
eggs	*les oeufs*	*Lbaidh*	البيظ
fruit	*les fruits*	*Lvawakih*	الفواكه
apple	*le pomme*	*Pompe* *Touvah*	بومب التفاح
peanuts	*les arachides*	*Guerte*	كرته
drinking water	*l'eau potable*	*Lmaa lbared*	الماء البارد
soft drink	*le jus*	*Mashroub tabi'II* *Assir*	مشروب طبيعي عصير
fruit juice	*le jus des fruits*	*Assis lvakiha*	عصير الفاكهة
beer	*la bière*	*Lkhamar*	الخمر
wine	*le vin*	*Lkhamar*	الخمر
coffee	*le café*	*Kave/kaffee*	كافه
tea	*le thé*	*Atay*	اتاي

	French	Hassaniya (phonetic)	Hassaniya (حسانية)
Getting around			
car	*la voiture*	*Wette*	وته
		Sayara	سيارة
bus	*le bus*	*Lbuss*	لبيس
		L'arrêt	الكار
		Lhavila	الحافلة
bus/taxi station	*le garage*	*Garage*	كراج
	la gare routière	*Lmahatta*	المحطة
four-wheel drive (4x4)	*le quatre-quatre*	*Quatquat (lool)*	كتكت
bush taxi	*le taxi-brousse*	*Taxi*	تكسي
private taxi	*le taxi*	*Taxi Khoussoussi/ Prive*	تكسي خصوصي/بريفي
aeroplane	*l'avion*	*Tayra*	طايرة
boat	*le bateau*	*Bakhra*	باخرة
canoe (dug-out or larger narrow fishing boat)	*le pirogue*	*Valougua*	فالوكة
		Kanoutt	كانوط
boatman	*le piroguier*	*Hawatte*	حواتة
Is it very far?	*C'est très loin?*	*Ba'iid*	بعيد
What time?	*A quel'heure?*	*Lwaghet Shenhou*	الوقت شنهو
morning	*le matin*	*Essbah*	اصباح
		Edh'haa	اظحى
afternoon	*l'après-midi*	*Lgayla*	القايلة
evening	*le soir*	*Limsaa*	لمسى
petrol/gas	*l'essence*	*Essence*	اسانس
diesel	*le gazole*	*Gazole*	كزوال
roundabout, crossroads	*le rond-point, le carrefour*	*Kareffour, Eddewar*	كرفو ,الدوار
street	*la rue*	*Atarigh*	اطريق
		Eshare'e	الشارع
road	*la route*	*Trigh*	طريق
police	*la police*	*Polis*	بوليس
		Shourta	شرطة
post office	*la poste*	*Maktab lbarid*	مكتب البريد
city, town	*la ville*	*Bleyda*	بليدة
		Madina	مدينة
		Gharya	قرية
desert	*le désert*	*Sahraa*	الفيافي الصحراء
forest	*la forêt*	*Ghabah*	الغابة
river	*le fleuve*		النهر
mountain	*la montagne*	*Lkedya*	الكدية
		Ljebel	الجبل
		Lgualb	القلب
valley	*la vallée*	*Lbatha*	البطحة
lake	*le lac*	*Dhaya*	الظاية
ocean	*l'océan*	*Libhar*	لبحر

	French	Hassaniya (phonetic)	Hassaniya (حسانية)
Days of the week			
Monday	*Lundi*	*Lethneyn*	لثنين
Tuesday	*Mardi*	*Ethlathe*	اثلاثة
Wednesday	*Mercredi*	*Lerib'aa*	لربعه
Thursday	*Jeudi*	*Likhmiss*	لخميس
Friday	*Vendredi*	*Ljemouaa*	الجمعه
Saturday	*Samedi*	*Essebet*	السبت
Sunday	*Dimanche*	*Lhad*	الحد
Numbers			
one	*un*	*Wahed*	واحد
two	*deux*	*Ethneyn*	اثنين
three	*trois*	*Ethlathah*	اثلاثة
four	*quatre*	*Arba'ah*	اربعه
five	*cinq*	*Khamsah*	خمسة
six	*six*	*Sitah*	ستة
seven	*sept*	*Sab'ah*	سبعة
eight	*huit*	*Thamaniyah*	اثمانية
nine	*neuf*	*Tis'ah*	تسعه
ten	*dix*	*Asharah*	عشرة
eleven	*onze*	*Ethda'ish*	اثدعش
fifteen	*quinze*	*Akhmista'is*	اخمسطعش
twenty	*vingt*	*Eshrin*	عشرين
twenty-five	*vingt-cinq*	*Khamsah wa ishrin*	خمسة و عشرين
fifty	*cinquante*	*Khamseen*	خمسين
one hundred	*cent*	*Miyah*	مية
five hundred	*cinq cents*	*Akhmiss miyah*	اخمس مية
one thousand	*mille*	*Eliv*	الف
five thousand	*cinq mille*	*Akhmiss t'alav*	اخمس ت الاف
ten thousand	*dix mille*	*A'eshar t'alav*	اعشر ت الاف

Pulaar vocabulary *Courtesy of Alassane Ba*

	French	Pulaar
Greetings		
Good morning	*Bonjour*	*Jam waali*
Good evening	*Bonsoir*	*Jam hiiri*
Good night	*Bonne nuit*	*Mbaalen e jam*
Goodbye	*Au revoir*	*Haa gongol*
See you later	*À plus tard*	*Haa ɓooya*
How are you?	*Comment allez-vous (polite)*	*No mbad-ɗon (more formal)*
	Ça va (informal)/Comment tu vas (informal)?	*No mbad-daa*
I'm fine	*Je vais très bien/ça va bien*	*Jam tan/ ko mawɗum*
Basics		
yes	*oui*	*Eey*
no	*non*	*Alaa*
please	*s'il vous plaît*	*Sabu Alla*
thank you	*merci*	*A jaaraama (sing), On njaaraama (pl)*

	French	Pulaar
thank you very much	*merci beaucoup*	*A jaaraama no feewi*
you're welcome	*de rien/je t'en prie*	*Alaa baasi/Enen ndendi*
excuse me	*excusez-moi, pardon*	*Yaafo*
I would like…	*je voudrais…*	*Njiɗnoo-mi ko…*
there	*là*	*ɗaa*
here	*ici*	*ɗoo*
stop	*arrêtez*	*Daro, Ndaro ɗee (Pl)*
Help!	*Au sécours!*	*Mballee kam*
Do you speak English?	*Parlez-vous anglais?*	*Ada nani Engele*
I don't understand	*Je ne comprends pas*	*Mi faamaani*
I don't speak French / Arabic	*Je ne parle pas Français / Arabe*	*Mi naanaani Farayse/Aarabe*
A bit	*un peu*	*Seeɗa*
Where is…?	*Où est…?*	*Holto…woni*

Health

chemist	*la pharmacie*	*Farmasi*
doctor	*le médecin*	*Doktoor*
hospital	*l'hôpital*	*Opital*
malaria	*le paludisme/le palu*	*Jontinooje*
mosquito net	*moustiquaire*	*Arkille/fabiyoŋ*

Accommodation

toilet	*la toilette, le WC*	*Taarode*
How much is it?	*C'est combien?*	*No foti Jarata?*
It is too much!	*C'est trop cher!*	*Ina seeri*
air conditioning	*climatisé*	*kilimatiseer*
May I see the room?	*Puis-je voir la chambre?*	*Mbele mbido waawi yiide suudu ndu?*
hotel	*l'hôtel (all sorts of accommodation), l'auberge (inexpensive)*	*Otel*

Food

restaurant	*le restaurant, le maquis (small, informal eatery)*	*Paasioŋ*
market	*le marché*	*Jeere*
bakery	*la boulangerie*	*Fuur mburu*
supermarket	*le supermarché*	*Superemarse*
some food	*de la nourriture/quelque chose à manger*	*ñaamde*
breakfast	*le petit-déjeuner*	*Kaccitaari*
lunch	*le déjeuner*	*Bottaari*
supper	*le diner*	*Hiraande*
bread	*le pain*	*Mburu*
butter	*le beurre*	*Boor*
sandwich	*un sandwich*	*Sandiis*
chocolate bread	*pain au chocolat*	*Mburu e sokola*
vegetables	*les légumes*	*Lijimaaji*
meat	*la viande*	*Teewu*
beef	*le boeuf*	*Teewu nagge*

	French	**Pulaar**
pork	*le porc*	*Teewu mbabba tugal*
chicken	*le poulet*	*Gertogal*
fish	*le poisson*	*Liŋngu (sing), Liɗɗi (pl)*
grilled meat/fish	*les grillades*	*Teewu/Liŋngu Juɗaaɗo*
I don't eat meat/fish	*je ne mange pas de viande/poisson*	*Mi ñaamata teewu/Liŋngu*
bush meat	*la viande de brousse*	*Teewu Waaño*
only vegetables	*juste des légumes*	*Lijimaaji tan*
eggs	*les oeufs*	*ɓoccooɗe*
fruit	*les fruits*	*ɓiɓɓe leɗɗe*
apple	*le pomme*	*Pom*
peanuts	*les arachides*	*gerte*
drinking water	*l'eau potable*	*Ndiyam laaɗam*
soft drink	*le jus*	*Jii*
fruit juice	*le jus des fruits*	*Jii ɓiɓɓe leɗɗe*
beer	*la bière*	*Saŋngara*
wine	*le vin*	*Saŋngara*
coffee	*le café*	*Kafe*
tea	*le thé*	*Ataaya*

Getting around

car	*la voiture*	*Oto*
bus	*le bus*	*Biis*
bus/taxi station	*le garage, la gare routière*	*Gaaraas*
four-wheel-drive (4x4)	*le quatre-quatre*	*Oto kaat kaat*
bush taxi	*le taxi-brousse*	*Otooji ladde*
private taxi	*le taxi*	*Taksi*
aeroplane	*l'avion*	*Abiyoŋ*
boat	*le bateau*	*Laana ndiyam*
canoe (dug-out or larger narrow fishing boat)	*le pirogue*	*Laana ndiyam*
boatsman	*le piroguier*	*Jom laana ndiyam*
Is it very far?	*C'est très loin?*	*Ina woɗɗi*
What time?	*A quel'heure?*	*Hol waktu*
morning	*le matin*	*Subaka o*
afternoon	*l'après-midi*	*Kikiiɗe*
evening	*le soir*	*Jamma*
petrol/gas	*l'essence*	*Esaas*
diesel	*le gazole*	*Gaasuwaal*
roundabout, crossroads	*le rond-point, le carrefour*	*Korosma*
street	*la rue*	*Bolol/ kallu/ laawol*
road	*la route*	*Tali*
police	*la police*	*Poliis*
post office	*la poste*	*Posto*
city, town	*la ville*	*Teeru o*
desert	*le désert*	*Ceernde /Geseejo*
forest	*la forêt*	*ladde*
river	*le fleuve*	*Maayo*
mountain	*la montagne*	*tulnde/ƴeeŋde*
valley	*la vallée*	*Weendu*
lake	*le lac*	*Weendu*

	French	Pulaar
ocean	*l'océan*	*Maayo*

Days of the week

Monday	*Lundi*	*Altine*
Tuesday	*Mardi*	*Taalaata*
Wednesday	*Mercredi*	*Allarba*
Thursday	*Jeudi*	*Alkamese*
Friday	*Vendredi*	*Aljuma*
Saturday	*Samedi*	*Aset*
Sunday	*Dimanche*	*Alet*

MAP TERMS GLOSSARY

Just as with the hackneyed old saying about Inuit and words for snow, there exists an entire specialised vocabulary developed to describe the Mauritanian landscape. There are many terms for types of dune alone: *aklé*, *khwâreg*, *elb* and *barkhane*, to name a few. This subtle and discerning vocabulary was an important tool, enabling nomads to exchange critical information to help navigate this enormous, empty landscape over many centuries.

Mauritanian place names are often descriptive, so below we've included a number of the most common geographical terms you might encounter around the country.

Adrar	mountain
Aftout	seasonally flooded depression
Aïn/aïoun	spring/springs
Aouker	dunes separated by easily accessible *goûd* valleys
Batha	a large, sandy oued/valley
Bediyya	the countryside/pastures, bush
Bir	well
Chehama	floodplains along the Senegal River
Dhar	escarpment
Erg	dune sea
Foum	river mouth
Goûd	valley between parallel dunes
Guelb/gleib/galb	peak
Guelta	pool
Hammada	high *reg* plateau
Hassi	well
Kedia	hill
Ksar	fort
Oued	seasonal watercourse
Oumm	head of valley
Ras	peak/summit/cape
Reg	flat rocky desert plain
Sebkha	salt pan
Tamourt	floodplain/waterhole
Tarf	ridge/point

Numbers

English	French	Pulaar
one	*un*	*Go’o*
two	*deux*	*ɗiɗi*
three	*trois*	*Tati*
four	*quatre*	*Nayi*
five	*cinq*	*Joyyi*
six	*six*	*Jeegom*
seven	*sept*	*Jeedidi*
eight	*huit*	*Jeetati*
nine	*neuf*	*Jeenayi*
ten	*dix*	*Sappo*
eleven	*onze*	*Sappo go’o*
fifteen	*quinze*	*Sappo joyyi*
twenty	*vingt*	*Noogaas*
twenty-five	*vingt-cinq*	*Noogaas e joyii*
fifty	*cinquante*	*Cappanɗe joyi*
one hundred	*cent*	*Teemeder*
five hundred	*cinq cents*	*Teemedde joyi*
one thousand	*mille*	*Ujunero*
five thousand	*cinq mille*	*Ujunnaaje joyi*
ten thousand	*dix mille*	*Ujunnaaje sappo*

Three issues of Wanderlust®

Use code
BRADT3
OR
at checkout

shop.wanderlust.co.uk

CONNECTING
TOURISM
TO AFRICA

Join us today! info@atta.travel www.atta.travel

ATTA's Official Airline Partner
Ethiopian
የኢትዮጵያ

Appendix 2

FURTHER READING

The corpus of work on Mauritania available in English is quite small, but this list is nonetheless not intended to be comprehensive, and there is a fair amount of academic scholarship available in addition to the works listed below. Some of the books below are out of print, but for the most part all are still relatively easily available through online booksellers.

LITERATURE

Beyrouk, Mbarek Ould *The Desert and the Drum* (*Le Tambour des larmes*) Dedalus, 2015
Beyrouk, Mbarek Ould *Pariahs* (*Parias*) Schaffner Press, 2023
Beyrouk, Mbarek Ould *The Silence of the Horizons* (*Le silence des horizons*) Schaffner Press, 2025
Ebnou, Moussa Ould *Barzakh: The Land In-Between* (*Le Barzakh*) Iskanchi Press, 2022
Slahi, Mohamedou Ould *The Actual True Story of Ahmed and Zarga* Ohio University Press, 2021

BIOGRAPHY AND TRAVELOGUE

Abeiderrahmane, Nancy Jones *Camel Cheese – Seemed Like a Good Idea* Createspace, 2013
Baird, Katherine *Growing Mangos in the Desert: A Memoir of Life in a Mauritanian Village* Apprentice House Press, 2022
Edwards, Ted *Beyond the Last Oasis: A Solo Walk in the Western Sahara* Oxford University Press, 1985
Hudson, Peter *Travels in Mauritania* Flamingo, 1990
Hudson, Peter *Under an African Sky: A Journey to Africa's Climate Frontline* New Internationalist, 2014
Puigaudeau, Odette du *Barefoot through Mauretania* (*Pieds nus à travers la Mauritanie*) George Routledge & Sons, 1937
Saint-Exupéry, Antoine de *Wind, Sand and Stars* (*Terre des hommes*) Reynal & Hitchcock, 1939
Slahi, Mohamedou Ould *Guantánamo Diary* Little, Brown & Company, 2015

NATURE The only birding guide specific to Mauritania is the 2010 *Oiseaux de Mauritanie – Birds of Mauritania* by Paul Isenmann et al, which can be hard to find; try the Natural History Book Service (**w** nhbs.com) for a copy. Otherwise, ornithologists should pick up the second edition of *Birds of Senegal and The Gambia* by Nik Borrow and Ron Demey (Princeton University Press, 2023) or *Birds of Western Africa* (2nd edition, Princeton University Press, 2014) by the same authors.

HISTORY AND CULTURE

al-Jannah, Aḥmad ibn Tuwayr *The Pilgrimage of Ahmad, Son of the Little Bird of Paradise: An Account of a 19th Century Pilgrimage from Mauritania to Mecca* Aris & Phillips, 1977
Cleaveland, Timothy *Becoming Walāta: A History of Saharan Social Formation and Transformation* Heinemann, 2002

Corréard, Alexandre and Savigny, J B Henry *Narrative of a Voyage to Senegal in 1816* Marlboro Press, 1986
Davidson, Basil *Lost Cities of Africa* Little, Brown, 1987
Fauvelle, François-Xavier *The Golden Rhinoceros: Histories of the African Middle Ages* Princeton University Press, 2018
Goodsmith, Lauren *The Children of Mauritania: Days in the Desert and by the River Shore* Lerner, 1993
Hamdun, Said and King, Noël *Ibn Battuta in Black Africa* Markus Wiener Publishers, 2009
Himpan, Brigitte and Himpan-Sabatier, Diane *Nomads of Mauritania* Vernon Press, 2019
Miles, Jonathan *The Wreck of the Medusa: The Most Famous Sea Disaster of the Nineteenth Century* Grove Press, 2008
Norris, H T *The Arab Conquest of the Western Sahara* Longman, 1986
Pazzanita, Anthony G *Historical Dictionary of Mauritania* (3rd edition) Scarecrow Press, 2008

POLITICS AND CURRENT EVENTS

Moctar, Hassan Ould *After Border Externalization: Migration, Race, and Labour in Mauritania* Bloomsbury, 2024
Pettigrew, Erin *Cries of the Oppressed: Leftists, Arab Nationalism, and National Identity in Early Post-Independence Mauritania* Forthcoming
Pogue, James *Gold Fever in the Coup Belt: The Mines of Mauritania* Granta 168, 2024

MUSIC, ART AND PHOTOGRAPHY

Gutberlet, Marie-Hélène and Kuster, Brigitta (eds) *1970–2018 – Interviews with Med Hondo* Archive Books, 2021
Gutberlet, Marie-Hélène and Kuster, Brigitta (eds) *On the Run: Perspectives on the Cinema of Med Hondo* Archive Books, 2021
Lam, Aïssata *Mauritanie: Carnet de voyage* 2023
Legarra, José Javier *Nouakchott Grande* Hades Consulting, 2020
Shackleton, Paula *Mauritania* Kinross, 2012. Coffee-table book published on behalf of Kinross Gold Corporation.
Vium, Christian *Ville Nomade* Actes Sud, 2016

RELIGION

Pettigrew, Erin *Invoking the Invisible in the Sahara: Islam, Spiritual Mediation, and Social Change* Cambridge University Press, 2023

ENSLAVEMENT

Cotton, Samuel *Silent Terror: A Journey into Contemporary African Slavery* Writers & Readers, 1999
Ruf, Urs Peter *Ending Slavery: Hierarchy, Dependency and Gender in Central Mauritania* Transcript, 2001
Segal, Ronald *Islam's Black Slaves: The Other Black Diaspora* Farrar, Straus & Giroux, 2002
Wiley, Katherine A *Work, Social Status, and Gender in Post-Slavery Mauritania* Indiana University Press, 2018

LANGUAGE There are a few relevant dictionaries and primers available on Amazon, but to get started, an eminently worthwhile resource is the Live Lingua Project (w livelingua.com/peace-corps-language-courses.php), which offers a free archive of downloadable Peace Corps language lessons which includes courses in Hassaniya, Pulaar, Soninké, Wolof and others.

Further Hassaniya resources (also originally meant for Peace Corps volunteers) can be found here:

Hassaniya Trainee Manual (ed. Chris Paul, Maylén Rafuls; 2009) **w** researchgate.net/publication/281747462_United_States_Peace_Corps_Islamic_Republic_of_Mauritania_Training_Program-_Language_component_Hassaniya_Trainee_Book

Mauritanian Arabic (Timothy P Francis and Stephen Hanchey; 1979) **w** archive.org/details/ED294423/ED290326

FRENCH TITLES A few specialised titles only available in French are also worthy of mention here. For a comprehensive French-language bibliography, see **w** mauritanie-au-gps.fr/Liens.y.htm.

Boulay, Sébastien *Pêcheurs imraguen du Sahara atlantique – mutations techniques et changements sociaux des années 1970 à nos jours* Karthala, 2013

Cheikh, Abdel Wedoud Ould *Eléments d'histoire de la Mauritanie* Centre Culturel Français Nouakchott, 1988

Choplin, Armelle *Nouakchott: au carrefour de la Mauritanie et du monde* Karthala, 2009

Daddah, Mokhtar Ould *La Mauritanie contre vents et marées* Karthala, 2003

Gandini, Jacques *Pistes et hors pistes en Mauritanie* Extrem-Sud, 2023

Kane, Ndiawar *Le fleuve refuse de séparer* Harmattan Sénégal, 2023

Kane, Ndiawar *Le sentier sinueux* Harmattan Sénégal, 2017

Mohameden, Mohamedou Ould and Ebnou, Moussa Ould *Contes et proverbes de Mauritanie (I: Contes d'animaux; II: Contes merveilleux; III: Maximes et proverbes)* Harmattan, 2008

Monod, Théodore *Méharées, exploration au vrai Sahara* Éditions Je sers, 1937

Puigaudeau, Odette du *Arts et coutumes des maures* Ibis Press, 2005

Puigaudeau, Odette du and Sénones, Marion *Mémoire du pays Maure, 1934–1960* Ibis Press, 2005

Thouzery, Michel and Vall, Abdellahi Ould Mohamed *Plantes médicinales de Mauritanie. Remèdes traditionnels et guérisseurs du Sahara au fleuve Sénégal* Association Plantes et nomades, 2011

Vernet, Robert and Naffé, Baouba Ould Mohamed *Dictionnaire archéologique de la Mauritanie* Université de Nouakchott, 2003

Vignote, Nicole and Meyer, Nicole *Couleurs et motifs. L'art des teinturières soninké* Centre Culturel Français Nouakchott, 2003

Finally, the *Découverte de la Mauritanie* series from Éditions Sépia (in partnership with the Centre Culturel Français) was published in the early 2000s and includes four impressively detailed, full-colour titles (out of a planned six), written by Abdallahi Fall, André Cormillot and Mohamed Adnan Ould Beyrouk:

L'Adrar 1 [Atar et ses environs]
L'Adrar 2 [Les villes anciennes: Chinguetti, Ouadane et le Guelb er Richât]
La vallée du fleuve [du Guidimagha au Parc National du Diawling]
Sur la route des caravanes [d'Atar à Néma par Rachid, Tidjikja et Oualata]

Index

Page numbers in **bold** indicate main entries; those in *italics* indicate maps.

INDEX OF ADVERTISERS

THE BRADT STORY

In the beginning

It all began in 1974 on an Amazon river barge. During an 18-month trip through South America, two adventurous young backpackers – Hilary Bradt and her then husband, George – decided to write about the hiking trails they had discovered through the Andes. *Backpacking Along Ancient Ways in Peru and Bolivia* included the very first descriptions of the Inca Trail. It was the start of a colourful journey to becoming one of the best-loved travel publishers in the world; you can read the full story on our website (**bradtguides.com/ourstory**).

Getting there first

Hilary quickly gained a reputation for being a true travel pioneer, and in the 1980s she started to focus on guides to places overlooked by other publishers. The Bradt Guides list became a roll call of guidebook 'firsts'. We published the first guide to Madagascar, followed by Mauritius, Czechoslovakia and Vietnam. The 1990s saw the beginning of our extensive coverage of Africa: Tanzania, Uganda, South Africa, and Eritrea. Later, post-conflict guides became a feature: Rwanda, Mozambique, Angola, and Sierra Leone, as well as the first standalone guides to the Baltic States following the fall of the Iron Curtain, and the first post-war guides to Bosnia, Kosovo and Albania.

Comprehensive – and with a conscience

Today, we are the world's largest independently owned travel publisher, with more than 200 titles. However, our ethos remains unchanged. Hilary is still keenly involved, and **we still get there first**: two-thirds of Bradt guides have no direct competition.

But we don't just get there first. Our guides are also known for being **more comprehensive** than any other series. We avoid templates and tick-lists. Each guide is a one-of-a-kind expression of an expert author's interests, knowledge and enthusiasm for telling it how it really is.

And a commitment to wildlife, conservation and respect for local communities has always been at the heart of our books. Bradt Guides was **championing sustainable travel** before any other guidebook publisher. We even have a series dedicated to Slow Travel in the UK, award-winning books that explore the country with a passion and depth you'll find nowhere else.

Thank you!

We can only do what we do because of the support of readers like you – people who value less-obvious experiences, less-visited places and a more thoughtful approach to travel. Those who, like us, take travel seriously.

TRAVEL TAKEN SERIOUSLY